52,50

D0083018

THE PAPERS OF
THOMAS JEFFERSON

THE PAPERS OF
Thomas Jefferson

Volume 19
24 January to 31 March 1791

JULIAN P. BOYD, EDITOR

RUTH W. LESTER, ASSISTANT EDITOR

PRINCETON, NEW JERSEY
PRINCETON UNIVERSITY PRESS

1974

Printed in the United States of America by
Princeton University Press, Princeton, New Jersey

DEDICATED TO THE MEMORY OF

ADOLPH S. OCHS

PUBLISHER OF THE NEW YORK TIMES

1896-1935

WHO BY THE EXAMPLE OF A RESPONSIBLE

PRESS ENLARGED AND FORTIFIED

THE JEFFERSONIAN CONCEPT

OF A FREE PRESS

ACKNOWLEDGMENTS

As indicated in the first volume, this edition was made possible by a grant of $200,000 from the New York Times Company to Princeton University. Since this initial subvention, its continuance has been assured by additional contributions from the New York Times Company; by the grant of the Ford Foundation to the National Archives Trust Fund Board as explained in Volume 17; by the Fellowship bestowed on the Editor by the John Simon Guggenheim Memorial Foundation; and by other benefactions from the Charlotte Palmer Phillips Foundation and from such loyal supporters of the enterprise as James Russell Wiggins and David K. E. Bruce. In common with other editions of historical documents, *The Papers of Thomas Jefferson* is a beneficiary of the good offices of The National Historical Publications Commission, tendered in many useful forms through its Chairman, James B. Rhoads, its Executive Director, E. Berkeley Tompkins, and its dedicated staff. For these and other indispensable aids generously given by librarians, archivists, scholars, and collectors of manuscripts, the Editors record their sincere gratitude.

GUIDE TO EDITORIAL APPARATUS

1. TEXTUAL DEVICES

The following devices are employed throughout the work to clarify the presentation of the text.

[. . .], [. . . .]	One or two words missing and not conjecturable.
[. . .]¹, [. . . .]¹	More than two words missing and not conjecturable; subjoined footnote estimates number of words missing.
[ ]	Number or part of a number missing or illegible.
[roman]	Conjectural reading for missing or illegible matter. A question mark follows when the reading is doubtful.
[*italic*]	Editorial comment inserted in the text.
⟨*italic*⟩	Matter deleted in the MS but restored in our text.
[ ]	Record entry for letters not found.

2. DESCRIPTIVE SYMBOLS

The following symbols are employed throughout the work to describe the various kinds of manuscript originals. When a series of versions is recorded, *the first to be recorded is the version used for the printed text.*

Dft	draft (usually a composition or rough draft; later drafts, when identifiable as such, are designated "2 Dft," &c.)
Dupl	duplicate
MS	manuscript (arbitrarily applied to most documents other than letters)
N	note, notes (memoranda, fragments, &c.)
PoC	polygraph copy
PrC	press copy
RC	recipient's copy
SC	stylograph copy
Tripl	triplicate

All manuscripts of the above types are assumed to be in the hand of the author of the document to which the descriptive symbol pertains. If not, that fact is stated. On the other hand, the following types of manuscripts are assumed *not* to be in the hand of the author, and exceptions will be noted:

FC   file copy (applied to all forms of retained copies, such as letter-book copies, clerk's copies, &c.)

Tr   transcript (applied to both contemporary and later copies; period of transcription, unless clear by implication, will be given when known)

3. *LOCATION SYMBOLS*

The locations of documents printed in this edition from originals in private hands, from originals held by institutions outside the United States, and from printed sources are recorded in self-explanatory form in the descriptive note following each document. The locations of documents printed from originals held by public institutions in the United States are recorded by means of the symbols used in the National Union Catalog in the Library of Congress; (explanation of how these symbols are formed is given above, Vol. 1: xl). The symbols DLC and MHi by themselves will stand for the collections of Jefferson Papers proper in these repositories; when texts are drawn from other collections held by these two institutions, the names of the particular collections will be added. The list of symbols appearing in each volume is limited to the institutions represented by documents printed or referred to in that and previous volumes.

CLSU	University of Southern California Library, Los Angeles
CLU	William Andrews Clark Memorial Library, University of California at Los Angeles
CSM	Colonial Society of Massachusetts, Boston
CSmH	Henry E. Huntington Library, San Marino, California
Ct	Connecticut State Library, Hartford
CtHi	Connecticut Historical Society, Hartford
CtY	Yale University Library
DeHi	Historical Society of Delaware, Wilmington
DLC	Library of Congress

DNA	The National Archives, with identifications of series (preceded by record group number) as follows:

AL	American Letters
CD	Consular Dispatches
DCI	Diplomatic and Consular Instructions
DD	Diplomatic Dispatches
DL	Domestic Letters
FL	Foreign Letters
LAR	Letters of Application and Recommendation
MLR	Miscellaneous Letters Received
MTA	Miscellaneous Treasury Accounts
NL	Notes from Legations
NWT	Northwest Territory Papers
PC	Proceedings of Board of Commissioners for the District of Columbia
PCC	Papers of the Continental Congress
PDL	Printing and Distribution of the Laws
SDC	State Department Correspondence
SDR	A Record of the Reports of Thomas Jefferson, Secretary of State for the United States of America
SWT	Southwest Territory Papers

G-Ar	Georgia Department of Archives and History, Atlanta
ICHi	Chicago Historical Society, Chicago
IHi	Illinois State Historical Library, Springfield
IMunS	St. Mary of the Lake Seminary, Mundelein, Illinois
InHi	Indiana Historical Society, Indianapolis
MdAA	Maryland Hall of Records, Annapolis
MdAN	U.S. Naval Academy Library, Annapolis
MeHi	Maine Historical Society, Portland

MB	Boston Public Library, Boston
MBA	Archives, State House, Boston
MBAt	Boston Athenæum, Boston
MH	Harvard University Library
MHi	Massachusetts Historical Society, Boston
MHi:AM	Adams Manuscripts, Massachusetts Historical Society
MiU-C	William L. Clements Library, University of Michigan
MoSHi	Missouri Historical Society, St. Louis
MWA	American Antiquarian Society, Worcester, Massachusetts
NA	New York State Library, Albany
NBu	Buffalo Public Library, Buffalo, New York
NcD	Duke University Library, Durham, North Carolina
NcU	University of North Carolina Library, Chapel Hill
NhD	Dartmouth College Library, Hanover, New Hampshire
NhHi	New Hampshire Historical Society, Concord
NHi	New-York Historical Society, New York City
NjHi	New Jersey Historical Society, Newark
NjP	Princeton University Library
NjMoW	Morristown National Historical Park, Morristown, N.J.
NK-Iselin	Letters to and from John Jay bearing this symbol are used by permission of the Estate of Eleanor Jay Iselin.
NN	New York Public Library, New York City
NNC	Columbia University Libraries, New York City
NNP	Pierpont Morgan Library, New York City
NNS	New York Society Library, New York City
O	Ohio State Library, Columbus
OCHP	Historical and Philosophical Society of Ohio, Cincinnati
OHi	Ohio State Archaeological and Historical Society, Columbus
PBL	Lehigh University Library
PHC	Haverford College Library

PHi	Historical Society of Pennsylvania, Philadelphia
PP	Free Library, Philadelphia
PPAP	American Philosophical Society, Philadelphia
PPL	Library Company of Philadelphia
PU	University of Pennsylvania Library
PWW	Washington and Jefferson College, Washington, Pennsylvania
RPA	Rhode Island Department of State, Providence
RPAB	Annmary Brown Memorial Library, Providence
RPB	Brown University Library
Vi	Virginia State Library, Richmond
Vi:USCC	Ended Cases, United States Circuit Court, Virginia State Library
ViHi	Virginia Historical Society, Richmond
ViRVal	Valentine Museum Library, Richmond
ViU	University of Virginia Library
ViU:McG	McGregor Library, University of Virginia
ViU:TJMF	Manuscripts deposited by the Thomas Jefferson Memorial Foundation in the University of Virginia Library
ViW	College of William and Mary Library
ViWC	Colonial Williamsburg, Inc.
VtMC	Middlebury College Library, Middlebury, Vermont
VtMS	Secretary of State, Montpelier, Vermont
WHi	State Historical Society of Wisconsin, Madison

4. OTHER SYMBOLS AND ABBREVIATIONS

The following symbols and abbreviations are commonly employed in the annotation throughout the work.

Second Series   The topical series to be published at the end of this edition, comprising those materials which are best suited to a topical rather than a chronological arrangement (see Vol. 1: xv-xvi)

TJ Thomas Jefferson

TJ Editorial Files   Photoduplicates and other editorial materials in the office of *The Papers of Thomas Jefferson*, Princeton University Library

TJ Papers   Jefferson Papers (applied to a collection of manuscripts when the precise location of a given document must be furnished, and always preceded by the symbol for the institutional repository; thus "DLC: TJ Papers, 4:628-9" represents a document in the Library of Congress, Jefferson Papers, volume 4, pages 628 and 629)

RG   Record Group (used in designating the location of documents in the National Archives)

SJL   Jefferson's "Summary Journal of letters" written and received (in DLC: TJ Papers)

SJPL   "Summary Journal of Public Letters," an incomplete list of letters written by TJ from 16 Apr. 1784 to 31 Dec. 1793, with brief summaries, in an amanuensis' hand except for six pages in TJ's hand listing and summarizing official reports and communications by him as Secretary of State, 11 Oct. 1789 to 31 Dec. 1793 (in DLC: TJ Papers, at end of SJL)

V   Ecu

ƒ   Florin

£   Pound sterling or livre, depending upon context (in doubtful cases, a clarifying note will be given)

s   Shilling or sou. (Also expressed as /)

d   Penny or denier

₶   Livre Tournois

℣   Per (occasionally used for pro, pre)

5. SHORT TITLES

The following list includes only those short titles of works cited with great frequency, and therefore in very abbreviated form, throughout this edition. Their expanded forms are given here only in the degree of fullness needed for unmistakable identification. Since it is impossible to anticipate all the works to be cited in such very abbreviated form, the list is appropriately revised from volume to volume.

Adams, *Works*   Charles Francis Adams, ed., *The Works of John Adams*, Boston, 1850-56, 10 vols.

Adams, *Diary*   *Diary and Autobiography of John Adams*, ed. L. H. Butterfield and others, Cambridge, 1961, 4 vols.

AHA   American Historical Association

AHR   *American Historical Review*, 1895-

Ammon, *Monroe*   Harry Ammon, *James Monroe*, New York, 1971

Annals   *Annals of the Congress of the United States: The Debates and Proceedings in the Congress of the United States . . . Compiled from Authentic Materials by Joseph Gales, Senior*, Washington, Gales & Seaton, 1834-56, 42 vols. All editions are undependable and pagination varies from one printing to another. The edition cited here has this caption on both recto and verso pages: "History of Congress." Another printing, with the same title-page, has "Gales & Seatons History" on verso and "of Debates in Congress" on recto pages. Those using the latter printing will need to employ the date or, where it is lacking, to add approximately 52 to the page numbers of *Annals* as cited in this volume.

ASP   *American State Papers: Documents, Legislative and Executive, of the Congress of the United States*, Washington, Gales & Seaton, 1832-61, 38 vols.

Atlas of Amer. Hist.   James Truslow Adams and R. V. Coleman, eds., *Atlas of American History*, New York, Scribner, 1943

Bear, *Family Letters*   Edwin M. Betts and James A. Bear, Jr., eds., *Family Letters of Thomas Jefferson*, Columbia, Missouri, 1966

Bemis, *Jay's Treaty*   Samuel Flagg Bemis, *Jay's Treaty: A Study in Commerce and Diplomacy*, New Haven, 1962, rev. edn.

Bemis, *Pinckney's Treaty*   Samuel Flagg Bemis, *Pinckney's Treaty: America's Advantage from Europe's Distress, 1783-1800*, rev. edn., New Haven, 1960

Betts, *Farm Book*   Edwin M. Betts, ed., *Thomas Jefferson's Farm Book*, Princeton, 1953

Betts, *Garden Book*   Edwin M. Betts, ed., *Thomas Jefferson's Garden Book, 1766-1824*, Philadelphia, 1944

Beveridge, *Marshall*   Albert J. Beveridge, *The Life of John Marshall*, Boston, 1916

Biog. Dir. Cong.   *Biographical Directory of the American Congress, 1774-1949*, Washington, 1950

B.M. Cat.   British Museum, *General Catalogue of Printed*

Books, London, 1931-; also *The British Museum Catalogue of Printed Books, 1881-1900*, Ann Arbor, 1946

B.N. Cat. Bibliothèque Nationale, *Catalogue général des livres imprimés. . . . Auteurs*, Paris, 1897-1955

Brant, Madison Irving Brant, *James Madison*, Indianapolis, 1941-61, 6 vols.

Bryan, *National Capital* W. B. Bryan, *History of the National Capital*, New York, 1914-1916, 2 vols.

Burnett, *Letters of Members* Edwin C. Burnett, ed., *Letters of Members of the Continental Congress*, Washington, 1921-1936, 8 vols.

Butterfield, *Rush* *Letters of Benjamin Rush*, ed. L. H. Butterfield, Princeton, 1951, 2 vols.

Cal. Franklin Papers I. Minis Hays, ed., *Calendar of the Papers of Benjamin Franklin in the Library of the American Philosophical Society*, Philadelphia, 1908, 6 vols.

Carter, *Terr. Papers* *The Territorial Papers of the United States*, ed. Clarence E. Carter, Washington, 1934-62, 26 vols.

Cutler, *Cutler* William Parker Cutler, *Life, Journals, and Correspondence of Rev. Manasseh Cutler*, Cincinnati, 1888, 2 vols.

CVSP William P. Palmer and others, eds., *Calendar of Virginia State Papers . . . Preserved in the Capitol at Richmond*, Richmond, 1875-1893

DAB Allen Johnson and Dumas Malone, eds., *Dictionary of American Biography*, N.Y., 1928-1936

DAE Sir William A. Craigie and James Hulbert, eds., *A Dictionary of American English*, Chicago, 1938-1944

DAH James Truslow Adams, ed., *Dictionary of American History*, N.Y., 1940, 5 vols., and index

DeConde, *Entangling Alliance* Alexander DeConde, *Entangling Alliance; Politics & Diplomacy under George Washington*, Durham, N.C., 1958

DNB Leslie Stephen and Sidney Lee, eds., *Dictionary of National Biography*, 2d ed., N.Y., 1908-1909

Dumbauld, *Tourist* Edward Dumbauld, *Thomas Jefferson American Tourist*, Norman, Oklahoma, 1946

Elliot's *Debates* Jonathan Elliot, ed., *The Debates of the Several State Conventions on the Adoption of the Federal Constitution . . . together with the Journal of the Federal Convention*, 2d ed., Philadelphia, 1901, 5 vols.

Evans   Charles Evans, comp., *American Bibliography*, Chicago, 1903-1955

Ford   Paul Leicester Ford, ed., *The Writings of Thomas Jefferson*, Letterpress Edition, N.Y., 1892-1899, 10 vols.

Freeman, *Washington*   Douglas Southall Freeman, *George Washington*, N.Y., 1948-1957, 6 vols.; 7th volume by J. A. Carroll and M. W. Ashworth, New York, 1957

Fry-Jefferson Map   Dumas Malone, ed., *The Fry & Jefferson Map of Virginia and Maryland: a Facsimile of the First Edition*, Princeton, 1950

Gottschalk, *Lafayette, 1783-89*   Louis Gottschalk, *Lafayette between the American and the French Revolution (1783-1789)*, Chicago, 1950

Greely, *Public Documents*   Adolphus Washington Greely, ed., *Public Documents of the First Fourteen Congresses, 1789-1817: Papers Relating to Early Congressional Documents*, Washington, 1900

HAW   Henry A. Washington, ed., *The Writings of Thomas Jefferson*, N.Y., 1853-1854, 9 vols.

Hening   William Waller Hening, ed., *The Statutes at Large; Being a Collection of All the Laws of Virginia*, Richmond, 1809-1823, 13 vols.

Henry, *Henry*   William Wirt Henry, *Patrick Henry, Life, Correspondence and Speeches*, N.Y., 1891, 3 vols.

Humphreys, *Humphreys*   F. L. Humphreys, *Life and Times of David Humphreys*, New York, 1917, 2 vols.

JCC   Worthington C. Ford and others, eds., *Journals of the Continental Congress*, 1774-1789, Washington, 1904-1937, 34 vols.

Jefferson Correspondence, Bixby   Worthington C. Ford, ed., *Thomas Jefferson Correspondence Printed from the Originals in the Collections of William K. Bixby*, Boston, 1916

Jenkins, *Records*   William Sumner Jenkins, ed., *Records of the States of the United States of America* (Library of Congress and University of North Carolina, 1950)

JEP   *Journal of the Executive Proceedings of the Senate of the United States . . . to the Termination of the Nineteenth Congress*, Washington, 1828

JHD   *Journal of the House of Delegates of the Commonwealth of Virginia* (cited by session and date of publication)

JHR   *Journal of the House of Representatives of the United States*, Washington, Gales & Seaton, 1826-

JS   *Journal of the Senate of the United States*, Washington, Gales, 1820-21, 5 vols.

JSH   *Journal of Southern History*, 1935-

Ketcham, *Madison*   Ralph Ketcham, *James Madison*, New York, 1971

Kimball, *Jefferson*   Marie Kimball, *Jefferson*, New York, 1943-1950, 3 vols.

King, *King*   C. R. King, ed., *The Life and Correspondence of Rufus King, Comprising His Letters, Private and Official, His Public Documents, and His Speeches, 1755-1827*, New York, 1894-1900, 6 vols.

L & B   Andrew A. Lipscomb and Albert E. Bergh, eds., *The Writings of Thomas Jefferson*, Washington, 1903-1904, 20 vols.

L.C. *Cat.*   *A Catalogue of Books Represented by the Library of Congress Printed Cards*, Ann Arbor, 1942-1946; also *Supplement*, 1948-

Library Catalogue, 1783   Jefferson's MS list of books owned or wanted in 1783 (original in Massachusetts Historical Society)

Library Catalogue, 1815   *Catalogue of the Library of the United States*, Washington, 1815

Library Catalogue, 1829   *Catalogue: President Jefferson's Library*, Washington, 1829

Loubat, *Medallic history*   J. F. Loubat, *The Medallic History of the United States of America, 1776-1876*, New York, 1878, 2 vols.

Maclay, *Journal*, ed. Maclay   Edgar S. Maclay, ed., *Journal of William Maclay, United States Senator from Pennslyvania, 1789-1791*, New York, 1890

Madison, *Letters and Other Writings*   James Madison, *Letters and Other Writings of James Madison*, Philadelphia, 1865

Malone, *Jefferson*   Dumas Malone, *Jefferson and his Time*, Boston, 1948-1970, 4 vols.

Mason, *Papers*   Robert A. Rutland, ed., *Papers of George Mason, 1725-1792*, Chapel Hill, 1970, 3 vols.

Mathews, *Andrew Ellicott*   Catharine Van Cortlandt Mathews, *Andrew Ellicott, his life and letters*, New York, 1908

Mayo, *British Ministers*   Bernard Mayo, ed., "Instructions to

the British Ministers to the United States 1791-1812,"
American Historical Association, *Annual Report*, 1936

Mays, *Pendleton*   David John Mays, ed., *Letters and Papers of Edmund Pendleton, 1734-1803*, Charlottesville, 1967, 2 vols.

Miller, *Hamilton*   John C. Miller, *Alexander Hamilton Portrait in Paradox*, New York, 1959

Mitchell, *Hamilton*   Broadus Mitchell, *Alexander Hamilton*, New York 1957, 1962, 2 vols.

MVHR   *Mississippi Valley Historical Review*, 1914-

Notes, ed. Peden   William Peden, ed., *Notes on the State of Virginia*, Chapel Hill, 1955

NYHS, *Quar.*   New-York Historical Society *Quarterly*, 1917-

NYPL, *Bulletin*   New York Public Library *Bulletin*, 1897-

OED   Sir James Murray and others, eds., *A New English Dictionary on Historical Principles*, Oxford, 1888-1933

Padover, *National Capital*   Saul K. Padover, ed., *Thomas Jefferson and the National Capital*, Washington, 1946

Peterson, *Jefferson*   Merrill D. Peterson, *Thomas Jefferson and the New Nation*, New York, 1970

PMHB   *Pennsylvania Magazine of History and Biography*, 1877-

Randall, *Life*   Henry S. Randall, *The Life of Thomas Jefferson*, N.Y., 1858, 3 vols.

Randolph, *Domestic Life*   Sarah N. Randolph, *The Domestic Life of Thomas Jefferson, Compiled from Family Letters and Reminiscences by His Great-Granddaughter*, Cambridge, Mass., 1939

Rowland, *George Mason*   Kate Mason Rowland, *Life of George Mason, 1725-1792*, New York, 1892, 2 vols.

Sabin   Joseph Sabin and others, comps., *Bibliotheca Americana. A Dictionary of Books Relating to America*, N.Y., 1868-1936

St. Clair, *Narrative*   Arthur St. Clair, *A Narrative of the Manner in which the Campaign against the Indians . . . was Conducted . . .* , Philadelphia, 1812

St. Clair, *Papers*   William Henry Smith, ed., *The St. Clair Papers. The Life and Public Services of Arthur St. Clair*, Cincinnati, 1882, 2 vols.

Setser, *Reciprocity*   Vernon G. Setser, *The Commercial Reciprocity Policy of the United States*, Philadelphia, 1937

Shipton-Mooney Index   Clifford K. Shipton and James E. Mooney, comps., *National Index of American Imprints through 1800, The Short-Title Evans*, 1969, 2 vols.

Sowerby   E. Millicent Sowerby, comp., *Catalogue of the Library of Thomas Jefferson*, 1952-1959, 5 vols.

Sparks, *Morris*   Jared Sparks, *Life of Gouverneur Morris*, Boston, 1832, 3 vols.

Swem, *Index*   Earl G. Swem, comp., *Virginia Historical Index*, Roanoke, 1934-1936

Swem, "Va. Bibliog."   Earl G. Swem, comp., "A Bibliography of Virginia History," Virginia State Library, *Bulletin*, VIII (1915), X (1917), and XII (1919)

Syrett, *Hamilton*   *The Papers of Alexander Hamilton*, ed. Harold C. Syrett and others, New York, 1961–, 17 vols.

TJR   Thomas Jefferson Randolph, ed., *Memoir, Correspondence, and Miscellanies, from the Papers of Thomas Jefferson*, Charlottesville, 1829, 4 vols.

Tucker, *Life*   George Tucker, *The Life of Thomas Jefferson*, Philadelphia, 1837, 2 vols.

Turner, *CFM*   F. J. Turner, "Correspondence of French Ministers, 1791-1797," AHA, *Ann. Rept.*, 1903, II

U.S. Statutes at Large   *The Public and General Statutes Passed by the Congress of the United States of America from 1789 to 1836*, edited by George Sharswood. Second edn., Philadelphia, 1837-40, 4 vols.

Van Doren, *Franklin*   Carl Van Doren, *Benjamin Franklin*, New York, 1938

Van Doren, *Secret History*   Carl Van Doren, *Secret History of the American Revolution*, New York, 1941

VMHB   *Virginia Magazine of History and Biography*, 1893-

WMQ   *William and Mary Quarterly*, 1892-

CONTENTS

CONTENTS

CONTENTS

[xxi]

CONTENTS

CONTENTS

CONTENTS

CONTENTS

[xxv]

CONTENTS

CONTENTS

CONTENTS

CONTENTS

ILLUSTRATIONS

Following page 348

JEFFERSON'S DESCRIPTION OF THE NATURAL BRIDGE

Jefferson may have set down this diagram and account of the Natural Bridge when he was in the vicinity in the summer of 1767, but it was not until 1774 that he purchased the tract embracing what he regarded as "the most sublime of Nature's works" (*Notes*, ed. Peden, p. 24). He was probably inspired to do so by the account written by William Carmichael and published in newspapers a few months before he acquired the site. The sketch here reproduced is the earliest known attempt at a delineation of the Natural Bridge, but Jefferson tried several times to induce artists to depict it (see note, TJ to Trumbull, 20 Feb. 1791; TJ's description in *Notes*, ed. Peden, p. 24-5, is based on the data presented in the 1767 Account Book from which this reproduction is made). In 1817 he made the following correction to the manuscript of his *Notes on Virginia*: "This description was written after a lapse of several years from the time of my visit to the bridge, and under an error of recollection which requires apology. For it is from the bridge itself that the mountains are visible both ways, and not from the bottom of the fissure as my impression then was" (MS note dated 16 Aug. 1817, quoted in *Notes*, ed. Peden, p. 263). Jefferson once thought "of building a little hermitage at the Natural Bridge," but he never did (TJ to Carmichael, 26 Dec. 1786). He regarded his ownership of this natural phenomenon as "in some degree a public trust, and would on no consideration permit the bridge to be injured, defaced or masked from the public view" (TJ to Caruthers, 15 May 1815). This was a trust that he held inviolate even in the face of bankruptcy.

PROPOSED SITES FOR THE FEDERAL DISTRICT ON THE UPPER POTOMAC

Sharpsburg. This plat "of Land proposed by the Inhabitants of Washington County [Maryland] in the Neighbourhood of Sharpsburgh to Erect the Federal City on" was submitted to Washington late in 1790 as a result of his tour up the Potomac ostensibly to examine various potential sites for the capital (see p. 22, note 43). But in fact Washington had already made his decision about the location some time before he began his up-river tour of inspection (see Editorial Note and group of documents on the location of the Federal District at 24 Jan. 1791). One of the arguments against placing the capital on tidewater was that it might be exposed to naval attack, as indeed was the case in 1814. But if the site indicated in the Sharpsburg plat had been chosen, lying at the confluence of the Potomac and Antietam Creek, the bloody engagement that followed the invasion of the Army of Northern Virginia into Maryland in 1862 would have occurred at the very seat of the national government.

[xxxi]

ILLUSTRATIONS

Williamsport. This plan of the small village of Williamsport, situated at the mouth of Conococheague Creek which marked the upper limit of permissible sites under the Residence Act of 1790, was submitted to Washington late in 1790 by General Otho H. Williams, who had served with him during the Revolution (see p. 24, note 47). Both this and the Sharpsburg plat are in the Washington Papers in the Library of Congress. (*Courtesy of the Library of Congress*)

WASHINGTON AND JEFFERSON FIX THE BASE POINT FOR THE FEDERAL DISTRICT

The President and the Secretary of State, both experienced surveyors, employed these notes of courses and distances "From the head of the Canal at the Great Falls, to the tail of the Canal at the little Falls" in order to fix the point of beginning of the first of the "lines of experiment" on Hunting Creek below Alexandria and for determining its bearing and extent to the northwest (see Editorial Note to group of documents on the location of the Federal District, at 24 Jan. 1791). The document is in Washington's hand, while the calculation of the distance and course "from the Courthouse in Alexandria" to the lower end of the canal is in that of Jefferson. (*Courtesy of the Library of Congress*)

THE BREACH IN THE GOVERNMENT BECOMES PUBLIC KNOWLEDGE

Although historians generally regard the conflicting opinions of Hamilton and Jefferson on the constitutionality of the Bank Bill as marking the beginning of partisan opposition, the cleavage in the administration—which in fact had long since been a political reality—was not noticed when these two opinions were submitted to Washington. Unpublished at the time, they could not have become the subject of public discussion. This was not the case with the *Report of the Secretary of State, on the subject of the Cod and Whale Fisheries . . . published by order of the Senate* (Philadelphia, John Fenno, 1791). It was that notable document which first publicly revealed to the nation and to the rival European powers that such a division in the cabinet existed and that it was indeed irreconcilable. Jefferson's *Report* was published officially in pamphlet form by Childs & Swaine, surprisingly at the direction of the Senate. What is even more surprising is that Hamilton's ardent supporter, John Fenno, not only published it in the *Gazette of the United States* but also brought it out in pamphlet form (the title-page of the latter is here reproduced from Washington's copy in the Boston Athenæum). This was possibly because Jefferson's defense of the fisheries momentarily obscured for the Senators and for Fenno, as indeed it has subsequently for historians, the real thrust of his argument. This, employing the depressed state of the fisheries as a political instrument, called unequivocally for a navigation act aimed at retaliation against Great Britain's "exparte regulations . . . for mounting their navigation on the ruins of ours" and for establishing "friendly relations towards those nations whose arrangements" were friendly to the United States. Such an argument, couched in unusually blunt language, caused a public sensation on both sides of the Atlantic. There can be little doubt that Jefferson, having failed completely in his appeal to Hamilton to reach an accommodation on the matter of the French protest on the tonnage acts, approved if he did not inspire the fairly extensive reprinting of his *Report*. The attempt by this means to stimulate an informed public discussion of so important an issue as the navigation bill, which he intended to propose at the opening of the Second Congress, was quite characteristic. So, too, was the realistic political strategy by which he, a southern planter, appeared as the champion of an important northern interest. (*Courtesy of the Boston Athenæum*)

PROCLAMATION AGAINST JAMES O'FALLON

James O'Fallon (1749-1794?), native of Ireland, student of medicine at the University of Edinburgh, and agent of the South Carolina Yazoo Company in Kentucky, was an adventurer and intriguer who first courted Spanish favor and then, discredited by James Wilkinson, offered to act as an intelligence agent for the United States. During the winter of 1790 O'Fallon was able to enlist in support of his enterprise the name of that redoubtable figure in western annals, George Rogers Clark, to whom he gave the command of his battalion and whose sister he soon married. But even the knowledge of this fact could not have brought anxiety to the administration, for both Washington and Jefferson were aware that Clark, now an inebriate, had lost the capacity for brilliant leadership he had once possessed (TJ to Innes, 7 Mch. 1791). Although it was known that O'Fallon was "levying an armed force" and suspected that his aim was an offensive mission against territory claimed by Spain, the confidence of the President and Secretary of State that such an adventurer would not be supported by westerners is evidenced by the fact that no action was taken save the issuance of this proclamation and the instruction that prosecutions against O'Fallon not be for treason unless clearly warranted by the testimony (original in DNA: RG 11; endorsed: "Proclamation of the President . . . requiring an observance of his Proclamations of August 14th. & 26th. 1790. Issued the 19th March 1791"). Having collaborated in drafting the opinion of the Attorney General on which this action was based, Jefferson also presumably prepared the text of this proclamation (see Opinion of the Attorney General, 14 Feb. 1791). Although the government had known about O'Fallon's plans at least as early as January, the proclamation was not issued until two weeks after Congress adjourned, another evidence of the absence of any real concern. Also, only fifty copies of the proclamation were issued in broadside form, though it was reprinted in newspapers (Vol. 17: 365). (*Courtesy of the National Archives*)

REPRESENTATIVE JOHN BROWN OF KENTUCKY

While the romantic intrigues of James O'Fallon received at the very outset a well-merited rejection even by such accomplished practitioners of deceit as James Wilkinson, the support given by Kentuckians over a long period of years to John Brown (1757-1837) reflected the confidence of the majority of the electorate in his probity, ability, and character. Well connected with the Prestons, Clays, Breckinridges, and other leading Kentucky families, Brown deserves to be known as the principal architect of his state's admission to the union. Despite the obloquy cast upon him by partisan opponents at the time and too readily accepted by historians since, he was one of the most formidable obstacles to western separatism. Brown was a confidant and respected friend of Jefferson, Madison, Monroe, and other leading southerners. As a student at the College of New-Jersey in 1776, he had joined Washington's retreating army, but Washington remained aloof toward his fellow Virginian, perhaps because, like others who represented the Kentucky District in the Virginia ratifying convention of 1788, he had voted against the Constitution. It has been mistakenly supposed that Brown studied law under Jefferson. He was in fact trained by Jefferson's own preceptor, George Wythe (see Editorial Note, group of documents on the threat of western disunion, at 10 March 1791).

The miniature here reproduced was executed by John Trumbull in 1792, the year that Brown became United States Senator from the new state of Kentucky. (*Courtesy of Yale University Art Gallery*)

INTERACTION OF POLITICS AND LEARNING AT THE DEATH
OF FRANKLIN

Joseph Sansom's Silhouette of Franklin, 1789. "Though Houdon's is as near as we are likely to get, there is still no one, standard Franklin face," wrote that preeminent authority on Franklinian iconography, Charles Coleman Sellers, "and I should like to think that not only the multiplicity of interpretations by the enduring, sensible, ever-various humanity of the man himself created this situation. It is as impossible to sum him up in a single portrait as in an epigram. He cannot be approached with reverence: as some images of the saints of old are said to have responded to their worshipers' adoration with physical movement, so would Franklin's big body have begun to shake with amusement at what was going on. Franklin is not to be worshiped but to be understood, and the portraits are true to him in the measure of their honesty and candor" (Sellers, *Benjamin Franklin in portraiture*, New Haven, 1962, p. 179).

This painted silhouette by Joseph Sansom, executed from life in the last few months of Franklin's life, quite obviously qualifies both for truth and candor. Sansom was twenty-two when he drew the profile of the aged philosopher-statesman, whose appearance in 1789 no doubt was much as Manasseh Cutler had described it a short while before on being introduced to Franklin, surrounded by friends in the garden at Franklin Court: ". . . a short, fat, trunched old man, in a plain Quaker dress, bald pate, and short white locks, sitting without his hat under the [mulberry] tree . . . [who] rose from his chair, took me by the hand, welcomed me to the city, and begged me to seat myself close to him. His voice was low, but his countenance open, frank, and pleasing.

ILLUSTRATIONS

He instantly reminded me of old Captain Cummings, for he is nearly of his pitch, and no more of the air of superiority about him" (Sellers, same, p. 182, citing Cutler, *Cutler*, I, 267-8; see also, Sellers, "Joseph Sansom, Philadelphia Silhouettist," PMHB, LXXXVIII [1964], 395-438). Sansom's sensitive profile was the last likeness of Franklin to be done from life. Within a few months after it was executed, Franklin's death produced panegyrics with political overtones on both sides of the Atlantic, the excesses of which he no doubt would have viewed with the same bemused detachment with which he regarded most human endeavors (see Editorial Note and group of documents, at 26 Jan. 1791). (*Courtesy of The Historical Society of Pennsylvania*)

State-House Square, 1790. This view of the buildings on what is now Independence Square was published in *The Columbian Magazine* for January 1790. On this historic spot there originated in 1791 the eulogies and consequent political repercussions evoked by the death of Franklin, involving the Congress of the United States, the legislature of Pennsylvania, and the oldest of American learned societies that had been founded by Franklin. The building on the left, no longer standing, was that of the Episcopal Academy, not quite finished when this engraving was published. The next, newly remodelled in 1790, was the building in which the Senate and House of Representatives assembled for the final session of the First Congress after the removal of the seat of government from New York. The State-House in the center (Independence Hall) housed the Pennsylvania legislature at this time. To the right of the State-House, the Hall of The American Philosophical Society, just completed and first used for a regular meeting of the officers and members in November 1789, remains the only structure on the Square still used for its original purpose. To the right are shown the Library Company of Philadelphia, a subscription library which Franklin founded in 1731, and Carpenter's Hall, where the first Continental Congress met in 1774. Officials of the federal and state governments, as well as officers and members of The American Philosophical Society, participated in one way or another in the events originating within this city block in 1791 that gave political connotations to the Society's memorial tribute to its great founder. Jefferson's role in these proceedings was undoubtedly more active than the records indicate (see Editorial Note and documents, at 26 Jan. 1791). (*Courtesy of The Boston Athenæum*)

THE SECRETARY OF STATE COMMENDS THE FIRST PUBLICATION OF AMERICAN STATE PAPERS

Jefferson's commendation of Ebenezer Hazard's proposed publication of historical manuscripts and public records was far from perfunctory. From early youth Jefferson himself had been an avid collector of books and manuscripts pertaining to the history of America, and as a young lawyer on the circuits he had transcribed and collected manuscript laws of his native state that might otherwise have perished. Even before the Revolution he had given encouragement and assistance to Hazard (see

ILLUSTRATIONS

Hazard to TJ, 23 Aug. 1774; TJ to Hazard, 30 Apr. 1775; Samuel
Huntington to TJ, 27 Apr. 1781). It is therefore understandable that
his testimonial in support of Hazard's undertaking, written in the knowledge that it would be published, should have emphasized the importance
to the public of collecting, preserving, and publishing historical documents. As he so often did, Jefferson caused what in other hands might
have been a routine acknowledgment to assume timeless verity because
of its assertion of fundamental truths.

A copy of Hazard's *Proposals* in the Library of Congress shows the
broadside as it was printed, without any appended sheet for subscribers'
names. The remarkably interesting copy here reproduced is a scroll to
which Hazard added one blank sheet and part of another to receive the
names of subscribers, with only that of the President being placed on the
broadside itself. It is important to note that, while the original scroll
is intact, measuring 94 by 33.5 cm., the reproduction is here presented
in two parts, being separated at the point where the sheet containing
subscribers' names is attached to the bottom of the broadside. (*Courtesy
of The Historical Society of Pennsylvania*)

Volume 19

24 January to 31 March 1791

JEFFERSON CHRONOLOGY
1743 · 1826

1743.	Born at Shadwell, 13 Apr. (New Style).
1760	Entered the College of William and Mary.
1762	"quitted college."
1762-1767	Self-education and preparation for law.
1769-1774	Albemarle delegate to House of Burgesses.
1772.	Married Martha Wayles Skelton, 1 Jan.
1775-76.	In Continental Congress.
1776.	Drafted Declaration of Independence.
1776-79.	In Virginia House of Delegates.
1779.	Submitted Bill for Establishing Religious Freedom.
1779-81.	Governor of Virginia.
1782.	His wife died, 6 Sep.
1783-84.	In Continental Congress.
1784-89.	In France as commissioner to negotiate commercial treaties and as minister plenipotentiary at Versailles.
1790-93.	U.S. Secretary of State.
1797-1801.	Vice President of the United States.
1801-09.	President of the United States.
1814-26.	Established the University of Virginia.
1826.	Died at Monticello, 4 July.

VOLUME 19
24 January 1791 to 31 March 1791

23 Jan.	Birth of Anne Cary Randolph, his first grandchild
24 Jan.	Proclamation locating Federal District
1 Feb.	Report on whale and cod fisheries
9 Feb.	Lands at Elk Hill advertised for sale
15 Feb.	Opinion on constitutionality of the Bank Bill
21 Feb.	Recommendations on consular vacancies
4 Mch.	Opinion on appointment of Joseph Anderson
10 Mch.	Decision to confront Spain on Mississippi question
15 Mch.	Search for European collaboration on navigation laws
26 Mch.	Experiments in desalination of sea water

THE PAPERS OF
THOMAS JEFFERSON

◅━━━━━▻

Locating the Federal District

EDITORIAL NOTE

The two great questions of funding the debt and fixing the seat of government . . . were always considered by me as questions of the most delicate and interesting nature which could possibly be drawn into discussion. They were more in danger of having convulsed the government itself than any other points.
—*Washington to La Luzerne, 10 Aug. 1790*

In the fall of 1790 competition for the Federal District—the second of three stages in the delicate task of providing a permanent location for the seat of government—stirred enterprizing citizens to activity

[3]

along the entire stretch of the Potomac comprehended in the terms of the Residence Act.[1] From Carrollsburg on the Eastern Branch to Williamsport at the mouth of the Conococheague, merchants, speculators, and landowners manifested an eager desire to serve the public interest and themselves by urging the selection of a site on or adjacent to their own holdings. As many others did during the first stage—for example, Robert Morris, who had hoped the capital would be fixed at Philadelphia, the center of his far-flung business enterprises, and William Maclay, who was ready to give up half of his acreage at Harrisburg

[1] For notes and documents on the first and most crucial stage of the contest over the location of the capital, see Vol. 17: 163-208; 452-72. This first stage, of course, was the culmination of an intermittent conflict that began as early as 1783.

The Editors are indebted to Kenneth R. Bowling for generously sharing his knowledge of the sources on this important question. In his 1968 doctoral dissertation, Bowling accepted in general the account of the assumption-residence compromise of 1790 as given by TJ, but corrected it in important respects ("Politics in the First Congress, 1789-1791," University of Wisconsin). In 1970 Jacob E. Cooke challenged Bowling's modification of the accepted view, going so far as to say that the bargain arranged by TJ, Madison, and Hamilton was not consummated; that the passage of the assumption and residence bills depended upon different negotiations and compromises that did not interconnect the two measures; and that, indeed, if Hamilton made any efforts to assure passage of the residence bill, either in the Senate or the House, he did not succeed ("The Compromise of 1790," WMQ, XXVII [Oct. 1970], 523-45). In a reply rejecting this interpretation, Bowling restated his original thesis in expanded form and, on the basis of fresh information, argued that the compromise TJ and Madison arranged with Hamilton assured passage of the assumption bill, first, by such modifications of its terms as to make it palatable to the South, and, second, in linking it to the residence bill, by preventing such a defeat of the Pennsylvania-Virginia coalition as had occurred in 1789 (Kenneth R. Bowling, "Dinner at Jefferson's . . ."; same, XXVIII [Oct. 1971], 629-40, with a rebuttal by Cooke reaffirming his view, p. 640-8). The Editors find Bowling's modification of TJ's version of the compromise convincing. They also believe that Cooke's interpretation is not sustained by the evidence.

The crucial fact is that the assumption bill could not have been passed had not Lee and White of Virginia and Gale and Carroll of Maryland changed their votes. Bowling, the first to point out that these Congressmen all represented districts lying on the Potomac, was also the first to discover accounts written immediately after consummation of the compromise by two able Congressmen which substantially corroborate TJ's remembered account. Both men—William L. Smith of South Carolina and John Brown of Kentucky, the one an opponent and the other a confidant of TJ and Madison—testified that assumption was passed by this switch in votes. Both gave as the cause the promise of a Potomac location for the capital. Neither mentioned the modification of the assumption bill as a part of the bargain, though it almost certainly was. Smith, whose account was detailed and obviously informed, said that the Senators from Massachusetts prevented defeat of the residence bill—that is, they declined to join in efforts to weaken the majority already available for the Potomac location under the arrangement between Pennsylvania and Virginia. Smith's letter, written to Edward Rutledge and dated 25 July 1790, is quoted by Bowling in WMQ, XXVIII [Oct. 1971], 639. That of John Brown, written to James Brown and dated 11 Aug. 1790, is quoted in another article by him, "The Bank Bill, the Capital City, and President Washington," *Capitol Studies*, I (1972), p. 69, note 1.

The Editors wish to thank Bowling for an early opportunity to read this article, which arrives independently at some of the conclusions set forth in this Editorial Note. Though their interpretations differ in detail, the Editors agree with Bowling that Madison's advice was sought soon after the residence bill was passed, that Washington had already decided upon the site for the Federal District before he left New York, and that the bank bill and the bill to amend the residence act were interconnected in political trading in a way somewhat comparable to the assumption-residence bargaining.

for a like motive—Maryland and Virginia landowners now displayed on a smaller scale the same kind of competition that had characterized the long struggle in Congress among conflicting sectional, local, and individual interests. Once the Federal District became fixed somewhere between the Eastern Branch and the Conococheague, a third and similar contest would ensue among those who dreamed of fortunes to be made from lands owned or bought on speculation at the site where the Federal City would be located and its public buildings erected. The decision as to choice of sites in these last two stages lay with the President. It was therefore to be expected that, under age-old promptings of cupidity, interested individuals would try to penetrate the profound secrecy with which he shrouded his preferences.

I

Washington, long experienced in land negotiations and reserved even with members of his official family, deepened the fog of secrecy by his tour up the Potomac. It has been assumed that the object of this journey, extending from his departure on the 12th of October to his return to Mount Vernon on the 24th, was to make an "examination of what was being done in the improvement of the Potomac by the company he had organized and headed."[2] Washington was indeed deeply interested in the operations of the Potomac Company. But even an ostensible tour of inspection of the works could scarcely have been undertaken at this particular juncture without creating the public impression that its real object was to enable the President to weigh the advantages and disadvantages of all possible sites within the allowable limits of the law. Secrecy as to the ultimate decision was indispensable and disinterested impartiality was what the public expected of Washington. But there is reason to suppose that he deliberately assumed the posture of one engaged in making a considered appraisal of all permissible sites. Even before the President left New York, James Madison—who was also personally interested in the improvement of the upper Potomac—advised that he "inform himself of the several rival positions; leaving among them inducements to bid against each other in offers of land or money."[3] This is precisely the strategy that Washington later employed with respect to the rivalry between the landowners of Georgetown and Carrollsburg, first to excite competition for the prize of the Federal City and then to combine their interests with that of the public, "lest in contending for the shadow they might loose the substance."[4] It was also the strategy that he followed on the journey that took him exactly to the upper limit set by law. This calculated expedition did in fact produce excited speculation that the Federal District might be placed some distance above Georgetown, the most powerful contender for the prize.

It is not surprising that this should have been so. Revolutionary ex-

2 Freeman, *Washington*, VI, 283; the *Maryland Journal and Baltimore Advertiser*, 26 Oct. 1790 (under a Georgetown date-line of the 20th), said that the tour was made "in order to fix upon a proper situation for the Grand Columbian Federal City." On the recent improvements in Potomac navigation, see notes 33 and 146.
3 See Document I.
4 Washington, *Diaries*, ed. Fitzpatrick, IV, 154-5.

perience, particularly in Virginia, had already demonstrated the vulnerability of tidewater cities. Several state capitals had been moved or were about to be moved inland at least to the head of navigation. Thus in the public mind it was by no means a foregone conclusion that the national capital would be fixed at or below that indefinite area commonly known as the fall line. Manasseh Cutler in 1788 had dreamed that the Federal City might eventually be erected on the banks of the Scioto, but this was the talk of a land speculator.[5] Fisher Ames in the debates of 1789 had declared that he would vote for placing it at Pittsburgh if that proved to be in the national interest, but this was merely thrown out in opposition to the Virginia effort to cloak the Potomac site under an appeal to general principles, or what Madison called "luminous truths."[6] During this struggle, in which hidden political coalitions were formed and dissolved and at times exposed in the debates, an "abundance of petitions" from towns far inland such as Carlisle, Lancaster, York, and Reading had been received.[7] The peripatetic experience of Congress during the Revolution had also prepared the public for a location away from tidewater.

But two salient facts, one obvious to all and the other hidden in the murk of political maneuvering, made such a location seem realistic, just, and indeed necessary for the preservation of the expanding union. The first of these was the spectacular trans-Allegheny migration of the preceding five years, an extraordinary movement of people and goods into a region of great fertility and promise. Washington was by no means the only Virginian who saw the Potomac as the best means of tapping the immense resources of the western settlements and connecting them with the seaboard states. But his considerable investment in lands in the upper valley of the Ohio and his awakening interest in commerce in the post-war years made him the most powerful and one of the most zealous advocates of a waterway connection with that region. For the same reason he could not be a disinterested observer of the efforts of James Madison, Henry Lee, and others in 1789 to bring the Federal District to the Potomac. He did in fact lend the immense weight of his influence to theirs more directly than has been supposed.[8]

[5] Cutler's representation is nevertheless revealing: he predicted that within twenty years there would probably be more people on the western than the eastern waters of the United States and that, in consequence, a tract of land would no doubt be set aside "for a federal town that will be central to the whole." He thought this and other legislative measures would be adopted in order to prevent westerners from forming schemes of independence and making connections with other nations ([Manasseh Cutler], *An explanation of the Map which delineates that part of the Federal Lands, comprehended between Pennsylvania West Line, the rivers Ohio and Sioto, and Lake Erie* [Newport, 1788], p. 40). *A Federalist* in the New York *Daily Advertiser*, 3 June 1790, argued that it would be better to have the permanent seat fixed at Marietta than to have the government "everlastingly moving about."

[6] *Annals*, I, 816, 818, 868-9, 870, 872, 873, 874.

[7] *Annals*, I, 819.

[8] Bryan, *National Capital*, I, 105, writes that Washington "took no recorded part in the partisan and sectional struggle"; Freeman, *Washington*, VI, 265, in describing the maneuvers of 1790, states that Washington's relation to legislative proceedings and to the Hamilton-Jefferson bargain was one of "almost monarchical detachment." Madison's full report of the conduct of Morris in 1789 shows how closely Washington kept in touch with the situation (Madison to Washington, 20 Nov. 1789, DLC: Washington Papers).

In the midst of those critical debates Robert Morris had a long talk "with a great Personage," who could only have been the President. At that time, Morris wrote confidently to his wife, the "Grand question for the permanent Residence seems to the Public Eye as if it were fixed on the Susquehanna, but it has yet to go through much Agitation and I still think as before." The great personage was very cautious in expressing himself but, Morris added, "he is much dissatisfied with what is doing in this business and I think not a little Angry at my Agency in it."[9] Washington's anger, pointed enough to be felt, was understandable. For what Madison described later to the President as "the Southern project of an arrangement with Pennsylvania" had been defeated by Morris through a coalition with New Englanders looking toward the location of the Federal District near Trenton.[10] From that time forward Virginians, though well aware that a Potomac site could not be achieved without acquiescence on the part of Pennsylvania, were cautious and skeptical in dealing with the great merchant. Even in 1790 when the coalition with Pennsylvania was revived and resulted in the award of the temporary residence to Philadelphia, the urgency and determination of Washington, Jefferson, and Madison to establish the Potomac location beyond recall reflected their fear that Morris and "the Philadelphia interest" would ultimately nullify the compromise. It was pointed out in the debates that a future Congress might repeal the law and Fisher Ames declared that, while the Pennsylvanians abhorred the bargain with the Virginians, they were "pretty sure of preventing the future removal to the Potomac."[11] In this distrust of Morris and the Philadelphia influence may be found a key to the second and less obvious factor entering into the location of the Federal District.

For after Madison had thwarted Morris in the first session by amending the bill so as to throw it back into the Senate, Virginia strategy proceeded on the assumption that the understanding with Pennsylvania would be revived in the next session but could not be trusted and that, if Virginia and the states farther south stood firm, any move for a location to the eastward of the Susquehanna could be defeated. Several weeks after the end of the session Madison reported to Washington Morris' overture for a revival of the Pennsylvania-Virginia alliance:[12]

> I reminded him of the conduct of his state, and intimated that the question would probably sleep for some time in consequence of it. His answer implied that Congress must not continue at N. York, and that if he should be freed from his engagements with the Eastern States . . . he should renounce all confidence in that quarter, and speak seriously to the Southern states. I told him they must be spoken to very seriously after what had passed, if Pennsylvania expected them to listen to her; that indeed there was probably an end to further intercourse on the subject. He signified that if he should speak it would be in earnest.

[9] Morris to his wife, 9, 11, 15 Sep. 1789; Morris to Francis Hopkinson, 6 Sep. 1789 (CSmH).
[10] Madison to Washington, 20 Nov. 1789 (DLC: Washington Papers).
[11] Brant, *Madison*, III, 277.
[12] Madison to Washington, 20 Nov. 1789 (DLC: Washington Papers).

Madison was certain that this would be done only after Morris had attempted to win over New York and the New England states by holding out Philadelphia and the Potomac as the alternative. The response of New England and New York would be to delay by threatening the South with Trenton, Germantown, or the Susquehanna. That threat, he believed, would be carried into execution rather than "suffer an arrangement to take place between Pennsylvania and the Southern States." The candid and accurate forecast of Morris' strategy in the next session could not have diminished Washington's earlier displeasure.

Such were the prospects from the northward just a fortnight before Virginia ceded an area ten miles square for the Federal District. Hidden in the terms of this timely legislation were hints of a strategy that looked to western Pennsylvania for allies whose regional interests would bind them to a Potomac location with ties more dependable than the sectional intrigues of Robert Morris had proved to be. These terms bear a remarkable resemblance to the resolution offered by Thomas Scott of western Pennsylvania that had opened the debates of 1789. That resolution had declared that "a permanent residence ought to be fixed for the General Government of the United States at some convenient place, as near the center of wealth, population, and extent of territory, as may be consistent with convenience to the navigation of the Atlantic Ocean, and having due regard to the particular situation of the Western country."[13] A few days later, Richard Bland Lee had moved in behalf of the Virginians his resolution of general principles which ended with this passage: "That a place as nearly central as a convenient water communication with the Atlantic Ocean, and an easy access to the Western Territory will permit, ought to be selected and established as the permanent seat of the Government of the United States."[14] This appeal to general principles, as opponents were quick to discern, seemed to point to the westward if not to a particular location. Would such opponents argue, Lee replied, "that our Western brethren are to be disregarded?"

Roger Sherman and others observed that the Lee resolution was essentially the same as that introduced earlier by Scott. Both resolutions had emphasized the fact that the growing West should be reckoned among the factors affecting a position of centrality for the capital and no member of Congress had argued to the contrary. John Vining of Delaware, acknowledging his participation in the Virginia-Pennsylvania alliance, had made this attention to the westerners his central argument for a Potomac site:[15]

I wish the seat of Government to be fixed there, because I think the interest, the honor, and the greatness of this country require it. I

[13] Scott introduced his motion on 27 Aug. 1789; the principal debates took place on 3, 4, 5, and 7 Sep. 1789 (*Annals*, I, 816, 817-21, 867-915).

[14] *Annals*, I, 868-9.

[15] *Annals*, I, 881. Sherman also said Lee's resolution of general principles "selects a place" on a navigable river, whereas some location affording only a land communication might be more just and expedient. Lee, Stone, and Madison stressed the growth of the western settlements, the danger of separation, the need to guard against foreign intrigue, and the fact that the Potomac offered a unique key to the vast resources of the West. Stone, angered by the opposition, flatly predicted that, however the issue was decided in that session, "it will not be long before the seat of Government must be carried thither."

look on it as the centre from which those streams are to flow that are to animate and invigorate the body politic. From thence, it appears to me, the rays of Government will most naturally diverge to the extremities of the Union. I declare that I look on the Western Territory in an awful and striking point of view. To that region the unpolished sons of earth are flowing from all quarters. Men, to whom the protection of the laws, and the controlling force of the Government, are equally necessary.

Apparently there were some even in the environs of Philadelphia who might be trusted to maintain a bargain when the promise of the West was invoked.

It was therefore natural that the Virginia act of cession, coming hard on the heels of the bitter contest in Congress and the distrust engendered by Morris, should have held up to view a western appeal against which none had argued in the debates. The preamble of the act declared that the benefits of government would be best diffused and its operations more prompt and certain by placing it in "such a situation . . . as will be most central and convenient to the citizens of the United States at large, having regard as well to population, extent of territory, and a free navigation to the Atlantic ocean, through the Chesepeake bay, as to the most direct and ready communication with our fellow-citizens in the western frontier." It further pointed out that a situation combining all of these considerations and advantages was to be found "on the banks of the river Patowmack, above tide water, in a country rich and fertile in soil, healthy and salubrious in climate, and abounding in all the necessaries and conveniences of life, where in a location of ten miles square, if the wisdom of Congress shall so direct, *the states of Pennsylvania, Maryland and Virginia may participate in such location.*"[16] The indication of a site above tidewater obviously ruled out Georgetown as a location for the Federal District. But Congress in its wisdom might not scrutinize this restrictive phrase with due regard for its literal meaning. Hence the point was reiterated with unmistakable emphasis. Pennsylvania, Maryland, and Virginia were not merely to enjoy the general diffusion of benefits resulting from a Potomac location. They were actually to participate in a "location of ten miles square." Legislative intent could not have been expressed with greater precision. The carefully chosen language pointed to a single spot on the map.

This explicit phraseology was not accidental. Neither was the glowing tribute to the salubrious climate and the fertile soil. Both came from the pen of Henry Lee, who was allied with James Madison in a speculative venture on the upper Potomac. No one could have been more aware of their interest than the President himself. In 1788 Lee had bought 500 acres at the Great Falls and had invited Madison to join him. Madison, well aware of Lee's fervor in pursuing such objects, sought Washington's advice. The response came immediately and with an optimism matching even that of Lee. If the navigation of the river were fully improved, Washington wrote, all sorts of manufactories would make the place exceedingly valuable; even if the canal improve-

16 MS text of bill, in clerk's hand with insertions in the hand of Henry Lee (Vi); Hening, *Statutes*, XIII, 43-4; emphasis added.

ments from thence to tidewater were not carried out, a town would emerge and the lots would be of great value; and—he added in confidence—the difficulties of canal construction below the Great Falls made the completion of that stretch dubious if not insurmountable. Beyond this, the prospect that this spot would become the funnel through which would pour the commerce from the Shenandoah, from western Maryland and Pennsylvania, and from the waters of the Ohio would open "a field almost too extensive for imagination; and . . . induce the Merchants of Alexandria, George Town and perhaps other places to establish their advanced posts at the Falls to catch the produce on its passage."[17]

This appraisal, sanguine beyond expectation, had given a spur to imaginations already at full gallop. Without telling Lee that he had consulted Washington, Madison met him in Alexandria and the two men quickly came to an understanding. Each of them would take two of the eight shares of the £4,000 venture; they would sell the remainder in Europe in order to raise capital for warehouses and other improvements; and Lee, who already knew Washington's views, would procure a testimonial from him to be sent to Jefferson in Paris. No greater cachet of respectability was obtainable, and Washington promptly gave it. His letter, while avoiding mention of the partners and their aims, actually enlarged upon the radiant vision he had already shared with Madison. Meanwhile, Madison had prepared for European capitalists a prospectus that echoed Washington's glowing words. Besides being such a site for manufactures as could scarcely be imagined, he pointed out, this would become the center for an extensive commerce with the fertile country of the Ohio if not of the lakes beyond. The navigation above was already open, while that below the Great Falls was "not likely to be opened for some time, and on account of its peculiar difficulties, perhaps a long time." If, therefore, proper measures were promptly taken, this site would "have the habit of Commerce in its favour and might be continued as the Entrepôt from causes not otherwise entirely equal to the effect." The undefined measures and the vague allusion to other causes may have referred to nothing more than the inertia of habit and when Lee, forwarding this prospectus and other papers to Jefferson, remarked that "the easy intercourse which this channel of communication affords between the atlantic, and our grow-

---

[17] Lee wrote Madison that the site was valued at £4,000 and had an encumbrance of rentals at £150 per annum (Lee to Madison, 29 Oct. 1788; Madison to Lee, 30 Nov. 1788, DLC: Madison Papers; Madison to Washington, 5 Nov., 2 Dec. 1788, DLC: Washington Papers; Washington to Madison, 17 Nov. 1788, Washington, *Writings*, ed. Fitzpatrick, xxx, 128-31). Lee had suggested that northerners such as Jeremiah Wadsworth and Robert Morris be allowed to join the venture. Madison, unable to command more than £100 or £200, said that he dared not become involved unless "arrangements can be engrafted in the Bargain which will make the bargain contribute itself the means of fulfilling its obligations, and its objects." Clearly the plan to raise additional capital was not merely to provide warehouses and to discharge the encumbrance of accumulated rents, but also to make the speculation itself supply the investment capital that Madison lacked. Before Madison had responded to Lee's invitation but after he had asked Washington's opinion, Lee wrote him again and said the value of the spot was "above present calculation. In this all agree, and no man more highly estimates it than General Washington, who is one of the best judges of property and is intimately acquainted with the place" (Lee to Madison, 19 Nov., 8 and 17 Dec. 1788, DLC: Madison Papers).

ing settlements in the West, will cement the union," he may have had in mind only the bonds of commerce.[18]

But the arguments in Congress that had taken the claims of the western settlements into account had also stressed the unifying effect that a central location for the capital would have. Such arguments for the Potomac had coincided in every respect save one with the promotional appeal that Lee and Madison made to Jefferson in the spring of 1789. That exception—the security enjoyed by a location above tidewater against an enemy attack by sea—was added to stern admonitions given to Madison as soon as news reached the upper Potomac that the question of the permanent seat had arisen. At the time he heard this alarming news, magnified by the threat that the capital might be located on the Susquehanna, Lee was in the Shenandoah valley. He opened his long letter to Madison with a sanguine account of the commerce on the Potomac from Fort Cumberland to their favored site at the Great Falls. The idea of connecting the seaboard with the western settlements, he wrote, had seized the minds of all orders. Men of substance no longer feared that the land of their choice beyond the Alleghenies was severed by nature from the land of their birth. "The discovery recently and universally received," Lee declared, "that the east and the west may and ought to continue members of the same government has done away this bar to emigration, and men respectable in character, family and fortune begin to leave us in every quarter. They go now with the persuasion that we shall continue long to be one people and that the Potomack will strengthen our connexion by the easy exchange it affords of those things mutually wanted. But I believe their reasoning on this subject presumes that the national policy will lend its aid to the accomplishment of this happy event. They consider the fixture of the imperial city on the Potomac as indubitable. Suggestions to the contrary fill every mind with passions indicative of disagreeable consequences to our peace and harmony."

Lee's hint of the possibility of disunion, a threat voiced so often from so many quarters during the debates in Congress and in the public press over the selection of the permanent seat, testified to the strength of the passions this issue had aroused. From the glowing prospects for their site at the Great Falls, Lee now turned to the foreboding consequences of a premature, uninformed, and mistaken choice—that is, a choice falling elsewhere than on the Potomac. His fears mounting as

[18] It should be noted, however, that in all of the debates about the seat of government, from 1783 on, the general if not the universal view was that the capital would also be a center of commerce (draft of Madison's prospectus, undated but after 14 Jan. 1789, DLC: Madison Papers; Madison, *Writings*, ed. Hunt, v, 321-4). Lee had earlier suggested that Madison take George Gilpin's observations and plat of the canal and have them "properly dressed and put into the American monthly magazines"; he added that Madison was "known to some few as part owner of the place" (Lee to Madison, 17 Dec. 1788, 14 Jan., 10 June 1789, DLC: Madison Papers; Lee to Washington, 9 Feb. 1789, DLC: Washington Papers; Washington to TJ, 13 Feb. 1789; Lee to TJ, 6 Mch. 1789; Madison to TJ, 13 June 1789; TJ to Lee, 11 Sep. 1789). During the time that Lee was seeking Washington's intercession with TJ, he was engaged in exchanging 5,000 acres of Kentucky lands, valued at £500, for the President's great stallion, Magnolio (Lee to Washington, 2, 11, 12, and 23 Dec. 1788; 27 Jan. and 6 Feb. 1789, DLC: Washington Papers).

he wrote, he concluded in language unusually blunt to be addressed to so astute and informed a representative as Madison. Lee could not predict what would be the result if the imperial city were not located on the Potomac: [19]

> Perhaps the moderation peculiar to American character would soon get the better of early disgust. But in the present unsettled state of the fœderal government danger is to be apprehended from a discussion of the question concerning the permanent seat. Better would it be in my mind to wait a little longer, let the influence and good of the new constitution be felt among the people, and let the edge of opposition be blunted. No injury can result from delay and much mischief may be done by precipitation. Indeed the public mind ought to be gradually prepared for the event and if possible should go hand in hand with the measure, otherwise discontent and great discontent will ensue, decide as you may.
>
> It is not conceivable to you at a distance, how the inhabitants of the So. Potomac country feel on this subject. I am told their brethren on the north side are if possible more impressed with hopes and fears. Together they form a most respectable body and I really believe are the most wealthy set of husbandmen in proportion to the extent of country within these States. They inhabit a region as delightful and as fertile as bounteous heaven ever gave to man. They enjoy the highest health and are hardy in war and industrious in peace. My thoughts have taken this turn on hearing yesterday that Mr. White was summoned to Congress from a presumption the seat of Government would be fixed. If precipitation or evident trick should be connected with the decision, clamor and mischief will proportionately increase. Carlisle is the most suitable spot in Pennsylvania for the interest of Potomac, if hard necessity should force you to fix in that state.
>
> How happens it that your house should determine to rise on the 22, much important business, essential indeed, not done, and yet this question so full of thorns, so inopportunely introduced, many gentlemen from the south too absent and the union not completed. What will No. Carolina say, the very moment she is about to unite, a matter of the highest consequence is unseasonably determined, for if you rise agreeable to your vote, the decision must be not only unseasonable but puerile.—Already has the hopes of some of the best friends to government abated. Pray be careful how you add to the causes of disgust.

Lee's fears must have been multiplied in conversations with another veteran officer, General Adam Stephen, whom he encountered during the visit of the Lees to the Berkeley springs beyond the Blue Ridge. For four days later, writing from the same place, Stephen restated Lee's arguments in even blunter language and added to this the argument against a tidewater location, mixed with an unconcealed animus against New Englanders. He, too, thought Scott's resolution premature: [20]

[19] Lee to Madison, 8 Sep. 1789 (DLC: Madison Papers).
[20] Adam Stephen to Madison, 12 Sep. 1789 (DLC: Madison Papers).

The Western country is daily moving into greater importance, and many members of Congress are not sensible of its Consequences to the United States. Perhaps until they now met, they never had occasion to bestow a thought upon it. Proper attention to that country is Absolutely Necessary. In time it will give law to America. . . . The Middle States could do better without the Territory to the East of Hudson River, than without the friendship and intimate Coalition with the Inhabitants of the Trans-appalachan Country. . . . In the Cities, and on Tidewater, Commerce, Agriculture, Speculation, pleasure and dissipation Seem to engross the Minds of the People. The Strength and Vigour of the United States lie in the Mountains and to the Westward. Our Coasts are as liable to be insulted and Ravaged as those of the Spaniards were less than a Century ago. . . . For that Reason the Seat of Government . . . is not Safe on Tide Water. . . . If a place that is nearly Central and convenient as can be expected to the Back country is pitched upon, the people have reason to be pleased. In the discussion of this affair we shall discover whether our Confederacy is well or ill combined. It is my Wish that the matter may be postponed to a future day, perhaps till after the next Election, when men will be better acquainted with the General Interests of the rising empire.

The deep-seated sectional bias and the strong hints of disunion voiced by this veteran of frontier and revolutionary battles—one whom Lee must have had in mind when he alluded to those husbandmen who were hardy in war and industrious in peace—revealed in unmistakable terms the feelings of one on the Virginia side of the Potomac. If, as Lee indicated, the brethren on the northern bank entertained even greater hopes and fears, the passions of inhabitants on the upper Potomac ran very deep indeed on this important matter.

But James Madison had no need of such counsels of delay and inaction. He was as greatly alarmed and as apprehensive of the fateful consequences of a premature decision as were his two military friends. He had, in fact, saved the day by adroit parliamentary tactics, thus gaining a brief breathing spell. But the issue would not wait. The time had now come to devise strategy for the next session of Congress against Robert Morris' declared determination to take up immediately on its convening "the Bill *only postponed*."[21] Lee's warning, unnecessary as it was, nevertheless provided an opening for a response that produced an abrupt abandonment of his pleas for postponement. Every circumstance during the altercations in Congress, Madison replied, betrayed "the antipathy of the Eastern people to a south-western position" for the capital:[22]

[21] Daniel Carroll to James Madison, 4 Oct. 1789 (DLC: Madison Papers), reporting that Morris had made this statement to Grayson; he added that "this Idea may possibly be thrown out here [Philadelphia] to brake his [Morris'] fall in this business." Carroll also stated that he and Grayson, believing that the opposition would be at work, thought it would be prudent during the recess of Congress "to have some papers published on the question respecting the permanent Seat of Congress."

[22] Madison to Lee, 4 Oct. 1789 (DLC: Madison Papers); emphasis added.

It can no longer be doubted in my opinion that they view the country beyond the mountains with an eye that will every day see fresh objections against carrying the Government into its neighborhood. I am not able to suppress my apprehensions that some begin already to speculate on the event of seperation of that part of the Union, and if measures be taken on that supposition, they will soon and of themselves realize it. Add to these unfavorable ideas that the presumptive successor to the presiding magistrate has been brought to a vote and an explanation which will render his administration an ominous period for the Potomac. *If a proper decision of the question be attainable, it must be under the auspices of the present Chief Magistrate and by some arrangement with Pennsylvania.* . . . I am extremely alarmed for the Western country. I have within a few days seen fresh and striking proofs of its ticklish situation. Mr. Brown thinks that the Susquehanna would for the present satisfy them on the subject of the seat of government, and in his own judgment prefers it to delay. There are others even from Virginia who could with difficulty be prevailed on to contend for the Potomac, with so little chance of success and against the danger of plans which would be fatal to the harmony, if not to the existence of the union. Several of the more Southern members, tho attached to the object of Virginia, do not view the rival of it precisely with her eyes. I make these remarks for yourself alone, and to prepare you for a disappointment, which I hold to be very possible, but which I shall certainly be among the last to concur in.

Henry Lee received this alarming communication just as he was about to attend the legislature as a member of the House of Delegates. In the light of Madison's forecast of the political realities, he instantly abandoned his impassioned arguments for postponing the issue. One could scarcely call for delay while facing an enemy who had already opened the engagement and who, Madison insinuated in a letter less calculated to prepare Lee for disappointment than to spur him to action, was about to triumph. If such a staunch Virginia Congressman as John Brown of Kentucky would rather see the capital on the Susquehanna than to have the decision postponed, it was obvious that prompt and decisive measures were needed.

The immediate result of Madison's revelations and Lee's newly-aroused fears was the passage of the Virginia act of cession. Now leading the advance instead of holding back, Lee introduced the bill soon after the legislature met. It was referred to a committee of which he was chairman and he reported it the next day.[23] Though there was "considerable opposition from the South side of James river" and from some of the Anti-Federalists, the bill passed without amendment.[24] A week later—the week during which Jefferson arrived in Richmond from France, perhaps soon after Lee received his letter with its dis-

[23] Lee reported the bill on 6 Nov. 1789 and it was passed without amendment (JHD, Oct. 1789, 1827 edn., p. 43, 58, 67, 68, 71, 75, 76, 79, 81, 82, 86, 99; MS bill in clerk's hand, with insertions in Lee's hand, in Vi; John Dawson to TJ, 17 Dec. 1789).

[24] John Dawson to James Madison, 17 Dec. 1789 (DLC: Madison Papers).

couraging news that not even the weight of Washington's name could raise capital in Europe for Potomac improvements[25]—the General Assembly added a more substantial inducement for the choice of a Potomac site by pledging $120,000 for public buildings in the Federal District and by inviting Maryland to make a like contribution of at least three-fifths of this amount. The sense of urgency behind both measures is revealed in the directive to Governor Randolph to transmit this resolution to the General Assembly of Maryland "without Delay."[26] John Dawson, who had kept in touch with Madison during the proceedings both in New York and in Richmond, gloomily expressed the fear that the money would never be demanded.[27] The disappointment which Madison had predicted might yet become a reality. But Henry Lee, the most zealous advocate of an up-river location, had exerted himself promptly, vigorously, and with as substantial a bulwark against such an eventuality as could be devised.

The ultimate decision, so Lee's statute declared, lay in the wisdom of Congress. But Madison was closer to reality when he said that a proper decision would have to be made "under the auspices of the present Chief Magistrate." Thus, while spurring Lee on to achieve legislative aids and inducements, Madison at the same time employed a very different kind of strategy with the President. This took the form of a letter recounting his conversations with Robert Morris, the general tenor of which could only have heightened Washington's earlier displeasure over the intrigues of the Senator from Pennsylvania. In this calculated brief it would have been presumptuous to include such a preparation for disappointment as Madison had given Henry Lee. But it was necessary to impress upon the President the fact that Morris was disappointed over his recent defeat, that he was determined to "call up the postponed Bill as soon as Congress should be reassembled," and that, despite his professed desire to keep alive "the Southern project of an arrangement with Pennsylvania," he was not worthy of Virginia confidence. Such a warning was as far as a prudent adviser dared go in approaching the indispensable source of a proper decision. But, coming so soon after Madison had won a narrow victory by parliamentary tactics, this warning was made all the more forceful by his open hint that in the coming session such a defense might be the only reliance against Morris' determination:[28]

I observed to him [Madison wrote] that if it were desirable to have the matter revived we could not wish to have it in a form more likely to defeat itself. It was unparliamentary, and highly inconvenient; and would therefore be opposed by all candid friends to his object, as an improper precedent, as well as by those who were opposed to the object itself: And if he should succeed in the Senate,

25 TJ to Lee, 11 Sep. 1789. TJ arrived in Richmond on 5 Dec. 1789, two days after the Virginia act of cession was passed, and left there on the 10th, the day the joint resolution pledging funds for the public buildings was adopted.
26 Beverley Randolph to the Governor of Maryland, 16 Dec. 1789, enclosing the act of cession of 3 Dec. and the joint resolution of 10 Dec. 1789 (Vi).
27 John Dawson to James Madison, 17 Dec. 1789 (DLC: Madison Papers).
28 Madison to Washington, 20 Nov. 1789 (Dft in DLC: Madison Papers; RC in DLC: Washington Papers).

the irregularity of the proceeding would justify the other House in withholding the signature of its Speaker, so that the Bill could never go up to the President. He acknowledged that the Bill could not be got through unless it had a majority of both Houses on its merits. Why then, I asked, not take it up anew? He said he meant to bring the gentlemen who had postponed the bill to the point, acknowledged that he distrusted them, but held his engagements binding on him, until this final experiment should be made on the respect they meant to pay to theirs.

Coupled with Madison's astute prediction of the strategy of the opposition and his assumption that a Potomac site could not be assured without the cooperation of Pennsylvania, this confident assertion that the "final experiment" between Morris and the northeastern states could easily be defeated on parliamentary grounds is scarcely convincing. Had the confidence been well-founded, there would have been no need to mention the matter, much less to describe this strategy of defense in such explicit terms. The real meaning could not have been lost on the President. Champions of a Potomac site in the House of Representatives would need a much safer defense in the coming session than the parliamentary device of having the Speaker withhold his signature.

But what Madison did not say reveals far more than his actual words. He left the President with the impression that Senator Grayson and others had confirmed his account of Morris' threat. This was true, but the statement withheld all else in Grayson's report. After conversing with Morris and others, Grayson had said that the conduct of the Pennsylvania delegation was much reprobated in Philadelphia; that "the real sentiments of Morris & Co." were as favorable to Virginia as could be wished; that the Pennsylvanians feared their own weakness, counted on the loss of three votes from South Carolina with certainty, and were doubtful of others; that Thomas Scott thought the Pennsylvania delegation was so irritated as to be willing to "go unconditionally to Potowmack by way of spiting N. York"; and that Thomas McKean, Benjamin Rush, and other leading Philadelphians thought that the Potomac was "a marvelous proper place," required by the good of the union. Grayson had concluded: "our contest about the Potowmack has been of infinite consequence; she is gaining friends daily, by being brought into view; and I agree with you that we played a great game and staked nothing. I would now (though never before) bet her against the field." He thought that the proper strategy for Virginia would be to "play the Precieux, and hold out the idea of *nolo episcopari*—but in such a manner as not to discourage advances. Our great danger is in stirring the subject, and frightening the Yankees into measures which (if left to themselves) they abhor: when we strike it should be in full conviction of success."[29]

But Madison had no intention of adopting such a strategy of confidence and coquetry. He therefore concealed Grayson's optimistic report, conveying to Washington only Morris' threat. By such suppression of the overly confident opinion and by giving warning of Morris'

[29] William Grayson to Madison, 7 Oct. 1789 (DLC: Madison Papers); the allusion is to Molière's *Les Précieuses ridicules*.

intentions, Madison clearly intended to prompt the President to let his influence be felt in the next session. But his real fear came from the West, not from Robert Morris. He revealed to Lee, but not to Washington, that he was "extremely alarmed for the Western country." He had full reason to know how restive John Brown and the Kentuckians were over such matters as the closed navigation of the Mississippi, the inadequacy of federal measures for frontier defense, and the long-pending question of Kentucky's admission to the union. In western eyes, these problems were now becoming intolerable. If Brown pressed for an early settlement of the residence question and preferred the Susquehanna to further delay, hope for the Potomac might well vanish forever. Thus the issue of the location of the permanent capital attached itself to the grave threat of western separation, just as it had for so long become enmeshed in almost all major questions. In Madison's alarm over the situation in the West, therefore, may be found the origins of his rejection of counsels of delay and stratagems of expediency. By frightening Lee, by subtly forewarning Washington, by preventing defeat through adroit parliamentary maneuvering in 1789, and by boldly planning for the contest of 1790 in an acute understanding of the requirements for victory, Madison became the foremost strategist in the organized campaign that ultimately placed the capital on the Potomac.

When the issue was joined in the summer of 1790, the uneasy alliance between Virginia and Pennsylvania held firm under the compromise that was initiated by Hamilton, made possible by Jefferson's good offices, and carried through with Madison's influence and the crucial switch of four Virginia and Maryland Congressmen from opposition to support of the assumption bill. Robert Morris, busy at his intrigues, was prudently absent when Pierce Butler introduced a new bill, had it referred to a committee composed with a single exception of southern Senators, and promptly brought in a report recommending that the permanent seat be located "on the eastern or northeastern bank of the Potomac."[30] In the Senate debates on the 28th of June the range of choices on the Potomac was defined for the first time as lying "between the Eastern branch and the Connococheague."[31] Three days later Oliver Ellsworth moved that these words be deleted and that "within thirty miles of Hancock Town" be substituted.[32] In this amendment—which failed like all others, save one permitting the President to borrow up to $100,000 for the erection of public buildings—one catches a glimpse of the spot to which Henry Lee's carefully chosen language in the Virginia act of cession clearly pointed. In the House, Richard Bland Lee, opposing Roger Sherman's motion to strike out the Potomac location and substitute Baltimore, declared that that city was as far southward "as *the place proposed*, besides being exposed by its frontier position on the sea." This, too, called attention to a precise location well

[30] *Annals*, I, 1017, 1019; JS, I, 148, 149. Butler's report was brought in on 8 June 1790; the vote was a tie and Adams broke it by voting against the report (*Annals*, I, 1022; JS, I, 152).

[31] *Annals*, I, 1032-3; JS, I, 167.

[32] Maclay, *Journal*, ed. Maclay, p. 313, names Ellsworth as the one who offered the motion; *Annals*, I, 1039; JS, I, 173.

above the tidewater vicinity of Georgetown. Moreover, Lee declared, "we are not confined . . . to a particular spot on the Potomac; we may fix it on a spot as far north as the gentleman from Connecticut wishes." Lee then "referred to a map of the Potomac and the adjacent country which lay on the table, and which had been sent from the Executive of the State of Virginia."[33]

This map cannot be identified and probably is not extant, having no doubt been lost along with most of the papers of the First Congress. It is plausible to suppose that it was a copy of Jefferson's *A Map of the Country between Albemarle Sound and Lake Erie* that he had caused to be engraved in London in 1787, since this was the most recent and most accurate map of Virginia and the middle states and since copies of it were readily available in Richmond.[34] But there can be no doubt about the geographical area to which Richard Bland Lee pointed. His own district lay on the upper Potomac.[35] He was also one of those substantial planters to whom his brother Henry Lee had referred in his urgent letter to Madison. He had indeed been the bearer of that plea for postponment and in 1789 he no doubt shared with others on both sides of the river the hopes and fears that it expressed. Now he was not only a spokesman for the Potomac location and for the interests of the author of the Virginia act of cession that were so closely identified with his own: he had also been one of the principal figures in the bargain for votes arranged by Hamilton, Madison, and Jefferson. He must have directed Roger Sherman's attention to a spot on the map well above tidewater, farther upstream even than the mouth of the Conococheague. For the fact is that the only site on the Potomac in which the states of Pennsylvania, Maryland, and Virginia could actually participate in the location of the Federal District as defined with such

[33] Emphasis added; *Annals*, II, 1716, 1718-19. The map (see note following) may have been among some unidentified "papers . . . to be presented to the view of the fœderal Legislature" that Gov. Beverley Randolph sent to the Virginia delegation on 29 Jan. 1790 (Vi). These papers also included the report of Thomas Johnson, president of the Potomac Company, stating that navigation on the Potomac was "now constantly performed by Batteaux of ten tons burthen, and upwards . . . to the Great Falls, within nine miles of Tide Water" (Thomas Johnson to Gov. Randolph, 16 Jan. 1790, enclosing printed statements of merchants of Alexandria and Georgetown concerning navigation and distances on tidewater, CVSP, V, 99). The French chargé reported to Montmorin that a resolution of the Virginia legislature had "again fanned the fire which was on the point of going out" and had transmitted a plan to make the Potomac navigable (Otto to Montmorin, 12 Jan. 1790, WMQ, XXI [July 1964], 415). John Dawson had already sent Madison copies of the act of cession and of the resolution pledging funds for public buildings (Dawson to Madison, 17 Dec. 1789, DLC: Madison Papers). It is clear, therefore, that, under Madison's leadership, the whole strength of Virginia was mobilized for the coming struggle.

[34] As he passed through Richmond on his way to assume office in 1790, TJ deposited with Augustine Davis 69 copies of this map to be sold. The map was also available in some copies of *Notes on Virginia* that TJ had earlier distributed to friends in Virginia, of which 57 copies had been sent to Alexander Donald, 40 of them for sale (TJ to Donald, 17 Sep. 1787; TJ to Madison, 17 Sep. 1787; Coolie Verner, "Mr. Jefferson Distributes his *Notes*," NYPL, *Bulletin*, LVI [Apr. 1952], 159-86).

[35] Kenneth R. Bowling has pointed out that Lee and White of Virginia and Gale and Carroll of Maryland represented the four districts lying along that part of the Potomac designated by Congress (WMQ, XXVIII [Oct. 1971], 634). Lee's home, "Leesylvania," was in Loudoun county.

precision in the Virginia act of cession was one centered on the little town of Hancock, hard by the Pennsylvania boundary, lying strategically at a meeting of lines of communication that afforded easy access by land into the heart of Pennsylvania and by water between the tidewater cities and the western settlements. For a century and more Indian warriors and emissaries, passing along the Tuscarora Path between the northern and southern provinces, had branched off a few miles above this place to visit the nearby warm springs. For more than a generation Scots-Irish and Germans from Pennsylvania had moved past this junction into the valley of the South Branch. Now hundreds of French immigrants, joined to far greater numbers of English farmers from the seaboard and piedmont, were passing this Potomac crossroads on their way to the Ohio Valley. Political strategy and personal interests may have caused the Virginia act of cession to point unequivocally to this spot, but nature had indeed made it a plausible as well as an inviting seat for the capital of a rising empire.

Richard Bland Lee could have been no stranger to the intent of the law drafted by his brother. In saying to Roger Sherman that the capital might be placed as far northward on the Potomac as the gentleman from Connecticut desired, he may even have been insinuating that an amendment extending the limits north of the Conococheague would be welcomed. Such an amendment as that offered in the Senate which confined the permissible choices within a thirty mile radius of Hancock would have been in accord with the Virginia act of cession. But, however much he may have desired it, Lee himself could not offer such an amendment. Bound by the bargain to which he was pledged, he could go no farther upstream than the Conococheague, unable even to counter the ridicule of New Englanders who found the Indian name ludicrous but might have been silenced by that of Hancock. For on this volatile issue defenders of the Potomac interest, who possessed even with the Pennsylvania-Virginia alliance only a bare majority in either house, dared not bring forth any amendment. All such attempts by others were voted down by the coalition with immovable intransigence. Congress in its wisdom had not gone all the way to the junction of national pathways at Hancock, but it had gone a long distance toward it. Conococheague, too, was at a junction of lines of communication running north into the heart of Pennsylvania, south into the Shenandoah valley, east to the tidewater, and west beyond the Alleghenies. Above all, it was up-river from the Great Falls. The threat to a manufacturing and commercial metropolis at that place, so it appeared to Madison, would come only from an entrepôt—or a national capital—located below on tidewater. Richard Bland Lee thought, mistakenly, that his shift on the issue of assumption would cause his defeat at the next election. But if he took comfort in the supposition that Conococheague augured well for his brother's dreams, he was no less mistaken.[36]

Such confidence would have been natural. The Virginia act of cession and the debates in Congress had exhibited such strong sentiment against a tidewater location and in favor of the claims of the western settlements as to give rise to newspaper reports, even in England, that

[36] Lee to TJ, 19 Aug. 1790.

a site "in the neighbourhood of Shepherd's Town for the permanent seat of the federal government" had already been decided upon and announced.[37] Nowhere were such expectations more keenly felt or more actively pursued than on both sides of the river in that area to which Virginia legislators expressly hoped their offer of jurisdiction and of funds would apply. It is not surprising, therefore, that the prosperous husbandmen, merchants, and artisans of the upper Potomac should have welcomed the President on his tour of inspection with banquets, illuminations, bonfires, and the ringing of bells. Nor is it surprising that, even in the midst of the glowing tributes, Washington should have betrayed his well-founded apprehension that the permanent seat of government on the Potomac might, after all, prove to be only the temporary residence. At Hagerstown he proposed to the assemblage this toast, revealing nothing about his preferred site but much about his continuing anxiety: "The River Patowmac. May the residence law be perpetuated and Patowmac view the Federal City."[38] The fear would persist even after the Federal City had been laid out and the public buildings erected.

II

Henry Lee, Adam Stephen, and other advocates of a location for the Federal District at or above the Great Falls could not, of course, bring to bear upon the President such bluntly expressed arguments as they had given to Madison in 1789. But their cause could be and was so pointedly sustained in the public press before and during Washington's inspection of the rival sites as to raise the question whether Henry Lee and his brother were among the anonymous writers. Certainly they could have applauded the correspondent of the *Maryland Journal and Baltimore Advertiser* who, in calling for a location above tidewater, argued that Baltimore was not suitable for the permanent seat because

[37] William Gordon to George Washington, 31 Jan. 1791 (DLC: Washington Papers); Gordon thought one advantage of such a location would be that, because of the falls beyond Shepherdstown, reservoirs for fire protection and sewage disposal could be erected upstream from the capital; among his other interesting suggestions was the following: "The securing of original records and state papers being of the utmost consequence, might it not be proper to have the apartments destined for them, at a distance from all other buildings; and so constructed as to be in no danger of suffering by fire, water, damps, or other enemies?" The public expectation in Virginia is also reflected in the fact that James Monroe, writing from Charlottesville shortly after the Residence Act was passed, said it was reported there that "the subject of residence . . . has terminated in favor of the headwaters of the Potowk." (Monroe to TJ, 26 July 1790).

[38] *Washington Spy* (Hagerstown), 21 Oct. 1790, quoted in Bryan, *National Capital*, I, 112. Serious attempts to move the capital were made throughout the next quarter of a century. In 1808 Representative James Sloan of New Jersey moved that the capital be transferred to Philadelphia because the experience of fifteen years had proved the Potomac plan to be "absurd, extravagant, and hopeless" ([James Sloan], *Reasons offered to the consideration of the citizens of the United States, in favor of the removal of the Seat of Government . . . to Philadelphia*, [Washington, 1808]). Representative Jonathan Fisk of New York made a similar proposal in 1814 after the burning of Washington (William Barlow, "Jonathan Fisk's Attempt to Relocate the Nation's Capital," NYHS, *Quar.*, LIII [Jan. 1969], 64-7).

it was too remote from the western settlements and lay too much exposed to attack from the sea:[39]

> By moving farther up the Potomac, that thoroughfare to the western region, the situation will be more healthy, it will add to the cultivation of an extensive, fertile, and populous country, and it will be more accommodated to our fellow-citizens west of the mountains and more so to almost one half of Pennsylvania, than if the seat of government was at Philadelphia. . . . Mr. [Ædanus] Burke [of South Carolina] is requested to attend to a sketch of the country which he designated a wilderness.
>
> Within four or five miles of Conegocheague is Hagers-Town, with twelve or eighteen stores and some manufactures: within ten miles down the river is Shepherds-Town and Sharpsburg with as many stores: within twelve miles farther southwest is Martinsburg with ten stores in it: within twenty-four miles northeast is Chambers-Town, the capital of Franklin County: within thirty-four miles southwest is Winchester, in which is sold about 80,000 pounds sterling worth of goods annually.—Within fourteen miles of Conegocheague there are upwards of thirty pair of bur mill stones employed in manufacturing wheat: within the same distance there are four furnaces and three forges for making iron.

The sectional bickering which produced the legal requirement that the capital be placed on the Maryland side of the river did not preclude the possibility that the Federal District could be located partly on both sides. This, in fact, was made logical if not obligatory by the terms of the Virginia and Maryland acts. Thus the up-river promotional activity was intense in both states, being at times carried on in collaboration. The tiny village of Shepherdstown, twelve miles above Harper's Ferry, was denied the hope of becoming the Federal City because it lay on the Virginia side of the Potomac. But just across the river to the northeast was the small settlement of Sharpsburg. Leading citizens of both towns met Washington on his tour of inspection and he made known his readiness to receive offers of land and money, just as he had encouraged such pledges from landowners in the vicinity of Georgetown. He also requested Colonel William Darke and Captain Joseph Chapline to have a plat made of the lands lying between Sharpsburg and the Potomac. Subscription forms were accordingly circulated in the neighborhood of that place and within a few weeks after Washington's appearance, donations of 475 acres of land on the Maryland side between Antietam Creek and the Potomac had been pledged, together with subscriptions amounting to $4,839 payable in eight annual instalments.[40] Individuals in and about Shepherdstown, of course, offered no donations of land but they were active in pledging funds. "The late visit of our illustrious president," one of the promoters declared in a public appeal, "encour

[39] 24 Sep. 1790, quoted in Bryan, *National Capital*, I, 108; Otho H. Williams, a Baltimore advocate of a location at the mouth of Conococheague, may have inspired this piece.

[40] Henry Bedinger and William Good to Washington, 1 Dec. 1790 (DLC: Washington Papers); for donations of lands, see illustration of plat in this volume.

ages a hope that the permanent seat of the federal government will be fixed opposite to this town on the Maryland shore and one half of the ten mile square will be located in Virginia.—This event will, however, depend much on donations from the inhabitants to defray the expenses of the federal buildings, especially as the president has informed us large offers have been made at other places on the Potomac. . . . Our friends in Maryland are making every possible exertion to effect this important purpose, and as the inhabitants in the Virginia part of the valley will be equally benefited, they request our cordial concurrence and aid."[41] Within a few weeks after Washington's visit, Virginians in and about Shepherdstown had pledged $20,662 toward the cost of the public buildings.[42]

Unavoidable accident, the Sharpsburg leaders informed the President, had prevented them from completing the plat of land that he had requested. However, if he could "with propriety postpone the decision . . . a few days," it would enable them "to shew at one View the situation and Donations in Lands." Early in December the plat, laid out in accordance with Washington's directions, was forwarded to the President. He was informed that no alterations in the pledges of money had taken place, that there had been a small but advantageous shift in the donations of land, and that the ascertainable prices of land in the vicinity had been recorded on the plat. But the next day there was disclosed the significant fact that a new clause in the Shepherdstown subscription form had been added to that previously shown to him. The revised form, which agreed in substance with that employed on the Maryland side, declared that the pledges had been made "Expressly on . . . Condition that the Town of McLinburg allias Sheapheards be included in the district and that the Federal Seat of Government be Located on any of the Lands between Thomas Sheapheards plantation and Capt. Joseph Chaplines Mansion."[43] All of these lands, donated principally by Joseph and Jeremiah Chapline, lay along the road between Sharpsburg and the ferry leading to Shepherdstown. Thus, through the collaboration of these towns on opposite sides of the Potomac and by the explicit terms of their pledges there emerged the real possibility, so it seemed, that the terms of the Virginia act of cession calling for a site above tidewater might be honored.

Nor were these the only overtures that Washington felt it expedient to encourage on his tour up the river. At the extreme upper limit of choices the infant town of Williamsport set forth its pretensions to future glory. Its founder, General Otho H. Williams, had served with

[41] *Gazette of the United States*, 27 Nov. 1790 (with Shepherdstown date-line of 5 Nov.), quoted in Bryan, *National Capital*, I, 114. There had been offers of land at Georgetown but, so far as known, no individual pledges of money. The equivocal expression about "large offers" that had been made at other places on the Potomac, though attributed to Washington, may have been that of the newspaper to encourage pledges of money. Even so, the donations up-river were far more impressive than those below.

[42] Henry Bedinger and William Good to Washington, 1 Dec. 1790 (DLC: Washington Papers).

[43] Same; Joseph Chapline and William Good to Washington, 4 and 5 Dec. 1790 (DLC: Washington Papers), enclosing plat in the former (see illustration in this volume) and at the head of the latter the text of the revised subscription form dated "Berkley County Novr. 1790."

repute during the whole of the Revolution. Deeming him "a sensible man, but not without vanity," Washington had appointed him collector of the port of Baltimore and had also sought his counsel in respect to other appointments.[44] In 1787, under authority granted by the Maryland legislature, Williams had laid out the town of Williamsport at the mouth of the Conococheague where he was a landowner and where he had spent most of his youth. When Washington arrived there in 1790 the rectangular plan of the town and its streets eighty feet in width were more discernible on the surveyor's plat than on the terrain.[45] About the 19th of October General Williams' brother had an interview with the President, who again indicated his readiness to receive offers of land and money. Williams himself arrived on the scene the next day. Immediately thereafter a handbill signed *An Inhabitant* was circulated in Washington county, its style and circumstances revealing beyond doubt that the collector of the Port of Baltimore was the author. "The Residence Act and the recent visit of the President," the handbill declared,[46]

encourage the Citizens of Washington County to hope that the Seat of the Federal Government will be located therein; And while the Citizens of other Counties on the Patowmack, have the same expectations, and will probably contribute considerably towards the construction of the necessary buildings, an inhabitant of Washington County invites his Country-men to make similar exertions. Partial or limited conditions annexed to a Subscription on this occasion, would divide the interest of the County into so many parts, favouring particular places, as to render the amount of any one of the Subscriptions of small consideration; He therefore recommends that the only condition to be annexed be 'that the permanent Seat of the Federal Government be located by the President in Washington County. . . .'

Concealed behind the flawed pseudonym, Williams called upon the real inhabitants of the county to meet on November 3 at Hagerstown, Williamsport, Sharpsburg, or Hancock to appoint proper persons to receive subscriptions. The annexed form hinted at the order of sums expected by showing that "A*** B***" had pledged $1,000. No mention was made of soliciting subscriptions among Virginians on the opposite bank of the river, but the form explicitly set forth the condition mentioned in the handbill.

General Williams sent a copy of the handbill to the President, together with the surveyor's plat of the town of Williamsport. He thought that all property owners ought to contribute lands on an equitable basis, but because of the difficulty of achieving this he announced his intention to promote legislation by Maryland "to appropriate to Congress, a district of ten miles square, in either of the Counties bounding on the river Patowmack, and between the eastern branch and Conoco-

44 Washington's "Opinion of the General Officers," 9 Mch. 1792 (Washington, *Writings*, ed. Fitzpatrick, XXXI, 512); Williams to Washington, 18 Apr., 5 and 14 July 1789; Williams to David Humphreys, 12 May 1789 (DLC: Washington Papers).
45 See illustration in this volume.
46 Printed handbill, Hagerstown, 26 Oct. 1790 (DLC: Washington Papers).

cheague creek; And to condemn and grant to Congress   acres of Land any where within the said District that the President of the United States will please to accept for the purpose of erecting public edifices and building a City," the cost of lands so condemned to be borne by an equitable apportionment among all citizens of the district. Williams had no desire to know the President's determination before it was communicated to Congress, he wrote, but he thought the Residence Act ambiguous. The policy of requiring private contributions did not accord with his ideas of public justice and the dignity of government. Yet he had stimulated the citizens of Washington county to exert themselves and he thought no terms more liberal than those set forth in the handbill could be obtained. Even so, he offered his own lands on the river or in Williamsport without compensation if no legislation on general principles should be adopted. "The town, although small," he concluded, "is upon a large scale, the streets, and alleys, being wider than common: and it is so disposed that it may be extended by the same lines, over the most suitable grounds in the vicinity to a great distance."[47]

But Williams' promotion of legislation granting power to condemn was scarcely needed. Maryland had already in 1788 offered to cede jurisdiction over a ten mile square, Jefferson had anticipated the need for powers of condemnation, and Daniel Carroll was the channel through which the administration handled this and other matters involving the Maryland legislature.[48] The inhabitants of Washington county had also proved themselves to be more liberal in donating land than Williams had supposed they would be. His hopes for his bantling town were soon dashed by competition from Sharpsburg and Shepherdstown. In addition, another location at the mouth of the Monocacy advanced its modest claims, being one of the "three plats of different parts on the Potomac" that the President had ordered to be laid out.[49] Thus, to a greater degree than has been supposed, inhabitants of the upper Po-

---

[47] Williams to Washington, 1 Nov. 1790; Williams to Francis Deakins, 8 Nov. 1790 (DLC: Washington Papers). A petition from Washington county, Maryland, asking the legislature to cede a district of ten miles square for the seat of government appeared in Bache's *General Advertiser*, 9 Nov. 1790.

[48] See TJ's report to Washington, 14 Sep. 1790 (Vol. 17: 462); proposals for legislation conveying the power of eminent domain also came from others who reported to Washington that, "as like difficulties occur at almost every probable place on the River . . . no doubt such a law will pass . . . there being a disposition in the majority of both Houses to promote the residence on Patowmack" (William Deakins, Jr. and Benjamin Stoddert to Washington, 9 Dec. 1790, DLC: Washington Papers). The Maryland act granting power to condemn was passed on 22 Dec. 1790.

[49] Francis Deakins, sending Washington a plat of the terrain about Monocacy and a list of those offering lands for public use, expressed "faint expectation of its possessing superior advantages to any other place" and spoke apologetically of the modest pledges of support (Francis Deakins to Washington, 12 Nov. 1790; William Deakins, Jr. to Washington, 18 Nov. 1790, DLC: Washington Papers). This anticipation of disappointment, perhaps reflecting private hints derived from his brother, distinguishes Deakins' effort from the vigorous promotion carried on by Williams and other up-river property owners. It was reported in the *Maryland Journal and Baltimore Advertiser*, 16 Nov. 1790, that Washington had "ordered three plats of different parts on the Potomac to be laid out." Bryan, *National Capital*, I, 115, identifies these as being in the vicinity of Conococheague, Monocacy, and Georgetown; but the three places indicated by the paper were perhaps the first two of these and the lands about Sharpsburg.

tomac exerted themselves with vigor as well as liberality. Washington was obliged to listen to them and even to encourage them. He would perhaps have had to do this if the journey up the Potomac had never been undertaken. Once it became public knowledge that he had welcomed offers of land and money in the vicinity of Georgetown, he had no choice but to extend this welcome to rival sites from Carrollsburg to Conococheague. Moreover, given the widespread public interest and the importance of the decision to any landowner fortunate enough to have possessions within the ten mile square, such enterprising men as General Williams and Captain Chapline would doubtless have come forward with proposals in any case.

But the strategy that Washington had adopted posed a serious difficulty. While it was generally expected that he would announce the choice of site in his annual message and while his own sense of urgency in getting the Federal City established called for as little delay as possible in announcing the decision, his silence on the topic at the opening of Congress was unavoidable. Having encouraged offers of land and money from Virginians and Marylanders all the way to the mouth of the Conococheague, he naturally could not proclaim the location of the Federal District until their responses had been received. Washington was not only obliged to postpone the announcement for several weeks after Congress convened: he was also bound even in his proclamation to sustain the appearance of having made the decision only after "duly examining and weighing the advantages and disadvantages of the several situations within the limits" prescribed by the law.[50] This is undoubtedly what Congress expected him to do.

Another conspicuous silence in the documents describing this eager competition on the upper Potomac—the letters, the handbills, the petitions, the town plats, and the reports in the press—is that of Henry Lee, theretofore the most vigorous advocate of a site above tidewater. Only ten months earlier he had given this purpose the stamp of law, not binding upon the President to be sure but creating a strong presumption that such an unequivocal expression of preference by Washington's native state would be weighed in the balance. Now, however, while Williams, Chapline, and others were busily urging their claims upon the President, there was no trace of such activity on the part of Lee. It is scarcely plausible to suppose that this was because the foremost leader in the movement for an up-river location had abandoned his former position or had become a minor and hidden participant in the efforts of others. It is still less so to suppose that he had suddenly abandoned his dream of a metropolis at the Great Falls, despite his failure to raise capital in Europe or to borrow it in America. But Lee's impressive silence during the clamor in the fall of 1790 does suggest that, unlike those who accepted the President's tour of inspection as a genuine attempt to weigh the advantages and disadvantages of the various sites, he had penetrated the reality of the situation and had drawn the obvious conclusion. Through his brother's connection with Madison and Jefferson in the arrangement which brought the capital to the Potomac, Lee must have been admitted to the secret. If so, he

50 See Documents VI and VII.

would have known at once that such promotional effort had become worse than futile. It now involved the risk of displeasing the President, perhaps even of jeopardizing the great object. The tidewater threat to the metropolis at the Great Falls had thus become a reality. But all was not lost. If Virginians stood united and quiescent under the indispensable leadership of the Chief Magistrate, the imperial city might yet remain on the Potomac in perpetuity.

III

There can be little doubt that Washington did consider all factors with characteristic thoroughness. He was acutely aware of the vulnerability of a tidewater location, of the importance of attaching the western settlements to the union more securely, of the danger of adding to the widespread indignation that had greeted the bargaining in Congress. But the fact is that the decision had already been made some weeks before Washington began his tour up the Potomac. What seems to be the earliest hint of this appears in Jefferson's letters immediately after the passage of the Residence Act and before the President signed it stating unequivocally that the government would be placed at Georgetown.[51] This may have been only an assumption and it was certainly an indiscretion. Nevertheless, long before Washington left Mount Vernon for his tour of the upper Potomac, all of the essential questions involved—the precise location of the Federal District on tidewater, its arrangement in the form of a square,[52] the definition of its bounds, its position straddling the river so as to embrace a part of the cessions of both Maryland and Virginia—had already been answered. This is proved beyond doubt by the newly-established dates of the three earliest documents on the subject, by the details set forth therein as to the location of the capital, by the propositions suggested (and only partially disclosed) to the landowners of the vicinity, by the specific mode of conveyances submitted to them alone so as to enable the Federal City to be laid out at once without further authority, and, conclusively, by the fact that Washington's decision to go below the allowable limits called for amending legislation.[53]

This last element of the decision is particularly revealing. Hitherto, Washington and Jefferson had proceeded under the conviction that it would be hazardous to appeal again to Congress. Yet this was done. When the decision was finally announced and coupled with a proposal for further legislation, William Maclay declared in astonishment that this was "the most imprudent of all acts"—one that seemed likely to unsettle the whole business.[54] The fact that Washington embraced the risk only a few weeks after the narrow victory in Congress suggests that the object was of such importance as to justify all hazards, includ-

[51] TJ to Monroe, 11 July 1790; TJ to Randolph, 11 July 1790; TJ to Short, 26 July 1790, note 2; see also TJ to Mason, 13 June 1790.

[52] TJ had supposed that the district might be "100 square miles in any form" (see Vol. 17: 460).

[53] See Documents I and II, Vol. 17: 460-3; Document I in the present group, which was identified and dated only after the preceding documents were published.

[54] Maclay, *Journal*, ed. Maclay, p. 378.

ing that of disappointing the up-river inhabitants. Had Washington seriously considered any other location, such a gamble would not have been necessary.

It now appears that James Madison may have made one indirect effort to forestall these dangers. In 1790, of course, such an overt attempt to influence the President as he had made during the previous autumn was denied to him. This was not merely because the situation had changed from one of devising an offensive strategy to one of executing a law. It was also because Madison was no longer the close confidant of the Chief Executive that he had been during the early months of the administration. But he was on terms of complete confidentiality with the Secretary of State. Jefferson was well aware of Madison's own personal interest in the proposed developments at the Great Falls. He was equally conscious of the implications of their joint role as collaborators on the Virginia side of the bargain with Hamilton. As Jefferson had pointed out while the event was still fresh in mind, it was Madison who had agreed to approach Richard Bland Lee and Alexander White "to consider how far the interests of *their particular districts* might be a sufficient inducement to them to yield to the assumption."[55] Jefferson's choice of words plainly reveals how well he and Madison understood the nature of the sweet coating that would make the bitter pill palatable.

For not only did Lee and White represent constituencies on the upper Potomac: they were both interested in efforts to improve its navigation and they shared the desire of their constituents to have the capital located above tidewater. Now, as a result of Madison's appeal, their votes had been indispensable in bringing the capital to a location somewhere between Carrollsburg and Conococheague. No one could have understood better than Madison the significance of the part played by these two men. Only a few months earlier he had lamented with Henry Lee the impediment to their own arrangements at the Great Falls, an enterprise he viewed as beneficial in a public as well as a private sense. "It gives me much concern," he had written, "that it is not more in my power to forward our object."[56] Suddenly, however, the outlook had brightened, all "from a fortuitous coincidence of circumstances which might never happen again."[57] But a political obligation had resulted from the compromise and Lee and White might well have believed that their constituents' preference would be honored, particularly since this preference had been explicitly declared by law to be that of the state of Virginia.

They were to be disappointed. But in any event, as shown by a document previously attributed to Jefferson but written by Madison, the latter did in fact urge a succession of steps to be taken in executing

[55] TJ's account of the bargaining for votes [1792?], Document x (Vol. 17: 207); emphasis added. It should be noted that TJ said "Lee came into the measure without hesitation," though it was with reluctance that White—a friend and legal adviser of Adam Stephen, who had argued for locating the capital above tidewater—agreed.
[56] Madison to Lee, 13 Apr. 1790; this was in response to Lee's letter of 3 Apr. 1790 in which he expressed the fear that the union was in danger of dissolution (Madison, *Writings*, ed. Hunt, VI, 10-12).
[57] Madison to Lee, 4 July 1790 (same, VI, 18).

the provisions of the Residence Act. This document contained two strong hints that seemed to point toward the choice of an up-river site. In the first Madison deemed it essential that the commissioners of the Federal District "be men who prefer any place on the Potowmac to any place elsewhere." In the second he urged that "the President inform himself of the several rival positions; leaving among them inducements to bid against each other in offers of land or money."[58] Madison had personal as well as public reasons for urging a careful weighing of the competing sites, not to mention his political obligation to Lee and White. He may have wished to focus attention on an up-river location at the time that he, Jefferson, and several citizens of Georgetown, inspecting lands in that vicinity on behalf of the President, journeyed by boat to the foot of the Little Falls.[59]

Yet, in view of his intimate and confidential relations with Jefferson, it is implausible to suppose Madison unaware of the fact that the decision had already been made. His advice about inspecting the rival claims could have been prompted by the same regard for public appearances that led Washington to make the tour of inspection. Moreover, this important document, which appears to have had substantial influence on other matters affecting the founding of the capital, contains evidence that he was aware of the nature of the President's decision. It raised the question, for example, whether it would not be convenient in the first instance to "accept . . . so much less than 10 miles square as will allow places to be afterwards taken in, *which may not now be attainable, or it may not be prudent now to accept.*"[60] In this and other respects, its cogent suggestions seemed not only to rest upon a knowledge of Washington's decision, but also to accord in various ways with what was eventually done. In only one significant respect—the hint that it might be advisable to make an appointment to the commission "with a view to attach particular parts of the Union to the object"—did Madison's memorandum fail to accord with suggestions advanced by Jefferson or with actions later taken. It is obvious why this suggestion was not adopted. To have appointed only one of the three commissioners from Massachusetts or South Carolina "after securing a majority near at hand" would have exposed at once the purely political reason for which it was done.

The parallel between this important document and that drawn up by Jefferson for a comparable purpose is so obvious as to raise immediate questions about their relationship.[61] The date, the recipient, and the use of Madison's memorandum can only be conjectured. Except for the coincidence between its suggestions and subsequent actions, there is no evidence that it was drawn up at the request of the President or indeed that it was received and used by him. It may be that Washington had solicited the opinion of one and then had shown it to the other with a request for comment, as he sometimes did.[62] Such an explanation

58 See Document I.
59 See Document III (Vol. 17: 465).
60 See Document I; emphasis added. Those places taken in after the passage of amendatory legislation were not at this time legally attainable. See note 69.
61 See Document I (Vol. 17: 460-1) and Document I in the present series.
62 See, for example, TJ's opinion on fiscal policy, 26 Aug. 1790, note.

would seem implausible in this instance. Since Madison's memorandum remained among his own papers, it is more logical to suppose that Jefferson had it before him while composing his own, eliminating much, borrowing parts, and adding other suggestions. As had happened after the passage of the Residence Act, Washington may have urged Jefferson to consult Madison and thus the resultant report represented their concurrent views.[63] This seems all the more plausible since Jefferson's memorandum is recorded in his register of public papers as a formal opinion, indicating that the President had requested it.[64] Furthermore, it omits most of Madison's suggestions as to the appointment of commissioners, though it seems to embrace his point about the dangers of interested decisions and about the delays that would result if they resided at a distance.[65] Madison's memorandum may never have been submitted to Washington, but it was certainly prepared just prior to the 29th of August 1790 and its author, like Jefferson, could scarcely have been unaware that by then Washington had decided. It would indeed have been politically imprudent in the extreme not to have informed Virginia's leader in the House of Representatives at the outset about what was intended. For, as indicated above, Washington's choice involved the very considerable gamble as to what Congress might do in response to a request for amending legislation. Along that hazardous course the legislative influence of Madison, who clearly was prepared to accept any site on the Potomac in preference to any location elsewhere, would be as indispensable as it had been in the recent compromise.

IV

The risk was great enough under any circumstances. But the remarkable fact is that Washington, keenly aware as he was of the powers of disruption that lay in this issue, was willing to embrace the hazard so soon after the uneasy settlement.[66] If he had not done so, both of the "two objects" mentioned in his first recorded statement about the location of the Federal District would certainly have been lost.[67] This fact alone indicates the importance that he attached to those objects. He had no need to define them in writing to Jefferson, but there can be no doubt as to their nature. The first, as proved by Jefferson's suggestions, was to include the town of Alexandria. That thriving Virginia port, county seat, and commercial rival of Georgetown lay some distance below the mouth of the Eastern Branch, thus being outside the limits defined by law. Having accepted the risk that this object involved, Washington was prompted to gamble on another. This second object, as described by a contemporary, required an arrangement of the Federal District so as to "make the River a diagonal through the square, leaving a right angled triangle on each side of it, thereby taking

[63] See Documents II, III, IV, V, and VI (Vol. 17: 193-200).

[64] Document I (Vol. 17: 461, note).

[65] Madison's memorandum appears to have had influence in other respects on actions taken at this time and subsequently—for example, the offering of premiums for architectural designs.

[66] See Washington to La Luzerne, 10 Aug. 1790, quoted in part at head of Editorial Note (Washington, *Writings*, ed. Fitzpatrick, XXXI, 84).

[67] See Document II.

in the greatest quantity of tide water."[68] This explanation is entitled to consideration because it came from Andrew Ellicott, to whom Washington confided the task of running the district lines. But it fell short of the mark. Months before the President asked Congress to amend the law, Madison urged it "as essential that the District should comprehend the water adjoining the establishment, and eligible that it should comprehend the opposite shore."[69] Jefferson's report to Washington outlined the Federal District so as to include both Alexandria and land on the Maryland side of the Potomac below the mouth of the Eastern Branch.[70] Once this was achieved and once the diagonals of the ten mile square were aligned with the cardinal points of the compass,[71] the maximum amount of tidewater would of course be comprehended, as perhaps was desired. But the important fact is that both of the two objects required amendment of the Residence Act. Having impressed upon local landowners the fear that, once lost, this opportunity of fixing the seat of government on the Potomac "could never more be regained," Washington deliberately chose a course that involved the risk of losing it.[72]

The danger of having Congress reopen the whole question was all the greater because of the widespread public indignation over the legislative bargaining that had brought the capital to the Potomac. To this could now be added the fact that Washington had construed the law as conferring upon himself alone the authority to decide upon the location, the size, and indeed the bounds of the Federal District. The second section of the Act had authorized the President to appoint commissioners who, under his direction, should survey and "by proper metes and bounds define the limit" of the district. The memoranda by Jefferson and Madison, both of which recognized the possible influence on the commissioners of local or interested views, indicate that they considered them to be vested with some discretionary power. Senator Maclay was in no doubt about the matter. For the President to take upon himself to establish the location by his own authority "when he might have placed the three commissioners in the post of responsibility," he declared, "was a thoughtless act." The general sense of Congress, he added, "certainly was that the commissioners should fix on the spot, and it may be a query whether the words of the law will warrant a different construction. The commissioners are now only

68 Jonathan Williams, Richmond, to Henry Knox, 18 Apr. 1791 (MHi: Knox Papers). By this arrangement Georgetown would of course be included.

69 See Document I in the present group. This is perhaps the best evidence that Madison knew of Washington's intentions before 29 Aug. 1790. Both of his suggestions could have been achieved *above* the mouth of the Eastern Branch without amendatory legislation, but not below it. It is possible, however, that in making these suggestions Madison was thinking of the requirement of the law which placed the seat of government on the Maryland side of the Potomac and thus he may have apprehended that the entire Federal District would be placed in that state. But, as argued above, Madison could scarcely have been unaware of the President's choice by late August. He certainly knew what it was in mid-September.

70 See Document II (Vol. 17: 463).

71 This arrangement of the district must have been suggested by TJ; compare his suggestions in 1786 for republishing the map of South America by Juan de la Cruz (Vol. 10: 216-17).

72 See Document II (Vol. 17: 461).

agents of demarkation, mere surveyors to run four lines of fixed courses and distances."[73]

The courses and the distances were indeed fixed. The President and the Secretary of State, both experienced surveyors, were the real delineators of the Federal District. The cessions of Virginia and Maryland had imposed upon the President an almost unavoidable obligation to cause the Federal District to fall in both states. This political if not moral obligation was strengthened by other practical considerations. "The matter, I believe," wrote Senator Maclay, "stands thus in fact: Virginia is not fully satisfied without having half of the ten miles square. She gives the one hundred and twenty thousand dollars, perhaps, on this very principle of having Alexandria included."[74] The Pennsylvanian erred both as to fact and motive. The Virginia act of cession had indeed suggested that both states, as well as Maclay's own, should participate in a location far above tidewater. But neither Virginia nor Maryland had actually appropriated funds when Congress assembled in December. The Virginia appropriation of $120,000 came only at the very end of 1790.[75] Five days later Washington was pressing forward in the preparation for the public announcement. Working together in inviolable secrecy, the President and the Secretary of State planned the Federal District essentially in accord with suggestions made by Jefferson and Madison on the basis of their knowledge of Washington's choice.

In defining the bounds so as to include the two objects, Washington first selected a point of departure on Hunting Creek, knowing full well that this point lay below the boundaries of Alexandria because in 1748 he had himself helped survey them.[76] This established, he sent some notes to Jefferson that appear not to have survived but were certainly such descriptions of the boundaries of the district as to comprehend the "two objects."[77] Immediately thereafter he discovered other papers, perhaps drawn from the records of the Potomac Company, that made it possible to proceed with more precision. He sent for Jefferson and made these papers available to him. Among them was one in Washington's own hand showing the courses and distances from "the head of the Canal at the Great Falls, to the tail of the Canal at the little Falls."[78] This, the President pointed out, would make it possible to ascertain the courses and distances from the court house in Alexandria to these two terminals of the canal "with as much accuracy as can be shown from *Common* Surveying if not to Mathematical truth."[79] Jefferson took Washington's field notes and calculated that the distance "from the Courthouse in Alexandria to the end of the course S. 8½ E. 14"—that

[73] Maclay, *Journal*, ed. Maclay, p. 378.
[74] Same, p. 395.
[75] 27 Dec. 1790 (Hening, *Statutes*, XIII, 125); Beverley Randolph to Washington, 15 Feb. 1791, enclosing a copy of the act, DNA: RG 69, MLR).
[76] Document II; Freeman, *Washington*, I, 232-3.
[77] Document II; see following note.
[78] It is generally assumed (Padover, *National Capital*, p. 36; Washington, *Writings*, ed. Fitzpatrick, XXXI, 189) that these notes of courses and distances were enclosed in Washington's letter to TJ of 2 Jan. 1791 (Document II); but they were among the papers referred to in that of 4 Jan. 1791 (Document III).
[79] Document III.

is, the course designated by Washington as terminating at the lower end of the canal—was "17¼ miles-15 poles." Thus, as shown by this highly interesting joint product of the pens of the President and the Secretary of State, the court house in Alexandria was the datum for fixing the point of beginning on Hunting Creek for the first of the "lines of experiment" and for determining its bearing and extent to the northwest.[80]

No obstacle now stood in the way of public announcement save the need for texts of the acts of cession and resolutions of Virginia and Maryland. Where, asked the President of Jefferson, were these "to be met with? If to be brought from the Archives of these States, much time will be required in obtaining them:—but query, are they not among the deposits of the General Government?"[81] The urgent inquiry reveals the secrecy as well as the haste with which the two men addressed themselves to this problem. For these essential documents were indeed among the deposits of the government, as Richard Bland Lee or any member of the Virginia delegation could have pointed out. Copies of the Virginia act and resolution of 1789 and at least the Maryland act of 1790 were also in the private papers of James Madison.[82] From one source or another Jefferson was soon in possession of the acts of cession of both states and thus was able to include their operative provisions in the text of the President's proclamation.[83] There was of course no need to disclose in this state paper the embarrassing conflict between the final decision on the site and the express preference recited in the Virginia statute. But, as Washington's request reveals, the astonishing fact is that the President had arrived at his decision and then had gone through the motions of inspecting the up-river sites without even having before him the text of the act of cession in which his own state had so explicitly declared its desire for a location above tidewater. Few episodes in his administration could reveal more clearly the often insuperable insularity with which he exercised the presidential powers. Congress, by permitting a range of choices as far up-river as Conococheague, had paid more attention to Virginia's expressed wish than did her most famous son.

Nevertheless, Washington adroitly diminished the risks he had so boldly embraced. The nature of this strategy suggests the influence of the Secretary of State. It was certainly his hand that framed the documents. In the opening line of the communication to Congress, Jefferson had the President say that he had acted in "execution of the powers with which Congress were pleased" to invest him.[84] Senator Maclay might expostulate in his diary, but none could question this executive construction of the law without challenging the immense personal authority of the President. Also, Washington did not actually request amendatory legislation. He merely presented an opportunity for Congress to consider an extension of the lower limit. If that body should

[80] See illustrations in this volume.
[81] Document II.
[82] John Dawson to Madison, 17 Dec. 1789 (DLC: Madison Papers), enclosing the Virginia act and resolution; Daniel Carroll to Madison, 26 Nov. 1790 (same), enclosing draft of Maryland bill pledging funds for public buildings.
[83] See Document IV, note; Document VII.
[84] Document VI.

refuse to permit the projected lower part of the district to be added, the ten mile square would still be completed on the northwest sector. In brief, within the limits of existing law, Congress was presented with an accomplished fact. The precise boundaries and a large part of the Federal District lying in both Maryland and Virginia were already "fixed upon, and directed to be surveyed, defined, limited and located. . . ."[85] The commissioners who Maclay thought were reduced to the stature of mere surveyors had not even been appointed until after this major part of the district had been defined.[86] The President's proclamation, which only announced actions taken and made no effort to explain the choice or to counter the arguments that had been advanced in Congress and in the press against a tidewater location, was issued the very day that Washington sent his communication to Congress—a communication in which the text of the proclamation was enclosed merely for the "more particular information" of the members.[87] Broadsides of the proclamation were struck off the same day. The moment the President received them, he dispatched copies to William Deakins, Jr. and Benjamin Stoddert just in time to catch the southbound post. Another indication of his sense of urgency appears in his covering directions:[88]

> I wish you to have [the proclamation] made public with all expedition. And in the most general and extensive manner that you can to prevent any kind of speculation. Let them be published in the News-Papers, put up in public places and otherwise so disposed as to answer my object as fully as possible.

Congress in its wisdom might or might not act, but the nation would be informed forthwith what the President had decided—though neither the legislators nor the public would be told why.

Yet even this adroit initiative in the use of power, to say nothing of the heroic proportions of the personage wielding it, could not silence the opposition. The legislative struggle that followed not only invalidates the supposition that the decision met the sanction of public opinion and that "no record of a dissenting voice" was to be discovered even in Congress:[89] it also posed a real danger that fruits of the bargain with Hamilton and the alliance between Virginia and Pennsylvania would be lost. William Maclay, so independent that he had once dared confront the President in person on the manner in which the Senate should exercise its right to advise and consent, declared to that body that, so far as he had had an opportunity of knowing the public mind,

[85] Document VII.

[86] Document IV; the text of the commission, dated 22 Feb. 1791 and issued to Thomas Jefferson, Daniel Carroll, and David Stuart, is printed in Washington, *Writings*, ed. Fitzpatrick, XXXI, 200.

[87] See Document VII; the proclamation appeared in Bache's *General Advertiser*, 25 Jan. 1791, in Brown's *Federal Gazette*, 25 Jan. 1791, and in many other newspapers. Bradford's *Pennsylvania Journal* kept it running from 9 Feb. to 20 Apr. 1791. A copy of the broadside of the proclamation is in DLC: Daniel Carroll Papers.

[88] Washington to Deakins and Stoddert, 24 Jan. 1791 (Washington, *Writings*, ed. Fitzpatrick, XXXI, 204-5).

[89] Bryan, *National Capital*, I, 120.

"the people had been disappointed."[90] Respect for the opinions of the people and a shrewd capacity for gauging them were distinguishing marks of Maclay's character and in this instance, despite the absence of comment in the press, there is every reason to accept his judgment. Certainly Henry Lee and the inhabitants up-river who had pledged their lands and considerable sums of money had no reason to rejoice when they read the President's proclamation. It is true that no such outburst as had greeted the Residence Act occurred at this time, but this was perhaps because of the angry debate over the militia, the excise, and the bank bills, to say nothing of the clamors of the western settlements for protection. The furore over these administration measures and inept military operations was enough to eclipse all opposition to the Potomac site. Those who were disappointed—and there were many—were perhaps awed into silence by the fact that they could only challenge the prudence, not the legality, of the President's decision. This placed a challenger of ground none was bold enough to occupy, at least openly.

Yet the opposition in Congress was so strong and so threatening as to give serious concern to both Washington and Jefferson. The first warning came when the legislators responded to the President's haste with calculated deliberation. More than three weeks elapsed before Charles Carroll, on the 16th of February, asked leave of the Senate to bring in a bill at once. Ellsworth objected, and Carroll was obliged to respect the rule requiring a one day's notice of such a motion. The next day Carroll's request was granted. But seven senators, all save William Maclay being from New York and New England, voted against the motion—an ominous sign that the old sectional cleavage on this issue still posed a threat.[91] Robert Morris had voted with the majority, but he had been dilatory in attending—Maclay thought him never "otherwise when a debate was expected."[92] The response of the administration to these signals of trouble ahead was immediate. Before the Senate assembled the next morning the Secretary of State called on Maclay, who later recorded an account of the visit almost as an afterthought: "Oh, I should note that Mr. Jefferson with more than Parisian politeness, waited on me at my chamber this morning. He talked politics, mostly the French difference and the whale-fishery; but he touched the Potomac, too, as much as to say 'There, oh there.'"[93] Maclay was too shrewd a judge of men not to discern the real object of the visit. His views on the difference with France and on the fisheries, to be sure, were not those of the Secretary of State. But in neither case was his vote of critical importance. With respect to the permanent seat of government, the situation was quite different. If Maclay continued to ally himself with the northeastern states and if a single southern senator went astray, the whole Potomac arrangement might be thrown into jeopardy. On this issue Butler and Izard of South Carolina were particular sources of concern. In the previous session the latter had often

[90] Maclay, *Journal*, ed. Maclay, p. 397.
[91] JS, I, 269, 272-3.
[92] Maclay, *Journal*, ed. Maclay, p. 396.
[93] Same, p. 397.

voted with the northern states and the former, in Maclay's words, had "bounced between them" and his southern colleagues.

Under these circumstances, it is not at all surprising that Washington himself, just four days before he sent his message to Congress, began to show marked attention to the dour Scot from the Susquehanna, who had voted "dead against the [Potomac] measure from the beginning."[94] Theretofore Maclay had considered himself to be disfavored and even neglected by the President. If so, he had earned the distinction. No one in or out of government had been so unflinching in opposition to the style as well as to the measures of the administration. Now, however, he was not only invited to dinner, but shown such marked attention by Washington as to arouse Maclay's wonder. At table on the 20th of January, Maclay noted in his journal, the President "asked me to drink a glass of wine with him. This was readily accorded to, and, what was remarkable, I did not observe him drink with any other person during dinner."[95] In the drawing room afterwards, somewhat to his embarrassment, Maclay found himself thrust before the President, who arose and made room on the sofa. But Maclay, already in motion for another seat lest he disclose the faintest trace of behaving like a courtier, took a place among some legislators from the New England states, with whom he was voting on the amending bill but against whom his prejudices ran deep and strong. Embarrassed at what he supposed might be taken as an act of discourtesy, he was generous enough to attribute Washington's unusual attentions to compassion.[96] The appraisal may have been as just as it was generous. But neither Washington nor Jefferson could have been unaware that, on this question and to the very hour of adjournment, Maclay's vote might be of critical importance. If their unusual marks of politeness to him at this time arose from such a concern, they ill conceived the nature of the man. Maclay, stubbornly independent and believing that presidential dinners and attentions had been used in order to influence votes, fled from sycophancy as from a plague. Wrapped in the mantle of his uncompromising republicanism, he believed that no man and no power on earth could cause him to change his vote. At once his strength and his weakness, this was in fact the chief reason why he now stood isolated in the Senate and repudiated by his constituents. In any event, such attentions by the President and the Secretary of State had no effect whatever on Maclay's course. "I have drowned Jefferson's regards in the Potomac," he reflected as he continued unwaveringly to the end to cast his vote with the opposition.[97]

When Carroll's bill came up for debate on the 18th of February, Robert Morris strongly hinted that if anyone should propose a postponement he would vote for it. Langdon of New Hampshire and Schuyler of New York then moved that the bill be postponed "to this

[94] Same, p. 397.
[95] Same, p. 374.
[96] Same, p. 375. Maclay's two-year term ended on 4 Mch. 1791. Always an individualist, he was at this time alone, embittered, and isolated from his colleagues in the Senate.
[97] Same, p. 398.

day se'ennight."[98] If successful, this move would have deferred further debate until the very last week of the session. Gunn of Georgia flatly accused Morris of using this indirect means of "getting rid of the measure."[99] But in fact the motion was carried by a substantial majority of 15 to 10. Every senator to the north of Maryland voted for postponement and all to the south of Pennsylvania voted against it. Langdon, Schuyler, and Morris voted with the majority. "They might as well have voted against the bill," Maclay acutely observed, "for the postponement is equally ungrateful at court."[100] The decisive vote revealed that the sectional cleavage had deepened. It also showed beyond doubt that Pennsylvania, without whose cooperation the Potomac was doomed, was now aligned with New York and New England. The final outcome would be determined when the bill came up for consideration on the 25th, with only seven crowded legislative days left of the session.

In 1789, for such a defection as this, Robert Morris had been made to feel the President's pointed displeasure. But at that time the issue was confined to the legislative branch and now, with the President inviting specific legislation, the situation was quite different. Having been a principal figure in the bargain that had brought the capital to the Potomac, Morris, by casting his vote with the New Englanders, appeared at once to repudiate that arrangement and to offer a challenge to the President himself. What happened to resolve the conflict in the week following the postponement is not reflected in the records, but it would have been remarkable indeed if Washington's anger had been less apparent under these circumstances than on the former occasion. The legislative actions that followed seem to speak eloquently of the force with which influence was brought to bear. When the bill came up on the 25th the determined opposition again moved a postponement —this time indefinitely. If carried, this would certainly have delayed action until the next Congress. The motion, however, was defeated by the narrow margin of 14 to 12. The sectional lines were clear and the margin slight, but the administration could now count on passage so long as its adherents remained firm and undivided. In the first vote on the bill itself that same day there was an identical alignment of 14 to 12. On Saturday the 26th the bill was approved without a roll call vote.[101] In the House there was no recorded debate but the opposition was substantial, the bill being passed by a sectional vote of 39 to 18. The President signed it on the final day of the session.[102]

The vote in the Senate may afford a plausible explanation for this sudden abandonment of what appears to have been a determined move on the part of Morris, the New Yorkers, and the New Englanders to defeat the bill by inaction. Four Senators who had voted for postpone-

[98] JS, I, 273.
[99] Maclay, *Journal*, ed. Maclay, p. 397.
[100] JS, I, 274; Maclay, *Journal*, ed. Maclay, p. 397.
[101] JS, I, 287-8, 289.
[102] Same, I, 298, 306; JHR, I, 392, 393, 397-8, 401, 408; *Annals*, I, 2024, 2025-6. In the House on 1 Mch. 1791, Gerry, Sherman, Trumbull, and Wadsworth were the only New Englanders who voted for the bill. The delegations of New York and Pennsylvania were divided. Of the 25 votes south of Pennsylvania, only one—Seney of Maryland—was against the measure.

ment on the 18th had for some reason changed their votes and given support to the administration. These were Morris, Langdon, Schuyler, and Read, the first three of whom had been the chief instigators of postponement. "This," declared a shocked Maclay, "is astonishing, indeed. It is plain the President has bought them. I know not their price, but that is immaterial." He then went on to describe the varying prices that he believed had been affixed:[103]

> I think the city [interest of Philadelphia] must see Morris in a new point of view. Were I to give such a vote, I certainly dared not walk the streets. Mr. Morris wishes his namesake, Gouverneur (now in Europe selling lands for him) placed in some conspicuous station abroad. . . . As to Langdon[104] I am at no loss; the appointment of his brother Woodbury is sufficient explanation. Schuyler is the supplejack of his son-in-law Hamilton. . . . As to Read I have heretofore known him to have been shaken by something else besides the wind.

The accuracy of the appraisal is open to doubt. Much too prone to attribute motives of venality, Maclay did not perceive that large questions of policy rather than mere desire for office might have influenced votes. This was true of the bargain that brought the capital to the Potomac in the first place and it seems equally so of the effort to keep it there.

The opportunity for another such compromise requiring a shift in votes may have occurred in respect to the excise bill that had aroused general hostility, especially in the South and the West. During this week in which the fate of Carroll's bill was held in suspense, the House and Senate were deadlocked over an amendment to the excise bill. Neither would recede from its position. On the 23rd the Senate requested a conference and appointed Ellsworth, King, and Morris as managers. The House agreed the same day, appointing Boudinot, White, and Livermore.[105] The deadlock was broken on the very day that Carroll's bill was taken up, when Morris and his three colleagues shifted positions and came to its support. The House forced a significant limitation on the patronage powers of the Secretary of the Treas-

103 Maclay, *Journal*, ed. Maclay, p. 401.

104 Several months earlier Woodbury Langdon had been recommended by Hamilton for appointment as commissioner of loans for New Hampshire. Washington appointed him, but he declined to serve (Washington to Langdon, 15 Oct. 1790; Langdon to Washington, 9 Nov. 1790; DNA: RG 59, MLR). John Langdon then warmly recommended Keith Spence. This was opposed by Nathaniel Gilman, who strongly urged William Gardiner for the place. Hamilton, undecided between the Langdon and Gilman factions, urged Washington to postpone the matter until "the arrival of the Eastern members." Soon thereafter—long before Washington's message on the Federal District—this post was given to Gardiner and Woodbury Langdon was awarded that of commissioner for settling accounts between the states and the United States, a more important office (Hamilton to Washington, 6 and 26 Oct., 1 Nov., and 2 Dec. 1790; Washington to Hamilton, 15 and 26 Oct., 8 Nov. 1790, Syrett, *Hamilton*, VII, 96-7, 115, 124-5, 135, 143-4, 187-8; JEP, I, 64; TJ to Woodbury Langdon, 24 Dec. 1790, enclosing commission, DNA: RG 59, PCC No. 120; Langdon to TJ, 14 Jan. 1791, DLC: Washington Papers).

105 JS, I, 237, 238, 239, 240, 247, 262, 263-6, 279, 288, 289, 292; JHR, I, 388, 391, 394, 395, 398.

ury and came within one vote of defeating the compromise.[106] "The third reading was given this day," Maclay lamented, "to [Carroll's] detestable bill of yesterday, and the last hand was put to the more detested excise law. All of these, however, were condemned as trifles in political iniquity."[107]

The bargain of 1790 had left few records of its existence, but the public suspected that it had taken place and bitterly condemned legislators for engaging in such trading.[108] Perhaps for this reason the comparable arrangement in 1791 on the amending bill, if such it was, appears to have left none. Nevertheless, the marked attentions shown to Maclay by Washington and Jefferson and the sudden shift on the part of Morris and his colleagues—one of them the father-in-law of Alexander Hamilton—suggest that influence was brought to bear at a crucial moment. If so, the Secretary of the Treasury, whose Walpolean tactics are to be discerned in the history of the major legislative achievements of Washington's administration, was in a strategic position to exert pressures to attain what both he and the President desired.

What Hamilton desired at the moment was not merely the passage of the excise and bank bills but their enactment into law under the cachet of the President. On the day that Carroll asked and was denied leave to bring in his bill, Washington sent to Hamilton the opinions of the Attorney General and the Secretary of State against the constitutionality of the bank bill. During the week that the Potomac bill was in suspense, Hamilton labored heroically to refute their arguments. On the 23rd he transmitted the result to the President, explaining that it had occupied him "the greatest part of last night."[109] Washington received the opinion at noon and acknowledged it immediately with a question that carried disturbing implications: "To what precise period, by legal interpretation of the constitution, can the president retain it in his possession, before it becomes a Law by the lapse of ten days?"[110] The question carried two strong implications—first, that the President, faced with conflicting cabinet opinions, might by a veto side with the majority, and, second, that if he were unable to decide between them, he might allow the bill to become law without his sanction. The ominous overtones of the query were heightened by the fact that it

[106] The section of the bill at issue placed no limit on the total compensation allowed all supervisors, inspectors, &c.: it merely provided that the total compensation of collectors and others be limited to 5% of all duties collected. The House altered this to 7% of the duties on spirits distilled *within the United States* and also limited such compensation to a period of two years, carrying its amendment by a vote of 34 to 20. The compromise accepted the House amendment, added a limit of the total allowance to $45,000 per annum, and permitted authorization to stand until "further ascertained by law." The House accepted this compromise reluctantly—by a vote of 30 to 29 (JS, I, 266, 288, 289-90; *Annals*, II, 2018, 2019, 2021, 2022, 2023-4; White, Madison, Lee, and other opponents of the excise were in the minority on this sectional vote). The aim of the opposition to curtail patronage is reflected in the remark of Maclay that Hamilton and his adherents would not stop "till, perhaps, as in Britain, ten men may be employed to guard one distillery" (Maclay, *Journal*, ed. Maclay, p. 387).

[107] Maclay, *Journal*, ed. Maclay, p. 401.

[108] See Editorial Note and Document X, Vol. 17: 170-1, 205-8.

[109] Washington to Hamilton, 16 Feb. 1791; Hamilton to Washington, 23 Feb. 1791 (Syrett, *Hamilton*, VIII, 50, 62-3).

[110] Washington to Hamilton, 23 Feb. 1791 (same, VIII, 134-5).

was addressed to the Secretary of the Treasury, since it was the particular duty of the Attorney General to advise the President on questions of constitutional interpretation—as shown by the fact that Washington had sought Randolph's opinion on the bank bill before consulting
anyone else. Hamilton replied at once: if the bill should be returned
on Friday the 25th "at any time while Congress are setting," it would
be in time.[111]

Also on the 23rd, when the supplement to the bank bill came before
the Senate and its adherents desired it to pass at once to a second reading, Carroll administered to them the same obstructionist tactics accorded him earlier. He refused consent, forcing the bill to lie over
another day. Hamilton, informed of this by Schuyler, relayed the
information to the President in a letter on the 24th that not only disclosed his annoyance but also carried a bold hint. The bill, he said,
would "doubtless pass, if there are not *studied* delays on the part of
the opposers of the Bank."[112] Soon thereafter he reported that the bill
had passed its second reading with "only three or four *dissentients*:
among these, Mr. *Carrol* and Mr. *Monroe*." He added that the roll call
vote had been taken "in order to *pledge* the members" and that it would
be passed the first thing on the 25th.[113] So it was and so, on that day,
did Morris, Langdon, Schuyler, and Read change their votes and the
President return the signed bank bill to the Senate. So far as the
record shows, only the Secretary of the Treasury was bold enough to
call the President's attention to delaying tactics on the part of opponents of the bank. He did so while Washington's decision on the
bank bill was still in doubt. If this was a threat that the bill to amend
the Residence Act might be defeated unless Washington signed the
bank bill, it was an act of youthful audacity almost equalling the outburst that had caused a temporary parting of the ways between the
two men during the war. But in the end it was Hamilton's chief supporters in the Senate who, yielding an important point on the excise
bill and perhaps fearful that the bank bill might be vetoed or allowed

[111] Hamilton to Washington, 23 Feb. 1791 (same, VIII, 135). The fixing of
the bank at Philadelphia during its existence gave additional force to Washington's query. "This," John Rutledge wrote after the bank bill had been signed,
"the Virginians and Marylanders regard as a thing which would retard the
moving of the seat of government southwardly. The President, it was imagined,
would discover local attachments. He had never done so on former occasions but
there were strong reasons for imagining he would on this." It was reported that
he would neither assent nor dissent to the bill and, Rutledge concluded, "this
gave great uneasiness" (John Rutledge to William Short, 30 Mch. 1791, DLC:
Short Papers). Maclay also thought that "the Potomac interest" regarded the
bank bill "as a machine, which, in the hands of the Philadelphians, might retard
the removal of Congress" (Maclay, *Journal*, ed. Maclay, p. 373). The obvious
inference is that Washington intended his pointed query to focus attention on
both bills, that Hamilton grasped this, and that the resultant shift in votes accommodated the wishes of both men—all without such bald bargaining as that of
1790 and also without causing the President "to discover local attachments."
Kenneth R. Bowling has analyzed the relations between the amending bill and
the bank bill from a different point of view ("The Bank Bill, the Capital City,
and President Washington," *Capitol Studies*, I [1972], 59-71).

[112] Same to same, [24] Feb. 1791 (same, VIII, 142-3).

[113] Gunn was the only other senator who voted against the bill (JS, I, 280,
288); Hamilton to Washington, 24 Feb. 1791 (Syrett, *Hamilton*, VIII, 143).

to become law without the sanction of Washington's name, suddenly abandoned their effort to thwart for a time if not to defeat the President's hopes for the Federal District. By persisting, they would have gained nothing and might have brought on a direct confrontation with Washington.

V

Immediately on the arrival of Washington's proclamation in Alexandria, the leading citizens of that place set out to determine where the first of the district lines began. What they discovered was that the closeted calculations of the President and the Secretary of State had resulted in an error. From their quick verification it appeared that a course from the Alexandria court house due southwest 160 poles and another thence southeast would strike the Potomac at a marshy place well above Hunting Creek. But an initial course of 220 poles from the starting point would cause the southeast line to "strike Hunting Creek at the first point of firm land which comes down the West side of Jones' or Fishing Point."[114] William Hunter, mayor of Alexandria, dispatched this information to the President by express, but it arrived too late to affect Jefferson's instructions to Andrew Ellicott, whom Washington had chosen to run the district boundaries. Ellicott, regarded by the President as a "man of uncommon talents," was urged to undertake the preliminary survey with all possible dispatch.[115] He arrived in Alexandria early in February and found the inhabitants "truly rejoiced at the prospect of being included in the Federal district."[116] Having confirmed what was already known about the miscalculation, he reported to Jefferson on the 14th and recommended that the starting point be fixed at the upper cape of Hunting Creek, or Jones' Point. He also suggested that the first line be run from that location northwesterly at an angle of 45° from the meridian, with each subsequent line setting off at a right angle to the terminus of its predecessor instead of by compass bearings as the proclamation directed.[117] That same afternoon he began "the first rough essay to furnish data" for the final survey, running the lines in accordance with his own suggestion without waiting for an answer.

By the end of a week Ellicott had completed the first of the four lines and "had crossed the river Potowmack, below the Little Falls, on the second line."[118] Three weeks later a Georgetown newspaper re-

[114] William Hunter to Washington, 28 Jan. 1791; George Gilpin to Washington, 28 Jan. 1791 (DLC: Washington Papers).

[115] Washington to David Stuart, 20 Nov. 1791 (Washington, *Writings*, ed. Fitzpatrick, XXXI, 420, 506); Document X, note. In 1789 Ellicott had also applied to Washington for appointment as successor to Thomas Hutchins, geographer of the United States (Ellicott to Washington, 16 May and 20 Aug. 1789, with testimonials to Ellicott's competence and character from John Ewing, Robert Patterson, Robert Andrews, and David Rittenhouse, DLC: Washington Papers).

[116] Ellicott to his wife, 14 Feb. 1791 (C.V.C. Mathews, *Andrew Ellicott* [New York, 1908], p. 83).

[117] Ellicott to TJ, 14 Feb. 1791 (Document XII). Ellicott also wrote TJ on 2, 23, and 27 Feb. 1791 and 12 and 24 Jan. 1793, as shown by entries in SJL, but none of these has been found.

[118] Davis' *Virginia Gazette*, 9 Mch. 1791, quoting the Georgetown *Times, and Patowmack Packet* of 23 Feb. 1791.

ported that he hoped soon to finish this preliminary survey. It added this tribute to one of his assistants: "He is attended by Benjamin Bannaker, an Ethiopian, whose abilities, as a surveyor, and an astronomer, clearly prove that Mr. Jefferson's concluding that race of men were void of mental endowments, was without foundation."[119] Ellicott

[119] *Hampshire Gazette* (Northampton, Mass.), 30 Mch. 1791, quoting a Georgetown paper of 12 Mch. 1791. TJ, of course, had not made such an assertion.

Recent biographical accounts of Benjamin Banneker (1731-1806), a mulatto whose father was a native African and whose grandmother was English, have done his memory a disservice by obscuring his real achievements under a cloud of extravagant claims to scientific accomplishment that have no foundation in fact. The single notable exception is Silvio A. Bedini's *The Life of Benjamin Banneker* (New York, 1972), a work of painstaking research and scrupulous attention to accuracy which also benefits from the author's discovery of important and hitherto unavailable manuscript sources. However, as Bedini points out, the story of Banneker's involvement in the survey of the Federal District "rests on extremely meager documentation" (p. 104). This consists of a single mention by TJ, two brief statements by Banneker himself, and the newspaper allusion quoted above. In consequence, Bedini's otherwise reliable biography accepts the version of Banneker's role in this episode as presented in reminiscences of nineteenth-century authors. These recollections, deriving in large part from members of the Ellicott family who were prompted by Quaker inclinations to justice and equality, have compounded the confusion. The nature of TJ's connection with Banneker is treated in the Editorial Note to the group of documents under 30 Aug. 1791, but because of the obscured record it is necessary here to attempt a clarification of the role of this modest, self-taught tobacco farmer in the laying out of the national capital.

First of all, because of unwarranted claims to the contrary, it must be pointed out that there is no evidence whatever that Banneker had anything to do with the survey of the Federal City or indeed with the final establishment of the boundaries of the Federal District. All available testimony shows that he was present only during the few weeks early in 1791 when the rough preliminary survey of the ten mile square was made; that, after this was concluded and before the final survey was begun, he returned to his farm and his astronomical studies in April, accompanying Ellicott part way on his brief journey back to Philadelphia; and that thenceforth he had no connection with the mapping of the seat of government.

Bedini, relying upon the best of the recollected accounts and contributing his own scientific expertise, indicates that, before leaving Philadelphia, Ellicott offered the post of scientific assistant to his young Maryland cousin, George Ellicott, who declined and may have recommended Banneker; that TJ, in subsequent conversations with Andrew Ellicott, encouraged him to employ Banneker; that Ellicott then rode southward from Philadelphia on horseback, stopping several days at Ellicott's Upper Mills to visit his widowed mother, to see Banneker, and to complete arrangements; that Banneker, newly outfitted with a wardrobe selected by the wife of George Ellicott, accompanied Andrew Ellicott to Alexandria, arriving there probably on the evening of 7 Feb. 1791; and that during the survey Banneker served as scientific assistant having charge of the instruments in the observation tent and being responsible for making astronomical observations. These instruments included a brass circumferentor, a surveying compass made especially for Ellicott by Benjamin Rittenhouse, a transit and equal altitude instrument made by Ellicott himself in 1789, a small zenith sector with a radius of 20 inches, a much larger one—almost six feet in length—made by David Rittenhouse and modified by Ellicott, a tall-case astronomical clock, several sextants, three telescopes, thermometers, drafting instruments, two copper lanterns of Ellicott's design with special slits for tracing meridian lines, and of course the usual chains, rods, and other surveying equipment. The clock, a particularly sensitive instrument that had to be protected against ground vibrations, changes in temperature, and any contact causing inaccuracy, was normally set on the stump of a tree and the observation tent erected over it and the other instruments. By far the most important of these was the larger of the two zenith

was also assisted by three others, all inexperienced. He confided to his wife that, in addition to a very severe attack of influenza, he had met with

sectors—"probably the most accurate scientific instrument in America at that time" —which was employed to determine latitude by observations of stars crossing the meridian. Thus, according to the traditional account, Banneker was engaged in making astronomical observations at different times during the night through the whole of the survey (Bedini, *Banneker*, ch. v, "The Great Adventure," p. 103-36; the compass, the transit and equal altitude instrument, and the large zenith sector are illustrated).

The difficulty with this account is, first, that it collides with chronology and, second, that it confuses the preliminary and the final survey. Ellicott was in Philadelphia on 2 Feb. 1791 when he received TJ's directions and presumably acknowledged them in a (missing) letter of the same date. If he traveled to Alexandria "by the first stage," as TJ directed, and if he left on Thursday, the 3rd, as Washington desired, his passage was remarkably swift for a winter's journey (he arrived in Alexandria perhaps on the evening of the 7th but more likely on the 8th; TJ sometimes covered the same ground in six days, but usually in seven, the time required for Ellicott's letter of 14 Feb. 1791 to reach TJ). It follows of course that Ellicott had no time to receive his cousin's refusal of the post and his presumed recommendation of Banneker; that TJ thus could not have known of such a recommendation or have encouraged its acceptance in subsequent conversations; and that Ellicott could not have spent several days at Ellicott's Upper Mills to engage Banneker and make other arrangements, if indeed he had time to stop there at all. The implication is obvious: Banneker must have been engaged later than has been supposed. Since George Ellicott had been Banneker's mentor, it is plausible to suppose that he sent Banneker forward to join his cousin after he had arrived in Alexandria, perhaps even after he had made observations fixing the latitude of that place on the 11th, had run the first two lines to establish the base point on Hunting Creek on the 12th, and had begun the rough survey on the afternoon of the 14th. Ellicott was able to recruit only five or six inexperienced men in any case and his cousin must certainly have known of this difficulty. Thus even the time at which Banneker joined the survey is clouded in uncertainty.

In any case, Banneker's participation in the surveying of the Federal District was unquestionably brief and his role uncertain. In less than seven working days after establishing the base point, Ellicott had run the first of the "lines of experiment" and had crossed the Potomac after completing more than a third of the second line. In other words, in this brief period he had finished a full third of rough survey, averaging one-twentieth of the total distance per day. Thus, even allowing for the attack of influenza which did not entirely interrupt his progress and from which he had fully recovered by the 21st of March, it is probable that the rough survey was completed within four weeks. It was certainly finished in less than six, for on the 28th of March Washington was able to inspect Ellicott's plat when he arrived in Georgetown.

The significance of this progress, which was in accord with TJ's urgent directions, lies not so much in its rapidity as in its value as corrective. Obviously, on Ellicott's swift journey from Philadelphia, whether on horseback or by stage, he could scarcely have brought with him a large assortment of scientific instruments, including his six-foot zenith sector and the bulkier astronomical clock, to say nothing of tents, stores, and other equipment. Nor indeed was this necessary. In authorizing the preliminary survey, Washington desired only that "the general view" of the location of the ten mile square be ascertained (Washington to TJ, 1 Feb. 1791; Document x). In giving directions to Ellicott, TJ required accuracy only in establishing the base point on Hunting Creek: the four lines of experiment could then be run with "only common exactness" (TJ to Ellicott, 2 Feb. 1791; Document xi). Thus speed and not absolute accuracy was the desideratum. The observation tent with its instruments of precision and with a scientific assistant engaged during the whole of the survey in recording astronomical observations, an elaborate surveying camp with tents for dining and sleeping, supported by experienced assistants such as Ellicott's younger brothers, Benjamin and Joseph, chain bearers, rodmen, woodcutters, and having in train horses, wagons, supplies, and other equipment—these all belonged to the measured pace of the

many difficulties for the want of his old hands.[120] Exaggerated and even fanciful accounts of the contributions of the ingenious and worthy Banneker have proliferated, but the fact is that—as Maclay had pointed out—all who were involved in the measurement of the bounds, whether in this hasty effort to produce a rough plat or in the definitive survey, had been reduced to the status of mere surveyors. Not even the commissioners could have made any substantial alteration in what the President and the Secretary of State had planned in such secrecy at the beginning of the year. The district had been defined so explicitly

---

final running of the boundaries. At this initial stage such would have been unwieldy and unnecessary encumbrances. The small, portable zenith sector, together with any reasonably accurate timepiece, would have enabled Ellicott to fix the base point on Hunting Creek with tolerable exactness. Thereafter his transit and equal altitude instrument, which he regarded as being "of all others the most perfect, and best calculated for running straight lines," would have sufficed for this rough survey. This, in fact, was the instrument that he employed (Andrew Ellicott to Robert Patterson, 2 Apr. 1795; Am. Phil. Soc., *Trans.*, IV [1799], p. 49). Since Ellicott chose to run each of the four lines at a right angle to its predecessor instead of by compass bearings as called for in the proclamation, his circumferentor would have served to establish these horizontal angles. There is no evidence to show which of the two zenith sectors he employed on the 12th of February to trace the meridian lines at Jones' Point, but it is plausible to assume that he used the smaller one because it had the advantage of portability. This is indicated by the fact that on the 14th Ellicott could not give the precise latitude of Alexandria (Document XII). Indeed, it was not until April, after the completion of the preliminary survey, that he "ascertained the precise point" of beginning (see note 130, below). Presumably by then his astronomical clock and the larger, more accurate zenith sector, together with other instruments needed for the definitive survey, had been brought from Philadelphia.

Since, therefore, there was no need for a scientific assistant engaged in continuous astronomical observations during the course of the rough survey, the traditional view of the role of Banneker requires revision. Bedini, describing Banneker as aged and inexperienced as a surveyor, concluded that he was "neither capable nor qualified to run the lines" (Bedini, *Banneker*, p. 115-16). What other function, then, could he have performed? Ellicott may have employed him because of his desperate need for helpers, possibly training him in the use of the transit and equal altitude instrument.

But, considering Banneker's infirmity and the nature of the preliminary survey, the most plausible explanation is one that has little if any relation to the task itself. As Bedini has demonstrated conclusively, abolitionists and friends of free Negroes assisted Banneker in the compilation of his almanacs, promoted their publication, prompted him to enter into correspondence with TJ, and in general brought him before the public, as they did others, to demonstrate the potentialities of his race. The allusion in Georgetown and other newspapers to Banneker's participation in the survey as a refutation of TJ's purported views on the intellectual capacity of Negroes seems to support this inference. If this explanation is correct, Banneker's actual function in the mapping of the Federal District, like that as compiler of almanacs and as correspondent of the Secretary of State, was less as surveyor than as symbol. But in his effort to penetrate the mass of errors and exaggerations that have accumulated around the symbol, Bedini gave Banneker's achievement a truer and more worthy evaluation: "Better than any other lesson to be derived from Banneker's life and work is the one he so admirably exemplified: that the thirst for knowledge is not limited to youth, and that the process of learning recognizes no barriers of race or creed" (Bedini, *Banneker*, p. xvii). The example was the creation of Banneker himself: the symbol largely that of others.

[120] Ellicott to his wife, Georgetown, 21 Mch. 1791 (Mathews, *Andrew Ellicott*, p. 86). Ellicott said that he had "worked . . . many days in extreme pain" but had fully recovered. He did not say whether this illness had actually interrupted the survey. Presumably it was completed about this time.

that Ellicott himself could propose only a technical variation in the manner of running the lines. Ellicott's suggestion arrived on the morning of the 21st of March, just in time for Jefferson to incorporate it in the proclamation that he hastily drafted and handed to the President on his departure shortly before noon on his southern tour.[121]

In addition to the ideas submitted in his first two reports, Jefferson offered three suggestions affecting the survey, the name, and the government of the Federal District, all of which failed to be adopted. The first, set forth in the President's proclamation of the 30th of March, was evidently a result of Ellicott's information about the unusual magnetic variations he had found in the vicinity of Alexandria. After accepting Ellicott's proposal to run the first line at an angle of 45° from the true meridian at the northern cape of Hunting Creek, or Jones' Point, Jefferson stated in the proclamation that the second line would start at the same place and run at a right angle with the first in a northeasterly direction, the third and fourth lines being carried ten miles from the terminals of the first two lines so as to meet in a point.[122] This mode of running the district lines appears in no other document and, in fact, it was not observed in the final survey. Both in that and in the preliminary survey the lines were run in the consecutive order prescribed in the original proclamation.[123] Jefferson's second suggestion about the name of the district evidently evolved out of his early texts in which he employed the terms "federal seat," "federal district," and "federal territory" in a synonymous sense. In the fullest amplitude of meaning which he gave to the last term, he intended that the inhabitants of the Federal Territory should enjoy full rights of self-government. This is proved by the fact that Jefferson later drafted a bill that would have provided an even more autonomous form of government than that enjoyed by other territories under the Ordinance of 1787 and its confirming act. This bill was never enacted.[124] Jefferson's suggestion that the district be called the Federal Territory was formally approved by the commissioners, but popular usage caused this official designation to give way to that ultimately confirmed, first by custom and then by law: the District of Columbia.[125]

Jefferson's third proposal, set forth in a memorandum prepared for the President's use in the discussions to take place at Georgetown on his way South in 1791, is the most surprising of all. In this document he suggested that the district square be tilted to the eastward, regardless of the bearings of its four lines as defined in the original proclama-

---

[121] Documents XII and XIII; Washington departed from Philadelphia "about 11 o'clock to make a tour through the Southern States" (Washington, *Diaries*, ed. Fitzpatrick, IV, 149). Hence TJ's draft of the proclamation, incorporating the suggestion made by Ellicott in a letter received on the 21st, was drafted early in the morning of that day. TJ and Knox accompanied the President "part of the way on his journey" (*Virginia Gazette* [Davis], 6 Apr. 1791).

[122] Document XIII.

[123] See note 118; also Ellicott's affidavit of 1 Jan. 1793, describing the running of the final lines (Mathews, *Andrew Ellicott*, p. 95).

[124] "An act for establishing the Government of the territory of Columbia," MS in TJ's hand, undated but probably written ca. 1800-1802 (DLC: TJ Papers, 232: 42012-13).

[125] Commissioners to L'Enfant, 9 Sep. 1791 (Padover, *National Capital*, p. 74).

tion. These courses, whatever interpretation the inhabitants of Alexandria and the public generally might have placed upon them, had not been fixed by the amending legislation and Jefferson concluded that his new arrangement would be legal. In a strict sense this was no doubt correct, since the district would still lie to the north of the Hunting Creek as the law required. But the legislative intent undoubtedly had been to authorize the President to fix the district in accordance with the explicit terms of his message and the proclamation, neither of which conveyed any hint that other alternatives might be in contemplation. What makes the suggestion all the more surprising is that Jefferson thought it would require further legislation by Maryland.[126] He offered no reason for proposing such a change in the district at this late date except that it would permit the inclusion of Bladensberg. This was perhaps a tribute to the desire of inhabitants along the Potomac to be included in the district, but Ellicott objected and Washington sustained him after he had inspected the survey and made his own observations. To have included Bladensberg, Washington informed Jefferson, "would have occasioned the exclusion of more important objects."[127] He did not explain what these were.

Despite illness and difficulties, Ellicott was able to place the results of the preliminary survey before the President when he arrived in Georgetown on the 28th of March. On that day Washington appointed the three commissioners, examined Ellicott's surveys, and was given a public dinner at Suter's tavern. The next day he brought the Georgetown and Carrollsburg landowners together, told them that their fears and jealousies of each other were "counteracting the public purposes and might prove injurious to its best interests," and urged them to make common cause of it lest they endanger the whole enterprise through procrastination and delay. Such a blunt warning, backed by the commanding presence of the Chief Executive, could not be disregarded. "This business being thus happily finished," Washington wrote in his diary, "and some directions given to the Commissioners, the Surveyor and Engineer with respect to the mode of laying out the district—Surveying the grounds for the City and forming them into lots, I left Georgetown, dined in Alexandria and reached Mount Vernon in the evening."[128] He carried with him Jefferson's draft of the proclamation, the principal paragraph of which Washington now thought unnecessary and indeed improper to disclose to public view. The very success of his negotiations at Georgetown had enabled him to suppress for the time being his intended announcement of the location of the public buildings. Washington inserted the date in Jefferson's draft of the proclamation and directed that it be signed, sealed, and published. With its principal passage deleted, the proclamation conveyed nothing to the public of which it was not already aware save the requirement of a mode of running the lines that everyone thenceforth disregarded. This rendered the proclamation almost meaningless, though on the day after Washington signed it information about the extent of the Federal

[126] See TJ's memorandum to the President, 11 Mch. 1791.
[127] Washington to TJ, 31 Mch. 1791. One of these objects may have been to avoid exclusion of George Mason's tract of land at the Little Falls.
[128] Washington, *Diaries*, ed. Fitzpatrick, IV, 154-5.

City was unofficially communicated to the press. This was in a "letter from a gentleman at George-town to his friend" in Baltimore, which concluded: "The spot for the public buildings is not yet fixed."[129] Suppression of this key passage in the proclamation left Washington uncommitted in case the Georgetown and Carrollsburg proprietors should fail, after all, to make common cause of it.

Shortly after this proclamation was issued, two of the commissioners arrived in Alexandria to preside over the fixing of the first of the stones marking the bounds of the Federal District. The mayor, the commonalty, and the members of different lodges of freemasons waited on the commissioners and drank this toast: "May the stone which we are about to place in the ground remain an immovable monument of the wisdom and unanimity of North-America." The company then proceeded to Jones' Point. There Ellicott ascertained the precise point from which the first line of the district was to proceed, the master of the lodge and his brethren placed the stone and made a deposit of corn, wine, and oil upon it, and then the Rev. James Muir struck this note of peace, plenty, and unity in his invocation:[130]

> May this Stone long commemorate the goodness of God and those uncommon events which have given America a name among the nations. Under this Stone may Jealousy and Selfishness be forever buried! From this Stone may a superstructure arise whose glory, whose magnificence, whose stability, unequalled hitherto, shall astonish the World and invite even the Savage of the wilderness to take shelter under its roof!

But the stone, like Washington's toast at Hagerstown to the perpetuity of the Federal City on the Potomac, was a testimonial also to the fears, the jealousies, and the threats of disunity that had marked the history of this effort to locate the capital of a growing empire. The commissioners and the surveyor of the Federal District thus contributed to the defining of its boundaries chiefly a symbolic act, one not only reflecting the divisions of the past but also anticipating those that would ensue at the next stage of the enterprise.

Amid the rejoicings along the tidewater and the silences up-river, Andrew Ellicott proceeded with the final survey of the boundaries, clearing a swath forty feet wide and setting up squared milestones numbered progressively from the beginning at Jones' Point and bearing on the interior face the inscription "Jurisdiction of the United

---

[129] Document XIII; the letter from Georgetown was published in *Virginia Gazette* (Richmond), 13 Apr. 1791, from a Baltimore paper of 1 Apr. George Mason, writing to his son after Washington's proclamation had been issued and giving him an exact description of the district boundaries, remarked: "The spot for the public buildings (which is the most important point) is not yet fixed" (George Mason to John Mason, 16 Apr. 1791, Rowland, *George Mason*, II, 336).

[130] *Pennsylvania Journal*, 4 May 1791; the account of the ceremony carried an Alexandria date-line of 21 Apr. 1791. After liquid refreshments at Jones' Point, the assemblage returned to Alexandria where "a number of toasts were drank, and the following . . . was received with every token of approbation: 'May "Jealousy, that green-eyed Monster," be buried deep under the work which we have this day completed, never to rise again within the Federal District!'" The account of the ceremony was carried in various newspapers, including the *Independent Chronicle* (Boston), 22 May 1791.

States" and on the opposite side, as required, "Virginia" or "Maryland."[131] On running the first line he was shocked to find the country so poor that every house encountered in a seven-mile stretch had only an earthen floor. "This country intended for the Permanent Residence of Congress," he wrote to his wife in surprise that such poverty could exist in the vicinity of Alexandria and Georgetown, "bears no more proportion to the Country about Philadelphia, and German-Town, for either wealth or fertility, than a Crane does to a stall-fed Ox." Then, matching the silence of Henry Lee and others who had experienced either disappointment or wonderment at the President's final decision, he also pledged his wife to secrecy: "As the President is so much attached to this country, I would not be willing that he should know my real sentiments about it."[132] Many of his countrymen must have felt the same.

VI

Washington was indeed profoundly attached to the environment in which he had grown up and to which he was bound by all of the ties of affection and interest. But the inference drawn by Ellicott, Maclay, and others at the time and since that his choice for the permanent seat of government was determined by his attachment to the pleasant countryside surrounding his own seat at Mount Vernon is one that cannot be sustained by proof and is difficult to defend on grounds of plausibility. There is, to be sure, little if any reason to doubt that, had Washington consulted only his own personal interests and preferences, the choice would have been the same as that he made on behalf of the nation. It is true also that later, when he was seeking to put his affairs in order and to lease all save one of his plantations to English farmers, he was at pains to point out that his estate—the most pleasantly situated of any in the United States and located on one of the finest rivers of the world, he thought—had indeed increased in value by its proximity to the capital. "The federal city . . . will, I have no doubt," he wrote, "from the advantages given to it by nature, and its proximity to a rich interior country, and the western territory, become the emporium of the United States."[133] It must also be conceded that, if any of Washington's decisions as President bears on its face marks of having been influenced by such personal considerations, this choice of location for the seat of government was surely the one. But this very fact presents the strongest reason for rejecting the inference. For if any should be led to believe that the President had permitted this important decision to be determined on grounds other than the national interest, then Washington's renown as Cincinnatus incarnate—his unique reputation as an incorruptible leader that extended throughout the western world and even into Siberia[134]—would unquestionably be tarnished. The asser-

[131] Ellicott's affidavit, 1 Jan. 1793 (Mathews, *Andrew Ellicott*, p. 95).
[132] Ellicott to his wife, "Surveyors Camp, State of Virginia," 26 June 1791; on 9 Aug. 1791 he also wrote his wife from camp near Georgetown: "a most eligant Camp and things are in fine order," though one of his hands had been killed the preceding week by a falling tree (same, p. 88-90).
[133] Washington to Arthur Young, 12 Dec. 1793 (Washington, *Writings*, XXXIII, 175-6).
[134] John Ledyard to TJ, 29 July 1787.

tions of William Maclay, Andrew Ellicott, and others provide proof enough that some harbored the suspicion but dared not voice it in public. It is scarcely credible to suppose that the President was not aware of this risk and that he did not take it into account.

For Washington was painfully cognizant that the eyes of Argus were upon him.[135] He had accepted the presidency despite his "invincible attachment to domestic life" and because he saw the beginning of the new government as a most solemn crisis in which the central question was whether the United States would "survive as an independent Republic, or decline from . . . fœderal dignity into insignificant and wretched fragments of Empire."[136] He was also aware that his countrymen expected too much of him and that their extravagant praises could be replaced by "equally extravagant . . . censures."[137] But he set out determined to act justly and solely for the public good, regardless of this danger. "I am conscious," he wrote, "that I fear alone to give any real occasion for obloquy, and that I do not dread to meet with unmerited reproach. And certain I am, whensoever the good of my country requires my reputation to be put in risque; regard for my own fame will not come in competition with an object of so much magnitude."[138] Viewed in the whole tenor of his presidency, an overwhelming amount of evidence has produced a general concurrence with Jefferson's estimate that, though Washington might err as other men, he erred with integrity and did not sacrifice the public good in order to maintain his own fame and popularity.[139] Nevertheless, one of the cardinal traits of his character was his profound concern not merely to be disinterested in the conduct of public office but also to maintain the appearance of being so. Once, in a fit of blazing anger before his cabinet, he "defied any man on earth to produce one single act of his since he had been in the government, which was not done on the purest motives."[140] The challenge was impossible to meet on probative grounds, of course, but the significance of the outburst lay not in his consciousness of purity but in the nature of his response to public obloquy. As his administration wore on and divisive politics emerged, responses of a similar if less vehement nature multiplied—as, for example, when he learned that his levees were reported in Richmond to be conducted with more pomp than at St. James' palace and that Patrick Henry had refused a place in the Senate because he affected to be "too old to fall into those awkward imitations" of monarchical manners.[141] Washington was indeed so inordinately concerned about the need to sustain his public reputation for impeccable conduct that he was even aware of the danger of exhibiting a seemingly false or "ostentatious disinterestedness."[142]

Yet this is the precise error, one of a fundamental nature affecting almost every aspect of his administration from its outward etiquette

[135] Washington to Bushrod Washington, 27 July 1789 (Washington, *Writings*, ed. Fitzpatrick, xxx, 366).
[136] Washington to Henry Lee, 22 Sep. 1788 (same, xxx, 95-6).
[137] Washington to Edward Rutledge, 5 May 1789 (same, xxx, 309).
[138] Washington to Henry Lee, 22 Sep. 1788 (same, xxx, 95-6).
[139] TJ to William Branch Giles, 31 Dec. 1795.
[140] TJ's memorandum of a cabinet meeting, 2 Aug. 1793.
[141] David Stuart to Washington, 2 June 1790 (DLC: Washington Papers).
[142] Madison to TJ, 22 Jan. 1786.

to its major decisions, into which Washington fell. His glowing letter to Jefferson early in 1789 about the importance of the Potomac connection with the northwest, for example, professed to be nothing more than a continuation of a long series of communications on the subject. In actuality, as Jefferson must have surmised, it was written solely and upon request in order to promote the speculation of Lee and Madison at the Great Falls, though this fact and their names were nowhere mentioned in it.[143] This concealment was intentional and it was done solely in order to avoid any imputation of improper motives. "For I hold it necessary," Washington explained to Lee, "that one should not only be conscious of the purest *intentions*; but that one should also have it in his power to demonstrate the disinterestedness of his *words* and actions at all times, and upon all occasions."[144] In brief, it was necessary to be able to make the demonstration even if, as in this case, deception as to purpose and means had to be employed. But of the many examples of this trait in Washington's character no further proof is needed than that offered by his tour of inspection up the Potomac in the autumn of 1790—a journey which, undertaken after the decision had been made, could have served no purpose save that of preserving the appearance of an impartial weighing of all factors affecting the public interest. So powerful was this trait that in this instance Washington encouraged false hopes and expectations among some of his fellow citizens in order to preserve his own posture of incorruptible conduct.

This, far from being the result of venality or of a devious temperament, was an impossible burden under which Washington, showered with the adulation of the world, labored in an earnest effort to meet the standards that the public expected him to meet. Hence the tragedy, as well as one of the principal keys to his conduct in the presidency, lies in this preoccupation with an outward demonstration of purity. For once the shield borne by the popular hero had been or appeared to have been blemished, as was inevitable, many concluded erroneously that the inner integrity did not exist and thus were led at the close of his administration to heap extravagant and unjust obloquy upon him. In the light of this very conspicuous aspect of his character, it is implausible to assume that Washington was not aware of the risk of being charged with having chosen the location of the Federal District because of personal interest and attachment. This was a risk that he faced and accepted.

[143] Washington to TJ, 13 Feb. 1789 (see notes 17, 18, and 144).
[144] The emphasis is Washington's; Washington to Lee, 13 Feb. 1789 (Washington, *Writings*, ed. Fitzpatrick, 202-3); Washington enclosed his letter to TJ of the same date, sending it under a flying seal so that Lee could read it before sending it on. Lee either enclosed this in his letter to TJ of 6 Mch. 1789 or sent it by the same conveyance, for TJ received both letters on the same day. Under these circumstances, he could scarcely have failed to grasp the real point of a communication that added nothing to Washington's previous letters on the Potomac navigation except to describe the potentialities of the site at Great Falls. It is this fact, together with Madison's involvement, that probably caused TJ to make a genuine effort to raise capital for the partners; for, in approaching Gouverneur Morris on the subject, he exhibited to him the letters of both Lee and Washington. Morris gave the proposition "the go bye" (Morris, *Diaries*, ed. Davenport, I, 58-9).

What powerful reasons, then, prompted the decision which seemed to ignore the wishes of the men on the western waters, which discounted the arguments about the vulnerability of a tidewater location, and which flouted the legislative expression of preference of his own state? The answer to these questions must remain conjectural, since Washington never disclosed the reasons for his choice. It must also include the supposition that, always cautious, deliberate, and thorough in arriving at a conclusion, he weighed all such factors in the scales of the national interest. What could have counterbalanced them? One of the factors most likely to exert a compelling influence over his judgment—the preference stated so explicitly in the Virginia act of cession —evidently was not known to him at the time the decision was made. As for the question of security, Washington seems to have been unduly optimistic about the possibility of providing adequate defenses against a naval assault on a tidewater capital. L'Enfant, for whose talents he had an exaggerated respect, may have led him into this error by suggestions advanced in 1789.[145] He may also have been convinced that a location near such active ports as Georgetown and Alexandria, lying on the main post road of the nation, would accommodate the western settlements quite as readily as an up-river site, besides being more acceptable to the northern and southern states. Since writing his glowing appraisal of the prospects of the site at the Great Falls, he had received encouraging reports that the difficult obstructions to the canal from that place to tidewater would undoubtedly be removed.[146]

By far the most powerful influence affecting his choice, however, appears to have arisen not from strategic or geographical considerations but from the realm of partisan politics. During the preceding three years Washington had been repeatedly alarmed by obstructionist tactics on the part of the Virginia opponents of the new government. Their response in 1788 to the New York circular letter calling for a second federal convention he regarded as a move "to set every thing afloat again."[147] George Mason's part in this gave him acute concern. A "respectable Neighbour of mine," he wrote at this time, "has said, the Constitution cannot be carried into execution, without great amendments."[148] Washington indeed considered the country to be in danger

[145] L'Enfant to Washington, 11 Sep. 1789 (DLC: Washington Papers).

[146] See note 33 above; George Gilpin to Washington, 2 Sept. 1789 (DLC: Washington Papers); Washington to Gilpin, 14 Sep. 1789 (Washington, *Writings*, ed. Fitzpatrick, xxx, 403). Gilpin had just returned from a tour of inspection of about 200 miles above tidewater and concluded: "If we allow 10 miles from the Tide to the big falls and 17 from the mouth of Savage [which he estimated to be 210 miles above tidewater] to deep Creek, 27 Miles Carriage unites Potomack with the Waters of Yohogany in their present State and the Ten Miles I have no doubt will be removed" (for Washington's earlier views on these obstructions below the Great Falls, see his letter to Madison, 17 Nov. 1788; same, xxx, 128-31).

[147] Washington to Benjamin Lincoln, 28 Aug. 1788 (same, xxx, 62).

[148] Washington to James McHenry, 31 July 1788 (same, xxx, 29); Washington conceded that some amendments might be necessary, but nevertheless feared that it would be "a point of no common delicacy" to do this "without producing or at least fostering such a spirit of innovation as will overturn the whole system." Long before the Federal Convention Madison had found Mason "too little impressed with either the necessity or the proper means of preserving the confederacy" (Madison to TJ, 10 Dec. 1783).

of political shipwreck because of such acrimonious partisanship and
the intrusion of local feuds and politics into the discussion of this great
national question. "A just opinion, that the People when rightly informed will decide in a proper manner, ought certainly to have prevented all intemperate or precipitate proceedings on a subject of so
much magnitude," he wrote, "nor should a regard to common decency
have suffered the zealots in the minority to stigmatize the authors of
the Constitution as Conspirators and Traitors. . . . Nor did the out-
rageous disposition, which some indulged in traducing and villifying
the members, seem much calculated to produce concord or accommodation."[149] The vilification rankled all the more because some of the
shafts had come from Mason, his former friend and political ally, and
had been more pointedly directed toward Washington than he affected
to think.[150] Only in the early weeks of 1789, when Virginia elected a
majority of Federalist representatives and when the two senators, Lee
and Grayson, professed a willingness to give the new government a
fair field, did Washington experience relief from the profound anxiety
for the fate of the union that the politics of his native state had induced in him.

But this was only a momentary relief. Washington had scarcely assumed office when he learned that Patrick Henry's comment about
proposed titles for the President and the Vice-President as squinting
towards monarchy was "in every mouth and . . . established him in the
general opinion as a true Prophet."[151] A few months later a further
cause for concern arose when a minority of the Virginia Senate, including a nephew of George Mason, declared that the people of Virginia

[149] Washington to Charles Pettit, 16 Aug. 1788 (same, XXX, 41-2).
[150] From 1787 onward Mason seems to have shown a tendency to impute treasonable motives to political opponents. An authentic example of this is his characterization of Edmund Randolph as "a young A—ld"—a traitor to his native
Virginia—because he had shifted from opposition to support of the Constitution
(George Mason to John Mason, 18 Dec. 1788, Rowland, *George Mason*, II, 304).
Mason is also reported to have given vent to his "envy and hatred for Genl.
Washington" during the debate over ratification by making a speech in Stafford
county in which he is alleged to have said that "Speculators, place-hunters, and
horse-jockeys composed that infamous body of traitors" who had drafted the Constitution (*Decius's letters on the opposition to the new Constitution in Virginia*
[Richmond, Augustine Davis, 1789], with marginal identification of Mason as
the speaker: see Vol. 16: 143). It is worth noting also that Mason thought there
were few clauses in the Constitution more dangerous than that giving Congress
exclusive jurisdiction over the Federal District. This unlimited authority, he
thought, might enable the government to set at defiance the laws of the surrounding states and "become the sanctuary of the blackest crimes" (Rowland, *George
Mason*, II, 416). This tendency to extreme viewpoints, to the imputation of unworthy motives, and to a fear of sapping influences at work on the pillars of republicanism (Mason to TJ, 10 Jan. 1791) was no doubt exacerbated in late years
by age and ill health. But of its existence there can be no doubt.
[151] David Stuart to Washington, 14 July 1789 (DLC: Washington Papers);
Edward Stevens told Madison that the Senate action on titles "had alarmed their
best friends. . . . It gave a great opening to the enemies of the Constitution to
insult its friends" (Stevens to Madison, 25 June 1789; Joseph Jones to Madison,
28 May 1789, DLC: Madison Papers).— On Washington's brief period of confidence in the strength of nationalist sentiment, see his letters between 1 Jan. and
2 Mch. 1789 to Howard, Innes, Knox, Lafayette, Lincoln, Powel, and Rochambeau
(Washington, *Writings*, XXX, 173, 185-7, 189-90, 194, 195, 213, 218, 219). See
also TJ to Madison, 29 July 1789.

would never have ratified the Constitution if they had thought it would
not be more materially altered than by the twelve amendments that had
been proposed by Congress.[152] By the spring of 1790 Washington
had even more striking symptoms of the kind of opposition in Virginia
that would soon be characterized as "a spirit which must either be
killed or will kill the constitution of the United States."[153] Federal
measures, he was informed, had produced a fast-growing "spirit of
jealousy which may become dangerous to the Union. . . . It is represented, that the Northern phalanx is so firmly united, as to bear down
all opposition, while Virginia is unsupported, even by those whose interests are similar to hers."[154] Washington, in reply, warned against
"malignant, designing characters, who miss no opportunity of aiming a
blow at the Constitution."[155] There can be little doubt that the characters whom he had in mind were the two principal leaders of the opposition in Virginia, Patrick Henry and George Mason. The latter had
so flatly refused the vacancy in the Senate created by the death of
William Grayson that Governor Randolph, in a proclamation designating John Walker, pointedly called attention to Mason's refusal.[156] "I
always expected the Gentleman, whose name you have mentioned,"
Washington had written about Mason, "would mark his opposition
to the new government with consistency. Pride on the one hand, and
want of manly candor on the other, will not I am certain let him

[152] The explanation given by the minority for withholding assent to four of
the proposed amendments because of their "defects and dangerous tendency"
appeared in the *Virginia Independent Chronicle*, 13 Jan. 1790. Stevens Thomson
Mason, one of the signers, was a nephew of George Mason, "whose principles he
had made thoroughly his own" (Rowland, *George Mason*, II, 319).

[153] Alexander Hamilton to John Jay, 13 Nov. 1790 (Syrett, *Hamilton*, VII,
149); it should also be noted that, long before he announced his decision on the
Federal District, Washington was well aware of the Virginia resolutions that had
provoked Hamilton's remark. He could scarcely have missed the publication of the
resolution, as originally introduced, in Davis' *Virginia Gazette*, 17 Nov. 1790, or
in Bache's *General Advertiser* of 28 Dec. 1790 which, quoting *The American
Mercury*, described Virginia as "stark mad with the assumption, declaring it . . .
a dangerous measure and unconstitutional" and as "proud without power, and
wise without decency."

[154] David Stuart to Washington, 15 Mch. 1790 (DLC: Washington Papers).

[155] Washington to David Stuart, 28 Mch. 1790 (Washington, *Writings*, ed.
Fitzpatrick, XXXI, 28-30); over a year earlier Washington had said that Henry
gave law to the legislature and that it had "displayed the most malignant (and
. . . unwarrantable) disposition toward the New Government, in all its acts"
(Washington to Madison, 17 Nov. 1788); Washington to Stuart, 2 Dec. 1788
(same, XXX, 131, 146-7).

[156] Beverley Randolph to George Mason, 25 Mch. 1790, transmitting his commission and entreating his acceptance because the "very important subjects now
before Congress, so interesting to America in general, and more especially to your
native State, call for the counsels of the wisest of her citizens." The *Virginia Independent Chronicle*, 31 Mch. 1790, announced Mason's appointment and that
same day Randolph issued a proclamation stating that Mason, "who was duly
chosen a senator . . . refused to act during the recess of the Legislature" (Rowland, *George Mason*, II, 324-5). One Virginian who hoped Henry would succeed
Grayson named Mason as his second choice because, "independent of his great
abilities, his interest dictates the propriety of his using his utmost endeavours, to
get the seat of the federal Government established [. . .] on the Potowmack"
(John Briggs to Richard Blow, 18 Mch. 1790; ViW: Blow Family Papers).

acknowledge an error in his opinions respecting it though conviction should flash on his mind as strongly as a ray of light."[157]

The warnings of multiplying disaffection in Virginia continued to come to the President in the spring and summer of 1790. On the question of assumption, he was told, "there would be as nearly an unanimity of opinion for an opposition, as perhaps could ever be expected on any subject." The "Catalogue of Public Discontents," Washington's friend David Stuart wrote after compiling the list of grievances, "really pains me much, and I believe every friend to the government, to think that there should be so much cause for them; and that a spirit so subversive of the true principles of the Constitution, productive of jealousies alone, and fraught with such high ideas of . . . power, should have manifested itself at so early a period of the Government. If Mr. Henry has sufficient boldness to aim the blow at it's existence, which he has threatened, I think he can never meet with more favorable opportunity if the assumption should take place on the principles on which it has been contended for."[158] Virginia, Washington declared just before he signed the Residence Act, "seems to be more irritable, sour and discontented than . . . any other State in the Union, except Massachusetts."[159] Threats of disunion had come from both states over the issue of assumption. On the question of the permanent seat of government—one that Washington had long regarded as "pregnant with difficulty and danger"[160]—the very arguments for a location that would help cement the union betrayed latent fears of disunion. It was at this precise moment when opposition to assumption was at its height in Virginia, with even Henry Lee hinting at separation and talking as if he were in the camp of Henry and Mason, that Washington prepared to make his choice of site for the capital. He had already urged that Virginia dissidents reflect upon a question he deemed of the greatest magnitude—whether, if it were dangerous to live in union with the northern phalanx, it would be less so to live in separation.[161] Yet sectional animosities and opposition to federal measures continued to grow. Now, with the public clamors augmented greatly by the legislative bargaining that had brought the capital to the Potomac, Washington

157 Washington to James Craik, 8 Sep. 1789 (Washington, *Writings*, ed. Fitzpatrick, XXX, 395-6).

158 David Stuart to Washington, 2 June 1790 (DLC: Washington Papers). In addition to Virginia opposition to assumption itself, the governor and council formally declared their want of confidence in two of the commissioners for settling accounts with the states, John Kean of South Carolina and John Taylor Gilman of New Hampshire, whose speculations and zeal for assumption were thought to have influenced their report, called by Madison "a libel on the State." This episode brought considerable embarrassment to Washington just as he was about to decide the location of the Federal District (Beverley Randolph to Washington, 4 Aug. 1790, with enclosed reports, DNA: RG 59, MLR; Washington to Randolph, 24 Aug. 1790, *Writings*, ed. Fitzpatrick, XXXI, 95).

159 Washington to David Stuart, 15 June 1790 (Washington, *Writings*, ed. Fitzpatrick, XXXI, 50).

160 Washington to Henry Lee, 22 Sep. 1788 (same, XXX, 95-6).

161 Washington to Stuart, 28 Mch. 1790 (same, XXXI, 28-30); this is one of the longest and most revealing letters that Washington wrote after the opposition had emerged in an unmistakable manner. On Lee's fear of disunion, see his letter to Madison, 3 Apr. 1790 (DLC: Madison Papers).

had at his disposal only the choice of its exact location as a possible means of placating some of the disaffected in his own state.

A choice on tidewater might add to the growing discontent of Henry Lee but, as Washington had reason to know, it could have a very opposite effect on George Mason. Lee, a known advocate of the Constitution and loyal supporter of the President, was genuinely dissatisfied with federal measures, but this was of recent origin and had been privately expressed. He had also directed his animus primarily at the northern states, not at the new system of government. The opposition of George Mason, on the other hand, had begun with the framing of the Constitution and was a matter of continuing public record. It was also, quite obviously, a source of genuine concern to Washington. As between these two Virginia malcontents, there was no doubt that Mason could command the more powerful political arsenal. If he could be won over as the sort of ally he had been during the Revolution, the opposition would be deprived of one of its most persuasive voices.

It is not surprising, therefore, that, soon after being elected, Washington had made friendly gestures toward his former friend.[162] Later, contrary to his firm and oft-repeated rule of making no appointments to office except for merit, he had yielded to Mason's importunings for patronage. This he did in an obvious effort to placate, for it was no secret among the political leaders of Virginia that, along with his undeniably great abilities as legislator, Mason possessed a shrewd and unabashed talent for improving his own interests through public office and political connections. At this juncture of events, zealously engaged in promoting the mercantile partnership that his son had formed with John Fenwick in Bordeaux, he was urging his former acquaintances in public life to patronize the firm and thus help augment American commercial connections with France.[163] So pronounced was this trait of character that, despite his hostility to the national government and his embittered attitude toward Washington himself, Mason had solicited the appointment of his son's partner as consul at Bordeaux. Washington, at first non-committal, finally acquiesced when the dissatisfaction

[162] Mason was entertained at dinner at Mount Vernon on 2 Nov. 1788 and, after being elected, Washington declined to consider Mason's coachman for employment unless released first by his employer (Washington, *Diaries*, ed. Fitzpatrick, III, 440-1; Washington to Mason, 23 Mch. 1789, *Writings*, ed. Fitzpatrick, XXX, 249-50; Mason to Washington, 23 Mch. 1789, DLC: Washington Papers).

[163] Mason, supplying his son with numerous letters of introduction in the United States and abroad, repeatedly urged him to cultivate the attentions of ministers, governors, legislators, members of the Federal Convention, and other public figures who could be useful to the firm of Fenwick & Mason. "I have written to most of my friends in the different States, informing them of your plan, and recommending the house," he wrote. "From the answers I have received, I have reason to think you will meet with encouragement, both from the eastward and southward; I think it would be proper for you to write to the gentlemen of your acquaintance in the late Federal Convention, and in Boston" (George Mason to John Mason, 18 Dec. 1788, Rowland, *George Mason*, II, 307; see also p. 298-9, 300, 301, 305, 316, 317, 331, 337-8). A typical letter of this sort is that from Mason to TJ, 21 July 1788, which he sent open to his son and added that "a letter of recommendation from our Minister, Mr. Jefferson, would have a good effect" (same, II, 299, 305).

in Virginia continued to mount and when Mason left no doubt in the public mind that he was still in the opposition.[164]

The political nature of this bestowal of patronage is revealed in the hard choice it presented between the competing claims of genuine merit and bald self-interest. "No nomination occasioned more difficulty, nor hung longer suspended than this," an embarrassed Secretary of State was obliged to report to John Bondfield, who had been displaced by Fenwick in the Bordeaux consulship after long and faithful service to the United States. Jefferson suffered in silence the affecting response from Bondfield, whom he had earlier recommended as well qualified for the office on grounds of service and ability.[165] But to George Mason he was careful to say that the appointment of Fenwick had been made "according to your desire." To this he added other placatory advances. Amendments to the Constitution that would place the new government on a more republican basis, he wrote in full awareness that he was voicing Mason's own views, should be sought by "pressing forward with constancy." As for the assumption issue, he professed to be excluded by his office from intermingling in such legislative matters, but urged the opposition to seek a compromise, adding almost casually that, in general, it was "necessary to give as well as take in a govern-

[164] Mason really wanted the post for his son, but felt that Fenwick's age and experience made it prudent to advance his candidacy. He was also well aware of the fact that his opposition to the Constitution might have impaired his influence with Washington (same, II, 304-5, 313). He nevertheless applied directly to the President soon after he had assumed office (Mason to Washington, 19 June 1789, DLC: Washington Papers; Mason's son also asked the Vice-President to support Fenwick's candidacy: George Mason, Jr. to John Adams, 25 June 1789; Adams to Mason, 4 July 1789, MHi: AM). Washington had Lear respond, pleading his recent illness, though he was sufficiently recovered at this time to engage in other correspondence. Lear stated that the President had from the beginning made it a rule to appoint only those qualified for office and had "in no instance departed from it"; that Bondfield had been appointed by Franklin and favorably commended by TJ; and that, since TJ was returning, he could be consulted on the point (Lear to Mason, 6 July 1789, DNA: RG 59, MLR). Only a few days before he refused to serve as senator, Mason applied again for the consulate for Fenwick, this time to TJ (Mason to TJ, 16 Mch. 1790). He believed the appointment was made because of his "Interest with our Friend Mr. Jefferson" (George Mason to John Mason, 26 July 1790; Mason, *Papers*, ed. Rutland, III, 1204).

[165] TJ to Bondfield, 31 Aug. 1790; Bondfield to TJ, 8 Oct. 1790. Not only was George Mason accorded this political favor: his son's firm was also given commercial patronage of the highest rank—that of the President and the Secretary of State. From the time he arrived in France in 1784, TJ had patronized Bondfield, whom he regarded as a good judge of wines. He recommended that Virginians consign their tobacco to him, ordered wines through him, purchased from him gifts of anchovies, olives, and other delicacies for Americans, and on one occasion asked him to testify to his credit with owners of vineyards. Now, just after Bondfield had been deprived of his consulate, TJ sent a large order of wines for Washington and a small one for himself—not to the merchant who had so long enjoyed his custom but to the newly established firm of Fenwick & Mason (TJ to Eppes, 24 Jan. 1786; TJ to Cary, 12 Aug. 1787; TJ to Bondfield, 18 Dec. 1787 and 22 Feb. 1788; TJ to Fenwick, 6 Sep. 1790; TJ to Short, 6 Sep. 1790). True, Fenwick was only to transmit the orders to owners of vineyards and to receive and forward the wines "ready packed" for shipping. Nevertheless, the commission on behalf of the President was a gesture of friendliness to the firm of Fenwick & Mason that—as those who bestowed it could not have been unaware—would almost certainly come to the attention of George Mason.

ment like ours." These carefully calculated observations to one who did not hesitate to ask favors of the government he had declined to serve were made even more pointed when Jefferson insinuated a comment about the vote of the House of Representatives to remove to Baltimore. "Some," he added, "hope an opening will be given to convert it into a vote of the temporary seat at Philadelphia, and the permanent one at Georgetown."[166] Long familiar with George Mason's readiness to identify his own private interests with those of the public, Jefferson also knew that he owned a considerable amount of land in the vicinity of Georgetown.[167] The seemingly casual remark must have been intended to awaken in the mind of the recipient such prospects of personal benefit from the location of the capital as had once stirred the hopes of Henry Lee.

No response, either by letter or by a change of attitude toward the national government, resulted from this bestowal of patronage or from these characteristic hints of the Secretary of State. But in the autumn of 1790 the bait was once more, unmistakably, dangled before Mason's eyes. Jefferson and Madison, after leaving Mount Vernon, stopped at Gunston Hall for a visit. Jefferson's prompt report of the ensuing conversation allows little room for doubt that its primary purpose was an attempt at conciliation and that the question of the location of the Federal District was the chief means employed. Mason, perhaps suspecting already that patronage had been given him for such a reason, backed away from the subject whenever it was broached. But the visitors kept returning to it, always keeping their host in doubt as to what the President's ultimate decision would be.[168] More reticent than usual, Mason yet said enough to make it clear that his decided preference was Georgetown. He also countered the arguments of those who advocated a site above tidewater by suggesting that the high hills surrounding Georgetown made it easily defensible. The whole tenor of his comments indicated a preoccupation with the commercial advantages of such a location. Jefferson's explicit report, which omitted the name of their host and even that of his residence, proves that the President was cognizant of the object of the visit and suggests that it was the result of a plan that had been concerted when Jefferson and Madison were at Mount Vernon.

George Mason, the only person outside of government whose counsel on the comparative merits of different sites is known to have been solicited, was also the only one who is known to have had the temerity to ask about the decision before the announcement was made.[169] His inquiry was soon answered by the President's proclamation and he was able to transmit the information to his son at Bordeaux. In doing so he did not allude to the effect of the choice upon the great question of national unity. But he did take pains to define the lines of the Federal

[166] TJ to Mason, 13 June 1790.

[167] See for example, Mason's influence on the Virginia bill for settling titles to unpatented lands, legislation about which he was deeply concerned and which directly affected his own interests (Vol. 2: 133-67).

[168] TJ to Washington, 17 Sep. 1790 (Document IV, Vol. 17: 466-7).

[169] Mason to TJ, 10 Jan. 1791.

District in detail so as to show that it would include all of his tract of some two thousand acres at the Little Falls. He did not need to point out that it also included his island in the Potomac and his property on the shore opposite Georgetown. His animus toward Alexandria—one of those local feuds and divisions that had deeply troubled Washington because of their effect on great national questions[170]—caused him to derive another sort of satisfaction from the President's decision:[171]

> The Alexandrians, as usual, are very much buoyed up on the occasion and think their fortunes made forever, although it is evident to any cool, impartial, sensible man, that if the inland navigation of Potomac and Shenandoah is effectually completed and the seat of the federal government fixed near the harbor of the Eastern branch, Alexandria must become a deserted village.

No comment escaped him that touched even remotely on the meaning of the decision for the nation.

In another year Mason, watching the development of the Federal City with sanguine expectations, would be urging his son to consult L'Enfant about his land opposite Georgetown whereon the projected Potomac bridge would rest, cautioning him to keep the move secret from the people of Georgetown.[172] Almost at the same time, in a private and confidential letter to Alexander Hamilton, Washington would be reporting that even the sensible and moderate friends of government in Virginia had been alarmed by national policies and that others, "less friendly, perhaps, to the government, and more disposed to arraign the conduct of its officers (among whom may be classed my neighbor and *quondam* friend Col. M[ason])," went further and complained of a long train of measures. These, Washington concluded, seemed in the minds of some to point to the most incalculable of all evils—"the breaking of the Union into two, or more parts."[173] The words that the President thus paraphrased were those of the Secretary of State, but the lengthy catalogue of public measures that had brought the greatest of evils into clear view over the horizon amounted, in sum, to an indictment of that philosophy of government which held that the true bonds of union were the ligaments of self-interest. If, as seems most likely, Washington had been largely influenced in selecting a site for the permanent seat of government in the hope that such ligaments would bind George Mason, his aim, it seems equally clear, was not to win over an individual, much less to decide an important public question on grounds of private interest. It was rather to seek in this exercise

170 Washington to Charles Pettit, 16 Aug. 1788 (Washington, *Writings*, XXX, 41-2), a letter evidently composed under the influence of Mason's charges (see notes 149 and 150).

171 George Mason to John Mason, 16 Apr. 1791 (Rowland, *George Mason*, II, 336). It is obvious from this letter that TJ, in his conversations with Mason the preceding September, had not disclosed to him his sketch showing the location of the Federal City on the Eastern branch.

172 George Mason to John Mason, 20 Aug. 1792 (same, II, 360).

173 Washington to Hamilton, 29 July 1792, "(Private and Confidential)" (Washington, *Writings*, ed. Fitzpatrick, XXXII, 95-100).

of choice another answer to the central question—whether the United States would survive as an independent nation or "decline . . . into insignificant and wretched fragments of Empire."[174]

The choice which fixed the imperial city on the Potomac was evidently that of the President alone. If it was made to placate an avowed dissident with appeals to private motives, it revealed a willingness to employ means—the appeal to self-interest—that were at the root of much of Virginians' discontent with national measures. Both in the making of the choice and in the means employed, it seems clear, Jefferson filled the role of an acquiescent agent. Had the choice rested with him, he might in this instance have resorted to the principal argument he had employed a few years earlier in advocating the removal of the capital of Virginia to a safer and more central location—that a due regard be paid to the rights of the western people.[175] Washington, of course, was also attentive to such claims. He had long felt that a free and easy commercial intercourse with the westerners was "the *best*, if not the *only* cement" that could bind the East and West and that, with interest so linked to policy, only parsimony and contracted views could prevent such a bond from being created.[176] But Jefferson, who also understood the relation of commerce to policy, rested his hope of avoiding the incalculable evil of disunion on other grounds. Seeing the danger arise not from disaffection and opposition but from a philosophy of administration that placed its reliance on interested motives, he might have placed the capital of the rising empire closer to the men on the western waters in whose loyalty to the principles of the Revolution he found the strongest bonds of union. If his role in the decision was merely acquiescent, he could have drawn from his *Notes on Virginia* the consoling reflection that it was the spirit and manners of the people and not the site of their capital on which the preservation of the republic depended.[177]

[174] Washington to Henry Lee, 22 Sep. 1788 (same, XXX, 95-6).
[175] See TJ's heads of argument for removal of the capital from Williamsburg to Richmond (Vol. 1: 602-3); see also his notes of 1783 (Vol. 6: 364) and his letter to George Rogers Clark, 4 Dec. 1783, saying that the southern states had urged the Potomac "as the only point of union which can cement us to our Western friends when they shall be formed into separate states."
[176] Washington to William Irvine, 31 Oct. 1788 (Washington, *Writings*, XXX, 123).
[177] The observation, it is worth noting, occurs in a discussion of manufactures and commerce (*Notes on Virginia*, ed. Peden, p. 165).

I. James Madison's Advice on Executing the Residence Act

[Before 29 Aug. 1790]

"The act for establishing the temporary and permanent seats of the Government of the U. States" requires the following steps for carrying the latter into effect.

1. The appointment of three Commissioners
     of sufficient respectability
          having good will to the general object without any par-
          ticular bias of private interest. Quer. If local situation
          or interest be an objection outweighing the advantage
          of proximity and zeal for the object, as the President
          is to prescribe the place, and the Commissioners only
          to define the district, and as the subsequent discretion
          in the Commissioners will give no opportunity of
          sacrificing their trust to local considerations. The es-
          sential point seems to be that the Commission should
          be filled by men who prefer any place on the Potowmac
          to any place elsewhere. On this supposition, it may be
          easy to find men who would suit.[1]
          residing (a majority at least) so conveniently to the scene
               of business as to be able to attend readily and gratis
     Should it be adviseable after securing a majority near at
     hand to make an appointment with a view to attach par-
     ticular parts of the Union to the object, N. England, particu-
     larly Massachusetts, first occurs—and next, S. Carolina and
     Georgia.

Mr. Ellicott	Mr. Gorum	
Mr. Fitzhugh (of Chatham)	[Gorham]	Mr. Bull
Mr. Loyd (of Annapolis)	Mr. O. Wolcott	Mr. Tucker
Revd. Mr. Lee Massey	Mr. of R.Isd.	Mr. Baldwin

2. That the President inform himself of the several rival po-
     sitions; leaving among them inducements to bid against each
     other in offers of land or money. As the location when
     compleated by the survey will not be mutable by the Presi-
     dent, it may be well to have the offers so framed as to be-
     come ipso facto absolute in favor of the U. S. on the event
     which they solicit.

3. That the President direct the survey of the District which
     he shall ultimately elect. It seems essential that the District
     should comprehend the water adjoining the establishment,
     and eligible that it should comprehend the opposite shore.
     The legality of this seems to be decided by the clause con-
     fining the purchase or acceptance of land for the use of
     U. S. "to the East side of the river within the said district"
     which <*would see*[*m to*]> imply that the *whole* district was
     not *necessarily* to be on *that* side.—Quer: whether it will
     not be convenient to accept in the first instance so much less

than 10 miles square as will allow places to be afterwards taken in, which may not now be attainable, or it may not be prudent now to accept.

4. The district being defined and the requisite quantity of ground secured, the next step must be to fix the site for the public buildings—and provide for the establishment or enlargement of a town within the district. As no special authority is given for the latter purposes the consent of proprietors will be necessary: but as they will have a common interest with the public, voluntary arrangements between them and the Commissioners may be readily procured in favor of any plan which the President may patronize. Should any difficulties be apprehended on this point they can be guarded against in the negociations preliminary to the actual location of the district.

5. The plan for the public buildings is to be approved by the President. The Commissioners will no doubt submit different ones formed by themselves, or obtained from ingenious Architects. Should it be thought proper to excite emulation by a premium for the best, the expence is authorized, as an incident to that of the buildings.

6. The completion of the work will depend on a supply of the means. These must consist either of future grants of money by Congress, which it would not be prudent to count upon, of State Grants, of private grants, or the conversion into money of lands ceded for public use which it is conceived the latitude of the term "use" and the spirit and scope of the act will justify.

MS (DLC: Madison Papers); entirely in Madison's hand; undated (for a discussion of probable date, recipient, and use, see Editorial Note above). The above text, which in a technical sense must be removed from the Jefferson corpus, was nevertheless beyond doubt a result of the close collaboration that existed between TJ and Madison on this as on other important questions.

This document came to be attributed to TJ through an error made in 1889 in preparing copies of documents from the Jefferson, Madison, and other collections then in the Department of State for use in the so-called Potomac Flats Case. To these copies were added others drawn from other departments of government, from the Library of Congress, and from the private collection of the Special Assistant United States Attorney, Hugh T. Taggart, who conducted the case for the government (Hugh T. Taggart to John Blair Hoge, 21 June 1889, DNA: RG 59), The resultant record of the case, which obviously reflects Taggart's zeal and interest in the history of the District of Columbia, is a very valuable historical source containing some documents not elsewhere available but is unfortunately extremely rare (*United States* v. *Martin F. Morris et al*: *The Record in the Potomac Flats Case, Equity No. 10,306, Supreme Court of the District of Columbia* [Washington, 1898], 7 vols.). Taggart searched the files himself, made a careful list of the documents desired, identified their sources, and, since copies were to be drawn from other repositories than the Department of State, was careful to point out that "perspicuity in the record will best be subserved by an arrangement of them in chronological order, and to accomplish this it will be necessary for the copies to be made separately, and not attached in any manner to each other" (Taggart to Hoge, 21 June 1889, DNA: RG 59, enclosing a list in which the third item clearly describes two undated memoranda by TJ as being a single one—the two documents printed in Vol. 17: 460-3; there is nothing in Taggart's descriptive note of this third item applicable to the above document by Madison; the list of copies actually transmitted to Taggart merely described this third item as "Proceedings to be had under the Residence Act"; enclosure in William F. Wharton to the Attorney General, 30 July 1889, DNA: RG 60). Despite Taggart's care, the two texts by TJ and that by Madison became consolidated as one in the preparation and printing of the record of the Potomac Flats Case. This was probably because all three are undated but the text of Madison's memorandum was also inexcusably garbled (see *Record*, VII, 2155-9; Padover, *National Capital*, p. 30-6, especially p. 32 for comparison with passage indicated in note 1, below). Thus in a historically important legal record prepared by an attorney with a meticulous regard for textual accuracy there came to be imbedded a consolidation and garbling of texts that has misled subsequent scholars.

For searching various series in the National Archives and collections in the Library of Congress and for locating the above text in the Madison Papers, the Editors are indebted to Mr. H. B. Fant of the National Hisorical Publications Commission.

[1] The text of this query, anchored to the main body of the text by a cross, is written in the margin of the first page except for the two concluding lines which are on the verso of the third page—a fact which accounts for the garbled passage referred to above.

II. The President to the Secretary of State

DEAR SIR   Sunday, 2d. Jany. 1791

The enclosed Notes are sufficiently descriptive to comprehend the *two* objects fully; but it is necessary to remark, that if the *first* line begins at a point on Hunting Creek, the *fourth* line cannot, in any part, *touch* (Though it will *include*) the Town of Alexandria; because Huntg. Creek is below the boundaries of the Town. —And, if it could be so ordered as for the *first line* to avoid *touching* the town—that is, to allow room for its extending backwards, as well as up and down the River, without throwing too much of the district into Virginia, it would be a desirable measure.—Where are the Acts, or Resolutions of the States of Virginia and Maryland (respecting the Cession of the ten miles Square) to be met with? If to be brought from the Archives of these States, much time will be required in obtaining them: —but quere, are they not among the deposits of the General Government? The presumption is, that they were transmitted by the two States above mentioned. Yrs. Affectly.   GO: WASHINGTON

RC (DLC); endorsed by TJ: "Washington Presidt." Enclosures not identified; one of them is usually, and mistakenly, identified as that referred to in the following document.

III. The President to the Secretary of State

Tuesday [i.e., Wednesday, 4 Jan. 1791]

The P. begs to see Mr. Jefferson before he proceeds further in the Proclamation.—From a more attentive examination of some Papers, in his possession, he finds that it is in his power to ascertain the course and distance from the Court House in Alexandria to the upper and lower end of the Canal at the little Falls with as much accuracy as can be known from *Common* Surveying if not to Mathematical truth.

If Mr. Jefferson is not engaged with other matters the President will be at home at nine Oclock.

RC (DLC); undated, but date is established by entry in SJPL recording under 4 Jan. 1791 receipt of a letter of that date from "G. W. to Th: J. on the 10. mile square" (actually an entry by ditto for that of 2 Jan. 1791). For one of the papers referred to, but not enclosed, see illustration in this volume; see also Editorial Note, note 78.

IV. Daniel Carroll to the Secretary of State

SIR   [Philadelphia] Jany. 22d. 1791.

I do myself the honor of incloseing a Resolution No. 1 of the Genl. Assembly of Maryland acceding to the proposition made by the General Assembly of Virginia on the 10th of Novr. 1789, likewise several resolutions No. 2. establishing a fund for the moneys pledg'd by the first resolution, and an Act No 3 to Condemn land if necessary for the public buildings of the United States.

By a letter lately receivd from our Governor I expect these papers are on their way to you officially.

It will be observd, that the whole of the first payment to be made the Treasurer of Maryland, is to become due on the first of Jany. 1792. From the information I receivd at Annapolis there is I believe money now in the Treasury of Maryland, which has arisen from the funds specified, and that the Treasurer in that Case wou'd pay the money if he shou'd not think himself precluded by the Terms, which declare the whole of the 1st payment to become due on the 1st of Jany. 1792.—At any rate I am confident there will be no difficulty in obtaining the money thro' individuals for the purposes mentiond, if any obstacle shou'd occur on the part of the Treasurer under the Law.—I have, Sir, the honor to be with great respect Yr most Obt. Servt.,   DANL. CARROLL

RC (DLC: Washington Papers); endorsed by TJ: "⟨Federal⟩ ⟨Geo. t.⟩ Washington, city of." Not recorded in SJL. On this same day, writing from Annapolis, Governor Howard sent Washington a copy of the acts passed by the Maryland General Assembly ceding a district ten miles square and granting right of condemnation, together with resolutions authorizing an advance of $72,000 for the erection of public

buildings (J. E. Howard to Washington, 22 Jan. 1791, same, with enclosures). The act authorizing condemnation and designating the procedure to be followed by the Commissioners in the case of lands owned by minors, married women, non-residents, or persons refusing to sell or accept "a reasonable compensation" for lands was passed on 22 Dec. 1790.

V. The Secretary of State to Daniel Carroll

DEAR SIR   Philadelphia January 24th. 1791

The President of the United States desirous of availing himself of your assistance in preparing the federal Seat on the Potomac, [is in hopes you will act as one of the Commissioners directed by the Law for that purpose. I have the honor now to enclose a joint commission for yourself and two others, together with][1] a Copy of the Proclamation meant to constitute your first direction. The President will from time to time communicate such further directions, as circumstances shall call for.—I have the Honor to be with great esteem Dear Sir Your most obt. & most h'ble Servt.

PrC (DLC); in Remsen's hand, unsigned; at foot of text: "Honorable Daniel Carroll." FC (DNA: RG 59, PCC No. 120). Enclosure: (1) Commission designating Thomas Johnson and Daniel Carroll of Maryland and David Stuart of Virginia "Commissioners for surveying the District of Territory accepted by the . . . Act for the Permanent Seat of the Government of the United States and for performing such other Offices as by Law are directed, with full authority for them or any two of them to proceed therein according to Law, and to have and to hold the said office with all the powers, priviledges and Authorities to the same of right appertaining each of them, during the pleasure of the President of the United States, for the time being" (FC in DNA: RG 42, PC, in clerk's hand including signature of Washington and attestation by TJ, dated 22 Jan. 1791; in the minutes of the proceedings of the Commissioners the commission is preceded by the text of the Residence Act). (2) Proclamation of 24 Jan. 1791.

On this same day TJ wrote Thomas Johnson and David Stuart identical letters (save as indicated below) but not enclosing commissions (PrC in DLC, in Remsen's hand, unsigned; FC in DNA: RG 59, PCC No. 120). Carroll did not accept the appointment until the session closed, for the reason given in the proceedings of the Commissioners: "Daniel Carroll Esquire, one of the aforesaid Commissioners, at the time of the issuing the Commission, being one of the delegates from the State of Maryland . . . refusing to Act, there were only two commissioners from that time until the 4th day of March 1791 when Mr. Carrolls time of serving in Congress having elapsed, a new Commission was sent him, and he agreed to serve" (FC in DNA: RG 42, PC). TJ sent Carroll his commission on that day (TJ to Carroll, 4 Mch. 1791; same, RG 59, PCC No. 120).

[1] The text of the letters to Johnson and Stuart differs from that in square brackets (supplied) and reads as follows: "has appointed you one of the

three Commissioners directed by the Law for that purpose. A joint Commission is made out and deposited in the hands of the honorable D. Carroll, who is named second therein. I have the honor to enclose you" &c.

VI. The President to the Senate and the House of Representatives

GENTLEMEN [24 Jan. 1791]

In execution of the powers with which Congress were pleased to invest me by their act intituled 'an Act for establishing the temporary and permanent seat of the Government of the United States' and on mature consideration of the advantages and disadvantages of the several positions within the limits prescribed by the said act, I have, by a proclamation bearing date this day,[1] directed Commissioners, appointed in pursuance of the act, to survey and limit a part of the territory of ten miles square on both sides the river Patowmack so as to comprehend Georgetown in Maryland and to extend to the Eastern branch. I have not by this first act given to the said territory the whole extent of which it is susceptible in the direction of the river: because I thought it important that Congress should have an opportunity of considering whether by an amendatory law they would authorize the location of the residue at the lower end of the present so as to comprehend the Eastern branch itself and some of the country on it's lower side in the state of Maryland, and the town of Alexandria in Virginia. If however they should think[2] that the federal territory should be bounded by the water edge of the Eastern branch, the location of the residue will be to be made at the upper end of what is now directed. A copy of the proclamation is inclosed for your more particular information.[3] I have thought it best to await a survey of the territory before it is decided in what part of it the public buildings shall be erected.[4]

Dft (DLC: Washington Papers); entirely in TJ's hand; undated, but FC (DLC: Washington Papers), which varies in other particulars—some of which are noted below—is dated "United States, January 24, 1791" (text in Washington, *Writings*, ed. Fitzpatrick, XXXI, 201). It seems very likely that the alterations in phraseology made in TJ's draft, particularly those indicated in notes 3 and 4, were by Washington.

[1] FC and text in JS, I, 285, read: "(a copy of which is herewith transmitted)."

[2] FC reads: "If, however, they are of opinion. . . ."

[3] This sentence is not in FC.

[4] FC reads: ". . . decided on what particular spot on the North Eastern side of the River the public buildings shall be erected."

VII. The Proclamation by the President

By the President of the U. S. of America.
A Proclamation.

Whereas the General assembly of the state of Maryland by an act passed on the 23d. day of December in the year 1788. intituled 'An act to cede to Congress a district of 10 miles square in this state for the seat of the government of the U. S.' did enact that the representatives of the said state in the house of representatives of the Congress of the U. S. appointed to assemble at New York on the 1st. Wednesday of March then next ensuing, should be, and they were thereby authorized and required on the behalf of the said state to cede to the Congress of the U. S. any district in the said state not exceeding ten miles square which the Congress might fix upon and accept for the seat of government of the U. S.

And the General assembly of the commonwealth of Virginia by an act passed on the 3d. day of December 1789. and intituled 'An Act for the cession of ten miles square, or any lesser quantity of territory within this state, to the U. S. in Congress assembled, for the permanent seat of the General government' did enact that a tract of country not exceeding ten miles square, or any lesser quantity, to be located within the limits of the said state and in any part thereof as Congress might by law direct, should be, and the same was thereby for ever ceded and relinquished to the Congress and government of the U. S. in full and absolute right, and exclusive jurisdiction as well of soil, as of persons residing or to reside thereon, pursuant to the tenor and effect of the 8th. section of the first article of the constitution of government of the U. S.

And the Congress of the U. S. by their act passed the 16th. day of July 1790. and intituled 'an act for establishing the temporary and permanent seat of the government of the U. S.' authorised the President of the U. S. to appoint three commissioners to survey, under his direction, and by proper metes and bounds to limit a district of territory, not exceeding ten miles square, on the river Potomac, at some place between the mouths of the Eastern branch, and Connogocheque, which district so to be located and limited, was accepted by the said act of Congress as the district for the permanent seat of the government of the U. S.

Now therefore, in pursuance of the powers to me confided, and after duly examining and weighing the advantages and disadvantages of the several situations within the limits aforesaid, I do hereby declare and make known that the location of one part of the said district of ten miles square shall be found by running four lines of experiment in the following manner, that is to say, running from the Courthouse of Alexandria in Virginia due South West half a mile, and thence a due South East course till it shall strike Hunting creek to fix the Beginning of the said four lines of experiment:

Then beginning the first of the said four lines of experiment at the point on Hunting creek where the said South East course shall have struck the same, and running the said first line due North West ten miles: thence the second line into Maryland due North East ten miles: thence the third line due South East ten miles: and thence the fourth line due South West ten miles to the beginning on Hunting creek.

And the said four lines of experiment being so run, I do hereby declare and make known that all that part within the said four lines of experiment which shall be within the state of Maryland[1] and above the Eastern branch, and all that part within the same four lines of experiment which shall be within the commonwealth of Virginia,[2] and above a line to be run from the point of land forming the upper cape of the mouth of Eastern branch due South West, and no more, is now fixed upon, and directed to be surveyed, defined, limited and located for a part of the said district accepted by the said act of Congress for the permanent seat of the government of the U. S. (Hereby expressly reserving the direction of the survey and location of the remaining part of the said district to be made hereafter contiguous to such part or parts of the present location as is, or shall be agreeable to law.)

And I do accordingly[3] direct the said Commissioners, appointed agreeably to the tenor of the said act to proceed forthwith to run the said lines of experiment, and the same being run, to survey, and by proper metes and bounds to define and limit the part within the same which is herein before directed for immediate location and acceptance, and thereof to make due report to me under their hands and seals.

In testimony whereof I have caused the seal of the U. S. to be affixed to these presents, and signed the same with my hand. Done at the city of Philadelphia the 24th.[4] day of January[5] in the year of our lord 1791. and of the independance of the United States the fifteenth.

By the President   GEORGE WASHINGTON
     TH: JEFFERSON

Dft (DLC: Washington Papers); entirely in TJ's hand, including signatures; the date, blank when TJ submitted Dft to Washington, was inserted later by Washington and TJ (see notes 4 and 5). Tr (DNA: RG 42, PC); text as finally proclaimed, differing from Dft in one particular (see note 3).

¹ In Dft preceding five words are in-terlined in substitution for "on the North side of the river Potomac," deleted.

² In Dft preceding five words are interlined in substitution for "on the South side of the said river," deleted.

³ Tr reads "hereby" instead of "accordingly."

⁴ Figures are in Washington's hand.

⁵ TJ inserted "January" after Dft had been prepared.

VIII. Daniel Carroll to the Secretary of State

SIR   Jany. 27th. 1791.

I had the ho[nour to re]ceive your favor, covering the Commission which includes my name in the appointment, for carrying into effect the Location of the permanent Seat of Government. It wou'd be as unnecessary, Sir, to confess the pleasure I shou'd feel in giving my Little aid for a purpose so consonant to my wishes for the public good, as I hope it is, to assure the President of the Value I place on every mark of his attention, and confidence. But notwithstanding these sentiments, I find myself constrain'd by several existing circumstances, to decline a service, which under other circumstances, wou'd be undertaken with no other reluctance than what might proceed from the apprehension of being in a place, which might be filled by some other better capable of executing its duties.

I have accordingly inclosed the Commission with which I have been honored, and have to request the favor of you, Sir, that in communicating these my sentiments to the President, you will at the same time assure him of my fervent attachment, and profound respect.—I beg you, Sir to believe that I am with great esteem & regard, Yr. most Obt. & Hble. Servt.,   DANL. CARROLL

RC (DLC: District of Columbia Papers); endorsed by Remsen as "received same day" and so recorded in SJL.

IX. The Secretary of State to the Commissioners of the Federal District

SIR   Philadelphia 29th. Jany. 1791.

Mr. Carroll, supposing that Doubts may arise, whether he can act as one of the Commissioners for the federal Seat, while a Member of Congress, has declined, and has returned me the Commission, which had been deposited with him as one of the Members; I have now the Honor to enclose it to Mr. Johnson, first named therein,[1] and to observe that two Members suffice for Business. It will be some Time before a Third will be named. The President, having thought Major L'Enfant peculiarly qualified to make such a Draught of the Ground as will enable himself to fix on the Spot for the public Buildings; he has been written to for that Purpose, and will be sent on, if he chuses to undertake it.[2]—I have the Honor to be, Sir, Your most obedient, & most humble Servant,

TH: JEFFERSON

RC (DLC: photostat of unlocated original); in clerk's hand, signed by TJ. PrC (DLC); at foot of text: "Thomas Johnson Esqr.," this being a clerk's copy, unsigned, of the letter to Johnson with the single variation indicated in note 1 below. FC (DNA: RG 59, PCC No. 120). Tr of Extract (DLC: Digges-L'Enfant-Morgan Papers); see note 2.

[1] PrC contains this note at foot of text: "Note. In the Letter to Mr. Stuart these words were comprised in the Brackets instead of [you] viz. Mr. Johnson first named therein." A similar note is appended to FC.
[2] The Extract comprises this sentence only.

X. The President to the Secretary of State

MY DEAR SIR   Tuesday Evening [1 Feb. 1791]

Nothing in the enclosed letter superceding the necessity of Mr. Ellicot, proceeding to the work in hand, I would thank you, for requesting him, to set out on thursday; or as soon after as he can make it convenient; also for preparing such instructions as you may conceive it necessary for me to give him for ascertaining the points we wish to know; *first*, for the *general* view of things, and *next* for the more accurate and final decision.—Yrs. sincerely & Affly.,   GO: WASHINGTON

RC (DLC); addressed: "Mr. Jefferson"; endorsed by TJ as received 1 Feb. 1791 and so recorded in SJL, with date attributed. Enclosure: Andrew Ellicott to the President, 1 Feb. 1791, applying for appointment as surveyor of the boundary authorized by the treaty with the Creeks, a post he later filled (DLC: Washington Papers).

XI. The Secretary of State to Andrew Ellicott

SIR   Philadelphia, February 2, 1791.

You are desired to proceed by the first stage to the Federal territory on the Potomac, for the purpose of making a survey of it.

The first object will be to run the two first lines mentioned in the enclosed proclamation to wit:—the S.W. line 160 poles and the S.E. line to Hunting creek or should it not strike Hunting creek as has been suggested then to the river. These two lines must be[1] run with all the accuracy of which your art is susceptible as they are to fix the begining either on Hunting creek or the river. If the second line should strike the river instead of the creek take and lay down the bearing and distance of the nearest part of the creek and also of any of its waters if any of them should be nearer than the creek itself; so also should either of these two lines cross any water of Hunting creek let it be noted. The termination of the Second line being accurately fixed, either on the creek or river, procced to run from that as a beginning the four lines of experiment directed in the proclamation. This is intended as the first rough essay to furnish data for the last accurate survey. It is desirable that it be made with all the dispatch possible and with only common exactness, paying regard however to the magnetic variations. In running these lines note the position of the mouth of the Eastern branch, the point of your first course there will receive[2] the S.W. line from the Cape of the Eastern branch, the canal and particular distance of your crossing it from either end, the position of Georgetown, and mouth of Goose Creek, and send by Post, a plat of the whole on which ultimate directions for the rest of the work shall be sent you, as soon as they can be prepared. Till these shall be received by you, you can be employed in ascertaining a true Meridian, and the latitude of the place, and running the meanderings of the Eastern branch, and of the river itself, and other waters which will merit an exact place in the map of the Territory. You will herewith receive a draft on the Mayor of Georgetown to cover your expenses.

TH: JEFFERSON

P.S. The President writes by Post to Mr. Beall Mayor of Georgetown to furnish you with money for your expenses for which therefore you may apply to him without further order.

MS not found; text taken from *Records of the Columbia Hist. Soc.*, II (1899), 170-1. Not recorded in SJL or SJPL. The text is obviously defective. Punctuation, spelling, and capitalization have been altered to conform to TJ's normal usage and one word has been supplied (see note 1 below). Enclosure: Proclamation of 24 Jan. 1791. Instead of enclosing the draft as stated, TJ was doubtless informed by Washington that he preferred to send the following letter to Thomas Beall, Mayor of Georgetown: "Sir: In consequence of your letter of the 26th of January to Daniel Carroll Esquire informing him that the order of the President of the United States upon you, as Mayor of George Town, would be paid on sight, I have to request that you will answer the demands of Andrew Ellicot Esquire, within the sum of fifty guineas, as he may have occasion to make them without further advice" (Washington to Beall, 3 Feb. 1791, *Writings*, ed. Fitzpatrick, XXXI, 209). It was Beall's communication of 26 Jan. 1791 that evidently caused Washington to ask TJ to prepare instructions and to direct Ellicott to proceed (see Washington to TJ, 1 Feb. 1791).

Although Washington's note of the preceding day had requested TJ to prepare Ellicott's instructions to be signed by himself, the above draft was allowed to stand. This, together with the fact that TJ did not record the letter in SJL, is perhaps another evidence of the desire for "all the dispatch possible" that the President so clearly manifested in all of the pro-ceedings at this time concerning the Federal District.

On 4 Feb. 1791 David Stuart wrote to TJ from Alexandria, no doubt concerning the proceedings there, but the text has not been found (recorded in SJL as received on the 14th).

¹ This word supplied.
² Thus in printed text, evidently garbled. What TJ meant, of course, was that Ellicott was to mark the point at which a southwest course from the northern cape of the mouth of the Eastern Branch would intersect the first of the four lines of experiment (i.e., a line running northwest ten miles from the beginning point on Hunting Creek).

XII. Andrew Ellicott to the Secretary of State

SIR   [Alexandria, 14 Feb. 1791]

I arrived at this Town on Monday last¹ but the Cloudy weather prevented any observations being made untill friday evening which was very fine. [On Saturday the two first lines were completed. You will see by the enclosed plat that the second line does not touch any part of Hunting Creek unless the spring drain noted in the plat is to be considered a part of it. It appears to me that in order to make the plan as complete as possible it will be proper to begin the survey of the ten miles square at the Eastern inclination of the upper cape of Hunting Creek, marked on the plat. This plan will include all the Harbor and wharfs of Alexandria, which will not be the Case if the two first lines mentioned in the proclamation are to remain as now.]² I shall submit to your consideration the following plan for the permanent location which I believe will embrace every object of Advantage which can be included within the ten miles square (Viz)—Beginning at the most   ³ inclination of the upper cape of Hunting Creek and running a streight line North westerly ten miles making an angle at the beginning of 45° with the Meridian for the first line. Then by a streight line into Maryland north easterly at right angles to the first, ten miles for the second line. Thence by a streight line at right angles to the second south easterly ten miles for the third line. Thence for the fourth line at right angles to the third south westerly ten miles to the beginning on the upper cape of Hunting Creek—Or the beginning may be expressed more in the spirit of the Proclamation thus 'Running from the Court House in Alexandria due south west and thence a due south east course till it shall strike the River Potomac.' [—as marked in plat A. The magnetic variations at this place is somewhat uncertain, arising no doubt from some local cause. It was 20 easterly when the second line struck the river and at the end of the first line, it was nearly as much Westerly. The Latitude of Alexandria, I find to be about 33 48 20 N.[4] This afternoon I intend beginning the rough survey which shall be executed with all possible dispatch,][5]

. . . You will observe by the plan which I have suggested for the Permanent Location a small deviation with respect to the courses from those mentioned in the Proclamation, the reason of which is that the courses in the Proclamation strictly adhered to would neither produce straight lines nor contain quite the ten miles square besides the almost impossibility of running such lines with tolerable exactness. I am Sir with the greatest Respect and esteem your Hbl. Servt.   ANDREW ELLICOTT

MS not found; the above text is a composite drawn from two printed sources, each of which relied on Ellicott's manuscript draft and each of which is incomplete and otherwise defective. These two sources nevertheless complement each other so as to permit the reconstruction of almost if not all of the original text. The first of these sources, which provides the basic text above and is the more reliable and more comprehensive of the two, is Mathews' *Andrew Ellicott*, p. 84-5; the second is Alexander's "Sketch of the Life of Andrew Ellicott," *Records of the Columbia Hist. Soc.*, II (1899), 172-3. Two paragraphs or passages from the latter have been interpolated at the appropriate points of the above text as indicated in note 2 and 4 below. TJ's entry in SJL shows that he received Ellicott's letter on 21 Mch. 1791.

[1] On the same day, writing to his wife, Ellicott said that he had arrived the preceding Tuesday (Mathews, *Andrew Ellicott*, p. 83). This was probably correct (see Editorial Note).

[2] The matter in brackets (supplied) is drawn from the second of the two printed sources indicated above. Since Mathews indicated an omission that coincides exactly with this passage as shown by what precedes and follows, it is clear that no part of the text has been lost at this point.

[3] Blank in Mathews' text; it is clear from the passage drawn from Alexander as indicated in note 2, however, that Ellicott meant and may have written "easterly."

[4] The error is obviously attributable to the copyist, not to Ellicott. The latitude of Alexandria is 38° 48.2'.

[5] The matter in brackets (supplied) is drawn from the second of the two printed sources indicated above. Since this passage in Alexander is followed by an editorial indication of "more erasures" (perhaps deletions made by Ellicott in the course of composition) and since at the corresponding point Mathews' text indicates an ellipsis, it is possible but by no means certain that a part of the original text is missing from both of the printed sources.

XIII. The Proclamation by the President

By the President of the U. S. of A.   a Proclamation

Whereas by a proclamation bearing date the 24th. day of Jan. of this present year, and in pursuance of certain acts of the states of Maryland and Virginia, and of the Congress of the U. S. therein mentioned, certain lines of experiment were directed to be run in the neighborhood of George town in Maryland for the purpose of determining the location of a part of the territory of 10. miles square for the permanent seat of government of the U. S. and a certain part was directed to be located within the said lines of experiment on both sides of the Potomac and above the limit of the Eastern branch prescribed by the said act of Congress:

And Congress by an amendatory act, passed on the 3d. day of this present month of March, have given further authority to the President of the U. S. 'to make any part of the territory below the said limit and above the mouth of Hunting creek, a part of the said district, so as to include a convenient part of the Eastern branch, and of the lands lying on the lower side thereof, and also the town of Alexandria.'

Now therefore for the purpose of amending and completing the location of the whole of the said territory of ten miles square in conformity with the said amendatory act of Congress, I do hereby declare and make known that the whole of the said territory shall be located and included within the four lines following, that is to say:

Beginning at Jones's point, being the upper cape of Hunting creek in Virginia, and at an angle, in the outset, of 45. degrees West of the North; and running in a direct line ten miles for the first line: then beginning again at the same Jones's point, and running another direct line, at a right angle with the first, across the Potomac, ten miles for the second line: then from the terminations of the said first and second lines, running two other direct lines, of ten miles each, the one crossing the Eastern branch aforesaid, and the other the Potomac, and meeting each other in a point.

And I do accordingly direct the Commissioners named under the authority of the said first mentioned act of Congress to proceed forthwith to have the said four lines run, and by proper metes and bounds defined and limited, and thereof to make due report under their hands and seals: and the territory so to be located, defined and limited, shall be the whole territory accepted by the said acts of Congress as the district for the permanent seat of the government of the U. S.

<*And Whereas the said first mentioned act of Congress did further enact that the said Commissioners should, under the direction of the President of the U. S. provide suitable buildings for the accomodation of Congress and of the President and for the public offices of the government of the United States; I do hereby further declare and make known, that [the highest summit of lands in the town heretofore called Hamburg, within the said territory, with a convenient extent of grounds circumjacent, shall be appropriated for a Capitol[1] for the accomodation of Congress, and such other lands between George town and the stream heretofore called the Tyber, as shall on due examination be found convenient and sufficient, shall be appropriated for the accomodation of the President of the United States for the time being, and for the public offices of the government of the United States.][2] And I do hereby direct the said Commissioners[1] accordingly.>[3]*

In testimony whereof, I have caused the seal of the U. S. to be affixed to these presents, and signed the same with my hand. Done at Georgetown aforesaid the 30th. day of March, in the year of our Lord 1791, and of the Independence of the U. S. the fifteenth.

MS (DNA: RG 59, MLR); entirely in TJ's hand except as indicated in notes below; endorsed by Lear: "Proclamation March 30th. 1791"; not signed. PrC (DLC). Tr (DLC: Washington Papers).

TJ received Washington's revised text of the proclamation on the night of the 5th of April, too late to be inserted in *Dunlap's American Daily Advertiser* and Bache's *General Advertiser* of the next morning, both of which were already filled. But he did succeed in getting it inserted in "Brown's evening paper of the 6th," the *Federal Gazette* (TJ to Washington, 10 Apr. 1791). From that printing the text of the proclamation as issued over Washington's name and TJ's attestation— none of the manuscript texts is signed —was reprinted in various newspapers, including the *New-York Journal*, 13 Apr. 1791, and Davis' *Virginia Gazette*, 20 Apr. 1791. Although officially published as of 30 Mch. 1791, the proclamation was drafted by TJ on the morning of 21 Mch. 1791 (see Editorial Note).

[1] This word capitalized by Lear.

[2] Brackets in MS, preceded by an asterisk keyed to this note at foot of text by TJ: "The part within [ ] being conjectural, will be to be rendered conformable to the ground when more accurately examined." In MS Lear drew lines through this paragraph and also that indicated in the following note.

[3] This paragraph in angle brackets (supplied) has lines drawn through it by Lear and was deleted from the text of proclamation as issued (for explanation of this deletion, see Editorial Note and Washington to TJ, 31 March 1791).

To Stephen Cathalan, Jr.

DEAR SIR   Philadelphia Jan. 25. 1791.

I duly recieved your father's favor of Sep. 25. and am happy that the Vice-consular commission which you must have recieved soon after was made to his liking. He desires me to say whether I still wish to have the commission executed as to the olives. I wish it, Sir, extremely. My honour is somewhat compromitted in that matter with the state of South Carolina, as it was on my earnest sollicitations they undertook it, and sent me about 30. Louis for that purpose, the balance of which (after paying the parcel you sent) has laid at Paris ever since. I must entreat you then at the commencement of the proper season to send one half the adventure of olive berries and olive plants to Bordeaux to Mr. Fenwic American Consul there to be forwarded directly to Charlestown, and to endeavor to find for the other half a vessel coming from Marseilles to Charlestown direct. Let the two adventures make up thirty Louis with what you furnished before, and draw for the balance on Mr. Short. Should you ever have direct opportunities to this place I will thank you to send me supplies from time to time of Brugnols and dried figs, say about 25 ℔. of each, yearly, and draw for the amount on our chargé or minister at Paris. These two articles cannot be got good here. Present my friendly respects to your father and the ladies, not forgetting the youngest, and be assured of the sentiments of sincere esteem & attachment with which I am Dear Sir your most obedt. humble servt.,

TH: JEFFERSON

PrC (DLC); at foot of text: "M. Cathalan le fils."

From John Harvie, Jr.

DR SIR   Richmond Jany. 25th. 1791

Your Letter dated so far back as the 2nd. of November has been withheld till the 12th. of this Month when it was deliver'd to me by Colo. Bell from Charlottesville. I should then have Immediately Answer'd it but as I Conceive there must be the want of Recollection, or some Misunderstanding in Circumstances either in you or Colo. Randolph respecting the 490 Acres of Land near Edge Hill, I thought it best to Address a Letter to Colo. Randolph on the Subject, and to await his Answer previous to my Writing to you. The Information that I now Collect from him is that about

Eighteen or twenty Years past, you told him that you had made an Entry for him with the Surveyor of Albemarle he thinks Staples for a parcel of Vacant Land Adjoining his Edge Hill tract, and that you would have it Survey'd for him, that either before or soon after your Departure for Europe, James Marks Located a Land Office Treasury warrant upon the same Land, which Location if Carry'd into Survey Colo. Randolph threatened with a Caveat. This threat alarming Marks he propos'd a Division of the Land which was Acceeded to and Colo. Randolph Consented that the Survey should be made upon Marks's Warrant. It was in this Stage of the Business that I became the purchaser of Mr. Marks's Lands, Including his Moiety in this Survey, as well as his Original tract and gave him what was thought a high price for the whole, every Shilling of which has been long since paid. At the time of my purchase from Mr. Marks or at any Subsequent period till you did me the honour of Writing to me on the Subject, I am positive I never heard a Whisper of your Claim from any person, and indeed as I was told that Colo. Randolphs Entry had been made for him by you I entertained no Suspicion of their being a Contending Right, and I really must believe that Mr. Marks Considered your Entry and Colo. Randolphs as one and the same thing, as I can no otherways Account for his Agreeing to Divide the Land with that Gentleman, and it was under the Influence of this Agreement I am told that Anderson Bryan Consented to have the Survey made upon Marks' location, for let his pretences now be what they may the Survey return'd to the Land Office is every word in his own hand Writing. He was Guilty of a very Reprehensible Breach of his duty if he Survey'd for Marks knowing that you had a better legal Right Unsatisfy'd at the time. The Survey was return'd to the Land Office in December 1784. and Continued Open to the Objection and Caveat of every person till June 1786 when a Grant issued not in my Name only, but in my name and Thomas M. Randolphs being the Assignees of James Marks as Tenants in Common. Within all that time no Information was given me by either of your Agents of your having any Right Infring'd by the Survey. If I had Suppos'd the Title questionable, it was then in my power to have held so much of the purchase Money as would have been equal to an Indemnification for the loss of the Land. What Induces me strongly to Suppose that you have Considered Colo. Randolphs Entry as a distinct Interest from Mr. Marks's Survey is that after seeing and holding some Conversation with you about Marks's Survey last Winter I made proposals to Colo. Randolph for the purchase of part of his Edge Hill tract and upon Confirming of that Bargain he offer'd me his Moiety of the 490 Acres Survey. I mention'd your pretentions to it. He then told me he believ'd that Matter was all set right for he had reminded you of his Entry, which you Recollected and had Admitted its priority. Considering this as a Relinquishment of your Claim, I became the purchaser of his Moiety and actually paid him for it the sum of Seventy five pounds. I very well know when a Grant has been fraudulently or surreptiously Obtain'd it will not stand in Equity, but throughout this whole Business my Title wore a very different Aspect, and cannot be shaken by any legal Discussion. But this is not the footing upon which I wish this or any other Subject to stand between you and me. I am willing the Matter should be referr'd to Mutual friends and if under all its Circumstances it shall appear Right for me to Surrender the whole or any part of it to you, I shall Conform to such Opinion. If on the other hand upon this Statement of my Claim, my Equity appears more Substantial than your own, I know you two well to entertain any doubt of your being ready to declare it. If the 490 Acres of Land did not lye Immediately back of the Land I purchas'd of Mr. Marks Colo. Randolph and my Mother I should Consider it of very little Value for of the whole I am told not more than 150 Acres can be Cultivated and that lyes upon the steepest part of the Mountain. The rest is so pav'd with Rock and Stone and runs on the very Top of the Mountain as to be Altogether a Barren. I have been oblidg'd to Write part of this Letter so hastily that I would be at the trouble of transcribing it if I was not fearful that you may have already Suppos'd that I had been backward in Answering yours and therefore as this is now ready for the Stage I am [obliged to] let it go. Your favoring me with a Letter now and then will Afford me very high Satisfaction, for I at all times shall be with the highest Esteem Dr Sir Yr Most Obt. & Affec. Servt.,   JNO. HARVIE.

RC (MHi); addressed: "The Honble Thomas Jefferson Esqr. Secretary of State Philadelphia"; postmarked "RICH-MOND, Jan 27" and "FREE"; endorsed by TJ as received 3 Feb. 1791 and so recorded in SJL, though with the erroneous date of 5 Jan.

To Adrien Petit

à Philadelphie ce 25. Janvier 1791.
A mon depart de Paris, mon cher Petit, vous m'aviez proposé et meme avec de l'empressement, de m'accompagner en Amerique.

Je ne m'y suis pas consenti, parceque je croyois toujours à ma très prochaine retour, et que je souhaitois de laisser mes affaires dans vos mains. Quand je suis convenu de rester ici, et que je me voyois dans le cas d'etablir une maison, j'aimois de me persuader, et sans y douter meme, que, vu le desir que vous m'aviez temoigné de visiter ce pays-ci, vous ne balanceriez pas de venir me joindre, et de demeurer chez moi au meme pié où vous etiez à Paris. Quels donc ont eté mes regrets à la reception de la lettre de Monsieur Short, qui m'a annoncé votre refus. Si les offres qu'il vous auroit fait de ma part ne vous ont pas convenus, peutetre qu'il les auroit arrangé plus à votre gré, connoissant le desir que je lui avois marqué de vous posseder. Il ne m'en a pas donne les details. Je ne pretends pas etre assez riche pour vous proposer de vous faire un sort ici. Mais certainement j'aurois souhaité de vous voir à votre aise ici autant que vous l'étiez à Paris. Je suis sur qu'etant ici, vous trouveriez des facilités à ameliorer votre sort qui ne peuvent pas exister en Europe, et des occasions de vous preparer un etablissement ou en terres, ou en commerce. Et en tout cas si, après l'avoir vu et essayé, le pays ne vous plaisoit pas, je vous aurois renvoyé en France à ma propre charge. Pensez-y, mon cher ami, et venez me joindre ici. M. Short prendra des arrangemens avec vous pour cet effet, et j'espere que vous en serez content. Vous trouverez ici Monsieur et Madame Adams, qui sont etablis à Philadelphie, et qui sont de vos amis. Mes enfants restent chez moi en Virginie. L'ainée est mariée. La cadette reste avec elle, et toutes les deux parlent de vous avec beaucoup d'amitié. Soyez sur qu'il n'y a personne qui en a plus que lui qui est avec beaucoup d'attachement, mon cher Petit votre veritable ami,   TH: JEFFERSON

PrC (DLC).

Death of Franklin
The Politics of Mourning in France and the United States

I. THE SECRETARY OF STATE TO THE PRESIDENT, 9 DECEMBER 1790
II. TOBIAS LEAR TO THE SECRETARY OF STATE, 26 JANUARY 1791
III. THOMAS JEFFERSON TO THE REV. WILLIAM SMITH, 19 FEBRUARY 1791
IV. THOMAS JEFFERSON TO JOHN VAUGHAN, 22 FEBRUARY 1791
V. THE SECRETARY OF STATE TO THE PRESIDENT OF THE NATIONAL ASSEMBLY OF FRANCE, 8 MARCH 1791

EDITORIAL NOTE

> We have assisted them in repulsing their enemies and vindicating themselves into freedom. In return they have taught us a just and humane spirit of toleration. . . . A nation actuated by such ideas can boast of being more than the conquerors of a world. They are at once our great example and support. Into their ports and marts of trade then, to the peaceable and happy country they inhabit, should it be our great endeavour, in preference to all others, to introduce our merchants, to inform themselves in the nature of their commerce, and imbibe the virtues which alone can cause it to flourish . . . economy, simplicity, purity of morals, integrity, and honesty.
> —*Report to the National Assembly of France,*
> *2 June 1791*

News of the death of Benjamin Franklin arrived in New York City on 22 April 1790. That same day James Madison arose in the House of Representatives, voiced a brief, moving tribute, and proposed that the members wear badges of mourning for a month. This, he said, should be done in respect for "a citizen whose native genius was not more an ornament to human nature, than his various exertions of it have been precious to science, to freedom, and to his country."[1] The motion was promptly adopted. This, the first tribute from the government to one of its private citizens, was of course reported in the press.

The next day Charles Carroll urged a similar gesture on the part of the Senate. Oliver Ellsworth spoke in opposition even before the motion could be seconded. Rufus King and William Samuel Johnson joined the attack. Ellsworth, addressing himself to the chair, said that the motion was certain to be lost and that it might as well be withdrawn. "This," Maclay confided to his diary, "was really insulting. But as the matter, strictly speaking, was not senatorial or such as belonged to us in our capacity as a public body, Carroll looked at me and I nodded assent, and it was withdrawn."[2] Butler, Izard, Lee, and

[1] JHR, I, 198; *Annals*, II, 1586.
[2] Maclay, *Journal*, ed. Maclay, p. 247. On the day before, Maclay, noting that

[78]

Adams—all inveterate in their dislike of Franklin—had no need to speak when others spoke for them.

In both houses the act of homage had been proposed by southerners. In the Senate all who are known to have spoken in opposition were, like Franklin himself, natives of New England. But the differing attitudes of the two houses and of the representatives of the two sections on this purely formal matter reflected far deeper political cleavages than those arising from mere personal animosities. The flawed gesture, presaging storms to come, assumed quite another aspect in Europe. When news of it arrived there, Madison's simple tribute to a venerated citizen lost every trace of ambiguity attached to it by the Senate's failure to act. It appeared instead as another clear trumpet call out of the West, shattering monarchical tradition and rallying the forces of reason, virtue, and liberty. Thus transformed, it resounded back across the Atlantic as an echo wholly changed in meaning and multiplied many times in power. In this altered form it again entered American politics, grating with even harsher intensity on the nerves of those who, like Senator Paterson of New Jersey, thought republicanism fine in theory but something else in practice. It thereby exacerbated deep divisions in the nation that were nowhere more sharply discernible than behind the closed doors of the Senate. The episode, perfectly symbolizing the revolutionary tides that had flowed eastward from America to Europe and were now beginning to return with redoubled force, illumines the nature of the breach between those who welcomed the new day and those who resisted it.

I

Early in June, Benjamin Vaughan in London wrote to inform the Duc de la Rochefoucauld of Franklin's death and to urge him to convey the news to Lafayette, Mirabeau, and others. But his object was to inspire action, not just to report the event. Congress and other corporate bodies, he stated somewhat loosely, had resolved to mourn a month for Franklin, "an honor not shown to any person before out of

---

"the House of Representatives voted to drape their arms for a month" and reflecting on the difference between Franklin's public fame and private character, had said that he would offer no objection if any Senator should propose a similar motion since it was "probably for the good of society that patterns of perfection should be held up for men to copy after." He also noted, however, that the Senate had taken no notice of the death of one of its own members, William Grayson (same, p. 246). Far from being an instigator, therefore, Maclay was on the defensive at the beginning of this episode, readily yielding at this time but later goaded to more determined measures by the actions of the Senate.

The refusal of the Senate so impressed TJ that he reported the fact to Short in France: "The house of representatives resolved to wear mourning, and do it. The Senate neither resolved it nor do it" (TJ to Short, 27 Apr. 1790). Indeed, its action made such an indelible impression on him that he recalled it many years later, along with the proposal that he was thereby prompted to make to the President: "I proposed to Genl: Washington that the Executive department should wear mourning. He declined it, because he said he should not know where to draw the line, if he once began that ceremony" (TJ to Benjamin Rush, 4 Oct. 1803).

office."[3] The letter had a remarkable effect in France, beginning with Mirabeau's electrifying announcement to the National Assembly on the 11th of June, the opening words of which produced a stunned silence: "Franklin est mort. . . ."[4] In this brief, eloquent, and carefully prepared speech, Mirabeau enlarged upon Vaughan's inaccuracies. But the terse eloquence was his own, its effect heightened in the stilled chamber by the voice wrung from a body so wracked with pain and so weakened from illness that the speaker could scarcely support himself. For ages, Mirabeau declared, cabinets and courts had ostentatiously mourned those who were great only in the eulogies of their flatterers. Nations should do homage to their true benefactors. The American Congress had set the example by decreeing a period of mourning to be observed for two months throughout the fourteen states in tribute to the man who had emancipated his country and had framed her Constitution. The National Assembly should unite with America in this act of veneration, paying homage before the whole world to the rights of man and to the philosopher who had contributed most to insure the rule of these rights throughout the earth. He therefore proposed that the members of the National Assembly wear mourning for three days and that "the President write to the American Congress" informing them of these proceedings. La Rochefoucauld and Lafayette spoke in support of the motion and all of the members on the left arose in a tumultuous ovation. A sober voice on the right, that of Montlosier, wondered if Franklin was actually dead and inquired whether the National Assembly had been informed of his death by Congress. Mirabeau answered that the news was private, not public, but impossible to doubt. His motion was adopted by acclamation. Many on the right abstained, for Mirabeau's speech and the support given by such moderates as Lafayette and La Rochefoucauld had drawn the mantle of the idolized American sage over their cause

[3] Vaughan to La Rochefoucauld, 4 June 1790 (full text in Gilbert Chinard, "The Apotheosis of Benjamin Franklin," Am. Phil. Soc., *Procs.*, XCIX [Dec. 1955], 441; an extract, provided by La Rochefoucauld or perhaps by Lafayette, appeared in *Journal de Paris*, 12 June 1790, and is to be found with the full text in Chinard's expanded and revised study, *L'Apothéose de Benjamin Franklin* [Institut Français de Washington, 1955], p. 14-16, referred to in notes below as Chinard, *L'Apothéose*). On 24 Apr. 1790 Benjamin Rush wrote Richard Price that "the government of the United States have shared in the general sympathy, agreeing to wear mourning for one month . . . thus proclaiming to the world that republics are not deficient in gratitude to those men who have deserved well of their country for wisdom and virtue" (Rush, *Letters*, ed. Butterfield, I, 564). The erroneous impression conveyed by Vaughan must, therefore, have originated in America in such letters as Rush's in order to create a favorable impression in Europe. Members of Congress were themselves inexact in stating the facts (Henry Wynkoop to Reading Beatty, 22 Apr. 1790, PMHB, XXVIII [1914], 194). So, understandably, was the French *chargé*, who reported that Franklin's death "imposed silence on his enemies and to honor his memory Congress adopted mourning for a month" (Otto to Montmorin, 10 May 1790, DLC: Henry Adams Transcripts; this dispatch arrived in Paris after the National Assembly had acted). Historians have also assumed that it was an act of homage taken by both houses.

[4] William Short to John Browne Cutting, 11 June 1790 (DLC: Short Papers), shows that Mirabeau had worked on the speech the night before. Vallentin, *Mirabeau*, p. 440, states that Mirabeau spoke at Lafayette's request.

and over the proposed constitution of France, then under discussion.[5]

The unprecedented tribute touched off a whole series of proceedings in the French capital that amounted to nothing less than a republican apotheosis of Franklin. Those conducting the solemnities identified the event with their own revolutionary aims. Franklin, the native genius who had risen from obscurity to the most elevated stations in science and statecraft, became in this outpouring of emotion the very symbol of universal aspirations, an example furnished by a free America of what any man might dream of becoming. On the same evening that Mirabeau delivered his stirring tribute, the members of the commune of Paris met and authorized a public eulogy of Franklin, selecting for the purpose Abbé Fauchet, a popular orator. Fauchet's eulogy was delivered in the Halle-aux-blés on the 21st of July before some three thousand persons, including Lafayette, Mirabeau, Sieyès, and others of the National Assembly. It was immediately printed and later issued in a second edition. The President of the commune of Paris, Abbé Benière, was directed to transmit an account of the proceedings to the American government.[6]

Late in October, at Monticello, Thomas Jefferson received Short's dispatch of the 14th of June informing him that the National Assembly had directed their President to "write to Congress to notify them the part they take in the melancholy event" and that a kind of enthusiasm had spread through the capital, with various societies and organizations manifesting their concurrence in the sentiments that Mirabeau had led the nation to express.[7] Jefferson forwarded this dispatch, along with others from Short, to Washington at Mount Vernon. Two months earlier, American newspapers had widely reported the action of the National Assembly and had reprinted garbled versions of Mirabeau's speech, those portions alluding to the action of Congress being perhaps pointedly omitted.[8] Thus neither the Presi-

[5] Text of the speech and of the decree directing the President to write "au Congrès américain" in *Archives Parlementaires*, XVI, 170-1; the reporter noted "un profond silence" after Mirabeau's opening words. Chinard, *L'Apothéose*, p. 18-28, includes the texts of Mirabeau's speech and other documents and extracts showing its contemporary reception in France.

[6] Fauchet, *Éloge civique de Benjamin Franklin . . . au nom de la Commune de Paris* (Paris, 1790); partial text in Chinard, *L'Apothéose*, p. 101-12. Fauchet's holograph manuscript has recently been acquired by the Library of Congress, which also has four drafts of Condorcet's *Éloge de M. Franklin, lu à la séance publique de l'Académie des Sciences, le 13 Nov. 1790* (Paris, 1791); partial text in Chinard, *L'Apothéose*, p. 129-43. TJ possessed Condorcet's eulogy but apparently not that of Fauchet (Sowerby, No. 519; see also Chinard, "The Apotheosis of Benjamin Franklin," Am. Phil. Soc., *Procs.*, XCIX [Dec. 1955], p. 448-9).

On 4 Oct. 1790 Bache's *General Advertiser* gave an account of the funeral ceremonies and described Fauchet's eulogy as "abounding with all that energy of sentiment, elegance of style, and animation of utterance peculiar to the Nation that almost idolizes whatever is American." Three weeks before TJ arrived in Philadelphia, Bache quoted a part of the eulogy and said that "a number of copies had been transmitted to Congress" (same, 1 Nov. 1790).

[7] Short to TJ, 14 June 1790.

[8] TJ to Washington, 27 Oct. 1790. Partial texts of Mirabeau's speech and the substance of the decree of the National Assembly—including the directive that "a letter of condolence be sent . . . to the Congress of America"—arrived in Boston on 15 Aug. 1790, were printed in the *Independent Chronicle* four days

dent nor the members of Congress could have been unprepared for the communications from France that arrived early in December at the opening of the session. These outpourings of veneration for Franklin, accompanied by expressions of friendship for the United States and of hope for a continuance of amicable relations between the two countries were received, ironically, just at the time that Otto, the French chargé, made a formal representation to the Secretary of State on the effect of the tonnage acts of 1789 and 1790.[9]

The first of these expressions of condolence was a letter from Abbé Sieyès, President of the National Assembly, enclosing a copy of its decree.[10] The second, a letter accompanied by a bulky packet, was addressed to "The President and Members of the American Congress."[11] This style of address, appropriate enough under the Articles of Confederation, was no longer so. In an action interpreted then and since as arising from a feeling of delicacy and respect for the principle of separation of powers, Washington declined to open it.[12] But he did not transmit it to the Congress. He sent it instead to the President of the Senate. There was no written message, but Washington's secretary, Tobias Lear, delivered the letter and packet to John Adams on the 7th of December and perhaps explained in person why neither had been opened. No entry in the journals testifies to what transpired in the Senate, but the next day Adams returned both the letter and the packet unopened. Again there was no formal communication, but Lear brought back "an opinion of the Senate that they might be opened with more propriety by the President." The Senate, he added, requested that Washington do so and "communicate such parts as he might think proper to the Legislature."[13] But even after receiving this particular request, Washington seemed bound by his scruples. Presumably neither he nor his secretary could open the letter or the packet without violating constitutional proprieties—but the Secretary of State might do so. Washington therefore directed Lear to send to Jefferson the "Letter and packet from the President of the National Assembly of France" with the request that he report what, if anything, should be communicated to Congress. Jefferson replied immediately that the letter con-

---

later, and from there spread generally through the American press (e.g., N. Y. *Daily Advertiser*, 23 Aug. 1790; *New-York Journal*, 24 Aug. 1790; *Federal Gazette*, 24 Aug. 1790; *Gazette of the United States*, 25 Aug. 1790; *Pennsylvania Mercury*, 26 Aug. 1790). On 1 Nov. 1790 Bache, who as Franklin's grandson was especially interested, reported: "We hear every day of additional marks of respect paid by the French nation to Dr. Franklin" (*General Advertiser*, 1 Nov. 1790).

[9] See Editorial Note and documents on the French representation on the tonnage acts, under 19 Jan. 1791.

[10] See Document II, enclosure II. Sieyès left the presidency on 20 June 1790 and his letter bears that date, but it was probably written afterward since he did not deliver it to William Short for almost a month (Short to TJ, 16 July 1790).

[11] See Document I, enclosure; also Lear to TJ, 8 Dec. 1790 (Document I in group of documents on proceedings in the Northwest Territory, under 14 Dec. 1790).

[12] Maclay, *Journal*, ed. Maclay, p. 350; Freeman, *Washington*, VI, 303 and note 138; Chinard, *L'Apothéose*, p. 61.

[13] Lear's entry in his record of legislative proceedings (DLC: Washington Papers, under 10 Dec. 1790).

veyed condolences on the death of Franklin and he recommended that it be laid before Congress. He also indicated that the letter—contrary to what Lear seemed to think and what has been supposed since[14]— was actually that of President Benière of the Commune of Paris. The accompanying packet contained twenty-six copies of Abbé Fauchet's *Éloge civique de Benjamin Franklin.* Jefferson said that these were intended for members of Congress and that, on the whole, this was "an evidence of . . . marked respect and friendship towards these United States."[15]

Washington chose, however, to disregard the opinion of the Senate, the recommendation of Jefferson, and indeed the intent of the communication itself. He sent Benière's letter and the copies of Fauchet's eulogy not to the Congress but to the Senate only, perhaps because only the Senate shared with the President a constitutional role in foreign affairs. This time, however, Washington sent a formal message. "I am commanded by the President of the United States," Lear wrote, "to deliver to the Senate a letter and sundry pamphlets which have come to his hands from the President of the Assembly of Representatives from the Community of Paris, addressed to the President and Members of Congress of the United States."[16] Punctilio was threatening to become tiresome. John Adams, whose opinion of Franklin was poles apart from that expressed by the French nation, must have thought less of the letter and packet opened than sealed. Senator Maclay described the scene that followed:[17]

> Our President looked over the letter some time and then began reading the additions that followed the President's name. He was Doctor of the Sorbonne, &ca. &ca. to the number of 15 (as our President said). These appelatives of Office, he chose to call titles, and then said some sarcastic things against the National Assembly for abolishing Titles.
>
> I could not help remarking that this whole Matter was received and transacted with a coldness and apathy that astonished me, and the letter and all the Pamphlets were *sent* down to the Representatives, as if unworthy the attention of our body. I deliberated with myself whether I should not rise and claim one of the copies in right of my being a Member. I would however only have got into a wrangle by so doing, without working any change on my fellow-Members. There might be others who indulged the same sentiments. But 'twas silence all!

[14] See Lear to TJ, 8 Dec. 1790 (Document I in group of documents on proceedings in the Northwest Territory, under 14 Dec. 1790); Chinard, *L'Apothéose,* p. 62.

[15] Document I.

[16] Lear to the President of the Senate, 10 Dec. 1790 (DLC: Washington Papers); JS, I, 220.

[17] Quotation from MS journal, DLC; Maclay, *Journal,* ed. Maclay, p. 350. Maclay erred in thinking that Fauchet's eulogy was given under the auspices of the National Assembly. The Speaker of the House directed the clerk to send two copies "to the President, for his own use" (John Beckley to Tobias Lear, 11 Dec. 1790; DLC: Washington Papers). Muhlenberg was a friend of Maclay and may also have given him a copy.

The House received Benière's letter and the twenty-six copies of Fauchet's eulogy on the 10th and immediately returned half of the pamphlets to the Senate, which took no official notice of them. The next day Smith of South Carolina, usually a strong supporter of Federalist measures, suggested that the House request the President to answer Benière's letter or that a joint committee of the House and Senate do so. He did not express preference for either form, but thought it "highly proper to take some notice of the polite attention shewn to the federal legislature by the President of the Commonalty of Paris." Boudinot thought that the matter should be left to the Speaker and that no notice of it should appear in the minutes. On the 13th, on Smith's motion, the House directed the Speaker to express its appreciation for this "tribute to the distinguished merit of Benjamin Franklin, a citizen of the United States." The French chargé incorrectly reported that the Senate had taken similar action.[18]

It can scarcely be supposed that Jefferson was unaware of this second and more glaring display of coldness on the part of the Senate, still less so that he was indifferent to the question of what response, if any, would be made to the similar communication from a body representing the whole of France. Abbé Sieyès' eloquent tribute to Franklin as a man of universal humanity and his hope that this solemn act of homage would strengthen the bonds between the two nations, thus laying the foundation for the enjoyment of liberty in "an indissoluble chain of connexion among all the people of the earth," could not have left him as unconcerned as Johnson, Ellsworth, King, Paterson, Schuyler, and others of the Senate majority obviously had been. But, so far as the records reveal, Washington had not asked Jefferson to draft an acknowledgment of these friendly sentiments. All that is known with certainty is that Sieyès' letter was transmitted by the President's secretary merely for the "perusal" of the Secretary of State.[19] If in fact Washington did not discuss it with Jefferson, his action in this instance stands in stark contrast to the kind of close consultation on drafts of dispatches, letters, messages, and proclamations that had prevailed ever since Jefferson entered office. Such collaboration between the President and the Secretary of State had never been more intimate than at this particular moment, as the documents on the French representation, on the British impressments, on the mission of Gouverneur Morris, and on the fixing of the seat of government clearly indicate.

[18] Smith's motion originally referred to "the illustrious memory of Benjamin Franklin," but Vining of Delaware moved an amendment to make the resolution read as above (proceedings of the House, 11, 13 Dec., as reported in Bache's *General Advertiser*, 13 and 14 Dec. 1790). The resolution does not appear in JHR, I, 334, 336. In *Annals*, II, 1838, Boudinot's objection to entering the matter in the journals is not mentioned, Smith's resolution is likewise omitted, and it is merely noted that the "business was specially committed to the Speaker." Otto, who had just been received cordially by Washington but somewhat coolly by Adams, deduced from his erroneous information of the Senate's action that the Vice President had been given "the mortification of being present at the triumph of the reputation of a man of whom he had always been jealous and who had been the principal cause of his disaffection for France" (Otto to Montmorin, 12 Dec. 1790, DLC: Henry Adams Transcripts). See below, at note 70.

[19] Lear to TJ, 8 Dec. 1790 (Document I in group of documents on proceedings in the Northwest Territory, under 14 Dec. 1790).

Yet the draft reply to Sieyès' letter was not prepared by the Secretary of State, who happened to possess a personal knowledge of the leaders of the National Assembly and who was highly respected by the moderates among them. For that duty the President turned instead to the Secretary of the Treasury, who had no first-hand knowledge or experience of the revolutionary movement in France and who, of course, had no responsibility for the conduct of foreign affairs. This remarkable procedure was not only a striking departure from customary practice: it was also a violation of Washington's own declared principles of administration.[20] Jefferson had drafted the President's response to a letter from the French monarch some months earlier. He would do the same a year later.[21] Why, then, was the Secretary of State apparently disregarded in a matter involving the legislature of France? Why indeed should this departure from administrative principle and practice have been compounded by another obvious impropriety in diplomacy? For, as head of state making an official response to a communication from the parliamentary body of another nation, Washington by this act not only flouted time-honored diplomatic tradition: he also committed his own office to the risk of affronting the monarch of France and, more important, his ministers. The tradition had not arisen out of an exaggerated concern for mere diplomatic protocol. It had developed over the centuries out of the need of sovereign states in their relations with each other to observe recognized rules of comity. Washington, as prudent and just as he was courteous, was not likely to disregard either his own accustomed administrative procedures or the necessary rules of diplomatic discourse without good and sufficient reason. Why did he do so in this instance?

II

The answers to these questions may lie in the circumstances surrounding the episode. On the 26th of January Washington transmitted to both houses of Congress—not to the Senate alone, as he had done six weeks earlier with Benière's letter from the commune of Paris—a translation of Sieyès' letter and the decree of the National Assembly. He did not inform either body of the fact that he had already responded to this communication. He did not suggest that any action be taken. He did not comment upon the form of address employed by Sieyès, except to say that his letter was "from the President of the National

[20] Washington to De Moustier, 13 Oct. 1789 (*Writings*, ed. Fitzpatrick, XXX, 440).

[21] Washington to Louis XVI, 6 Apr. 1790; Washington to Louis XVI, 14 Mch. 1792, the latter responding to the King's letter of 19 Sep. 1791, addressed "À Nos très chers grands amis et alliés les Etats-unis de l'Amérique Septentrionale"—a form of address which caused the House of Representatives to doubt the propriety of preparing its own response since it assumed the President would reply. It is worth noting that, on this occasion, Washington had taken so little note of the address that, on learning of the doubts raised in the House, he was obliged to ask TJ to look at the cover and inform him of its address (Lear to TJ, 5 Mch. 1792; TJ to Washington, 13 Mch. 1792; Washington to Louis XVI, 14 Mch. 1792; JHR, I, 527, 532-4; *Annals*, III, 456-7; JS, I, 404, 408, 409-10, 448). The Senate on this occasion also displayed the same kind of apathy toward France that it had exhibited in the present instance. See TJ's memoranda of conversations with Washington under 12 Mch. 1792 (Ford, I, 187-9).

Assembly of France to the President of the United States."[22] On that same day, Washington had his secretary send to Jefferson four documents. The first three of these—the letter from Louis XVI in response to Washington's letter recalling Jefferson, the letter from Sieyès, and the decree of the National Assembly—were to be placed among the departmental files. The fourth was Washington's response to the President of the National Assembly. As to it, Lear offered no explanation but gave an order: it was a communication from the President "which the Secretary of State will transmit accordingly." Presumably the letter —in Washington's holograph—was signed, sealed, addressed, and ready to be dispatched.[23] Jefferson carried out the directive in silence.

The obvious inference to be drawn from these circumstances is that Washington's supposed scruples about receiving improperly addressed communications were, to say the least, inconsistent. For if a sense of delicacy about constitutional bounds had kept him from opening Benière's letter, why should he not have applied the same principle to that of Sieyès? Despite Lear's statement to Jefferson and Washington's assertion to both houses of Congress indicating that that letter had been directed particularly to the President, it was in fact as improperly addressed as that from Benière. The decree of the National Assembly had obligated their President to write "au Congrès."[24] The translation of the decree as published in the American press made this directive plain for all to read. The text of Sieyès' letter itself showed that he had been charged by the National Assembly "to communicate their resolution to the Congress of the United States."[25] The original letter evidently has not survived, but there can be no doubt that, in keeping with the form of address that had long prevailed in official communications from France and would continue to be employed for some time to come, it bore some such superscription as "Le Président du Congrès des États-Unis."[26]

French officials and legislators were by no means alone in continuing to use a mode of address that had been rendered obsolete by the adoption of the Constitution. Even some Americans did so after 1789.[27]

[22] Washington to the Senate and House of Representatives, 26 Jan. 1791, DLC: Washington Papers; JS, I, 236; JHR, I, 363; *Annals*, II, 1932-3. A week earlier Washington had sent to the Senate only the letter from Louis XVI of 11 Sep. 1790, "addressed to the President and members of Congress of the United States of America" (Washington to the Senate, 17 Jan. 1791, JEP, I, 65).

[23] Document II; William Short recognized Washington's hand on the address cover (Short to TJ, 30 Mch. 1791).

[24] *Archives Parlementaires*, XVI, 171; *Procès-Verbal de l'Assemblée Nationale* (Paris, 1790), No. 317, 11 June 1793.

[25] See note 8 above. In reporting proceedings of the House, Bache's *General Advertiser*, 27 Jan. 1791, as well as other papers, printed both Sieyès' letter and the decree. Document II, enclosure II.

[26] Chinard says that it was addressed to the "Président du Congrès" but does not cite authority ("The Apotheosis of Benjamin Franklin," Am. Phil. Soc., *Procs.*, XCIX [Dec. 1955], p. 450).

[27] See, for example, David Mead to William Maclay, 24 Aug. 1790, enclosing a petition headed: "To His Excellency the President, the Members of the Senate, and Representatives of the United States in Congress Assembled at Philadelphia." Mead confessed that he was "totally unacquainted with matters of Form in such cases" and apologized for any impropriety "in the Address or Otherwise." Maclay

For some time to come and from as far away as India Washington continued to receive other communications that failed to recognize the constitutional independence of his office.[28] All save two of these, it appears, were opened and acted upon by him evidently without scruple and certainly without deference to Congress. The first of these exceptions was the letter from Benière. The second was a communication from the President of the Provincial Assembly at Cape François addressed to "Messieurs Le Président et les respectable membres de L'Auguste congrès des Etats unis de L'amerique."[29] Washington sent this letter to the Senate unopened, according to a memorandum by Lear, "with a request that if it contained anything of an Executive Nature it might be communicated to the President of the United States. The Senate declined opening the letter and returned it to the President . . . as being more proper, in their opinion, to be opened by him and such parts as he might think best communicated to the Senate." On opening this letter, Washington "found . . . that it did not contain matter which it was necessary to lay before Congress."[30] This episode occurred just ten days after that involving Benière's letter. Quite obviously, the President had purposely presented to the Senate a request identical with the one he had received from that body on the former occasion. Thus he had twice deferred to the Senate—each time concerning a letter bearing a superscription in French—and twice he had received the same negative response. This ended such exchanges. Thenceforth Washington did not hesitate to open and act upon letters that bore the obsolete form of address.

But the significant fact to be observed about these deferential transactions between the President and the Senate is that Washington had also not scrupled to open such improperly addressed letters *before* these two instances. This is amply demonstrated by the treatment accorded the letter from President Sieyès, not to mention earlier ex-

placed the petition before the President, not the Senate (DNA: RG 59, MLR). A petition from John Tanner to the President, 1 Jan. 1791 was similarly addressed (same). On variant forms of address, see J. B. Moore, *Digest of International Law*, IV, 462. See note 64 below.

[28] See, for example, the addresses on letters from Louis XVI of 11 Sep. 1790 and 19 Sep. 1791: the former was addressed "À nos très chers grands Amis et Alliés les Président et Membres du Congrès général des Etats-Unis de l'Amérique Septentrionale" and the latter—perhaps reflecting a confusion caused by TJ's instructions to Short (see below and TJ to Short, 8 Mch. 1791)— altered this form to: "À nos très chers grands Amis et Alliés les Etats-Unis de l'Amérique Septentrionale." Both of these communications were opened by Washington (see note 22). Other examples, both earlier and later, showing that he did not hesitate to receive, open, and act upon improperly addressed communications, can be found in DLC: Washington Papers and in DNA: RG 59, MLR.

[29] Dated at Cape François, 7 Sep. 1790, describing the alarming situation in Santo Domingo and asking for assistance (RC in DNA: RG 59, MLR). Washington dismissed the matter at this time but was obliged to face the more urgent appeals some months later. See also Cutting to TJ, 6 July, 4 and 9 Aug. 1790.

[30] Memorandum on legislative proceedings by Lear under date of 17 Dec. 1790 (DLC: Washington Papers); the letter and message accompanied a list of nominations of that date (JEP, I, 63). There is no mention of this in the journal of the Senate (JS, I, 223).

amples.[31] The procedures followed with respect to the letters from
Benière and Santo Domingo therefore stand as exceptions to the prevailing practice. Thus the generally accepted view that Washington
sent Benière's letter unopened to the Senate because of a scrupulous
regard for the boundaries set by the Constitution becomes no longer
tenable. Some other explanation for his action must be found. When
Washington sent Benière's letter to the Senate on the 7th of December,
he knew perfectly well that he had not conveyed the official tribute
that had been paid to the memory of Benjamin Franklin by the representatives of the French nation. That tribute lay open before him,
signed by Sieyès. He knew with equal certainty that soon or late he
would be obliged to transmit that letter not just to the Senate but to
both houses of Congress. This duty was imposed upon him by a fact
widely known on both sides of the Atlantic—that the gesture of
homage to Franklin had been made by the National Assembly of
France to the Congress of the United States. Yet for six weeks Washington retained open in his hands the more significant of the two
communications from France after sending unopened to the Senate
that of lesser importance. The most plausible explanation for this is
to be found not in the trivial question of protocol concerning forms of
address but rather in the deep political cleavages within the country,
within the administration, and within the Congress.

Washington was well aware of the existence and nature of these
cleavages. They were of long standing and, in respect to the two great
powers of Europe, involved deep affections and antipathies. "You know
we have two parties with us," Hamilton told the British agent Beckwith
soon after news of the French tribute arrived in the United States,
"there are gentlemen, who think we ought to be connected with France
in the most intimate terms, and that the Bourbon compact furnishes
an example for us to follow; there are others who are at least as
numerous, and influential, who decidedly prefer an English connexion."[32] The nation was indeed divided, though not equally and not
over a question of alliances and compacts. But if an Anglican interest
existed in the sense meant by Hamilton, it was surely to be found in
its most concentrated form in the Senate. There its protagonists were
overwhelmingly in the majority, including the father-in-law of Hamilton whom Maclay, with ample cause, thought "amazingly fond of the
old leaven" of monarchy.[33] Against this majority Maclay, Monroe, and
Carroll stood almost solitary against those who argued that interest
alone governed the policies of nations, that this had been the motive of
France in helping the states win their independence, and that gratitude to such an ally therefore had no place in national decisions. Hamilton was the accepted leader of the Senate majority, his whole system
looked toward a rapprochement with England, and he had made it
plain that, out of personal predilection as well as on grounds of national policy, he had "always preferred a connexion with [her] to that

[31] Document II; see note 28.
[32] Report of George Beckwith, enclosed in Dorchester to Grenville, 10 Nov.
1790 (PRO: CO 42/69, f. 16-25, 61-8, 69-72); Syrett, *Hamilton*, VII, 70.
[33] Maclay, *Journal*, ed. Maclay, p. 167.

of any other country."[34] The prevailing attitudes of the Senate majority were of the same general character, devoid of enthusiasm for republican principles and especially for manifestations of these coming from revolutionary France. The first clear evidence of the former tendency came in the Senate's discussion of honorific titles, which produced a profound feeling of revulsion in the country. The first overt act indicating a preference for England over France emerged in the Senate's action on the tonnage duties in 1789, which laid the foundation for protest and possible retaliation.[35] These were unmistakable evidences of feelings in the Senate that affected even its attitude toward the death of Benjamin Franklin, an American little regarded in England but idolized in France.

Facing these realities, Washington may well have hesitated to subject the condolences of the National Assembly to the chilling kind of response that the Senate had accorded Carroll's original motion to follow the House in paying homage to Franklin. To have done so would have been to invite an almost certain affront to a friendly ally. Such a gratuitous rejection of a significant expression of friendship would have been especially damaging at this moment, when France was formally protesting American legislation that Washington himself had regarded as being contrary to justice as well as policy.[36] It is therefore quite plausible to suppose that Washington deliberately chose the unopened letter from the commune of Paris—perhaps in full knowledge of its precise character, certainly in awareness that it did not speak for the whole of France—as a means of testing the temper of the Senate. If so, the answer was immediate and unequivocal. The Senate coldly dismissed the friendly gesture as of no concern to itself, even though it did request the President to lay before it such of the substance of Benière's letter as might be deemed worthy of consideration. The same kind of response was accorded the letter from Santo Domingo, the submission of which was in effect an invitation to the Senate to take the initiative.

These two well-concealed tests, if such they were, provided as exact a gauge as could be desired for estimating what action the Senate would take on the letter from Sieyès. To avoid the risk of an affront to the National Assembly that could not be concealed and to insure a decent reciprocation of friendly sentiments by the government of the United States, only one course seemed open—that is, for the President himself to make the response. Yet Sieyès' letter would still have to be laid before Congress. What if the Senate should persist in its intransigent attitude? Again only a single unexceptionable course seemed likely to insure at least the outward appearance of friendliness. The response would have to be drafted by that member of the cabinet whose leadership the Senate accepted virtually without question—the Secretary of the Treasury.

[34] Syrett, *Hamilton*, VII, 70, 440-1.
[35] Short to TJ, 4 Aug. 1790.
[36] Washington to David Stuart, 26 July 1789; *Writings*, ed. Fitzpatrick, XXX, 363; see Editorial Note, French protest against the tonnage acts, under 18 Jan. 1791.

Such, at any rate, was the course that Washington adopted, thereby seeming to ignore the member of the cabinet in whose province these matters fell and at the same time violating both administrative practice and diplomatic tradition. But for these very reasons it becomes implausible if not incredible to suppose that Washington, then in habits of close and intimate consultation with his Secretary of State, did not consult him at every stage of this delicate episode. All that preceded and all that followed the adoption of this strategy to circumvent the Senate majority—particularly the choice of a quiet, adroit, and effective means of achieving a desired end—points convincingly to the source of Washington's invitation to Hamilton to draft the response.[37] Such finesse seems easily attributable to the hand of the Secretary of State.

III

The Senate promptly confirmed the prudence of such a strategy by behaving precisely as Washington and Jefferson had every reason to fear it might. When the President's terse message transmitting Sieyès' letter to both houses came to the Senate on the 26th of January, that body gave it the same treatment it had accorded the letter from Benière. William Maclay, isolated and embittered at the end of his long and futile contest with an unyielding majority, thus again described the frigid atmosphere:[38]

> . . . a Letter from the National Assembly of France on the Death of Doctor Franklin was communicated from them and Recieved with a Coldness that was truly amazing. I cannot help painting to myself the disappointment that awaits the French Patriots, while their warm fancies are figuring the raptures that we will be thrown into, on the Reciept of their letter, and the information of the honors which they have bestowed on our Countryman, and anticipating the complimentary echos of our Answers, when they find that we, cold as Clay, care not a fig about them, Franklin or Freedom.

Maclay's esteem for Franklin and his regard for France were not unqualified. But he had been goaded beyond endurance when Ellsworth and others proclaimed the doctrine that gratitude had no place in the affairs of nations and that interest alone should serve as the basis of national policy. Franklin might be imperfect and France not disinterested, but a generous gesture of friendliness deserved to be met with a decent respect for the amenities.

Such a response, by a prompting from some source disclosed neither in its journal nor in that of Maclay, the Senate was finally persuaded to make. On the 22nd of February, with full control over its emotions,

[37] Washington must have made the request shortly before 25 Jan. 1791, when he transmitted Sieyès' letter to Congress. Hamilton prepared the draft in time for Washington to copy it and have it ready for TJ to forward it that same day (see Document II, enclosure III; since Washington's letter is dated the 27th, Lear may have made a mistake in the date of his letter to TJ or he may have held it until Washington finished copying the reply).

[38] Entry for 25 Jan. 1791 (Maclay's MS journal, DLC; Maclay, *Journal*, ed. Maclay, p. 379-80).

it adopted the following resolution: "*Resolved,* By the Senate and House of Representatives of the United States of America in Congress assembled, That the President of the United States be requested *to cause to be communicated* to the National Assembly of France, the peculiar sensibility of Congress, to the tribute paid to the memory of Benjamin Franklin, by the enlightened and free Representatives of a great nation, in their decree of the eleventh of June, one thousand seven hundred and ninety."[39] The House immediately concurred. Since the Senate originated the resolution, it is plausible to suppose the Secretary of the Treasury let it be known to his friends that, although the President had responded for himself, a formal expression from the Congress was nevertheless expected. This unexpected thawing of the Senate's chilly attitude coincided exactly with the crisis over the navigation bill which resulted in its being referred to the Secretary of State, a move that created much anxiety among the defenders of the British interest.[40] When this important issue was joined, Sieyès' letter had been lying unnoticed on the Senate table for almost a month.

But Jefferson's strategy of indirection, if it was his, resulted in another and more serious violation of diplomatic propriety. This lay in the nature of the response Hamilton drafted, a text that Washington adopted almost without change except for such alterations in phraseology as were made necessary in a reply addressed to Sieyès' successor in office. While adhering stylistically and superficially to conventional usage in such matters, Hamilton's draft contained two substantive passages that were as gratuitous as they were improper. The first was an allusion to Louis XVI. The whole of Sieyès' letter—its magnanimous tribute to Franklin, its testimony to the empire of reason and virtue, its expressions of hope for amity between the two nations, its salute to Washington and Lafayette—had voiced only the sentiments of the National Assembly. That body and its supposed counterpart in America—the Congress of the United States—were declared to be the first to exhibit the spectacle of two free nations existing in perfect concord. Nowhere in this optimistic expression of hope for the sway of reason was the monarch of France mentioned, either directly by title or indirectly by allusion. The tribute to great men like Franklin as the parents of universal humanity made it plain, as did the politically-inspired eulogy by Mirabeau, that the omission was intended. Men of wisdom and virtue, regardless of national boundaries, were the true benefactors to whom expressions of filial gratitude were due from "all the tribes of the great human family," not hereditary rulers claiming authority as of divine right.

A polite and ritualistic response, to be sure, did not require that notice be paid to these eloquent and intentional silences in the French tribute. It did not even impose a need to salute the National Assembly as a body representative of "Twenty-six millions of men, breaking their chains, and seriously occupied in giving themselves a durable constitution." These allusions in Sieyès' letter, if embarrassing, could have

---

[39] JS, I, 278; emphasis added.

[40] JHR, I, 387, 389, 398; *Annals,* II, 2021; JS, I, 295. The resolution appeared in the *Federal Gazette,* 23 Feb. 1791, as the only item under Senate proceedings. See Vol. 18: 237.

been easily avoided or obscured by the kind of rhetoric that characterized so many formal responses of that era, not excluding the text that
Hamilton had drafted. But what the Secretary of the Treasury caused
the President of the United States to say on this head was neither
evasive nor clouded in fine phrases. The breaking of chains he attributed not to the efforts of the elected representatives of the French
people, but in general to undefined "circumstances" and in particular
to the "patronage of a Monarch, who has proved himself to be the
friend of the people over whom he reigns." This gratuitous comment
over the signature of the head of one state about the ruler of another
was not only improper in form: its substantive assertion was also
belied by almost every action that had been taken by the legislative
body to which it was addressed. It was wholly at variance with the
tone and purpose of the communication to which the President was
responding. Indeed, that letter only epitomized the fact that the demonstrations of homage to Franklin in France were, in the final analysis,
demonstrations against monarchism if not against the monarch.

The second impropriety in Hamilton's text was its allusion to the
French constitution. Sieyès had said only that the people of France
were seriously engaged in providing themselves with a durable constitution, doing so in emulation of a generous people who had preceded
them in that noble endeavor. This surely called for a reciprocation of
generous expressions and Hamilton supplied them. But it by no means
required the offering of unsolicited advice about the kind of constitution suitable for France. That, on the contrary, was proscribed by
every principle of comity between nations. Yet Hamilton proceeded to
contribute such counsel, embedding it in his polite phrasing of solicitude for the welfare of the French people. He caused the President to
express the wish that the labors of the National Assembly would
"speedily issue in the firm establishment of a Constitution, which by
wisely conciliating the indispensable principles of public order, with
the enjoyment and exercise of the essential rights of man," would
perpetuate the freedom and happiness of the people of France. The
two texts of the draft prepared by Hamilton reveal very clearly the
emphasis that was intended. Only in the second was the word "indispensable" added to the phrase "the principles of public order."
Similarly, while the earlier text had referred to "the principles of
liberty," the second modified this to mean "the *true* principles of
liberty."[41] Sieyès, of course, had said nothing at all about the need to
incorporate principles of public order in the constitution of France.
He had spoken only of a durable constitution. Hamilton's reciprocal
allusion to "the firm establishment of a Constitution" would have provided a polite, appropriate, and sufficient response, had he been content to stop at that point. The proclaimed purposes of the revolutionists
in France, as in the United States, had made the rights of man the
first object of all government. But Hamilton in this reply to the National Assembly, as indeed in his whole system of policy, placed primary emphasis upon public order, characterizing this as indispensable
while viewing the rights of man as limited to those of an essential

41 See Document II, enclosure II and textual notes (emphasis added).

nature. The tribute to the benevolence of the monarch of France and the emphasis on public order undoubtedly reflected his own convictions, but the gratuitous advice about the internal affairs of another nation was nevertheless a serious breach of diplomatic courtesy.

This remarkable departure from recognized rules of diplomacy has been interpreted as a calculated move on the part of the President. "Washington," wrote Gilbert Chinard, "went as far as he possibly could to express his full approval of the new constitution at a time when [it] had not yet been signed by the King of France. . . . The President of the United States had established a very dangerous precedent in expressing an opinion about the domestic affairs of a foreign country. In that sense the letter was an epoch making document."[42] While demonstrating beyond doubt that the tribute to Franklin had been affected by the aims of the constitutionalists in the National Assembly, Chinard was not aware that Hamilton had drafted the response to Sieyès' letter. Hence the conclusions he drew—that Washington did not consult his Secretary of State, that neither he nor Jefferson had fully realized the danger of departing from diplomatic rules observed by older governments, and that "the attempt to establish direct communications between parliamentary bodies . . . was in part frustrated by Washington's taking the initiative to write personally to the Assemblée nationale"[43]—collide with the fact that the French tribute mixed with revolutionary aims also became involved in American partisan politics of a very contrary tendency. The aim of the President and the Secretary of State, far from being a deliberate effort to intervene in the affairs of France, must instead be regarded as an attempt to prevent injury to Franco-American relations arising from the hostile attitude of the Senate. The allusions to the French constitution were the genuine views of Hamilton, going as far as he dared in urging the French to respect their monarch and to frame a funda-

[42] Chinard, "The Apotheosis of Benjamin Franklin," Am. Phil. Soc., *Procs.*, XCIX (Dec. 1955), p. 452. It should be pointed out that Chinard modified this interpretation in the revised and expanded edition of his useful monograph, indicating only that this seemed to mark "une date dans l'histoire des relations diplomatique entre la France et les États-Unis" and that a precedent, though an isolated one, had been created in communications between parliamentary bodies (Chinard, *L'Apothéose*, p. 67). Nevertheless, Washington's reply to Sieyès was a commentary on the internal affairs of France in a very different sense from that advanced by Chinard in the English version of his monograph and to a far greater degree than that indicated by him in his revised interpretation.

[43] These interpretations were also revised in Chinard's *L'Apothéose*, p. 65 (see preceding note), for there it is stated that Washington's letter ". . . reprenait les thèmes développés par le Président de l'Assemblée nationale, sur un mode mineur, ce qui prouve que Washington ou son Secrétaire de État étaient loin d'être ignorants des formes employées traditionnellement par les diplomaties européennes."

TJ's scrupulous regard for delicacy in such matters was characteristic, being based both on an exact knowledge of the forms of diplomacy and on his own inherent respect for civilized discourse, whether between nations or individuals. In 1792, for example, when he drafted Washington's response to the letter of Louis XVI transmitting the completed French constitution, he "avoided saying a word in approbation of the constitution, not knowing whether the King, in his heart, approved it" (memorandum of conversation with Washington, 12 Mch. 1792; Ford, I, 188).

mental law that would place first emphasis on "the indispensable principles of public order." These sentiments were certainly not intended to support the views of Mirabeau, La Rochefoucauld, and Lafayette. In so far as Hamilton addressed himself to those sitting in the French legislature, he voiced the convictions of the members on the right, speaking for the majority of the American Senate but to the minority of the National Assembly. The characteristically bold expedient was dangerous not so much because it broke with diplomatic tradition or constituted an ill-conceived precedent, but because it involved the risk of injuring the friendly relations existing between the United States and France. Since the destruction of the alliance was a cardinal point in Hamilton's policy, the bold allusions must have been calculated.

If so, the effort failed. Washington allowed the two improper statements to stand, perhaps because he shared their sentiments, perhaps because, in their matrix of polite and even friendly language, he found them unexceptionable. When Washington's letter arrived in France, William Short recognized his handwriting on the cover, assumed that it was a reply to that of Sieyès, and delivered it to Montmorin. That minister, as if to call attention to the impropriety of such a communication, declined to receive it and recommended that Short deliver it to La Rochefoucauld. This he did. When La Rochefoucauld was called upon by the President to read the letter to the National Assembly, his translation was hurried and he had the misfortune to use an expression to which those on the right attached a meaning "by no means favourable." Worse, this occurred in that part of Washington's letter intended as a particular compliment to Lafayette himself. The marquis, immensely vain and known throughout the capital of France as one for whom Washington had a paternal affection, was crushed.[44] The members on the right were delighted.

Thus La Rochefoucauld and Lafayette, the two who had induced Mirabeau to make his dramatic eulogy of Franklin in the hope of benefiting the constitution, witnessed the embarrassing denouement, the one an unwitting cause and the other his mortified victim. The majority of the Senate of the United States, had they been present, could scarcely have enjoyed the spectacle less than did the opposition. Washington's letter, according to the official proceedings, was received with "vifs applaudissemens" testifying to the desire of strengthening the bonds between the two free peoples. It was ordered to be printed and inserted in the minutes.[45] But the seemingly calculated and certainly

[44] Short to TJ, 30 Mch. 1792. TJ made an extract of this passage of the letter and gave it to Washington, perhaps to inform him of Lafayette's wounded feelings and perhaps also to call attention to Montmorin's refusal to accept the letter (Tr of Extract in TJ's hand, DNA: RG 59, MLR, endorsed by Washington). Short identified the passage for TJ: "The expression in English is as the Duke de la R[ochefoucauld] tells me '*May he* ever continue to have the public good in view &c.' In French it is '*Puisse-t-il* &c.'" (Short to TJ, 30 Mch. 1791; emphasis in MS). In the extract that TJ copied and sent to Washington, he delicately omitted the French equivalent, thereby providing an indirect commentary on his relations with Washington and perhaps with Short.

[45] The French translation is given in Chinard, *L'Apothéose*, p. 72-4, from the *Procès-Verbal de l'Assemblée Nationale*, No. 602, p. 17-19, 26 Mch. 1791. Lafayette never mentioned the embarrassing incident to Washington, nor did he.

improper advice that Hamilton had offered about the kind of constitution he thought fitting for France had also been drowned in the ribaldry.

IV

The coldness of the Senate inspired a countervailing warmth among those who embraced a very different set of political convictions. During the month in which that body allowed Sieyès' letter to lie undisturbed on its table, two significant events in Pennsylvania provided ample proofs of this resentment. That they were directly inspired by the failure of the Senate to reciprocate the friendly gesture scarcely admits of doubt. In the first of these incidents, indeed, may be found a reflection of William Maclay's indignation over the behavior of those in the Senate who seemed to care "not a fig about [France], Franklin or freedom." For it was his brother, Samuel Maclay, who arose in the House of Representatives of Pennsylvania on the 14th of February and offered the following resolution:[46]

> *Whereas*, the National Assembly of France have testified their regard to the memory of our late venerable fellow-citizen, Doctor Benjamin Franklin, in terms equally respectful to him, and honorable to themselves: And as it is for the general interest of humanity, that a tribute of respect should be paid to virtue in every clime, and that such benevolent actions as those of the National Assembly, founded on general philanthropy, should be reciprocated through the civilized world:
>
> *Resolved*, therefore, That a committee be appointed to draught a letter to the President of the National Assembly of France, expressing the high satisfaction of the Representatives of Pennsylvania derive from the proceedings of that august body, who have paid so honorable a tribute to the memory of our late venerable president, Benjamin Franklin; and also expressing the exalted respect they entertain for that illustrious band of patriots, who forgetting localities and national distinctions, considered mankind as members of the same family, and have nobly exhibited so great a pattern of universal benevolence.

This was indeed a proposal for a communication between legislative bodies that was unprecedented. But, as someone must have pointed out, the tribute to Franklin had not been addressed to the legislature of Pennsylvania and for that body to act while the Senate remained silent might have an effect in France quite the opposite of that intended. Yet the feelings that had been aroused were too strong to be stifled. The next day James McLene, who had seconded Maclay's motion, proposed that a congratulatory address be sent to the National Assembly to express "the sympathetic feelings of this House on the subject of their virtuous exertions in the cause of freedom, and on the flattering prospect of their success in effecting a revolution, which will restore to the blessings of equal liberty so many millions of our fellow-men."

[46] Extracts from *Journal*, House of Representatives, printed in Chinard, "The Apotheosis of Benjamin Franklin," Am. Phil. Soc., *Procs.*, XCIX [Dec. 1955], p. 454-5, and *L'Apothéose*, p. 70-2.

THE POLITICS OF MOURNING

This substitute motion was adopted unanimously. At first a committee was authorized to prepare the address, but on the 26th of February the House directed its Speaker, William Bingham, to do so. Bingham's own political convictions could have given him little pleasure in the task, but the address, as reported by him on the 8th of April, was immediately approved. Its tenor was as different from the response drafted by Hamilton as were the two parties in the nation that each of these documents reflected. Its allusions to monarchy were cast in the still vibrant rhetoric of the American revolution:[47]

> We fondly hope that no untoward or inauspicious circumstances may intervene to interrupt your glorious career, until you have effactually restored to the blessings of equal liberty, civil and religious, so many millions of our fellow men; until you have abolished the odious and arrogant distinctions betwixt man and man, and until you have implanted in the minds of the people a generous and passionate enthusiasm for their country, instead of a confined, though romantic, attachment to the person of a King.

Its expressions of gratitude to France for her assistance during the struggle for independence, mingled with sympathy and admiration, were the very opposite of what Ellsworth and other Federalists in the Senate had been saying:

> A nation which has been actuated by such magnanimous policy, which, with a noble enthusiasm, so generously interposed its power, so profusely poured forth its treasures, and mingled its blood with ours, in the defense of the liberties of America, is entitled to a grateful return of our regard, and to the warmest wishes that sensibility or attachment can express.
> It was under the operation of these feelings that we have always lamented that a brave and gallant people, who had become the voluntary champions of our freedom, should not themselves be free; —that after having assisted in erecting for us a temple of liberty, they should return to the house of bondage. Fortunately, the scene has changed, and your present situation awakens the most amiable sympathies of the human heart.
> We now view with a greateful exultation, your glorious triumph

[47] Extracts from *Journal* of 14, 15, 16, and 26 Feb. and 6 and 8 Apr. 1791 and full text of address, signed by Bingham and addressed "To the President of the National Assembly of France," together with French text as printed in Le Hodey's *Journal des Etats-Generaux* for 2 June 1791, are in Chinard, *L'Apothéose*, p. 69-72, 76-8.

In view of Bingham's position as a strong Federalist, speculator, banker, and friend of England, the question immediately arises whether he could have produced an address so ardent in its expression of devotion to revolutionary principles and to France. It is possible that the text was provided for him and even that William Maclay, whose ready and gifted pen can easily be imagined as producing it, was the one responsible for its impassioned rhetoric. Maclay dined with Bingham on the 6th of January and thought him his political though not his personal enemy (Maclay, *Journal*, ed. Maclay, p. 366). Since William and Samuel Maclay were attending legislative bodies in the same city—indeed in the same group of buildings—and were perhaps even rooming together, it is scarcely conceivable that they did not collaborate during this episode.

of reason over prejudice,—of liberty and law over flattery and
despotic will. You have nobly broke the fetters that bound you to
your former government, and have, in the view of astonished Europe,
undertaken a revolution, founded on that pure and elementary principle, that the people are the source of power—that in them it is
naturally inherent, and from them can alone be derived.

This remarkable address nowhere mentioned the indispensable principles of public order. It did not defend the use of titles and other
artificial distinctions as arising out of the natural inclinations of men,
as John Adams had done in the Senate and in his correspondence at
this time with Samuel Adams—an exchange that epitomized the deep-
ening divisions within the nation.[48] On the contrary it stamped such
distinctions as odious and arrogant, altogether inimical to the aims of
those seeking the blessings of equal liberty. As if to make the thrust of
its meaning all the more unequivocal, the Pennsylvania address—
voicing expressions of respect and concern for the success of an ally
in the cause of freedom and presuming to speak for the united suf-
frages and sentiments of the citizens of the United States—said not a
word about the events that had given rise to it, the death of Franklin
and the tribute of the National Assembly. But, as the French chargé
reported, the address was inspired by the homage paid to Franklin.
"It is the first step of the kind that has been taken by a sovereign
state," he wrote. "They tell me that other states of the union will at
once follow the example of Pennsylvania."[49] Clearly, the aroused opposition was beginning to organize.

The second event that was prompted by the indifference of the
Senate was less obviously political in purpose, at least in its outward
manifestations, but it was rooted in the same profound cleavages. This
episode involved the scientific institution that Franklin had founded,
The American Philosophical Society Held at Philadelphia for the
Promotion of Useful Knowledge. Two days after Franklin's funeral,
a memorable spectacle witnessed by some twenty thousand persons, a
special meeting of the Society was called to consider some testimonial
"to the Memory of their late illustrious President."[50] The members of
the Society, as well they might, no doubt regarded this extraordinary
manifestation of respect and affection as being all that was requisite
in the nature of a public ceremonial. They therefore voted that a
eulogy "be prepared by one of their members, to be pronounced before

[48] John Adams to Samuel Adams, 12 Sep. and 18 Oct. 1790; Samuel Adams
to John Adams, 4 Oct. and 20 Nov. 1790. Copies of these famous letters (two
versions of the last) are in DLC: TJ Papers, f. 9796-9807, 9888. They were
printed in a pamphlet in 1802, *Four letters: being an interesting correspondence
between those eminently distinguished characters, John Adams, Late President
of the United States, and Samuel Adams, late Governor of Massachusetts. On
the important subject of Government* (Boston, Adams & Rhoades, 1802); see
Sowerby, No. 3287.
[49] Otto to Montmorin, 4 Apr. 1791 (DLC: Henry Adams Transcripts).
[50] This event was widely noticed in America and in Europe. Vaughan told La
Rochefoucauld that the procession extended half a mile and "was viewed by
such a concourse of people as was probably never before assembled in America"
(Vaughan to La Rochefoucauld, 4 June 1790; Chinard, *L'Apothéose*, p. 16); see
Van Doren, *Franklin*, p. 779-80.

this Body, as soon as may be convenient." The purpose obviously was to provide a tribute by the learned society as distinguished from a public testimonial. This is proved both by the phraseology employed and by what followed.

When the members came to choose an orator, David Rittenhouse and the Rev. William Smith received an equal number of votes. Both were vice-presidents of the Society and Rittenhouse would soon succeed Franklin in the presidency. He was also the nearest American claimant to his mantle in the realm of science. But despite the assurance given by the two men that one of them would deliver the eulogy, ten months elapsed before anything was done. Rittenhouse and Smith, active and zealous in their official duties, continued during the summer and autumn to attend the Society's meetings and to take part in its various functions. There is no evidence that either claimed the honor for himself or that the other would not yield. On the contrary, both appeared deferential. In the end Smith accepted only on Rittenhouse's assurance that he would furnish notes on Franklin's attainments in science.[51] During this interval of ten months, while public and scientific bodies in France proclaimed the virtues of the Society's founder, its two vice-presidents and members remained silent and preoccupied with its usual concerns, including the acceptance of a bequest of books from Franklin.

The breaking of the silence came with dramatic suddenness—just a week after the Senate of the United States, sitting within stone's throw of the Hall of the Society, had received with such cold indifference the tribute by Sieyès. The full texts of Sieyès' letter and the decree of the National Assembly appeared in Bache's *General Advertiser* on the 27th of January. On the 4th of February the Society began to act with a celerity in remarkable contrast to its previous lethargy. It appointed a committee of three—including John Vaughan, brother of Benjamin Vaughan whose letter to La Rochefoucauld had inspired the French tributes—to call upon Rittenhouse and Smith in order to obtain "a determinate answer with respect to the Eulogium." From that point forward the Society concentrated its full force upon this single object, transforming it from a simple testimonial by the Society for its members to a public ceremony in the presence of all of the dignitaries of city, state, and nation. The timing, the enlarged plans, the urgency, the measures taken to insure the presence of both the Senate and the House of Representatives—all provided convincing proofs that the political purposes implicit in the testimonials to Franklin both in France and in the United States had finally affected the councils of this oldest of the nation's learned societies.

On the 18th the committee on the eulogy reported "the Business . . . in forwardness."[52] A meeting of the Society was called on the 25th to consider "special and important business." At that time a committee on arrangements was directed to extend invitations to the President, the Vice-President and Senate, the Speaker and House of Representatives, the Governor and legislature of the state, the "Ministers of the United

[51] Brooke Hindle, *David Rittenhouse*, p. 311; minutes, 21 and 23 Apr. 1790 (Am. Phil. Soc., *Procs.*, XXII [July 1885], pt. iii, p. 181).
[52] Same, p. 188, 189.

States for State, Treasury, and War," the diplomatic corps, the judges of the Supreme Court of the United States, and other officials, dignitaries, and citizens. The committee was also instructed "to have letters to the Houses of Congress ready, early to-morrow morning."[53] On Saturday the 26th, the committee met as required, presented invitations to the President, the Senate, and the House, and received their replies.[54] On that day in the Senate the report of the Secretary of State on the French representation on the tonnage acts was under debate and Maclay listened to a "burst of abuse . . . against the French by Ellsworth in the most vituperative language that fancy could invent." Maclay himself received the brunt of the attack and, finding no protection from Adams in the chair, left the room.[55] The Society's particular invitation to the two houses of Congress, the selection of the date for the ceremony, and the choice of an hour early in the morning indicate clearly that those managing the affair particularly wished members of Congress to be present. The date chosen was the 1st of March, two days before the close of the session. The Senate's consideration of the report by the Secretary of State on the French complaint—marked by the bitterest invective since the debates on the assumption of state debts—formed an appropriate counterpoint to the suddenly urgent proceedings of the Society, with the climax taking place in the last hectic hours before the members of Congress dispersed.

When the Society's committee on the eulogy reported that the business was in forwardness, it may or may not have provided a full explanation of its activities. But both the record of the proceedings and the silences in the documents indicate the close involvement of the Secretary of State, Franklin's successor as minister to France and one of the most active and interested members of the American Philosophical Society. There is no indication that Jefferson had any part in the selection of the orator. But it is interesting that the choice did not fall on Rittenhouse, a friend of Jefferson and one who, in general, shared Franklin's philosophical and scientific as well as political interests. It fell instead on Smith, who had once been a bitter enemy of Franklin and whose loyalist inclinations had led him to oppose American independence as "illusory, ruinous, and impracticable."[56] Smith's qualifications for the honor, therefore, would seem to have been about as

[53] Bache's *General Advertiser*, 25 Feb. 1791; Am. Phil. Soc., *Procs.*, XXII [July 1885], pt. iii, p. 181.

[54] Same, p. 191, with full text of Washington's acceptance, dated 26 Feb. 1791 and addressed to the Rev. Samuel Magaw (not in Fitzpatrick); JS, I, 289, mentions the invitation but records no action; not referred to in JHR, I, 392-4, but included in proceedings of the House as given in *Federal Gazette*, 26 Feb. 1791. The committee announced on the 28th that the eulogy would be pronounced the next day "at half past 9 o'clock" (*General Advertiser*, 28 Feb. 1791; *Federal Gazette*, 28 Feb. 1791).

[55] Maclay, *Journal*, ed. Maclay, p. 405.

[56] DAB. Benjamin Rush, who knew Smith well, considered him a man of genius, taste, and learning who, in his role as educator and preacher, was an influential figure in Pennsylvania politics. But he also characterized him as offensive in company, irascible, profane, avaricious, irreligious, immoral, and, in the years before his death in 1803, such a habitual drunkard that he "descended to his grave . . . without being lamented by a human creature" (Rush, *Autobiography*, ed. G. W. Corner, p. 262-5).

inappropriate as those entitling Alexander Hamilton to draft the response of the President of the United States to the President of the
National Assembly. The committee certainly conferred with Jefferson
and asked his aid in the preparation of the eulogy. This he readily
gave, at least in the form of a letter addressed to Smith and perhaps
in other ways as well. All of the committee's proceedings—the choice
of Smith as orator, the solicitation of Jefferson's assistance, the emphasis on the public character of the ceremony, and particularly the nature
of the aid given—suggest that Jefferson was much more intimately
involved in the planning than the record reveals.

His letter to the eulogist, like his ostensible letter to James Madison
in 1789 on the doctrine that the earth belongs to the living, was addressed to William Smith only in form. In actuality it was framed for
a particular occasion and a particular assemblage. In both instances
such indirection was thoroughly characteristic and, at bottom, political
in purpose. As soon as Jefferson dispatched his recollections of Franklin in France, he transmitted a copy of the letter to his friend John
Vaughan, as if to insure that those in charge of the affair guarantee
the inclusion of its central point.[57] On its surface Jefferson's letter
seemed to confirm the characterization he gave it in his note to Vaughan.
Its dismissal of Franklin's *bon mots* as too incongruous for the occasion,
its associating him with such a minor technological matter as Argand's
lamp, its accrediting him and others with giving the death wound to
"that compound of fraud and folly" in Mesmer's theory of animal
magnetism, its assurance that nothing of interest in philosophy or politics took place thereafter—all of these comments fully deserved Jefferson's description of them as small offerings. But their very triviality
served to accent all the more the central point of his tribute to
Franklin:[58]

> No greater proof of his estimation in France can be given than the
> late letters of condolence on his death from the National Assembly
> of that country, and the community of Paris, to the President . . .
> and to Congress, and their public mourning on that event. It is I
> believe the first instance of that homage having been paid by a
> public body of one nation to a private citizen of another.

The occasion for which the American Philosophical Society had so
long waited was a distinguished one. On the morning of the 1st of
March, Thomas Jefferson, Alexander Hamilton, and forty-three other
members assembled "at their Hall and proceeded in a body to the
German Lutheran Church in Fourth street."[59] There the President of
the United States and Mrs. Washington, the Vice-President and Mrs.
Adams, the members of the Senate and the House of Representatives,
the Cabinet officers, and a large number of citizens listened to the

[57] See Document IV.   [58] See Document III.
[59] Minutes, 1 Mch. 1791 (Am. Phil. Soc., *Procs.*, XXII [July 1885], p. iii, p.
191-2). Alexander Hamilton was elected a member of the Society on 21 Jan.
1791. The diploma was delivered to him in person on the 18th of February
(same, p. 188, 191, 192; MS journal, Corresponding Secretary, PPAP). This
meeting at Philosophical Hall prior to the eulogy was evidently the only one
that Hamilton ever attended.

Reverend Dr. Smith's long, hyperbolic tribute to his former enemy.[60] The only elements of enduring interest in the oration are the passages on Franklin's scientific achievements contributed by Rittenhouse and the pointed political allusions of the Secretary of State. The whole of Jefferson's letter was incorporated in the eulogy as "from [Franklin's] illustrious Successor" in France, but its text was presented in curiously garbled form, with phraseology altered and paragraphs inverted. In the form ultimately published and presumably as delivered on the occasion, the key passage about the tributes of the commune of Paris and the National Assembly was paraphrased and presented without quotation marks as the orator's own commentary. Embarrassing as it always was for Jefferson to be brought upon the center of the stage, he must nevertheless have been gratified that Smith focused the climax of his effort on the unique gesture of respect and tribute by the French nation and on the expression of gratitude for Franklin's being spared to contribute his wisdom and virtue to the establishment of freedom in his own country and to "view . . . its *Dawn* in the *East,* where Men seem'd till now to have learned every thing—but *how to be free.*"[61]

The eulogy, according to William Maclay, caused much comment of a favorable nature. He himself disliked it, but conceded that he might have been too censorious because he despised Smith as "certainly a vile character." As the audience dispersed, the Senate went back to its hurry of business at a time when, as Maclay expressed it, "the immature resolve and ill-digested law often escape examination while nothing but home occupies the minds of the departing members."[62] The next day Washington received the enrolled joint resolution requesting him to respond on behalf of the Congress to the condolences of the National Assembly. That task he assigned to the Secretary of State, who in executing it employed some of the same phrases that he had given to the eulogist of the day.

V

The letter that Jefferson addressed to the President of the National Assembly a week later over his own signature stood in marked contrast to the one that Hamilton had drafted for the President. It was half as long, its style was elevated but plain, and its substance was as apposite as its form, being completely devoid of any improper or gratuitous offer of political advice. It spoke with conviction the language of amity and respect, while concentrating upon the distinguishing feature of the action taken by the National Assembly—an action that had "set the first Example of the Representatives of one Nation, doing Homage by a public Act to the private Citizen of another, and, by withdrawing arbitrary Lines of Separation, to reduce into

[60] *Federal Gazette,* 1 Mch. 1791. Governor Mifflin was absent on account of illness.

[61] See Document III and compare the relevant passages with William Smith, *Eulogium on Benjamin Franklin* (Philadelphia, 1792), p. 32-4, 35; on verso of second leaf Smith acknowledged his indebtedness to Rittenhouse, TJ, Jonathan Williams, and Benjamin Rush for assistance in preparing the eulogy. See Sowerby No. 520.

[62] Maclay, *Journal,* ed. Maclay, p. 408.

one Fraternity the Good and the Great, wherever they have lived or died."[63]

In transmitting to William Short this response to a letter "to Congress," Jefferson gave instructions about the proper constitutional distinction to be observed in future communications. "Let it be understood," he wrote, "that Congress can only correspond through the Executive, whose organ in the case of foreign nations is the Secretary of state. The President . . . being co-ordinate with Congress, cannot personally be their scribe."[64] He was very clear about the principle involved. A year later, when the Virginia legislature emulated Pennsylvania by adopting a resolution and congratulatory address to the National Assembly, Governor Henry Lee asked the Secretary of State to advise him whether these should be transmitted to that body or to the French monarch.[65] "I am of opinion," Jefferson replied, "that all communications between nations should pass through the channels of their Executives." This was the long-established rule of diplomacy, but in a time of revolution it could not be considered as absolute and Jefferson pointed to the exceptions: "in the instance of condolance on the death of Doctr. Franklin, the letter from our General government was addressed to the President of the National assembly: so was a letter from the legislature of Pennsylvania, containing congratulations on the atchievement of liberty to the French nation." He had not heard that the ministry took it amiss in either instance. "Perhaps therefore," he advised Lee, "this method may at present be the safest, as it is not quite certain that the sentiments of their executive and legislative are exactly the same on the subject on which you have to address them."[66]

Jefferson's response, made for the President on behalf of the Congress, was read to the National Assembly on the 2nd of June together with the address from the Pennsylvania legislature. Both of these expressions of friendship and good will happened to arrive at a moment when the National Assembly, angered by a letter from Abbé Raynal, was disposed to accord them a favorable reception. The delegates, to the accompaniment of loud applause on the left, immediately decreed that the letter and the address be spread upon its minutes and printed, that President Bureaux-Pusy respond to the legislature of Pennsylvania, that he express to the American minister the desire of France to strengthen as much as possible the fraternal bonds between the two peoples, and that, in order to promote their mutual interests, a new commercial treaty with the United States should be negotiated.[67] "The

63 See Document v.

64 TJ to Short, 8 Mch. 1791. In 1793 Genet requested an exequator for a consul whose commission was addressed to Congress. TJ refused to grant the request because of the constitutional impropriety or even to enter into a discussion of the matter with Genet. From the outset he held firmly to the principle that the transaction of business with foreign nations was "Executive altogether" (TJ's opinion, 24 Apr. 1790; TJ to Genet, 2 Oct. and 22 Nov. 1793).

65 Henry Lee to TJ, 23 July 1792.

66 TJ to Lee, 13 Aug. 1792.

67 Texts of TJ's letter, the Pennsylvania address, Bureaux-Pusy's reply to the latter, Fréteau Saint-Just's report for the diplomatic committee, and the decree of the National Assembly are given in Chinard, L'Apothéose, p. 75-81. The committee, Saint-Just reported, thought the National Assembly should "use every possible means to cherish and encourage a reciprocal commercial inter-

moment," Short informed Jefferson, "was exceedingly favorable for your letter and the address of Pennsylvania."[68]

It seems fitting that these events—the Senate's dismissal of President Benière's letter and Fauchet's *Eloge civique*, its equally cold treatment of President Sieyès' communication on behalf of the National Assembly, the bitter resentment of William Maclay over such hostile dispositions toward an ally, the impassioned address of the Pennsylvania legislature that must have been inspired by him, the urgent arrangement of the long-deferred ceremonies of the American Philosophical Society in honor of its founder—all occurred within the limits of a single city square, a spot symbolizing more than any other the unity of the nation. There, in the center of a small cluster of buildings used by city, state, and nation as well as by an institution of learning, stood the one in which Thomas Jefferson, only a decade and a half earlier, had compressed into a single sentence a philosophy of government that many in America and Europe believed had ushered in a new era in human affairs.

But in the cabinet and behind the closed doors of the Senate there were proofs enough of an enduring skepticism about the brave new order, manifesting itself in legislation as well as in these matters of merely ritualistic significance. These evidences, beginning with anachronistic proposals for honorific titles, levees, birthday rites, and other formal trappings of monarchy, could not be hidden from public view and the popular response could scarcely avoid being as political in character as the attitudes which provoked it.[69] John Adams, a veritable "Colossus . . . of independence" when the ideals of 1776 were being formulated but now revising his views of equality and liberty, de-

---

course between France and America." Significantly, and no doubt because of this recommendation by the committee, texts of the committee's report and of the decree of the National Assembly, as translated by Philip Freneau, appeared in Freneau's *National Gazette* on 17 Nov. 1791, together with TJ's letter to the President of the National Assembly. Bache's *General Advertiser*, 19 Nov. 1791, published the same texts. This must have been done at TJ's prompting, for the Second Congress had just convened, Ternant had arrived as minister from France, and TJ was prepared to make his report to Congress recommending a navigation bill aimed at Great Britain.

[68] Short to TJ, 6 June 1790. Immediately after the reading of the Pennsylvania address, one delegate cried out that a copy of it should be sent to the Abbé Raynal (Chinard, *L'Apothéose*, p. 78).

[69] It is significant also that, at this time, the celebrations of Washington's birthday in Philadelphia and elsewhere revealed similar divisions. In New York the Cincinnati toasts exhorted the rising generation to emulate Roman virtues and their fathers' love of country, saluted American agriculture and commerce, and said not a word about friendship for France. In Philadelphia, at one of the most elegant assemblies ever held in the city and attended by Washington in military dress, the toasts included "The King and National Assembly of France," "The nations in alliance with the United States," and "The Marquis de la Fayette" (*Federal Gazette*, 23 and 24 Feb. 1791; the full text of the French Declaration of Rights appeared in the latter issue). At another "elegant entertainment" given by the merchants and citizens of Philadelphia to the Vice-President and members of both houses of Congress—attended also by members of the Cabinet—the same three toasts were offered, together with one to "The Memory of Doctor Franklin" (same, 5 Mch. 1791).

scribed the political reaction only a few weeks after the American
Philosophical Society paid its homage to Franklin.[70]

> That there is and will be a Rival [to himself as presumed successor
> to Washington] I doubt not. There is a French interest at work to
> this purpose as deep as it is wicked. My countrymen with all their
> sagacity and all their vigilance are not enough acquainted with the
> World, nor with the History of their own Revolution to be upon
> their guard against political inventions concealed with infinite art,
> urged with unwearied diligence, multiplied and varied with fruitful
> ingenuity, and pursued with long perseverance. Panegyricks upon
> panegyricks come from Europe upon some characters in order to
> lessen others; Politicks are carried on instead of Philosophy in
> learned and scientific Academies; Newspapers from Georgia to
> New Hampshire Magazines &ca. are Cooked and dress'd. The pop-
> ulace are made the dupes of their own feelings, Aristocrats are
> bloated with their own pride.

Thus at this early date, even before Jefferson had praised Paine's
The Rights of Man and charged some in the United States with political heresies, Adams thought he perceived the identity of his ambitious rival. Like Hamilton, he saw danger arising only from the
intrigues of a French interest. By 1797 his faith in the sagacity of the
people was so qualified that he could place little reliance in it to
prevent an English or French puppet from succeeding him in the
presidency.[71] But Adams no less than Hamilton, as Maclay said of
Ellsworth at this time, had "mistaken the genius of the people."[72]
Historians have also mistaken the spirit of the American people
in this critical decade, holding that the tide of revolutionary ideas
began in 1789 to flow westward from France instead of eastward from
America; that, in response to this new force, parties and the two-
party system emerged, to say nothing of the claim of a political opposition to legitimacy; and that, paradoxically, by creating parties theretofore neither conceived in idea nor recognized as need, the impact of
the French Revolution may have enabled the United States to with-
stand the real dangers of subservience to foreign powers and to survive as a republic, thereby becoming in an age of revolution the only
country in which a peaceable transfer of power took place in a
democratic direction and without a *coup d'etat.*[73] The impact of events
in France on American politics was indeed powerful. But the claims

[70] John Adams to John Trumbull, 31 Mch. 1791 (MHi: AM); for a discerning
appraisal of Adams' altered point of view about America and about government,
see John R. Howe, Jr., *The Changing Political Thought of John Adams* (Princeton, 1966), p. 133-92.
[71] John Adams to Abigail Adams, 17 Mch. 1797 (*Letters of John Adams,
addressed to his wife*, ed. C. F. Adams, I, 252).
[72] Maclay, *Journal*, ed. Maclay, p. 405.
[73] This generalized interpretation, unavoidably simplified, is conveniently summarized in R. R. Palmer, *The Age of the Democratic Revolution*, II (Princeton,
1964), 509-34, particularly p. 510, 522, 524-7, and 531; the works of Hazen,
Jones, Faÿ, and others accept more or less the same general premises. Modifications and variants of these views are presented in Eugene P. Link, *Democratic-
Republican Societies, 1790-1800* (New York, 1942) and in W. N. Chambers,
Political Parties in the New Nation: The American Experience, 1776-1809 (New
York, 1963). Roy F. Nichols, *The Invention of the American Political Parties*

are too sweeping and overlook too much. For a generation the American people, long schooled in governing themselves even as colonials, had debated on a national scale the most fundamental principles of government. Their awareness of the need of political parties—indeed, of their indispensability to the success of a legitimate opposition and so of self-government itself—was rooted in this profound and innovative experience. Their divisions on the propositions of equality and government by consent had existed even before these were proclaimed as the national ideal. Their views of policy respecting the two great powers of Europe and their fears of foreign subversion divided them when the Constitution had not as yet been framed. Their cleavages and their parties were thus in process of development long before the reciprocal influence of the French Revolution was felt and made use of by those of opposing convictions. These alignments began to assume more definite, if unorganized, form soon after the new government came into being and provided, both in its constitutional framework and in the tone and tendency of the acts of those in power, fresh stimulus for their coherent growth. The tide sweeping in from France intensified the divisions and hastened the development.

Thus the real significance of these outpourings of homage for Franklin and friendship for France, genuine as they were, is to be found not in the overt expressions but in the ominous undertone of resentment toward the Senate because of what its actions revealed. The anger was as unmistakable as the developments it foreshadowed. The address of the legislature of Pennsylvania illumined as by a flash of lightning the nature of the divisions in the political fabric. Its accompanying thunderclap was a warning whose rolling reverberations would increase in volume as the dangers of disruption of the union multiplied in the next few years. Its meaning, even if mistaken by some in government, was clear. Such a manifestation of friendship for France was, at bottom, a message of encouragement to revolutionists there lest, as Jefferson and many other Americans feared, their failure should furnish "a powerful argument with those who wish to introduce a king, lords and commons here, a sect which is all head and no body."[74] It was, in short, an affirmation of attachment to American revolutionary principles. Soon it would become an admonition, voicing openly the opinion that "a dissolution of the honorable and beneficial connection between the United States and France, must obviously be attempted with a view to forward a plan of a more intimate union and connection . . . with Great-Britain, as a leading step towards assimilating the American government to the form and spirit of the British monarchy."[75]

The amplified warnings were no more heeded than its first discernible undertones had been. But these, coming long before the full

(New York, 1967), traces party roots far back into colonial and even into English backgrounds.

74 TJ to Edmund Pendleton, 24 July 1791; see also TJ to George Mason, 4 Feb. 1791; TJ to Edward Rutledge, 25 Aug. 1791.

75 Resolves of Caroline county (based almost wholly on James Madison's composition), 10 Sep. 1793 (text in Mays, Pendleton, II, 608-10; see also Madison to TJ, 2 Sep. 1793; Pendleton to Washington, 11 Sep. 1793, enclosing a copy of the resolves, same, II, 613; Washington to Pendleton, 23 Sep. 1793, Writings, ed. Fitzpatrick, XXXIII, 94-6).

force of the French Revolution had been felt, testified to the accuracy of Hamilton's assertion that two parties existed in the nation. The issues that divided them, as Tocqueville saw more clearly than the Secretary of the Treasury, rested on the moral and philosophical propositions the American people had embraced. No officer of government or representative of the people had dared openly to challenge these propositions, thereby providing eloquent if silent testimony to their hold on the American mind. But this was the bond that held the union together in this divisive decade when principles of administration and of policy seemed, if not to betray political heresies, at least to admit the people only to "an essential *share* in the sovereignty."[76] The strength of the bond, as well as the political means for employing it so as to effect a peaceable transfer of power, was not created suddenly out of necessity because of the cataclysmic events in France. It was drawn from the deep wells of American revolutionary experience and purpose.

Benjamin Franklin would doubtless have been amused to find that his own demise had provided the earliest and most illuminating glimpse of the coming political ordeal. But he could scarcely have been surprised, for the divisions that manifested themselves in matters of inconsequence as well as in great issues of finance and foreign policy were clearly discernible to him and his contemporaries. Historians would also discover this in time.[77]

[76] John Adams to Samuel Adams, 18 Oct. 1790, defining a republic as one "in which the people have, collectively or by representation, an essential *share* in the sovereignty" (DLC). To this Samuel Adams replied on 20 Nov. 1790: "Is not the *whole* sovereignty, my friend, essentially in the people? . . . That the sovereignty resides in the people is a political doctrine which I have never heard an american politician seriously deny" (DLC).

[77] Mary P. Ryan, "Party Formation in the United States Congress, 1789 to 1796: A Quantitative Analysis," WMQ, XXVIII [Oct. 1971], 523-42, analyzes all roll call votes for the period studied on the assumption that only a comprehensive view of voting behavior on all issues, important and inconsequential, would indicate party alignments. She presents as her fundamental discovery "the emergence in the first session . . . of two voting blocs which remained remarkably stable in the eight sessions that followed." Her arbitrarily-designated blocs ultimately became identifiable as Federalists and Republicans, having as their "most immediately apparent characteristic . . . their sectional composition."

I. The Secretary of State to the President

SIR   Department of State. Dec. 9. 1790.

I have now the honour to return you the letter from the President of the Assembly of representatives for the community of Paris to the President and members of Congress, which you had recieved from the President of the Senate with the opinion of that house that it should be opened by you, and their request that you would communicate to Congress such parts of it as in your opinion might be proper to be laid before the legislature.

The subject of it is the death of the late Dr. Franklin. It conveys expressions from that respectable city to the legislature of the United States, of the part they take in that loss, and information that they had ordered a solemn and public Oration for the transmission of his virtues and talents to posterity; copies of which for the members of Congress accompany their letter: and it is on the whole an evidence of their marked respect and friendship towards these United States.

I am of opinion their letter should be communicated to Congress, who will take such notice of this friendly advance as their wisdom shall conceive to be proper. I have the honour to be with the most profound respect, Sir, Your most obedient & most humble servant,   TH: JEFFERSON

RC (DNA: RG 59, MLR); at foot of text: "The President of the U.S."; endorsed by Lear: "The Secy of State respecting a letter and pamphlets from the President of the Community of Paris." PrC (DLC). Tr (DNA: RG 59, MLR); lacks complimentary close. Entry in SJPL reads: "Th: J. to G. W. on the letter of communauté of Paris on death of Dr. Franklin."

ENCLOSURE

President of the Commune of Paris to the President and Members of Congress

Mr. President—Gentlemen,   Paris, 29 July 1790

We have learned that Franklin, the man of all nations, is no more—having enlightened them all, and in every species of knowledge, they ought to share in a loss, which is common to them all.

The august Legislators of our nation have hastened to set the example; but the assembly of representatives of the Commons of the Capital believed it their duty to add to this universal mourning a new tribute of honor, in decreeing that the virtues and the talents of this true Philosopher should be transmitted to posterity, in a public and solemn eulogium, the first that has been rendered among us to civic virtue. The assembly charges me to transmit it to you. I felicitate myself in having this occasion to render homage to men who are free, and are truly worthy to be so. May that homage be acceptable, as well as the sentiments of brotherhood and respect, with which I am Mr. President, Gentlemen, Your very humble and very obedient Servant,

BENIÈRE, Doctor in Theology of the house and Society of the Sorbonne,
honorary Canon of the metropoli[tan] Church of Rouen.
Pastor of the Parish of St. Peter of Chai[llot]
One of the Electors of Paris.
Supplying Deputy to the National Assem[bly]
President of the Commons of Paris.

Tr (DNA: RG 59, MLR); at foot of text: "Messrs. The President and Members of the American Congress"; in Lear's hand; docketed by Lear: "The Presdt. of the Assembly of Repts. for the Community of Paris to the Presdt. and Members of the American Congress." The letter appeared in a slightly different translation in the proceedings of the House as reported in Bache's *General Advertiser*, 14 Dec. 1790.

II. Tobias Lear to the Secretary of State

United States January 26th 1791

By the President's command T. Lear has the honor respectfully to transmit to the Secretary of State, to be lodged in his Office, a letter from His most Christian Majesty to the President and Members of Congress dated Septr. 11th 1790 a letter from the President of the National Assembly of France to the President of the United States and a decree of that Assembly dated June 20 1790. And a letter addressed to the President of the National Assembly of France which the Secretary of State will transmit accordingly.

TOBIAS LEAR.
Secretary to the President
of the United States.

PrC (DNA: RG 59, MLR). Not recorded in SJL.

ENCLOSURE I

Louis XVI to George Washington

TRÈS CHERS GRANDS AMIS ET ALLIÉS. Nous avons reçu la lettre par la quelle vous nous avez informés de la nouvelle marque de confiance que vous avez donnée au Sieur Jefferson, et qui met fin aux fonctions de la place de votre Ministre plénipotentiaire auprès de nous. La maniere dont il s'est conduit pendant tout le tems qu'il a résidé à notre cour, Lui a mérité notre estime et une entiere approbation de notre part. C'est avec plaisir que nous lui rendons ce témoignage. Nous en avons un bien Sincere à profiter de cette occasion pour vous renouveller les assurances de l'affection et de l'amitié que nous portons aux Etats-Unis en général et à chacun d'eux en particulier. Sur ce Nous prions Dieu qu'il vous ait, TRÈS CHERS GRANDS AMIS ET ALLIÉS, en sa sainte et digne garde. Ecris à Paris le 11. Septembre 1790. Votre bon Ami et Allié,   LOUIS
MONTMORIN

RC (DNA: RG 59, Ceremonial Letters); in clerk's hand except for signatures of Louis XVI and Montmorin; addressed: "A nos très grands Amis et Alliés les Président et Membres du Congrès général des Etats-Unis de l'Amérique Septentrionale"; docketed by Remsen: "11 Septr. 1790. rect. of letter recalling Mr. Jefferson"; at foot of text: "Aux Etats-unis de l'Amérique Septentrionale."

Montmorin sent the above letter to Otto, together with his own response to TJ of 31 July 1790, and added this comment: "Je vous prie de faire parvenir l'une et l'autre à leur destination. Nous regrettons veritablement M. Jefferson: ses principes de justice, son caractère conciliant et son attachement à l'alliance lui ont mérité l'estime du Roi et de son Ministère: nous desirons qu'il Serve de modèle pour le choix qu l'on fera de Son Successeur" (Montmorin to Otto, 11 Sep. 1790;

Dft in Arch. Aff. Etr., Corr. Pol., E-U., xxxv, photostats in DLC). Montmorin perhaps intended Otto to make use of this comment when he delivered the letters and it is worthy of note that, though Montmorin's letter to TJ was written in July and the King's in September, the former—presumably the latter also—was delivered in mid-January in the midst of the discussions with Otto over the tonnage acts.

ENCLOSURE II

The President of the National Assembly of France to "The President of Congress"

MR. PRESIDENT   [Paris, 20 June 1790]

The National Assembly has worn, during three days mourning for Benjamin Franklin, your fellow citizen, your friend, and one of the most useful of your co-operators in the establishment of American Liberty. They charge me to communicate their resolutions to the Congress of the United States. In consequence, I have the honor to address to you, Mr. President, the extract from the proceedings of their session of the 11th, which contains that deliberation.

The National Assembly have not been stopped in their decree by the consideration that Franklin was a stranger;—great men are fathers of universal humanity;—their loss ought to be felt, as a common misfortune, by all the tribes of the great human family; and it belongs, without doubt, to a nation still affected by all the sentiments, which accompany the achievements of their liberty, and which owed its enfranchisement essentially to the progress of the public reason, to be the first to give the example of filial gratitude of the people towards their true benefactors;—besides that these ideas, and this example, are so proper to disseminate a happy emulation of patriotism, and thus extend more and more the empire of reason and virtue, which could not fail promptly to determine a body, devoted to the most important legislative combinations; charged with assuring to the French the rights of men and citizens; it has believed, without doubt, that fruitful and great truths were likewise numbered among the rights of man.

The name of *Benjamin Franklin* will be immortal in the records of Freedom and Philosophy, but it is more particularly dear to a country, where, conducted by the most sublime mission, this venerable man knew very soon to acquire an infinite number of friends and admirers, as well as by the simplicity and sweetness of his manners, as by the purity of his principles, the extent of his knowledge, and the charms of his mind.

It will be remembered, that every success, which he obtained in his important negociations, was applauded and celebrated (so to express it) all over France, as so many crowns conferred on genius and virtue.

Even then the sentiment of our rights existed in the bottom of our souls. It was easily perceived, that it feelingly mingled in the interest which we took in behalf of America, and in the public vows, which we preferred for your liberty.

At last the hour of the French has arrived:—we love to think, that the citizens of the United States have not regarded with indifference our first steps towards liberty. Twenty-six millions of men, breaking their chains, and seriously occupied in giving themselves a durable constitution, are not unworthy of the esteem of a generous people, who have preceded them in that noble career.

We hope, they will learn, with interest, the funeral homage, which we have rendered to the Nestor of America. May this solemn act of fraternal friendship serve more and more to bind the tie, which ought to unite two free nations. May the common enjoyment of liberty shed itself over the whole globe, and become an indissoluble chain of connexion among all the people of the earth. For ought they not to perceive, that they will march more steadfastly and more certainly to their true happiness, in understanding and loving each other, than in being jealous and fighting.

May the Congress of the United States, and the National Assembly of France, be the first to furnish this fine spectacle to the world! and may the individuals of the two nations connect themselves by a mutual affection, worthy of the friendship which unites the two men, at this day most illustrious by their exertions, for liberty—WASHINGTON, and LA FAYETTE.

Permit me, Mr. President, to offer, on this occasion, my particular homage of esteem and admiration.

I have the honor to be, With respectful consideration, Mr. President Your most humble And Most obedient servant

SIEYES, President.

Tr (DNA: RG 59, MLR); in Lear's hand. On the form of address, see Editorial Note.

ENCLOSURE III

The President to the President of the National Assembly of France

SIR   United States January 27. 1791

I received with particular satisfaction, and imparted to Congress[1] the communication made by the Presidents letter[2] of the 20th of June last in the name of the National Assembly of France. So peculiar and and so signal an expression of the esteem of that respectable body for a citizen of the United States, whose eminent and patriotic services are indelibly engraved on the minds of his countrymen cannot fail to be appreciated by them as it ought to be.[3] On my part I assure you, Sir, that I am sensible of all its value.

The circumstances,[4] which, under the patronage of a monarch, who has proved himself to be the friend of the people over whom he reigns, have promised the blessings of liberty to the French Nation, could not have been uninteresting to the free Citizens of the United States; especially when they recollected the dispositions, which were manifested by the individuals as well as by the Government of that Nation towards their still recent exertions, in support of their own rights.[5]

It is with real pleasure, Sir, that I embrace the opportunity now afforded me, of testifying through you to the National Assembly, the sincere, cordial and earnest wish, I entertain, that their labours may speedily[6] issue in the firm establishment of a Constitution, which by wisely conciliating the indispensable[7] principles of public order with the enjoyment and exercise of the essential rights of man, shall perpetuate the freedom and happiness of the People of France.

The impressions naturally produced by similarity of political sentiment are justly to be regarded as causes of national sympathy;[8] calculated to confirm the amicable ties which may otherwise subsist between nations. This reflection, independent of its more particular reference, must dispose every benevolent mind to unite in the wish, that a general diffusion of true principles of liberty,[9] assimilating as well as ameliorating the condition of Mankind and[10] fostering the maxims of an ingenuous and virtuous policy, may tend to strengthen the fraternity of the human race, to assuage the jealousies and animosities of its various sub-divisions, and to convince[11] them more and more, that their true interest and felicity will best be promoted by mutual good will and universal harmony.[12]

The friendship to which the President alluded in the close of his letter has caused me to perceive with particular pleasure, that ONE who had endeared himself to this Country by an ardent zeal and by useful efforts in the cause of liberty, has by the same titles acquired the confidence and affection of his own. May it ever be his chief aim to continue to be beloved as one of her most virtuous and most faithful Citizens!—I beg you to accept my acknowledgments for the sentiments in the same letter which relate more particularly to myself, and at the same time to be assured of the most perfect consideration, on my part.

GO: WASHINGTON

FC (DLC: Washington Papers). Tr (DLC: Hamilton Papers); in an unidentified clerk's hand; lacks concluding paragraph (see note 12 below). MS (DLC: Hamilton Papers); entirely in Hamilton's hand (printed in full in Syrett, *Hamilton*, VII, 459-61). MS clearly represents a revised version of the (missing) draft from which Tr was copied. FC follows MS except in minor changes in phraseology such as that indicated in note 2. The more significant variations between Tr and MS are indicated in textual notes below.

[1] The corresponding phrase in Tr is at the close of the sentence and reads: ". . . which I took an early opportunity of making known to Congress."
[2] MS reads: "your letter"; the alteration and another of the same sort were made necessary by the fact that Bureaux de Pusy had succeeded Sieyès as President of the National Assembly.
[3] Tr reads: ". . . whose memory will be ever justly dear to his countrymen has a strong claim upon their acknowledgements."
[4] Tr reads: "The progress of the Events which . . . ." (see Editorial Note).
[5] Tr reads: ". . . of that Nation in favor of the success of their still recent exertions for the preservation of their own rights."
[6] This word is not in Tr and is interlined in MS.
[7] This word is not in Tr.
[8] Tr reads: ". . . as causes of sympathy between free nations."
[9] Tr reads: ". . . of the principles of liberty." In MS this was first altered to read ". . . of the principles of natural

liberty" and then was changed to read as above, except that the definite article was retained.

10 Preceding ten words are not in Tr.

11 Tr reads "teach."

12 Tr ends at this point.

III. Thomas Jefferson to the Rev. William Smith

DEAR SIR   Philadelphia Feb. 19. 1791.

I feel both the wish and the duty to communicate, in compliance with your request, whatever, within my knowledge, might render justice to the memory of our great countryman Dr. Franklin, in whom Philosophy has to deplore one of it's principal luminaries extinguished. But my opportunities of knowing the interesting facts of his life have not been equal to my desire of making them known. I could indeed relate a number of those bons mots, with which he was used to charm every society, as having heard many of them. But these are not your object. Particulars of greater dignity happened not to occur during his stay of nine[1] months after my arrival in France.

A little before that, Argand had invented his celebrated lamp, in which the flame is spread into a hollow cylinder, and thus brought into contact with the air within as well as without. Doctr. Franklin had been on the point of the same discovery. The idea had occurred to him; but he had tried a bull-rush as a wick, which did not succeed. His occupations did not permit him to repeat and extend his trials to the introduction of a larger column of air than could pass through the stem of a bull-rush.

The Animal magnetism too of the Maniac, Mesmer, had just recieved it's death's wound from his hand in conjunction with his brethren of the learned committee appointed to unveil that compound of fraud and folly.[2] But after this, nothing very interesting was before the public, either in philosophy or politicks, during his stay: and he was principally occupied in winding up his affairs there.

I can only therefore testify in general that there appeared to me more respect and veneration attached to the character of Doctor Franklin in France than to that of any other person in the same country, foreign or native. I had opportunities of knowing particularly how far these sentiments were felt by the foreign Ambassadors and ministers at the court of Versailles. The fable of his capture by the Algerines, propagated by the English news-papers, excited no uneasiness; as it was seen at once to be a dish cooked up to the palate of their readers. But nothing could exceed the anxiety of his diplomatic brethren, on a subsequent report of his death, which, tho' premature, bore some marks of authenticity.

I found the ministers of France equally impressed with the talents and integrity of Doctr. Franklin. The Ct. de Vergennes particularly gave me repeated and unequivocal demonstrations of his entire confidence in him.

When he left Passy, it seemed as if the village had lost it's Patriarch. On taking leave of the court, which he did by letter, the king ordered him to be handsomely complimented, and furnished him with a litter and mules of his own, the only kind of conveyance the state of his health could bear.

No greater proof of his estimation in France can be given than the late letters of condoleance on his death from the National assembly of that country, and the community of Paris, to the President of the U.S. and to Congress, and their public mourning on that event. It is I believe the first instance of that homage having been paid by a public body of one nation to a private citizen of another.

His death was an affliction which was to happen to us at some time or other. We had reason to be thankful he was so long spared: that the most useful life should be the longest also: that it was protracted so far beyond the ordinary span allotted to man, as to avail us of his wisdom in the establishment of our own freedom, and to bless him with a view of it's dawn in the east, where they seemed till now to have learned every thing, but how to be free.

The succession to Dr. Franklin at the court of France, was an excellent school of humility.[3] On being presented to any one as the Minister of America, the common-place question, used in such cases, was 'c'est vous, Monsieur, qui remplace le Docteur Franklin?' 'It is you, Sir, who replace Doctor Franklin?' I generally answered 'no one can replace him, Sir; I am only his successor.'

These small offerings to the memory of our great and dear friend, whom time will be making greater while it is spunging us from it's records, must be accepted by you, Sir, in that spirit of love and veneration for him in which they are made: and not according to their insignificance in the eyes of a world, who did not want this mite to fill up the measure of his worth.—I pray you to accept in addition assurances of the sincere esteem and respect with which I have the honor to be, Sir, your most obedient & most humble servant,   TH: JEFFERSON

RC (PHi); endorsed; docketed by Robert Gilmor, famous collector of autographs, showing that he received the letter in 1826 from William Smith's son. Tr (PPAP); at foot of page TJ wrote "Copy." PrC of Tr (DLC); lacking TJ's note on last page.

On the tradition to which this letter gave rise concerning TJ's response to queries upon his succeeding Franklin as minister, see TJ to De Blome, 19 May 1785, note. TJ's remarks about Franklin's experiments on the principle of the ARGAND . . . LAMP may have reminded him that he had not yet acknowledged young Rutledge's gift of a "Keirs patent hydrostatical lamp" fitted to a Wedgwood reproduction of an Etruscan candelabra (see Rutledge to TJ, 20 Nov. 1790; TJ to Rutledge, 20 Feb. 1791).

¹ In RC and Tr, TJ first wrote "eight" and then corrected it to read as above. Actually, Franklin did not leave French soil until almost a year after TJ arrived.

² As an example of Smith's alteration of TJ's phraseology within quotation marks, the following is his version of the foregoing sentence: "About that time, also, the King of France gave him a signal testimony of respect, by joining him with some of the most illustrious men of the nation, to examine that *Ignis fatuus* of philosophy, the *Animal Magnetism* of the *Maniac*, Mesmer; the pretended effects of which had astonished all Paris. From Dr. Franklin's hand, in conjunction with his Brethren of the learned Committee, that compound of Fraud and Folly was unveiled, and received its death-wound."

³ At this point Smith added the words "to me."

IV. Thomas Jefferson to John Vaughan

[Philadelphia] Feb. 22. 1791.

Th: Jefferson presents his compliments to Mr. Vaughan and incloses him a copy of a letter he has just sent to Dr. Smith. There was so little within his particular knowlege, worthy of being noted in memory of Dr. Franklin, that he communicates it only in proof of his respect for the desire of the committee who did him the honor of calling on him, and of whom Mr. Vaughan was one.

RC (PPAP); addressed: "Mr. Vaughan"; endorsed: "A note from Mr. Jefferson . . . Inclosing a Letter to Dr. Smith relative to an Eulogium on Dr. Franklin"; docketed: "No. 1." Not recorded in SJL.

V. The Secretary of State to the President of the National Assembly

SIR,   Philadelphia March 8th. 1791.

I have it in Charge from the President of the United States of America to communicate to the National Assembly of France the peculiar Sensibility of Congress to the Tribute paid to the Memory of Benjamin Franklin by the enlightened and free Representatives of a great Nation, in their Decree of the 11th. of June 1790.

That the Loss of such a Citizen should be lamented by us, among whom he lived, whom he so long and eminently served, and who feel their Country advanced and honoured by his Birth, Life, and Labors, was to be expected. But it remained for the National Assembly of France to set the first Example of the Representative of one Nation, doing Homage by a public Act to the private Citizen of another, and, by withdrawing arbitrary Lines of Separation, to reduce into one Fraternity the Good and the Great, wherever they have lived or died.

That these Separations may disappear between us, in all Times and Circumstances, and that the Union of Sentiment, which mingles our Sorrows on this Occasion, may continue long to cement the Friendship and the Interests of our two Nations, is our constant Prayer. With no one is it more sincere than with him, who, in being charged with the Honour of conveying a public Sentiment, is permitted that of expressing the Homage of profound Respect and Veneration, with which he is, Sir, Your most obedient, and Most humble Servant, TH: JEFFERSON

RC (Archives Nationales, Paris, Ser. C—71, dossier 701, pièce 11); in Remsen's hand, except for signature; at foot of text: "The President of the National Assembly of France"; at head of text: "Renvoye au Comité Diplomatique J[ean] X[avier] B[ureaux de] P[usy] Presid." and, in pencil in another hand: "La traduction est au Comité diplomatique et sera rapportée." Tr (PU); in TJ's hand, except date and docketing, which are in Remsen's hand; unsigned. PrC of missing Tr (DLC); in Taylor's hand, unsigned. FC (DNA: RG 59, DCI). Recorded in SJL but not in SJPL.

From Childs & Swaine

SIR   Philada. Jany. 27th. 1791.

The late application of Mr. Brown to Congress which has been referred to you, induces us respectfully to state, That sometime in December last, we commenced the publication of a new or Second edition of the Acts of Congress passed at the first session; that this publication is nearly completed, and that another, smaller edition, is considerably advanced upon; that it is our intention to publish like editions of the Acts, Treaties &c. of the Second Session, and so to continue for the present and all future Sessions like publications as they shall become necessary:—From whence we beg leave to submit, how far the result of any decision on Mr. Brown's case may include ours, or others similar thereto, or establish any particular or exclusive indulgence in his favor. Being with every sentiment of the most perfect regard and esteem, Sir, Your most obedt. and very hble. Servts., CHILDS & SWAINE

RC (DNA: RG 59, PDL); endorsed by TJ as received 27 Jan. 1791 and so recorded in SJL. See TJ's report on Andrew Brown, 7 Feb. 1791. On the contract Childs & Swaine made in 1789 for printing the laws, see J. H. Powell, *The books of a new nation* (Philadelphia, 1957), p. 87-8.

From Tench Coxe

SIR   January 27th. 1791

I had the honor to receive this afternoon your note relative to the value of the transportation of the whole produce of the United States to foreign markets. By this I understand the amount of the freight money that would be paid by the owners of our produce to the owners of the vessels in which they are laden, if they were always different persons.

In the very imperfect state of the documents in the public offices it is impossible to speak with any degree of certainty on this point, and our freights are not yet settled to their former rates. Opinions may be formed however by which a Statesman may venture to be guided in his political reasonings. I have attempted to make up such an opinion and I submit it to you as my best judgment under my present information. It is ascertained that the Tonnage employed in the foreign trade for one year, had North Carolina and Rhode Island been in the union, would have been 650,000 Tons of carpenter's measurement. These vessels may be considered as going away fully laden, for till last year it was always the case, and the certainty of the increase of our crops renders it safe to omit any deduction from this casual consideration. The medium freight of the above tonnage from all parts of the Union to all parts of the world may be estimated at nine dollars per ton, including deck freight and passage money, which is essentially freight, or 5,850,000 dollars; even six millions of dollars would not be an exaggeration.

If the tonnage contemplated in your note is the vessels tonnage, or carpenter's tonnage as it is termed, the above 650,000 tons being exclusive of coasters and fishermen give a pretty certain answer. If the cubic measurement of our exports, which in Europe is applied to goods, were intended, my opinion is that every 100 tons of carpenter's measurement gives about 100 Tons of cubic measurement, on a medium of the construction and size of our present carriers.

I very much regret that the return of the quantity of goods shipt to the several parts of the world promised so confidently yesterday cannot be yet furnished by reason of the frequent and necessary avocations of the Clerks. As soon as it is made up, which must be tomorrow or next day, it shall be transmitted. I have the honor to be, with the highest respect, Sir, Your most obedt. humble Serv., TENCH COXE

RC (DLC). Not recorded in SJL. TJ's note has not been found and is not recorded in SJL. But see TJ's Report on the Fisheries, 1 Feb. 1791, Document IX, Appendix No. 18.

From William Short

DEAR SIR   Amsterdam Jan. 28. 1791

Since my last of the 24th. the inclosed letter has been recieved here. It is of so important a nature that I copy it to send it to you by the post of this morning as it is possible it may arrive in London in time for the Packet. It is generally believed here to be authentic though no body knows how it has got into the public. It is said also that it was printed in an accredited Parisian gazette the 21st. inst. No letters here from Paris of that date which are the latest by post, speak of it. I have letters also myself of that date from a person much in the way of information who mentions nothing of such a letter. These circumstances added to my opinion that the King would not have kept it so long uncommunicated to the national assembly, make me doubt its authenticity though I find few in that sentiment.—I am the more disposed to think it fictitious also because I learn that a forged *bref du Pape* circulated in some parts of France has been denounced to the assembly. This may come from the same source and be intended for the same purpose. The present moment may be chosen also for publishing it on account of a very extraordinary petition to the assembly signed by two thousand citizens of Strasburg who ask the re-establishment of the nobility and clergy. This gives uneasiness at Paris. It is the first thing of the kind which has happened and makes many fear that the tide is turning.—Letters will arrive from Paris this evening; but it will be after the departure of the English post, which is the last that can possibly be in time for the packet. I will give you further information however respecting this letter by another conveyance. Should it be true there can be no longer any doubt of the intention of the Empire to interfere in the French affairs.

This renders the present misunderstanding between the servants of Vienna and Berlin in the affairs of Liege the more interesting. Since my last we have seen the answer of the Marechal de Bender to M. Dohm in which he says that his instructions from Vienna

do not allow him to listen to the representations of this minister.—
An animated correspondence has also taken place between M. de
Pilsack the Prussian minister at Liège, and M. de Keuhl the
Austrian commandant. It ended it is said by the latter returning
a letter to the former without opening it. M. de Pilsack in a letter
to the Marechal de Bender which is public, after complaining of
M. de Keuhl adds "Mais je ne suis pas moins indigne que M. le
Leut. Gen. de Keuhl s'est permis de dementir une piece lui remise
officiellement d'un ministre de Prusse (the letter of M. de Dohm
mentioned in my last) sans entrer préalablement avec celui-ci en
explication. J'informe incessament Le Roi, mon maitre, d'un
evénément aussi extraordinaire, et m'empresse d'avoir l'honneur
d'en faire part a V.E. en lui demandant les reparations promtes
et publiques, qu'une offense pareille faite à ma cour, en ma personne, exige."

We know nothing further of this business as yet. The King
of Prussia seems to have acted very impolitically in the affair of
Liege. By taking part with the people against the Prince he has
alienated the affections or lost the confidence of those who formed
the Germanick league and added much to his force. This happens
also without his having attained his end since the Austrian troops
are in Liege and the ministers of the circles employed in enforcing
the decrees of the chamber of Wetzlaer. I am with sentiments of
the most most perfect respect & attachment, Dear Sir your most
obedient & most humble servant,   W: SHORT

PrC (DLC: Short Papers); at head
of text: "No. 54"; at foot of text:
"Thomas Jefferson Secretary of State."
Tr (DNA: RG 59, DD). Recorded in
SJL as received 9 Apr. 1791. Enclosure: Text of letter from Leopold II
to Louis XVI, Vienna, 14 Dec. 1790,
expressing his concern over decrees of
the National Assembly abolishing the
privileges of the nobility and clergy
which are considered to be violative of
rights granted by former public treaties, such as that of Munster of 1648,
and transmitting the demand of the
Electoral College that the empire and
its members be excepted from such decrees and the *status quo ante* restored
in order that "tous les ordres de notre
empire connoissent combien les dispositions de V. M. pour notre empire sont
amicales, et combien sont respectés les
traités subsistant entre sa nation et
notre empire" (Tr in DNA: RG 59,
DD). See Short to TJ, 7 Feb. 1791.

From Tench Coxe

Sunday Evening [30 Jan.? 1791]

Mr. Coxe has the honor to inform Mr. Jefferson that pitch is certainly 11/ ⅌ 112℔. i.e. dutied to exclusion as a manufacture.
Tar 11d. ⅌ barrl. and turpentine 2/3 ⅌ Cwt.

Mr. Remsen's copy of Mr. Coxe's very rough minutes, corrected, is enclosed, also the amount of fur duties in England equal to 15 and 20 ℔ Ct. ad valorem at the medium prices.

Mr. Coxe will not fail to send the Return of Exports the Moment Mr. Hamilton shall have done with it.

RC (DLC); undated and unrecorded in SJL, but evidently written just before Coxe transmitted the return of exports (see Coxe to TJ, 1 Feb. 1791). Enclosures not identified.

The RETURN OF EXPORTS may have been enclosed in the above, for TJ sent it back to Coxe in a (missing and unrecorded) note which the latter acknowledged in his of 1 Feb. 1791. The return covered the period 10 Aug. 1789 to 30 Sep. 1790 and is printed in ASP, *Commerce*, I, 23-34, as submitted by Hamilton to Congress on 15 Feb. 1791.

From Madame de Rausan

Marg[au]x en medocq Le 30e [de Janvier] de Lan. *1791*

J'ay Recu, Monsieur, La Lettre que vous m'avés fait L'honneur de M'ecrire dattée du 6e 7bre dernier par Laquelle vous me demandés dix douzaines de Bouteilles de mon vin de Margaux première Calitée. Quoy que je Sois dans L'usage de Le vendre en nouveau, je m'en trouve une petitte partie de 3 tonneaux de L'année *1785* qui, quoy que bon, n'est pas une des meilleures Années. Il est tiré en bouteilles depuis plus d'un an, il doit donc avoir acquis à present le Bouquet qu'il peut avoir pour l'année. Je vous en envoye 4 Caisses de 25 Bouteilles chacunne à raison de 50 S. la bouteille, elles sont en verre de france, et une 5e Caisse de 25 Bouteilles de *1786* en verre Englais, à raison de 3ᵗ la bouteille. Je n'ay gardé q'un tonneaux de Cette Qualité, je l'ay fait tirer tout Exprès pour vous. Cette Espèce de vin a besoin de Séjourner quelques tems en Bouteilles, Comme vous Scavés, Monsieur. Apprès le tems que vous Croirés nécessaire pour en juger, vous pourrois me mander Si vous en voulés d'autre. Je pourrois aussi vous faire part d'une Barrique que j'ay gardé de L'année *1788*, Et d'une autre Barrique de L'année *1790*. Seulement, pour que vous puissiés juger Ces differentes années, Lorsqu'il Sera en Boitte, Si vous le jugés à propos, Monsieur, je me ferois un vray plaisir de Conserver toutes les années une partie de ma recolte pour entretenir la Correspondance que vous voulés bien etablir avec moy. Allors je Serais plus Surveillante que jamais pour qu'il Soit bien Conservé. En tout Cas vous pouvés Compter, Monsieur, qu'il n'y a aucune fraude ny Mélange dans mon vin, Ce qui fait qu'il est très Sain pour la Santé.

J'envoye, Celon votre intantion, les 5 Caisses de vin chés Mr. Fenwick, Consul des Etats unis de La Nouvelle Engleterre, aux Chartrons. Puisque vous le voulés Comme Cela, Monsieur, je Luy ferois passer avec ma lettre pour vous ma quittance de 325^{tt} pour le montant des 5 Caisses de vin, qui sont arrangées aussi Solidement qu'il a Eté possible. J'ay L'honneur dêtre avec La Consideration la plus parfaite, Monsieur, votre très humble et très obeissante Servante,   BRIET DE RAUSAN

Toutes Les dittes Bouteilles Sont Cacheptées de mon Cachet pareil à Celuy de ma Lettre. Mon adresse est: Mde. Briet de Rausan, Locataire au Couvent de Notre dame, rue Dutra, à Bordeaux.

J'ay Monsieur environ 2 ou 3 mille Bouteilles de Ce vin de *1785* de *50* S. la bouteille, il est tout en Caisse de *25* Bouteilles, par Conséquent tout pret au Cas que vous en ayés besoin. Pour Celuy de *1786* à 3^{tt} la bouteille, je n'en ay plus que 3 Barriques.

RC (MHi); addressed: "A Monsieur Monsieur Th: Jefferson a philadelphie"; endorsed by TJ as received 21 Jun 1791 and so recorded in SJL.

From Noah Webster, Jr.

SIR   Hartford Jany. 31st 1791

The bearer of this, Mr. John Jenkins, will present with this, a Method of teaching the art of penmanship, which appears to me to be in some measure novel and very ingenious. If his plan should make the same impression on you, I flatter myself it will receive your patronage and encouragement.—I have the Honor to be Sir, with great respect your obedt hum Servt

NOAH WEBSTER JUN

RC (NNP); endorsed by TJ as received 18 Feb. 1791 and so recorded in SJL.

John Jenkins' *The art of writing* (Boston, 1791) apparently did not make the same impression on TJ that it had on Webster and other leading educators of New England. In his *The art of writing reduced to a plain and easy system on a plan entirely new* (Elizabethtown, N.J., 1816), Jenkins explained that he had been an instructor of writing in ten states since 1781, that his system was under the patronage of the Massachusetts legislature and the American Academy of Arts and Sciences, and that the first edition of 1791 was "highly approved by the first characters" (p. iii). The foundation of his system was the assumption that "nearly the whole alphabet was composed of six principal strokes or lines," which he arranged and classified by number. In the second edition Jenkins published a list of fifty-four subscribers under date of 21 Feb. 1791 in addition to those already obtained in New England—for example, John Hancock, Jeremy Belknap, Fisher Ames, Ezra Stiles, and Noah Webster, Jr. The subscribers in Philadelphia included William Samuel Johnson, Robert Morris, Ebenezer Hazard, Arthur St. Clair, and Benjamin Franklin Bache (same, p. viii-x). Three medical men—Benjamin Rush, James Hutchinson, and Benjamin Say—after examining Jenkins' directions for the position of the body and limbs declared themselves satisfied that the system was "easy and natural; and that the action of the muscles, and the circulation of the blood . . . less interrupted by it than by any of the usual positions in writing" (same, p. xii). TJ, who was much interested in tachygraphy and various forms of multiplying texts, evidently was not enamored of systematic forms of handwriting that stifled individuality. He was not a subscriber to Jenkins' *The art of writing* and, so far as is known, did not lend his patronage to the man or to his system.

Memoranda and Statistics on American Commerce

I. JEFFERSON'S NOTES ON SHEFFIELD'S *OBSERVATIONS ON THE COMMERCE OF THE AMERICAN STATES,* [1783-1784?]

II. JEFFERSON'S NOTES ON COXE'S *COMMERCIAL SYSTEM FOR THE UNITED STATES,* [ca. 1787]

III. EXTRACTS FROM SPEECH OF WILLIAM PITT, APRIL 1790

IV. NOTES ON AMERICAN TRADE WITH IRELAND, [1790?]

V. ESTIMATE OF AMERICAN IMPORTS, [1785-1786?]

VI. ESTIMATE OF AMERICAN EXPORTS, [1785-1786?]

VII. EXPORTS FROM EIGHT NORTHERN STATES BEFORE 1776, [ca. 1784]

EDITORIAL NOTE

The present situation is interesting and critical. The policy, which the United States ought to observe, *in the legislation of commerce,* is likely to be formally discussed. At such a moment, facts, accurately ascertained and candidly stated, are of the utmost importance; for how shall we so well reason, as from what we know? It is to be desired, that *the light of indisputable truth* may enable our own legislators, and those of foreign nations, to discover the ground of common interest, and that no erroneous maxims, however sanctioned, may close one avenue of mutually beneficial communication.
—Tench Coxe, *The American Museum,*
March, 1791

This appeal to the legislators of America and Europe to base their commercial regulations on facts accurately ascertained and candidly stated could not have met with a more interested or more receptive public official than the American Secretary of State. Nor could it have found one better grounded, both by habit of mind and by legislative and diplomatic experience, in the art of political arithmetic. From early youth onward, stimulated by an insatiable curiosity and by the climate of rational inquiry fostered by the philosophy of Bacon, Newton, and Locke as well as by the unfolding wonders of a new continent,

Jefferson had been indefatigable in gathering and organizing factual knowledge. Everything that could be weighed, measured, mapped, or calculated—whether an animal, a building, a plantation, a canal, or the weather—aroused his almost compulsive interest in recording data. It was because of long years spent in accumulating exact information about every measurable facet of his native state that he was able to produce in his *Notes on Virginia* a compilation of statistics not equalled for any other American state in the eighteenth century. It would be difficult if not impossible to refute the considered judgment of James H. Cassedy that "probably no one in America was more imbued with the statistical spirit than was Jefferson. If his mind was concerned with the most elevated political and philosophical issues of the day, it was also concerned with building a firm base of quantitative information upon which such concepts could rest."[1]

Jefferson, of course, was familiar with and gathered data from the leading European writers on population, finance, trade, and other aspects of political economy. But he was no American counterpart of Sir John Sinclair, who surpassed him in the mere accumulation of data but lacked his political acumen in employing statistics as an effective instrument of policy. Jefferson always kept the main object in view, just as he kept on enlarging, verifying, and refreshing his reservoir of facts. Even after his *Notes on Virginia* was published he continued to add to it such new accretions of data that it could never be regarded as completely finished. So it was also with his continuing effort to obtain reliable statistics about the trade, shipping, and fisheries of the United States. The present group of documents exemplifies all of the habitual traits—the patient searching for precise data, the readiness to revise the factual foundation in the light of new information, and the steady concentration on the great objects of policy. Some of these compilations were made during Jefferson's years in France, others soon after he became Secretary of State, and all formed a continuing and growing base for the report on commerce that he handed in at the end of his term of office.

The first number of Tench Coxe's *A brief examination of Lord Sheffield's Observations on the commerce of the United States* made its appearance in the March, 1791, issue of *The American Museum*. Jefferson undoubtedly welcomed its candor, its moderation, its rational argument, and its freshly marshalled statistics. He certainly could not have disagreed with the assertion that the Americans were a nation *sui generis* whose peculiar relationship with Great Britain called for mutual accommodation and an effort "to discover the ground of common interest." Coxe's proposition that erroneous maxims—that is, the immensely influential doctrines of Sheffield that had been given the sanction of law—should not be allowed to foreclose beneficial communication on commercial policy had in fact been central to Jefferson's efforts of the past decade to loosen the British hold on American trade. Jefferson possessed both the first and sixth editions of Sheffield's *Observations* and he may have compiled his notes on it soon

---

[1] James H. Cassedy, *Demography in early America: beginnings of the statistical mind, 1600-1800*, p. 255; see also, Edwin T. Martin, *Thomas Jefferson: Scientist*, p. 3-18.

after the former came out in 1783. He certainly made these notes available to Madison in 1790 when retaliatory measures were under discussion.[2] He had known as early as 1786 that Sheffield was aided with information supplied by Silas Deane, but he thought the commercial data provided in Alexander Clunie's *The American traveller* more reliable.[3] He was perhaps the more disposed to do so because Clunie, like Coxe, argued in favor of moderation and urged the advantage of mutually beneficial trade arrangements. The data that Jefferson drew from both Sheffield and Clunie, corrected in part from other sources, were also made available to Madison during their effort to achieve commercial reciprocity.[4]

While Jefferson undoubtedly approved Coxe's dispassionate use of facts in refuting Sheffield, he understood his character and was less intimate with him than is generally supposed. The two men did not meet until the summer of 1790 when Benjamin Rush gave Coxe a letter of recommendation to Jefferson, praising him as a zealous advocate of the new government but being discreetly silent about his behavior during the Revolution.[5] Three years earlier Jefferson had received a copy of Coxe's *An enquiry into the principles, on which a commercial system for the United States of America should be founded.*[6] He was sufficiently impressed by it to lend it to his friend Morellet, who found it a mixture of good and bad principles.[7] Jefferson also made a few notes of facts presented in the pamphlet, but did not comment on Coxe's ideas. He unquestionably agreed with the view that agriculture was the bulwark of the national economy, that the cultivation of the soil promoted virtue, that the fisheries were in need of encouragement, and that the foundations of national wealth and consequence were "so firmly laid in the United States, that no *foreign* power" could undermine or destroy them. But the expressed fears that internal disorders threatened to disrupt the union and that the spirit of disobedience to law was alarming could have evoked no sympathetic response. Also, in this pamphlet published at the very moment the Federal Convention had convened and after the American people had been discussing the fundamental principles of government for a generation, he must have been surprised to find Coxe confused over the distinction between a legislative and a constituent assembly.[8] He must

2 See note, Document I; Sowerby, Nos. 3616 and 3618.

3 TJ to Brissot de Warville, 16 Aug. 1786; see note, Document VI.

4 See Documents V and VI.

5 Rush to TJ, 4 May 1790; the recommendation was solicited by Coxe. Madison, perhaps also at Coxe's request, had recommended him in 1787 (Madison to TJ, 19 Aug. 1787; Coxe to TJ, 3 Sep. 1787, both received the same day and both missing).

6 TJ received at least two copies of the pamphlet, one evidently sent by John Browne Cutting in 1788 and the other perhaps by Edward Carrington or Benjamin Hawkins (Sowerby, No. 3623; Carrington to TJ, 9 June 1787, and Hawkins to TJ, 9 June 1787, both received just before TJ lent the pamphlet to Morellet). Coxe's *Enquiry* was first presented on 11 May 1787 at a meeting of the Society for Political Enquiries, held at the home of Benjamin Franklin.

7 Morellet to TJ, 1 Aug. 1787.

8 Coxe later said that the *Enquiry* was "inscribed to the members of the convention at an early period of their business" (Coxe, *A view of the United States of America* [Philadelphia, 1794], p. 4). While his *Enquiry* set out to discuss the principles of an American commercial system, Coxe limited his proposals largely

have been equally surprised at the argument that American commerce was more adversely affected "by the distractions and evils arising from the uncertainty, opposition and errors of . . . trade laws [of the states], than by the restrictions of any one power in Europe." Grounding his argument on this premise, Coxe had concluded that merely giving Congress power to veto state laws on trade would enable the federal government "to prevent every regulation, that might oppose the general interests, and by restraining the states . . . gradually bring our national commerce to order and perfection." This narrow concept, coming from a prominent merchant who had been a delegate to the Annapolis Convention, was advanced at the culmination of the long and widely discussed effort to grant Congress general powers over commerce.

Limited as his proposals were, Coxe nevertheless did cautiously hint that the "article in the British trade laws, which confines the importation of foreign goods to the bottoms of the country producing them, and of their own citizens, appears applicable to our situation." This, too, was a proposition that Jefferson had long since urged, not to establish an American mercantilism, but to achieve through retaliation such a "system . . . as should leave commerce on the freest footing possible," as had been contemplated originally in the plans of 1776 and 1784 for commercial treaties.[9] Early in 1791, after the idea of retaliation had been embodied in proposed legislation as a result of the collaborative efforts of Madison and Jefferson, Coxe again advocated it.[10] At that time, and thereafter for the next few years, Jefferson found him a useful source of statistical information. He respected Coxe's talents and would no doubt have agreed with William Maclay that he possessed "persevering industry in an eminent degree." He esteemed Coxe's commercial knowledge enough to consult him in the preparation of his Report on Commerce and to submit an early draft for his verification and criticism.[11]

But it is a mistake to suppose that Jefferson's reliance upon Coxe extended much beyond a natural desire on his part to augment and correct his own considerable body of data, which was of such range and depth that Coxe was able to make additions to it chiefly because he had access to customs records in the Treasury. Jefferson's ideas of American policy toward other nations, in commerce as in all else, had been formed long before he became acquainted with Coxe. It is necessary to state the obvious fact only because Coxe's influence, which was confined almost exclusively to the supplying of data, has been exaggerated.[12] Jefferson soon found that the prolix, discursive, and

---

to specific remedies, such as duties to promote the fisheries, regulations favoring American shipping, encouragement to manufactures, and so on. He later conceded that the grant of a general power over commerce was better than his more limited proposals (same, p. 11n.).

[9] TJ to Adams, 19 Nov. 1785.

[10] "Thoughts on the Navigation of the United States," enclosed in Coxe to TJ, 5 Mch. 1791.

[11] Maclay, *Journal*, ed. Maclay, p. 258; Editorial Note to TJ's Report on Commerce, 16 Dec. 1793; Coxe to TJ, 5 Feb. 1793; TJ to Coxe, 5 Feb. 1793.

[12] See, for example, Harold Hutcheson, *Tench Coxe: A Study in American economic development*, p. 29-35.

repetitive memoranda and offers of assistance that Coxe showered upon him fully merited Maclay's observation that their author suffered from "the literary itch, the *cacoethes scribendi*." He also found that, although the over-zealous Coxe needed to be treated with caution, his special talents as a pamphleteer could on occasion be useful.[13]

The relationship that began in 1790 was closest during the years when Jefferson was Secretary of State, being carried on largely through a correspondence that owed more to Coxe's initiative than to anything else. It was never a bond of intimacy or confidence. The supposition that Coxe's ultimate shift of political allegiance from the Federalists to the Republicans can be traced to these beginnings, that in this and other ways Jefferson sought to manipulate him for partisan purposes, and that indeed he made Coxe his confidant in order to have an informer in the Treasury cannot be sustained by the facts.[14] Jefferson was too reserved, too penetrating a judge of character, and too committed to the principles of the Revolution to be anything but guarded in his relations with one whose support of the American cause had been dubious at best. He may not have known the full story of Coxe's career of vacillation, but it is scarcely possible that Madison, Monroe, and others in a position to know could have failed to acquaint him with its general nature. This went far beyond the position of neutralism that Coxe professed to Madison in 1789 when he was seeking office under the new government.[15] Indeed, though Coxe has generally been given the benefit of the doubt, it has now been established beyond question that his allegiance to the new nation was as easily transferable as his partisan affiliations were later. It was not characteristic of him to seek the neutral middle ground, always exposed in a time of revolution, but rather to find favor with those in power. When power alternated, so could he, but he was also capable of cultivating simultaneously the good will of those in opposition as well as those in authority. During the war he was fortunate enough to have on both sides influential connections that first brought him large profits as a merchant during the British occupation of Philadelphia and then, after he had been adjudged guilty of high treason by a proclamation of attainder, enabled him to escape confiscation and other penalties.[16]

Although he avoided these punishments, Coxe ultimately suffered a harsher fate. It was his tragedy always, in the end, to earn the distrust of those whose favor he had gained. Thus it was with Sir William Howe who allowed him lucrative military contracts, with Alexander Hamilton who appointed him to the Treasury, with John Adams whose election as Vice President he labored to achieve, with the Federalists whose cause he first espoused, and with the Republicans

[13] Maclay, *Journal*, ed. Maclay, p. 252, 258. Coxe's letters to TJ were more numerous in 1790 and 1791 than at any other time except in 1801 when he was seeking office. See Editorial Note to group of documents under 15 Mch. 1791.

[14] Hutcheson, *Tench Coxe*, p. 28-9; Leonard D. White, *The Federalists*, p. 224-5; see Coxe to TJ, 16 Apr. 1791, note.

[15] Coxe to Madison, 17 Sep. 1789 (DLC: Madison Papers).

[16] Jacob E. Cooke, "Tench Coxe: Tory Merchant," PMHB, XCVI (Jan. 1972), 48-88, is the definitive account of Coxe's role during the Revolution, being based in part on the voluminous but hitherto inaccessible papers of Coxe.

who held his allegiance longest, perhaps because, after being abandoned by both parties, he had no other to claim. In 1790 when he was appointed to the Treasury such prominent Philadelphians as Robert Morris, Thomas FitzSimons, and James Wilson—all of whom knew him well as a person, as a merchant, and as a political aspirant—maligned his character "with great asperity."[17] In 1797 Adams dismissed him from office as a person of partisan duplicity.[18] Hamilton thought him "too cunning to be wise."[19]

The opinion of Jefferson must rest largely on inference. It is clear that he was aware of Coxe's shifting allegiances, that he did not hold the past against him, that he respected his assiduity in accumulating data on matters of public concern, and that, on occasion, he was willing to make discreet use of him as an ally. Their connection was never closer than in this period when Jefferson was preparing his reports on commerce and the fisheries, as those documents reveal.[20] But even then Jefferson relied on him chiefly for factual information, not for ideas of policy or for anything approaching the kind of creative and confidential relationship that made his collaboration with Madison so productive. During his presidency, when Coxe showered him with unsolicited offers of advice, importunate pleas for office, and charges of injustice and neglect, Jefferson took umbrage and for a number of years would not answer his letters.[21] In fact, in the quarter of a century after 1801 he responded only three times to Coxe's numerous letters, though in the end he spoke of their ancient friendship and said that they had been "fellow laborers indeed in times not to be forgotten."[22] Jefferson must have been thinking of Coxe's genuine assistance in supplying statistics in the early months of their acquaintance.

But these amiable expressions assume their true meaning only when judged in context. They were in acknowledgment of a letter from Coxe delivered by John S. Skinner, publisher of the *American*

[17] Maclay, *Journal*, ed. Maclay, p. 255; Maclay added that George Clymer "rather supported him."
[18] White, *The Federalists*, p. 289, quoting George Cabot's remark to Adams that Coxe was "a traitor . . . who never deserved to have been trusted." See Adams' endorsement, made at a later date, on Coxe's letter to Adams, 15 June 1791 (Vol. 18: 261, note 111).
[19] Hamilton to Wolcott, 5 Aug. 1795 (CtHi: Wolcott Papers).
[20] See documents and Editorial Note, Report on the Fisheries, 1 Feb. 1791; Report on Commerce, 16 Dec. 1793. For comment on TJ's influence on Coxe's reply to Sheffield, see Editorial Note to group of documents under 15 Mch. 1791.
[21] TJ to Coxe, 27 Mch. 1807, in which TJ candidly told Coxe why he had not responded theretofore. Early in TJ's administration Coxe wrote him more than two dozen letters applying for office, in addition to his insistent appeals to Madison and Gallatin (DNA: RG 59, Applications for Office, M/418). "I submit, sir," one of his typical letters ran, "whether . . . there is any man who has labored more, or with more effect, or with more injury to himself *to prevent a counter-revolutionary operation* from 1792 to 1801 than I. . . . I have received nothing yet from your justice or your friendship" (Coxe to TJ, 18 Apr. 1801; same). It was on Gallatin's recommendation that Coxe in 1803 was appointed Purveyor of Public Supplies. Gallatin felt that justice demanded this but he added: "personal predilection for him I have not" (Gallatin to TJ, 21 June 1803). TJ made the appointment but persisted in his silence toward Coxe for the next four years. The only letters he is known to have written him after 1801 are those of 27 Mch. 1807, 21 Sep. 1807, and 13 Oct. 1820.
[22] TJ to Coxe, 13 Oct. 1820.

Farmer with whom Jefferson had recently been in correspondence.[23] In his brief reply, Jefferson explained that writing was so slow and painful for him as to prevent his engaging in regular correspondence. This polite but obvious effort to forestall further communication brought an immediate response from Coxe asking for support in obtaining a federal appointment and enclosing another letter to Madison making a similar request.[24] Jefferson did not respond. Also, in forwarding the letter to Madison as requested, he ignored the appeal for patronage. But he did express in emphatic terms what he thought the application exemplified. This, he wrote, was "a sample of the effects we may expect from the late mischievous law vacating every 4. years nearly all the executive offices of the government. It saps the constitutional and salutary functions of the President, and introduces a principle of intrigue and corruption. . . . It will keep in constant excitement all the hungry cormorants for office, render them, as well as those in place sycophants to their Senators, engage these in eternal intrigue to turn out one and put in another, in cabals to swap work; and make of them, what all executive directories become, mere sinks of corruption and faction."[25] This was an eloquent, if implicit, appraisal that placed Coxe—talented, industrious, and informed as he was—among the sycophants and the office-hungry cormorants. The long and tragic record seems to render this a just estimate.

23 Coxe to TJ, 4 Aug. 1820 (missing); see Skinner to TJ, 30 Jan. and 4 May 1820; TJ to Skinner, 24 Feb. and 16 May 1820.
24 Coxe to TJ, 11 Nov. 1820; Coxe to Madison, 12 Nov. 1820 (DLC: Madison Papers).
25 TJ to Madison, 29 Nov. 1820.

I. Jefferson's Notes on Sheffield's
Observations on the Commerce of the American States

[1783-1784?]

[Is the navigation act of Gr. Br. beneficial to her when applied to the U.S.? Will she not lose more than she will gain by it?

We never carried more than 25 ship loads from the W. Indies whereas the carriage of the U.S. is probably 6. or 800 shiploads of which Gr. B. would participate.

Is it for our advantage to make this a mutual participation? If it is, it can only be made so by their opening valuable and free markets to us.

Gr. Br. might apply the principles of that act advantageously against other states who would have only manufactured and not raw materials to carry; but the American materials are raw.

If U. S. retaliate by passing a navigation act we shall be gainers in point of carriage.

No nation will exclude our commodities in our own bottoms, because they are raw, nor forbid us to bring theirs in our own bottoms, because they are manufactured.

Can Russia be substituted by England instead of America to advantage.
    Argument against
        her ports are shut up by ice
        her tar is thinner
    Argument for it.
        she has not inhabitants to manufacture
        she will make quicker paiments.
Treaty between G. B. and Russia expires in 1786.
Will Russia and the U. S. be competitors? Examine the articles
    particularly
        Iron.   We do not make enough for ourselves.
        hemp. do.
        cordage. do.
        sail duck. We make some.
        tobo. They cannot pretend to a competition.
        tar.
        pitch.
        turpentine
        masts
        furs

Ld. Sheffd. pa. 54. The whale fishery even to Hudson's bay cannot be carried on to greater advantage from Nov. Scot. St. John's and N.F.L. than from the Eastern states: because the difference of distance is but a few hours sail, besides the whales had left that ground before the war.

    pa. 58. He is wrong in saying that the Americans being possessed of the greater part of the carrying trade to and from the W.I. could employ in that their fishing vessels during the winter. The last fare of fish is coming in from Oct. 20. to Dec. 25. They recommence their fishing about 20th. Feb. of the ensuing year. A voiage to the W.I. takes 3 months. It is obvious then that the interval of fishing is not long enough to admit a W.I. voiage unless it be for the few who bring in their last fare very early. The rest are either laid up for the winter, or go to Virginia for corn. It would be miserable economy to suffer the fishing of the ensuing year retarded a moment by their vessels being out on a W.I. voiage. Besides the fishing vessels are totally improper to go to the W.I. because they are too small to carry lumber.][1]

The soil of N.F.L. is a barren. They never can farm it. They raise good roots. They are furnished with cattle, sheep &c. from the Eastern states. In N.F.L. at the Northern end are good masts and other timber for ships. St. John's has very little timber. Nova Scotia none or little. What vessels they build are mostly of pine. They have built their new town of Shelburne with timber boards &ca. from the Eastern states. The soil of the island St John's is excellent. The climate is softened by being surrounded by the sea. This is capable of real improvement. Halifax and Shelburne are not more liable to freeze than Boston which is shut up from one to 4 weeks only comm[unibus] ann[ibus].

pa. 62. He is mistaken probably in supposing that the British can undersell the Americans in their Spermaceti candles in the W.I. Both must perform double voiages. i.e. one to catch the whale and bring home the Spermaceti to be manufactured, and a second to carry it to market. The manufacture requires very little labour, and therefore any difference in the price of labour will be scarcely sensible and will be counterbalanced by our propinquity[2] to the market. Seven eighths of the Spermaceti candles made, go to the W.I. where the heat of the climate renders them cheaper than tallow. The other eighth supplies Europe, Africa and America.

pa. 64. The Canadians cannot succeed in manufacturing flour; because as soon almost as the season in the fall admits of manufacturing their streams freeze up, the transition being immediate from extreme heat to extreme cold.

pa. 65. Neither France nor Engld. can prevent our supplying their fisheries with provisions. The run between the banks and continent is so short that their vessels can come for it or we carry to them without a possibility of detection.

pa. 68. He sais 'timber for pipe staves may be found in Canada and Nov. Scot.' Red oak holds molasses but not rum. White oak holds rum but not molasses. As to rum, the pores of the red oak are so large that the liquor escapes and even the white oak must be of the very best. As to molasses, it does not escape thro' the pores of the white oak, but it is so heating that it occasions the staves to shrink and then it escapes at the joints. But in red oak by entering and distending the pores it counteracts the shrinkage at the joints and keeps them tight.

Canada has white oak but it's ports are shut up 8 months in the year. Nova Scotia has no white oak or next to none. Tho he sais they have at Passamaquaddy and St John's river. There is none in the province of Maine. The white oak grows worse the farther North which induces a doubt on the quality of that in Canada.

pa. 69. Tar before the war cost only 4/sterl. the barrel in N. Car and not 6/

Pitch cost in N.C. 5/sterl. and not 7/6

The bounty on tar was 5/6 sterl. the barrel.

Russia tar costs 5/6 to 6/ the barrel at the port of exportation. The freight from thence is as high as from N.C. The navigation is more dangerous and open only a few months in the summer.

Swedish tar is dearer than that from Archangel.

72. There is a duty of 1/ a barrel on foreign pitch and tar which has not yet been extended to that of the U. S. A duty also on foreign turpentine.[3]

pa. 84. No American vessels ever went to the W. Indies for freight except those newly built for sale in the Eastern states, and of these only a part. Ld Sheffd. supposes built in the Eastern states in 1769. 71. topsail vessels, 200 sloops and schooners the tonnage of the whole 13,435 tons. Of these about 35 topsails of from 220 to 250 tons each went to the W.I. for freight. Of course the whole portage between W.I. and Gr. Br. which we took from the latter was but 8000 tons annually. This would maintain 533 seamen (at 1. to every 15 tons). The worth of one of these ships, with the freight would make a remittance of 2500£ which was in exchange for British manufacture[s]. Then the whole 35 ships remitted 62,500£. Suppose labourers and manufacturers on an average require *25£[4] for their support. Then these 35 ships maintained §2500[5] labourers and manufacturers. [If this] carriage is taken from us, remittances to that amount are suppressed and of course purchases of [Bri]tish manufacture. So that Gr. Br. gaining 533. seamen loses §2500[5] labourers and manufacturers.

[pa. 89. What an insult to suppose we shall carry our tobaccos to Gr. Br. to be sorted and reexported to the different markets, as if we could not sort it at home. If it were necessary to bring it all to one place, the nearer home the better, and Norfolk should be the place, because there is not a pound of tobacco exported from Maryld. Virga. or N. Carola. but what must pass Norfolk. There too it may be collected in small craft.][1]

The portage of the produce of the U.S. to market and the returns, as calculated by Mr. Tracy on Ld. Sheffield's tables is worth 750,000£ sterl. [or 1,000,000£ lawful,][1] which at the average of 50/ the ton sterling employs 400,000 tonnage of ships. Suppose these ships to be of 200 ton each and to make two

---

* Champion sais £5. pa. 25.   § Should then be 12,500.

voiages a year i.e. to carry out 200 tons and bring back 20 tons (equal to their proceeds) twice a year it will give constant em-

ploiment to $\dfrac{400,000}{220 \times 2}$ = 909 ships. Allow 12 men to each of these

and it maintains 10,818[2] seamen. I had produced nearly the same result thus.

The tobacco of Virga is about	30,000	tons
1,000,000 bush. wheat (@ 60 ℔. pr. bush)	30,000	
600,000 bush. Ind. corn and every thing else	30,000	
Returns about one tenth in weight	10,000	
	100,000	
The other states afford about three times as much	300,000	
	400,000	tons

At 2 voiages each this gives constant emploiment to 1000 ships.

At 12 men to each this supports	1200	seamen
The Cod fisheries support	3000	
The whale fishery	2500	
Other coasting business	2500	
	20,000	

[It is only the first article however which Gr. Br. will participate with us if we do not pass a navigation act, that is the 12,000 seamen, as before the war she possessed and may possess again all the carrying business Southward of Baltimore. This amounts to 2/3 of the whole; of course it maintained for her 8000 seamen, in return for the 533 which we maintained in the carriage between the W.I. and Europe. The portage between the U. S. and W.I. is about 1/3 of the whole, i.e. it amounts to 250,000£ sterling.][1]

MS (DLC: TJ Papers, 59: 10128-9); in TJ's hand; undated but ca. 1785-1786 (see Editorial Note). Tr (DLC: Madison Miscellany); in James Madison's hand; at head of text: "1790. Extracts from MSS. remarks by Mr. Jefferson—on Ld. Sheffield."; text omits passages in brackets as indicated below (see note 1) and includes the following at its close that is not in TJ's text: "Stat: 5. Ric. 2. c. 3. 'none of the King's liege people shall ship any merchandize out of or into, the realm, but only in ships of the King's leigeance, on pain of forfeiture.'—The British Statutes prohibit foreigners to carry on the coasting trade, that is, to go from one part to another in G. Britain."

[1] Passage in brackets (supplied) was not transcribed by Madison.

[2] Thus in MS; in Madison's text the word is "proximity."

[3] In Madison's text there is an asterisk at this point connected with the following, not in TJ's MS: "[see London price current for 1788 where this is better stated]."

[4] In the footnote in MS "Champion" appears to be struck out, but Madison text has neither footnote and at this point reads: ". . . require (according to Champion) 5£ for their support."

[5] Madison texts reads "12,500."

II. Jefferson's Notes on Coxe's
Commercial System for the United States

[ca. 1787]

pa. 8. Exports but 1/4 or 1/5 of home consumption, i.e. 1/5 or 1/6 of the whole produce.

9/10 of people in Amer. employed in Agriculture.

10. 7/8 of people in New Engld. employed in agriculture, the remaining 1/8 in manufactures, fisheries, navigation and trade.

13. Coasting vessels entered at Phila. in 1785 were 567 sail. All the others, i.e. sea vessels were 501.

15. 5000 barr. mackarel, salmon, pickled cod sold in Philada. annually.

21. An argument in favor of manufactures to a certain degree is that we may turn to profit the *natural* powers of the country, viz. *water, fuel, sun, air*

24. European manufactures come to Amer. under a charge of 25.p.cent. for commission, package, custom house papers, porterage, freight, insurance, damage, interest of money, waste, loss on exchange, and the impost proposed of 5. pr. cent. This operates as bounty on our manufactures.

30. Cotton (before the revolution) cost but 9 d. sterl. a lb. in the W. Indies. The perfection of European factories and consequent increase of demand has raised it 50. p.cent. This year's price in Phila has been 2/ sterl.

40. He thinks we shall soon make the following articles so cheap as to throw foreign ones out of competition, viz. beer, spirits, potash, gunpowder, cordage, loaf sugar, paper, snuff, tobo, starch, anchors, nail rods, and many other articles of iron, bricks, tiles, potters ware, millstones, cabinet work, corn fans, Windsor chairs, carriages, sadlery, shoes, boots, coarse linens, hats, a few coarse woollens, linseed oil, Wares of gold, silver, tin and copper, some braziery, wool cards, worms and stills.

Federal farmer

pa. 158. Waste of labour and property during war 300,000,000 dollars

157. In 10. years has been actually paid by the states 24. million dollars bounty money to souldiers and contributions to federal treasury.

162. The State governments cost about 4. times as much as the federal. The State debts nearly equal to federal debt. Imposts since the peace nearly equal to all other taxes.

MS (DLC: TJ Papers, 36: 6230); in TJ's hand; at head of text: "Tench Cox's enquiry into the principles of American commerce"; undated, but presumably drawn up about the time TJ received a copy of Coxe's pamphlet in July 1787.

The FEDERAL FARMER was Richard Henry Lee, whose letters in opposition to the Constitution, *Observations leading to a fair examination of the system*

of government, proposed by the late Convention (New York, 1787), went through three editions and sold thousands of copies throughout the states. Lee then brought out *An Additional number of letters from the Federal Farmer* (New York, 1788), largely a repetition of the first. TJ owned the edition of 1788 that included both titles. It was from this that he extracted the above data (Sowerby, No. 3020).

III. Extracts from Speech of William Pitt

Extracts from a Speech of Mr. Pitt's in the British house of Commons published in a London Gazette of April—1790.

The exports of GBritain . . . . Sterg. £18.513.000
   N.B. of this Sum £13.494.000. was Bh. Manufactures.
Imports £17.828.000
Manufactures exported in 1774 were £10.342.000.0.0, so that article is increased £3.152.000
9224 Vessels in 1773 navigated by 63,000 Seaman. ⎫
11.085 do. in 1778 83000   do. ⎬ Tonnage
not mentioned. N.B. It is remarkable that he did not give the Navigation or Seamen of 1790.
Revenues of 1788-9—£15.723.000
   Do. . .1789.90. .15.846.000
A statement of the Duke of Portlands of 1783 states the manufactures of G.Britain to have then been £54.000.000 of which sum £17.000.000 were for the Woolen Branch and near £11.000.-000 in that of Leather.

The exports of G.Britain by an actual return of the Inspector Genl. of their customs was in 1764. £16.512.403 and the imports £10.364.307 balance of trade therefore in 1764 £6.148.096 and as above stated by Mr. Pitt in 1790 £685.000, or about three millions of dollars.

MS (DLC: TJ Papers, 54: 9285-6); endorsed in the same unidentified hand as that of the text: "Mr. Pitt's statement of exports, imports, ships & seamen of G. Britain."

IV. Notes on American Trade with Ireland

Ireland [1790?]

West
Coast Dublin, the emporium, more flax ceed and potash, exported from the U.S. than to all the other ports put together—and also more linen imported than from all the other ports together, altho the vessells generally return, in only a small part loaded, as a full cargo of Linnen would amount to £80,000 Sterling, and the Cargoes of seed, and Ashes seldom to more than 3. or 4000 Currency. It is found by experience that at the Dublin Wharehouses, the linens are purchased cheaper than from the manufacturer owing to necessity the Merchants are under of selling them, at whatever price they will sell for, being generally in advance to the manufactures.

West
Coast Newry, is the next place in point of importance there being an inland Navigation into a lake Called Lough Neigh and from thence to Colerain in the North. This place is also a repository for the Linnen manufactures have a large magazine, for the unpacking and examination and stamping the Linnens.

North West Belfast, has an inferior proportion also of the American trade.

North London Derry has at least an equal proportion to Newry of the export trade from this Country but as they do not in that neighbourhood manufacture little else than the 3¼ Linnens, the produce of the Cargos which are of principally Flax seed and some pot ashes, is placed in Dublin Newry or Belfast for Linnens or the vessells nearly return in Ballast.

Nth East
Coast Sligo—Some export trade to these places, but little or no imports.

Limerick
on the East
Coast Considerable export of Seed and ashes, but no imports scarcely, the proceeds being transmitted to Dublin or London.

South
West
Coast Cork. Before the War and for a short time since, there were considerable proportions of provisions imported from thence but at present very little. However the lumber from the Chesepeke, forms rather an extensive export trade to this place, and the proceeds are lodged either in Dublin or England.

S. W. Coast Waterford and Wexford Port intermediate between Cork and Dublin. Very little done either in exports and imports with America.

New York and Philadelphia are supposed to engross 7/8 of the trade of the U.S. with Ireland. There is besides some export from Wilmington North Carolina—Virginia and Maryland principally in the article of flax seed.

MS (DLC: TJ Papers, 59: 10178-80); in an unidentified hand.

V. Estimate of American Imports

[1785-1786?]

From Europe and Africa

Woollen cloths of every description.
Linens of every description.
Hosiery. Hats.
Gloves, shoes, boots, sadlery, & other things of leather.
Silks, gold & silver lace, jewellery, millinery, toys.
India goods.
Porcelain, Glass, Earthen ware.
Silver, copper, brass, tin, pewter, lead, steel, iron, in every form.
Upholstery, Cabinet work, Painter's colours
Cheese, Pickles, Confitures, Chocolate.

Wine. 2000 tons @ £100. = £200,000. Brandy. Beer.
Medicinal drugs, Snuff, Bees wax.
Books, Stationary.
Mill stones. Grindstones. Marble.
Sail-cloth. Cordage. Ship chandlery. Fishing tackle.
Ivory. Ebony. Barwood. Dyewood.
Slaves!

Salt. 521,225 bushels @ 1/. £ 26,061 - s 5

£. sterl.
3,039,000

£. sterl.	
350,000.	Massachusets
250,000	New Hampshire / Rhode island / Connecticut
531,000	New York / New-Jersey
611,000.	New-Jersey / Pennsylvania / Delaware
865,000	Maryland / Virginia
18,000	N. Carolina
365,000.	S. Carolina
49,000.	Georgia
3,039,000.	

From the West Indies

			£ s
Salt.	500,484 bushels	@ 1/	25,024-4
Fruits			2,239-10
Cocoa.	576,589 ℔	@ 6d	25,798-10
Coffee.	408,494 ℔	8d	15,249-12
Sugar.	10,232,432 ℔		168,007
Molasses.	3,645,464 galls.	1/	186,281-16
Rum.	3,888,370 galls.	2/3	437,441-12-6
Ginger. Pimenta.			1,395-1
Cotton.	356,591 ℔	1/	17,829-11
Hides.			7,870-5
Indigo	4,352 ℔	4/6	979-4
Ivory. Turtle-shell			247-4
Lignum vitae. Sarsaparilla. Fustic. Annattas.			5,170.
Logwood.			13,624-17-6
Mahogany.			20,280.

927,438 7

3,966,438-7

MS (DLC: 59: 10427v); in TJ's hand, undated, but probably compiled about 1785-1786. Tr (DLC: Madison Miscellany); in Madison's hand, with following at head of text: "Estimate [by Mr. Jefferson] of the imports of the U. S. those from W. Indies are taken from Ld. Sheffield. those from other parts from the American Traveller (1769)."

TJ's figures for imports from the West Indies are taken from Table No. IV of the second (1784) edition of Sheffield's *Observations on the commerce of the American states*, compiled by Thomas Irving, Inspector General of the Imports and Exports of North America, and Register of Shipping. Irving's tabulation, dated at the Custom House, Boston, 1 Oct. 1771, covers the period from 5 Jan. 1770 to 5 Jan. 1771. TJ combined articles and also lumped together importations from all of the West Indies, whereas Irving's table distinguished between the British and foreign islands. TJ also failed to note that the figures included importations into Newfoundland, Bermuda, the Bahamas, and all of "the several provinces in North America," which of course included Canada.

[135]

VI. Estimate of American Exports

[1785-1786?]

Estimates of the annual exports of the United States.
Those of the American traveller are taken as the basis, but corrected.

	Massachusetts	N. Hampshire Rhode Island Connecticut	New York New Jersey	Pennsylvania New Jersey Delaware
Fish.	£. sterl. 150,000²	£. sterl 7,000	. . . .	. . . . .
Fish-oil	bar. 30,000. £ 45. 168,750³	tons 1500. £. 15 22,500		. . . .
Fish-bones	ton 28. £ 300. 8,400	. . . . . .	. . .	. . . .
Salt-meat.	bar. 9000. 30/ 13,500	15,000	£. sterl. 48,000⁷	£. sterl 15,000
Live-stock.	12,000	25,000	17,000	20,000
Butter. Cheese.	. . . . . .	. . . . . .	8,000	10,000
Flour. Bread.	. . . . . .	. . . . . .	bar. 250,000 250,000	bar. 350,000 350,000
Wheat.	. . . . . .	. . . . . .	bush. 560,000. 3/ 84,000⁸	bush. 800,000 120,000
Indian corn. Pulse.	. . . . .	. . . . .	40,000	12,000
Rice.	. . . . .		. . .	. . . .
Indigo.	. . . . .			. . . .
Tobacco.	. . . . .	. . . . .	. . . .	. . . .
Potash.	bar. 8000. 50/. 20,000	bar. 6000. 15,000	hhds 7000 40/ ⸜14,000	. . . . .
Peltry.	5,000⁴	2,400⁴	35,000	50,000
Flax-seed	. 20,000⁴	bush. 15,000. 2/. 1,500⁴	hhds 7000 40/ 14,000	hhds. 15,000 30,000
Hemp.	. . . . .	.		. . . .
Iron. Copper	. . . . .	. . . .	20,000	35,000
Turpentine &c.	bar. 1500. 8/ 600	. . . . . .	. . . .	. . . .
Timber. Lumber.	45,000	40,000⁵	25,000	35,000
Ships.	70. £ 700 49,000	100,000⁶	20. £ 700 14,000	17,500
Miscellanies	9,000	. . . . . .	1,500	1,000

Virginia Maryland	N. Carolina	S. Carolina	Georgia	Total	Exported to Europe	Exported to the West Indies
. . . .	. . . .	. . . .	. . . . .	£157,000	£107,000	50,000
. . . .	. . . .	. . . .	. . . . .	191,250	181,688	9,562
. . . .	. . . .	. . . .	. . . . .	8,400	8,400	. . . .
£. sterl 15,000	. . . .	£. sterl. 25,000	. . . . .	131,500	. . .	131,500
. . . .	£. sterl 5,000	15,000	5,000	99,000	. . .	99,000
. . . .	. . . .	. . . .	. . . . .	18,000	. . .	18,000
bar. 0,000. 60,000⁴ bush.	. . . .	. . . .	. . . . .	660,000	330,000	330,000
50,000. 127,500¹¹	. . . .	. . . .	. . . . .	331,000¹	331,000¹	. . . .
20,000¹²	7,000	12,000	. . . . : .	91,000	30,000	61,000
. . . .	bar. 2000. 40/. 4,000	bar. 110,000 220,000	bar. 18,000 36,000	260,000	189,350	70,650
. . . .	. . . .	℔ 500,000. 2/. 50,000	℔ 17,000 1,700	51,700	51,700	. . . .
hhds. £ 5,000 15. 1,275,000¹³	hhds. 2000. 30,000¹⁴	. . . .	. . . . .	1,305,000	1,305,000	. . . .
. . . .	. . . .	. . . .	. . . . .	49,000	49,000	. . . .
25,000	5,500	45,000	17,000	184,900	184,900	. . . .
14,000	. . . .	. . . .	. . . . .	79,500	79,500	. . . .
tons £ 000. 21. 21,000	. . . .	. . . .	. . . . .	21,000	21,000	. . . .
35,000	. . . .	bar.	. . . . .	90,000	84,000	6,000
10,000⁴	bar. 51,000. 7/. 17,850.	bar. 8000 2,800¹⁵	. . . . .	31,250	29,410	1,840
55,000	15,000	20,000	11,000	246,000	82,000	164,000
0. 1000. 30,000	. . . .	10. £ 600 6,000	. . . . .	216,500	216,500	. . . .
7,000	. . . .	. . . .	3,500	22,000	22,000	. . . .
				4,244,000	3,302,448	941,552

MS (DLC: TJ Papers, 59: 10427); in TJ's hand; undated but probably compiled about 1785-1786. Tr (DLC: Madison Miscellany); in Madison's hand, with following at head of text: "Estimate [by Mr. Jefferson 17   ] of the annual exports of the U. States, those of the American Traveller (1769) taken as the basis but corrected. This statement refers to the exports prior to the Revolution." Dft (DLC: TJ Papers, 2: 207-208); in TJ's hand; at head of text: "Exports of the United states. According to the American traveller"; containing a list of "corrections" on verso; for variations between Dft and MS, see notes below.

THE AMERICAN TRAVELLER: [Alexander Clunie], *The American traveller: containing observations on the present state, culture and commerce of the British colonies in America, and the further improvements of which they are capable; with an account of the exports, imports and returns of each colony respectively,—and of the numbers of British ships and seamen, merchants, traders and manufacturers employed by all collectively . . . by an Old and Experienced Trader* (London, 1769; see Sowerby, No. 3611). Clunie, who argued on the eve of the American Revolution in favor of moderation and claimed that mutual advantage in commerce was "the most solid Basis, the strongest Cement of Union," grounded his observations on his own experiences as a trader and on travels in the preceding quarter of a century in which he had traversed the whole coast of America from 68° north latitude to the tip of Florida and "penetrated some thousands of miles westward, into the Wilderness, many Parts of which were never before trodden by European feet." TJ regarded him as more reliable than Sheffield (TJ to Brissot de Warville, 16 Aug. 1786). He may, in fact, have made use of his work as early as 1784 when he was engaged in preparing his own statistics on American commerce (see Vol. 7: 323-49). This conjecture is supported by the fact that the figures in Dft correspond with those given by Clunie, whereas the corrections as indicated in the notes below were drawn principally from his own later researches, particularly in respect to the tobacco monopoly and the fisheries. The obvious intent of the corrections was to enable TJ to approximate the volume and value of American exports in the postwar years. Clunie, for example, valued tobacco at £8 per hogshead, whereas TJ increased the figure to £15, approximately what it was in France in 1786 (TJ to Maury, 24 Dec. 1786). Only for Georgia were TJ's final figures the same as those of Clunie, as the following comparison of totals will show:

	Cluny	TJ
Massachusetts	£370,500	£501,250
New Hampshire, Rhode Island, and Connecticut	114,500	228,400
New York, New Jersey	526,000	570,500
Pennsylvania, New Jersey, and Delaware	705,500	695,500
Virginia, Maryland	1,040,000	1,694,500
North Carolina	68,350	84,350
South Carolina	395,666	449,800
Georgia	74,200	74,200
	£3,294,716	£4,244,500

(Clunie, *American Traveller*, pp. 47-8, 51, 57, 60, 62, 66, 70, and 74).

1 Thus in MS, an error for 331,500.
2 Dft reads £100,000; correction on verso reads as above.
3 Dft reads "7,000 tons @ 15£. 105,000"; correction on verso reads as above.
4 Dft blank.
5 Dft reads 30,000; correction on verso reads "£50,000 sterl."
6 Dft blank; correction on verso reads "10,000 tons @ 7£ lawful."
7 Dft reads 18,000.
8 Dft reads "560,000. [@] 2/6. 70,000."
9 Both Dft and Clunie give the figure as 45,000 and TJ at first placed this figure on MS, then, surprisingly, corrected it to read as above. It will be noted that the totals for Pennsylvania, New Jersey, and Delaware provide the only instance in which Clunie's figures exceed those of TJ.
10 Dft reads "100,000."
11 Dft reads "320,000 bush. 40,000."
12 Dft reads 30,000.
13 Dft reads "96,000. [hhds.] 8£ 768,000"; correction on verso reads "87,000 @ 15£. 1,305,000."
14 Dft reads "2000. hhds. 7£. 14,000."
15 Dft reads "8000. bar. 6/5. 2,666."

VII. Exports from Eight Northern States before 1776

[ca. 1784]

Before the late revolution, the eight states, from Delaware to New-Hampshire inclusive, exported to the West Indies, Great Britain and Ireland

	£ sterl.		
Flaxseed	60,000		These articles are still received
Pot-ash	50,000	210,000	in Gr. Britain and Ireland, as
Furs	100,000		formerly.
Naval stores	75,000	75,000	Bounty taken off, but not subject to Aliens duty.
Shipping	200,000	200,000	Prohibited.
Whale-oil	200,000	200,000	Pays a duty amounting to a prohibition.
Lumber	80,000		These articles we formerly carried to the West Indies: but being now restrained to British bottoms, they are scarcely carried there at all and may be considered as prohibited.
Live-stock	100,000		
Flour	360,000		
Wheat	50,000		
Indian corn	20,000	610,000	
Spermaceti	20,000		Articles formerly carried to the West Indies, but now expressly prohibited.
Fish	125,000		
Beef and Pork	30,000		
Slaves	50,000	225,000.	
Total		1,445,000	£ sterl.

The same states exported moreover to other parts of the world

	£ sterl.		
Flour	240,000		
Wheat	100,000		
Indian corn	7,000		
Fish	125,000	472,000	£ sterl.

Great-Britain Ireland and the West-Indies then took off three fourths of the exports of these eight states. They now take the three first articles only, being one tenth.

MS (DLC: TJ Papers, 36: 6238); in TJ's hand; undated but perhaps compiled about 1784. PrC (DLC: TJ Papers, 59: 10125-6).

Report on the Fisheries

EDITORIAL NOTE

It is obvious that all the Powers of Europe will be continually maneuvring with Us, to work us into their real or imaginary Ballances of Power. They will all wish to make of Us a Make Weight Candle, when they are weighing out their Pounds. Indeed it is not surprising for we shall very often if not always be able to turn the Scale.
—*John Adams, in conversation with Richard Oswald, 1782*

I

During the peace negotiations of 1782, John Adams not only feared that the fisheries would be used as a makeweight by European powers: he also saw this nursery of seamen as a source of internal contention and discord. The bitter sectional debates in Congress—a "long struggle over cod and haddock," one delegate called it—convinced him that his fellow New Englanders regarded treaty protection of the fisheries as a "Point . . . so tender and important that if not secured it would be the Cause of a Breach of the Union of the States."[1] To Adams the debates had shown very clearly how one European power

---

[1] Adams, *Diary*, ed. Butterfield, III, 65; the epigraph is at p. 61. Adams was quoting New England delegates in Congress who, he said, had put their ultimatum in writing. He was probably referring to the instructions of 27 Oct. 1781 from the General Court to the Massachusetts delegates in Congress, directing them "to use their utmost influence that instructions be given to the ministers appointed by Congress for negociating a Peace, in the most pressing terms to insist, that the Free and unmolested Exercise of this right be continued and Secured to the Subjects of the United States" (DNA: RG 360, PCC No. 74).

tried to intervene in the parties and policies of the United States. Yet his apprehensions were more than matched by his confidence. England might be mistress of the seas and the royal navy might sink an occasional fishing schooner off Newfoundland, but, he warned, no amount of power could succeed in restraining the New England fishermen, "the boldest men alive, from fishing in prohibited Places."[2] Furthermore, while France and England might use the makeweight in pursuing their own interests, the United States could place it on either side of the scales as her interest dictated. Adams longed for just two hours with Charles James Fox or any of the king's ministers in order to explain what the fisheries meant to the future relations of Great Britain and the United States.[3]

Four years later all of Adams' vigorous pronouncements about the fisheries—their importance as a nursery of seamen, as a profitable commerce, as an instrument of foreign manipulation, as a cause of internal divisions, as an American counter in the European balance of power, even as a symbol of national pride in the bold, enterprising fishermen—were echoed by the authors of *The Federalist* in their powerful plea for union. In the eleventh number Hamilton asserted that the fisheries constituted one of those "rights of great moment to the trade of America" that might be jeopardized if the states were disunited. Just as Adams had warned Englishmen, so he warned his countrymen:[4]

> France and Britain are concerned with us in the fisheries; and view them as of the utmost moment to their navigation. They, of course, would hardly remain long indifferent to that decided mastery of which experience has shewn us to be possessed in this valuable branch of traffic; and by which we are able to undersell those nations in their own markets. What more natural, than that they should be disposed to exclude, from the lists, such dangerous competitors?
>
> This branch of trade ought not to be considered as a partial benefit. All the navigating States may in different degrees advantageously participate in it. . . . As a nursery of seamen it now is, or when time shall have more nearly assimilated the principles of navigation in the several States, will become an universal resource. To the establishment of a navy it must be indispensible.

Also like Adams, Hamilton believed that a united America might hope

James Lovell was the delegate who referred to the long struggle over cod and haddock (quoted in Richard B. Morris, *The Peacemakers*, p. 19. Morris' account of the problem of the fisheries in the peace negotiations is the best treatment of the subject; see especially, p. 18-20, 324-6, 346-51, 373-9, 387-91, 400, 407-8. See also E. C. Burnett, *The Continental Congress*, p. 433-7).

[2] Adams, *Diary*, ed. Butterfield, III, 73.

[3] Same, III, 74.

[4] *The Federalist*, ed. Jacob E. Cooke, p. 69-70; see also the fourth essay by John Jay, published in November, 1787 (same, p. 19, 21). Jay, like Hamilton, recognized that the fisheries were inseparably connected with the broad question of navigation.

"to become the arbiter of Europe in America; and to be able to incline the ballance of European competition in this part of the world" as her interest might dictate. But if she remained disunited and impotent, her trade would be snatched from her and used to enrich her "enemies and persecutors."[5]

In France, within a few days after these remarks were published, Jefferson used similar language with the king's ministers, warning that prohibitory duties on American whale oil would shift a "useful body of seamen out of our joint scale into that of the British."[6] He, too, looked upon the fisheries as a means of building that maritime strength which he regarded as the only instrument by which the United States could act on Europe. He agreed with Adams and Hamilton that this was not a sectional interest but a national resource that could be effective in tipping the European scales one way or the other. In 1788 he argued in his *Observations on the Whale-Fishery* that England's restrictive commercial policies had not merely destroyed the primacy of the American whaling fleet but had brought on a critical choice for France—the "danger of permitting five or six thousand of the best seamen existing to be transferred by a single stroke to the marine strength" of her enemy.[7] Now, in 1791, his report on the fisheries reiterated these arguments. France, he indicated, had become sensible of the need to balance the power of England on the water, but she seemed not sufficiently aware that her encouragement of the American fishery would abridge "that of a rival nation whose power on the ocean has long threatened the loss of all balance on that element."[8] This was a softened version of what Jefferson had first expressed. In a passage subsequently deleted, England was portrayed unequivocally as a "nation aiming at the sole empire of the seas."[9] One can scarcely suppose that this moderation of the language was due to a lack of conviction about British aims. On the contrary, the suppressed passage offers an important key to Jefferson's attitude and conduct toward England in the quarter of a century following the Treaty of Paris of 1783.

It is understandable that he and many other Americans should have held such convictions, for the roots of British compulsions to achieve maritime supremacy ran deep. England, of course, was no less ardent than France in professing a desire for the equilibrium of Europe and no less zealous in searching for the makeweights needed to attain it. But after her triumph in 1763, the scales that had never achieved more than a fleeting and uncertain balance under the best of circumstances seemed fixed in her favor. From that time forward the nation that was so dependent on naval power was propelled irresistibly toward the goal of dominion of the seas. Being the first empire on earth and daily enlarging her hegemony in both hemispheres, she could scarcely afford to be second upon the ocean. Indeed, before Jefferson was born, one of

5 Same, p. 68, 69.
6 TJ to Montmorin, 6 Dec. 1787; see also, TJ to Lambert, 6 Dec. 1787.
7 *Observations on the Whale-Fishery*, printed in Vol. 14: 242-54, at p. 244.
8 See Document IX.
9 See Document IX, note 2.

the most popular British poets of the century gave to the idea of primacy on the ocean the sanction of a command from on high:[10]

> When Britain first, at Heavn's command,
>   Arose from out the azure main,
> This was the charter of the land,
>   And guardian angels sung this strain:
> Rule, Britannia! Britannia, rule the waves!
>   Britons never will be slaves.

To the youthful Jefferson and other loyal subjects of the king who were stirred by the refrain, it must have seemed unthinkable for Britons not to acquiesce in the divine dictate. But after the Revolution, those bred in the tradition were confronted with one of the harshest realities of independence—unilateral rule of the waves ruled out the very concept of that balance of power on which the commercial interests of the young nation so greatly depended. In the face of this towering fact, it is not surprising that Adams in the peace negotiations, Jefferson in his *Observations on the Whale-Fishery*, and Hamilton in *The Federalist* should have voiced substantially the same views about the importance of the fisheries, both as an element in American trade and as an instrument of policy. Such a concurrence of opinion reflected the general desire expressed in all quarters for a stronger union to counterbalance the effect of British trade restrictions. This desire had indeed been the primary impetus if not the most effective force in bringing about what contemporaries called the revolution in government of 1787.

But in 1791 the situation was vastly altered. The old and bitter clamors over the fisheries that had once seemed to Adams to threaten a separation of the states were now muted. This was not because there had been any essential change in the plight of the fishermen. Only a few months before Jefferson submitted his report, George Beckwith reported to the British ministry that New England seafarers had "suffered more by the Act of Independence, than any part of the Country, from the decay of their ship building, and the effect which the dismemberment of the Empire has produced on their oil and fish in foreign markets."[11] Nor had there been any substantial change in the European desire for a makeweight in the political scales, with the consequent danger of foreign interference in the internal parties and policies of the United States. But the general agreement about where the national interest required the American makeweight to be placed had been dissolved. Hamilton, formerly a powerful and effective defender of the fisheries on the grounds of national interest, showed by his policies that his advocacy of their cause in *The Federalist* had been basically forensic in nature. Adams, once the foremost champion of the fishermen, had suffered such a sea change in

[10] James Thomson, *Alfred*, Act II, Sc. 5 (*The Works of James Thomson* [London, 1788], ed. Patrick Murdock, III, 130). TJ possessed the London, 1766, edition of Thomson's *Works* in four volumes (Sowerby, No. 4547).
[11] Dorchester to Grenville, 25 Sep. 1790 (PRO: CO 42/69, f. 14).

his political thought that he seemed less concerned about their distress than about the importance of titles and distinctions among men. Although he knew from experience how difficult it was to obtain exact information on the fisheries, there is no evidence that any of the data he possessed was made available to Jefferson.[12]

Perhaps most revealing of all, the former sectional roles were altered. The conflict over the fisheries in Congress in 1781 had been between northern delegates who insisted upon their protection by treaty and southern delegates who were equally determined not to jeopardize peace arrangements by such a precondition. But now, less than a decade later, it was a southern planter in the Cabinet and his fellow Virginian in the House of Representatives who plead the cause of the cod and whale fisheries, those exclusively northern enterprises which, as Jefferson expressed it, differed in everything except "in being as unprofitable to the adventurer, as important to the public."[13] His views of the fisheries as a political institution had been sharpened and strengthened by the change in circumstances since he presented his *Observations on the Whale-Fishery* to the French ministry, but he had not abandoned the ground he occupied in that notable treatise. Indeed, before he went to Europe in 1784 to help negotiate treaties of commerce his purpose was essentially the same as that expressed in 1791— to try to open a new and memorable epoch in the history of the freedom of the ocean.[14] When that system of treaties failed, he had grasped at once the implications of the failure. Always preferring amicable to adversary means, he had yet not hesitated to advocate use of a weapon bearing the hallmark of old-world politics. This, as Adams had predicted, could not only be a makeweight in the political scales of Europe, but also a source of partisan conflict at home. Indeed the partisan differences on this question made their appearance even before Jefferson assumed office as Secretary of State. This occurred in the very capital of the cod and the haddock, the General Court of Massachusetts.

II

Less than a week before Jefferson reported on the distressed plight of the fisheries, Governor Hancock addressed the Massachusetts legislature in rhapsodic terms: "The happiness of the people . . . is everywhere acknowledged: their field has in the year past, yielded its increase in great abundance: our fishery and commerce have been prospered, and . . . the public securities of the United States are very fast approximating in their real, to their nominal value." Two years

[12] Adams, of course, had no official responsibility in the matter, but in presiding over the Senate he did not hesitate at times to try to influence legislative measures, both directly and indirectly (see, for example, Maclay, *Journal*, ed. Maclay, p. 2-3, 10-12, 17, 24, 55-6, 92, 94, 115, 116, 243, 385). His opinion on matters of policy was also occasionally sought by Washington. For his difficulties in trying to get information on the state of the fisheries during the peace negotiations, see Adams, *Diary*, ed. Butterfield, III, 75, 83, 85.

[13] Document IX.

[14] See TJ's Report on treaties of amity and commerce, 20 Dec. 1783 and his resolution on such treaties [Apr.? 1784]; also, his letters to Carmichael, Humphreys, and Short in group of documents under 15 Mch. 1791.

EDITORIAL NOTE

earlier Hancock had hailed the commencement of "a new and important Æra" in which the principles of the Revolution would be given full sway by the new government—but he had not even mentioned the fisheries.[15] The Massachusetts delegation in Congress had done somewhat better. Fisher Ames, Benjamin Goodhue, and Elbridge Gerry—the last representing the impoverished fishermen of Marblehead—spoke of the fisheries much as John Adams had during the peace negotiations. All argued that they were important as a nursery of seamen and as an indispensable link in the trade with the West Indies. All were agreed as to their languishing state. "I contend," declared Fisher Ames in a sharp clash with James Madison, "that [the fishermen] are very poor, they are in a sinking state, they carry on their business in despair." He argued that the duty of six cents a gallon on molasses would be a ruinous tax upon them since dried and pickled fish were essential as articles of barter in the West Indian trade.

But Madison, equally a friend of commerce and navigation, believed that the opposition to the modest duty was actually made in the interest of the New England rum distilleries, which were far from languishing. He exposed the true nature of the arguments of the opposition by showing that Ames' own state levied 17 cents a gallon on rum. This, he charged, caused the fisheries to "labor under greater discouragement from the policy of Massachusetts, than . . . from the policy of the United States." Ames made no response to the telling observation and, when Madison called attention to the omission, he still failed to do so. When pressed, he fell back on the argument that the fishermen were too poor to pay a 6 cent duty on an estimated per capita consumption of 12 gallons of molasses per year.[16] Nor had Ames, Goodhue, Gerry, Wadsworth, and other New Englanders defended the fisheries when FitzSimons proposed a doubling of the duty on imported cables and cordage to protect the domestic manufacturers of those articles. Madison, who from the outset had doubted the policy of levying any duty on cordage or hemp, could only achieve a compromise that reduced the increase by half.[17]

The impost Act of 1789 did, to be sure, permit an allowance on the export of dried and pickled fish in lieu of duty paid on imported salt used in the fisheries. But this was woefully inadequate, being an estimated one-fiftieth of the value of the fish.[18] Further, the allowance went to the exporters, not to the fishermen who needed salt for curing their catch, hence was of slight benefit to them.[19] There was, of

[15] Addresses of John Hancock to the General Court, 27 Jan. 1791 and 8 June 1789 (Journal of the House of Representatives, MBA). The former address appeared in Bache's *General Advertiser*, 11 Feb. 1791. In it Hancock advanced only one recommendation. Because of the assumption of state debts, he called for provisions for the payment of interest on state obligations.

[16] Debates of 27-28 Apr. 1789 (*Annals*, I, 216, 217, 218-19, 220, 222, 223-5, 227-30, 230-5, 236-7, 240).

[17] *Annals*, I, 217.

[18] Raymond McFarland, *A history of the New England fisheries* (New York, 1911), p. 135. McFarland's treatise is confined almost exclusively to the cod fisheries; that of Harold A. Innis, *The cod fisheries* (Toronto, 1954), is concerned with the international aspects of the trade.

[19] See report of John Glover and others from Marblehead, 1 Feb. 1790 (Document IX, Appendix No. 5).

course, no allowance made for duties paid on cables, cordage, twine, hooks, lead, iron, duck, woolens, and other articles that were as necessary to the fisheries as salt, not to mention duties on sugar, rum, and molasses. Even the minimal benefits that the impost Act of 1789 sought to confer upon the fisheries extended only to the pursuers of cod and haddock, not to the whalemen. "Do gentlemen flatter themselves," Benjamin Goodhue asked during the debate on the duty that he said would destroy the distilleries and ruin the fishermen, "it will be borne without murmuring? It certainly will not."[20] The prediction was well founded. The champions of the distilleries, using the plight of the fishermen as a powerful argument, had caused the duty on molasses to be reduced from 6 to 2.5 cents per gallon. Madison thought this put the interests of a few distillers above those of the nation, but the victory was none the less impressive. While the depressed state of the cod fisheries had greatly helped New England representatives to argue for and obtain substantial benefits for the distillers of rum and the manufacturers of cordage, the fishermen had received only token relief. The whale fishermen, whose mastery of their craft made them the prized makeweight in the European scales, had not been given even that much national support. It was obvious that those engaged in both branches of the fisheries—"carried on by different persons, from different Ports, in different vessels, in different Seas, and seeking different markets"[21]—had this in common: the Massachusetts delegation in Congress, like Governor Hancock, had been more concerned about the assumption of state debts, the settlement of accounts with the national government, and the rise in the value of federal securities than about their place in the national economy. The murmurings that Goodhue predicted were soon heard in the General Court of Massachusetts.

The first petition came from the inhabitants of Nantucket, who declared themselves to be "greatly allarmed at the declining and Embarrassed state of the Whale-Fishery." The petitioners, considering the fishery as the birth-right of their country, pointed to its prosperous state before the war—150 sail, mostly square-rigged, yielding from the British market £150,000 sterling annually. This "Source of Wealth from the Great deep," they declared, "gave great Aid to the Merchants of Massachusetts by remittance, Afforded large sums of Specie from the West India Islands, Arrising from the Spermaceati Candles and Straind Oil (which to that Market was well adapted)," and employed upwards of 2,000 seamen—objects of such national consequence that Great Britain, in order to encourage and retain a branch of commerce little known to other European powers, had imposed an alien duty of £18-3-0 sterling per ton on the importation of whale oil. Then, the memorialists pointed out, came the destructive effect of the war and the deprivation of their market. France, however, was well disposed, new efforts were made to encourage the use of whale oil there, the General Court added its spirited support, and these facts gave "new life and Ardour to the business." But these hopes were soon blasted by the competitive inducements of France and England, to which some whalemen had yielded:[22]

[20] *Annals*, I, 221.   [21] Document IX.
[22] Petition of the inhabitants of Nantucket, in town meeting at Sherburn, 6 Jan. 1790 (MS in MBA, Ch. 124, Resolves of 1789; signed by Frederick Folger,

When the citizens of our Own Country not regarding her truest Interest Had, first recourse to Great Britain, but not Meeting with Encouragement adequate to their wishes, repaired to the Court of France, who . . . did not fail to embrace so favourable an Opertunity in using their Endeavours by appropriations of large sums of Money for the express purpose of Establishing that Valuable branch in their own Kingdom. At the same time repeated Solicitations have been made to the Inhabitants of this Island for their Removal from hence to Dunkirk for the purpose of Establishing the Fishery at that place, but being by them rejected, altho Strongly urged by the Abettors of this Ruinous plan, who finding themselves disappointed in their expectations of a General remove, have themselves removed to France, and with them they have taken (and others have sent and still are sending) their Ships to be bottomed in France, to Avail themselves of a Bounty of Forty shillings sterling for every Ton, which is given as encouragement in the fishery of that Kingdom, and have so far Succeeded, that they have already Employ'd in that Fishery about 4000 Tons of Shipping which are mostly from this Country and principally navigated by it's Citizens. This Injurious proceedure will not only destroy the sale of our Oil at the French Market, but must end in the ruin and total loss of the Whale-fishery to this Country forevermore.

The Nantucket petitioners closed by viewing "with great concern the Potent Powers of Europe aided by the Citizens of our own Country, thus industriously endevouring our Rivalry." They could scarcely have given a more graphic illustration of the way in which France and England, contending over an American makeweight, had fomented internal discord and dissension. Indeed, they felt themselves so victimized that they designated Josiah Barker and Stephen Hussey, together with their elected representatives, to present and reinforce their appeal.

The Nantucket petition was referred to a joint committee of the legislature that was soon enlarged to include representatives interested in the cod fishery. This committee was instructed to take into "serious consideration the state of the Fisheries at large, and report such measures, as may be best calculated to relieve those important branches of commerce from their present embarrassments."[23] Those engaged in the cod fisheries soon made themselves heard. The redoubtable Revolutionary veteran John Glover and twelve others of Marblehead listed the handicaps under which they suffered—first among them the duty on salt, followed by those on other necessities. The only relief they asked was the payment of the allowance on the salt duty directly to owners of fishing vessels.[24] A similar petition on behalf of the shoremen of Gloucester presented "facts as melancholy as uncontrovertible"

Town Clerk; endorsed by David Cobb, Speaker of the House of Representatives, 22 Jan. 1790, as read and referred to a committee of three; endorsed the same day by Samuel Phillips, Jr., President of the Senate, as read and referred to Benjamin Austin, Jr. and Joshua Thomas).

[23] Resolution of the House of Representatives, 26 Jan. 1790 (MS in MBA, Ch. 124, Resolves of 1789; endorsed as read and concurred in by Senate, 27 Jan. 1790).

[24] This petition is printed in full below, Document IX, Appendix No. 5.

about the decline of the fishery of that town from 83 schooners in 1774 to 45 fifteen years later. The petitioners requested that the bounty on the export of fish be replaced by one for the benefit of fishermen and shoremen, that a drawback on the duty paid on salt used in the fishery be allowed, and that the Massachusetts poll tax on "these distressed (tho' most serviceable) Citizens" be waived.[25] A few days later the selectmen of Marblehead submitted to the General Court a listing of 458 widows and 866 orphans of that town—"poor widows, and fatherless Children . . . in a Most Distressing Situation without fuel, provisions, and but Very Little Cloathing to guard them against the inclemency of the Season." In addition, they reported almost 300 fishermen whose families were "in the most malloncolly Circumstances, not haveing even the Common necessarys of Life to Support them; nor . . . any prospect of their ever being in a better Situation, while the fishing business remains under so many Disadvantages, as it at present Does; *and no incouragement given to that important branch of business.*"[26]

The committee to which these affecting documents were referred represented both chambers, but the leadership came from the Senate and its dominant figure was Benjamin Austin, Jr. This fact made it certain that the result would be quite different from the kind of defense of the fisheries that Fisher Ames and his Massachusetts colleagues had made in Congress. Austin was a devoted disciple of Samuel Adams. He was known, feared, and ridiculed by Bostonian Federalists for his articles in the *Independent Chronicle* attacking the Cincinnati, the practice of the legal profession, and all manifestations of aristocratic retreat from the principles of the Revolution. He was indeed one of the earliest and most vociferous critics of the general tendency of Washington's administration.[27] Austin naturally became an ardent Jeffersonian. His later writings over the pseudonym *Old South*, bluntly reminding Bostonian merchants of their circular of 1785 calling upon all of the states to enable Congress to counteract British restrictions that were so destructive of American ship-building, fisheries, and naviga-

[25] Petition of Daniel Rogers, Winthrop Sargeant, and David Pearce on behalf of the shoremen of Gloucester, 2 Feb. 1790 (MS in MBA, Ch. 124, Resolves of 1789; endorsed as read in the House of Representatives on 4 Feb. 1790 and referred to the joint committee on the fisheries; also endorsed as read and concurred in by the Senate, 8 Feb. 1790).

[26] "A return of the widows; Male, and female, fatherless Children, in, and belonging to the Town of Marblehead," 9 Feb. 1790 (MS in MBA, Ch. 169, Resolves of 1789; signed by Isaac Mansfield, John Glover, Richard Harris, Nathaniel Lindsey, Burrill Devereux, and Samuel Hooper, Selectmen of Marblehead; emphasis added).

[27] The sketch of Benjamin Austin, Jr. (1752-1820) by Samuel E. Morison in DAB concludes that he was regarded as a dangerous radical, but was "essentially a conservative always opposing local improvements and changes." Austin was in fact one of those who, like Jefferson, grasped at once and consistently supported the implication that the republican principles of the Revolution meant a continuing commitment to change. He could have been regarded as a dangerous radical only by those who had not been so consistent. The famous exchange between Austin's mentor Samuel Adams and John Adams in 1790 epitomizes the consistency of the one and the change of attitude in the other (*Four letters: being an interesting correspondence between those eminently distinguished characters, John Adams, late President of the United States; and Samuel Adams, late Governor of Massachusetts* [Boston, 1802]). See Sowerby, No. 3287.

tion, reflected the same consistent view he had upheld from the time of Shays' rebellion onward.[28] There could be no doubt about the position he would take in behalf of suffering fishermen. Austin drafted the report for the joint committee:[29]

> ... they find that the Whale and Cod Fisheries are very important branches of Commerce not only to this State, but to the United States in general.—That the embarrassments now attending these branches arise principally from the political regulations of some European Nations.—And as Congress is by the Constitution vested with the power to counteract those Regulations, the Committee think it necessary, that a representation of the Value, importance, and declension of the Fisheries should be made to that Honourable Body.

There was not a word in the report about such palliatives as drawbacks and bounties. Austin stood on the same ground once occupied by the Boston merchants who argued that, unless the United States adopted expedients similar to the trade restrictions of Great Britain, the commerce and perhaps the union itself would "become victims to the *artifice* of a nation, whose *arms* have been in vain exerted to accomplish the ruin of America."[30]

The committee joined to its report the draft of a representation from the General Court to Congress. This draft, while comparing the prosperous state of the fisheries before the war with their depressed circumstances afterwards, focused its attention on the chief cause of the decline and on the grant of power that made remedial measures possible:

> That the exclusive right of regulating trade, must be vested in one supreme Legislature whose jurisdiction extends throughout every part of the nation is obvious on the least reflection; and experience has taught us that partial regulations, and provisions of this nature, are not only injurious in their consequences to the States that adopt them, but do not in any view forward those beneficial effects intended to be produced by them.—The decisive Remedy therefore, for evils resulting to our commerce from the Political systems of

[28] Benjamin Austin, Jr., *Constitutional republicanism, in opposition to fallacious Federalism; as published occasionally in the Independent Chronicle, under the signature of Old-South* (Boston, 1803). TJ had read and admired *Old South* even before Austin sent him the collected essays (TJ to Austin, 28 June 1803; Austin to TJ, 7 July and 24 Aug. 1803). See Sowerby No. 3534.

[29] Report of joint committee on the fisheries, dated Feb. 1790 (MS in MBA, Ch. 169, Resolves of 1789; signed by Austin and entirely in his hand).

[30] Circular letter of a committee of fifteen merchants, 22 Apr. 1785, signed by John Hancock, Samuel A. Otis, Samuel Breck, Stephen Higginson, Perez Morton, and others. This committee, representing the Boston mercantile community, had been directed to correspond with merchants in seaports throughout the United States "on the alarming situation of . . . commercial intercourse with Great-Britain." The appeal, echoing the rhetoric of committees of correspondence a decade earlier, called for "mature deliberation, as well as the *most spirited* and vigorous exertions." It concluded that "nothing short of vesting Congress with full powers to regulate the internal, as well as external commerce of all the States," could remedy the situation (quoted in Austin, *Constitutional Republicanism*, p. 163-4; see note 28).

other Kingdoms, and Nations: and the adequate encouragement for supporting, and sustaining its various branches, must be provided for by the Wisdom of Congress.

The draft representation stated that the whale fishery, because of local advantages and fishermen whose perseverance and performance had astonished the world, had achieved such a phenomenal growth before the war that it consisted of 24,000 tons of shipping, 4,000 seamen, and products worth £350,000 sterling annually. But the British duty and the French inducements to American whalemen to settle at Dunkirk, added to the bounties granted by both nations, had reduced the number of whaling vessels to 70, employing 950 men, and producing only about £60,000 annually. As for the cod fishery, it had employed 28,000 tons of shipping, engaged 4,000 seamen, and produced about £125,000 annually before the war. But since then the English and French encouragement of their own fishery, the closing of the British West Indies, the enormous duties in the French West Indies, and the inaccessibility of the Mediterranean because of "the allowed piracy of the Algerines" had subjected that branch of the trade to such embarrassments that by 1789 it employed only 20,000 tons of shipping and 3,500 seamen, with the prospects of being reduced by a third in the next season. The committee's draft representation raised the question whether the duty on salt, despite the allowance to exporters of codfish, would not "add to the other discouragements which have arisen from the policy of rival Nations." It declared that the combined fisheries employing 8,000 men and yielding products worth at least £600,000 sterling were important to the entire union as a nursery of seamen, a ready defense in time of war, a market for agricultural produce and manufactures, and a "means of a circuitous trade important to the General Commerce and Revenue of the United States." The draft concluded with a final passage in which the Massachusetts legislature expressed its reliance "on the wisdom of the National Legislature to devise, and their disposition to pursue those measures which the policy of rival Nations have made necessary." The draft had been prepared up to this point in the hands of two members of the Senate.

But Benjamin Austin was clearly not satisfied with the closing paragraph, even though it did place responsibility directly on the policy of rival nations. He therefore struck it out and substituted a longer passage which, while recognizing the dangers posed by European nations' encouragement of their own fisheries, declared it to be "incumbent on the Congress of the United States, in order to prevent a total annihilation of these important branches in America, to give the most ample encouragement to our own Citizens, engaged in these employments. . . . We are the more earnest in our request, as we conceive them to be the great staples of our Commerce, by employing the largest quantity of shipping, and the most numerous Body of Seamen, than any other Mercantile Business pursued by us." Then, as so often in his writings, Austin called attention to the expectations that had been aroused by the movement for a more perfect union. He seemed to be reminding Congress, and John Adams in particular, of the issue once considered "so tender and important" as to threaten a breach of the union if neglected:[31]

> The fisheries, were considered of such importance, that it excited the particular attention of our Ambassadors in the treaty of Peace. They were Objects so highly contemplated by the Northern states, that the purposes of Independance, would have been considered by them but half accomplish'd unless they had obtained an express declaration in favour of their Fisheries.
>
> The People of the northern States anticipated an enlargement of their Commerce, by the adoption of the fœderal Constitution. They confidently relied on Congress, that they would pursue such measures, as would counteract the policy of rival Nations. Among the Objects of our National Commerce, our Whale and Cod Fisheries stand foremost; and the advantages arising from the fœderal Government, as it respects the Northern states, essentially depend on the promotion and establishment of these important branches.
>
> During the War a regiment of hardy Troops was composed of men who were formerly employed in our Fisheries. The widows of many of those Veterans are now suffering every misfortune of human Life. Their Consolations depend on the Assistance of Government to enable their Children to follow those paths of Industry, so steadily pursued by their Fathers. We earnestly hope they will not plead in vain, but flatter ourselves that Congress will adopt such regulations as will encourage them in their laudable exertions, and enable them to obtain a comfortable subsistance for their indigent Families.
>
> The happiness and prosperity of Individuals, we acknowledge, are but secondary motives to influence public measures, yet . . . we cannot but rest assured, that Congress will embrace the Object of our Fisheries upon those extensive principles which evidently influence the European Powers—Vizt. an increase of our Agriculture, Manufactures, and National Commerce.

Austin's impassioned appeal did not prevail. Another and briefer memorial to Congress, evidently drafted by one of the House members of the joint committee, was substituted for it. The substitute representation, briefer and less forceful, included the same general statistics comparing the whale and cod fisheries before and after the war, referred to the article in the Treaty of Peace as an evidence of the value attached to the fisheries, and concluded:[32]

[31] Draft of representation from the General Court to Congress (MS in MBA, Ch. 124, Resolves of 1789; in three different hands with the concluding paragraphs in the hand of Austin; undated but drawn between 9 and 23 Feb. 1790).

[32] Representation from "The Legislature of the Commonwealth of Massachusetts To the Congress of the United States," 23 Feb. 1790 (MS in MBA, Ch. 124, Resolves of 1789; endorsed as approved by the Senate on 23 Feb. 1790 as amended and as concurred in by the House on the 24th). The Senate amendment only offered a more generalized statement about the bounties and encouragements given to the cod and whale fisheries by France and Great Britain.

The General Court had merely asserted "We think that Markets for fish oil abroad . . . ought to be obtained." This was both weak and ambiguous, for the

To support the fisheries we think that Markets for fish oil Abroad much more advantageous to our Citizens ought to be obtained; and that many of the duties laid on several articles particularly consumed in these fisheries, and by those employed in them, ought to be lessened or taken off. Perhaps instead of a small bounty to the exporting merchant on fish a bounty to the fisherman and shoremen may be found beneficial.

This representation, slightly amended in the Senate, was approved late in February. There was no suggestion about how the markets abroad were to be obtained. Every hint that the depressed state of the fisheries was due to the rival policies of foreign powers had been eliminated. There was in it no such allusion as that in Austin's draft to the power that had been granted Congress to enable it to counteract "the political regulations of some European Nations." The weakened version, echoing the disinclination of New England representatives in Congress to support retaliatory measures against Great Britain, was immediately approved by both houses. That same day the General Court adopted a resolution directing the Massachusetts Senators to introduce the representation, together with the accompanying petitions from Nantucket and Marblehead, and to use their influence to have the matter "taken up and duly considered."[33] The hidden political contest that brought about the defeat of Austin's draft and the substitution of one lacking all traces of its imperative nature deprived Jefferson of the opportunity —one that obviously would have been gratifying to him and would have greatly reinforced his argument—of being able to say in his report that Massachusetts, the state whose enterprising citizens had created and fostered the fisheries, had again echoed the sentiments of her merchants in 1785 and, in behalf of an important national interest, had called for retaliatory measures against Great Britain. Clearly, the issue, at least for the elected representatives of Massachusetts in the General Court and in the Congress, was not so tender and important as it had been during the peace negotiations just a few years earlier.

Two weeks after this weakened memorial had triumphed, a second petition on behalf of the merchants, shoremen, and fishermen of Marblehead was presented to the General Court, accompanied by statistics on the annual income and expenses of a fishing vessel in the preceding three years and by a statement of individual distresses during the preceding year testifying to "the rapid decline of an important branch of Commerce, and the danger . . . of the depopulation of the town of Marblehead." The petitioners were aware that many of the difficulties could only be removed by Congress, but they felt that relief would be "more seasonably obtained, if the representations from the

French market for oil was already open. But TJ, in paraphrasing the statement, gave it the force of a request and extended its meaning as far as he could to indicate support for affirmative use of national power over foreign commerce. The Massachusetts legislature, he asserted in words that reflected his own inclination rather than the literal terms of the representation, "asks that . . . the national influence be used abroad for obtaining better Markets for their produce" (see Document IX).

[33] Senate resolution, 23 Feb. 1790, concurred in by the House on 24 Feb. 1790 (MS in MBA, Ch. 124, Resolves of 1789).

more immediate sufferers, should receive the sanction" of the General Court. Further, while pointing to the duties on salt, tonnage, and other necessary articles for the fisheries as being unequal and impolitic levies, the petitioners declared:[34]

> . . . these extraordinary expences cannot be reimbursed in the Sale of the Fish, while prevented in the Market by the Policy of foreign nations, rivals in the same business, and discouraged by their heavy exactions. A Release or Mitigation of the duties of Tonnage, in favor of Fishing Vessels, and a prohibition upon the importing of the Fish cured by foreign nations, will in a small degree counteract their bounties, which have effected a large increase of their Fisheries, and threaten the entire loss of the Fisheries of the United States.

> If the long exercise of an employment, the riches and extent of profitable commerce heretofore gained by it, the numbers of people which it has supported, their hardy habits, their readiness and bravery in time of War, and Public danger, and an increase of Navigation from the same source, in time of Peace, may be considered, as proofs of the national importance of such employment, the importance of the Codfishery can evidently be proved. The early and later History of New-England, and especially of the period of the late War, afford the most striking proofs.

The Marblehead petitioners hoped that, on inquiry by the General Court into "the national Advantages, and present embarrassments of the Codfishery . . . and recommended under their authority, to the attention of the Congress," remedies and relief would be forthcoming. The legislature directed the Massachusetts Senators to add this petition and its two enclosures to the other representations already transmitted.[35] At the same time it appointed a committee to correspond with the Massachusetts delegation in Congress on the subject of the fisheries.[36] Shortly thereafter *A Real Republican*, whose indignant comments seem to echo Benjamin Austin's blunt remarks that had failed of adoption by the General Court, asked publicly whether the commercial and other benefits promised under the new Constitution had been realized:[37]

[34] Memorial of Jonathan Glover and Samuel Sewall to the General Court, 1 Mch. 1790 (MS in MBA, Ch. 169, Resolves of 1789, signed by Glover and Sewall).

[35] The resolution of the House of Representatives, dated 8 Mch. 1790, requested the governor to transmit the memorial and its enclosures to the Massachusetts Senators and ask them "to use their influence that the same be taken up and considered together with the other representations . . . already transmitted." The Senate, perhaps because this language appeared to be a repetition of that in the earlier one, substituted another draft, approved by the House on the 9th, which merely requested that the memorial and its documents be sent to the Senators and "laid before Congress with the representation . . . relative to the subject of the Whale and cod fisheries" (MS of both resolutions in MBA, Ch. 169, Resolves of 1789).

[36] Journal of the House of Representatives, 8 Mch. 1790 (MBA). Since the General Court adjourned on the 9th, this committee had been appointed to correspond during the recess. Apparently no communication took place between the committee and the delegation.

[37] *Independent Chronicle*, 29 Apr. 1790.

Has their commerce been extended by the revival of the *Carrying-Trade*?—Have our *Whale* and *Cod Fisheries*, those staples of the northern States, been duly attended to?—While other nations are encouraging their Fisheries by bounties, and other encouragements —wherein have we given a support to ours? On the contrary, we have cramped them with duties which operate almost as prohibitions. So essential are these important branches of commerce to the northern States, that we have a right to *demand* the assistance of congress; for should government fail to support these great commercial branches, the present constitution will prove but of little advantage to us. . . . The patience of the citizens is almost exhausted; they no longer look with assurance to that body, in whom, a few months since, they placed implicit confidence.

Similar comments continued in the press.[38] These were reinforced by appeals to the Vice President, the stalwart defender of the fisheries during the peace negotiations. Thomas Crofts reported to John Adams that commerce had not been so sluggish since the closing of Boston port in 1774, ship carpenters were wholly out of business, and the "sound of the Ax or the Hammer . . . hardly to be heard" in the city. "Cannot something be done to Encourage the Cod and Whale Fisheries?" he asked. "Must the ship building be wholly Annihilated in the Eastern States?"[39] "If no measures could ever be carried in the State

[38] Same, 27 May 1790; a writer in the *Massachusetts Centinel*, 22 May 1790, thought that southern opposition would mean that "the fishery must be annihilated, the carrying trade distressed, the seamen and manufacturers turned graziers, and the value of every foot of property in every seaport in New-England sunk . . . one half in its value." Another, under the pseudonym *Numbers*, rejected this conclusion, spoke for national as opposed to sectional interest in a trade of which four-fifths was carried in foreign vessels, and declared that the seamen and manufacturers had been "a great instrument . . . indeed the axis of the late revolution." He asserted that the time had come to speak plainly and that "the multiplied petitions and remonstrances with which the congressional table has been piled, from the eastward of the Hudson" had made clear the sufferings of the people (*Independent Chronicle*, 27 May 1790).

[39] Thomas Crofts to John Adams, 17 May 1790 (MHi: AM). That same day John Hurd wrote to Adams: "The Publick Papers may puff up the increasing trade of America, but you may rely on it in this state it is on the decline. Our Fishery is discourag'd and is lessen'd one hundred sail this spring. Much was expected from the Carrying Trade. . . . But wherever we go, we find the Harbours crowded with British shipping which have the preference—whilst our own ships sail the coast from Boston to Georgia begging a freight. . . . Why cannot Congress say that no Goods Wares or Merchandise shall be imported in British ships but what are the growth or manufacture of Great Britain. Surely we have a right to retaliate when it is so much for our interest" (MHi: AM). But Adams, once so ardent in urging Americans to "unite, retaliate, prohibit, or trade with France," now seemed to listen more to the counsel of Stephen Higginson, who wrote: "Should we at once adopt a resentful, restrictive System, the effect may be to increase the Evil. . . . I should hope more from open and calm negotiation than retaliation" (John Adams to James Bowdoin, 9 May 1787, and to Isaac Smith, 20 June 1786; Stephen Higginson to John Adams, 21 Dec. 1789; MHi: AM). Higginson also took a complacent view of the state of commerce and the fisheries, thinking that "habits of dissipation and expense contracted during the war" were largely responsible for their decline, that the frugality and industry of those pursuing the fisheries on the south shore of Cape Cod would cause the trade to be transferred from Marblehead, Gloucester, and other distressed towns —a fact he thought "in a national View, of no great importance"—and that

Legislature to encourage the fisheries," Adams replied, "I leave you to judge whether it is probable that bounties can be obtained from the general government." He reminded Crofts that the Massachusetts navigation act, which he thought might have given full employment to shipwrights, had been repealed. "If Congress should make a similar law," he added, "it will be opposed by powerful interests who will continually grumble against it and there is neither vigor nor constancy enough in the government, I am afraid, to persevere."[40] Adams had reason to be pessimistic, presiding as he did over the very center of opposition to all retaliatory measures against Great Britain.

The Massachusetts representation, together with the urgent appeals from Nantucket, Marblehead, and Gloucester, with their accompanying documents, were laid before the House of Representatives on 14 April 1790.[41] The great issue at the moment was Hamilton's report on public credit and the matter of the fisheries was tabled. Not until the 9th of August, only three days before adjournment and long after the bargain arranged by Hamilton, Jefferson, and Madison had assured passage of the assumption and residence bills, did the House of Representatives refer the Massachusetts representation and accompanying documents to the Secretary of State and direct him to report at the next session.[42] Ames, Goodhue, and Gerry, eloquent and determined champions of the suffering fishermen when the question of a duty on molasses was under consideration, had for four months sat indifferent to their pleas while engrossed in the question of the assumption of state debts. The two Massachusetts Senators, Tristram Dalton and Caleb Strong, had been specifically requested to use their influence to have Congress take the fisheries under consideration. But they, too, had remained silent. The *Independent Chronicle* expressed its regret that the whale fisheries, on which depended thousands of hardy and industrious citizens, had been deferred to the next session "when so much other business had been attended to, the greatest part of which is of the most trifling and uninteresting nature. . . . People here do not inquire whether Congress are to sit at Philadelphia or the Potowmack, whether the Quakers are gratified in their absurd memorial, or whether the petition of John Twining has been attended to; but whether measures have been adopted to extend our commerce and enlarge our navigation."[43]

But one citizen of distressed Marblehead did receive prompt relief from the federal government. General John Glover, whose boatmen had done such heroic work in putting the American army across the

---

Americans had so many advantages over Europeans in carrying on the fisheries they would not lose this branch of trade (Stephen Higginson to John Adams, 24 Mch. 1790. MHi: AM).

[40] John Adams to Thomas Crofts, 25 May 1790 (MHi: AM).

[41] Although both the resolution of the General Court of 23 Feb. and 9 Mch. 1790 had specified that the representation and accompanying petitions be laid before Congress by the Massachusetts Senators—with the former requesting that they use their influence to have the matter considered—they left it to an unidentified "member from Massachusetts" to present the materials in the House (JHR, I, 193).

[42] JHR, I, 296.

[43] Quoted in New York *Daily Advertiser*, 2 Sep. 1790, from the *Independent Chronicle*, 26 Aug. 1790.

Delaware in 1776 when even Washington had almost given up hope, was now poor and distressed. When the President was in Boston on his northern tour, Glover had a personal interview with him and asked to be considered for public employment because of his considerable "Loss of property in pursueing the fishing business since peace." Subsequently he made two written appeals, asking to be considered for appointment as collector of the port of Marblehead. But that post, with the support of John Adams and on the personal recommendation of Elbridge Gerry and all of the principal merchants of that port, went instead to Samuel Russell Gerry, brother of the Congressman.[44]

III

The representation of the Massachusetts General Court and the accompanying petitions and documents came to the Secretary of State in mid-August at the close of the second session. But if these materials had been received with indifference by the Massachusetts delegation, their effect upon Jefferson was quite otherwise. No one in America, whether in or out of public office or whether engaged in the trade as fisherman or merchant, had devoted as much study to the history of the cod and whale fisheries and the effect of British policy upon them as he had. His own data as set forth in his *Observations on the Whale-Fishery* in 1788 was both more exact and more complete than that in the documents submitted to him. Even without benefit of Benjamin Austin's suppressed draft, he could not have failed to note that the General Court had not followed the Nantucket and Marblehead peti-

[44] John Glover to Washington, 24 Feb. and 15 July 1790 (DLC: Washington Papers). Glover appealed to his old comrade in arms, Henry Knox, in more personal terms than those used with Washington: "After giveing to my Country Eight years Service, for which have received but a small Compensation; I returned to my family, Consisting of a wife and Eight Children, who Lookt up to me for Support. I was under the necessity of resuming the fishing business again, or Let them Starve, that part of my pay, not spent in the Services at that time, being not Worth more than 2/6 in the pound; and in persuing the fishery, the three past years, have Sunk of my property three thousand pounds; that with my Constitution being Very much impair'd, while in the Services, has induced me to offer myself a Candadate, to the president, for the appointment of Collector . . . for the Port of Marblehead" (Glover to Knox, 15 July 1790, MHi: Knox Papers). The same day Glover's brother-in-law wrote to Knox supporting the application: he believed that the President "would appoint Genl. Glover, even without solicitation, but it will not be amiss for his Friends to mention him" (B. Hubbard to Henry Knox, 15 July 1790; same).

Robert Hooper and fifty-seven merchants and traders of Marblehead petitioned the President to appoint Samuel R. Gerry, calling attention to his relation to Elbridge Gerry and saying that he was "in every respect qualified" (petition of Hooper and others, 16 July 1790, DLC: Washington Papers). Samuel R. Gerry, perhaps at his brother's prompting, applied to Alexander Hamilton. Elbridge Gerry recommended him to Washington, describing the petition of the merchants as "voluntary" and saying that other testimonials supporting him as "a man of strict honor, probity, and assiduity" could be acquired if necessary (Gerry to Washington, 26 July 1790; same). At the same time Gerry wrote to the Vice President, reminding Adams that he had promised his support. He said that his brother had a large family to maintain and that the voluntary petition of the merchants testified to his popularity—a qualification scarcely essential for the post of collector in a port in which, as elsewhere, TJ declared frauds existed in the importing and exporting of produce of the fisheries (see Document IX; Gerry to Adams, 26 July 1790; MHi: AM).

tions in pointing to the policy of foreign powers as the basic cause of the decline in the fisheries. Perhaps in the hope of eliciting support for his policy, Jefferson wrote at once to Governor Hancock asking for precise information about the numbers of vessels and seamen, the kinds and amounts of fish taken, and the markets available. The nature of the questions reflected the views Jefferson had long since expressed, both in his *Observations* and in his support of Madison's effort to discriminate in favor of nations in treaty with the United States. Indeed, his object was implicit in the reason he gave Hancock for desiring statistics showing the prosperity of the fisheries before the war and their decline afterwards. Such a comparison, he wrote, would enable Congress "to discover the cause of that decline, and provide either a remedy for it, *or something which may countervail it's effect*." He knew that Hancock disliked communicating through departmental heads, and so flattered him by saying that the information could be obtained nowhere else "and under no other auspices so likely to produce it." He hoped to submit his report at the beginning of the session and therefore urged Hancock to make the information available by the first of November.[45]

Hancock, having just called the General Court into special session, laid Jefferson's communication before that body. "I thought it my duty to communicate it to you," he informed the Senate and House of Representatives, "and to do every thing in my power to carry into effect the valuable purposes of the Secretary of State."[46] The legislature at once appointed a joint committee—Benjamin Austin was one of the Senate members—to select men experienced in the fisheries as a committee of inquiry. Captain Peleg Coffin, Jr. was designated head of the latter committee.[47] Despite the difficulties of obtaining precise information—none was available from official records prior to the Revolution or from the newly established federal offices—the committee's report, based largely "on the recollection and Knowledge of men Conversant in the fishing business," was promptly compiled. That report and its accompanying documents, transmitted by Governor Hancock, were awaiting Jefferson when he arrived in Philadelphia on the 20th of November.[48] Considering the circumstances, the statistics gathered were a tribute to the painstaking efforts of the committee. But, useful as the information was, Coffin's report was even more remarkable in the manner in which, almost literally, it echoed Benjamin Austin's analysis of the causes of the decline of the fisheries: "The embarrass-

[45] TJ to Hancock, 24 Aug. 1790; emphasis added. The letter to Hancock served another purpose. Later, in discussing procedures governing official correspondence between the President and governors of the states, TJ said that Hancock was the only one who had refused to correspond with the heads of departments, but that, in a particular case, his legislature obliged him to do so (TJ to Monroe, 29 May 1801). This was perhaps the instance TJ had in mind, since, due to TJ's inquiry, the General Court asked Hancock to report the results of the investigation to the Secretary of State.

[46] Hancock's address to the General Court, 15 Sep. 1790 (MS Journal of the House of Representatives, MBA).

[47] MS Journal of the Senate, 17 Sep. 1790 (MBA).

[48] See Document I and the enclosed report of the committee headed by Peleg Coffin, Jr.; also Document IX and Appendices Nos. 2 and 12.

ment and difficulties under which the business now labours is principally caused by the Political regulations of rival Nations. We must depend for relief on the power and disposition of Congress to counteract these regulations." Also, while pointing to adverse political regulations, it hailed the removal of the duty on American fish in the French West Indies, theretofore the chief cause of embarrassment to the cod fishery. Jefferson must have been gratified, even though the appeal for countervailing measures had not come from the General Court. In his report he did not allude to his efforts to procure additional information through Governor Hancock. Nor, of course, did he reveal that even before the House referred the Massachusetts representation to him, he had urged the American consul in London to procure general political intelligence, particularly that respecting the state of the British fisheries. Such continuing search for factual data in anticipation of political need was thoroughly characteristic.[49]

Jefferson's hope of submitting the report early in the session was not to be realized. But when at last he sent it to the Speaker he explained that it was not delayed "a moment longer than the difficulty of procuring and digesting the materials necessarily occasioned."[50] In this arduous business the Assistant Secretary of the Treasury, Tench Coxe, proved a valuable coadjutor whose aid Jefferson had sought even before he departed for Monticello. While Coxe had had no mercantile experience with the fisheries and was aware that those engaged in the business had little knowledge of it or facility in communicating what they knew, he was an assiduous compiler of statistics and a

[49] TJ to Johnson, 7 Aug. 1790. Johnson was not able to procure the information desired until early in 1791 (see Johnson to TJ, 4 Apr. 1791). TJ had also asked Nathaniel Barrett to keep him informed of the exact state of the French and English fisheries. Even at that time he feared that Congress might cause France to put American whale oil on a worse footing—a fear which anticipated the French protest against the tonnage acts (TJ to Nathaniel Barrett, 27 July 1790).

[50] Document VIII. The fact that TJ had desired to submit the report at the beginning of the session lends further support to the supposition that he had suggested the paragraph in Washington's message calling for encouragement to navigation and the fisheries (see note 56). Had he been able to do so, the connection between Madison's draft of the response to the message and his own advocacy of retaliatory measures would have been all the more obvious.

Washington had also received an appeal from *A Sailor* of Georgetown—actually a captain of a vessel—who wrote anonymously: "Of all the different classes of people in this country our new constitution and subsequent laws has provided for the encouragement of all but sailors. Why those people should be neglected I cannot conceive. They certainly are necessary to every commercial country, and ought to meet the Patronage of the Government. Our harbours are crowded with foreign ships to carry our produce to market, and our own Ships are commanded by foreigners. There is more than two thirds of the commanders of Ships from this country foreigners, some of whom even refuse to do what is necessary for their being allowed to clear out their ships themselves, but are under the necessity of letting their mates do it for them. This I conceive to be a most scandalous imposition on Americans. . . . I am pretty certain two thirds of our produce are shipped from the Southern States in British bottoms while our ships always return from England empty and meet with difficulty to procure freight even in this country." The anonymous mariner urged that the President recommend remedial measures to Congress (*A Sailor* to the President, 25 June 1790, Georgetown, DNA: RG 59, MLR). For a similar appeal from Massachusetts, see note 39 above.

practical theorist on the subject. Most important of all, he had access to
the records of the Treasury. He not only assisted Jefferson with facts
about the fisheries, but was also a useful ally in furnishing official
statistics concerning exports, imports, and tonnage. He was indeed so
zealous that, by the time Jefferson returned in November, he was able
to place in his hands several useful documents bearing on the fisheries.[51] Jefferson made careful note of Coxe's facts and recommendations, which in some degree were reflected in the final report.[52] But
the special emphasis given to it and the policy it advocated had long
since been shaped by Jefferson himself. On the strategic objective the
collaboration of James Madison was indispensable, for Jefferson's proposed solution to the plight of the fisheries was only an administrative
counterpart of Madison's efforts to obtain a navigation bill. His advocacy of the use of force against the Algerines in order to open the
Mediterranean for American fish and other products was another aspect
of the same coherent policy.[53]

Both men must have discussed these interrelated aspects of foreign
trade when they visited Mount Vernon just before Congress convened.
In 1789, in what apparently was intended as an inaugural address,
Washington had hailed the enterprising seamen navigating their "Vessels to almost every region of the known world" and had called for
legislative encouragement to the fisheries and the carrying trade. If
this were given, he declared, "we shall possess such a nursery of Seamen and such skill in maratime operations as to enable us to create
a Navy almost in a moment."[54] That address Washington had dis-
carded and with it the recommendation of support for the fisheries.
But at the opening of the third session, facing the danger of war between nations engaged in commerce with the United States, he presented to Congress an emphatic recommendation that could not be disregarded:[55]

> I recommend it to your serious reflexion how far and in what mode,
> it may be expedient to guard against embarrassments . . . by such
> encouragements to our own Navigation as will render our commerce
> and agriculture less dependent on foreign bottoms, which may fail
> us in the very moment most interesting to both of these great ob-
> jects. Our fisheries, and the transportation of our own produce offer
> us abundant means for guarding ourselves against this evil.

Jefferson must have composed this paragraph of the message as he
did two others immediately following it.[56] He had consistently advocated support for navigation and the fisheries as necessary means of
lessening American dependence on British carriers, and in the report

[51] Documents II, III, and IV and their enclosures. See also TJ to Coxe, 30
Nov. 1790.

[52] Document VII.

[53] See Document V; also TJ's reports on Mediterranean trade and the Algerine
captives, 28 Dec. 1790.

[54] Washington, *Writings*, ed. Fitzpatrick, XXX, 302, 305.

[55] Same, XXXI, 167.

[56] See note to TJ's recommendation of topics for the President's annual message, 29 Nov. 1790. See also note 50.

his reference to these "materials of indemnification" echoed the language employed in Washington's message.

The Senate response to this part of the President's message was formal and non-committal: "The navigation, and the fisheries, of the United States, are objects too interesting not to inspire a disposition to promote them, by all the means which shall appear to us consistent with their natural progress and permanent prosperity."[57] The response of the House did not mention the fisheries, no doubt because Madison, who drafted it, was well aware that Jefferson's report would connect both subjects just as the President had done. On the question of encouraging American navigation, Madison's draft so far committed the House as to cause vigorous opposition by William L. Smith of South Carolina, who desired to avoid what he considered a pledge to enact legislation that might exclude all foreign carriers.[58] But Madison's language prevailed and Smith, hoping to postpone action, moved that the subject be deferred because of its intimate connection with the fisheries, about which a report was expected in a few days.[59] Benjamin Goodhue of Massachusetts, a merchant and defender of the shipping interests, objected. He "imagined" that the anticipated report would be confined to the fisheries and therefore moved that a committee be appointed to bring in a bill for the encouragement of navigation. As Smith immediately indicated by reading the pertinent paragraph in the President's message, navigation and fisheries had been pointedly connected. Goodhue's motion, benefiting from Madison's leadership, was adopted. But his attempt to separate the two subjects reveal the particular interests for which he spoke, as did his allusion to the report on the fisheries that was expected "from the Secretary of the Treasury."[60] Smith again corrected Goodhue, but the slip was understandable.

For it was about this time that Alexander Hamilton, knowing well what a dependable supporter of his measures Goodhue was, sent him a letter "of consequence to the Whale Fishery" and indicated his desire to discuss it with him the next day.[61] The important letter that Hamilton enclosed has not been identified and the nature of its contents can only be surmised. It may have contained information similar to that sent by Christopher Gore early in December to inform the administration that an emissary then in New England was believed to have been sent to the United States "by the direction of Lord Hawkesbury and Mr. Grenville, for the express purpose of knowing what priviledges, from the british government, would induce the inhabitants of Nantucket to remove from that island to Great Britain,

[57] Response of the Senate to the President's address, 10 Dec. 1790 (JS, I, 220-1).

[58] Response of the House of Representatives to the President's address, 11 Dec. 1790 (JHR, I, 334-5). See Editorial Note to group of documents on commercial and diplomatic relations with Great Britain, under 15 Dec. 1790.

[59] Annals, I, 1840-3.

[60] Annals, I, 1847, 1949. Goodhue's statement that he "imagined" the report would be confined to the fisheries is not in Annals but is in the proceedings of the House as reported in Bache's General Advertiser, 16 Dec. 1790.

[61] Hamilton to Goodhue, [1790] (Syrett, Hamilton, VII, 407).

and carry on their whale fishery from thence."⁶² Gore's report about the British agent was transmitted to Jefferson, who made use of it in his report. But there is no evidence that either Hamilton or Goodhue shared with him the "letter of consequence to the Whale Fishery." Goodhue's inadvertent slip revealed the direction in which he looked for leadership just as his motion betrayed his lack of concern for the fisheries as a national interest. But if he believed that Jefferson would confine his report strictly to the depressed state of the fisheries, urging only such meager remedies as the Massachusetts legislature had suggested, he was grievously mistaken. Hamilton, after Jefferson had forced him to declare himself on the French protest against the tonnage acts, could not have so greatly misgauged his intent.

During January Jefferson labored under extraordinary pressures to complete the report which he had hoped to submit at the opening of the session.⁶³ Its postponement was in some respects an advantage, for it enabled Tench Coxe to furnish statistics from the customs records that reinforced but went considerably beyond those relating exclusively to the fisheries. Also, a few days before the report was submitted, Jefferson received a letter from William Short that he extracted and transmitted at the same time that he submitted his report to the Speaker. In preparing the extract Jefferson carefully omitted Short's remark about the extreme ignorance of the members of the National Assembly on commercial matters. He also deleted another sentence that might have given offense to particular interests in France. But he found very useful Short's observation that some in the National Assembly thought experience had proved commerce with the United States to be a losing business, supposing as they did that Americans were "so much attached to England and to English manufactures, that every sacrifice which France could make to encourage commercial connexcions . . . would be lost."⁶⁴ The favors already bestowed on

⁶² Christopher Gore to Tobias Lear, 10 Dec. 1790 (Document VI). It is possible, though not likely, that this was the letter sent by Hamilton to Goodhue. The debate took place five days after the date of Gore's letter and it usually required six days for a letter to go from Boston to Philadelphia.

The British secret agent, Peter Allaire, reported that "Congress" had proofs that the British government had sent an emissary to Nantucket to try to induce the whalemen to come under the British flag (Yonge to Aust, 3 May 1791, "Private," enclosing Allaire's memorandum of "Occurrences" in the United States from 6 Feb. to 2 Mch. 1791; PRO: FO 4/10, f. 11).

⁶³ See Document VIII. Three days after submitting the report, TJ wrote: "a particular and pressing business obliged me to suspend all correspondence for some weeks past" (TJ to Powell & Fierer, 4 Feb. 1791). The business he referred to was undoubtedly the report on the fisheries. See note to Short to TJ, 7 Nov. 1790, for an account of the household difficulties and pressures of public business that TJ had to contend with in the weeks preceding.

⁶⁴ Short to TJ, 21 Oct. 1790 (see notes 1, 2, and 3 for identification of the extract; also, Document VIII, note). The extract as enclosed in TJ's report is printed in full in ASP, Commerce, I, 22, but of course without indication of the alterations and omissions made by TJ. Short's letter was received on 27 Jan. 1791; his next letter of 6 Nov. 1790 would have furnished other useful information, but it arrived too late. TJ must have received copies of The Times (London) for 14, 15, and 16 Dec. 1790 containing an account of the debate in Parliament in which there was some discussion of the English whale fishery,

American commerce by France—particularly the one that Jefferson had been instrumental in obtaining and which he regarded as the sheet anchor of the alliance—were clearly in danger. Jefferson's fear that the sheet anchor, resting not on treaty but on the will of France, would give way if no reciprocal concessions were made in response to the French protest against the tonnage acts was manifest in his anxious appeal for Hamilton's cooperation. That attempt had failed, but it did help define the nature of the cleavage in the Cabinet. More important, Hamilton's flat rejection of the overture undoubtedly prompted Jefferson to present his policy in the challenging language that he gave to the report.

With the door opened by Washington's emphatic recommendation of support for navigation and the fisheries, Jefferson made the most of the opportunity. He laid the completed report before the President and Washington gave his approval on the first of February.[65] This guaranteed that the division in the administration would become public, with the lines being drawn on the broad question of policy on which, at the time the eleventh *Federalist* was published, Hamilton and Jefferson had been in such apparent agreement.

IV

Jefferson's report on the fisheries has been characterized by the leading authority on the maritime history of Massachusetts as being friendly to the fishermen but non-committal.[66] It was indeed the most friendly—and the best informed—defense that the fishermen had ever received at the hands of a public official. But no one in government and certainly no emissary of France or Great Britain at the time so far misconceived its salient feature as to think Jefferson had not committed himself in unequivocal terms. Senator Maclay, to be sure, did confide to his diary that Jefferson's "great object seems to be the making . . . a nursery for Seamen that we, like all the nations of the earth, may also have a Navy."[67] While the creation of a small naval force had long been advocated by Jefferson, Maclay erred in thinking this the

but these also arrived too late for him to make use of the information (see Robert Crew to TJ, 17 Dec. 1790).

It was the decree of 29 Dec. 1787 that TJ considered to be the sheet anchor of the connection with France (TJ to Short, 15 Mch. 1791). In his report TJ appended copies of that and two other French decrees favoring American commerce (Document IX, Appendices Nos. 8, 9, and 10).

[65] On 1 Feb. 1791 TJ recorded in SJPL receipt of a message of that date from the President approving his report on the fisheries. Washington's note of approval has not been found.

[66] Samuel E. Morison, *Maritime History of Massachusetts 1783-1860* (Boston, 1921), p. 134.

[67] Maclay, *Journal*, ed. Maclay, p. 384. TJ called on Maclay late in February and "talked politics, mostly the French difference and the whale-fishery" (same, p. 397). Maclay had mistakenly thought TJ a party to an administration design led by Washington to quarrel with France (same, p. 386; see Editorial Note to group of documents on French protest against the tonnage acts, under 18 Jan. 1791). But the real purpose of TJ's visit—which Maclay also misunderstood—was evidently to gain support for the bill to amend the Residence Act (see Editorial Note to group of documents on the location of the Federal District, under 24 Jan. 1791).

great object of the report, just as he failed to perceive that the administration, at this time, was divided even on the question of establishing a navy. Though circumstances were greatly altered, Jefferson's purpose was essentially the same as that set forth so clearly in his *Observations on the Whale-Fishery* two years earlier—to promote countervailing measures against Great Britain's restrictive commercial system. While the object of his policy remained unchanged, Jefferson responded to the altered circumstances in such a way as to indicate a conscious desire to make his intent clear beyond all doubt. In his *Observations*, writing as a diplomat urging a particular course upon a foreign nation, he had taken unusual precautions to impress upon the French government that his views were "intended for the perusal of his Majesty's ministers only, the matter . . . being improper to be communicated further." He had repeated this injunction to secrecy in his official report to John Jay and, without exception, in his letters to Washington, Lafayette, Adams, and others to whom he had sent copies of the treatise.[68] These precautions were not intended to protect information about the fishery and its product, but rather to conceal from public view his treatment of this part of American commerce as "a Political institution." In doing so, he had argued that France held the balance and that, by opening or closing the French markets, she could tilt the scales as she pleased.

But now, in 1791, Jefferson was employing basically the same facts to argue that the power of determining the European balance rested with the United States and should be exercised. He was addressing himself not in a confidential communication to a foreign ministry, but openly to the legislative branch of the government and, in a very real sense, to the world at large. These altered circumstances induced him to make some slight changes in the form of presentation. While the report was an unmistakable effort to counter the mercantilist doctrines of Sheffield and Hawkesbury, it did not describe these—as Jefferson did in his draft—as being the "crooked maxims of interest and jealousy, which have so long misled the short-sighted statesman." It pointed to the benefits conferred on the fisheries by France, but did not employ the praise first bestowed upon that nation as one "setting so remarkable an example of taking the pure principles of right and reason for their guide."[69] These were mere modifications on unessential points, characteristically muted in order to avoid needless offense to adversaries. But, by contrast, the kind of language Jefferson used in substantive matters was far blunter than any he had previously employed. Great Britain, he declared, had not only placed a prohibitive duty on foreign oil, but had recently sent an emissary among American whalemen at Nantucket to induce them to settle where "a sameness of language, religion, laws, habits and kindred" gave them a preference—that is, to emigrate to Halifax under the British flag rather than to Dunkirk under that of France. Such inducements were compounded by the fact that oil from this competitive fishery was brought into American ports and reshipped fraudulently under the United States

[68] TJ to Jay, Lambert, La Luzerne, Montmorin, and Necker, all written on 19 Nov. 1788; TJ to Washington, 4 Dec. 1788; TJ to Adams, 5 Dec. 1788.
[69] Document IX, note 6.

flag "into ports where it could not be received under theirs," thus endangering the market that France had opened to American fishermen.[70] A "particular interest"—the Nantucket whalemen settled at Dunkirk—had been perpetually soliciting the French government to exclude the oil of those Americans who had not forsaken country and friends for foreign bounties, but France had resisted these pressures:

> The late Government there saw well that what we should lose thereby would be gained by others, not by themselves. And we are to hope that the present Government, as wise and friendly, will also view us, not as rivals, but as co-operators against a common rival. Friendly arrangements with them, and accomodation to mutual interest, rendered easier by friendly dispositions existing on both sides, may long secure to us this important resource for our seamen.

Using the same statistics and rephrasing the argument he had so recently employed in his appeal to Hamilton and in his report on the French protest against the tonnage acts, Jefferson emphasized that this was not in the interest of the fishermen alone: France was a market for a fourth of American tobacco, three-fourths of her livestock, an increasing proportion of her rice, a large amount of grain, and, in time, would be a market for ships, ship timber, potash, and peltry. France had met the United States in fair arrangements by treaty, whereas England had shown no disposition "to arrange this or any other commercial matter to mutual convenience." The loss of seamen, a natural consequence of British obstructions, called for timely attention. It would be too late, he argued, when the fisherman had changed his occupation "or gone over to another interest"—that is, the British side of the scales. To those who opposed retaliatory measures as being likely to result in commercial warfare, he argued in effect that the question was moot—such a conflict had already been initiated by the British:[71]

> The exparte regulations which they have begun for mounting their navigation on the ruins of ours, can only be opposed by counter-regulations on our part. . . . If regulations exactly the counterpart of those established against us, would be ineffectual, from a difference of circumstances, other regulations equivalent can give no reasonable ground of complaint to any nation. Admitting their right of keeping their markets to themselves, ours cannot be denied of keeping our carrying trade to ourselves. And if there be any thing unfriendly in this, it was in the first example.

Unlike Benjamin Austin, Jefferson did not point to the general agreement on the need for retaliatory measures that had led to the formation of a government capable of adopting them. Nor did he charge

[70] Document IX. TJ evidently added the statistics set forth in Appendix No. 4 in order to emphasize this point. He had particularly called the frauds to the attention of Washington during the preceding summer: "In France, where we have considerable privileges denied to the English, the government has been much perplexed and defrauded by British ships under false American colours. And these suspicions have produced embarrasments to vessels really ours" (see Document I in group of documents on consular establishment, under 21 July 1790). See also Fenwick to TJ, 2 Aug. 1790.

[71] Document IX.

that some in office now condemned measures they had once vigorously promoted. But his goal—"to force Gr. Britain by a navigation act, to come forward in fair treaty," as he expressed it a few weeks later[72]— was unmistakable. Nothing could have been less non-committal than the extraordinarily blunt words of the report.

Speaking as if for the administration, Jefferson confidentially explained his policy to the French chargé in the hope that concessions made by France to the American whale fishery would not be withdrawn. "Our object," he informed Otto, "is to establish a navigation act. . . . The House of Representatives having charged me to make a report on this subject has sufficiently declared its opinion, for my sentiments are known. I have particularly declared them in my report on the fisheries. . . . You may be certain that this great stroke will be carried in the next session."[73] With the publication of the report officially and in several other editions, including newspaper reprintings, those who had a few years earlier argued for retaliatory measures— Hamilton, King, Jay, and others—were left in no doubt about Jefferson's object. Indeed, they feared that his prediction about the great stroke was well-founded.[74] King endeavored to postpone action on the report to the next Congress.[75] Other supporters of Hamilton in the Senate were alarmed, for Jefferson as presumed head of "the French interest" seemed to be gaining an ascendancy in the administration—

[72] TJ to James Innes, 13 Mch. 1791.

[73] See Otto's account of the confidential conversation—more likely a transcription of a memorandum supplied by TJ—in his dispatch to Montmorin, 10 Mch. 1791 (DLC: Henry Adams transcripts; see also Editorial Note to group of documents on the French protest against the tonnage acts, under 18 Jan. 1791).

[74] On 5 Feb. 1791 the Senate directed 200 copies of the report to be printed (JS, I, 239). Childs & Swaine issued it under the title *Report of the Secretary of State, on the subject of the cod and whale fisheries, made conformably to an order of the House of Representatives of the United States, referring to him the representation of the General Court of the Commonwealth of Massachusetts on those subjects; February 1, 1791.* (Philadelphia, 1791); Childs & Swaine brought out another edition in 1792. Fenno issued the *Report* in pamphlet form and also published it, in somewhat delayed and fragmented form, in *Gazette of the United States,* from 4 May through 2 July 1791. The report appeared in Childs & Swaine's *New-York Daily Advertiser* in the issues of 22-25 Feb. 1791 (it was this version that Bond enclosed in his dispatch to Leeds of 14 Mch. 1791; PRO: FO 4/10, f. 183-200). TJ apparently did not retain a copy of the report in his own library, but it is almost certain that it was he who prompted the widespread public dissemination of the report (see note to TJ to Mason, 4 Feb. 1791).

[75] King did this under guise of correcting the journal of the Senate for 5 Feb. 1791 which had directed the report to be printed "for the use of the members of Congress" and which he claimed was an error. He desired the report to be postponed "to the 28th of December next, and corrected the minutes . . . to read so." Maclay thought this "not correcting matter of form, but total alteration and adjection of new matter." He opposed King and, though the alteration was adopted, it was "amended afterward and placed nearer the truth" (Maclay, *Journal,* ed. Maclay, p. 386). In 1786 Rufus King had "complained bitterly" to the French chargé about the exclusion of American fish from the French West Indies and, expressing regret that Congress lacked the ability to retaliate, had said that the United States would be willing to exclude Great Britain entirely if France would make concessions permitting trade with her islands (Otto to Vergennes, 20 May 1786; Arch. Aff. Etr., Paris, Corr. Pol., E-U., XXXI). TJ's report and its appendices showed what concessions France had made, but King, like Hamilton and others who had shifted positions, was now unwilling to make use of the power that had been granted.

indeed, to be aiming at the formation of a league with France and Spain.[76] Foreign observers confirmed their apprehensions. Phineas Bond, transmitting a copy of the report to the British government, saw it as an introduction to "a series of proceedings calculated to promote measures very hostile to the commercial interests of Great Britain." He interpreted the object of the report precisely as Jefferson had explained it to Otto. Besides revealing in form and scope Jefferson's policy of retaliation against Great Britain and his desire for a closer connection with France, it was also, Bond thought, "couched in a language of severity not practiced between nations at Peace with each other." He thought that the regulations advocated by Jefferson were such as a part of the administration was "anxiously disposed to promote." But the Lords of the Committee on Trade and Plantations, taking into account Madison's navigation bill, Jefferson's report on the French protest on tonnage, and especially Washington's message on the failure of Gouverneur Morris' mission, concluded that "the Executive Government of the United States are likely to give their whole Weight in support of such Measures, and that in the new elections . . . they will probably use their best Endeavours to obtain the return of such as are disposed to promote" them.[77]

Sir John Temple, like Bond and others, also perceived a calculated design on the part of the administration in the sequence of events beginning with the President's annual message. These moves, he thought, had "indeed caused a vast alteration in the minds and sentiments of the people in general," being apparently intended to leave the members of Congress with "impressions of coldness and dislike to Great Britain" as they returned to their constituents.[78] The French chargé was understandably as gratified as the British agents were alarmed. In an extended summary of the report, Otto declared that Jefferson had discharged his task "as an enlightened politician, a good patriot, and a man convinced that commerce with France was infinitely useful to the United States." He had not only done justice to the commercial favors granted by France, Otto thought, but, in pointing out that with two-fifths of total exports valued at $25 million being carried in British bottoms at an annual cost for insurance and freight of $2.25 million or an average of $1,392,857 more than Americans would have to pay transporting their own produce, he had expanded on the advantages that would be derived from a navigation act. This calculation, Otto concluded, "has caused a great sensation here."[79]

The extent of the sensation produced by this bold advocacy of a navigation act is indicated in part by the response that Jefferson knew would come from "a particular interest"—an interest centered in the

[76] See Editorial Note to group of documents on commercial and political relations with Great Britain, under 15 Dec. 1790, especially p. 238-43.

[77] Bond to Leeds, 14 Mch. 1791 (AHA, Ann. Rept., 1897, p. 477). The interpretation of Bond's letter by the Committee for Trade and Plantations is set forth in Cottrell to Grenville, 26 May 1791 (PRO: FO 4/10). For TJ's efforts to bring into Congress more representatives of the agricultural interest, see TJ to Mason, 4 Feb. 1791, and TJ to Innes, 13 Mch. 1791.

[78] Temple to Leeds, 19 Mch. 1791 (PRO: FO 4/9, f. 201-2).

[79] Otto to Montmorin, 6 Mch. 1791 (DLC: Henry Adams Transcripts).

Treasury.[80] One evidence of this appeared in the displeasure shown by two Senators toward Tench Coxe for his role in supplying Jefferson with information from the customs records.[81] But the most striking manifestation of opposition came from Hamilton himself, covertly as might have been expected but none the less revealing. On the 30th of December the House of Representatives directed the Secretary of the Treasury to report the amount of exports, the amount of duties paid on imports and on tonnage from 1 August 1789 to 30 September 1790, and, "as soon as may be," similar statistics for the last quarter of 1790.[82] This was probably at Madison's prompting and because of Jefferson's need for information going beyond the narrow limits of the fisheries and into the broad area of navigation and commerce. Hamilton immediately complied by submitting an abstract of duties on imports and tonnage.[83] This showed the tonnage of the fisheries and coasting trade but did not indicate the ports or countries to which vessels were cleared. However, the statistics were arranged by states and vessels were identified by countries of registry, thus permitting calculations to be made showing the proportion of American to foreign tonnage. Tench Coxe supplied Jefferson with supplementary information based on the Treasury returns.[84] He also transmitted to Madison for Jefferson's use a further analysis of these returns and an estimate of the number of seamen employed. Pointing out that a large proportion of American seamen had been British subjects, Coxe observed: "Should one third of our seamen appear to be drawn from Great Britain, these added to a proportion of landsmen would make the difference to them or us of ten or twelve sail of the line."[85] Jefferson went so far as to have one of his clerks transcribe the analysis, probably with the intention of adding it as an appendix to his report, but he did not include it. The bare tonnage statistics, which he presented in a greatly simplified form, showed Great Britain's share almost twenty times that of France. These figures, together with those showing "the mass of

[80] See TJ to Mason, 4 Feb. 1791; see note there.

[81] Coxe later told TJ that, shortly after the government moved to Philadelphia, he had expressed the opinion that the Secretary of State should stand second in line of succession to the Presidency, whereupon he was "called on next day by Mr. J. of the Senate and an earnest expostulation took place." He added: "Mr. Hamilton considered it as a preference of a person whom he called his Enemy. I found a like displeasure in two Gentlemen of the S[enate] who discovered . . . that I had contributed to the stock of information on which your report in favor of their own fisheries was founded" (TJ to Coxe, undated but evidently written early in 1801 when Coxe wrote numerous letters applying for public employment; DNA: RG 59, M/418; see also Editorial Note to group of documents on commercial statistics, at end of Jan. 1791). "Mr. J. of the Senate" was undoubtedly William Samuel Johnson. If the reference to "their fisheries" may be taken literally, the other two Senators were presumably Tristram Dalton and Caleb Strong of Massachusetts.

[82] JHR, I, 350.

[83] Secretary of the Treasury to the Speaker of the House, 6 and 7 Jan. 1791 (Syrett, Hamilton, VII, 418-19, 420-1; the enclosed abstract of duties paid on tonnage is printed in ASP, Commerce, I, 7-8; that for duties paid on imports is in ASP, Finance, I, 89).

[84] See Coxe's memoranda quoted in note to Document IX, Appendices Nos. 6 and 17; see also, Coxe to TJ, 27 and [30?] Jan., 1 Feb., and 15 Apr. 1791.

[85] See note to Document IX, Appendix No. 17.

Seamen . . . in distress," Jefferson observed simply, indicated "the materials for indemnification."

Even so, Jefferson particularly needed official statistics showing the amounts and kinds of exports. These were not forthcoming from the Secretary of the Treasury in response to the request of the House of Representatives. The session was far advanced when, on the 13th of January, Jefferson made his appeal to Hamilton for some concession to France and was refused.[86] That same day James Madison called at the Treasury seeking information from Tench Coxe in addition to that on imports and tonnage already sent to the House by Hamilton. Coxe sought an appointment at Madison's lodgings that night. Presumably the meeting occurred, for the next day he supplied further information to Madison, including a fairly accurate estimate of exports from Pennsylvania and returns relating to trade with France.[87] Perhaps at that time Jefferson also obtained from Coxe an abstract of exports of the American fisheries showing that France absorbed more than half of the whale oil and that the French West Indies took almost two-thirds of the produce of the cod fishery.[88] Within a few days he had received more complete returns covering a longer period of time and was able to present a detailed rather than a summary account of fishery exports to all countries.[89] Before the month was out he had also acquired statistics of American exports of livestock to the French West Indies amounting in value to three-fourths of the total exported to all countries. The source of this information Jefferson gave merely as "from Returns in the Treasury Office."[90] To this was added, in time to be included in his report, information about the amount of dried and pickled fish imported into the United States from British colonies. Figures were not available, however, to show the amount of whale oil brought in British bottoms into the United States "to be reshipped fraudulently . . . into ports where it could not be received" under the flag of Great Britain.[91] Statistics showing the value of all exports, the extent of American dependence on British vessels, and thus the amount "Taxed on . . . Agriculture by British Wars" could only be given on the basis of well-formed estimates made by Madison and Coxe.[92] Figures for the number and tonnage of vessels of all countries entering French ports from the United States and for American exports of flour to France were procured by Jefferson from French sources.[93]

It is obvious, therefore, that during the month that intervened between the time the House requested information from the Secretary of the Treasury and the completion of the report on fisheries, Jefferson gathered his most essential data on navigation and commerce not from his fellow Cabinet officer but through circuitous channels. Two

[86] See Documents VII and VIII in group of documents on French protest against the tonnage acts, under 18 Jan. 1791.

[87] Coxe to Madison, 13 and 14 Jan. 1791 (DLC: Madison Papers).

[88] Undated tabulation showing imports of products of the fisheries by France and the French West Indies as compared with the rest of the world (DLC: TJ Papers, 57: 9835; in TJ's hand).

[89] Document IX, Appendix No. 3.   [90] Document IX, Appendix No. 14.

[91] Document IX, Appendix No. 4; the quotation is from the text of the report.

[92] Document IX, Appendix No. 18.

[93] Document IX, Appendices Nos. 15 and 16. The returns of exports were being made up in the Treasury as early as November (see Document III).

weeks after he submitted his report, Hamilton handed in the abstract of American exports that had been requested a month and a half earlier. Its figures tallied exactly with those Jefferson, through indirect means, had obtained before the first of February. Clearly, had he been so inclined, Hamilton could have reported these statistics before that date. These facts, together with the resentment shown to Coxe by the two Senators for his role in making the figures unofficially available to Jefferson, confirm the supposition that the delay by the Secretary of the Treasury was deliberate.

The French chargé, pleased that "the friends of France" had come forward with a navigation bill aimed at Great Britain and that "the English party" had been defeated in their effort to have it referred to the Secretary of the Treasury, thought there was no doubt that Jefferson's policy would be supported. He believed that Hamilton, intentionally, had sought to discredit Jefferson's report by withholding essential information about the countries to which goods were exported.[94] The inference, based perhaps on an abbreviated newspaper summary, was unfounded.[95] But Otto, having the advantage of Jefferson's confidential conversation about his aims, penetrated the meaning of the report in a way that others did not. The "discussion of the navigation act, joined to the debates caused by Mr. Jefferson's report on the fisheries," he informed his government, "has divided the American government into two parties, one of which, directed by Messrs. Hamilton and R. Morris, tends to favor England, and the other, under the auspices of Mr. Jefferson and his friends, inclines toward France."[96] The report on the fisheries, with its bold declaration in favor of an American navigation bill to counteract that of Great Britain, did indeed give a powerful impetus to partisan conflict in the government, but not precisely in the sense that Otto understood it.

V

The division of opinion between those seeking a rapprochement with England and those who hoped, with Jefferson, to lessen American commercial dependence on a single nation had long existed within the government. What the report on the fisheries did was to force the contest into the open in a way that had not been possible theretofore. In calling for retaliatory measures against Great Britain, Jefferson in effect was abandoning such efforts as he made a fortnight earlier to seek an accommodation with Hamilton on the question of the French protest. As a realistic politician, faced by accumulating evidence of the tendency of Hamiltonian measures, he must have perceived that such hopes of unity were now illusory. His report on fisheries had the

[94] Otto to Montmorin, 6 Mch. 1791 (DLC: Henry Adams Transcripts).
[95] Hamilton's report of exports showed what countries received what goods (Secretary of the Treasury to the Speaker of the House, 15 Feb. 1791; Syrett, *Hamilton*, VIII, 39; MS of the enclosed table of exports from Aug. 1789 to 30 Sep. 1790 is in DNA: RG 233, 1st. Cong., H.R.; printed text in ASP, *Commerce*, I, 24-34). Newspapers, however, published only the quantity and value of each article, without indicating the countries importing American goods (Bache's *General Advertiser*, 2 Mch. 1791; Fenno's *Gazette of the United States*, 12 Mch. 1791). The newspaper version was the text submitted by Otto and by British consuls (Bond to Leeds, 14 Mch. 1791; PRO: FO 4/12).
[96] Otto to Montmorin, 10 Mch. 1791 (DLC: Henry Adams Transcripts).

sensational impact it did because it opened war on those largely un-
declared principles of administration which, in another context, he
would soon brand as political heresies.[97] The contest between Hamilton and Jefferson over the constitutionality of the bank bill, generally
accepted as the point at which parties began to coalesce under their
opposed principles, was in no public sense comparable to that induced
by the report on the fisheries. Their opinions on the bank bill, privately submitted to the President, did not bring them upon the public
stage as contestants in a divided administration.[98] The report on the
fisheries, on the other hand, was immediately and widely published in
the press. Even though Hamilton and his supporters made no overt
response to it—none could have dared to do so openly without risking
the disfavor of the President who had so strongly recommended that
encouragement be given to navigation and the fisheries—its meaning
was clear. As a reaffirmation of concepts of policy that had once provided so cohesive a force for national unity, the call for measures that,
in Hamilton's former words, could "incline the ballance of Europe,"
was no less a challenge because it could not be openly accepted. The
obligatory silence imposed upon those who had once employed similar
arguments to create a government strong enough to become the
"arbiter of Europe in America" could not conceal their awareness that
they had now been placed on the defensive. The sensations of alarm
created by the report were manifest in their urgent and covert appeals
to the British government to support its interest in the United States.[99]

The political nature of the report revealed itself similarly in its
sectional aspect. In this sense the conflict paralleled the sectional divisions that had marked the debates over the fisheries in 1781—but
now the roles of the North and the South were reversed. The Boston
merchants who in 1785 had made such a powerful appeal for national
unity in behalf of American navigation and the fisheries were, at this
time, focusing their attention almost wholly upon Hamilton's fiscal
measures. The point that Adams in 1782 had considered "so tender
and important that if not secured it would be the Cause of a Breach
of the Union" was not, at this juncture, the fisheries but the assumption of state debts and the settlement of accounts with the federal
government. Ames, Goodhue, Gerry, and other New Englanders, once
so eloquent in championing the distressed fishermen when only a
small duty on molasses was at stake, now received Jefferson's report in
silence. It was left to the two Virginians, one in the Cabinet and one
in the Congress, to reaffirm the obligation of the government to use
its powers in opening up free markets abroad. There can be little doubt
that both Jefferson and Madison sought to mobilize the southern representatives in support of their move for a navigation bill to aid the
fisheries and, of course, the agricultural exports. The immediate and
extensive publication of the report in the press suggests that such dis-

[97] Even before his famous note to the American printer of Paine's *The Rights
of Man* (see TJ to Jonathan B. Smith, 26 Apr. 1791), TJ had apprehended
"heresies preached now, to be practised hereafter" (TJ to James Innes, 13 Mch.
1791; see also TJ to George Mason, 4 Feb. 1791, mentioning a "sect" high in
office and its "heresies").

[98] See note to TJ's opinion on the bank bill, 15 Feb. 1791.

[99] See Editorial Note to group of documents on commercial and diplomatic
relations with Great Britain, under 15 Dec. 1790.

semination must have been inspired. Jefferson's effort to induce James Innes to become a candidate for Congress from Kentucky sufficiently testifies to the well-founded fears both of British agents in the United States and of Hawkesbury's Committee of the Privy Council for Trade and Plantations that efforts would be made to elect representatives favoring the principles that Jefferson had so bluntly stated.[100]

But nothing could more clearly reveal the reversal of the sectional roles on this issue or more precisely reflect Jefferson's perception of the political realities involved than his letter to Governor Hancock. That letter, on its surface, appeared to be nothing more than a polite transmittal of copies of the report on the fisheries, one of them directed to the committee of inquiry to demonstrate that Jefferson had not failed to present their testimony in a way that "might tend to procure a proper interference in this interesting branch of business." But in fact the letter was an appeal for political support from New England, whose representatives now appeared to have so little stomach for retaliatory measures and who believed that the Secretary of State, as one Senator expressed it, was "making every possible exertion to turn the commerce of this Country into the scale of France."[101] The letter to Hancock was a private one—Jefferson retained no copy of it in the departmental files in which he so scrupulously caused everything of an official nature to be recorded. In it he condensed the whole object of his report, his strong hint of sectional division on the issue, and his calculated political appeal into a single sentence:[102]

> From the disposition I see prevailing in the principal mass of the southern members to take measures which may secure to us the principal markets for the produce of the fisheries, and for rescuing our carrying trade from a nation not disposed to make just returns for it, I am in hopes something effectual will be done this session, if these principles are solidly supported by the members from your part of the Union, of which I trust there is no cause to doubt.

If Jefferson had actually believed that these principles would be supported by New England Congressmen, he would scarcely have expressed himself in these oblique and conditional terms. He no doubt was genuinely confident that the mass of the people—especially in the South where opposition to Hamiltonian measures had already become articulate—would support the measures he advocated. Even there, however, his inquiries of George Mason of Virginia and James Innes of Kentucky about the kind of reception a navigation bill would meet with in their states reveal some concern about the outcome.[103] He was too perceptive a politician, however, not to realize that the real danger of defeat would come from the North. It cannot be doubted, therefore, that his letter to Hancock was meant as both warning and appeal. The reversed attitudes of Northern representatives concerning the plight of the fisheries and the use of retaliatory measures must, for

[100] TJ to James Innes, 13 Mch. 1791.
[101] Memorandum of conversations between George Beckwith and various persons in government (enclosed in Beckwith to Grenville, 14 Mch. 1791; PRO: FO 5, 95/1). The Senator was probably William Samuel Johnson.
[102] Document X.
[103] TJ to George Mason, 4 Feb. 1791; TJ to James Innes, 13 Mch. 1791.

similar reasons, have been among the causes prompting Jefferson and Madison to make their Northern tour to gauge the political weather.

But out of the report on the fisheries there emerged one impressive and incontrovertible fact. Jefferson had declared his principles so clearly, emphatically, and publicly as to command attention on both sides of the Atlantic. None thenceforth could doubt that he stood on the same ground he had always occupied. The author of the eleventh *Federalist*, on the other hand, was confronted by a dilemma. Thrown on the defensive, he could not openly oppose these principles without standing self-confessed of having abandoned the position he had once defended in that powerful plea for national dignity and strength. Nor could he acquiesce without sacrificing his real objectives. Hamilton's response, therefore, was silence. Thus the partisan and sectional storms over the fisheries that had so greatly troubled the political seas when terms of the peace treaty were being debated were not to be resumed. Jefferson's open challenge, so alarming both to British representatives in the United States and to the defenders of the British interest in America, was not met in open debate. But Hamilton's hostility to the policies enunciated in the report was as ceaseless as it was covert. The metaphor that Jefferson once employed to describe the similar methods of Patrick Henry, another master of political deception, is singularly apposite. The minnows following in the wake of the whale that nourished them were mere parasites, Jefferson explained, but "the whale himself was discoverable enough by the turbulence of the water under which he moved."[104]

[104] TJ to Isaac Zane, 24 Dec. 1781.

I. The Governor of Massachusetts to the Secretary of State

SIR   Boston Oct. 25: 1790

Having laid your Letter of the 24th. of August last before the Legislature of this Commonwealth; an order passed that assembly appointing a Committee to meet as soon as may be, and consult, and determine the proper means of obtaining full, and authentic information respecting the Whale, and Cod fisherys as heretofore, and now carried on in this Commonwealth and to lay the same before the Governor, to be transmitted to you agreeable to your request. The Committee have since met, and made their report which is accordingly inclosed. The fisherys altho particularly beneficial to this State must at the same Time be of very great advantage, for obvious reasons, to the United States.—I flatter myself that due attention will be had to so interesting a Subject, and am with great Esteem, and respect Your obedient & very huml. Servt.   [JOHN HANCOCK]

FC (MBA). Recorded in SJL as received 22 Nov. 1790. Enclosures: (1) Resolution of the General Court of Massachusetts designating Peleg Coffin and others as a committee to gather information on the fisheries, 17 Sep. 1790. (2) Report of this committee to John Hancock, 13 Oct. 1790, printed below. (3) State of the cod fishery from 1765 to 1775 (for texts of this and following enclosure, see Report, Appendix No. 2). (4) State of the cod fishery from 1786 to 1790. (5) State of the whale fishery from 1771 to 1775 (see Report, Appendix No. 12). (6) Account of the whale fishery of Nantucket before and after the war, showing that from 1772 to 1775 there were 150 vessels having a tonnage of 15,000, employing 2,025 seamen and producing 30,000 barrels of whale oil, spermaceti oil, and headmatter selling at Nantucket at £22, £40, and £50 per ton respectively, most of which was exported to England. The Account further showed that in 1783 the Nantucket fleet had been reduced to 19 vessels having a tonnage of 1,485, employing 253 seamen and producing 2,649 barrels, with market values the same except that headmatter had increased to £60 per ton; that from 1784 to 1787 the fleet had averaged 28 vessels of 2,370 tonnage, employing 376 seamen and producing 4,813 barrels exclusive of headmatter, with Nantucket prices at £20 for whale oil, £20 for spermaceti oil, and £45 for headmatter; and that from 1788 to 1790 an average of 39 vessels having a tonnage of 4,207, and employing 349 seamen had produced 11,703 barrels, with a decline in prices to £13 per ton for whale oil and £50 per ton for headmatter, and no market at all for spermaceti. The account indicated that in 1788, 7,000 barrels of whale oil were exported to France and 1,620 barrels of spermaceti were shipped to France and London, while the next year the comparable figures were 6,000 and 2,897. In 1790 half of the production of the whale fishery remained on hand. This fact and the reduction in prices after 1783 were explained in the following marginal note: "The difference in the price of Spermo. Oil from 1783 to 1784 was Owing to the duty of £18-3-0 Sterlg. p Ton imposed on American (as foreign) Oil imported into the Ports of Great Britain. — Great Britain having lately prohibited the Importation of American Oil into their Ports, even in British Bottoms, there is therefore the greatest half Obtain'd on the present season now on hand."

ENCLOSURE

Peleg Coffin, Jr. and Others to John Hancock

SIR   Boston Oct. 13. 1790

Pursuant to a Resolution of the Legislature of Massachusetts passed the 17th Ultimo we have endeavoured to collect full and Authentic information respecting the Cod and Whale fisheries as heretofore, and now carried on in this Commonwealth. Your Excellency must be sensible that in executing the business assigned us we could derive no Aid from any Public office establish'd in this Government prior to the Revolution, neither can the present state of the Fisheries be accurately ascertained by recuring to the Offices now established under the Government of the Unites States; we were compelled therefore to rely principally for information on the recollection and Knowledge of men Conversant in the fishing business. The inclosed statements of the fisheries of this Commonwealth are the result of our enquiries from men whom we tho't best able to give us information on the subject—with such means of information we presume Accuracy cannot be expected—but we think the inclosed papers exhibit as true and exact a state of the fisheries as can at this time be Obtained.

After having collected and stated the Information requested by the Secretary of State, we beg leave agreeably to the direction of the

Legislature to mention to your Excellency some of the difficulties under which the fisheries of this State now labour, and the causes of the present decline.

Among the embarrasments of the Whale fishery, the regulation of the Government of Great Brittain may be considered as the principal cause of its present declension. When we were a part of the Brittish empire the Citizens of this State found a ready sale for all their Oil and Bone in the Brittish market. On the establishment of Peace the American Oil was subjected to a duty of Eighteen pounds three shillings Sterling ⅌ Ton when imported into the Brittish ports. To this discouragement has since been added a Prohibition of American Oil by the Brittish Government.

The liberal Bounties given by the Government of France and Great Brittain to those persons that shall prosecute the Whale fishery from their respective dominions has induced many of the Citizens of this and the other States in the Union enured to the danger and difficulty of encountering the Whale to remove with their families to France and Nova Scotia thereby contributing to the establishment of a fishery which if not counteracted we fear will rival the Whale fishery of the United States.

With respect to the Codfishery the following we think are the principal embarrasments.—The hostile disposition of the Algerines deprives the American fishery of a market in the Mediteranean which was formerly enjoyed.

The Prohibition of American Fish in the Brittish West India Islands.

The heavy duty heretofore imposed on American fish in the French ports in the West Indies.

The Bounties granted to the French and Brittish fishermen at Newfoundland.

The duty formerly imposed on the American fish in the French West India Islands has not been exacted during the last Year. This we are happy to observe has removed one principal embarrasment to the Cod fishery of this State, and should this regulation continue, will we think contribute to encrease the Cod fishery of the United States.

The Citizens of this State undoubtedly enjoy greater natural Advantages for prosecuting the business of the fisheries than any other People. The embarrasment and difficulties under which the business now labours is principally caused by the Political regulations of rival Nations. We must depend for relief on the power and disposition of Congress to counteract these regulations. When we consider the Importance of the Fisheries to the United States, as a Nursery for Seamen, which may be Necessary for the defence of Society in time of War, and facilitating the Exportation of their productions in time of Peace as creating a very considerable demand for the surpluss produce of the Country, thereby encouraging the Agriculture of the United States, we are led to hope that while other Governments are supporting their Fishery by Liberal Bounties, the Government of the United States will at least forbear imposing any duty of Tonnage, or any other duty on the Vessells employed or the Materials used in the American Fishery.

That your Excellency may have the happiness of Witnessing the

Prosperity of the Commerce, Fishery, and every other Interest of the People whom you Govern, is the wish of Your Excellencys Most Obedt. and most Humble Servants.

PELEG COFFIN Junr.
THOS: DAVIS
EBEN PARSON

NB Colo. Orne and Capt. Pearson two of the Committee were necessarily called from town before the copying of the papers but were present at the completion of the above business.

RC (MBA); in clerk's hand except for signatures; endorsed: "From the Committee to seek information respecting Cod & Whale fisheries. No. 2."

II. Tench Coxe's Notes on the Dutch and Prussian Fisheries

[ca. 23 Nov. 1790]

Notes on the Dutch Fisheries.
1st the Whale fishery.

The whale Fishery* was carried on previous to the year 1645 by the Groenland or northern Company, who had obtained an exclusive right from the Government for that purpose. Their charter expired in the Year 1741, after which the business declined so much, that the States found little enducement to renew the privilege, but declared the fishery in the Seas of Groenland and Davis's Strait a free trade.

From that period″ those enterprises became general, and were pursued by Individuals with great Spirit upon a new plan: for the company as well as other Nations had heretofore been accustomed to boil the oil on the coast and Bays, where the Fish was formerly caught in great abundance, for which purpose the necessary ware houses and apparatus were kept there; but as the whales became Scarce near the coast, the vessels were obliged to look for them among large fields of ice, many leagues from the Shore, and ever Since it has been the general practice to take the blubber in casks and to prepare the oil at home.†

* The Spaniards and the People inhabiting the Coast of the Bay of Biscay, were originally the first engaged in the whale fishery; from whom the dutch obtained their knowlege of that trade, by engaging some of the most experienced hands into their service.
″ From this fact may be drawn some conclusions against the expediency of commercial monopolies.
† The extraordinary goodness of the oil in the Southern whale fisheries however is said to be occasioned by the immediate extraction of the oil. In other Scenes they take every whale that offers, because they are scarce and have therefore frequently to employ several days in getting thro what have been sometime caught. But in the Southern Scenes where whales are plenty they take them

To give encouragement to this trade, the duties on imports, which had been imposed, during the existence of the company, were taken of from all the oil, blubber, whale bone, Sea horse teeth and Seal Skins imported: the experiment was well calculated to depreciate the Fisheries of other Nations and the Dutch soon experienced the advantage of the measure.§

In the Year 1750 several duties on Salt provision and beer were considerably reduced for the benefit of the Groenland and Davis's Strait fisheries;‡ and the Year following it was resolved, that in all cases where a vessel was lost, the duties which had been paid on the Stores of Such vessel should be returned.

In the Year 1775 a memorial was presented to the States general by a Committee from the principal persons engaged in the whale fishery, praying to be exempted from the duties on exportation* and that a premium of 40 guilders per head might be granted to each man, who should be employed on board of a whaling vessel. This memorial was under consideration 'till the year 1777 when a premium of 30 guilders, for a period not exceeding 2 years was allowed by government to each man so engaged; but the other point of having the duties″ on exportation remitted met with objections.

The very liberal bounties established in great britain in favor of their fisheries, and the effect it had produced, as will hereafter be shewn, were circumstances that could not but render a similar expedient in holland necessary and advantageous. The committee before mentioned represented in their memorial the necessity of it, in a Statement which furnishes *a perfect view of the Situation of the dutch and british fisheries in the Year 1775* in Substance as follows.

[The whale fishery is of great importance to holland, as the produce yielded by the Sea, may properly be considered as our Country produce,† which furnish employ for thousands of hands; all the apparatus being made and the vessels fitted out in our own country.

---

as they chuse and extract the oil of one before they catch another lest the oil from the death of the Animal should become rancid.

§ We have no duty on the imports, and should abstain from it, so far as regards our own at least.

‡ We have no duty on beer or salt provisions and the duty of the Salt is allowed on exportation. N.B. The duty on the Salt in the Stores of Vessels should be allowed on their departure with a fishing licence.

* We have not nor can we have a duty on exports by the Constitution.

″ See the duties page 13 [i.e., page 13 of MS; see below].

† It is in fact making something and that considerable—out of Nothing but— Labor or industry.

A new vessel from 110 to 116 feet,§ including
anchors cables rigging Sails &ca. cost from‡ 32 to 36000 guilders
    60 to 70 Lines, 6 or 7 *Sloops*,* Casks,
harpoons and other materials   8 to   9000
    Store rent, Lighters, victualing &ca.
for 42 *a* 48 men   4 to   5000

               Total"   44,000 to 50,000 guilders

From these outfits the country evidently derive real advantages, whereas those immediately concerned, risque their property, as has formerly been represented, that during a period of 47 years 14 millions† have been lost in this Traffick, besides the loss arrising from the decrease of Capital.§

The instances which have proved profitable to the owners are but few: greater losses are to be apprehended from the present high prices of all the necessaries and materials. To clear the expences of a voyage, each vessel must at least bring a return of 15,000 guilders exclusive of 1000 guilders for Insurance, besides the Yearly decrease of Capital, which may be calculated on an average at 30,000 guilders for every vessel completly equipped, making the Sum of 3,870,000 guilders for 129 vessels, which have been fitted out this present year, and which must each fetch out of the Sea 20 Tons of net goods to clear themselves: The prospect of doing this is very unfavorable, as all our neighbours use greater exertions in that trade than ever, to which they are encouraged by the aid of their respective governments, in particular the british who allow 40 Shilling Sterling per Ton (in 1775) to each vessel which is employed in the whale fishery, by which means the number of their whaling vessels have since the Year 1749 (when the bounty was granted) encreased from 2 to 109 vessels, which in the Spring 1775 sailed from England and Scotland, measuring in the whole 33,318 Tons, and amounting at 40 Shillings per Ton to £66,636—equal to 732,996 guilders, near 300,000 Dollrs. which amounts upon an average to 6725 guilders for each vessel.‡

The fisheries in Sweden and Denmark have also received additional Strength from the encouragements offered by their governments, without which they would have but little enducement to

§ about 350 Tons.
‡ On a medium 13800 Drs., a Dutch Ship of that size now would cost 21000 Drs. Our best live Oak 12500 Dollrs.
* These, it is presumed, are sloop-rigged open boats—i.e. pinnaces.
" On a medium 19000 Drs.
† Equal to 5,600,000 Dollars.
§ which being in ships, lines, casks and provisions must be very great.
‡ £1017 Pennsa. Curry. or near 3000 Drs. for a Vessel of 300 Tons: worth new here about 9 or 10,000 Drs. The best live Oak 10800 Drs.

that trade, so that instead of Holland formerly exceeding all the other Nation's together in the whale fishery, *they* at present exceed the dutch by one third in the number of vessels, nay England alone now sends out nearly as many vessels as Holland.

Another obstacle presents itself with regard to the whale bone trade. Of this article Holland formerly shipped 5/8 parts to great Britain, of which Sale we are now deprived, on account of the high duty imposed on all foreign whalebone imported into that kingdom and which may be considered as an additional premium on the Fishery of that nation amounting commonly to 50 guilders per 100 weight.*

Our exportation of whale oil is also on the decline. Hamburg and Bremen receive great supplies, partly from their own fisheries and partly from England and Russia, so as to be able to furnish the greatest part of Germany with that article. France and Spain are mostly supplied from England; and as it has been always computed that 3/4 of the product of our Fisheries are exported, the competition of those and other rival nations, will scarcely leave a foreign market for us: our own provinces and the river rhine will be our limits.

Another disadvantage ought not to pass unnoticed, which is that the prices of the produce of the fisheries are considerably reduced; The whalebone of the latest voyage having already been sold as low as 90 guilders" or less, which gives a loss. Oil may also, in case of a successful Season fall from 60 to 40 guilders per 12 Stekan (63 Gallons) and in that case vessels that return with one half or 2/3 of their cargo must sink money.

These are the most material circumstances, that impede the progress of our fisheries. The effect of the premium granted by the british parliament has already been severely felt by our groenland fleets, having since that period decreased one third in number."][1]

2dly Of the hering Fisheries

The vessels employed in this Fishery (Buizen) are from 40 to 60 Tons burthen, and cost new from 8 to 9000 guilders each.

8800ƒ equal to £800 Stg a Vessel of 60 Tons here worth on a medium new about £700 P.C.

Their outfits amount to about 6000 guilders for two voyages, or 3000 guilders per Voyage; for three voyages to 8000 each, or 2666 2/3 guilders each, and their complement of men is 13 or 14.

The hering Fishery is of less importance at present than it has been about a century ago, when 1500 vessels were employed;

* Equal to 20 Drs. per 100 ℔. Avoirdupois Value in the U. S. (   ) Dollrs.
" We sell as above mentioned at   Dollrs.

the number of vessels that are now in that trade is generally less than 200 annually. Notwithstanding it is said, that this business affords a Livelyhood for 20,000 Persons.

The following is a List of the number of vessels fitted out and in the hering fishery, vizt.

in the Year 1770	149 Buizen and 20 Yagers
1771	153	20	do.
1772	160	23	do.
1773	169	20	do.
1774	166	20	do.
1775	156	20	do.
1776	179	22	do.

As an encouragement to that trade, the States granted by a resolve of the 19th may 1775 a premium of 500 guilders to each vessel, for and during the term of two Years; and after the expiration of the said term, a premium of 400 guilders was allowed for another two Years to each vessel employed in that trade. But from the bad practice by persons frequently receiving the bounty, without sending their vessels again in that trade the second year, it was to be expected that some alterations would take place, which has happen'd since, the bounty being discontinued.

There are several good regulations in Holland respecting the hering trade, which are strictly observed. *The assorting, packing and pickling* is done in the open air, *by sworn Inspectors*. The casks are *branded* with different marks, according to the several kinds and qualities, which are distinguished by the time when they were caught, whence they receive their particular denomination. The season for the hering Fishery commences on the 24th. of June, before that time, no vessel is allowed to throw a net.†

Prussian Fishery

At Emden there is a Company who employed in the Year 1784 forty-three vessels in the hering Fishery, measuring 2560 Tons.

Of the yearly profits a certain sum is appropriated to the building of a few new vessels, which they annually add to their number.

The Stocks of the Company sold at that time at 220 guilders; their dividend has of late been 5, 6 and 7 percent, which might be higher, if the management was made less expensive, as the King presents the establishment with the yearly sum of 10,000 Rixdollar (7,500 Spanish Milld Dollars)§

---

† In the Laberdan or large pickled Fishery on the coast of Iceland were employed in the year 1763, 148 vessels, in 1768, 160 do. in 1773, 107 do.; 1775, 78 do.; 1776, 36 do. It is supposed in Holland that the declension of this trade was caused by the aid given to the British Fisheries in Parliamentary Bounties.

§ Equal to 3 dollars ℔ Ton on the whole of their Vessels.

Herring is sold in Holland and other northern Seaport towns by the Last and Barrels. A Last is 12 Barrels. A Barrel contains from about one thousand to twelve hundred herings, which depends upon the Size; Yet no regard is paid to the number contained in a Barrel.

The dutch hering of the first run is the smallest but at the same time by far the fattest.‡ This kind is caught from the 24th. of June to   July. The fleets dispatch their Yagers with all possible speed to the principal Seaport towns, where those first at market sell their cargoes at a high price, which is generally in all July. Immediately after the price settles itself, yet differs every year. In a price Currt. from Hamburg of August 1785 I find the following

			our money
Full hering from Holland	5 Dollars Currt. per Barrel equal	4¼ Dollars
Matjes*	do.	4 Dollars	3⅜ do.
Swedish		4 Dollars	3⅜ do.
Norway	4 a 5 Dollars	3⅜ to 4¼

This is nearly the lowest rate: in some Years the prices have been from 50 to 75 pCt. higher.

Duties on certain Articles, the produce of the Fisheries in Holland.

	Duties on importation	Duties on exportation
on foreign hering per Last of 12 Barrels	18 florins	18 ƒ
on hering of the dutch fishery	free	free
on Smoaked hering or bucking from Great Britain per Last of 12,000	7½ ƒ	1½ ƒ
Ditto from other foreign Countries per ditto	7½ ƒ	5 ƒ
Ditto dried in the Country per Last of 10,000 or 20 Straw		1½ ƒ
on all pickled fish, Cod &ca. of home fishery per Last of 12 Barrels	free	—
on foreign ditto	18 ƒ	—
on all ditto whether foreign or dutch per ditto		1½ ƒ
on Salmon pickled dried or Smoaked of the value of 100 florins	4 ƒ	1½ ƒ
on Cod fish dried per 100 ℔	1 Stuiver	2½ Stuiver
on Seahorse teeth of the home fishery per 100 ƒ	free	2 ƒ
on ditto from foreign fisheries do	8½ ƒ	2 ƒ
on whale bone, home fishery do	free	2½ ƒ
on ditto, foreign do	10 ƒ	2½ ƒ
on ditto Splitt do	12 ƒ	2 ƒ
on Whale oil, Seal or blubber of the home fishery per Quardel or 63 Gallons	free	10 Stuivers
on Ditto do foreign	3 ƒ	10 Stuivers

‡ Is this the Case with our fish?   * An inferior kind.

A View of the Groenland Fishery from the Year 1768 to 1777

	Number of Vessels	Number of Fish	Casks of Blubber	Quardels of Oil	Number of Vessels lost	Price of Whale oil	Price of Whale bone
1768	123	392 5/6	9,428	14,210.	5	62.64.48.54.	160.180.120.150.
1769	111	972 1/2"	18,784	28,461	4	54.40.45.	160.110.140.
1770	105	438 1/2	11,319	16,738		45.54.48.	140.156.150.140.
1771	110	105 2/3"	3,319	4,728	4	50.70.72.	125.176.150.
1772	93	546 1/12	15,442	23,335	2	80.53.50.60.	130.110.120.
1773	91	195	8,443	12,460	5	69.50.58.66.	135.117.114.
1774	82	281	9,158	13,680		66.60.64.	110. 90. 95.
1775	88	86"	3,055	4,541	5	65.85.80.	100.130.110.
1776	84	365	8,464	12,768	2	80.60.63.	90. 95. 90.
1777	75					60.62.57.	.87. 90.100.
						guilders per 63 Gallons	guilders per 100 ℔.

" From such variations the trade appears extremely precarious, which must render such long voyages and expensive outfits very distressing to the concerned.

of the Davis's Strait Fishery

	Number of Vessels	Number of Fish	Casks of Blubber	Quardels of Oil	Vessels lost
1768	36	207 1/2	8,729	12,812	
1769	42	155 1/2	6,899	10,009	
1770	45	85 1/2	3,815	5,547	1
1771	40	38	1,808	2,557	
1772	38	239 1/2	10,350	14,738	
1773	43	249 1/2	10,414	15,006	1
1774	48	179	7,821	11,313	2
1775	47	19	961	1,373	
1776	39	144 1/2	6,353	9,278	
1777	45	178	8,007	11,756	1

Prices of whale Oil in Hamburg

1785				Our money	
from Bergen in Norway	88	mark Curr'y per 63 Gallons equal		24¾ Dollars	
Hamburg	116	do.	do.	32⅝	do.
England	110	do.	do.	31	do.
Lissabon	90	do.	do.	25¼	do.
Archangel	96	do.	do.	27	do.
Swedish	84	do.	do.	23⅝	do.

MS (DLC: TJ Papers, 69: 12013-21); in clerk's hand except for marginal notes in hand of Tench Coxe and one note in TJ's hand (see note 1, below); endorsed: "[* *] On the Fisheries of the Dutch & Prussians"; undated, but evidently written shortly before Coxe enclosed it in his letter to TJ of 23 Nov. 1790, wherein he identifies it with the double asterisks employed in the endorsement and describes it as "a paper translated, in abridgment, by a very well informed and judicious German merchant from a Dutch Book, which he assures me is to be relied on." TJ's extract as identified in note 1 was submitted with his Report as Appendix No. 13 (see note there for description of texts of extract).

¹ The passage enclosed in brackets

(supplied) was marked off in pencil by TJ, who placed the following marginal note at head of the quotation: "Extract from a Memorial presented to the States General in 1775 by a Commee. of the merchants engaged in the Whale fishery"; (see Document IX, Appendix No. 13).

III. Tench Coxe's Notes on the American Fisheries

[ca. 23 Nov. 1790]

Since the discovery of the Compass every nation, adjacent to the Ocean, has manifested great and constant solicitude about the fisheries within their intermediate reach; and the skillful and enterprizing have extended their views to the most remote foreign Scenes. The two greatest naval powers of Europe have discovered very high ideas of this object by their free use of bounties and prohibitions, by encouraging the prosecution of it on the distant coasts of the United States, though separated from them by 3000 miles of a great Ocean, and by the most jealous attention to the otherwise worthless territories, which are in some degree the foundation of their respective rights, because they are useful to their fishermen. Facts like these afford sufficient admonitions to institute a close and judicious investigation of the Subject to a people as observing and to a government as vigilant as those of the United States. By such an enquiry we may learn how far our own immediate interests require the pursuit and how far policy forbids the relinquishment or neglect of the object.

It will be found useful to begin with ascertaining on certain ground, the principal facts which relate to the fisheries of the United States. The returns of exports now making up at the Treasury will assist in estimating the value of the commodities, which we draw from the water.* On these returns, it is to be remarked, that there should be a deduction of the piscatory Articles imported from foreign Countries. To make up the aggregate value of the commodities we derive from the fisheries we ought to add an estimate of that portion of them, which is never entered in the United States being carried immediately from the Scenes of the fisheries to foreign Markets; and a further estimate of the value of the commodities, which being consumed in our families,

* See the returns, paper A. [See Document IX, Appendix No. 3.—Ed.]

manufactories and public establishments, cannot appear in our list of exports.

A return of the vessels licensed to carry on the fisheries would help further to discover the importance of this object. It would shew how much tonnage, how much capital, and how many men must be employed and how many families of the Merchants and Mariners concerned must derive subsistence, comfort or wealth from the fisheries. The contiguity or nearness of some of the greatest fishing banks and waters in the world to our coast, when compared with their distance from the ports of the two European Nations, that have a right to fish in those Scenes, are advantages that need but to be suggested. Were other things only equal the competition there must from this circumstance eventuate in our favor; And in regard to the whale fisheries which are not on or near our coasts, it may be safely affirmed, that they are on a medium as convenient to the Citizens of these States as to those of any European Country; and consequently in the foreign, we have no particular inconvenience *arising from the situation*, to sustain in the competition with the other Maritime Nations.

The cost of Vessels, which are the great fishing instruments, is manifestly worthy of notice and here facts are much in favor of the United States. Our Merchant Ships, *fitted for taking in a Cargo*, compare with french, dutch and british Oak Ships as follows:

The prime live Oak and Cedar Ships of the United States

	♉ Ton	34 to 36 Drs.
The white Oak Ships of Do.	♉ do.	24 to 32
Those of france	♉ do.	54
Those of Great Britain	♉ do.	54 to 58
Those of the United Netherlands	do.	58 to 60

The common Oak Ships of the United States last from 12 to 20 years, if employed in the fishing trade, and from 8 to 15 Years in common Trades. As substitutes for these France might have recourse to purchases of us, which however is not yet the case or to Baltic Fir and Larch ships, which cost 32 to 34 Dollars ♉ Ton and last in common trades about seven years, but longer when employed in the Fisheries. England might do the same, but at present British built Ships alone are entitled to the enormous bounties, and the benefit of the restrictions and prohibitions imposed on foreigners, by which they support their fisheries. It is evident that by this rejection of the use of foreign built vessels the English Fisheries are so far sacrificed to their *manufactory of*

Ships. The same thing is observable in regard to the carrying Trade under the laws of that Nation.

The skill and activity of our Mariners and the capacity of our Vessels and (in the words of the Art) "their Excellency as *Sea boats*" exceedingly decrease the risque and produce an expedition that is very œconomical, and consequently profitable in a business, the whole outgoings of which are contingent expences.† In these particulars we have greatly the advantage of the English, and the deficiency of the French in activity, together with their want of Skill in Navigation, removes all apprehension about success in an equal Competition with them.

The Casks in which pickled fish, Oil &ca. are put are much cheaper in the United States than in France, Holland or England, which being a constant charge operates to render the neat profits greater to our fishermen than to theirs. The price of a white oak barrel, fit to hold pickled fish is in Great Britain and Ireland 3/6 to 6/ Stg. and in New England at a medium only 1/9 Stg. This difference upon Oil and fish worth on an average 18/Stg. is a saving to us, or an extra profit of 16. to 20 ₩ Cent.§

The portion of the fishing business carried on in the winter by the Eastern States is in some degree on the footing of a domestic Manufacture, which are most useful employments and exceedingly promotive of Industry. Small vessels are often owned by three and four persons, who navigate them with their Sons. They come in with their little cargoes salted down in the hold of vessels, and leaving them with their women and children to complete the curing, proceed to sea in quest of more. Their Bank fisheries are also by short runs from home, and equally short ones back in vessels of 60 to 90 Tons. Instead of this British and French Ships require the advances of large capitals, and are conducted by Masters, Mates and Petty Officers, hired at a great expence.

Such of our fishermen as are employed in taking small fish,

---

† (Note) The Exports from Great Britain in the Greenland fishing Vessels in 1780 were no more than £70 stg. and the imports amounted to £38.000 stg. That fishery was begun about 1720, and was trifling at first

in 1740 it produced £2800.　Exports that year £900
in 1750　　　　　　10.000.　　do. in that year　200 stg.
in 1760　　　　　　16.000.　　do.　　　　　　330
in 1770　　　　　　22.000.　　do.　　　　　　60
in 1780　　　　　　38.000　part of this was probably the extra war value.
[Playfair]

§ It is asserted by Champion that the cost of supplies to the British Ship at Newfoundland if from the United States are four parts in seven of the Cost of the same if from G Britain. The following facts confirm this assertion—
a barrel of pork in the U. S. 36/ stg. in G. Brit. 41 to 45/ in Holld. 50 to 53 f.
do. medium beef in Do. 27/ to 30/ .... 41 to 47/ ...... 45 to 46/6
a hundred wt. of Shipbread 8 to 10/ .... 15 to 16/
Casks as stated † [see preceding note—Ed.]
Rum less than half price—also melasses—

vizt. Mackrell, Alewives, Manhaiden &ca. run into Port on an approaching Storm, and consequently in those instances avoid the risque, which is in effect making a saving in the article of insurance, while their foreign Competitors are Subject to a Monthly premium from the time of their leaving one European Port, thro the whole of the fishing Season, 'till their arrival in another. This is rather a minute observation perhaps, but it encourages the poor in the prosecution of the business, and consequently keeps up the inclination and the habit.

It may appear perhaps at first view that we obtain our Salt upon worse terms than the European Nations, but this is not altogether the fact. The Commodities of the United States being generally unmanufactured and bulky the vessels that carry them abroad do not on a medium bring back a sufficiency of imports to *balast* them. We Ship less to Great Britain than to France or Spain, and we import more from thence; yet fine Salt and Coals are frequently the sole return Cargo, and the vessels never are filled with them. To France, Spain and Portugal we send many more vessels than to Great Britain and we import from them in the Aggregate, less than from the latter only; hence we very often find Vessels with a mere balast of salt returning from the three former kingdoms which manufacture it in great quantities. It is very beneficial to the timbers, and easily put in and out, and is upon the whole, an agreable cargo to owner and Seamen. It is so cheap that funds are never wanted to buy it, for the outward freight money alone is always sufficient to purchase more than a Ship can carry.

The English encourage their Newfoundland fisheries by
1st. A prohibition of all foreign piscatory articles.
2ndly. By Bounties of £25 to £50 Sterling ℔ man in the first 100 sail that take the first trip or fare 10.000 fish (equal to 500 Quintals) and then make a second trip. This is equal to £370 Stg. for a vessel that may not take more than 800 Quintals in the two trips, and will buy a New England Schooner of 80 tons that will in three of their fares take that quantity! For the second 100 sail they give Bounties of £18. to £19 to £35. Stg. equal to £260 Stg."

It may be of use to mention some of their regulations.

They prohibit fishing with Nets whose Meshes are not four inches wide.

They swear the Master of every Vessel to these facts—that the Oil is of Sea Animals and that it and the fish were taken by British

---

" Besides these immense bounties from 7 to 9/ ℔ bble of 50 Gallons have been granted to encourage the pilchard fishery and to vessels employed in the white herring fishery a large bounty. A reference to the British statutes will shew these grants and their variations from time to time.

built vessels, man'd ¾ by subjects of Britain usually resident in Europe and having a british Captain, or by british Subjects on the Shores or banks.

They inflict penalties on Seamen who absent themselves from fishing vessels.

They give the first class of bounties to men that go out on shares without wages.

They confine the advances to Seamen in this Trade at all times to one half of what is due 'till their final discharge at the end of the Season and Voyage, except in the case of "*green hands*" whose outfit may actually require more.

The use of the gun Harpoon in the whale fisheries merits attention. An account of this Invention and the experiments made with it are inserted in the Memoirs of the London Society of Arts, Manufactures and Commerce.

The emancipation of the human mind from religious Slavery seems to threaten the Cod fishery with the loss of those consumers, who eat fish to make themselves fit for divine worship. The banishment of pious follies from the great kingdom of France ensures the progressive extinction of superstition in Italy, Portugal and Spain. But on the other hand liberty in those Countries will introduce or extend the commercial spirit and manufactures among 50 Millions of people, and will call for much additional food and raw materials. Our Skill in Seamanship and the cheapness of our vessels give us reason to expect that we shall do much of the fishing business that will be necessary to procure the Supplies for such a demand. The more Manufactures extend beyond the Sphere of the *British* and *Dutch* Dominions, the greater will be our chance of a Market for such piscatory Articles as they require—for tho the latter do not prohibit, they rival and interfere.

The use of fish-Oil in France for lighting their cities will add greatly to the Market for the produce of the Whale fishery; but it is needless to enlarge on this topic, as no information can be given on a point that is accurately understood already.

If we enumerate the ordinary modes of promoting national Shipping and of enlarging the nurseries for seamen, we find they are

1st. the coasting trade.

2ndly. the trade with transmarine colonies.

3dly. the fisheries.

4thly. the carrying trade for other Nations, including the carriage of supplies to their Markets from our ports.

We have been too well instructed that the latter is not at our command further than it may be the precarious pleasure of foreign Nations to admit it. Of the second we do not possess, nor probably for many years shall we have any. The coasting trade is valuable, as the English Colliers and our numerous little coasters prove. But the whale, bank, bay and river fisheries are our greatest *certain* dependence. *Probabilities* are much in favor of our having a considerable share of the carriage of our own produce to Foreign Countries; but *the certainties* are greater in the case of Fisheries. To these remarks we may add that the nations which have figured most in private Shipping, fleets of ships of war, seamanship, and naval tactics have sedulously cultivated the fisheries and perhaps we may say that no Modern nation, that are not conspicuous as fishermen, have ever been eminent in the above respects.

The fisheries not being *the traffic in* but the creation of commodities by personal and manual operation, it seems almost proper to class them amongst the manufactures of our Country. If they may be placed with propriety under that head then it may be remarked that they are freer from the principal charge against the useful Arts than any other, vizt. that they tend to promote debility in their pursuers. Those who carry on the whale fishery are remarkably healthy, robust and active.

It may not perhaps be deemed a refinement if the fisheries should be recommended to public countenance, because they keep our rivals and competitors from rearing and employing so many more Seamen. For it is manifest that were the vessels, which we employ in all the fisheries, to be turned into other trades, and were the consumers which we supply with piscatory articles to be without our commodities, a greater number of British, Dutch and French Vessels and Sailors would be employed in the business. If we mean to pay any attention to Naval Objects, this consideration will not be found destitute of weight. It may be further remarked that our most severe restrictor, the most selfish conservator of rival commercial interests, will be the most likely to feel the favorable effects of a negligence of the fisheries on our part. And moreover in time of war they and all Nations will fear us in proportion as we preserve our nautical skill and abilities, for our distance from Europe will render the Ocean in a great degree our scene of military action.

It is said in England that the fisheries are more disadvantageous from their precariousness in some seasons than from their want of a medium profit thro' a series of years. Here then we have a considerable advantage in the Cod fisheries over the Europeans. They are obliged to come out in vessels of 200 Tons on an average, subject to insurance and other heavy charges, and if they do not succeed in their fares they lose their whole Expences. A great part of our fisheries is carried on in smaller, cheaper and less expensive vessels, three of which do not exceed the above number of Tons. Having a very short run out to the Banks and back again, they are very rarely so unfortunate as not to make a saving Voyage.

It will not be easy to procure a correct Statement of our former fishing trade. The returns, that may be obtained from the New England States, particularly the three Eastern ones, will give some idea of its situation prior to the revolution. Champion, de Warville and Sheffield may also be examined with due allowances. The former, whose prejudices are not against the United States, informs us, that by a Statement of Mr. Brooke Watson, a Member for London in the british House of Commons the number of Vessels employed in the *Whale fishery* in the year 1764 by the present United States was 150 Sail, in *the Cod fishery* 300 Sail, and in *the Mackarel fishery* 90 Sail. Watson is not to be suspected of over rating our importance, but he had opportunities and judgement enough to be relied on, excepting only the influence of the prejudices incident to his situation. I do not know how far these might be justly imputed to him. Champion states a wonderful encrease of the fisheries in the peace subsequent to the treaty of 1762. He supposes that 500,000 Quintals of Codfish and 53000 barrels of pickled fish were taken in 1772 by vessels belonging to the then british Colonies. The writers concerning those times say that Nantucket had from 140 to 200 Sail of Vessels and from 2000 to 2500 Seamen, and that their fisheries were worth £40,000 Sterling, and Marthas Vineyard 200 Sail and 2000 seamen.

It is asserted by some of the writers, that a British Whalemans expence is about £10 Stg. per Annum, which considering the coarseness of his Cloathing, his living on Fish of his own catching thro a great part of the year and free from house rent on Ship board, is not improbable; and that his earnings to himself and the Nation are £30. Sterling ℔ Annum.

The Paper [* *] contains some Account of the fisheries of the United Netherlands and the Prussian Port of Emden. With the facts and observations on the former, which are extracted from a Dutch work of considerable reputation, are intermingled some comparative remarks on the British regulations and fisheries. They are now furnished with a view to aiding in the complete developement of the Subject. From the admissions of this work, in regard to the Dutch, from similar admissions of Mr. Playfair in regard to the british and from general reasonings founded on the bounties, premiums, prohibitions, duties and restrictions by which these two Nations and the french support their fisheries, as also from a comparison of the value of these several grants and sacrifices with the actual produce of their fisheries there appears satisfactory reason to believe that neither of those three Nations make any Mercantile profit out of this branch of their Commerce. Should this be the case it is manifest that these direct and indirect expences add greatly to the positive expence of their Naval Armaments and Marine Wars, and that they raise new questions concerning their actual benefits from the carrying trade, seeing that their Navy and Merchant Ships are manned with Sailors produced at so great an expence. We ought to ask, if America also loses money by the fisheries, whether extreme measures to support them ought to be adopted should we deem a navy immediately necessary. On the other hand should we find that the fisheries are a source of actual profit to us alone we should comfort ourselves with the reflexion that we are in no danger of being outstript in a competition which is partly on our own Coasts, and which proves a losing business to our rivals.

From the view of the subject, which is presented in the foregoing observations and collection of facts, tho much unconnected, may be deduced the following means of improving, promoting and encouraging the fisheries of the United States. As these are the ends of the investigation, no reserve will be used in the suggestion of such as have *the color of expediency*, since the consideration which they are to undergo will ensure the rejection of those, which are of too small or of doubtful propriety, or which are likely to be injurious.

Those which occur are

1st. An advance of the allowance on the Salt exported in fishing Vessels, under due securities and regulations, instead of paying it six months after the exportation of the fish. The object of this is to aid the fishermen particularly the poorer part of them, by affording the immediate use of funds (the value of the Salt) which government is not to retain, but they or their successors in the ownership of the fish are finally to recover. The regulations may be so formed, that the salt duty on that part which shall be consumed at home, will be secured. If salt free of duty be estimated at 16 Cents, then when the new impost of 12 Cents shall be in operation, it may be estimated at 28 Cents, so that a fisherman, who could only take 100 Bushels without the advance of the allowance, might with it take 175 bushels. If vessels are lost, as the law now stands, they lose the allowance, i.e., pay the duty *without consumption*, which really is hard.

2ndly. The duty on that part which should be consumed at home might be relinquished by Government and would promote the consumption of salted and pickled fish. This should be well considered, however, as it involves the principle of inequality. The consumers and fishermen would probably divide the profit, but the non consumers, that is the body of agriculturalists, would not have a corresponding advantage. The best lights in which to place it are 1st. in that of a very moderate premium to encourage the fisheries, and secondly, a moderate premium to encourage the use of fish.

3rdly. Exempting fishing vessels from the Tonnage of 6 Cents. It has ever appeared to me, as inexpedient to lay any duty upon American Vessels, as upon American Working Waggons. It is taxing the transportation of our produce. A principal Argument in my mind has been that tho' as beneficial a difference between foreigners and our own Vessels would be made, it would appear to them more moderate. But this by the way. The question now is, whether *fishing vessels* and they *alone* can expediently be exempted; if not alone, then how far the exemption may be extended.

4th. The Casks that contain our pickled fish should be uniform and should be reduced (if larger than foreign) to the size of those foreign Casks, which are of most established reputation in the Markets where they and we compete. This honest œconomy would be an actual profit. Thin Staves make a tighter barrel than thick which we use, but more wood might be applied in the hooping than is our Custom. If on the other hand our Casks are too small they should be enlarged, as we shall suffer in reputation otherwise, and the known faults of commodities always produce a double loss to the seller.

5th. A Strict and uniform inspection, at the moment of Shipment, of the Casks, their Size, quality and condition and that of the fish in all essential particulars, and the branding every Cask with "the *United States*" would, if the inspectors should be honest and judicious, prove advantageous to the reputation of the commodities, and consequently beneficial to the fisheries. From experience I know the advantage Pennsylvania has derived from an honest and judicious inspection as well of her own produce as of the Article of Tobacco, tho' the latter has no legal establishment. Ireland also remarkably proves the Utility of a nice Inspection in her wet provisions.

6th. The attainment and communication of the knowlege of the best methods of pickling, curing and preserving fish, extracting and purifying Oil, and such other things as by inhancing the value of piscatory articles encrease the profits of the fisheries. A few Herring-curers from Holland would be a valuable emigration to New England. It appears from the Dutch publication abovementioned, that they borrowed their first information from a few Biscayans. This object seems a very proper one for individuals largely interested in the fisheries, yet if the Legislature should venture to grant a premium for anything relative to this branch it may be doubted whether a fitter Subject for reward than the introduction of Skilful Curers will present.

7thly. The introduction of improvements, by invention and importation, in the mode of fishing, and of implements that facilitate and give certainty to the business. The British *gun-Harpoon*, for example, is said to be very useful and is unknown in our practice. Where Whales are scarce, it enables the fishermen to strike them at a greater distance, by which they may often take a fish that will never be seen again by the same Vessel.

8thly. Promoting the consumption of the produce of the fisheries. Associations are a precarious mode, yet they give animation to the pursuers of an Object. The revenue Cutters, Ships of war, and troops on the Atlantic waters might without inconvenience be made to use fish as far as a fourth or a third of the animal food of which their rations are in part composed. The same idea may be applied to military and Naval assylums, when established, with such exceptions as medical advice should prescribe. The aged and maimed could not be injured by this kind of food, though the diseased and recently wounded generally would.

To draw into due public notice the actual cheapness of this kind of food compared with the flesh of land animals. The Table of prices is made up to elucidate this idea, and to shew the degree in which the fact exists. Tis plain that the prices of meat would be reduced by the use of fish in all families, that live near the Seaports, and that in those populated Scenes the price of labor and consequently of building, manufacturing &ca. would be reduced.

Since fish is a cheaper food than Butchers Meat, the Legislature might safely require that every American Vessel should take among her Sea Stores every fourth, fifth or sixth barrell of pickled fish, or 200 ℔. of dried fish as an equivalent. If some principal seaport (not interested in the fisheries) such as New York, Baltimore or Philadelphia could be brought to petition Congress on this subject upon the principle of encouragement to the fisheries, as our great marine nursery it would have a good effect in removing any doubts that might exist about the acceptation of such a measure.

A very considerable aid to the fisheries is even now derived from manufactures. Whalebone Cutters, Makers of Stays, Whips, Umbrellas, Fishing tackle, Millinary, Philosophical Apparatus, and other Articles, now use Whalebone; Ivory turners use the Sea Horse teeth; Druggists, Instrument and Watch Makers, sadlers, Shoemakers, Tanners, Hatters and others use the Skins and furs of various sea animals; Shipbuilders, Riggers, Soap and Candle makers, Leather Dressers and others use the Oils and Spermaceti; and our Towns and the Houses of Laborers and Manufacturers are lighted by the Oils. It is moreover true that large quantities of pickled and dry fish are used in our Towns by the workmen, in our Shops and factories. The extension of Manufactures, therefore, the encrease of Manufacturing Citizens, and the creation and growth of Manufacturing Towns are objects, the promotion of which will also greatly promote the fisheries by affording them a capital market for their various articles subject to no duties, very small charges of transportation, insurance &ca. even in time of war, and out of the reach of foreign caprice, jealousy, restriction and prohibition.

Before we pass from this point it may be well to advert to the utility of promoting by all due means those particular branches of Manufacture which are subservient to and requisite in conducting the fisheries. The encouragement of Ship Building, the care of the raw material, *timber* the growth of Hemp and flax for the Manufacturing of Sail Cloth and Cordage, lines, twine and Netts, coarse iron manufactures such as Anchors, harpoons, gigs, nails, Spikes and bolts are what are particularly contemplated here.

And further—the establishment of *the manufactory of fine and coarse Salt* on the coasts of the United States which would be in peace a considerable aid, and in the time of war infinitely important to the fishing branch of commerce.

9thly. The Prohibition of British piscatory Articles, or in more general terms, of the piscatory articles of those Nations that prohibit ours in ports whereto they admit our vessels. In general duties, equal to a prohibition, accompanied with a drawback appear better, than actual prohibitions, because they leave scope for advantages to be obtained in the foreign trade in the Articles. In this case however the prohibition seems most politic because we are distressed to find foreign Markets for our piscatory Articles and therefore ought not to aid in promoting the interference of theirs. The Nova Scotians &ca. cannot supply Cattle, Lumber and Vegetables to make up, with fish, Cargoes for the french Islands, for example, as we do; nor can they make, with equal advantage, the dryfish Voyage to Europe. The consequence is, that they use our channels of vents for their fish by sending them hither, and giving them an opportunity of being exported with a drawback on as good terms as our own. To deprive them of this privilege would discourage much the fishing spirit in the actual inhabitants of the Northern British Colonies, and probably produce their emigration hither. It would also discourage their Shipbuilding. It would likewise decrease the number of small vessels belonging to that adjacent Country, which certainly do, and, as they increase, will more and more injure our Revenue especially when the duties shall be encreased among us. The population of that Country is an engine which is convertible in war also to our injury. Their fishermen and the Bermudians and Providence-men, turned into Privateers, will be peculiarly able to annoy and injure our trade, both from their situation and skill. Witness the course of things in the late war. It appears to me a very unwise thing to give a people, thus circumstanced, benefits which it is acknowledged our own fishermen want. It is however certain that many of the best informed and most judicious persons in the Eastern States are favorable to the indulgences now allowed to them, and even wish there was no duty on their fish. The Reason given is, that they take cattle and other articles in return to the full amount. I answer, if they could not send *such goods* to pay for the Articles they take, they being of prime necessity, they must send less rival goods—or Cash—or they must emigrate hither. Each man's labor and consumption, who should emigrate, would count as two in our Scale, and would be equal in value to that portion, which we enjoy of supplying 6. 8 or 10 residents there. This point is of great importance. Due respect should be paid to the opinions and desires of the Eastern States, yet the use of the investigation, directed by the House of Representatives, is, inter alia, to ascertain and eradicate Errors in the public mind and in the existing laws. I do not feel disposed however to be decided in my Judgment on this head, tho' I have expressed myself so freely and strongly to bring the point into View.

Premiums of an honorary nature, or, which will be beneficial to the individual without expence to the Nation, if any such can be thought of, might have a favorable effect but it seems more than doubtful whether expensive bounties would be adopted by the legislature, or proper in themselves under the existing circumstances of the business and of the country.

In Great Britain, sailors who go on shares in their fishing Vessels without wages are particularly encouraged, it being supposed, I presume, that they make themselves more perfect Masters of the business and continue more steadily in the pursuit. Tis a fact of some importance therefore, that our fishermen are much in that habit and that they carry their immediate interest further by participating in the Vessels themselves. To encourage this practice appears to be desirable.

Some negative measures interesting to the fisheries also deserve notice. Monopolies being less œconomical in their execution as being more liable to negligence and fraud, and being also less beneficial to every branch of mere commerce than perfect freedom in it, should by no means be granted. The Dutch, who afterwards succeeded so well in the fisheries, labored without profit while they were conducted by an exclusive Company.

Heavy duties on the importation and excises on the consumption of piscatory Articles should be avoided, if it is intended to encourage this trade, as also duties on the exportation of them, which last however the constitution forbids. This favorable circumstance does exist in the same degree in Holland or England.

I will conclude this paper by observing—lastly, that our fisheries should be, and I trust always will be encouraged by the non impressment of the Seamen employed in them, for I hope this shocking outrage on the happiness of individuals and families and upon the rights of men and free Citizens will never be committed on the poorer members of our Community.

T.C.

MS (DLC: TJ Papers, 60: 10283-322); in clerk's hand save for notes, initialed signature, and one or two interlineations in Coxe's hand; caption at head of text: "Miscellaneous Notes on the Fisheries"; undated but enclosed in Coxe to TJ, 23 Nov. 1790.

IV. Tench Coxe to the Secretary of State

Nov. 29th. 1790

Mr. Coxe has the honor to enclose to Mr. Jefferson a letter containing some further information concerning the fisheries: also the table of prices refer'd to in his notes, and a little estimate of the profits of the cod fishery.

Mr. Anthony was bred to the Sea out of Rhode Island, is a man of judgment and probity, and is now a partner of one of the principal houses in Philadelphia, who do *half* the New England business of the port.

The Calculation of the fishery, which Mr. Coxe has hazarded, should be very strictly tested by the better information received from Massachusetts.

RC (DLC). Not recorded in SJL. Enclosures: (1) Joseph Anthony to Tench Coxe, 27 Nov. 1790, and its enclosure, both printed below. (2) Table of prices entitled: "A comparison of the prices of pickled and dried Fish in New England with those of Butchers Meat of common qualities in the Philadelphia Market, and of pickled Meats for Sea Stores" (MS in clerk's hand with final note by Coxe, undated, in DLC: TJ Papers, 69: 12022-3). All prices are in Pennsylvania currency (dollars) for bulk quantities, averaged at pence per pound, as follows: "Dried Codfish (not dumb'd [i.e. dunned or cured so as to give it a particular color and quality])" of the first, second, and third quality at 2 1/7, 1 1/2, and 1 3/8 pence respectively; "Seale fish" at 1 1/7 pence; pickled mackerel of the first, second, and third quality at 2 4/5, 2 1/7, and 1 3/7 pence; and pickled cod, alewives, New England shad, salmon, and menhaden at 1 3/7, 1 3/7, 1 11/14, 2 5/8, and 21/40 pence respectively. These prices were compared with those for fresh meats "as used by Families that can buy per carcase": mutton, "deemed low the Year through," at 3 to 3 1/2 pence; pork at 3 to 4 pence; veal at 3 1/2 to 4 1/2 pence; and beef "by the quarter . . . the year through" at 3 to 4 pence. Prices of pickled meats for sea stores were given as follows: pork "is deemed low at 3 1/10" pence; beef at 2 1/2 pence; and bacon ("Flitches, Shoulders & Hams") at 4 1/2 to 7 pence. The list concluded with this statement: "The charges on transporting fish from New England to the Middle and Southern States is scarcely to be considered, as Vessels from the Eastern Ports to those States are frequently at an expence for Ballast, but let 7 1/2 per Cent be added in lieu of all charges, and pickled and dried fish will still be a cheaper food for Families and Sea Stores than fresh, smoaked or pickled Meats." To this Coxe added: "Note. The fleshmarkets of the Southern Seaports, it is believed, are dearer, quality for quality, than that of Philada." (3) "Calculation of the Bank fishery in a Schooner of fifty Tons," estimating the cost of the vessel, stores, and advanced wages at £500, extra expences through the season covering all charges at £75, and the "profit in an employment which not lasting more than six months leaves time for two West India Voyages at £175. Against this total of £750 the calculation balanced the "fish and Oil taken in the several fares" at £450 and the cost of the vessel (£400) minus the deduction "for decays, wear and tear of Sails, rigging &c." (£100) at £300. To this estimate the memorandum added: "In the above business are comprehended the resulting benefits of food for the people and wages adequate to the Clothing and feeding of their families, and the nursing of Seamen to qualify us as a Nation for Naval establishments and the carrying trade. The Capital employed is such parts of the Vessel and outfits as actually occasion an advance of the Money before the Sales of the Fish from the first fare.—This will not be more than her Outfit to sea, but if it be extended to £525, then the sum of £175 leaves a profit upon the Capital employed of 33 1/3 per Cent, and the use of the Vessel in the Coasting, or West India trade for the remainder of the Year" (MS in DLC: TJ Papers, 69: 12009-10; in clerk's hand, undated).

ENCLOSURE I

Joseph Anthony to Tench Coxe

DEAR SIR   Philadelphia. 27th. November 1790

Your Letter of the 18th Instant to Hewes & Anthony was duly Receaved, the Contents of which; and of the Inclosures fell more Immediately under my Notice, from my being a Native of New England, and in Early life Conversant in the Business to which this Enquiry Relates, the whole of which I have had under Consideration, and here give you the most Correct and Early Information, that I can Recolect, or Discover from Enquiry. In answering your Queries, I have been as Particular as Possible. Before the Revolution, there was Very few Vessels Employ'd in the whale Fishery of Larger burthen than Sixty to Ninety Tons, and they did not Generally Cruise farther than about the Lattitude of 36." on this Coast. Some went to the River St. Lawrence, and Streights of Bellisle, a few years before the War; a few of the Largest Vessels went as far as the Western Islands, where for awhile, they had great Success, till the whales grew Shy there, and the worms Injur'd the Vessels much. Since then they have Extended the Fishery much further, and of Course, their Vessels fitted at much greater Expence. Formerly they Rig'd their Sloops Very Plain and Spareing. The Captain and Crew Drew one half, and agreed among themselves in what Proportion to Divide the fare. Sometimes the Owners hire the men by the month, and give them about Common Seamans wages, which at that time was Not more than Six Dollars ⅌ month throughout New England; at other times they would give them a fixed Sum for a Share, Success or Not, but they were generally found the most attentive, when their Dependence was on a Share of what they Caught. About that Period the whale Fishery was persu'd much more Extensive than Since the peace, tho' the oil and Headmatter did Not Command Near the price that they Now do. But was we *Now* to take an Equal Quantity to what was then Caught, I am Clearly of Oppinion there would Not be Vend for it, as Neither Sort is permitted to Entry in England or any of the British Islands in the west Indies, where Very Large Quantities used to be Sent, and the Same Prohibition Accounts for the Price of Different kinds of Codfish being Lower Now than before the war. We are So Restricted, we have no Market for half the Common Fish that are taken. The Better Kind, are Sent to Lisbon, Spain, and the Streights, where the Common and Midling Sort will Not bring any Price.

In the Price Current both formerly and the present time, I have been as Correct as my memory will Enable me to be. Codfish generally brought a better price before the Revolution than Since, but mackrel you will observe were Not worth So much. They have Not Latterly been taken in So great Quanties as heretofore, and the best kind Decreases Every year. Before the Revolution we were acquainted with only three Sorts of Oil Vizt. the Spermacete, Right Whale, or Bone Whale, and the Liver oil from the Codfish, but of Late years they being two other kinds of Oil from the Southern Climate, tho from the Same kind of *Bone whale*, as are Caught at the Northward tho by No means so large. If anything further is wanted that is within the Compass of my knowledge. It shall be Communicated with the greatest Cheerfullness by, Sir your Obedient and Very Humb. Servant, JOSEPH ANTHONY

RC (DLC); at foot of text: "Tench Coxe Esqr."

ENCLOSURE II

Answers to Queries on the Fisheries by Joseph Anthony

[ca. 27 Nov. 1790]

Queries

1. What is the most convenient and advantageous size or Tonnage for a Vessel proper for the *Cod* fishery?　　45 to 60 Tons Schooner Rigged.

2. What is such a Vessel worth with her provisions, *advanced wages*, and fishing implements on board, as she stands when cleared for the Banks the first voyage?　　About five to seven hundred pounds L[awful] Money. [A Vessel of 45 Tons costs (exclusively of extra Articles for the fisheries) in N. Engd. the cheapest £360., the best £450. Lawful N.Y.][1]

3. What are her monthly Expences: if possible note her Officers and Mens Wages, &c., particularly.　　The officers and men are Commonly on Shares. The Terms we are unacquainted with.

4. What is the most convenient and advantageous size or tonnage for a vessel proper for the *Whale* fishery?　　About 70 Tons for this Coast, and 150 to 200 Tons for Foreign Fishery.

5. What is such a Vessel worth with her provisions, advanced Wages and fishing implements on board, as she stands when cleared for her *first* whaling Voyage?　　The Smaller Size about £900. The Large £1,800 to £2,100 L.M.　　[N.B. This is all Lawful Money, at 6/ to the Dollar. The best New England Vessels (exclusively of the extra articles for the fishing Business) cost £2000 Lawful Money for 200 Tons, and the cheapest £1600 Lawful Money for [. . .] Tons. Shipbuilding however is rising in *all* our cheap ports.][1]

6. What are her Monthly expences? If possible the particulars are desired. The men are generally on shares and Draw about a 32d. barrel; the other monthly Expences Exclusive of the wear and Tear of Materials cant be above £12 to £15 per month.

7. It is supposed that the Cod fish on the American Banks have decreased.   By no means, tho its not pursu'd Nearly so Extensively as before the Revolution.

8. Is it not true that the Whales on the American Coast had become more rare before the war, and are now very scarce?   For some years before the Revolution the whales on the american Coast became so shy that there was No Encouragement for pursuing them. But in the Course of the war they got more Tame, tho they are not plenty now.

9. Is the gun Harpoon used by the whalers of the United States? We Cannot say with Certainty but believe Not.

MS (DLC); queries in the hand of a clerk, answers in the hand of Joseph Anthony; address leaf bears the following in Tench Coxe's hand: "The Honorable Thomas Jefferson Esquire" and the following notation by TJ (the first word being in the printed style similar to that used in the report on the fisheries of 1 Feb. 1791): "Fisheries. (*Cod & whale Fishery*) Papers from Mr. Coxe"; at head of text in Coxe's hand: "answered by Mr. Josh. Anthony of Philada."

1 Matter in brackets (supplied) is in hand of Coxe.

ENCLOSURE III
Joseph Anthony's Table of Prices

Dried Fish.		The average of 1770 to 1775 Not dumb'd Fish	in 1789 to 1790
Best Cod	℔ 112	18 /to 25/L.M.	16/L.Money
2nd. quality		14/ to 15/	12/ @ 13/
3rd. do. if any such		12/ @ 13/	10/ @ 11/
4th. do if any such Scale Fish.		10/ @ 11/	8/ @ 9/
Smoked Salmon		2/6 @ 7/b. Cask.	ditto
Pickled Fish.			
+ Worst Mackarel ℔ bbl of 30 to 32 Gs. contg 224. ℔ fish		15/	20/
+ middling do ℔ do		20/	30/
+ best do ℔ do		30/	42/
+ Manhaden ℔ do		12/	8/
+ Alewives ℔ do		15/	20/
+ Pickled Cod ℔ do		25/	20/
Pilchards ℔ do		none	
+ Salmon ℔ do		45/	40/
Herrings Qu: ℔ do		15/	20/
+ Shad ℔ do		20/	25/
Oils vizt.			
Spermaceti Oil		50/ @ 60/	90/ @ 110/
Whale Oil Northern best		40/ @ 45/	
Train Oil Southern or Brazil		Not known then	40/ a 45/
Blubber		18/	20/
Liver Oil (Tanners)		35/	42/
Spermaceti		2/ @ 2/1	3/2
Headmatter		£30 to £35 ℔ Ton	£45 @ £55
Whale Bone Short & Long		2/6 @ 6/	10d. @ 2/

What does a bbl of pickled fish usually weigh, exclusive of the Cask[?] About 2 Cwt.

What does a bble of do. usually gauge[?] 30 @ 32 Gallons.

MS (DLC: TJ Papers, 69: 12000-2); at head of text: "(N.B. 6/ ℔ dollar"; in clerk's hand; endorsed: "Mr. Joseph Anthony Price Currt."

This may have been accompanied by another document giving "Prices in London August 27, 1790," as follows:

		Price	Duty
"Whalefins, Greenland	per Ton	£150-0-0 }	97-18-0
South fishery		100-0-0 }	
Whaleoil, Greenland		£22 to 23*	ditto
South Fishery		£16 to 17*	ditto
Spermaceti Oil, Brown		£44 to 45	ditto
White		£52 to 54	ditto
Seal oil, brown		£21 to 22*	ditto
white		25 to 26*	ditto
Cod oil		21 to 22*	ditto

* These articles are, *in effect*, prohibited" (DLC: TJ Papers, 66: 11460; in hand of clerk except for note marked by asterisk, which is in that of Tench Coxe).

V. Memoranda by James Madison

[Jan. 1791]

G. Britain from		At war			At peace	
May 1689 to Sepr. 1697 =	8y. 4m.	to	May 1702 =	4y. 8m.
May 1702 to Aug. 1712 =	10. 3.	to	Decr. 1718 =	6. 4
Decr. 1718 to June 1721 =	2. 6	to	Mar. 1727 =	5. 8
Mar. 1727 to May 1727 =	0. 2	to	Octr. 1739 =	12. 4
Octr. 1739 to May 1748 =	8. 7	to	June 1755 =	7. 0
June 1755 to Novr. 1762 =	7. 5	to	June 1778[1] =	15. 7
June 1778 to Mar. 1783 =	4. 9	to	May 1789 =	6. 2
				3.	lost in broken months

42. War   58. peace

ho' these nates are n an Un-rwriter it y be well o consult T[ench] C[oxe] or thers, on them.

{ During war Insurance between U.S. & G.B. may be rated from 12 to 20 per Ct.[2]
       do.   U.S. & W. Inds.   from 12 to 20 do.
During peace   U.S. & G.B.   about 2 1/2 do.
          U.S. & W. Inds.   abt. 2 1/2 do.
During war insurance of freight beyond that of peace from 30 to 50 per Ct. }

*The annual value of exports from U.S. in British Bottoms =   [3] Dollars
    Freight of do. from do. in do. to Europe =   do.
        do. of do. from do. in do. to W. Inds. =   do.

Annual value of Imports in Brit: Bottoms [see Champion p. 51]   do.
[See Report of Impost & the 10 per Ct. discount in favr. of Amer.Botts.]

From these data result the expence of Insurance & freight taxed by Brit: Wars on the trade or rather agriculture of U.S. during their present dependence on British Bottoms.

* Champion p. 140.

From the same may be inferred the loss which war with Spain would have cost the U.S. During the prospect of it insurance in Some instances rose to near double the peace rate.[4]

To the wars of the above period, France was with little exception a party. So was Holland, excluding the war preceding the last. So in fact were the maritime nations in Genl.

Perhaps it may be easier to make the calculation for all our trade in Foreign Bottoms, than for that in British alone: or expedient to super-add the former to the latter calculation.[5]

MS (DLC: TJ Papers, 233: 41600); entirely in hand of James Madison (but see note 2, below); undated, but certainly written after 6 Jan. 1791 when Hamilton submitted his "General Abstract of Duties Arising on the Tonnage of Vessels entered into the United States" (ASP, *Commerce*, I, 7-8) and before 1 Feb. 1791 when TJ handed in his report. Dft (DLC: Madison Papers); at head of text in Madison's hand: "made for Mr. Jefferson, when preparing his report for Congress"; endorsed; containing variations in substance and phraseology from text of MS, some of which are indicated in notes below.

[1] Thus in MS; neither Madison in compiling this table nor TJ in using it included the two years of war after the colonies declared their independ-ence, the basis of the calculation obviously being that of the formal declaration of war against a sovereign nation, in this instance France.

[2] At this point the figure "16," probably in TJ's hand, is set down in MS.

[3] Blank in MS in this and following two entries. See Appendix No. 18 of TJ's Report.

[4] Dft reads: "During the late question between G. B. and Spain insurance rose in some instances to double or nearly double that of peace, being a tax at the rate of   dollars per annm. Had war taken place we see the tax ⟨we must have⟩ which would have been imposed by our dependence on Brit: Bottoms."

[5] Dft reads: "The Calculation may be extended to the *whole* of our trade in foreign bottoms."

VI. Christopher Gore to Tobias Lear

MY DEAR SIR   Boston December 10. 1790

A few weeks since, a gentleman by the name of Stokes, arrivd from Great Britain at some port in the Southern States on his way to Nantucket, to which place he went, and remained there some weeks. He then came to Boston, and embarked for Halifax.

From what I have heard I am induc'd to believe this gentleman came from England, by the direction of Lord Hawkesbury and Mr. Grenville, for the express purpose of knowing what priviledges, from the british government, woud induce the inhabitants of Nantucket to remove from that island to Great Britain, and carry on their whale fishery from thence.

It is well known, that many fishermen, who formerly went from Nantucket to Nova Scotia, return'd last autumn to that island—

that those who went to France and establish'd themselves at Dunkirk, under the patronage of the french government are dissatisfied with their situation—that Lord Hawkesbury has at all times regretted his inattention to William Rotch, who, at the conclusion of the war, went to London for the purpose of proposing to the british court a removal from Nantucket of its inhabitants to Great Britain, provided, suitable priviledges cou'd be granted them by that Government. Not meeting with the encouragement expected, he went to France and established the Whale fishery at Dunkirk, which has proved advantageous to the merchant and master of the ship, but otherwise to the seamen, that is to say, to the large proprietors in the produce of the adventure but not to the sailors, who are small sharers.

That William Rotch went to France in August last to obtain the promis'd bounty from that Government, and probably to adopt the most prudent means of either retaining the seamen there, or establishing them with the navigation of him self and friends in Britain, or possibly return them to America.

I am inform'd by several british merchants who are well acquainted with the sentiments of Lord Hawkesbury on this subject—that the establishment of the Nantucket Fishermen, in some part of England, is an object very near his heart—that he has ever regretted the inattention of the british court to the proposals of Mr. Rotch, as occasioning the loss of a favorable opportunity, to obstruct the rise of the American Nation, and promote the wealth and importance of Britain—and that he is intent on remedying this neglect by discovering an effectual method to seduce those expert navigators from France and America. Perhaps it may be of some importance, that the views of the brit. ministry, as discover'd in the errand of Mr. Stokes, shoud be known to those who administer the government of the U.S. and it is possible, that it may not be known. This my friend is the only apology I offer for troubling you to read this letter.

I will not detain you longer, but request you woud present the affectionate regards of Mrs. Gore and myself to Mrs. Lear and believe me to be very truly your friend & obed servt,

C: GORE

RC (DLC). Not recorded in SJL.

While TJ made use of this letter in preparing his report, he refrained from identifying by name or nationality the agent who had been among the Nantucket whalemen "for the purpose of renewing the invitations to a change of situation." Nor did he attribute this purpose to Hawkesbury and Grenville as did Gore, who doubtless reflected comments made by the emissary himself (see Document IX). The agent, Charles Stokes, was actually sent in the spring of 1790 by Charles Francis Greville (1749-1809), whose expensive tastes had led him by 1784 into such serious financial straits that he was obliged to offer for sale his collection of paintings and sculptures and to give up his liaison with Emma Hart in favor of his uncle, Sir William Hamilton, whom she married (Namier and Brooke, *History of Parliament*, II, 550-1). To recoup his finances Greville also sought from 1784 on to attract the Nantucketers to settle at the capacious harbor of Milford-Haven. He consulted both Hawkesbury and Grenville before dispatching Stokes to Nantucket. As a result the Committee for Trade and Plantations authorized him to "communicate to the Foreign Whale Fishers their resolution of 1790 that it would be expedient to renew the invitation [of 1786] to foreigners" (Greville to the Committee of South Whalers of London, 7 July 1792; British Museum: Liverpool Papers, XXXIX, f. 9-18). This, however, was not confirmed by the Privy Council until 1791 when the result of Stokes' mission was made known (Greville's Memorandum, 22 Apr. 1793; same, XL, f. 14-15). Even then its action only advised that the renewal of the invitation be recommended to Parliament. Greville, however, imprudently proceeded on the assumption that the British government was committed to extend and honor such an invitation.

Hawkesbury, who in 1790 was gathering data for his famous report on trade relations with the United States, very likely gave instructions that Stokes report on commercial and political affairs in America as well as on the whalemen, for Stokes in fact did so both then and later. In November, from Boston, he wrote directly to both Hawkesbury and Grenville but confided his political observations to the former. To Hawkesbury he said that he had gone to Nantucket "to collect the present situation of the Inhabitants, their expectations from the Legislature of the United States, and their sentiments towards G.B." He reported the Nantucketers to be in an extremely distressed situation, found them a virtuous, industrious people with a decency and sobriety of behavior quite uncommon among seafarers, and strongly recommended them as an object worthy of the attention of the ministry: "A colony of such men, My Lord, established at Milford Haven would be productive of

the greatest national benefit. It would be a school for Naval adventure in which Welch youth might learn to unite good morals with a perfect knowledge of their profession. I was led to inquire what provision the government of this country had made or intended to make to secure to herself so valuable a people. I found none had been made or in contemplation. On the contrary the situation of these Islanders was much worse than any under Government." Further, he thought favors granted by France to American oil had been or soon would be withdrawn. "Should a prohibition of this branch of the fishery either in British or American vessels take place," he added, ". . . these people will have no resource left. They are, My Lord, sensible of these truths. Indeed, the daily depreciation of their property convinces them beyond a doubt that an adherence to their present pursuit is utterly impossible." Stokes concluded with an accurate prediction of matters that would come before Congress—the bank, an excise tax, and a navigation bill discriminatory against Great Britain which, if adopted, would be followed with one designed to place the carrying trade of the United States in American vessels. However, he gave Hawkesbury the comforting assurance that the navigation bill would "receive a powerful and certain Negative from the Northern interest," which he thought was almost unanimously opposed to it. But he also reported serious violations of the British navigation act in the forgery of Mediterranean passes and the sale of blank certificates of British registry falsely used to cover American vessels (Stokes to Hawkesbury, 25 Nov. 1790; British Museum: Liverpool Papers, XXXVI, f. 342-5; see also Stokes to Hawkesbury, 14 Nov. 1791, same, XXXVIII, f. 131-8).

On the same day Stokes reported to Grenville on the situation of the Nantucketers. He found that the elder William Rotch had already returned to Dunkirk and that Samuel Rodman, his son-in-law who was concluding the family business at Nantucket, would soon follow. But the other inhabitants were more cautious. Stokes thought them generally uninformed "excepting what relates to the peculiarly beautiful system of sobriety and economy attached to their fishery," hence not likely to make new arrangements unless there were immediate prospects of gain. Nevertheless, they had so much confidence in Rotch that if his interview with Hawkesbury were successful, Stokes thought eight or ten vessels could immediately be attached to the Southern whale fishery out of Milford-Haven, to be increased to forty in a year or so. However, if Rotch could not be induced to settle there, it would be difficult to persuade the others. "If then, Sir, G.B. is determined upon securing to herself this valuable people," Stokes concluded, "now I think is the moment. . . . They have nothing to expect from their own Government. . . . The memorial they have presented has been unattended to, and these valuable people will be in the course of a few years entirely lost to every country." Stokes left with Rodman the plans and measures adopted by the British government for the development of Milford-Haven, to be used "only with confidential people" until Rotch's decision became known. He then departed for Halifax to try to persuade the fishermen there to use their influence with the Nantucketers (Stokes to Grenville, 25 Nov. 1790; British Museum: Liverpool Papers, XXXVI, f. 340-1).

But Greville's ambitious plans did not materialize beyond the settlement of a few Nova Scotia whalemen at Milford, for the earlier invitation was not renewed by the British government. Even that had been stoutly opposed by merchants who believed that the admission of "40 ships foreign built and navigated and owned by foreigners to privileges of British ship owners would be such an infringement of the Navigation Act as would scarcely admit of adequate compensation," besides being impolitic and unjust to unemployed British seamen (Samuel Green, Secretary of the Liverpool Chamber of Commerce, to Lord Penrhyn, 21 Apr. 1788; same, XXXIV, f. 39-40). But after Greville had set out to detach the Nantucketers and to build up his establishment at Milford, he ran into even more formidable obstacles in the form of the entrenched Committee of South Whalers from London. In 1792 in a blunt letter to the Committee, he charged that their influence with Hawkesbury in 1785 had "tended to limit the liberality and justice of this Country to the Nantucketers," thus depriving him of the opportunity to settle Rotch and his family at Milford. The result, he declared, confirmed his "prediction to the Privy Council in 1784 that France would gain a Whale Fish-

ery from our Folly and that we should lose that Market and establish a Competitor formidable if the fishery was established and the Trade conducted by Nantucketers." But he did not come as a supplicant and had not previously asked their cooperation because he "neither wanted your Weight of Interest nor your Capital." Further, he foresaw that the system of whaling "by Great Capitals who engage from the River with fresh Crews every voyage" would eventually fail for want of skilled and experienced whalemen, hence his own modest nursery at Milford would eventually benefit the whaling carried on by London capitalists. His own limited object was only to bring over the whalemen from Dunkirk and those Nantucketers connected by blood or property with those at Dartmouth whom he had agreed to settle at Milford-Haven. Thus, by destroying the competition from France and stifling those left at Nantucket, there would be "a common Interest existing between all the Whale Fishers of G.B. to embarrass and annihilate the Foreign and Colonial Whale Fishery, and a Nursery of Harpooners, Masters &ca. . . . be formed at home." He desired to cooperate in all "subsequent measures necessary to confine to G.B. the benefits of the Whale Fishery, which has taken Root in France, N. Scotia and survives in America from the contracted policy which has prevailed since the year 1786" (Greville to John St. Barbe, 7 July 1792, British Museum: Liverpool Papers, XXXIX, f. 19-20). The response was brief and emphatic: "You know the sentiments of our Committee. . . . We cannot join you on any account. The fishery being now perfectly established in Great Britain, we are under no apprehension of its being injured by the Trade carried on out of America. . . . If Government wishes to give encouragement to small ships fitting out on a frugal plan, it must be totally distinct and under a different head from that of the Southern Fishery" (St. Barbe to Greville; 2 Aug. 1792; same, XXXIX, f. 19-20).

Greville then appealed to Pitt and Hawkesbury, reminded the latter of the assurances given him in the spring of 1790, and urged government to meet what he regarded as an honorable engagement. But Hawkesbury, deeply interested in the Southern whale fishery in whose fleet one vessel was appreciatively named *The Lord Hawkesbury*, declined to intercede (see especially, Greville to Hawkesbury, 2 Jan., 4 May, 14 and 25 Aug., 11 Sep. 1792; 21 Jan., 1 Feb. 1793; and Greville's memorandum, 22 Apr. 1793; Hawkesbury to Greville, 29 Aug. 1792, 25 Jan. 1793; Greville to Sheffield, ca. Mch. 1793; Sheffield to Hawkesbury, 5 Mch. 1793; George Chalmers to Hawkesbury, 19 and 30 Apr. 1793; British Museum: Liverpool Papers, XXXVIII, f. 203, 330; XXXIX, f. 7-8, 9-18, 19-20, 21, 34-5, 51-2, 225-8, 235-6, 247-52, 351, 352; XL, 13, 14-15, 16-22).

The distressed Nantucket whalemen, Stokes had accurately predicted, had "nothing to expect from their own Government." Greville who had sent him on his mission now discovered too late that the British ministry was equally apathetic.

VII. Jefferson's Notes and Outline for the Report

[Jan. 1791]

Observations

Our advantages for the cod fishery are
1. Neighborhood. Woman and children salt.
2. Cost of vessels. But the half of that Baltic fir ships, considering price and duration
3. Mariners. Skill, activity, sobriety, order
4. Excellence of our vessels as sea-boats, decrease risk, and quicker returns.
5. Casks. Their cheapness. This alone is an extra profit of 15. to 20 percent.
6. Provisions. Cheapness
7. Winter fishing. Like domestic manufactures fills up odd times.
8. Small vessels, because voyages short. Requires small capital.
9. Shore fishery. Run into port in a storm and so lessen danger. Foreigners pay monthly insurance.

Champion says the cost of supplies to N.F.L. from U.S. and from Engld. are as 4:7

Resources for making seamen.
1. The coasting trade
2. The carrying trade
3. The fisheries.

We have no market for half of our common fish. Which renders W.I. markets so essential.

Fisheries are manufactures, because they create produce.
Preferable to other manufactures which debilitate those employed in them.

Every man we employ in fishing counts as 2. because withdraw
  him, and it leaves empty and so adds 1. of our enem[y].
Neither the French, Brit. nor Dutch make any mercantile profit
  from their fisheries.
We alone can do this.
T[ench] C[oxe] proposes
  1. An advance of the allowance on the salt exported in fishing
       vessels
  2. A relinquishment of the duty on salt used for fish consumed
       at home. Which would be a light premium to encourage
       the consumption of fish and consequently the fisheries
  3. An exemption of fishing vessels from the tonnage of 6.
       cents. To tax vessels is like taxing waggons which carry
       our produce to market.
  4. Promoting consumption of fish, making it part of the mili-
       tary ration, of ship stores.
  9. The prohibition of British fish.
Exempt fishermen from land militia duty in peace and war.
But may it not be required in return for all this that they be
  formed into a marine militia and be liable to be called on tours
  of marine duty in time of war?
Were we to refuse to Brit. vessels the exportation of our produce
  their N.F.L. vessels (by their own law) must be fed from Eur.
  which would increase that part of their expence in the proportion of 4:7 (Champion 119.) and so far operate as Duty on
  them.
If we do not exclude British from our carrying business
  1. Our shipbuilding suppressed
  2. Our ship carpenters go to other countries
  3. Our young men have no call to sea.
  4. Our produce must pay war freight and insurance in Brit.
       bottoms during war
  5. We lose the value of cabotage which would be immense in
       time of war as we should be carriers for belligerent powers

MS (DLC: TJ Papers, 233: 41654); entirely in TJ's hand; undated, but evidently drafted shortly before preparing the Report.

In DLC: TJ Papers, 233: 41656

there is a briefer outline that TJ employed in preparing his report. The above notes are based in part on the documents supplied by Tench Coxe.

VIII. The Secretary of State to the Speaker of the House of Representatives

Sir   [1 February 1791]

I have now the honor of enclosing you the Report on the subject of the Fisheries of the United States which the House of Representatives had required from me. However long the delay, I can assure you, Sir, with truth that it has not been a moment longer than the difficulty of procuring and digesting the materials necessarily occasioned.

I enclose at the same time extracts from a letter of Mr. Short the Chargé des Affaires of the United States in France which came to hand after the Report was finished. From this there is reason to apprehend that our whale oils will be excluded from the markets of that Country, and perhaps that they are so already. The measures necessary to prevent or to retrieve this loss rest on the wisdom of the Legislature.

I have the honor to be with sentiments of the most profound respect Sir Your most obedient and most humble Servant.

PrC (DLC); PrC in hand of Black-well; unsigned and all save the de-scenders in date eliminated by close cropping; entry in SJPL reads: "[1791. Feb. 1.] Th: J. to Sp. H. R. inclosing report." In addition to the report, TJ enclosed an extract from Short to TJ, 21 Oct. 1790 (see notes 1, 2, and 3 to that letter for identification of extract).

IX. Report on the American Fisheries by the Secretary of State

The Secretary of State, to whom was referred by the House of Representatives, the representation from the General Court of the Commonwealth of Massachusetts, on the subjects of the Cod and Whale Fisheries, together with the several papers accompanying it, has had the same under consideration and thereupon makes the following REPORT.

The representation sets forth that, before the late war, about 4,000 Seamen and 24,000 Tons of shipping were annually employed from that State in the Whale Fishery, the produce whereof was about £350,000 lawful money a year.

That, previous to the same period, the Cod Fishery of that

State employed 4000 men and 28,000 Ton of Shipping and produced about £250,000 a year.

That these branches of business, annihilated during the war, have been in some degree recovered since: but that they labour under many and heavy embarrassments, which, if not removed, or lessened, will render the Fisheries every year less extensive and important.

That these embarrassments are, heavy duties on their produce abroad, and bounties on that of their competitors: and duties at home on several articles particularly used in the Fisheries.

And it asks that the duties be taken off, that bounties be given to the fishermen, and the national influence be used abroad for obtaining better markets for their produce.

The Cod and Whale Fisheries, carried on by different persons, from different Ports, in different vessels, in different Seas, and seeking different markets, agree in one circumstance, in being as unprofitable to the adventurer, as important to the public. A succinct view of their rise, progress and present state with different nations, may enable us to note the circumstances which have attended their prosperity and their decline, to judge of the embarrassments which are said to oppress ours, to see whether they depend on our own will, and may therefore be remedied immediately by ourselves, or whether, depending on the will of others they are without the reach of remedy from us, either directly or indirectly.

Their history being as unconnected as their practice, they shall be separately considered.

Within 20 years after the supposed discovery of Newfoundland by the Cabots, we find that the abundance of fish on it's banks had already drawn the attention of the people of Europe. For as early as 1517 or 1519. we are told of 50 ships being seen there at one time. The first adventurers in that fishery were the Biscayans of Spain, the Basques and Bas Bretons of France, all united anciently in language and still in habits and in extreme poverty. The last circumstance enabled them long to retain a considerable share of the fishery. In 1577 the French had 150 vessels there, the Spaniards had still 100, and the Portuguese 50, when the English had only 15. The Spaniards and Portuguese seem at length to have retired silently, the French and English claiming the fishery exclusively as an appurtenance to their adjacent Colonies, and the profits being too small for nations surcharged with the precious metals proceeding from their mines.

3. Hakluyt 499. Herrera. Dec. 2. L. 5. c. 3.

Encyclop. ancienne. art. Morue. 8. Raynal. 15. edn. Geneve. 1780. Hakluyt.

8. Raynal. 408.

Without materials to trace the intermediate progress, we only know that so late as 1744 the French employed there 564 ships, and 27,500 seamen, and took 1,246,000 Kentals of fish, which was three times the extent to which England and her Colonies together carried this fishery at that time.

Sheffeild. Tab. 8.

The English in the beginning of the 17th. century, had employed generally about 150 vessels in the Newfoundland fishery. About 1670 we find them reduced to 80, and 100, the inhabitants of New England beginning now to supplant them. A little before this the British Parliament, perceiving that their Citizens were unable to subsist on the scanty profits which sufficed for their poorer competitors, endeavoured to give them some advantage by prohibiting the importation of foreign fish: and, at the close of the century, they formed some regulations for their Government and protection; and remitted to them some duties. A successful war enabled them in 1713 to force from the French a cession of the Island of Newfoundland. Under these encouragements, the English and American fisheries began to thrive. In 1731 we find the English take 200,000 Kentals of fish and the Americans 230,000 besides the refuse fish not fit for European markets. They continue to gain ground and the French to lose it, insomuch that about 1755 they are said to have been on a par: and in 1768 the French have only 259 vessels of 24,420 Tons, 9,722 seamen, taking 200,000 Kentals, while America alone for some three or four years before that, and so on to the commencement of the late war, employed 665 vessels of 25,650[1] Tons, and 4,405 seamen, and took from 350,000 to upwards of 400,000 Kentals of fish, and England a still greater quantity, 526,000 Kentals as is said.

Trade's increase. cited 2. Anderson's hist. comm. 353.

Sr. Josiah Child.

18. Car. 2. c. 2; 10. 11. W. 3. c. 25.

5. W.M. c. 7. &c.

Treaty of Utrecht. § 13.

3. Anders. 426.

Raynal.

Raynal. edn.

Statement by committee Massach.

Sheffeild 57. edn. 1784.

Sheffeild 57. edn. 1784.

Spain had formally relinquished her pretentions to a participation in these fisheries at the close of the preceding war; and at the end of this, the adjacent Continent and Islands being divided between the United States, the English and French, (for the last retained two small Islands merely for this object) the right of fishing was appropriated to them also.

Treaty of Paris. §.18.

Treaty of Versailles. §.4.

France, sensible of the necessity of balancing the power of England on the water, and therefore of improving every resource for raising seamen, and seeing that her fishermen could not maintain their competition without some public patronage, adopted the experiment of bounties on her own fish and duties on that of foreign nations brought into her markets. But notwithstanding this her fisheries dwindle from a change taken place insensibly in the character of her navigation, which from being the most economical, is now become the most expensive. In 1786 she is said to have employed but 7000 men in this fishery, and to have taken 426,000 Kentals; and in 1787 but 6000 men and 128,000 Kentals. She seems not yet sensible that the unthriftiness of her fisheries proceeds from the want of economy, and not the want of markets: and that the encouragement of our fishery abridges that of a rival nation whose power on the ocean has long threatened the loss of all balance[2] on that element. *1788. said by Grenville in parl.* *1788. said by Grenville in parl.*

The plan of the English Government since the peace has been to prohibit all foreign fish in their markets, and they have given from 18 to 50 pounds sterling on every fishing vessel complying with certain conditions. This policy is said to have been so far successful as to have raised the number of seamen employed in that business in 1786 to 14,000, and the quantity of fish taken to 732,000 Kentals. The Table No. 1. hereto annexed will present to the eye this history more in detail. *15. G. 3. c. 31; 18. G. 3. c. 55; 26. G. 3. c. 26.* *said by Pitt in parl. 1788.*

The fisheries of the United States annihilated during the war, their vessels, utensils, and fishermen destroyed, their markets in the Mediterranean and British America lost, and their produce dutied in those of France, their competitors enabled by bounties to meet and undersell them at the few markets remaining open, without any public aid, and indeed paying aids to the public:[3] Such were the hopeless auspices under which this important business was to be resumed. Yet it was resumed, and, aided by the more force of natural advantages, they employed during the years 1786. 7. 8. 9. on an average 539 vessels, of 19,185 Tons, 3287 Seamen and took 250,650 Kentals of fish: see No. 2. And an official paper (No. 3) shews that in the last of those years our exportation amounted to 375,020 Kentals, and 30,461 barrels, deduction made of 3701 Kentals and 6343 barrels of foreign fish received and re-exported. See No. 4. Still however the calculations in No. 5. which accompany the representation shew, that the profits of the sales in the years 1787.8. were too small to afford a living to the fisherman, and on those of 1789 there was such a loss as to withdraw 33 vessels of the Town of Marblehead alone from the further pursuit of this business: and the apprehension is that, without some public aid, those still remaining will continue to withdraw, and this whole commerce be engrossed by a single nation. *statement by committee of Massach.* *Report of Glover and others, a committee from the owners of fishing vessels*

This rapid view of the Cod-fishery enables us to discern under what policy it has flourished or declined in the hands of other nations, and to mark the fact that it is too poor a business to be left to itself, even with the nation the most advantageously situated.

It will now be proper to count the advantages which aid, and the disadvantages which oppose us in this contest.

Our advantages are

1. The neighbourhood of the great Fisheries, which permits our fishermen to bring home their fish to be salted by their wives and children.

2. The shore fisheries, so near at hand as to enable the vessels to run into port in a storm and so lessen the risk for which distant Nations must pay insurance.

3. The winter fisheries, which like household manufactures, employ portions of time which would otherwise be useless.

4. The smallness of the vessels, which the shortness of the voyage enables us to employ and which consequently require but a small capital.

5. The cheapness of our vessels, which do not cost above the half of the Baltic fir vessels, computing price and duration.

6. Their excellence as Sea-Boats which decreases the risk and quickens the returns.

7. The superiority of our mariners in skill, activity, enterprise, sobriety and order.

8. The cheapness of provisions.

9. The cheapness of Casks, which of itself is said to be equal to an extra profit of 15 per cent.

These advantages are of such force, that while experience has proved that no other nation can make a mercantile profit on the Newfoundland fishery, nor can support it without national aid, we can make a living profit, if vent for our fish can be procured.

Of the disadvantages opposed to us, those which depend on ourselves are

Tonnage and Naval duties on the vessels employed in the fishery.

Impost duties on Salt.
on Tea, Rum, Sugar, Molasses
hooks, Lines and Leads.   } used in the fishery
Duck, Cordage and Cables.
Iron, Hemp and Twine

Coarse woollens worn by the fishermen and the Poll tax levied by the State on their persons. The statement No. 6 shews the amount of these, exclusive of the State-tax and drawback on the fish exported to be 5.25 Dollars per man or 57.75 Dollars per vessel of 65. Tons. When a business is so nearly in equilibrio, that one can hardly discern whether the profit be sufficient to continue it, or not, smaller sums than these suffice to turn the scale against it. To these disadvantages add ineffectual duties on the importation of foreign fish. In justification of these last it is urged that the foreign fish received is in exchange for the produce of agriculture. To which it may be answered that the thing given is more merchantable than that received in exchange and that agriculture has too many markets to be allowed to take away those of the fisheries. It will rest therefore with the wisdom of the Legislature to decide whether prohibition should not be opposed to prohibition, and high duty to high duty, on the fish of other Nations: whether any and which of the naval and other duties may be remitted, or an equivalent given to the fisherman in the form of a drawback or bounty: and whether the loss of markets abroad may not in some degree be compensated by creating markets at home, to which might contribute the constituting fish a part of the military ration in stations not too distant from navigation,[4] a part of the necessary sea-stores of vessels, and the encouraging private individuals to let the fisherman share with the cultivator in furnishing the supplies of the Table. A habit introduced from motives of patriotism would soon be followed from motives of taste: and who will undertake to fix limits to this demand, if it can be once excited, with a nation which doubles and will long continue to double[5] at very short periods?

Of the disadvantages which depend on others are
1. The loss of the Mediterranean markets.
2. Exclusions from the markets of some of our neighbours.
3. High duties in those of others, and
4. Bounties to the individuals in competition with us.

The consideration of these will find its place more aptly after a review of the condition of our Whale fishery shall have led us to the same point. To this branch of the subject therefore we will now proceed.

The Whale fishery was first brought into notice of the southern nations of Europe in the 15th. Century by the same Biscayans

1. Hakluyt. (1598) 413. 414; 3. Pennant. Brit. zool. 52. 54.

and Basques who led the way to the fishery of Newfoundland. They began it on their own Coasts, but soon found that the principal residence of the Whale was in the Northern seas, into which therefore they pursued him. In 1578 they employed 25 Ships in that business. The Dutch and Hamburghers took it up after this, and about the middle of the 17th. Century the former employed about 200 ships and the latter 350.

The English endeavoured also to participate of it. *In 1672 they offered to their own fishermen, a bounty of six shillings a Ton on the oil they should bring home, and instituted, at different times, different exclusive companies, all of which failed of success. They raised their bounty in 1733,§ to 20 shillings a Ton on the admeasurement of the vessel. In 1740 to 30 shillings with a privilege to the fisherman against being impressed. The Basque fishery, supported by poverty alone, had maintained but a feeble existence before competitors aided by the bounties of their nation, and was in fine annihilated by the war of 1745, at the close of which, the English bounty was raised to 40 shillings. From this epoch their whale fishery went on, between the limits of 28 and 67 vessels till the commencement of the last war.

The Dutch, in the mean time had declined gradually to about 130 ships, and have since that fallen down to less than half that number; so that their fishery, notwithstanding a bounty of 30 florins a man, as well as that of Hamburg, is now nearly out of competition.

In 1715 the Americans began their whale fishery. They were led to it at first by the whales which presented themselves on their Coasts. They attacked them there in small vessels of 40 Tons. As the whale, being infested, retired from the Coast, they followed him farther and farther into the Ocean, still enlarging their vessels, with their adventures to 60, 100, and 200 Tons. Having extended their pursuit to the western Islands, they fell in accidentally with the Spermaceti whale, of a different species from that of Greenland, which alone had been hitherto known in Commerce: more fierce and active and whose oil and head matter was found to be more valuable, as it might be used in the interior of Houses without offending the smell. The distinction now first arose between the Northern and Southern fisheries; the object of the former being the Greenland whale, which frequents the Northern Coasts and Seas of Europe and America, that of the latter being

Marginal notes:
Encyclop. Meth. Planches. Cetologie, introdn. 23. ib. 24. Hakluyt. Sr. Joshua Child.
25 Car. 2. c. 7
6 G. 2. c. 33
13. G. 2. c. 28.
Encycl. Meth. Planches. Cetologie. Introdn. 24.
22. G. 2. c. 45.
5. Anders 308 (1778.)
6. Anders. 927.
Peleg Coffin's letter.
A tradition in Nantucket
Peleg Coffin's letter.
Tradition

* 25. Car. 2. c. 7
§ 6. G. 2. c. 33.

the Spermaceti whale, which was found in the Southern seas from the western Islands and Coast of Africa to that of Brazil, and still on to the Falkland Islands. Here again, within soundings on the Coast of Brazil they found a third species of whale, which they called the Black or Brazil whale, smaller than the Greenland, yielding a still less valuable oil, fit only for summer use, as it becomes opaque at 50 degrees of Farenheit's thermometer, while that of the Spermaceti whale is limpid to 41. and of the Greenland whale to 36. of the same Thermometer. It is only worth taking therefore when it falls in the way of the fishermen, but not worth seeking, except when they have failed of success against the spermaceti whale, in which case this kind, easily found and taken, serves to moderate their loss.

Pugh and others.

Pugh's experiments.

In 1771, the Americans had 183 vessels of 13,820 Tons in the Northern fishery, and 121 Vessels of 14,020 Tons in the Southern, navigated by 4059. men. At the beginning of the late war they had 177 vessels in the Northern and 132 in the Southern fishery.

Statement by committee of Mass. Statement given me at Paris

At that period, our fishery being suspended, the English seized the opportunity of pushing theirs. They gave additional bounties of 500. 400. 300. 200. 100 pounds sterling annually to the five Ships which should take the greatest quantities of oil; the effect of which was such as by the year 1786 to double the quantity of common oil necessary for their own consumption. Finding on a review of the subject at that time that their bounties had cost the Government £13-10 sterling a man annually, or 60 per cent on the cargoes, a part of which went consequently to ease the purchases of this article made by foreign nations, they reduced the Northern bounty from 40 to 30 shillings the Ton of admeasurement.

Seth Jenkins's examn. before the H. of Commons in 1775.

15. G. 3. c. Jenkinson in parl. 1786.

26. G. 3. c.

They had some little time before turned their attention to the Southern fishery, had given very great bounties in it, and had invited the fishermen of the United States to conduct their enterprizes. Under their guidance and with such encouragement, this fishery, which had only begun with them in 1784 or 1785, was rising into value. In 1788 they increased their bounties, and the temptations to our fishermen, under the general description of *foreigners who had been employed in the whale fishery*, to pass over with their families and vessels to the British Dominions either in America or Europe, but preferably to the latter. The effect of these measures had been prepared by our Whale Oils becoming subject in their market to the foreign duty of £18-5 sterling the Ton, which being more than equal to the price of the common oil,

26 G. 3. c. 50.

28 G. 3. c. 20.

operated as a prohibition on that, and gave to their own Sperma-ceti oil a preference over ours to that amount. The particulars of this history are presented to the eye more in detail in the table No. 7.

The fishermen of the United States left without resource by the loss of their market began to think of accepting the british invitation, and of removing some to Nova Scotia, preferring smaller advantages in the neighbourhood of their ancient Country and friends, others to Great Britain, postponing Country and friends to high premiums.

The Government of France could not be inattentive to these proceedings; they saw the danger of letting 4. or 5000 seamen, of the best in the world, be transferred to the marine strength of another nation, and carry over with them an art which they possessed almost exclusively. To give time for a counter plan, the Marquis de la Fayette, the valuable friend and Citizen of this as well as that Country, wrote to a Gentleman in Boston to dissuade the fishermen from accepting the british proposals, and to assure them that their friends in France would endeavour to do something for them. A vessel was then arrived from Halifax at Nantucket to take off those who had proposed to remove. Two families had gone aboard, and others were going. In this moment, the letter arriving, suspended their designs. Not another went aboard, and the vessel returned to Halifax with only the two families.

The plan adopted by the French Ministry very different from that of the first mover, was to give a counter-invitation to the Nantucket men to remove and settle in Dunkirk, offering them a bounty of 50 Livres (between 9. and 10. dollars) a Ton on the admeasurement of the Vessels they should equip for the whale fishery, with some other advantages. Nine families only of 33 persons, accepted this invitation. This was in 1785. In 1786 the ministry were led to see that their invitation would produce but little effect, and that the true means of preventing the emigration of our fishermen to the british Dominions, would be to enable them still to follow their calling from their native Country, by giving them a new market for their oils, instead of the old one they had lost; the duties were therefore abated on American whale oil immediately, and a further abatement promised by the letter No. 8, and in December 1787 the Arret No. 9 was passed.

The rival fishermen immediately endeavoured to turn this

Convention with the Nantuckois Dec. 5. 1785.

Rotch.

measure to their own advantage, by pouring their whale oils into the markets of France, where they were enabled by the great premiums received from their Government, perhaps too by extraordinary indemnifications, to undersell both the French and American fishermen. To repel this measure, France shut her Ports to all foreign fish oils whatever, by the Arret No. 10. The british whale fishery fell in consequence the ensuing year from 222 to 178 Ships. But this general exclusion had palsied our fishery also. On the 7th. of December 1788 therefore, by the Arret No. 11, the Ports of France, still remaining shut to all other Nations, were again opened to the produce of the whale fisheries of the United States, continuing however their endeavours to recover a share in this fishery themselves, by the aid of our fishermen. In 1784. 1785. 1786. they had had 4 Ships. In 1787 three. In 1788. 17. in the two fisheries, of 4500 Ton. These cost them in bounty 225,000 Livres which divided on 1550 Tons of oil, the quantity they took, amounted to 145 Livres (near 27 Dollars) the Ton, and on about 100 natives on board the 17 Ships (for there were 150 Americans engaged by the voyage) came to 2250 Livres, or about 416⅔ dollars a man. *Rotch. But Chardon says 6. in the Encycl. Meth. ubi supra. pa. 26. Rotch.*

We have had during the years 1787. 1788. 1789. on an average 91 vessels of 5820 Tons in the Northern, and 31 of 4390 Tons in the Southern fishery. See No. 12. *Statement by Committee of Mass.*

These details will enable Congress to see with what a competition we have to struggle for the continuance of this fishery, not to say it's increase. Against prohibitory duties in one country, and bounties to the adventurers in both of those which are contending with each other for the same object, ours have no auxiliaries but poverty and rigorous economy. The business, unaided, is a wretched one. The Dutch have peculiar advantages for the Northern fishery, as being within 6 or 8. days sail of the grounds, as navigating with more economy than any other nation in Europe, their seamen content with lower wages, and their merchants with lower profit. Yet the Memorial No. 13 from a Committee of the Whale Merchants to the States General of Holland in the year 1775. states that 14 millions of guilders equal to 5,600,000 dollars, had been lost in that fishery in 47 years, being about 120,000 dollars a year. The States General thereupon gave a bounty of 30 guilders a man to the fishermen. A person intimately *Pugh.* acquainted with the british whale fishery, and whose information merits confidence, has given assurance that the Ships employed in their Northern fishery in 1788, sunk £800 each on an average, more than the amount of the produce and bounties. An English ship of 300 Tons and 42 Seamen in this fishery generally brings home, after a four months voyage 25 Ton of Oil, worth £437.10 sterling. But the wages of the Officers and seamen will be 400. There remain but £37.10 not worth taking into account, towards the outfit and merchants profit. These then must be paid by the Government, and it is on this idea that the british bounty is calculated.

Our vessels for the Northern fishery average 64 Tons, and cost when built, fitted out and victualled for their first voyage about 3000 dollars. They have taken on an average the three last years, according to the statement No. 12. 18 Tons of oil, worth, at our market 900 dollars, which are to pay all expences, and subsist the fisherman and Merchant. Our vessels for the Southern fishery average 140 Tons, and cost when built, fitted out and victualled for their first voyage about 6500 dollars. They have taken on an average the three last years according to the same statement 32 Tons of oil, each, worth at our market 3200 dollars, which are in like manner to pay all expences and subsist the owners and navigators. These expences are great, as the voyages are generally of 12 months duration. No hope can arise of their condition being bettered by an augmentation of the price of oil. This is kept down by the competition of the vegetable oils, which answer the same purposes, not quite so well, but well enough to become preferable, were the price to be raised, and so well indeed as to be more generally used than the fish oils for lighting Houses and Cities.

The American whale fishery is principally followed by the inhabitants of the Island of Nantucket, a sand Bar of about 15 miles long and 3 broad, capable of maintaining by its agriculture about 20 families. But it employed in these fisheries before the war, between 5 and 6000 men and boys. And in the only harbour it possesses it had 140 vessels, 132 of which were of the larger kind, as being employed in the Southern fishery. In agriculture then they have no resource, and if that of their fishery cannot be pursued from their own habitations, it is natural they should seek others from which it can be followed, and preferably those where they will find a sameness of language, religion, laws, habits and kindred. A foreign emissary has lately been among them for the purpose of renewing the invitations to a change of situation. But attached to their native Country, they prefer continuing in it, if their continuance there can be made supportable.

Pugh.

Table No. 12.

Examination of Seth Jenkins

Gore's letter to Mr. Lear about Stokes

This brings us to the question what relief does the condition of this fishery require?

1. A remission of duties on the Articles used for their calling.

2. A retaliating duty on foreign oils, coming to seek a competition with them in or from our Ports.

3. Free markets abroad.

1. The remission of duties will stand on nearly the same ground with that to the Cod fishermen.

2. The only Nation whose oil is brought hither for competition with our own, makes ours pay a duty of about 82. dollars the Ton in their Ports. Theirs is brought here, too, to be reshipped fraudulently under our flag into ports where it could not be received under theirs, and ought not to be covered by ours, if we mean to preserve our own admission into them.

The 3d. and principal object is to find markets for the vent of oil.

Portugal, England, Holland, Sweden, Denmark, Prussia, Russia, the Hanse Towns, supply themselves and something more. Spain and Italy receive supplies from England, and need the less as their skies are clearer. France is the only Country which can take our surplus, and they take principally of the common oil, as the habit is but commencing with them of ascribing a just value to that of the Spermaceti whale. Some of this however finds it's vent there. There was indeed a particular interest perpetually soliciting the exclusion of our oils from their markets. The late Government there saw well that what we should lose thereby would be gained by others, not by themselves. And we are to hope that the present Government, as wise and friendly, will also view us, not as rivals, but as co-operators against a common rival. Friendly arrangements with them, and accomodation to mutual interest, rendered easier by friendly dispositions existing on both sides, may long secure to us this important resource for our seamen. Nor is it the interest of the fisherman alone, which calls for the cultivation of friendly arrangements with that Nation. Besides five eighths of our whale oil, and two thirds of our salted fish, they take from us one fourth of our Tobacco, three fourths of our live Stock (No. 14), a considerable and growing portion of our Rice, great supplies occasionally of other grain; in 1789. which indeed was extraordinary, four millions of bushels of wheat, and upwards of a million of bushels of Rye and Barley (No. 15.) and nearly the whole carried in our own vessels (No. 16). They are

Bureau of the balance of commerce in France.

a free market now, and will in time be a valuable one for our Ships and Ship timber, potash and peltry.[6]

England is the market for the greater part of our Spermaceti oil. They impose on all our oils a duty of £18.5. sterling the Ton, which, as to the common kind, is a prohibition as has been before observed, and as to that of the Spermaceti, gives a preference of theirs over ours to that amount, so as to leave in the end but a scanty benefit to the fisherman. And not long since, by a change of construction, without any change of the law, it was made to exclude our oils from their ports, when carried in our own vessels. On some change of circumstances it was construed back again to the reception of our oils, on paying always however the same duty of £18.5. This serves to shew that the tenure by which we hold the admission of this commodity in their markets, is as precarious as it is hard. Nor can it be announced that there is any disposition on their part to arrange this or any other commercial matter to mutual convenience. The exparte regulations which they have begun for mounting their navigation on the ruins of ours, can only be opposed by counter-regulations on our part. And the loss of seamen, the natural consequence of lost and obstructed markets for our fish and oil, calls in the first place for serious and timely attention. It will be too late when the seaman shall have changed his vocation, or gone over to another interest. If we cannot recover and secure for him these important branches of employment, it behoves us to replace them by others equivalent. We have three nurseries for forming seamen. 1. Our coasting trade, already on a safe[7] footing. 2. Our fisheries, which, in spight of natural advantages give just cause of anxiety. 3. Our carrying trade the only resource of indemnification for what we lose in the other. The produce of the United States which is carried to foreign markets, is extremely bulky. That part of it now in the hands of foreigners, and which we may resume into our own, without touching the rights of those nations who have met us in fair[8] arrangements by Treaty, or the interests of those who by their voluntary regulations, have paid so just and liberal a respect to our interests, as being measured back to them again, places both parties on as good ground perhaps as Treaties could place them, the proportion I say of our carrying trade which may be resumed without affecting either of these descriptions of Nations, will find constant employment for 10,000 seamen, be worth 2 Millions of dollars annually, will go on augmenting with the population of the United States, secure to us a full indemnification for the Seamen we lose,

Proclamation of Apr. 1 1790.

Proclamation of Oct. 5. 1790.

and be taken wholly from those who force us to this act of self-protection, in navigation.

Hence too would follow that their Newfoundland ships, not receiving provisions from us in their bottoms, nor permitted (by a law of their own) to receive in ours, must draw their subsistance from Europe, which would increase that part of their expences in the proportion of 4. to 7. and so far operate as a duty towards restoring the level between them and us. The tables No. 2. and 12. will shew the quantity of Tonnage, and consequently the mass of Seamen whose interests are in distress, and No. ⁹ the materials for indemnification.

If regulations, exactly the counterpart of those established against us, would be ineffectual, from a difference of circumstances, other regulations equivalent can give no reasonable ground of complaint to any nation. Admitting their right of keeping their markets to themselves, ours cannot be denied of keeping our carrying trade to ourselves. And if there be any thing unfriendly in this, it was in the first example.¹⁰

The loss of seamen, unnoticed, would be followed by other losses in a long train. If we have no seamen, our ships will be useless, consequently our Ship timber, Iron and hemp: our Ship building will be at an end, ship carpenters go over to other nations, our young men have no call to the Sea, our produce, carried in foreign bottoms, be saddled with war freight and insurance, in times of war; and the history of the last hundred years shews that the nation which is our carrier has 3. years of war for any 4. years of peace (No. 18.); we lose, during the same periods, the carriage for belligerent powers, which the neutrality of our flag would render an incalculable¹¹ source of profit, we lose, at this moment, the carriage of our own produce to the annual amount of 2 millions of dollars, which in the possible progress of the encroachment, may extend to 5. or 6. millions, the worth of the whole, with an increase in proportion to the increase of our numbers. It is easier, as well as better, to stop this train at it's entrance, than when it shall have ruined or banished whole classes of useful and industrious Citizens.

It will doubtless be thought expedient that the resumption suggested should take effect so gradually as not to endanger the loss of produce for the want of transportation: but that, in order to create transportation, the whole plan should be developed, and made known at once, that the individuals who may be disposed

Champion 119.

The whole tonnage from the U.S. would have been about 650,-000. had N. Carolina and R. isld. been included. This on a medium freight of D. to all parts of the world would be nearly 6. millions of dollars. T. Coxe. But in another view 25 millions of dollars worth of exports @ 20. pr. cent freight, would be 5 millions.

to lay themselves out for the carrying business, may make their calculations on a full view of all circumstances.

On the whole, the historical view we have taken of these fisheries proves they are so poor in themselves as to come to nothing with distant nations who do not support them from their Treasury. We have seen that the advantages of our position place our fisheries on a ground somewhat higher such as to relieve our Treasury from the necessity of giving them support, but not to permit it to draw support from them, nor to dispense the Government from the obligation of effectuating free markets for them: that for the great proportion of our salted fish, for our common oil, and a part of our Spermaceti oil, markets may perhaps be preserved by friendly arrangements towards those nations whose arrangements are friendly to us, and the residue be compensated by giving to the seamen thrown out of business the certainty of employment in another branch of which we have the sole disposal.

TH: JEFFERSON Secy. of state.
Feb. 1. 1791.

FC (DLC: TJ Papers, 60: 10413-65); text of Report is in Blackwell's hand except for signature, date, interlinear corrections, and marginal citations of authorities, which are in TJ's hand (texts of the 18 items in the Appendix are in various hands and for convenience citations for rough drafts and other texts are given individually for each of these items). It is important to note that *only* the four citations of authorities at the foot of the page were included in the *Report* as submitted, TJ's marginalia as shown above being set down only on his own file copy. With this exception FC agrees with text of report as submitted and as recorded in DNA: RG 59, Record of Reports of Thomas Jefferson, 175-252, in hand of Lambert who endorsed FC as "Recorded and Examined. February 1st. 1791." Dft (DLC: TJ Papers, 60: 10466-81); actually a fair copy of a (missing) composition draft, entirely in TJ's hand and endorsed by him: "Fisheries. Report on."; contains a number of deletions, some of which are indicated in notes below. Dft does not contain appendix; it consists of text of the *Report* only (but see notes to nos. 1-18).

1 Thus in all texts; but see Table (Appendix No. 1), where the figure is given as 25,000.
2 In Dft TJ first wrote: "a rival nation aiming at the sole empire of the seas," and then altered the passage to read as above.
3 At this point in Dft TJ first wrote and then deleted: "according to the example of other nations till corrected by experience."
4 Preceding seven words interlined in above text and also in Dft.
5 At this point TJ first wrote and then deleted: "every 25. years."
6 In Dft TJ first wrote and then deleted: "It is so reasonable too that they should permit their Colonies to seek the first necessaries of life where they can get them cheapest, that the indulgence, or rather right, will scarcely be refused by a nation setting so remarkable an example of taking the pure principles of reason and right for their guide, instead of the crooked maxims of interest and jealousy, which have so long misled the short-sighted ⟨politician⟩ statesman."
7 TJ first wrote and then deleted: "proper."
8 TJ first added "and equal" and then deleted the words.
9 Blank in MS; other texts read "No. 17."
10 TJ first wrote: ". . . it is in the example, not in the imitation," and then altered the passage to read as above.
11 This word interlined in Dft in substitution for "immense," deleted.

No. 1

An Historical View of the Cod-fisheries of France, England, and the United States.

	France					England					United States				
	Vessels	Tonage	Seamen	Kentals	Value Dollars	Vessels	Tonage	Seamen	Kentals	Value Dollars	Vessels	Tonage	Seamen	Kentals	Value Dollars
1577	150					15									
1615						150									
1626						150		8,000							
1670						80									
1676						102		9,180							
1731										1,738,800					
1744	564		27,500	1,441,500					200,000	540,000				230,000	621,000
1764											300				
1765											665	25,000	4,405	350,500	1,071,000
1766											665	25,000	4,405	350,500	1,071,000
1767											665	25,000	4,405	350,500	1,071,000
1768	259	24,420	9,722	200,000	861,723						665	25,000	4,405	350,500	1,071,000
1769											665	25,000	4,405	350,500	1,071,000
1770											665	25,000	4,405	350,500	1,071,000
1771											665	25,000	4,405	350,500	1,071,000
1772								25,000	486,561		665	25,000	4,405	350,500	1,071,000
1773	264	24,996	10,128						516,000		665	25,000	4,405	350,000	1,071,000
1774									516,000		665	25,000	4,405	350,500	1,071,000
1775						400	36,000	20,000	600,000	2,250,000	665	25,000	4,405	350,500	1,071,000
1785								7,000							
1786			7,000	426,000					470,000		539	19,185	3,287	250,650	609,900
1787			6,000	128,000				14,000	732,000		539	19,185	3,287	250,650	609,900
1788											539	19,185	3,287	250,650	609,900
1789											539	19,185	3,287	250,650	609,900
1790											539	19,185	3,287	354,276	865,207

MS (DLC: TJ Papers, 232: 41651); entirely in TJ's hand. PrC (DLC: TJ Papers, 60: 10432); in Taylor's hand except for "No. 1." inserted by TJ at head of text. Tr (DNA: RG 59, Record of Reports of Thomas Jefferson). Dft (DLC: TJ Papers, 233: 41643). The last differs from other texts in these particulars: (1) the columns are in different order ("America," England, France); (2) a fourth column lists "Authorities" for the figures given; (3) the value for the cod fishery for the United States in 1731 is expressed as "138.000 £ sterl."; (4) the figures for the United States for 1790 are listed as of 1789 and as derived from "Treasury Abstracts"; (5) the figures for the United States for the two periods 1765-1775 and 1786-1790 are not repeated as above but are bracketed under a single entry and are cited as having been derived from the "Massachusets commee."; and (6) one entry for 1605 listing 250 vessels for England, but giving no other statistic and citing "2 And[erson] 24. Cites Child" as authority, is deleted. All other authorities in final column of Dft for the figures for France and England for the years 1577-1787 are cited line by line in the following sequence:

"[1577] 2 Anderson. 192.
[1615] 2 And. 353. cites Trade's increas[e]
[1626] 2 And. 422. cites Golden fleece.
[1670] 3 And. 24. cites Child.
[1676] 3 And. 53. cites M. S.
[1731] 3 And. 426. cites Import[an]ce of Brit[ish] plan[tations]
[1744] Sheffield. Tab. 8.
[1764] 5 And. 242.
         Champion. 77. cites Brook Watso[n]
[1768] Raynal.
[1772] Shef. 57. Champion. 57.
[1773] 5 And. 920. Mr. Pitt.
[1774] Do.
[1775] 5 And. 242. Evid[en]ce on bill for rest[or]ing commerce of New Engld.
[1786] ib.
[1787] ib."

In DLC: TJ Papers, 233: 41653 there is another chronological account of the fisheries from 1496 to 1787 that TJ also prepared largely on the basis of *Anderson's historical and chronological deduction of the origin of commerce*, by Adam Anderson (TJ possessed the 6-vol. Dublin, 1790 edition; Sowerby, No. 3545). On the verso of this outline TJ recorded the chronology of events leading up to his report, beginning with the petition from Marblehead of 1 Feb. 1790 and concluding with the report of the committee of inquiry to Governor Hancock on 13 Oct. 1790. Other memoranda by TJ based on Anderson's work and on documents employed in preparing the report are to be found in DLC: TJ Papers, 233: 41654-5.

No. 2.

State of Code fishery of Massachusetts from 1765 to 1775.   From 1786 to 1790, Inclusive

	Vessels annually	Tonnage	Seamen	Kentals to Europe @ 3.5 D.	Kentals to W: Indies @ 2.6 D.	Vessels annually	Tonnage	Seamen	Kentals to Europe @ 3. D.	Kentals to West Indies @ 2. D.
Marblehead ..	150	7,500	1200	80,000	40,000	90	5,400	720	50,000	25,000
Gloucester ...	146	5,530	888	35,000	42,500	160	3,600	680	19,500	28,500
Manchester ..	25	1,500	200	10,000	10,000	15	900	120	3,000	7,500
Beverley	15	750	120	6,000	6,000	19	1,235	152	5,200	10,000
Salem	30	1,500	240	12,000	12,000	20	1,300	160	6,000	10,000
Newburyport .	10	400	60	2,000	2,000	10	460	80	1,000	5,000
Ipswich	50	900	190	8,000	5,500	56	860	248	3,000	6,000
Plymouth	60	2,400	420	8,000	16,000	36	1,440	252	6,000	12,000
Cohasset	6	240	42	800	1,600	5	200	35	1,000	1,500
Hingham	6	240	42	800	1,600	4	180	32	800	1,200
Scituate	10	400	70	1,000	3,000	2	90	16	400	600
Duxborough .	4	160	28	400	1,200	9	360	72	1,500	3,000
Kingston	6	240	42	800	1,600	4	160	28	700	1,300
Yarmouth ...	30	900	180	3,000	6,000	30	900	180	2,000	10,000
Wellfleet ...	3	90	21	300	600	—	—	—	—	—
Truro	10	400	80	1,000	3,000	—	—	—	—	—
Provincetown	4	160	32	500	1,100	11	550	88	3,000	5,200
Chatham	30	900	240	4,000	8,000	30	900	240	3,000	9,000
Nantucket ...	8	320	64	1,000	2,200	5	200	40	500	1,500
Maine	60	1,000	230	4,000	8,000	30	300	120	1,000	3,500
Weymouth ...	2	100	16	200	600	3	150	24	1,000	1,250
	665	25,630	4,405	178,800	172,500	539	19,185	3,287	108,600	142,050

PrC (DLC: TJ Papers, 60: 10433); in Taylor's hand except for "No. 2." inserted by TJ at head of text. Dft (DLC: TJ Papers, 233: 41643); entirely in TJ's hand. Tr (DNA: RG 59, Record of Reports of Thomas Jefferson). FC (DLC: TJ Papers, 233: 41646); entirely in TJ's hand. MS (MBA); in clerk's hand on two separate sheets; text differs from PrC in captions given to the columns and in following note at foot of the first table: "N.B. The quantity of fish consumed in the United States being inconsiderable the Committee have made no allowance for that consumption, but have considered the whole quantity taken as Exported." (Both sheets of MS comprise the text of enclosures Nos. 3 and 4 in Hancock to TJ, 25 Oct. 1790; see Document I above.)

For TJ's use of these statistics, together with other data furnished by Tench Coxe, in calculating the amount of duties paid by each fisherman on salt, cordage, and other items used in the cod fishery, see note to Appendix No. 6.

No. 3.

Abstract of the Produce of the Fisheries exported from the United States, from about August 20th. 1789, to September 30th. 1790.

	Fish dried		Fish pickled		Oil—Whale		Oil spermaceti		Whale bone		Candles spermaceti		Total Value
	Quantity	Value	Quantity	Value	Quantity	Value	Quantity	Value	Quantity	Value	Quantity	Value	
	Quintals	Dollars	Bbls.	Dollrs	Barrels	Dollrs	Barrels	Dollars	lbs.	Dollrs	lbs.	Dollars	Dollars
France	543	1,086	12	20	9,914	73,767	1,403	17,523	108,807	17,917	1,200	480	749,497
French West Indies	251,116	518,288	29,294	90,818	1,756	13,685	80	1,029	—	—	38,754	14,884	749,497
Amt. of 1st: Class	251,659	519,374	29,306	90,838	11,670	87,452	1,483	18,552	108,807	17,917	39,954	15,364	749,497
Spain	72,300	194,457	280	813	593	4,174	—	—	—	—	2,896	1,256	203,276
Spanish West Indies & Florida	824	978	300	886	5	38					1,685	674	203,276
Great Britain	5	10	—	—	1,738	21,048	3,840	60,000	1,075	215			89,859
British Wst. Indies	1,970	4,114	795	3,075	15	124					756	353	89,859
Nova Scotia	—	—	13	40	1	10	100	870					
Holland	—	—	15	45	807	5,683			5,220	1,050			79,404
Dutch Wt. Indies	23,822	48,631	4,778	13,404	179	1,317					23,162	9,274	79,404
Portugal	18,594	41,306	69	242	4	60					148	58	55,137
Portuguese Islands	5,432	11,307	292	801	139	1,243	8	120	6,150	1,230			55,137
Germany					470	2,990							4,220
Danish Wt. Indies	1,180	2,386	803	2,421	3	27							4,834
African Isl. & Coast of Africa	613	1,324	147	564	6	42					165	66	1,996
Mediterranean	2,314	4,628	6	36	135	700			29	5	328	150	5,519
Sweden	8	16											16
East Indies											1,285	529	529
Amt. of 2d: Class	127,062	309,157	7,498	22,327	4,095	37,456	3,948	60,990	12,474	2,500	30,425	12,360	444,790
Amt. of both Classes	378,721	828,531	36,804	113,165	15,765	124,908	5,431	79,542	121,281	20,417	70,379	27,724	1,194,287

PrC (DLC: TJ Papers, 60: 10434); in Taylor's hand except for "No. 3." inserted by TJ at head of text. Tr (DNA: RG 59, Record of Reports of Thomas Jefferson). MS (DLC: TJ Papers, 57: 9835); entirely in TJ's hand. The last is an abstract showing that TJ at first contemplated using this as Appendix No. 14 and that he intended to give a mere summary contrasting the total exports of the cod and whale fisheries to France and the French West Indies with those of the rest of the world.

No. 4.

Abstract of articles imported into the United States from British colonies for one year, commencing the 15th. August 1789 and ending on the 14th. of August 1790, as far as the accounts have been rendered.

      6,343 barrels of pickled Fish.

Cwt. 3,701. 2.20 ℔s. of dried Fish.

Note. Oil and Lumber imported, paying a Duty ad valorem, the quantity of each can only be ascertained by the several Collectors, having reference to the original Entries.

JOSEPH NOURSE Register.

Treasury Department Registers Office
23d. November 1790.

PrC (DLC: TJ Papers 60: 10435); in hand of Remsen except for "No. 4." inserted by TJ at head of text. Dft (DLC: TJ Papers, 233: 41643); entirely in TJ's hand, giving merely the figures. Tr (DNA: RG 59, Record of Reports of Thomas Jefferson).

No. 5.

Marblehead Feby. 1st. 1790.

We the Subscribers being a Committee appointed by the Owners of fishing Vessels in the Town of Marblehead, to take into Consideration the many Grievances and Burdens the Cod fishery now labors under, and to make a Statement of them, which Statement so made to be handed to Colo. Glover, by him to be laid before the Committee of the General Court appointed to consider the same, do report the said Statement as follows, Vizt.

1st.   Impost Duties on Salt
2d.   Impost Duties and Excise on Rum, Sugar, and Molasses
3rd.   Impost on Hooks, Lines, and Leads
4th.   on Coarse Woolens
5.   on Duck, Cordage, and Cables
6.   on Hemp, Iron, and Twine
7.   Tonnage and Naval Duties
8.   the ineffectual Duties on foreign Fish
9.   the Duties our Fisheries pay at foreign Markets, while the Fisheries of France and England receive large Privileges and Bounties from their Governments.
10.   the Heavy Poll tax laid on the Fishermen
11.   Excise on New England Rum.

It appears to the Committee from an exact Investigation that the Earnings and Expenses of the fishing Schooners of this Town for the Years 1787 and 1788 and 1789 were to the Earnings of each Schooner vizt.

For the Year 1787	£145
For the Year 1788	137
For the Year 1789	82
and that the Annual average Expenses of these	
Vessels inclusive of Insurance	124

It also appears that the Number of Schooners employed in the Grand bank fishery for the Year 1789 were one hundred and twenty four, nineteen of which were Property of Persons not belonging to the Town, and of which Number thirty three sail have been taken out of the Fishery from the Declension of the Business exclusive of the aforementioned Disadvantages.

That the Bounty granted to the fishery by Congress as a Compensation for the Duty on Salt, this Committee humbly Conceive will not operate to that Purpose so effectually, as if paid direct into the Hands of the Owners of the Vessells, instead of the Shippers of the fish.

Jno. Glover	Richard Pedrick
Israel Forster	Knott Pedrick
Edwd. Fetyplace	Samuel R. Gerry
William Knight	Richard James
Samuel Hooper	Joshua Orne
Robert Hooper junr.	Marston Watson
William R. Lee	

A true Copy Attest
JOHN AVERY JUNR. Secretary

PrC (DLC: TJ Papers, 60: 10436-8); in Taylor's hand except for "No. 5." inserted by TJ at head of text. MS (MBA: R169, Resolves of 1789). Tr (DNA: RG 59, Record of Reports of Thomas Jefferson).

No. 6.

An estimate of the Duties paid by the Proprietors and Navigators of a fishing Vessel of 65 tons and 11 hands.

	dolls.
Duty on Salt	80.25
Rum	14.
Tea	2.54
Sugar	3.3
Molasses	.99
Coarse woolens	7.33

Lines, lead and hooks	2.09
Sail cloth, yearly average	2.5
Cordage, cables do.	20.
Tonnage	3.9
Iron, yearly average	1.

138. divided on 11

Men, is 12.5 dollars per man. But deducting the drawback of the duty on Salt It remains 57.75 dollars on the whole. or 5.25 dollars on each man.

PrC (DLC: TJ Papers, 60: 10439); in Remsen's hand except for "No. 6." inserted by TJ at head of text. Dft (DLC: TJ Papers, 234: 41901); in TJ's hand, with calculations showing that he allotted to the eleven men 76 quintals of salt, 11 gallons of rum, 2 pounds of tea, and 20 pounds of sugar. MS (DLC: TJ Papers, 233: 41647); entirely in TJ's hand. Tr (DNA: RG 59, Record of Reports of Thomas Jefferson).

Tench Coxe assisted TJ in compiling these figures by furnishing the following document:

"100 bushels of Salt are used in curing 100 barrels of *pickled* fish, or one bushell per barrel. Duty 12 cents per bushel.

80 bushels of salt are expended in curing 100 Quintals of dried fish, or 4/5 of a bushel per quintal. Duty 12 Cents per quintal.

11 gallons of Rum per season of 8 months for each man, if of New England quality, proposed duty twelve cents per gallon.

2 lb. of Tea, duty 12 cents per lb. or coffee, or chocolate equivalent (per do. of do.) for each man.

20 lb. of sugar per ditto of do. for ditto, duty per lb. 1 1/2 Cents.

3 gallons of Melasses per do. of do. for do. duty 3 cents per gallon.

Coarse woolen cloth, hosiery &c. as purchased by the men, 10 dollars each. Prime-cost 60/ Stg., duty two thirds of a dollar per man.

Lines, lead and hooks 2 1/4 dollars per man duty about 19 cents per man.

Sailcloth for a vessel of 65 Tons—value 150 dollars—duty 7 1/2 dollars.

Cordage and Cables per vessel of 65 Tons 2 1/2 to 3 Tons, to fit out when new; duty, if imported, 20 dollars per ton. This would be better for the owners of fishing Vessels, than to allow the duty on hemp which is only 54 cents per Cwt. or 10 80/100 Dollars per Ton.

Tonnage 6 cents per ton, once per annum. No other naval duties.

Twine, trivial, in sails only—and it is made here.

Iron for this and many other reasons should be *free*—duty on the quantity used for a vessel of 65 Tons about six dollars.

There is no poll tax under the laws of the Union, but there is under those of Massachusetts.

A further remark relative to the abolition of the Tonnage of six cents.

It appears by the return of Tonnage for one year made from the Treasury, that the *foreign* Tonnage alone is 135,000 dollars per annum. The expences of the lighthouses, beacons, buoys and public piers for 1790 was less than 45,000 dollars or one third of the above sum, including 24,000 granted for the Chesapeak light house, and 1500 dollars for completing that at Portland Head. Whence it is manifest that the six cents on the fishing vessels might be abolished and that these would remain an abundant fund for those purposes" (MS in DLC: TJ Papers, 60: 10483; entirely in Coxe's hand except for the pencilled note by TJ at foot of text, quoted below; not recorded in SJL but endorsed as received 1 Feb. [1791]).

On the last page of Coxe's manuscript, TJ, basing his calculations on the statistics set forth in Appendix No. 2 in order to estimate the amount of duties levied on each fisherman on salt and the other items listed in Appendix No. 6, made the following pencilled note: "3,287 men to 19,185 tons gives near 6. ton to a man. 108,-600 + 142,050 K [i.e., Quintals] = 250,650 K to 3,287 men is 76 K. to a man. A vessel of 65. tons then has 11 men and takes 836 K."

No. 7.

An Historical View of the Whale Fisheries of Holland, England, and the United States.

	Holland	England	
1578			Basques 25.
1612		2	
1615	11	4	
1620		7	
1663	202		
1669	138		
1670	148		Hamburg abt. 350
1678	120		Eng. bounty 6/.
1683	242		
1686	189		
1688	214		
1692	32		
1702	224		
1713	93		
1715			Americans begin
1721	260		Hamburg 79. Basques. 20.
1725	226	12	
1726	218	14	
1727	202	16	
1728	182	18	
1729	184	20	Basques. 27.
1730	168	22	Basques 33
1731	164	22	America 1300, Tons on their own Coast
1732	176	21	
1733	184	2	Basques 15 to 20 Eng. bounty 20/
1736	191	1	Basques 10 to 12
1737	196		
1744			Eng. bounty 30/ Basques 5 or 6[1]
1748	94		
1755	181	66	Eng. bounty 40/
1756	186	67	
1757	180	55	

	Holland	England	United States North	United States South	Tons.
1758	159	52			
1759	155	34			
1760	154	40			
1761	161	31			
1762	165	28			
1763		30			
1764	161	32			
1765	165	33			America, 150.
1766	167	35			
1767	165	39			
1768	160	41			
1769	152	44			viz 13,820 North 14,020 South 4059 men.
1770	150	50	183	121	
1771	150	50			
1772	131	48			
1773	134	55			
1774	130	65			
1775	129	96	177	132	Eng. bounty 500£. 400£. 300£. 200£. 100£.
1776	123	91			Dutch bounty 30f a Man
1777	116	77			
1778	111	71			
1779	105	59			English bounty 30/
1780	82	52			
1781		34			English bounty 40/
1782		38			
1783	55	47			
1784	62	93			France 4. Ships
	North	South			
1785	65	154	18		
1786	67	153			Eng. bounty 30/
1787	67	217	38	91	31 viz. 5820 tons North. 4390 tons South. 1611. men. France 3 Ships
1788	69	222	54	91	31 France 17
1789		178		91	31 Hamburg 32

PrC (DLC: TJ Papers, 60: 10440); in Taylor's hand except for "No. 7." inserted by TJ at head of text. Dft (DLC: TJ Papers, 233: 41624); entirely in TJ's hand; contains one variation not in other texts (see note 1). FC (DLC: TJ Papers, 233: 41657); entirely in TJ's hand. Tr (DNA: RG 59, Record of Reports of Thomas Jefferson).

[1] Dft reads: "Basques 5. or 6. War begun. Here the English success begins."

No. 8.

[Text of Calonne to TJ, 22 Oct. 1786, here omitted (see Vol. 10: 474-6). In addition to texts cited there, an English translation is in DLC: TJ Papers, 60: 10441-6 (PrC in Blackwell's hand except for "No. 8." inserted by TJ at head of text) and also in DNA: RG 59, Record of Reports of Thomas Jefferson.]

No. 9.

["An Act of the King's Council of State, for the encouragement of the Commerce of France with the United States of America," 29 Dec. 1787, printed above Vol. 12: 468-70 and here omitted. In addition to the parallel-column text employed there, an 8-page official printing with English and French texts in parallel columns (not including the covering letter by Lambert) is in DLC: TJ Papers, 60: 10447-50, with "No. 9." at head of text and with the colophon "A Paris, de L'Imprimerie Royale, 1787." TJ submitted with his report only the English translation as taken from this official text (Tr in DNA: RG 59, Record of Reports of Thomas Jefferson).]

No. 10.

["Arret of the King's Council of State, prohibiting the importation of foreign Whale and spermaceti oil into his kingdom," 28 Sep. 1788, printed above Vol. 14: 216, note, and here omitted. In addition to the text employed there, a PrC in Blackwell's hand save for "No. 10." inserted by TJ at head of text is in DLC: TJ Papers, 60: 10451-2. Tr of English version as submitted with TJ's report is in DNA: RG 59, Record of Reports of Thomas Jefferson.]

No. 11.

["Arret of the Kings Council of State, expecting Whale and other fish Oil, and also Whale bone, the product of the fisheries of the United States of America, from the prohibition contained in the Arret of the 28th. September last," 7 Dec. 1788, printed above Vol. 14: 268-9 and here omitted. In addition to the text there employed, a PrC in Remsen's hand save for "No. 11." inserted by TJ at head of text is in DLC: TJ Papers, 60: 10453-5. Tr of English version as submitted with TJ's report is in DNA: RG 59, Record of Reports of Thomas Jefferson.]

No. 12.

State of the Whale Fishery in Massachusetts from 1771 to 1775.

Ports from which the Equipments were made.	The number of vessels fitted out Annually for the Northern Fishery	Their Tonnage	The number of vessels fitted out Annually for the Southern Fishery	Their Tonnage	The number of Seamen employed	Barrels of Spermaceti Oil taken annually	Barrels of Whale Oil taken annually
Nantucket	65	4,875	85	10,200	2,025	26,000	4,000
Wellfleet	20	1,600	10	1,000	420	2,250	2,250
Dartmouth	60	4,500	20	2,000	1,040	7,200	1,400
Lynn	1	75	1	120	28	200	100
Martha's Vineyard	12	720			156	900	300
Barnstable	2	150			26	240	
Boston	15	1,300	5	700	260	1,800	600
Falmouth in the County of Barnstable	4	300			52	400	
Swanzey	4	300			52	400	
	183	13,820	121	14,020	4,059	39,390	8,650

State of the Whale Fishery from 1787 to 1789 both inclusive.

Ports from which the Equipments were made.	The number of vessels fitted out Annually for the Northern Fishery	Their Tonnage	The number of vessels fitted out Annually for the Southern Fishery	Their Tonnage	The number of Seamen employed	Barrels of Spermaceti Oil taken annually	Barrels of Whale Oil taken annually
Nantucket	18	1,350	18	2,700	487	3,800	8,260
Wellfleet & other Ports at Cape Cod	12	720	4	400	212		1,920
Dartmouth	45	2,700	5	750	650	2,700	1,750
Cape Ann			2	350	28		1,200
Plymouth	1	60			13	100	
Martha's Vineyard	2	120	1	100	39	220	
Boston	6	450			78	360	
Rochester & Wareham	7	420	1	90	104	800	
	91	5,820	31	4,390	1,611	7,980	13,130

True Copy, Attest John Avery Junr. Secretary

N.B. About one quarter of the Spermaceti is head matter, the remainder manufactured into Candles. The Spermaceti Oil, previous to the Revolution, was mostly exported to Great Britain. The average price in that market for five years previous to the War, about forty pounds sterling for the Spermaceti Oil, and fifty pounds for Head. The Whale Oil was formerly about one half exported to the French and English West India Islands, the other half sold in the United States. The average price of this Oil, about seventy Dollars per Ton. A whale producing one hundred and twenty Barrels whale oil, will generally produce 2000 ℔. Bone, which was chiefly exported to Great Britain, the price about half a Dollar pr. pound. A whale producing 50 to 60 Barrels, will generally produce nearest ten pounds of bone to a Barrel of oil.—The average price of Oil for three years past, as follows, vizt. Spermaceti, one hundred dollars ⅌ ton. Whale Oil, fifty Dollars ⅌ ton. Head matter, one hundred and fifty do. ⅌ ton. Bone, about fifteen Cents ⅌ pound.

PrC (DLC: TJ Papers, 60: 10456); in hand of Lambert except for "No. 12." inserted by TJ at head of text. Tr (DNA: RG 59,

Record of Reports of Thomas Jefferson). FC (MBA). (Text of FC was enclosure No. 5 in Hancock to TJ; see Document I above.)

No. 13.

["Extract from a Memorial presented to the States General in 1775 by a Committee of the Merchants engaged in the Whale Fishery," printed above, Document II in the present group, where extract is identified (see note 1). In addition to the text there employed a PrC is in DLC: TJ Papers, 60: 10457, in Blackwell's hand save for "No. 13." inserted by TJ at head of text; Tr of text as submitted with TJ's report is in DNA: RG 59, Record of Reports of Thomas Jefferson. Another text of the extract, differing from these in its inclusion of Coxe's marginal notes, is in DLC: TJ Papers, 2: 211-2 (also in Blackwell's hand).]

No. 14.

Abstract of Live stock exported from the United States from about August 20th. 1789 to September 30th. 1790, from Returns in the Treasury Office.

	French W. Indies		All other countries		Total	
	Heads	Value	Heads	Value	Heads	Value
Horned Cattle	3573	66,915	1833	33,045	5,406	99,960
Horses	6970	263,281	1658	76,235	8,628	339,516
Mules	22	833	215	8,013	237	8,846
Sheep	5379	8 502	4679	8,537	10,058	17,039
Hogs	4185	9 580	1119	4,901	5,304	14,481
	20129 [i.e. 22,129]	349 111	9504	130,731	29 633	479,842

PrC (DLC: TJ Papers, 60: 10461); in Remsen's hand save for "No. 14." inserted by TJ at head of text. Tr (DNA: RG 59, Record of Reports of Thomas Jefferson). Dft (DLC: TJ Papers, 57: 9834); entirely in TJ's hand.

No. 15.

Grain and Flour imported from the United States of America into the Ports of France, in the Year 1789. from an official Statement.

	French kentals. lbs			
Rice	123,401	69		24,680 Tierces of 500 French pounds each.
Flour	256,545	94	equal to	140,959 American barrels.
Wheat	2,015,297	3		3,664,176
Rye	307,390	96		558,891 American bushels
Barley	260,131	52		520,262

PrC (DLC: TJ Papers, 60: 10461); in Remsen's hand except for "No. 15." inserted by TJ at head of text. Tr (DNA: RG 59, Record of Reports of Thomas Jefferson). Dft (DLC: TJ Papers, 233: 41645); in French, entirely in TJ's hand; this shows that the "official Statement" mentioned above was derived from the "Bureau de la balance du commerce," for (like the two following drafts) it is written on the same slip of paper with Dft of No. 16. Another Dft (DLC: TJ Papers, 53: 8983); in TJ's hand, with number undesignated and with the item of rice at the bottom of the tabulation. FC (DLC: TJ Papers, 53: 8993); in Remsen's hand except for the number inserted by TJ and the following note in pencil opposite the entry for rice: "make rice the first article in the table."

No. 16.

Office of the Balance of Commerce of France } Statement of the Vessels entered in the Ports of France from the U. S. of America in the Year 1789.

	Vessels	Tons
French	13	2,105
Imperial	3	370
English	43	4,781
Dutch	1	170
Hanseatic	1	200
American	163	24,173
	224	31,799

PrC (DLC: TJ Papers, 60: 10461); in Remsen's hand except for "No. 16." inserted by TJ at head of text. Tr (DNA: RG 59, Record of Reports of Thomas Jefferson). Dft (DLC: TJ Papers, 233: 41645); in French, entirely in TJ's hand. Another Dft (DLC: TJ Papers, 53: 8983); in TJ's hand, with the number undesignated. FC (DLC: TJ Papers, 53: 8993); in Remsen's hand, except for number inserted by TJ.

No. 17.

Abstract of the Tonnage of foreign Vessels entered in the Ports of the United States from October 1st. 1789 to September 30th. 1790.

France	13,435
Holland	8,815
Sweden	311
Prussia	394
Spain	8,551
Portugal	2,924
Denmark	1,619
Germany	1,368
British Dominions	225,495
	262,912

PrC (DLC: TJ Papers, 60: 10462); in Remsen's hand except for "No. 17." inserted by TJ at head of text. Tr (DNA: RG 59, Record of Reports of Thomas Jefferson).

The above figures represent TJ's highly simplified summary of the data contained in Hamilton's abstract of duties paid on tonnage of vessels entering American ports between the dates given (Secretary of the Treasury to the Speaker of the House of Representatives, 6 Jan. 1791, with tables; ASP, Commerce, I, 6-8). TJ's figures omit data for the tonnage of American vessels engaged in the fisheries and in foreign and coastal trade. Concerning the statistics furnished by Hamilton, Tench Coxe submitted the following document to James Madison who in turn transmitted it to Jefferson:

"The Tonnage duty, as appears by the abstract, was paid in the year between 1st. Oct. 1789 and 1st. Oct. 1790 on about 766,000 Tons of foreign and American vessels. The proportions belonging to the several nations are as follows, on a scale of 766.

United States, including coasters of 20 Tons and upwards and fishing vessels		502 8/10
Great Britain, exclusive of Ireland	222 5/10	
Ireland	3 2/10	
		225 7/10
France	13 4/10	
Spain	8 7/10	
Portugal	2 9/10	
Germany	1 4/10	
Denmark	1 6/10	
Sweden	0 3/10	
Prussia	0 4/10	
Holland	8 8/10	
		37 5/10
		766.

The American Tonnage including coasters and fishermen is near 2/3 of the whole, excluding both of them it is 18/31 parts; the British, including the Irish, something less than 1/3; the other foreign tonnage a little more than one twentieth. The British Tonnage about six times as great and all the rest of the foreign. In forming the above scale of the Tonnage, of all descriptions, employed in the commerce of the United States, an abstract from the books of the Treasury, for the year preceding the 30th. September 1790, was used as a guide. In order to do justice to the American proportion it is necessary to add to it twice 26,250 Tons for the fishermen and twice 113,000 Tons for the coasting vessels above 20 Tons. All vessels employed in the foreign trade pay Tonnage at each entry from abroad, which on a medium is about three times per annum, but the fishermen and coasters pay tonnage only once per annum, and therefore appear but once in the return, tho' constantly employed. Let however only 139,200 Tons or once the Sum of the Coasters and fishermens be added to the scale, and it will stand thus. The extent of the Scale will be 905 2/10, and the American Tonnage will be 642, the British will remain at 225 7/10, the French at 13 4/10 &c.

If it is found proper to encourage our fishermen, of which there can be no doubt, it must certainly be proper to encourage the coasters. The former are not 27,000 Tons, and the latter 113,000 Tons, to which something may be added for vessels under 20 Tons.

Until a return of vessels actually owned in the United States shall be made out, it may be safe to estimate the American Tonnage (including coasters of 20 Tons and upwards) at one Third of the American Tonnage stated to be entered through the year with the above addition—i.e. we may safely state our coasting, fishing, and merchant ships at 214,000 Tons.

The Seamen in the coasters are perhaps 6 for every 100 Tons, or for 113,000 Tons		6780 Men
For the fishing vessels 10 or 11 men per 100 Tons, or for 26,252 Tons say 10		2625
For merchantships 4 men per 100 Tons, or for 121,000 Tons, being 1/3 of the entries,		4840
		14245

Exclusive of officers.

The British seamen are stated, by Mr. Pitt, to have been 63,000 in 1774, and 83,000 in 1778, that is on a medium about five times the above number. Their subjects are not probably more than three or three and a half times the number of our citizens. Since 1774 and 1778 the above American Tonnage has been nearly all created, and a very large proportion of the seamen has been drawn from Britain. Should one third of our seamen appear to be drawn from Great Britain, these added to a proportion of landsmen would make the difference to them or us of ten or twelve sail of the line. It is therefore probable that more strict rules may be adopted by them on this subject.

A further nursery for seamen, than what appears in the above statement, exists in our coasters under 20 Tons which are very numerous, but paying nothing they are not noticed in the returns of the Collectors of the Revenue. This part of our coasters would be made the subject of a statement framed out of the documents in the Register's office, but they do not furnish the materials.

P.S. It appears certain, on consideration, that the coasters are much swelled by a practice which prevailed some time of Vessels, bound coastwise to load for foreign countries, taking out licences of which they availed themselves to avoid the 2d Duty on entry" (DLC: Madison Papers; in Coxe's hand, undated). TJ evidently intended to include this document in his report, for he caused one of his clerks to transcribe it from the text furnished Madison (DLC: TJ Papers, 59: 10200-01).

Since Hamilton's report of duties on tonnage did not indicate the ports or countries to which vessels had cleared, Coxe also supplied TJ with the following general estimate of the subdivisions of the carrying trade of the United States:

"The return of Tonnage does not shew to what ports or kingdoms the vessels are dispatched. But the documents from the custom houses shew those facts so that, with time, the statement might be effected. The proportion of each foreign and of our own flag cleared in each state is however shewn by the abstract laid before the house of representatives.

The following facts are to be relied on, and may be of some present Use.

1st. All vessels to the British insular and continental colonies are British.

2dly. All vessels to the ports beyond the Cape of Good Hope are American.

3dly. All the fishermen 26250 Tons are American, but the produce of the British fisheries is imported to the amount of 25 or 30,000 dollars per annum.

4thly. Of the vessels to the French Islands seven in eight are American, the rest chiefly French and English.

5thly. A large proportion of the vessels to the other West India islands (not British) are American.

6thly. The vessels to and from all the Spanish dominions except Spain and the wine Islands are Spanish.

7thly. A Great proportion of the vessels to and from Spain and her wine Islands are British owing to the share that nation holds of the Spanish Trade. Of the rest, which are numerous, the Americans are the greater part. There are a few Spaniards, and sometimes ships of other nations.

8thly. The English and Americans principally divide the trade of Portugal and their wine islands. But there are some Portuguese and a few ships of other nations.

9thly. The Traders with Britain and Ireland, especially those which import large cargoes of dry goods, are the greater part Americans, owing to the powerful operation of the 10 per cent duty. The remainder are British and Irish, as they do not permit foreigners to import goods, not of their country, into those Kingdoms.

10thly. The French Trade is principally in our bottoms. Of the remainder the British have the most—the French the next proportion—the rest is much divided.

11thly. Of the few ships from Holland, Denmark and Russia the greater part are American, the British the next, the rest are inconsiderable.

12thly. The British have the greater part of the Mediterranean trade, our vessels being unprotected by passes. The rest is divided in small portions among the French, Spaniards and ourselves. Occasionally a few Italians partake.

13th. Foreigners partake but little in the coasting trade" (MS in DLC: TJ Papers, 69: 12007-8; undated, in Coxe's hand).

No. 18.

That the encouragement of our carrying Business is interesting, not only to the carrying States but in a high degree also to the others, will result from the following Facts.

	Dollars.
The whole exports of the United States may be stated at	25,000,000
Great Britain carries $\frac{2}{5}$ of these in value, that is to say	10,000,000
Freight and Insurance on this in times of peace, are about $22\frac{1}{2}$ per Cent	2,250,000
The same charges in War are very various, according to the circumstances of the War. We may say however 55 per Cent	5,500,000
The difference between peace and war freight and insurance, then, is annually	3,250,000

Taxed on our Agriculture by British Wars, during their continuance, and our dependance on British Bottoms.

Of the last 100 years, Great Britain has had* 42 years of War and 58 of peace, which is 3 of War to every 4 of Peace nearly.

In every term of 7 years then we pay 3 times 3,250,000 dollars, or 9,750,000 which averaged on the years of peace and War, are annually and constantly 1,392,857 more than we should pay, if we could raise our own Shipping to be competent to the carriage of all our productions. Besides this many of our bulky articles, not bearing a War freight, cannot be exported if exposed to that; so that their total loss is to be added to that before estimated.

*Y. M.			Y. M.
Peace. 4.8	1689	May	
	1697.	Sep.	8.4 War
	1702.	May	
6.4	1712.	Aug.	10.3
	1718.	Dec.	
5.8	1721.	June	2.6
	1727.	Mar.	
12.4	1727.	May	0.2
	1739.	Oct.	
7.0	1748.	May	8.7
	1755.	June	
15.7	1762.	Nov.	7.5
	1778.	June	
6.2	1783.	Mar.	4.9
	1789.	May	42.0
57.9			

PrC (DLC: TJ Papers, 60: 10463); in Remsen's hand except for "No. 18." inserted by TJ at head of text. Tr (DNA: RG 59, Record of Reports of Thomas Jefferson). Dft (DLC: TJ Papers, 53: 9035); entirely in TJ's hand. For Madison's information on which this item is based, see Document III in the present group.

X. Thomas Jefferson to John Hancock

SIR   Philadelphia Feb. 20. 1791.

With many thanks for the papers and information you were pleased to have procured for me on the important subject of the fisheries, I do myself the honour of now inclosing you a copy of my report to the house of representatives. From the disposition I see prevailing in the principal mass of the Southern members to take measures which may secure to us the principal markets for the produce of the fisheries, and for rescuing our carrying trade from a nation not disposed to make just returns for it, I am in hopes something effectual will be done this session, if these principles are solidly supported by the members from your part of the Union, of which I trust there is no cause to doubt. Should nothing be done, I cannot say what consequences will follow, nor calculate their extent. May I take the liberty of presenting through you, sir, another copy of the report to the committee who were pleased to lend their assistance in the collection of materials; to shew them that I have not failed to present their testimony in that view which might tend to procure a proper interference in this interesting branch of business.—I have the honour to be [Sir with sentiments of the most] perfect respect and attachment, [Your Excellency's] most humble [and most obedient Servant,

TH: JEFFERSON]

RC (CSmH); mutilated; lacks complimentary close and signature, supplied from PrC (DLC), also mutilated.

From Tench Coxe

SIR   Feby 1. 1791

I have this moment the honor of your note with the Return of exports which is for about 13. Months and 20 days. The odd time is from about 10th. Augt. to 30th. Septr. when little Tobacco, rice, or grain is at market. When I conjectured the amount of our exports yesterday it was principally founded on an opinion that our imports came nearly to that sum, which was the result of a statement made by one of the writers in the office, who I find has been very inaccurate. I have however to observe that very large additions are to be made to this return for *merchandize* exported. I have *known* a single shipment of Nankeens six times as large as the whole quantity set down, and I have *known* a single sale of

dry goods for St. Domingo equal to all that is stated to be shipt thither. Steel is but 978 Drs. Gunpowder but 869 Drs. Ginseng but 90,000 ℔. Beer but 4600 Drs. and there appears to be but 1,300,000 wheat, which cannot be right. On the whole, Sir, I feel a confidence that this return is considerably short of the truth. I have the honor to be with perfect Respect Sir yr most obedt. & most hum. Servt.,
TENCH COXE

RC (DLC); endorsed by TJ as received 1 Feb. 1791 but not recorded in SJL. TJ's note with the return of exports is missing (see note to Coxe to TJ, 30 Jan. 1791).

The above letter proves that Coxe made the returns of exports available to TJ, just in time to be used in his report (see Document IX in group of documents on the fisheries, 1 Feb. 1791, and Editorial Note).

From Diego de Gardoqui

SIR   Madrid 1st. February 1791

Although I have not the honour of being personally acquainted with you, yet I flatter myself you will pardon the liberty I take in Introducing to you the Bearer Mr. Joseph Jaudenes, who returns to that Country and takes his Nephew Mr. Joseph Santayana with him, both having Commissions from His Majesty, and as their residence will be in that City, your politeness and attention to them will greatly oblige me, and in return I hope you will command me here, where I shall be particularly happy to serve you. Mean time I have the honour to be with the greatest respect Sir, Your Excellency's most obt. & very humble Servt.,
JAMES GARDOQUI

RC (DLC); endorsed by TJ as received at New York 16 June 1791 and so recorded in SJL.

To the President of the Senate

SIR   Philadelphia February 2d. 1791.

As the information contained in the enclosed extracts from a letter of Mr. Short's lately received, has some relation to a subject now before the Senate, I have thought it my duty to communicate them, and have the honor to be with sentiments of the most profound respect and attachment, Sir Your most obedient and most humble Servant:

PrC (DLC); in clerk's hand, unsigned. Not recorded in SJL but entry

in SJPL reads: "Th:J. to Pres. of Sen. inclosing Short's letter on commerce of France and US." Enclosure: Extracts from Short to TJ, 21 Oct. 1790 (see note 3 there). Texts of the Extracts are printed in ASP, *Foreign Relations*, I, 120-1. On TJ's editing and use of this extract, see Vol. 18: 544-5.

To Martha Jefferson Randolph

MY DEAR MARTHA   Philadelphia Feb. 2. 1791.

I have this moment recieved yours of January 16. and answer it by the first post. It is indeed an interesting letter to me as it gives me details which I am sure will contribute to your happiness, my first wish. Nothing is so engaging as the little domestic cares into which you appear to be entering, and as to reading it is useful for only filling up the chinks of more useful and healthy occupations. I am sincerely sorry that the mattrasses cannot yet be forwarded. But the state of the river here forbids it, and while it is incertain whether it will be found open or shut no vessels come here from Virginia. They shall go by the first possible opportunity. Whenever your letter to Bruny comes I will accompany it with the seeds: but you must inform me at the same time what kind of seeds to send her.—Congress will certainly rise the 1st. of March, when you will again have Colo. Munroe and Mrs. Monroe in your neighborhood. I write to you out of turn, and believe I must adopt the rule of only writing when I am written to, in hopes that may provoke more frequent letters. Mr. Randolph's letter of Dec. 27. and your's now acknowledged are all I have recieved from Monticello since I left it. Give my best affections to him and Poll, and be assured my dear daughter of the sincere love of Yours affectionately,   TH: JEFFERSON

PrC (MHi); at foot of text: "Mrs. Randolph."

From Thomas Mann Randolph, Jr.

DEAR SIR   Monticello Febr: 2d. 1791.

Polly has allready informed you of the addition of a little Grand Daughter to your family and of its unexpected arrival; which was pleasing to us as it was not in the least premature. Mrs. Fleming had been kind enough to offer her assistance to Patsy during her confinement which we expected would have commenced about the end of February, and I had gone down to accompany her up. But Mrs. Lewises attention and tender concern supplied the place of Mrs. Fleming and made some amends for the want of my Sympathy. Patsy has had one slight fever only which lasted for a very short time: the little girl is perfectly well and grows fast. The Father and Mother are anxious to know when she will have the honor of kissing her Grandpapas hand.

You shall no longer have reason to complain of our irregularity in the correspondence. We are ashamed to have made you repeatedly desire what was before strongly sollicited by Affection and commanded by Gratitude, respect and Duty. The Charlottesville post after an intermission of the whole of December, is continued again. The letter-carrier intends to remain in his office another year if he meets with encouragement, which I do not doubt of.

Polly is in fine health: her fondness for her little niece and attention to her Sister, have kept her back some pages in Don Quixote which she was on the point of finishing. I am Dear Sir, your most obedt. & affectionate Servt., THOMAS M. RANDOLPH

RC (MHi); endorsed by TJ as received 21 Feb. 1791 and so recorded in SJL.

To Robert R. Livingston

DEAR SIR   Philadelphia Feb. 4. 1791.

Unremitting business since the meeting of Congress has obliged me to a rigorous suspension of my correspondencies, and this is the first day I find myself at liberty to resume them, and to acknowledge the receipt of your favor of Dec. 10. The drawings &c. were immediately laid before the board of arts, who, adhering to a general rule, desire a model of your invention and a more ample description, as also more complete drawings. In the mean time a bill is prepared for altering this whole train of business and putting it on a more easy footing; this has rendered me the less uneasy under the delay of my answer. I am glad that the experiment you have tried has verified your calculations. The diminution of friction is certainly one of the most desireable reformations in mechanics. Could we get rid of it altogether we should have the perpetual motion. I was afraid that using a fluid for a fulcrum, the pivot (for so we may call them) must be of such a diameter as to lose what had been gained. I shall be glad to hear the event of any other experiments you may make on this subject.—On that of weight and measures I shall certainly be glad to have a communication of your ideas, and the rather as you suggest they would be so totally different from what has been proposed. It may seem as imprud[ent] as improper to provoke letters from you, when I am obliged to ask such indulgencies as to the time of answering. But the truth is I shall always be glad to hear from you and to have your ideas, which are always valuable, and I will answer you when I can. You have too much experience of the obstacles to an exact correspondence in such an office as I hold, to refuse me this indulgence. Are the people in your quarter as well contented with the proceedings of our government, as their representatives say they are? There is a vast mass of discontent gathered in the South, and how and when it will break god knows. I look forward to it with some anxiety. Adieu, my dear Sir, Your affectionate humble servt,   TH: JEFFERSON

PrC (DLC); at foot of text: "Honble Robt. R. Livingston."

To George Mason

DEAR SIR   Philadelphia Feb. 4. 1791.

I am to make you my acknowledgements for your favor of Jan. 10. and the information had from France which it contained. It confirmed what I had heard more loosely before, and accounts still more recent are to the same effect. I look with great anxiety for the firm establishment of the new government in France, being perfectly convinced that if it takes place there, it will spread sooner or later all over Europe. On the contrary a check there would re- tard the revival of liberty in other countries. I consider the estab- lishment and success of their government as necessary to stay up our own and to prevent it from falling back to that kind of Half- way-house, the English constitution. It cannot be denied that we have among us a sect who believe that to contain whatever is per- fect in human institutions; that the members of this sect have, many of them, names and offices which stand high in the estima- tion of our countrymen. I still rely that the great mass of our community is untainted with these heresies, as is it's head. On this I build my hope that we have not laboured in vain, and that our experiment will still prove that men can be governed by reason. You have excited my curiosity in saying 'there is a particular cir- cumstance, little attended to, which is continually sapping the republicanism of the United states.' What is it?—what is said in our country of the fiscal arrangements now going on? I really fear their effect when I consider the present temper of the Southern states. Whether these measures be right or wrong, abstractedly, more attention should be paid to the general opinion. However all will pass. The excise will pass. The bank will pass. The only corrective of what is amiss in our present government will be the augmentation of the numbers in the lower house, so as to get a more agricultural representation, which may put that interest above that of the stock-jobbers.

I had no occasion to sound Mr. Madison on your fears expressed in your letter. I knew before, as possessing his sentiments fully on that subject, that his value for you was undiminished. I have always heard him say that tho you and he appeared to differ in your systems, yet you were in truth nearer together than most persons who were classed under the same appellation. You may quiet yourself in the assurance of possessing his complete esteem.[1]—I have been endeavoring to obtain some little distinction for our useful customers the French. But there is a particular interest opposed to it, which I fear will prove too strong. We shall soon see. I will send you a copy of a report I have given in, as soon as it is printed. I know there is one part of it contrary to your sentiments: yet I am not sure you will not become sensible that a change should be slowly preparing. Certainly whenever I pass your road I shall do myself the pleasure of turning into it. Our last year's experiment however is much in favor of that by Newgate. I am with great respect & esteem, Dear Sir, Your friend & servt,   Th: Jefferson

PrC (DLC); at foot of text: "Colo. Mason."

It is significant that TJ knew when he wrote this letter that his report on the fisheries would be made public, for it was not until the next day that the Senate directed it to be printed (JS, I, 239). In promising to send a copy as soon as it appeared, he confidently relied on assurances evidently given him by someone in the Senate or in the House. Considering the nature of the report and the apathetic attitude of the Massachusetts Senators toward the fisheries, it is highly unlikely that they would have urged publication of so vigorous a call for countervailing measures against Great Britain. It is also significant that publication was authorized by the Senate rather than by the House, since the report was submitted to the latter.

These facts suggest that TJ himself must have consulted Madison in the House and Monroe in the Senate in a deliberately calculated effort to draw into the public arena A PARTICULAR INTEREST (the Secretary of the Treasury and his supporters) that had opposed TJ's efforts to obtain SOME LITTLE DISTINCTIONS for France—that is, the placing of French vessels on the same footing as those of American citizens in return for the monopoly given by France to American whale oil and the opening of the French West Indies to products of the cod fishery (see TJ's report on the French protest, under 18 Jan. 1791). Having first sought accommodation with Hamilton, TJ, after being refused, decided to declare himself unequivocally and publicly on this central question in foreign relations. The publication of the report was therefore essential to his purpose and TJ evidently set about achieving this in characteristic fashion. The result, aside from creating a sensation on both sides of the Atlantic, removed the issue from the closed debates of the Senate and opened it up to public discussion (see Editorial Note to TJ's report on the fisheries, under 1 Feb. 1791).

It seems clear from the context that that part of the report to which Mason objected was its call for countervailing measures that would seek to replace British with American vessels in the carrying trade. In the face of statistics that the report presented, Mason may have feared that American shipping was not adequate to the task of conveying the bulky native produce to market. Hence in assuring him that A CHANGE SHOULD BE SLOWLY PREPARING, TJ was only echoing the expedient

suggested in the report that the transition "should take effect so gradually as not to endanger the loss of produce for want of transportation." Since he knew when he compiled the report what Mason's sentiments were, he must have had him in mind when he composed this passage.

1 This sentence interlined in PrC.

From William Nelson, Jr.

SIR   Williamsburg February 4th. 1791.

I wrote to you by post on the 22d. of November, since which I have not had the pleasure of hearing from you. I then enclosed you attested copies of the resolutions and acts of Assembly, as well as those of proclamations and certain orders of council which affect the debts, or other property, or the persons of British subjects or American refugees. The day after the date of my letter, I sent the collection of the acts of Assembly printed in 1733. to York, to the care of Mr. T. Nelson, who was expected about that time to set off for Philadelphia.—Since that time, I determined to wait till I could make a more complete collection of the ordinances, and acts of the Assembly of this State, than could then be procured. I send you by this stage the edition abovementioned, together with those of 1752 and 1769: also the acts passed in 1769—

the ordinances passed in December		1775.
those	May	1776.
the Acts passed in	October	1776.
	May	1777.
	May and October	1778.
	May and October	1779.
	May and November	1781.
	May and October	1782.
	and of May	1783.

The acts, from October 1783 to October 1788 inclusive, are in your office, and I will send those which are required to make up the complement from the beginning of the revolution as soon as I can procure them. The Gentlemen, who copied the acts, proclamations, resolutions, and orders of Council, have presented the enclosed accounts for their services.—You will be pleased to send me an order for the amount on William Heth collector for the district of Bermuda Hundred and City-Point. I have sent also the journals of two conventions, as they may contain some information curious, and worthy to be filed in your office, relative to the immediate causes of the revolution.

I mentioned in the letter above referred to, that some members of the bar hold an opinion, that "the act to repeal so much of a former act as suspends the issuing of executions, upon certain judgments, until December 1783," which was passed in May 1782, (and which is No. 8. in the list sent you.); whilst it was in force, only prevented the recovery of debts which were assigned by British subjects to Citizens, and that, even if it *did* prohibit the recovery of british debts, which had *never* been assigned, it hath expired with the Act passed in Octr. 1782. to amend the former law.

From the marginal note, as well as the manner in which the judges of the Court of Chancery of this State have taken notice of the subject, in the table to the collection which is in your office, under the head of "British Debts," it would seem that they favored the opinion that the first law only prevented the recovery of debts assigned. To me, however, it is clear, that the recovery of all debts originally due to British subjects, was prohibited by it, and the words "altho' the same may be transferred to a citizen of this State and unless the assignment hath been made or may be made for a valuable consideration *bona fide* paid before the 1st. of May 1777. &c." were intended only to prevent fraudulent assignments, and can not restrain thte prior general expressions that no debt originally due to British subjects should be recoverable.

The act of Octr. 1782 prevented the recovery of those debts or demands even if contracted with or due to any other person, for the use of, or in common with, any British subject, altho' renewed, changed, and acknowledged to an agent, partner or assignee, or to any other person for their own use or benefit, or for that of such british-subject, since the 19th. of April 1775. By this act also citizen-partners might recover their proportion by attachment in the high Court of Chancery. It has been contended in the General Court of this state, in conformity with the opinion abovestated that the former act by this was rendered temporary, and, that this act having expired, the former hath also expired, it being the design of the legislature to embrace the whole subject of British debts in this and to comprehend in it the substance of the former, and hence that they making this temporary, intended that the other should be considered as temporary also. I think, however, that only the latter act is made temporary, and perhaps, even if a law at first perpetual, under an idea of its being temporary, is continued by a subsequent act, which is to expire at a particular period, when the latter goes out of force, the former is still in existence. The old doctrine, that, if a perpetual law is repealed by a temporary one, when the repealing law expires, the original law remains in force, is well known.

This rule of construction is now altered by the 9th. chapter of the Acts of 1789.

The question whether the Act passed in May 1782 was still in force arose before the passage of the Act of 1789; but, as it was only a collateral one before the court, it was not decided.—Whether the Act of October 1782 carried it out of existence with itself, or not; it appears to me that the Treaty with Great Britain has repealed it.

As your letter required information relative to the decisions on this subject, I have thought it not improper to state the question as it has arisen in one of our superior Courts, altho' it was not decided. I referred you in my last to Colo. Monroe, as to two decisions, which I heard had taken place in the State-District-Courts of Charlottesville and Fredericksburg, as that gentleman practised at that time in those Courts, and informed you, that the general Court, at their last session had ordered the papers in the British Suits, which were made dormant by the sequestration law, to be sent to the District-Courts. This, however, was not thought to prejudge the question "whether they were recoverable."—I beg'd also to be informed by you whether you wish for copies of the inquisitions, traverses, injunctions, judgments or decrees relative to escheated estates. As to the orders of council relative to sequestered estates or the persons of refugees prior to those which I sent, I informed you that the journals of the executive containing them, were in the hands of Colo. Davies, one of the commissioners for settling the accounts between the United States and the individual States. —I have the honor to be With great regard Sir Your mo: ob: servt.,   WM. NELSON JR

P.S. Upon reflection I fear that the books, if sent by the stage, may miscarry, and shall therefore send them to Norfolk, to the care of Colo. Lindsay, who will send them to you by water.   WN

RC (DNA: RG 59, MLR); endorsed by TJ as received 17 Feb. 1791 and so recorded in SJL.

To William Peachy

Dear Sir   Philadelphia Feb. 4. 1791.

Since the reciept of your favor of Dec. 7. I have been endeavoring to recollect the transactions which were the subject of your letter: but this is rendered impracticable by the lapse of time, the variety of events which have since passed thro' the mind, a six years absence and total abstraction from my private transactions, and my present separation from my letters, memorandums and accounts of that date. What little therefore seems to recur to me I am afraid to hazard, lest it should be wrong. I remember paying you a sum of interest at your request, and sending you another sum by Mr. Robt. W. Carter, but I do not remember either the dates or sums, nor in the latter instance at whose request. In both cases I paid as executor of Mr. Wayles who was administrator of Reuben Skelton, to you as executor of Doctor Flood, and as to myself I know that I paid to Mr. Wayles's creditors the identical money I received from his debtors for old debts, for he died 2. years before there was any continental money. I have some expectation that I may go to Albemarle in the month of April. If I should, and that should be in time to give you an explanation, I may perhaps be able to do it on recurring to my books and papers of that date which are there. I remember your endeavors to save the estates of Mr. McCaul and his daughter, and my giving you a passport for one or both to come to America. This is all I can say with certainty till I go home, when if it will serve you, you shall hear further from Dr. Sir Your most obedt. humble servt,

Th: Jefferson

PrC (DLC); at foot of text: "Colo. William Peachy."

To Powell & Fierer

Gentlemen   Philadelphia Feb. 4. 1791.

A particular and pressing business having obliged me to suspend all correspondence for some weeks past it is not till this day that I am at liberty to answer the letters I have received. Among these are your favours of Dec. 23. and Jan. 26. the first of which covered a subscription paper for the glass works you propose to erect in Virginia. If the object of this was to procure subscriptions among the citizens of this place, I presume it would be a very hopeless attempt, and one which I could not undertake. If to procure them from the delegates of Virginia here, they are few, too distantly situated all of them from the intended works to be personally interested in them, and not in a situation here to spare contributions. As to myself, the distance of my possessions from the same works, places me under the impression of no other interest than a general one. In that point of view I am willing to yeild any aid which the situation of my affairs in Virginia will admit. These being left in the hands of Colo. Nicholas Lewis in Albemarle, and he being the only judge what can be done, I must refer the matter to him, and will write to him on that subject in my first letter to him. I return the subscription paper in hopes it may be useful in the hands of some one more in a situation to circulate it, and am with great esteem Gentlemen your most obedt. humble servt,   Th: Jefferson

PrC (DLC).

To William Vernon

Sir   Philadelphia Feb. 4. 1791.

Your letters to Mr. Short and Mr. Fenwick on the subject of your son were duly forwarded, and I have now the pleasure of inclosing you their answers, shewing that they will be ready to do what shall depend on them to prevail on him to return. Your's of Dec. 14. was duly recieved, and this is the first moment it has been in my power to answer it. I shall be ready to do any thing else I can towards effecting your desires, being with great esteem Sir Your most obedt. humble servt,   Th: Jefferson

PrC (MHi); at foot of text: "Mr. William Vernon, Newport." Vernon's letter to TJ of 14 Dec. 1790 (RC in DLC) referred to that of 1 Sep. 1790, said that he had forwarded duplicates to Short and Fenwick, and expressed concern as to whether TJ had received that letter and its enclosures.

From Thomas Barclay

Dear Sir   5 Feby 1791

From the best information I can obtain the emoluments of the Consulship of Lisbon does not amount to three hundred pounds sterling ℔ Annum, and the place is a Very expensive one to live at. I therefore will not give you the trouble of mentioning me to the President on that subject.—If I Could be brought into his View for such appointment as he should think proper, under the Excise law that is likely to pass, it might prove of Consequence to Dear Sir Your Very Obed. Servant, THOS. BARCLAY

RC (DNA: RG 59, CD); endorsed by TJ as received 5 Feb. 1791 and so recorded in SJL.

From Henrietta Maria Colden

SIR   New York Febry. 5th. 1791

I am honor'd with your letter of the 20th. Janry.—If to know your Goodness be to deserve it, I might have some claim to the friendship you have extended to me; but the Benevolence of your Heart is the passport to that attention you have bestowed on my request and situation. In early life, and whilst my Sons were yet in Infancy, the Task to effect their Education, and to extricate their Property from embarrassments, devolved on me. In my endeavours to discharge this Duty, I was buoyed up by a Hope that their happiness and Success in Life, would Smooth the decline of mine, and retribute those days of Care to which my Youth was condemned.—Think then Sir, how interested I am to secure this Object? and think with what Satisfaction I perceive that my Son feels an additional incitement to distinguish himself, in being honor'd with your good opinion and Patronage. If he is so fortunate, as to do his Country service in the line he has chosen, the anxious moments his Fate may cost me, will be repaid.

I assure you Sir, I received with unfeigned pleasure the News of the late Pacification. Had I been certain we should have continued Neutral, to have been a Spectator of the Miseries attendant on War, is sufficient to cause a feeling mind to sympathise, with fellow Creatures involved in that Calamity. To have participate in them, is to be impress'd with Horror at the Approach of that Scourge to the human Race.

I am sorry the wants of this City have been so exaggerated as to excite a concern in our Friends; the price of Fuel has been uncommonly high, owing to the premature freezing of the Hudson; but there has been no *Want* of that necessary Article. From the same cause, we have been supplied with Wheat from the Southern States, but the plentiful Crops throughout the Continent renders the additional freight little felt. Our Stores up the Country are unusually full; when our navigation opens, this market will be overstock'd with Grain: an unpleasing prospect to *Us* Farmers.

The attention of the Good folks of this City was lately engrossed by the Choice of a new Senator to Congress, to the great Mortification of Mr. Schuyler's friends. The Gentleman brought in by Governor Clinton's party, *as they say*, "Not to Oppose, but to keep a Sharp look out on the Measures of the Government" is a Man of too considerable abilities, for the Side he has taken. If he moves on Antifederal Ground, he may do *harm*. But that business is now over. Our present Object is The National Bank: in confidence of that measures being adopted, large Subscriptions have been agreed upon amongst our Monied Men and Speculators; and Committee is sent to Boston to unite their Measures with the Stockholders in that City. I am credibly informed that Subscriptions to the amount of nearly two Millions of Dollars will be fill'd up in this City and to the Eastward. The confidence and unanimity amongst the Publick Creditors, in N. York and Boston will give them a powerful influence in the direction of the National Bank; to effect this, every Nerve will be strained by the Monied Men and Mercantile interest in these Cities. My Son requests me to offer his grateful acknowledgements to you Sir. He is very impatient to have the honor to be personally known to you, and to your Friend Mr. Rittenhouse. Having devoted himself this winter to the Study of Astronomy, he contemplates with pleasure the advantages to be derived from Mr. Rittenhouse, in that Science.—I have the honor to be Sir, With perfect esteem, Yours Most Obedient & Obliged Servant. HENRIETTA MARIA COLDEN.

RC (DLC); endorsed by TJ as received 9 Feb. 1791 and so recorded in SJL.

Mrs. Colden's observation about the great mortification of Schuyler's friends over his displacement in the Senate by Aaron Burr may have originated with her. In saying that "Our present Object is the National Bank" and that the monied interest of New York and Boston would strain every nerve to gain direction of it, she may have done nothing more than echo the views of aristocratic circles in which she moved. But, since she was a friend of Alexander Hamilton, the allusion to Burr may have been an indirect admonition and the confidence expressed that the bank bill would pass—a confidence that neither Hamilton nor his supporters felt—conceivably could have been prompted by the Secretary of the Treasury. In any case, TJ ignored the openings thus offered to discuss political matters of the greatest concern to Hamilton. But, in his earlier letter he had expressed regret that nothing had been done about a naval establishment —possibly a hint that, on this subject, "Mr. Schuyler's friends" had ignored his advocacy of force in opening trade with the Mediterranean (TJ to Mrs. Colden, 20 Jan. 1791). The above letter ended TJ's correspondence with Mrs. Colden.

From J.P.P. Derieux

MONSIEUR   CharlotteVille ce 5. fevrier 1791.

J'ai reçu il y a quelques jours une Lettre de Mde. Bellanger du 25. juillet. Elle me dit combien elle a eté fachée d'apprendre par celle que vous lui avés fait L'amitié de lui Ecrire que vous ne retourniés pas; cette mauvaise nouvelle a affligé, me dit-elle, tous vos amis en France, tandis que Ceux d'ici s'en rejouissent. Elle m'ajoute aussi que vous avés eu La bonté de lui ecrire en ma faveur, ce qui me pénetre encore de La plus vive reconnaissance; cette bonne parente, satisfaitte de l'interet affectioné que vous prenés à moi et ma famille, continue de me montrer les meilleures dispositions possibles, et elle a jusqu'à La bonté de me dire qu'elle fera un testament solide aussitot que Ses affaires seront finies avec Le succession de son mari; touttes ses Lettres sont remplies d'amitié; elle me parle beaucoup de Mr. Short, qu'elle voit très souvent et avec qui elle paroit très Liée.

Je n'ay encore rien de Satisfaisant pour moi à vous annoncer concernant La rentrée d'une partie de mes fonds, et je crains beaucoup que Le desordre et La Confusion qui ont eu lieu, et continuent peut etre encore aux Isles françaises, ne m'ayent eté très prejudiciables; quant à L'autre partie plaçée sur La maison que j'ai en ville, Le propriétaire est actuelement à Richmond occupé de La vente d'une quantité Considerable de Bestiaux, et on m'a informé qu'il devoit repasser par ici avec L'intention de redimer cette proprieté, ce qui me determine à prendre encore un peu de patience, car si, dans Les circonstances où je me trouve, j'allois cedder cet objet sur Credit, et que Mr. Mazzei vint à disposer de Colle avant que je me trouvas mieux dans mes affaires, je me trouverois alors sans maison, ny terres, au lieu qu'en attendant quelque nouveau Supplement, je pourrai Sans Craindre un deplacement desavantageux, remplir mon ardent desir de quitter La Ville.

J'espere toujours beaucoup, Monsieur, de La recommendation dont j'ose me flatter que vous aurés bien voulu accompagner La dernière que j'ai eu L'honneur de vous adresser pour mon Cousin P[ier]re Le Roy à Bordeaux. Je vous aurai une nouvelle obligation de voulloir bien adresser à Mde. Bellanger celle que je prends La Liberté de Joindre ici pour elle.

Mde. de Rieux vous prie d'agreer Les assurances de Son respect, et j'ay L'honneur d'etre avec les Sentiments de La plus parfaitte reconnaissance et attachement Monsieur Votre très humble et très obeist. Serviteur, PLUMARD DE RIEUX

RC (MHi); endorsed by TJ as received 28 Feb. 1791 and so recorded in SJL.

Report on Memorial of Andrew Brown

The Secretary of State, to whom was referred the memorial of Andrew Brown, Printer, of Philadelphia, has had the same under his consideration, and thereupon makes the following REPORT.

The Memorialist states, that he has in contemplation to publish a correct edition of the laws, treaties, and resolutions of the United States, and prays, that such measures may be adopted for giving a public authentication to his work as may ensure its reception throughout the United States.

The Secretary of State observes, that there exists, at present, but a single edition of the laws of the United States, to wit, the one printed by Childs and Swaine: that this edition is authentic, the proof-sheets thereof having been carefully collated by sworn clerks, with the original rolls, in his office, and rendered literally conformable therewith. That the first volume of this edition can now rarely be found, the copies originally printed, being mostly disposed of.

That it is desirable that copies of the laws should be so multiplied throughout the States, and in such cheap forms, as that every citizen of the United States, may be able to procure them. That it is important also, that such publications be rendered authentic, by a collation of the proof-sheets with the original rolls, by sworn clerks, when they are printed at the seat of government, or in its neighbourhood, and by a collation of the whole work, when printed at a distance, and a certified correction of it's typographical errors annexed to each volume.

That this, however, if done at the public expence, would occasion an inconvenient augmentation of the number of clerks, as the act of collation requires the presence of three clerks, one to hold the roll, a second a printed copy already authenticated, and a third the proof-sheet.

That it would be more reasonable, that persons of confidence should be employed at the expence of the editor, to be named and sworn as clerks, for the special occasion.

That, in this way, he is of opinion, it will be advantageous to the public to permit, that the laws to be printed by the Memorialist, be collated with, and corrected by the original rolls, and that a certificate thereof, by the Secretary of State, be annexed to the edition.

TH: JEFFERSON
Secretary of State

February 5th. 1791.

FC (DNA: RG 59, Record of Reports of Thomas Jefferson); accompanied by copy of resolution referring Brown's memorial to Secretary of State to examine and report, dated 17 Jan. 1791 and attested by John Beckley. PrC (DLC); unsigned; in Bankson's hand.

On 14 Jan. 1791 Andrew Brown, who had been recommended to TJ's patronage by Benjamin Rush and William Bingham, presented his memorial requesting that Congress "adopt some mode of authenticating a new edition of the Laws of the United States, which he is now about to publish" (JHR, I, 354; see note, Rush to TJ, 15 Aug. 1790). The memorial was tabled, but later referred to TJ (JHR, I, 355). TJ's report, transmitted under cover of a letter to the Speaker of 5 Feb. 1791 (PrC in DLC), was presented to the House on 7 Feb. 1791 and on the 15th a joint resolution was passed permitting Brown or any other printer at his own expense "to collate with and correct by the original rolls, the laws, resolutions, and treaties, of the United States, to be by him printed," provided that the persons to be employed in this task be approved by the Secretary of State, who would issue a certificate to be annexed to the edition concerning the collation and correction of the texts (JHR, I, 377, 379, 381; SJ, I, 269, 270, 273). This solution to the problem accommodated at once TJ's desire to restrain the growth of the bureau, to meet the objections of Childs & Swaine set forth in their letter of 27 Jan. 1790, and to promote the distribution of the laws. The report was not printed by Congress but, being of special interest to printers, was widely published in newspapers (e.g., Davis' *Virginia Gazette*, 23 Feb. 1791; *Gazette of the United States*, 8 June 1791).

On 14 Feb. 1791 Bache's *General Advertiser* intimated that Brown had asked for exclusive right to publish the laws. Brown denied this, saying that his memorial had only proposed a method of authenticating the text and that TJ's report, favorably to the object but "far from the design of granting this odious monopoly . . . evinced his impartiality and his attachment to the freedom of the press" (*Federal Gazette*, 14 Feb. 1791; on 23 Feb. 1791 Brown printed TJ's report and the joint resolution). Even so, his paper soon showed evidence of partiality for the Secretary of State. Within a month it included selections from the *Gazette de Leide*, just as TJ had persuaded John Fenno to do a year earlier. Brown was soon regarded as hostile by the Federalists and within another year Timothy Pickering was busy raking up old calumnies to try to "put the villain to silence" (Timothy Pickering to Jedediah Rogers, 12 Mch. 1792, MHi: Pickering Papers).

To John Garland Jefferson

DEAR SIR   Philadelphia Feb. 5. 1791.

I received a considerable time ago your favor of Nov. 12. and have been prevented from answering it by an extraordinary press of business from which I am but just now emerging. I think Mr. Carr and yourself have acted prudently in dropping your acquaintance with Mr. Rind. I am not acquainted with his character, but I hope and trust it is good at bottom; but it is not marked by prudence, and the want of this might often commit those who connect themselves with him. I hope that that affair will never more be thought of by any body, not even by yourself except so far as it may serve as an admonition never to speak or write amiss of any body, not even where it may be true, nor to countenance those who do so. The man who undertakes the Quixotism of reforming all his neighbors and acquaintances, will do them no good, and much harm to himself.—I am glad you are settled to your mind. I am persuaded that your present retirement is much more friendly to study than the situation of Charlottesville or it's neighborhood. I need not advise a close pursuit of your studies, I know you are disposed to that. Learning and judgment are the endowments which will carry you forward in the profession of the law. Imagination is of less value, therefore neither to be cultivated nor encouraged. Rigid integrity is the first and most gainful qualification (in the long run) in every profession. Be so good as to remember me affectionately to my sister [Carr and] family, including Peter among them, and to be assured of [the] sincere attachment with which I am Dear Sir Your affectionate f[riend & servt.],

Th: Jefferson

PrC (DLC); slightly mutilated, missing words from 19th century Tr (DLC) and indicated in brackets (supplied).

To James McHenry

Dear Sir   Philadelphia Feb. 5. 1791.

An extraordinary press of business ever since the meeting of Congress has obliged me to suspend all my correspondencies so that it is not till now that I am able to take them up, and among the first your favor of Dec. 14. On the subject of that I am obliged to ask you to name some person at Paris who may, as your agent, attend to all the details of sollicitation, as it would be impossible for Mr. Short to do that, and indeed contrary to a fixed rule which has been established of necessity to prevent his being used as the factor of individuals which would be more than he could do, and lead him often to what would be improper. I will write to him to support your claim by his interposition at proper occasions, as far as shall be right, and in this he will move in concert with M. de la Fayette. As soon as you shall advise me to whom to address your papers, I will forward them through Mr. Short and with a letter to him. In the mean time they remain in my hands. I have the honor to be with great esteem Dr. Sir Your most obedt. humble servt,   Th: Jefferson

P.S. No time is lost as yet he being at Amsterdam.

RC (DLC: McHenry Papers); addressed: "Doctr. James McHenry Baltimore"; postmarked: "6 FE" and "Free"; franked by TJ. PrC (DLC); mutilated.

On 14 Dec. 1790 McHenry also wrote Short asking his "protection of the enclosed memorial to the minister of the French marine, considering you as placed in a situation to convey to the court where you reside any well founded complaints by your fellow citizens for injury done them by the French nation or any of its subjects." McHenry stated that his loss had been considerable and added: "I see no other way of obtaining redress short of ministerial support. Let me therefore entreat you to countenance my application, shewing it before delivered to the Marquiss de la Fayette and conferring with him on the subject" (McHenry to Short, 14 Dec. 1790, OCHi: Short Papers, endorsed as received 28 May 1791). In response to the above letter announcing a rule which TJ himself had observed as minister and which he no doubt enjoined upon Short before leaving France, McHenry wrote TJ: "I thank you for your kind attention to my little business. I knew very well you could not have leisure at this season and rested satisfied that it would not be the least recollected. You will find among my papers a letter to Messrs. Le Couteulx & Cie. which you will be pleased to destroy and substitute the inclosed in its place. I request these gentlemen to present the memorial which Mr. Short is to deliver them, and countenance it; or if that is inconvenient to appoint some person to attend to the details of solicitation in their name. I rather suspect I ought not to rely on their putting themselves to much trouble, and must therefore place my dependance on Mr. Short and the Marquiss, and the letter you are so obliging as to say you will write to the former" (McHenry to TJ, 9 Feb. 1791, endorsed by TJ as received 14 Feb. and so recorded in SJL, OCHi: Short Papers). TJ forwarded this letter to Short with McHenry's papers (TJ to Short, 8 Mch. 1791). But instead of destroying McHenry's first letter to Messrs. Le Couteulx & Cie. he returned it to the author (TJ to McHenry, 28 Mch. 1791).

From David Humphreys

Sir   Lisbon Feby. 6th. 1791.

On the 24th. of Janry. I left Madrid, and arrived here this day. I remained a week beyond the time I had prescribed myself, in order that Mr. Carmichael might have an opportunity of confering fully with the Compte de Florida Blanca, after the King's return from hunting at Aranjuez. We were, however, disappointed in the expectation of sounding that Minister; for at the time when Mr. Carmichael waited upon him with that intent, so many Characters of a Superior Grade in the Diplomatic Corps attended in the Antichamber, that he found no possibility of having an audience for business, or even of speaking to him a single word of any kind. Although Mr. Carmichael, as Chargé des Affaires of the United States, has been treated with more attention and favor than any other; yet we laboured under a great mistake in supposing that His Most Catholic Majesty had so far dispensed with a general rule (under consideration of our peculiar circumstances as a Nation) as to place him on a level with Ministers of the first or second Order, in favorable treatment of person or advantageous situation for business. The contrary is so clear a truth, that no Chargé des Affaires is permitted to attend the King's Levees with Ambassadors and Ministers. Nor on other occasions, let them attend ever so early, can they address the Minister of State until all Diplomatic Characters of an higher grade shall have finished their business with him. It is true the privilege of appearing in the Royal presence with Ambassadors &c. is of little consequence to the welfare of the States in whose service they are employed. But it is a serious misfortune, when they have national affairs of an important nature to discuss with the Minister, not to be able to speak to him at all, or not until he has become so tired of conversing with others that he will not give them a patient hearing. This is exactly the case, in the transactions which Mr. Carmichael is obliged to have with the Compte de Florida Blanca. As the business with which he is now charged requires to be managed with uncommon address and delicacy, I have advised him to seize some good occasion for obtaining a particular Audience to explain our desires specifically, but in the most discreet manner, with the reasons and motives on which they are founded. And I have told him, that I apprehended the sooner this could be done; the better it would be; since the affairs of Europe; far from being settled, may soon produce a Crisis highly favorable to the promotion of our interests; and since our western Settlers cannot brook long delay. Hitherto he had only found a casual opportunity (that is to say, immediately after my arrival) to suggest to the Minister, in general terms without abruptness, our sincere disposition to be connected with Spain in the most liberal and friendly manner; and for this purpose the apparent expediency of making arrangements respecting the navigation of the Mississipi, before any ill adventures shall happen in that quarter.

During my whole journey and continuance in Madrid, I endeavoured, in the Character of a traveller, to keep a middle line between an ostentatious display of myself, and an affectation of entire privacy. But as I was known to some of the Diplomatic Corps in person, and, it seems, to the Compte de Florida Blanca by character, a general conclusion prevailed that I had come to Spain on some business of national concern. Nothing ever fell from me to countenance this idea; and, I entreat, you will be persuaded, that I have exerted myself to fulfill the Wishes of the Executive, to the best of my abilities.

I was sorry to find Mr. Carmichael's health had suffered very much by the climate. He had been severely attacked by bilious and nervous Disorders; insomuch that last fall he did not expect to survive. He is much mortified that so many of his Dispatches have miscarried. By the original Documents which I have seen in his hands, I am convinced he has been extremely assiduous and successful in procuring early and authentic intelligence. I have also seen the Cyphers formerly sent to him, and the Certificates of the manner in which he received them. It is difficult for a Person at a distance to form an adequate judgment of the embarrassments to which a public Man, situated as he was, is subjected in making written Communications, from such an inland Place, and under such a jealous Government. He appears disgusted with the Country, and the mode of life he is compelled to lead. He desires ardently to return to his native Land; but he wishes to distinguish himself first by rendering some essential service to it, if possible.

Just before I came from Madrid, an Ambassador from Morocco had arrived there.

In this Kingdom every thing remains very quiet: and so far as I can learn, the People enjoy much tranquility and happiness under the mild administration of the reigning Sovereign. With Sentiments of the highest esteem & respect I have the honor to be, Sir Your most obedient & most humble Servant,   D. HUMPHREYS

P.S. I have found the Memorandum, which I had misplaced, in my Cypher; and therefore shall not have occasion to trouble you with repeating it, as requested in my letter No. 7.

RC (DNA: RG 59, DD); at head of text: "No. 12"; endorsed by TJ as received 31 Mch. 1791 and so recorded in SJL. Tr (DNA: RG 59, DD).

To William Hay

DEAR SIR   [Philadelphia Feb. 7. 1791.]

I have been obliged by other [business to suspend for] some time past all private correspondencies. Y[our favor of] Dec. 2. is among the first I am able to take up. My friend Mr. Madison happening to be with me just as I was proceeding to consider the question you propose whether Dr. Currie stands bound to see that the printer of the Encyclopedie makes good his engagements as to that work? I was glad to associate Mr. Madison in considering the question, and we both conclude that Dr. Currie having sold out his subscription, is clear of it, and that the purchaser buys his right with all it's chances. We suppose it to resemble other cases of joint enterprise, where partners sell out, others buy in, and the purchaser, through ever so many degrees, stands in the shoes of the original partner whom he represents. The printing of a book is a joint enterprize of the subscribers, and the printer is their agent.

This is so well understood in Paris, and these transfers of subscriptions with all their rights so well ascertained, that Dr. Currie could not there maintain an action against the printer when it should be once understood that he had sold out. I recurred to your letter to me of Apr. 26. 1787. wherein you mention your acquisition of the right (Dr. Currie never mentioned it in any of his letters). The words of your letter are 'Dr. Currie our mutual friend has been so obliging as to *give up* to me the new edition of the Encyclopedie for which I am to furnish him &c.' I am not [without hopes] I may be able to relieve you from it, as I think it probable I may meet with a purchaser here. It will give me great pleasure to serve you in this or any other way. But I believe you must inform me how livraisons you have, for on searching I do not find my account of them against Dr. Currie, from whence I presume I gave it in to him. In the mean time I will put into the first order I give for books from Paris the 2d. part of your Tome 3d. of Arts and Mestiers. I would observe also that you are now free to continue to take any of the particular dictionaries you chuse, without taking the others.—I am with great esteem Dear Sir Your most obedt. humble servt, TH: JEFFERSON

PrC (DLC); mutilated, some missing words being supplied from 19th century Tr (DLC).

From William Short

DEAR SIR   Amsterdam Feb. 7. 1791.

In my last I sent you a copy of a letter, such as it then appeared in public, from the Emperor to the King of France. I mentioned at the same time the general opinion and my doubts as to its authenticity. A letter from M. de Montmorin to the assembly has since reduced this matter to certainty. He has sent them a translation of this letter which you will see in the journals of the assembly. He and a member of the diplomatick committee both gave the assembly to understand that the letter was merely a formal one which the Emperor had been obliged to write. You will find that it is somewhat different from that which I sent you.

The disturbances at Strasburg which I mentioned to you seem to have subsided for the present. At least nothing more is said about them in the assembly. The decree for displacing such of the clergy as refused the oath has begun to be carried into effect in Paris.—Successors are already appointed to some of them. Apprehensions seem still to be entertained that this will occasion uneasiness and disturbance in some of the provinces.

No other measure has been taken by the assembly with respect to the *droit d'aubaine* since that which I have already mentioned to you of referring it to several committees.

They have at length fixed the duties on the importation of several foreign articles. Instead of adopting the report of the committee in the mass as there was reason to expect, they discussed the articles separately. The committees of commerce and imposition adhered to their idea of subjecting the American oils to a moderate duty, in consequence of their second opinion, of which I have formerly given you an account. Finding that it would be opposed in the assembly they agreed to augment it in hopes of succeeding by that means. The opposition however still continued. It was finally decided to exclude all foreign oils except the American and to subject them to a duty of twelve livres the quintal.—This may be considered as a prohibitive duty, but the partisans of the plan knowing that a majority of the assembly would be against the exclusion of the American oils made use of this stratagem.—There are many who wish to make an experiment to see whether the national fishery can be made adequate to the national consumption, and others who wish to make us purchase by a general commercial treaty a market for this particular article.

The subject of tobacco has been also brought on. The committee of impositions had decided together with the committee of commerce to propose an impost of five sous a pound. Many of their best informed members were for a lower duty. The expected opposition in the assembly induced them the morning of the report to change the impost to ten sous a pound. Mirabeau to the astonishment of every body and contrary to the expectations of Clavière and Warville who are two of his council, supports the system of monopoly. He is for prohibiting the culture every where in France even in the provinces that formerly exercised this right. One of the reasons given in favor of his system also is the necessity of cultivating their commercial connexions with us, which he says would be lost if the culture of this article was permitted in France.—His speech produced a very great effect and revived the hopes which had for some time ceased of continuing the farm. The subject was adjourned for further consideration until friday last. As yet I know nothing further. It seems to me utterly impossible to prohibit the cultivation of this article in France under the present constitution and in the present situation of things. It is putting the province of Alsace at stake to attempt it there under the circumstances of the moment. Indeed the plan proposes that this should not be effected fully before the year 96. Such a decree would certainly excite much disorder there, and it is the part of France where of all others it is the most essential to preserve tranquillity and above all an attachment to the French government. It is impossible to form any reasonable conjecture of what the assembly will decide on relative to this matter. I will communicate the result however as soon as it is known. The variation in the assembly as well on this as on other subjects, will necessarily have produced a variation in my letters respecting them.

I have lately recieved a letter from M. de Montmorin in which he mentions that the King has named M. de Ternant as his Minister Plenipotentiary in America. He does not say when he will go there, but I take it for granted it will be in the spring.

The state of Europe in general is as when I last wrote to you. In the E. Indies the English have marched into the possessions of Tippo Saib and taken some places. An account came by the way of the Isle of France which mentioned their having recieved a check from the army headed by Tippo Saib himself. This is generally considered as premature.

This letter will be sent by the way of London, will contain one for the Secretary of the Treasury, and carries assurances of the sentiments of affectionate attachment with which I am, dear Sir, yours,   W: SHORT

PrC (DLC: Short Papers); at head of text: *"No. 55."* Tr (DNA: RG 59, DD). Recorded in SJL as received 23 Apr. 1791.

From Thomas Mann Randolph, Jr.

DEAR SIR   Monticello Feb. 8. 1791

Patsy continues in very good health and would have written to you herself had I not prevented her from the fear of her being fatigued. The little one is perfectly well and increases in size very fast. We are desirous that you should honor her and ourselves by confering a name on her and accordingly have deferred the christening till we can hear from you. Polly is very well and prepares to give you some account of her little niece by the next Post.

Tobacco is rising very rapidly: 20/ at Lynchburg may be got. Wheat continues low in Richmond. I am Dear Sir your most obedt. & aff. Servt.,   THOMAS M. RANDOLPH

RC (MHi); endorsed by TJ as received 12 Mch. 1791 and so recorded in SJL.

To Nathaniel Colley

DEAR CAPTAIN   Philadelphia Feb. 9. 1791.

I have received your favor of Jan. 22. by post that by Capt. Anderson being not yet arrived. In your account you have omitted freight and commission, and I was not merchant enough to know how much they should be. I have therefore by guess inclosed you a bank post note for seventy dollars, which if too little shall be corrected. Observe that by an arrangement between the bank and Treasury, any collector of duties gives ready money for their post-notes, so that you have only to present the inclosed to the Collector most convenient to you. I thank you sincerely for your attention to this little commission, and should I have any thing at any other time to be done in the same way at London, I will avail myself of your kind offer of service. My daughters are both in Virginia. I will convey by letter your kind remembrance of them. Pray drop me a line to inform me if you recieve this, so as to make me easy on that point. A thousand shorter and pleasanter voyages to you than that we had together. I am with great esteem Dear Captain Your most obedt. humble servt.,   TH: JEFFERSON

PrC (MHi). Colley's account by Captain Anderson was received by TJ two days after he wrote the above (see note, Colley to TJ, 22 Jan. 1791). The shipment arrived at the Philadelphia customs by the 16th (Sharp Delany to TJ, 16 Feb. 1791; RC in DLC).

From Delamotte

MONSIEUR   Havre 9e. fevrier 1791

Il y a longtems que Je n'ai eu l'honneur de vous écrire, faute de choses interessantes à vous Communiquer, Car depuis ma derniere nous n'avons pas eû un seul Navire Americain dans notre port, et l'assemblée Nationale ne s'est occupée de rien qui puisse interesser les Etats Unis. Si Elle l'eut fait, Je n'aurois pas manqué de vous écrire par la Voye d'Angleterre. Voici qu'Elle vient enfin de prendre un dernier parti sur la ferme du Tabac et Je profite de l'occasion d'un Navire françois qui va à Charlestown pour vous apprendre les decrets qui sont sortis à ce sujet.

La Culture du Tabac en france est libre.

La fabrication et la Vente le sont aussi.

Tous Tabacs fabriqués sont prohibés à l'importation.

Tous Tabacs en feuilles Etrangers seront admis sous un Droit de 25^{tt} ꝑ 100 ℔. Ceux qui seront importés en droiture par Navires françois ne payeront que les ¾ de ce Droit. Enfin les Tabacs Etrangers Jouiront de L'Entrepot pendant un an. Voilà, Monsieur, les articles decrettés Jusqu'à present sur cet objet. Il en seroit sans doute decrettés quelques autres, Comme la Distribution des Ports qui serviront d'Entrepôts, &c. Vous verrés par le Journal de Paris No. 45. qu'on a Conservé une Sorte de Regie pour Compte de la Nation, et Je ne puis que vous reporter à ce Journal pour vous donner une idée Juste de cet objet particulier. Cependant, Je puis vous ajouter qu'Elle ne trouve que fort peu d'approbateurs et qu'on est d'opinion qu'elle ne durera pas Longtems, parce que n'ayant point d'autres avantages que les particuliers, ou elle écrasera ceux ci, ou ceux ci réclameront tellement Contre Elle qu'on l'abolira, et Je prevois que ce sera sans peine, lorsque la ferme actuelle aura écoulé sous ce nom de Regie Nationale les Tabacs qu'Elle a.

Mr. Short est encore en Hollande et c'est peut-être son absence qui cause que le Roy n'a encore donné ses exequatur à aucune des Commissions de Consul.

Je remets au Capitaine Asselin, du Navire le Vendangeur, Porteur de la presente, 2 paquets que Mr. Short m'a envoyé pour vous, Monsieur. Si ce Capitaine n'avoit pas eu la folie de me demander 300^{tt} de fret pour chacune de vos voitures, Je les lui aurois données malgré sa destination, surtout par cette consideration que Je vois fort peu de Navires Americains dont les Ecoutilles (hatches) soient assez larges pour admettre un pareil volume. J'attends de Hambourg un Navire Americain qui doit aller à Baltimore et auquel Je donnerai vos Voitures s'il peut les prendre, celles de vos Caisses de meubles qui sont restées pour Philadelphie, 4 paniers de vin de Champagne, une Caisse Contenant le Portrait de Mr. De La fayette et 2 petites Boites Contenant 2 Cilindres et des habillements de Tafetas. Tous ces objets devroient être envoyés à Philadelphie, mais Je crains que l'occasion n'en Soit trop éloignée.

Voici, Monsieur, les documens des depenses que J'ai payées pour Nathaniel Huls, montant à £581. 16. O. Je m'entendrai de cette somme avec Mr. Short. J'ai L'honneur d'Etre avec une parfaite Considération, Monsieur Votre très humble & très obeissant Serviteur,   DELAMOTTE

RC (DNA: RG 59, CD); endorsed by TJ as received 22 June 1791 and so recorded in SJL. Enclosure: State-ment of account showing that Dela-motte, as vice-consul, had paid 581^{tt} 16s "in Order to send back to his native

Country Nath: Huls a maimed Seaman left at the hospital of this town by the Brig Wandering Jew . . . Come from New York in the month of March 1790 with a cargo of 732 Bbls. of flour ship'd by Messrs. Cunningham & Co" (same).

To Daniel L. Hylton

DEAR SIR   Philadelphia Feb. 9. 1791

Understanding that tobacco continues low in Virginia, whereas the price here for the best is about a guinea, I wish to make an experiment of bringing some of mine here. I have nobody at Richmond to act for me, and therefore on looking about for a friend to execute this commission, I feel a confidence in your being so good as to do it. I would wish to have 20 hogsheads sent to me by the first possible conveyance, because they are at present in want here, and as the river is now open they will soon get their supply. I would wish one half of it to be of the Albemarle and the other of the Bedford crops. In the last there are two qualities, to wit, some which was hurt by the fire, and the rest good. I should like a hhd. or two of the fired part merely as an experiment of this market. However if there be not of the three kinds enough already got down to allow choice, send 20. hhds. of such as is down. I am so little of a merchant as to know nothing of the expences necessary to be paid there. All that can be paid here, I would chuse should be drawn for on me: and for what must be paid of necessity there, I will return you a bank post note by the same post which brings me your information of what it should be. Be so good as to inform me by the first post whether this commission can be executed immediately, or when I may expect it. Present my respects to Mrs. Hylton and accept assurances of the esteem and attachment of Dr. Sir Your friend & servt,

                                   TH: JEFFERSON

P.S. If this adventure succeeds I think of having the residue of my crop brought here, which renders dispatch in the first essay, important.

PrC (MHi).

The above, together with TJ to Nathaniel Colley, 9 Feb. 1791, was enclosed in another of the same date to James Brown (missing). Robert Coventry acknowledged the last on 17 Feb. 1791, the evening of its arrival: "I expect to see Mr. D. Hylton tomorrow when I shall deliver him your letter with the order for the 20 hhds. Tobacco, and he will inform you how soon he can send it round to Philadelphia; but I am afraid this severe weather may prevent any Vessell from getting to Philada. for some time. I expect to forward your letter tomorrow to Capt. Colley by a safe conveyance.—Mr. Brown is at Norfolk dispatching some ships for Europe, or he would have done himself the pleasure of answering your letter by this Post" (RC in MHi; endorsed by TJ as received 26 Feb. 1791 and so recorded in SJL).

To Nicholas Lewis

DEAR SIR   Philadelphia Feb. 9. 1791.

I have been so closely engaged ever since the meeting of Congress as never to have had a moment to write to you. I think it might be well to advertize my lands at Elkhill for sale, and therefore inclose you the form of an advertisement, in which you will observe I have omitted the name of the proprietor, which as long as I am in public I would wish to keep out of view in every thing of a private nature. If you think any thing in the advertisement had better be omitted, or any thing else inserted be so good as to make it what you think it should be.

Understanding that tobacco is still low in Virginia, and the price here, for such as mine being from 26/ to 30/ Virginia money I have concluded to try an experiment of bringing part of it here, and if it suits the market the rest may come also. Not being able to wait till the order could go through you, I have written to Mr. Hylton to send me immediately 20. hhds. of it, as they are now in want here, and the river now opening they will soon have their supply. I am in hopes it may come in time to order on the residue, if the experiment succeeds. However I would not have the shipment of the rest to Mr. Maury delayed on that account, as perhaps I may find the bringing it here not to answer. The proceeds of these 20 hhds. shall be immediately remitted to Mr. Lyle or Hanson. Wheat is here at a French crown: tho' in truth there is little brought to market. I have no doubt it will fall as soon as the farmers come in.

Congress will rise on the 3d. of March. They have passed an excise bill, which, considering the present circumstances of the union, is not without objection, and a bill for establishing a ban[k] to which it is objected that they have transcended their powers. There are certainly persons in all the departments who are for driving too fast. Government being founded on opinion, the opinion of the public, even when it is wrong, ought to be respected to a certain degree. The prudence of the President is an anchor of safety to us.—I recieved Mrs. Lewis's letter of Jan. 22. and return her many thanks for it, as well as for her kind attention to my daughter, who expresses great sensibility for her goodness. I am with great esteem Dear Sir Your affectionate friend & servt,

TH: JEFFERSON

P.S. I must pray you to get the contract with Ronald completely executed, and particularly as to the mortgage of his Bever-dam lands. I observe part of my Cumberland lands advertised for the taxes of 1789. which I mention lest the advertisement should have escaped you.

PrC (DLC). Text of the enclosed advertisement is at foot of second page of PrC and reads: "FOR SALE. The lands called Elk-hill on James river and the Byrd [creek] adjacent to Elk-island in Goochland, containing 669. acres and consisting of [two] parcels, the one of 307. acres of low grounds and high-lands both of the first quality, the other of 362. acres of good grain land, mostly well timbered. The two parcels are 250 yards apart, a public road passing thro' that interv[al] and are cultivated as one plantation. On the former, and in a very handsome posi[tion] is a commodious dwelling house built by the late Reuben Skelton for his own residence, having 4. rooms below and 2. above, with good out-houses erected since his time. The price is 40/ sterling the acre, payable by installments in the years 1793. 4. 5. 6. with interest from the delivery of the land. Real security will be required. Capt. Henry Mullins, who lives adjoin-ing to the lands will shew them to any person wishing to purchase, and the subscriber in Albemarle has full au-thority to conclude the sale—[Nichs. Lewis]." The advertisement, dated 3 May 1791, ran in Davis' *Virginia Ga-zette* from 25 May 1791 to 13 July 1791. Lewis allowed the text to stand exactly as written by TJ, only adding his name, here given in square brackets (supplied) from the printed text.

To Martha Jefferson Randolph

MY DEAR MARTHA   Philadelphia Feb. 9. 1791.

Your two last letters are those which have given me the great-est pleasure of any I ever recieved from you. The one announced that you were become a notable housewife, the other a mother. This last is undoubtedly the key-stone of the arch of matrimonial happiness, as the first is it's daily aliment. Accept my sincere congratulations for yourself and Mr. Randolph. I hope you are getting well, towards which great care of yourself is necessary: for however adviseable it is for those in health to expose them-selves freely, it is not so for the sick. You will be out in time to begin your garden, and that will tempt you to be out a great deal, than which nothing will tend more to give you health and strength. Remember me affectionately to Mr. Randolph and Polly, as well as to Miss Jenny. Your's sincereley,   TH: JEFFERSON

RC (NNP); at foot of text: "Mrs. Randolph."

To William Tatham

SIR   Philadelphia Feb. 9. 1791.

I have not till now been able, since the meeting of Congress, to attend to my private correspondencies. I have forwarded to Mr. Short the subscription paper you sent for him, and should any opportunity occur of recieving subscriptions to the one you sent me, I will surely avail you of it, tho' it is not probable. Indeed I have thought of putting it into the hands of Colo. Griffin the representative of your district who would be more in the way of doing this. I inclose you the map of the Holston country, and am Sir Your very humble servt,   TH: JEFFERSON

PrC (MHi). Enclosure: Tatham's manuscript map of the "Holston, Wautauga, Nenoctuckie and Clinch Countries," which TJ had seen as early as 1780 and regarded as "a pretty good map" (TJ to Greene, 27 Dec. 1780; Tatham to TJ, 1 Nov. 1790).

Early in 1790 Governor Randolph, influenced perhaps by Tatham's zeal and his hope that Virginia would not much longer "yield the plaudit of foreign powers, to the industry of Her Eastern Sisters" in matters of improvement, granted him access to the public archives. In the ensuing months Tatham worked industriously at his task and late in September announced his proposals for publishing "a large and comprehensive map of the southern division of the United States" by subscription only. The announcement carried this impressive testimonial signed by Beverly Randolph, James Wood, James McClurg, John Tyler, William Nelson, Jr., William Hay, John Harvie, John Marshall, and Alexander Montgomery: "Being requested by Mr. Tatham, to view the Map . . . which he has begun, we attended at the mason's Hall, and after examining the progress he has made, and being fully informed of the materials he has collected, and the assistance he will derive from both public and private sources, our opinion is—That Mr. Tatham is fully adequate to the work he has undertaken; that he has made considerable progress in the Map, in a very neat and correct manner; and that when finished, we believe it will be the most useful and valuable Map yet published of the Southern parts of the United States; and in such opinion have each sub-

scribed for a copy" (Davis' *Virginia Gazette*, 29 Sep. 1790; Tatham to Randolph, 8 and 24 Feb. 1790, 13 Apr. 1790, and 10 Aug. 1790, CVSP, V, 111-2, 118-9, 133-7, 196-7).

In his first brief glance among the archives, Tatham noticed that the records for TJ's administration were far less full than they should have been. He thought some had perhaps been destroyed by Benedict Arnold, but, he added, "I would flatter myself it will appear they were preserved as your private Property, since I recollect some of them were so. My manuscript of the Holston, Wautauga, Nenoctuckie and Clinch Countries . . . would now be very usefull" (Tatham to TJ, 17 Feb. 1790). There is no evidence that TJ responded to this appeal. Some months later Tatham solicited a note from Governor Randolph to James Monroe, asking the latter to lend the map in TJ's absence. Monroe declined and Tatham repeated his request of TJ, promising to return the map (Tatham to TJ, 1 Nov. 1790). Tatham's unflattering assumption that TJ had converted public records to his own possession may in part account for the curt tone and the unresponsive nature of the above letter, so uncharacteristic of TJ's usual manner of lending encouragement to useful improvements. The fact that TJ returned the map to Tatham, without comment, would seem to indicate that he regarded it as Tatham's personal property—possibly as a loan that had been made to TJ as governor. But the real reason for TJ's habitual attitude of aloofness to Tatham is that, far from sharing the confidence in his capacity expressed by Randolph, Marshall, and others, TJ regarded him as an enthusiast more ready at conceiving ambitious plans than in executing them. His attitude toward Tatham's proposals should be compared with that expressed in his famous letter to Hazard of 17 Feb. 1791.

On this same day TJ did consult COLO. GRIFFIN and then sent him the following note: "Th: Jefferson presents his compliments to Colo. Griffin and sends him the subscription paper for Mr. Tatham's map which he was so kind as to say he would recieve and see if any thing could be done with it" (TJ to Samuel Griffin, 9 Feb. 1791; PrC in MHi).

From Fenwick, Mason & Co.

SIR   Bordeaux 10 feby. 1791.

We have the honor of your favor of the 6th. Sepr. addressed to our J. F. containing letters to several wine proprietors with a request to pay for and expedite the several parcels of wine you ordered, which shall be complyed with by the first vessel in Philadela. Tho' as oppertunities direct from here are very rare, we shall venture to expedite your Wines when received by the first good vessel to Boston N. York or Charleston with directions to our correspondent to send them immediately on to Philadelphia. This mode of conveyance we shall adopt as the most probable to insure their arrival this Summer.

We have received Madam de Rausan parcel and advice from the Countess de lus Saluce that she shoud immediately prepare and forward us the parcel ordered from her. M. de Miromenel has also wrote us that his Son in Law the Count de la Pallu, at present the proprietor of the Estate of Segur wou'd comply with your order but we have since seen his homme d'affair who says he has no wine on hand proper to ship as a sample that will do justice to his estate, therefore cannot execute your order. Shoud this prove to be the case we shall venture to send for the president some of our own chusing. We fear we shall be in the same situation respecting the frontignac as we have heard nothing of Mr. Lambert. We have wrote him twice to frontignac. Shoud we not hear from him before an oppertunity offers, we shall also send you the frontignac from among the best to be procured in Bordeaux.

Monsieur de Pechard is the proprietor of the Estate of *La fite* (formerly Segur) and monsieur de fumel of *Obrion* and *Chateaumargeaux*. These are three of the first four growths of wine in this provence, the owners of which are residents here and generally provided to supply their friends. The Miromenel Estate *La Tour* (formerly Segur also) is the fourth, of which there are three proprietors Count de la Pallu, Marquis de Beaumont and the Count de Segur. Their homme d'affaire here is M. Domenger who has the management of the Estate.

Mr. Vernon is now here and declares it is in his intention to embark for Am[eric]a this spring tho' he has let pass two or three oppertunities. We think he will embark after he finds he cannot have any advances made him here. As yet he has not felt the want of them having received at Paris the sum his father last remitted Mr. Short. We have the honor to be Sir Your most obd & Hble Servants, FENWICK MASON & CO.

P.S. Since writing the above we have received the frontignac Wine from Mr. Lambert. There is now a vessel here for Chas. Town. If none offers for Philadela. before this is ready, we think to ship your wines by her. We are F. M & Co.
18 feby.1791.

RC (MHi); addressed: "The Honourable Thomas Jefferson Esquire Secretary of State Philadelphia Minerva [Capt.] Cooper via London"; endorsed by TJ as received 6 July 1791. This was the duplicate: its original (not found) is recorded in SJL as received 21 June 1791.

From Lambert

MONSIEUR   Frontignan 10e. fevrier 1791

J'ai Reçeu avec un Plaisir infini La Lettre que vous m'avés fait L'honneur de m'ecrire Le 6. 7bre. Dernier et qui m'est heureusement parvenue depuis une quinzaine de jours.

J'étois fort desireux de sçavoir de vos Nouvelles, j'en avois demandé depuis peu à Mr. De Moustier, ambassadeur en Prusse. Je les attendois avec impatience quand Votre Lettre arrivée m'a paru un present du Ciel. Avec quel transport je l'ai Lue, je l'ai devorée, il m'a semblé vous voir, vous serrer dans mes Bras, et vous Renouveller L'assurance de mon attachement Respectueux, et qui ne s'éteindra qu'avec ma Vie.

Le Lendemain du jour où vous m'aviez fait L'honneur à Paris de me Recevoir parmi vos Convives en Xbre. 1788, je fus attaqué d'une Violente maladie, qui me Conduisit au Bord du tombeau et qui me priva du plaisir de vous Revoir avant mon Depart. J'y suis Revenu à Raison d'un Litige que j'avois devant L'Assemblée Nationale pour la Mairie de Cette Ville, et que j'ai Eu la Satisfaction de gagner; j'avois L'espoir de vous y voir Encore, mais vous Etiés deja bien loin de moi, et dans un autre Monde, d'où il m'est impossible d'avoir de vos nouvelles aussi souvent que je L'ambitionne ardament.

Je souhaite que votre ami Le Respectable General Washington trouve le vin que je vous Envoye aussi bon qu'il peut le desirer. D'après le gout de votre Pays que Mr. De Moustier m'a fait Connoître, j'ai choisi Ce vin moins Liquoreux que Celui de mon Precedent Envoy. Il est bien facheux pour moi que la mauvaise qualité du muscat Rouge de l'année, ne me permette pas de vous en Envoyer; s'il est bon à la prochaine Recolte, je vous en Conserverai.

La Caisse de 60. B[outei]lles pour vous est marquée T.J.N.1. et Les Deux qui sont pour votre illustre General sont sous la marque de G.W. N. 2. et 3. Les trois Caisses D'égalle Contenance L'une, se montent à £:232ᵗ.10s. que Mr. Fenwick me fera parvenir à sa plus grande Commodité. Veuillez presenter L'hommage de mon Respect au grand Washington et être bien Convaincu vous même de Ce Sentiment profond, qui est depuis longtemps melé dans mon Coeur à l'attachement le plus inviolable, avec Lesquels j'ai L'honneur d'être Monsieur Votre très humble et très obeissant Serviteur

LAMBÊRT D.m.—maire

RC (MoSHi); endorsed as received 21 June 1791 and so recorded in SJL.

From Fulwar Skipwith

MY DEAR SIR　　　　　Basse terre, Guadalupe 10th. Feby 1791

Owing to the long and obstinate continuance of the unhappy disputes of Martinique, and finding myself on that account no less than for want of instructions from you, unable to render much service in my official capacity, I have within the last fortnight been induced to make this my place of residence, meaning to await the reestablishment of order in that distracted island and likewise the necessary communication from you respecting my consular department. The awkward circumstance of having not as yet experienced this last and most pleasing gratification in addition to the unfavorable turn of affairs in these islands, have reduced my slender finances as well as patience to some little trial. The first obstruction to my establishment I am flattering myself cannot longer exist, than the second, which from a late decree of the National Assembly seems to portend an early period to the violent disorder predominating thro' out their American possessions. The leading feature in this decree is that there shall be four disinterested persons appointed from the body of the Nation to examine into the claims grievances &c. of all parties, with no other power however than that of making a representation thereof to the Assembly of the Nation, who will afterwards redress such wrongs, and remedy such evils in their old colonial system as may appear necessary. With these Commissaries also are to arrive a strong marine and land force in order to support government on its former basis untill the necessary changes can be made. So wise and prudent purposes can only be defeated by the Soldiery, should those to come be tempted by the same corruption, which has so effectually distroyed all subordination among the late established troops of these islands, a fatal confusion which the National change has and most likely will be long productive of.

The bearer Capt. Clifton has been so good as to promise the safe delivery of a half dozen pots of Guava jelly which I solicit your acceptance of and that you will rest assured that when relieved from the peculiar hardship of my situation, my fondest hope will be to make myself as useful in my department as I have been flattered by the delicate and honourable manner, in which I have been appointed to it. With the most feeling sentiments of friendship & Respect I remain Sir Your mo ob Servt,

FULWAR SKIPWITH

RC (DNA: RG 59, CD). Not recorded in SJL.

From Florida Blanca

SIR   Madrid, 12th. February 1791.

Mr. Carmichael will have informed you of the favorable reception he met with from the King when he was presented by me to His Majesty as Chargé des Affaires of the United States appointed by their President, being made known as such by the Letter which you sent to me through his hands, dated the 11th. of April last.

The change which has taken place in the destination of Don Diego de Gardoqui had induced me to expect that an earlier opportunity should have offered to answer Your Honour's Letter. And altho' the opportunity I looked for has not yet presented itself, His Majesty not having yet come to a determination respecting the Person he is to appoint to succeed the said Chargé des Affaires, I could not but avail myself of the return to your Capital of Don Joseph Jaudenes, one of the Secretaries of the said Chargé des Affaires, recommending him thro' you, by the King's Order, to the President and States, as I likewise recommend to them Don Joseph de Viar, who will introduce him to you and deliver you this Letter; the King hopes that these Spaniards will be considered as his Majesty's servants, and be distinguished and attended to on all proper occasions.

I am further ordered by His Majesty to request you to assure the President of the United States, that faithful to the maxims of moderation and good faith which he has been taught by his August Father, he does and will preserve towards your States that Esteem and friendship which ought to subsist between good Neighbours. And as to myself individually, I beg you will rest assured of the consideration and high esteem which I hold you in, & I pray to God that he may Preserve you many Years.

I kiss Your Honour's hands—Your most obedient humble Servant

Tr (DNA: RG 59, NL); in clerk's hand; at head of text: "(Translation)"; at foot of text: "To Mr. *Joseph* Jefferson, Minister of State to the United States for the Department of Foreign Affairs." RC (same); in Spanish. Recorded in SJL as received by TJ while in New York, 16 June 1791.

From David Humphreys

SIR   Lisbon Feby. 12th. 1791

The postponement of the sailing of the Vessel by which I wrote on the 6th instant affords me an opportunity of continuing my Correspondence to this day. Since I had the honor of addressing you last, a Packet has arrived from England in five days passage, and yesterday the ordinary Post came in with the Mails from different parts of the Continent. The summary of Intelligence received through these Channels is, that the Russians still continue to obtain great advantages over the Turks; that Ismael defended by a Garrison of 13,000 Men, was taken by assault on the 22nd of December; that Poland was forming a Treaty with the Porte; that Misunderstandings had arisen between the Emperor and the King of Prussia respecting the subjugation of Leige that it was probable the British would send a Fleet into the Baltic next Campaign; that the war rages vehemently between their forces and those of Tippo Saib in the East Indies; and that Major General Meadows, who has assumed the command of the large Army assembled in the Carnatic, has taken three or four garrisoned Places from the Enemy.

From France there is nothing of importance, except that many of the Clergy had taken the Civic Oaths. The disturbances in their West India Islands have occasioned an unusually great demand, and enhancement in the prices of Sugars. I have the honor to be, With perfect consideration Sir, Your most obedient & Most humble Servant,   D. HUMPHREYS

RC (DNA: RG 59, DD); at head of text: "(No. 13)"; endorsed by TJ as received 31 Mch. 1791 and so recorded in SJL. Tr (same).

From Mary Jefferson

DEAR PAPA   February 13

I am very sorry that my not having wrote to you before made you doubt of my affection towards you and hope that after having read my last letter you were not so displeased as at first. In my last I said that my sister was very well but she was not. She had been very sick all day without my knowing any thing of it as I stayed upstairs the whole day. However she is very well now and the little one also. She is very pretty has beautiful deep blue eyes and is a very fine child. Adieu my Dear Papa & beleive me to be your affectionate daughter,   MARY JEFFERSON

RC (ViU); endorsed by TJ as received 28 Feb. 1791 and so recorded in SJL. The style of the letter indicates that it was dictated and that this was probably done by Mary Walker Lewis. For Mary's LAST LETTER see note, Mrs. Lewis to TJ, 23 Jan. 1791.

From John Barry

SIR   Strawberry Hill February 14: 1791

I am informed it is in contemplation to have a few Ships of War built. Permit me Sir to give you my opinion what kind would be the most proper for this Country at present and for Years to come. I would have them almost in every respect like Frigates with this difference only that their should be a deck fore and aft insted of gang ways with wide gratings and the middle of a few of the Beams to unship to let down the large boats. The sides of the largest should be run up so as to form ports that they might occasionally be Frigates or Ships, with two tire of Guns. Those may carry twenty four pounders on there lower deck and nines or twelves on the upper deck, the smaller ones to carry Eighteens on the lower deck and Nines on the Quarter deck and forecastle. They will cost very little more then common Frigates of their dimensions and have this advantage, they will be Stronger and have more room for their Men. It is too frequently the case on board Ships of War, that the Men are crowded together and of course can not keep them selves clean, and is often attended with sickness. Those Ships have many other advantages. They carry their lower tire higher than Ships of the Line and it is to be presumed as they are not so broad nor so high out of water they will out sail them and in a high sea be equal to any and Superior to Fiftys or Sixtys. Fortys or Frigates they are at all times an over match for. There is another advantage should they be sent against any of the Barbary cruisers they will allways have a sufficient number of Men on the upper deck to prevent boarding which is a very great practice with them and will give us a Superiority as we can defend our Ships from being boarded at the same time keep our lower deck Guns playing on the Enemy. I have the Honor to be Sir Your Obedent Humle. Servt.,   JOHN BARRY

RC (DNA: RG 59, MLR); endorsed by TJ as received 18 Feb. 1791 and so recorded in SJL.

To Charles Hellstedt

SIR   Philadelphia February 14th. 1791

I now return you the papers you were pleased to put into my hands, when you expressed to me your dissatisfaction that our Court of Admiralty had taken cognizance of a complaint of some Swedish sailors against their Captain for cruelty. If there was error in this proceeding, the law allows an appeal from that to the Supreme Court; but the appeal must be made in the forms of the law, which have nothing difficult in them. You were certainly free to conduct the appeal yourself, without employing an advocate, but then you must do it in the usual form. Courts of Justice all over the world, are held by the laws to proceed according to certain forms, which the good of the suitors themselves requires they should not be permitted to depart from.

I have further to observe to you, Sir, that this question lies altogether with the Courts of Justice; that the Constitution of the United States having divided the powers of Government into three branches, legislative, executive and judiciary, and deposited each with a separate body of Magistracy, forbidding either to interfere in the department of the other, the Executive are not at liberty to intermeddle in the present question. It must be ultimately decided by the Supreme court if you think proper to carry it into that. You may be secure of the strictest justice from them. Partialities they are not at liberty to shew. But for whatever may come before the Executive relative to your Nation, I can assure you of every favor which may depend on their dispositions to cultivate harmony and a good understanding with them.—I have the honor to be with great esteem Sir Your most obedient & most humble Servant,   TH: JEFFERSON

PrC (DLC); at foot of text: "Charles Hellstedt esquire Consul for Sweden at Philadelphia"; lacks signature, which is supplied from Tr (DNA: RG 59, PCC No. 120).

Opinion of Attorney General on the Case of James O'Fallon

Feb. 14. 1791.

The opinion is,

1. That the attorney for the district of Kentucky do forthwith take the most effectual measures for prosecuting according to law O'Fallon; and that he be informed, that, unless the testimony within his reach will clearly subject him to the charge of treason, the prosecution be for a riot.

2. That a proclamation issue, reciting the treaties, law and former proclamation on this subject, and declaring the purpose of the executive, that the disturbers of the public peace shall be prosecuted with the utmost rigor of the law.

The measures fit to be taken by way of precaution to the commandant of Fort Washington, are not here noticed.

PrC (DLC); in handwriting of Edmund Randolph, except for date and some overwriting of blurred words which are in TJ's hand. Recorded in SJPL.

James O'Fallon, an Irish adventurer who acted as general agent of the South Carolina Yazoo Company in Kentucky, entered into correspondence with Governor Miró of New Orleans in 1790, claiming that his company intended to establish an independent government allied to Spain (see O'Fallon to Miró, 16 July 1790; Lawrence Kinnaird, "Spain in the Mississippi Valley, 1765-1794," AHA, Ann. Rept., 1945, III, pt. II, 359-60). He presented his plans under a different coloring in a

letter to Washington in September. But it was not until late in the session that Washington laid before the Senate a "volume of a letter from a Dr. O'Fallon . . . avowing the raising of a vast body of men in the Kentucky country to force a settlement with the Yazoo country" (Maclay, *Journal*, ed. Maclay, p. 378). Maclay interpreted this and other documents transmitted at the same time as meaning a desire for more troops to defend the western frontiers. But, as indicated by the above opinion of the Attorney General —actually a joint one as proved by TJ's part in the composition and by his recording it in SJPL—the response of the administration to the threat of potential treason in the West did not contemplate such a use of force as Hamilton would later advocate. Washington sent a copy of O'Fallon's missive to Henry Knox, who transmitted it to Senator Ralph Izard with the suggestion that, "as it contains insinuations which are most probably unfounded, against several gentlemen of respectable characters," it would be highly improper to publish it (Lear to Knox, 15 Jan. 1791, DLC: Washington Papers; Knox to Izard, 31 Mch. 1791, MHi: Knox Papers).

The President's proclamation was not issued until 19 Mch. 1791, just as Washington was setting off for the South (Washington, *Writings*, ed. Fitzpatrick, XXXI, 250). Since John Brown of Kentucky had departed at least ten days earlier and bore important letters from TJ, it would appear that if O'Fallon had given any real concern the proclamation would have been issued in time for him to convey it (see Editorial Note to group of documents on new approaches to Spain, under 10 Mch. 1791). O'Fallon's voluminous letter probably exposed his romantic nature enough to convince TJ that the men from beyond the mountains in whom he had such confidence would not support such a leader (on O'Fallon's intrigues, see A. P. Whitaker, *Spanish-American Frontier*, p. 132; J. C. Parish, "The Intrigues of Doctor James O'Fallon," MVHR, XVII [Sep. 1930], 230-63; see also, William Murray to TJ, 12 May 1791).

The text of the proclamation against O'Fallon conforms in substance to the advice given in the above opinion (see illustration in this volume). Although no text exists in TJ's hand, it was almost certainly drawn as well as attested and printed by the Secretary of State (see Volume 17: 365; 50 copies of the proclamation were issued). The FORMER PROCLAMATION ON THAT SUBJECT—that of 26 Aug. 1790—has been attributed to TJ (Washington, *Writings*, ed. Fitzpatrick, XXXI, 99, note 71). While it was attested by TJ and perhaps was also a collaborative effort, that proclamation is actually in the hand of Edmund Randolph (MS in MHi: Knox Papers).

From C.W.F. Dumas

[The Hague] 15e. fevr. 1791.

Les Gazettes ci-jointes diront à V.E. tout ce que l'on sait ici parmi les mieux instruits des affaires générales de l'Europe. Je m'apperçois, depuis quelques jours, que le parti Pr[ussie]n ici commence à s'allarmer sur la tournure que les affaires prennent en Allemagne. Par contre, les autres, incomparablement plus nombreux, s'en réjouïssent, en conçoivent l'espoir de voir humilier enfin leurs oppresseurs. Les fonds américains se soutiennent ici sur le pied le plus avantageux. Messrs. N. et Jb. v. Staphorst & Hubbard ont ouvert une nouvelle négotiation de ƒ 1200,000 fondés sur vos dettes consolidées à 6 p% d'intérêt sans plus. Un rentier, qui vient d'en faire venir d'Amst[erdam] 8 Obligations de ƒ 1000, m'a dit avoir dû payer ¾ p% de courtage pour les avoir au pair, et qu'on ne peut déjà plus les avoir à moins de 1½ p%, c'est à ƒ 1015 pour 1000; tandis que les anciennes sont toujours de 20 à 25 audessus du Capital, parce qu'elles valent 9 p% d'interet par an au moins.

J'espere de me voir bientôt favorisé par Votre Excellence de bonnes nouvelles Américaines; spécialement de ce qu'Elle pense avec toute la sage Administration de notre auguste Union, sur mon idée des Paquebots ou autre bâtimens *commissionnés*, pour cheminer *régulierement* chaque mois, tour à tour de Philadelphie, N. York, Baltimore à Helvoetsluis et vice versa. Je suis toujours fermement persuadé qu'il seroit de la dignité, de l'intérêt et de l'utilité de cette belle Union d'avoir au moins cette voie de correspondance non précaire, indépendante et sûre, tant qu'il existera une Puissance perpétuellement tendante à envahir, empiéter, se prévaloir, influer, dominer partout où elle peut. Mon Zèle est donc pur en proposant cette affaire, et sollicite votre indulgence pour la liberté que je prends d'y insister si souvent. Si ces bâtimens pouvoient être armés plus ou moins selon les temps, ils pourroient occasionellement servir d'escorte, et être d'autant plus respectés.

J'accomplis ce jour le 70e. anniversaire de ma naissance; celui du 19 Avril prochain me sera plus cher, parce qu'il sera mon 16e. anniversaire au service de la plus heureuse Confédération qui existe sur ce Globe. Tous les jours jusqu'au dernier de ma vie, je prierai Dieu de la bénir de plus en plus. De V.E. le t. resp. humble ob. & fid. serv.

FC (Dumas Letter Book, Rijksarchief, The Hague; photostats in DLC). Recorded in SJL as received 19 June 1791.

Opinion on the Constitutionality of the Bill for Establishing a National Bank

The bill for establishing a National Bank undertakes, among other things

1. to form the subscribers into a Corporation.
2. to enable them, in their corporate capacities to receive grants of land; and so far is against the laws of *Mortmain*.*
3. to make *alien* subscribers capable of holding lands, and so far is against the laws of *Alienage*.
4. to transmit these lands, on the death of a proprietor, to a certain line of successors: and so far changes the course of *Descents*.
5. to put the lands out of the reach of forfeiture or escheat and so far is against the laws of *Forfeiture and Escheat*.

* Though the constitution controuls the laws of Mortmain so far as to permit Congress itself to hold lands for certain purposes, yet not so far as to permit them to communicate a similar right to other corporate bodies.

6. to transmit personal chattels to successors in a certain line: and so far is against the laws of *Distribution*.

7. to give them the sole and exclusive right of banking under the national authority: and so far is against the laws of *Monopoly*.

8. to communicate to them a power to make laws paramount to the laws of the states: for so they must be construed, to protect the institution from the controul of the state legislatures; and so, probably they will be construed.

I consider the foundation of the Constitution as laid on this ground that 'all powers not delegated to the U.S. by the Constitution, not prohibited by it to the states, are reserved to the states or to the people' [XIIth. Amendmt.]. To take a single step beyond the boundaries thus specially drawn around the powers of Congress, is to take possession of a boundless feild of power, no longer susceptible of any definition.

The incorporation of a bank, and other powers assumed by this bill have not, in my opinion, been delegated to the U.S. by the Constitution.

I. They are not among the powers specially enumerated, for these are

1. A power to *lay taxes* for the purpose of paying the debts of the U.S. But no debt is paid by this bill, nor any tax laid. Were it a bill to raise money, it's origination in the Senate would condemn it by the constitution.

2. 'to borrow money.' But this bill neither borrows money, nor ensures the borrowing it. The proprietors of the bank will be just as free as any other money holders, to lend or not to lend their money to the public. The operation proposed in the bill, first to lend them two millions, and then borrow them back again, cannot change the nature of the latter act, which will still be a payment, and not a loan, call it by what name you please.

3. 'to regulate commerce with foreign nations, and among the states, and with the Indian tribes.' To erect a bank, and to regulate commerce, are very different acts. He who erects a bank creates a subject of commerce in it's bills: so does he who makes a bushel of wheat, or digs a dollar out of the mines. Yet neither of these persons regulates commerce thereby. To erect a thing which may be bought and sold, is not to prescribe regulations for buying and selling. Besides; if this was an exercise of the power of regulating commerce, it would be void, as extending as much to the internal commerce of every state, as to it's external. For the power given

to Congress by the Constitution, does not extend to the internal regulation of the commerce of a state (that is to say of the commerce between citizen and citizen) which remains exclusively with it's own legislature; but to it's external commerce only, that is to say, it's commerce with another state, or with foreign nations or with the Indian tribes. Accordingly the bill does not propose the measure as a 'regulation of trade,' but as 'productive of considerable advantage to trade.'

Still less are these powers covered by any other of the special enumerations.

II. Nor are they within either of the general phrases, which are the two following.

1. 'To lay taxes to provide for the general welfare of the U.S.' that is to say 'to lay taxes *for the purpose* of providing for the general welfare'. For the laying of taxes is the *power* and the general welfare the *purpose* for which the power is to be exercised. They are not to lay taxes ad libitum *for any purpose they please*; but only to *pay the debts or provide for the welfare of the Union*. In like manner they are not *to do anything they please* to provide for the general welfare, but only *to lay taxes* for that purpose. To consider the latter phrase, not as describing the purpose of the first, but as giving a distinct and independent power to do any act they please, which might be for the good of the Union, would render all the preceding and subsequent enumerations of power completely useless. It would reduce the whole instrument to a single phrase, that of instituting a Congress with power to do whatever would be for the good of the U.S. and as they would be the sole judges of the good or evil, it would be also a power to do whatever evil they pleased. It is an established rule of construction, where a phrase will bear either of two meanings, to give it that which will allow some meaning to the other parts of the instrument, and not that which would render all the others useless. Certainly no such universal power was meant to be given them. It was intended to lace them up straitly within the enumerated powers, and those without which, as means, these powers could not be be carried into effect. It is known that the very power now proposed *as a means*, was rejected *as an end*, by the Convention which formed the constitution. A proposition was made to them to authorize Congress to open canals, and an amendatory one to empower them to incorporate. But the whole was rejected, and one of the reasons of rejection urged in debate was that then they would have a power to erect a bank, which would render the great cities,

where there were prejudices and jealousies on that subject adverse to the reception of the constitution.

2. The second general phrase is 'to make all laws *necessary and proper* for carrying into execution the enumerated powers.' But they can all be carried into execution without a bank. A bank therefore is not *necessary*, and consequently not authorised by this phrase.

It has been much urged that a bank will give great facility, or convenience in the collection of taxes. Suppose this were true: yet the constitution allows only the means which are 'necessary' not those which are merely 'convenient' for effecting the enumerated powers. If such a latitude of construction be allowed to this phrase as to give any non-enumerated power, it will go to every one, for these is no one which ingenuity may not torture into a *convenience, in some way or other*, to *some one* of so long a list of enumerated powers. It would swallow up all the delegated powers, and reduce the whole to one phrase as before observed. Therefore it was that the constitution restrained them to the *necessary* means, that is to say, to those means without which the grant of the power would be nugatory.

But let us examine this *convenience*, and see what it is. The report on this subject, page 3. states the only *general* convenience to be the preventing the transportation and re-transportation of money between the states and the treasury. (For I pass over the increase of circulating medium ascribed to it as a merit, and which, according to my ideas of paper money is clearly a demerit.) Every state will have to pay a sum of tax-money into the treasury: and the treasury will have to pay, in every state, a part of the interest on the public debt, and salaries to the officers of government resident in that state. In most of the states there will still be a surplus of tax-money to come up to the seat of government for the officers residing there. The payments of interest and salary in each state may be made by treasury-orders on the state collector. This will take up the greater part of the money he has collected in his state, and consequently prevent the great mass of it from being drawn out of the state. If there be a balance of commerce in favour of that state against the one in which the government resides, the surplus of taxes will be remitted by the bills of exchange drawn for that commercial balance. And so it must be if there was a bank. But if there be no balance of commerce, either direct or circuitous, all the banks in the world could not bring up the surplus of taxes but in the form of money. Treasury orders then and bills of exchange may prevent the displacement of the main mass of the money collected, without the aid of any bank: and where these fail, it cannot be prevented even with that aid.

Perhaps indeed bank bills may be a more *convenient* vehicle than treasury orders. But a little *difference* in the degree of *convenience*, cannot constitute the necessity which the constitution makes the ground for assuming any non-enumerated power.

Besides; the existing banks will without a doubt, enter into arrangements for lending their agency: and the more favourable, as there will be a competition among them for it: whereas the bill delivers us up bound to the national bank, who are free to refuse all arrangement, but on their own terms, and the public not free, on such refusal, to employ any other bank. That of Philadelphia, I believe, now does this business, by their post-notes, which by an arrangement with the treasury, are paid by any state collector to whom they are presented. This expedient alone suffices to prevent the existence of that *necessity* which may justify the assumption of a non-enumerated power as a means for carrying into effect an enumerated one. The thing may be done, and has been done, and well done without this assumption; therefore it does not stand on that degree of *necessity* which can honestly justify it.

It may be said that a bank, whose bills would have a currency all over the states, would be more convenient than one whose currency is limited to a single state. So it would be still more convenient that there should be a bank whose bills should have a currency all over the world. But it does not follow from this superior conveniency that there exists anywhere a power to establish such a bank; or that the world may not go on very well without it.

Can it be thought that the Constitution intended that for a shade or two of *convenience*, more or less, Congress should be authorised to break down the most antient and fundamental laws of the several states, such as those against Mortmain, the laws of alienage, the rules of descent, the acts of distribution, the laws of escheat and forfeiture, the laws of monopoly? Nothing but a necessity invincible by any other means, can justify such a prostration of laws which constitute the pillars of our whole system of jurisprudence. Will Congress be too strait-laced to carry the constitution into honest effect, unless they may pass over the foundation-laws of the state-governments for the slightest convenience to theirs?

The Negative of the President is the shield provided by the constitution to protect against the invasions of the legislature 1. the rights of the Executive 2. of the Judiciary 3. of the states and state legislatures. The present is the case of a right remaining exclusively with the states and is consequently one of those intended by the constitution to be placed under his protection.

It must be added however, that unless the President's mind on a view of every thing which is urged for and against this bill, is tolerably clear that it is unauthorised by the constitution, if the pro and the con hang so even as to balance his judgment, a just respect for the wisdom of the legislature would naturally decide the balance in favour of their opinion. It is chiefly for cases where they are clearly misled by error, ambition, or interest, that the constitution has placed a check in the negative of the President.

TH: JEFFERSON
Feb. 15. 1791.

PrC (DLC); MS worn on right-hand edges and some parts of words are supplied from Tr (DLC: Washington Papers), which varies slightly in punctuation and capitalization. Entry in SJPL reads: "[Feb.] 15. Op[inio]n Th: J. on the Bank law.—Madison's speech on same subject." This would suggest that TJ enclosed Madison's argument against the constitutionality of the bank (see Madison, *Writings*, ed. Hunt, VI, 19-44).

Hamilton's creation of the Bank of the United States—one modelled on the Bank of England, privately directed but inseparably connected with government, capitalized largely on the pyramided public paper made possible by his funding and assumption measures, and believed by opponents to have been designed to support the special interests that controlled its policies—widened and deepened the partisan and sectional cleavage that had long since made its appearance within the government. Joseph Charles, *The origins of the American party system* (New York, 1961), p. 26, pointed out that historians had often concerned themselves with the impact of the bank bill on public opinion while neglecting to do so for the funding and assumption measures, which he regarded as the "first milestones in the growth of parties." There is still general agreement that "it was Madison's and Jefferson's opposition to the original charter [of the bank] that marked the birth" of the Republican

party and that "Jefferson's attack on the constitutionality of the Bank and his enunciation of a narrow interpretation of the 'necessary and proper' clause of the Constitution became articles of faith in the Republican dogma" (Edward C. Carter, II, "The birth of a political economist: Mathew Carey and the recharter fight of 1810-1811," *Pennsylvania History*, XXXIII [July, 1966], 280; for variant opinions on the politics of the bank issue, see Mitchell, *Hamilton*, II, 86-108; Malone, *Jefferson*, II, 337-50; Brant, *Madison*, II, 327-33; Schachner, *Jefferson*, I, 416-22; Miller, *Hamilton*, p. 255-77; see also, Stuart Bruchey, "Alexander Hamilton and the State Banks, 1789 to 1795," WMQ, 3rd. ser., XXVII [July, 1970], 347-78, the best analysis of Hamilton's attempt to reconcile—under the broad rubric of the public interest—his conflicting views about rival banking systems chartered under federal and state authority; while just to Hamilton, Bruchey concludes that, in the favoritism shown the Bank of New York, he "acted in ways that deserve to be questioned"; the definitive texts of Hamilton's proposal of the bank and his defense of its constitutionality are presented by Syrett, *Hamilton*, VII, 237-42; VIII, 62-134). Leonard D. White, *The Federalists*, p. 223, concluded that the "first substantial break over public policy occurred . . . when Jefferson declared Hamilton's plan . . . beyond the power of Congress to enact."

But it must be emphasized, first of

all, that the contest over the bank did not bring TJ and Hamilton into public view as protagonists of opposing views of public policy. Their opinions were solicited by the President in private and were not known to the contemporary public. Washington's long delay in signing the bill did, of course, cause much anxiety on the part of Hamilton and others; Madison's impassioned argument in the House of Representatives was a matter of public record; and the constitutional issue was discussed in the press (*Federal Gazette*, 21 Feb. 1791; *Va. Gazette* [Richmond], 16 Mch. 1791). Second, both Madison and TJ, as ardent and consistent nationalists, had frequently upheld the doctrine of implied or inherent powers advanced by Hamilton to defend the bank bill—Madison most conspicuously in *The Federalist* No. 44 and TJ most radically in arguing for a treaty that he considered beyond the powers of the Confederation (TJ to John Adams, 28 July 1785, enclosure; see also TJ's opinion on the constitutionality of the Residence Act, Vol. 17: 197). This very fact, which implied that TJ and Madison were in effect arguing against themselves, obliged TJ also to question the necessity of a national bank since state-chartered institutions were in existence. Third, the constitutional issue was raised belatedly. While both TJ and Madison were undoubtedly disturbed about the tendency of Hamilton's measures and resorted to a strict constructionist position to challenge that tendency, this was primarily a weapon of defense— a wholly inadequate one. Finally, though Washington's doubts may not have been entirely resolved by Hamilton's argument, there are grounds for supposing that southern—especially Virginia—opposition to a national bank chartered for twenty years rested on the suspicion that this was another means of keeping the government in Philadelphia (see Editorial Note to group of documents on the location of the Federal District, under 24 Jan. 1791).

Théophile Cazenove, representative of several Amsterdam firms, was not the only contemporary to observe a connection between the bank and the capital issues: "As those who desire that the seat of government be on the Potomac are united against the Bank, so the opposite party are united in its favor" (Cazenove to his principals, 5 Feb. 1791; Cazenove Letterbook). Fisher Ames declared that the "great point of difficulty was, the effect of the bank law to make the future removal of the government" from Philadelphia less likely. William L. Smith claimed that Virginians had indeed proposed "first by innuendo and finally in direct terms" that if the charter were limited to ten years the bill would be supported, but if not, the constitutional issue would be raised. "Had Pennsylvania acceded to the proposition, which the writer knows was made to this effect," Smith declared, "much discussion and ill humor might have been spared, a prodigious deal of debate respecting the constitutionality of the law would have been avoided, and the painful agitation and disturbed state of mind for many days of a great character [Washington] would not have been excited" (Fisher Ames to George Roberts Minot, 17 Feb. 1791, Ames, *Works*, ed. Seth Ames, I, 95-6; [William L. Smith], *The politicks and views of a certain party displayed* [1792], p. 17; both quotations from Ames and Smith are drawn from an article by Kenneth R. Bowling, "The Bank Bill, the Capital City, and President Washington" (*Capitol Studies*, I [1972]). These observations scarcely did justice to the convictions of those who advanced the constitutional argument and Madison categorically denied Smith's allegation about a proposition to limit the charter to ten years (Madison's "Outline of an Answer to a Pamphlet," 1792; DLC: Madison Papers, cited by Bowling). But there can be no doubt that political maneuvers in which both Washington and TJ were involved did connect the bank bill and the bill to amend the Residence Act (see note to group of documents on the location of the Federal District, under 24 Jan. 1791).

While the partisan and sectional cleavages were exacerbated by the bank issue, the first public break on a fundamental question of policy came with TJ's remarkably blunt report on the whale and cod fisheries. This was a deliberate and conscious effort on his part to force the issue into the open after the lines had been drawn in private. It brought him and Hamilton on the stage as contestants, being none the less a confrontation because TJ was the challenger and Hamilton, confronted with a dilemma, was his silent and covert opponent. Its nature, if not its purpose, was obvious to the public. It therefore created something of a public sensation in a manner that the bank issue did not, for it reaffirmed policies on which there had once been general agreement but on which there was now partisan and sectional divergence. Hamilton had won a crowning victory with his bank bill, but a costly one. He and his followers, at the moment of their triumph, were deeply concerned over the threat implicit in TJ's report and its legislative counterpart, Madison's navigation bill (see Edi-

torial Note to TJ's report on the fisheries, 1 Feb. 1791). Fiscalism, victorious on the domestic scene, was now faced with a serious challenge on a basic question of foreign policy, one not confined to the interests of a special group but concerned with the welfare of the whole economy. Hamilton was well aware that this was less a moment for celebrating triumph than for being politically circumspect. For the challenge that had been made by TJ was issued with the approval of the President, Hamilton's very essential aegis.

To Mary Jefferson

MY DEAR POLL   Philadelphia Feb. 16. 1791.

At length I have recieved, a letter from you. As the spell is now broke, I hope you will continue to write every three weeks. Observe I do not admit the excuse you make of not writing because your sister had not written the week before: let each write their own week without regard to what others do, or do not do.—I congratulate you my dear aunt on your new title. I hope you pay a great deal of attention to your niece, and that you have begun to give her lessons on the harpsichord, in Spanish &ca. Tell your sister I make her a present of Gregory's comparative view, inclosed herewith, and that she will find in it a great deal of useful advice for a young mother. I hope herself and the child are well. Kiss them both for me. Present me affectionately to Mr. Randolph and Miss Jenny. Mind your Spanish and your Harpsichord well and think often and always of, Your's affectionately,

TH: JEFFERSON

P.S. Letters inclosed with the book for your sister.

RC (ViU); addressed: "Miss Maria Jefferson Monticello." PrC (ViU). Enclosure: John Gregory (1724-1773), *A comparative view of the state and faculties of man with those of the animal world* (London, 1766). The letters enclosed with the book may have been those to Martha Randolph and Lewis Nicholas of 9 Feb. 1791, assuming that these missed the post of the previous week.

If TJ's sole purpose had been to furnish "a great deal of useful advice for a young mother," it is strange that he did not choose another work by the professor of medicine at the University of Edinburgh whose ideas he found so congenial. Gregory's *A father's legacy to his daughters* was an extremely popular treatise devoted to the improvement of mind and manners, going through many editions in both English and French. TJ owned a copy of the London, 1779, edition (Sowerby No. 1354). But Gregory's *Comparative view*, a series of discourses presented to the Philosophical Society of Edinburgh between 1758 and 1763, contains only one small passage that is strictly relevant to TJ's avowed purpose in sending it to Martha. Only the first of the discourses is devoted to reflections on infancy, "that period of life, where Instinct is the only active principle of our Nature, and consequently where the analogy between us and other animals will be found most compleat." It urged a "back to Nature and Common sense" approach to the care and nurture of infants, inveighing against the use of midwives, wet nurses, restrictive clothing, and in general any practice that disregarded the lessons of instinct "and the analogous Constitutions of other Animals."

All of the remaining discourses were devoted to those distinctions that set man apart from "the rest of the Animal Creation": his powers of reasoning, his social dispositions, his refinements of taste, and his capacity for religion. The second discourse developed the theme that talent and genius were not in themselves sufficient to place their possessor at the head of a useful art or profession or to make him more happy in himself. On the contrary, these endowments were "usually dissipated in such a way, as renders them of no account, either to the Public or the Possessor." Thus nothing was more likely to deprive the world of the fruits of great talents than "the passion for universal knowledge so constantly annexed to those who possess them." By this indulgence "the flame of Genius is wasted in the endless labour of accumulating promiscuous or useless facts, while it might have enlightened the most useful Arts by concentrating its force upon one object." Mere passive and undirected reading contributed to the same end and thus the "powers of Genius and Invention languish for want of exercise." Moreover, "All the public and social affections, in common with every taste natural to the Human Mind, if they are not properly exercised, grow languid." Yet in a situation withdrawn from the world, private and selfish feelings—especially "Envy and Jealousy, the most tormenting of all Passions"—flourished. Fail-

ure to mix with the world was often an insuperable obstacle to the advancement of men of merit, thus providing "a frequent source of their disgust to the World, and consequently to themselves." One of the principal misfortunes of talent exerted in a speculative and isolated rather than an active sphere was "its tendency to lead the Mind into too deep a sense of its own weakness and limited capacity." This naturally brought on "a gloomy and forlorn Scepticism." Under such handicaps, "Reason, that boasted characteristic and privilege of the Human Species," would produce little if any public or private good. Despite all of these and other limitations, however, those endowed with superior talents were "born to an ascendancy and empire over the Minds and Affairs of Mankind, if they would but assume it."

Such was the burden of the message in Gregory's *Comparative view*, and it contradicts TJ's declared purpose in sending it to his daughter. Even that fractional part of the discourses that treats of infancy seems under the circumstances somewhat superfluous for such an object. Martha Randolph had long been exposed to her father's faith in common sense and the healing power of nature. Moreover, she was at that moment under the capable guidance of Mrs. Mary Walker Lewis in facing the problems of infant care. By contrast, the principal burden of Gregory's discourses—the warning that the man of talent, withdrawn from society, might contribute little to the public good or to his own happiness—seems exactly suited to another member of the little audience to which the letter to Mary was addressed. In view of the sensitive web of relationships connecting father, daughter, and husband, a resort to a characteristically indirect means of persuasion may have seemed more appropriate for use by one who, under other circumstances, never hesitated to make direct appeals to young men of talent urging them to assume active roles in society. It is therefore difficult to avoid the conclusion that Gregory's *Comparative view* was chosen not for the stated reason, but because it contained a great deal of useful advice peculiarly fitted to the temperament and condition of the young father at Monticello. See TJ to Randolph, 24 Feb. 1791, note.

From William Blount

["Territory of the United States of America South of the River Ohio. At William Cobbs." *17 Feb. 1791*.] In December he appointed and commissioned civil and military officers for Davidson, Sumner, and Tennessee counties, which form the district of Mero. "The people of that district also appear much pleased with the change of the government.—The superior Court for the District of Washington is now setting. Judges Campbell and McNairy are present. Whether Mr. Perry accepts of his appointment or not. I am uninformed."

RC (DNA: RG 59, SWT); endorsed by TJ as received 11 Mch. 1791 and so recorded in SJL. For the officers commissioned, see Carter, *Terr. Papers*, IV, 432-42. Mero District was named for Don Estevan Miró, Spanish governor of Orleans. William Peery declined the appointment and Joseph Anderson was named to fill the vacancy (same, IV, 40, 45; see documents grouped at 4 Mch. 1791 on the Anderson appointment).

From Ebenezer Hazard

Thursday Morning. [17 Feb. 1791]

Mr. Hazard presents his respectful Compliments to Mr. Jefferson. It has occurred to him that if Mr. Jefferson would favor him with a Line or two recommendatory of his Undertaking, which he might be permitted to publish, it would expedite the printing of his Collection of State Papers, and render the public Appearance of that work less problematical than it will otherwise be, as the Sanction of Mr. Jefferson's Name will undoubtedly occasion considerable Additions to the List of Subscribers.

It cannot be expected that a first Attempt of this kind can be *complete*, especially as Mr. Hazard was prevented, by his Appointment to Office, from prosecuting the Business in the regular Manner he at first proposed:—the Collection, however, contains a great Variety of valuable and important State Papers, and authentic historical Documents; a Part of which Mr. Hazard has left for Mr. Jefferson's Inspection. These Records of the United Colonies of New England, though frequently refered to by Historians, have never been before published; and, including Mr. Hazard's, there are but three Copies of them in being.

As it is necessary to publish the Proposals prior to the Recess of Congress, Mr. Hazard will take the Liberty of waiting on Mr. Jefferson in a Day or two.

RC (DLC); endorsed by TJ as received 17 Feb. 1791 and so recorded in SJL. On Hazard's undertaking and the nature of the documents left for TJ's inspection, see note, TJ to Hazard, 18 Feb. 1791.

From James Monroe

DEAR SIR   Phila. Feby. 17. 1791.

This will be presented you by Mr. Yard at present residing in this city, but lately from St. Croix, whither also he proposes shortly to return. Presuming the establishment of consuls will be extended to that Island, and being willing to accept of such appointment, he has requested me to make his pretensions known to you. His connection with Mrs. Monroe's family has given me the pleasure of his acquaintance, and I am happy to assure you that I believe him to be possess'd, in a high degree, of all the qualifications necessary for the discharge of the duties of that office. As Mr. Yard is possess'd of an ample fortune, he is desirous of this trust more, in gratification of his feelings, as a proof of the publick confidence, than from any view of emolument. And as he is extensively connected in that Island and with those of the first estimation, this perhaps may furnish an additional reason for employing him. Having resided there for sometime he is well acquainted with its trade; information in this respect in detail, may perhaps be serviceable to you, and whether he succeeds or not in the above object he will be happy to possess you with whatever he knows on the subject. I am with the greatest respect & esteem Dr Sir your friend & servant,   JAS. MONROE

RC (DLC): endorsed by TJ as received 17 Feb. 1791 and so recorded in SJL.

George Washington to William Deakins, Jr., and Benjamin Stoddert

GENTLEMEN   Philadelphia Feb. 17. 1791.

I have recieved your favors of the 9th. and 11th[1] instant and shall be glad if the purchase from Burnes should be concluded before you recieve this at £15 or £15-10 as you hope. But as you mention that should he ask as far as £20. or £25. you will await further instructions before you accept such an offer, I have thought it better, in order to prevent delay, to inform you that I would wish his lands to be purchased even at those prices, rather than not obtain them.

The Maryland assembly has authorized a certain number of acres to be taken, without the consent of the owners, on making compensation as therein provided. This will be principally useful as to the old lots of Hamburg. However by purchasing up these lots or as many as we can, we shall be free to take on the terms of the act so much of any other lands in our way, and consequently those whose proprietors refuse all arrangement. I will therefore beg the favour of you to take measures immediately for buying up all the lots you can in Hamburg on the lowest terms you can not exceeding the rate of twenty five pounds the acre. I leave it to yourselves to dispatch a private agent for this purpose to treat with the proprietors wherever to be found, or to do it by any other means which in your discretion shall appear not too expensive, and which may not excite suspicions of their being on behalf of the public. I am with great esteem, Gentlemen, your most obedt. humble servt.

PrC (DLC: Washington Papers); entirely in TJ's hand except for docketing and dates (see note 1) in Washington's hand; at foot of text: "Messrs. Dickens and Stoddart." Not recorded in SJL or SJPL.

1 Dates inserted by Washington in RC (missing) before PrC was executed.

From Benjamin Hawkins

DEAR SIR   Mrs. Houses friday 18th. Feby. 1791.

I am very desirous of obtaining your opinion on the Constitutionality of the Treaties formed with the Indians at Hopewell on the Keowée. If I recollect right, you informed me you had yours in writing some time last summer.—If the request be not an improper one, and you have reserved a copy, you will oblige me by a gratification of my desire. I do not mean to ask the liberty of using your name with it.—I have the honor to be very sincerely Dear Sir, Your most obedient & hule. servant,

BENJAMIN HAWKINS

RC (DLC); endorsed by TJ as received 18 Feb. 1791 and so recorded in SJL. For TJ's opinion on the Treaty of Hopewell, see TJ to Knox, 26 Aug. 1790.

From William Hay

DEAR SIR   Richmond February 18th. 1791

Your Determination respecting the Encyclopédie in which Mr. Madison concurs with you, is perfectly satisfactory to me, and the more so, as you so obligingly offer your Services to dispose of it in Philadelphia. As I now consider myself bound to pay Doctr. Currie the Value of the original Subscription in standard English Books, perhaps you will be able to swap the Encylopédie with some of the Booksellers, for such Books as the Doctor may chuse. In this View, I shall call on the Doctr. for a List of the Books he wants and enclose it to you. As I know well you have very little Time to devote to private Correspondence, I must beg pardon for troubling you with this Business. Permit me, Sir, to inform you, that I would be happy to have it my Power to serve you, and to assure you that I am with great Esteem & Respect Dear Sir Your most Obt. Hbl. Sevt,   WM. HAY

P.S. The Account of the Livraisons and Doctr. Currie's List are enclosed.

RC (MHi); endorsed by TJ as received 16 Mch. 1791 and so recorded in SJL.

To Ebenezer Hazard

SIR   Philadelphia Feb. 18. 1791.

I return you the two volumes of records, with thanks for the opportunity of looking into them. They are curious monuments of the infancy of our country. I learn with great satisfaction that you are about committing to the press the valuable historical and state-papers you have been so long collecting. Time and accident are committing daily havoc on the originals deposited in our public offices. The late war has done the work of centuries in this business. The lost cannot be recovered; but let us save what remains: not by vaults and locks which fence them from the public eye and use, in consigning them to the waste of time, but by such a multiplication of copies, as shall place them beyond the reach of accident. This being the tendency of your undertaking be assured there is no one who wishes it a more complete success than Sir Your most obedient & most humble servt.,   TH: JEFFERSON

RC (PHi). PrC (DLC). Enclosure: The two unbound manuscript volumes (DLC: Hazard Papers) comprising Hazard's copy made in Plymouth in 1779 and 1781 of the Records of the United Colonies of New England, the text of which made up the major part of the second of the only two volumes to be published of Hazard's pioneering effort to preserve and publish American historical documents, *Historical collections; consisting of the state papers . . . intended as materials for an history of the United States* (Philadelphia, 1792-1794). See Sowerby No. 3044.

This brief, eloquent, and timeless philosophy for archivists, curators of historical manuscripts, and editors of historical documents sprang from TJ's own life-long concern to protect the sources of American history against loss and to disseminate them for use (see TJ to Wythe, 16 Jan. 1796). His interest in Hazard's bold undertaking went back to 1774 (see text of Hazard's first printed prospectus under 23 Aug. 1774; TJ to Hazard, 30 Apr. 1775). In *Notes on Virginia* TJ had printed the list of documents he had made in 1775 for Hazard's use, and stated: "An extensive collection of papers of this description has been for some time in a course of preparation by a gentleman fully equal to the task, and from whom, therefore, we may hope ere long to receive it" (*Notes*, Peden ed., p. 179, 296n.). Hazard's duties as postmaster-general from 1782 to 1789, among other obstacles, disappointed this expectation. Like his friend Charles Thomson, Hazard was not continued in office under the new government, but, unlike him, he was not given a glowing testimonial for faithful public services extending back to the beginning of the government (Washington to Thomson, 24 July 1789; *Writings*, ed. Fitzpatrick, xxx, 358-9). Indeed, Washington did not even inform the incumbent that another would take his place, but left Hazard to learn on the streets that Samuel Osgood would be his successor. The cause of this unceremonious dismissal is attributable, first, to Washington's mistaken belief that Hazard was opposed to the Constitution, and second, to opposition from the struggling stage lines that had been under contract to deliver the mail. The latter may have given TJ an additional motive for assisting Hazard, for he had long been concerned about the need for "speedy and frequent communication of intelligence" (TJ to Adams, 16 May 1777) and Hazard, thinking that owners of stage lines had sacrificed safe and expeditious handling of mails for the sake of greater gains through passenger revenue, had failed to renew their contracts (Fred Shelley, "Ebenezer Hazard: America's First Historical Editor," WMQ, 3rd. ser., XII [Jan. 1955], 60-1; W. E. Rich, *History of the United States Post Office to the year 1829*, p. 64-7). The historically minded intellectual was one of the few incumbents of his office to manage the postal service without a loss, but his zeal for dispatch and efficiency brought him into collision with those who believed mail contracts should be awarded to a young and struggling transportation industry in order to meet another public necessity. This was an enduring conflict, but the first manifestation of it left Hazard at 44 with no means of support for his young and growing family. TJ had been unable to supply him with the clerkship in the Department of State for which he applied early in 1790 (Hazard to TJ, 20 Feb. 1790). But Hazard, stunned by a dismissal for which he had been unprepared and whose causes he did not fully grasp, turned to his compilation of documents in the belief that a patriotic public would support a venture illuminating the political progress of the country and "clearly point[ing] out different advances from persecution to comparative liberty, and from thence to independent empire" (Hazard's memorial to Congress, 11 July 1788; JCC, XI, 682). The confidence was as bold as the long-pursued plan, and it was in the full tide of this hope that Hazard appealed to TJ.

To TJ's prompt response Hazard replied the same day: "Mr. Hazard presents his respectful Compliments to Mr. Jefferson.—He has received the Records of the United Colonies of New England, and is much obliged to Mr. Jefferson for his Letter which accompanied them" (RC in DLC; dated "Friday Evening" and recorded in SJL as received 18 Feb. 1791). The testimonial had been solicited for publication, was composed with that end in view, and of course was employed in newspaper advertisements and in Hazard's broadside, *Proposals for printing by subscription, a collection of state papers intended as materials for an history of the United States of America* (Philadelphia [Thomas Dodson], 24 Feb. 1791; *Gazette of the United States*, 5 Mch. 1791; Hazard to TJ, 17 Feb. 1791). Hazard's own copy of the prospectus, a scroll with a double-column appendage of signatures of subscribers, is now in the Historical Society of Pennsylvania, at once an object and a champion of the purposes of such indispensable repositories. Its list of signatures begins with the bold autograph of the President who had dismissed the faithful and competent public servant without grace or ceremony, and is followed by those of the Vice-President, members of the Cabinet, Senators, Representatives, and civil servants. TJ's signature is thirty-third on the list.

The apposite words of TJ's letter

were quoted by the Editor in the fore-front of the document that led to the present edition (*Report to the Thomas Jefferson Bicentennial Commission on the need, scope, proposed method of preparation, probable cost, and possible means of publishing a comprehensive edition of the writings of Thomas Jefferson* [Princeton, N.J.], mimeographed text, 25 Sep. 1943), and Hazard's copy of the prospectus with its imposing array of signatures of subscribers was reproduced in facsimile in the document that led to the first general appropriation by the Federal Government authorizing grants for the collection, reproduction, and publication of documentary source material significant to the history of the United States (*Hearing . . . on H. R. 6237*, 88th Cong., 1st. sess., Washington, 1963, p. 23). Thus TJ's timeless testimonial in support of the pioneer editor of historical sources in the eighteenth century continued to sustain the similar purposes of his successors in the twentieth. But Hazard, whose bold conception, self-sacrificing industry, and intellectual integrity won for him "a place of first rank in the roster of American antiquaries," was mistaken in his belief in public support. His two volumes served historians well for over half a century but their fate at the hands of the purchasing public was, as a business venture, "just short of disastrous." Hazard bore his loss with equanimity and even labored in the hope of issuing a third volume, but it never appeared (Shelley, "Ebenezer Hazard: America's First Historical Editor," WMQ, 3rd. ser., XII [Jan. 1955], 45).

From William Short

DEAR SIR   Amsterdam Feb. 18. 1791.

I learn that a change of wind which lasted a few hours only at length allowed three of the vessels which had my letters, to get out of the Texel some days ago. Others were less fortunate and still remain there. My several letters by the way of England will previously have explained the cause of this uncommon delay.

I mentioned to you in my last that the committee of commerce had wished to propose to the National assembly a duty on American oils even lower than those of the *arret du Conseil*, that against their sentiments and to obtain a majority they had at length consented to propose an higher one, that even this was rejected and the duty 12.ᵗᵗ the quintal decreed. From my No. 53. you certainly did not expect such an issue to this business: it is useless to repeat here what I have so often mentioned that it is temerity to form any conjecture where the decision depends on a vote of the national assembly.—I still think that a short experience will correct this error into which they have been drawn by the causes mentioned in my last. The duty on *Morues vertes et seches, harengs, maquereaux et sardines* is fixed at 20.ᵗᵗ the quintal.

The article of tobacco is discussed from time to time in the assembly and it is as impossible to say when it will be decided as what the decision will be, although the post of this evening from Paris may perhaps bring it. It is said that the deputies sent extraordinarily from the Belgick provinces on Mirabeau's speech (already mentioned to you) arriving there have changed his opinion and if so the assembly will certainly abandon even an attempt to prohibit the cultivation of that article. They certainly have not force enough to carry such a prohibition into effect. If they had I should rather they should do it and preserve the farm than permit the cultivation and embarass the importation by too heavy duties, which may perhaps take place from a desire to satisfy all parties and from a *mezzo termine* system which is frequently adopted by the assembly to extricate themselves from difficult questions.—I have not returned from hence to Paris during these discussions 1. because I knew the committees were as favorably disposed as I could have made them. 2. because the Secretary whom I employed was much to be relied on both on account of his dispositions and connexions and 3. because it was impossible to know whether I should not arrive too late, or whether any thing would be done in the assembly respecting these questions during the time I could have staid there. The term which had been prescribed to me to remain here now expiring I am preparing to return there.

Since the taking of Ismailow nothing remarkable has presented itself in that quarter. It is thought the Prince Potemkin will advance his army without taking winter quarters in hopes of forcing the Porte to a separate peace. The conferences at Szistow go on slowly. The circumstances of the Emperor and the King of Prussia have much changed since it was agreed to hold them. The affair of Liege is going on much against what is considered the honor and glory of the latter and there appears as yet no evidence of his intending to give active opposition. The English continue gradually equipping their fleet. It is thought that they will eventually send one into the Baltic and another into the Levant. It is not known what role Denmark will adopt. In fact the present state of politics in Europe continues much longer to be an uncertain one than could have been expected.—England and Spain are still corresponding on the means of carrying into execution their late convention. I have the honor of inclosing you a letter for the Secretary of the Treasury and of assuring you of the sentiments of attachment & respect with which I am, dear Sir, Your most obedient humble servant,   W: SHORT

PrC (DLC: Short Papers); at head of text: "*No. 56.*" Tr (DNA: RG 59, DD). Recorded in SJL as received 23 Apr. 1791. Enclosure: Short to Hamilton, 17 Jan. 1791, announcing the completion of the Holland loan (see Short's private letter to TJ, following).

From William Short

Dear Sir   Amsterdam Feb. 18. 1791.

I wrote to you on the 17th. of Jan. private. Whenever I begin a letter of that kind I find an almost irresistible impulsion to apologize for the repeated *ennui* that you must have recieved from my several letters written posterior to June last. I am prevented from it only by the consideration that it is now too late to prevent it and from a desire to avoid importunity.—Since my last the Secretary I left at Paris has forwarded me a letter which Petit wrote to him. In it he says *qu'il meure d'ennui*, wishes to know whether any successor has yet come to take your place, and adds that I had promised him to write to you to know whether you would give him an 100.^{tt} a month, and that he would be willing to go for that sum. His *ennui* where he is and his desire to go to America at present I suppose have made him wish he had made that proposition to you. On the contrary he first balanced about going. As soon as the letter from you fixing the wages arrived he determined not to go in the beginning on that account, and finally on account of his mother and other reasons, then leaving the affair of wages quite out of the question. I suppose the most weighty was his persuasion that your successor would employ him. I have written to him that you were sorry he had determined not to go and still wished it but that you had not authorized me to augment the wages, that if you do not get a maitre d'hotel at Philadelphia I am to send you one and that I am to wait until I hear farther from you. that in the mean time, I will write to you respecting his proposition at present, that I had not done it before because he never said any thing to me which even tended to authorize it, and desire him to recollect what he told me about his mother, his family &c. &c. I add to him from your letters what you say about your successors not arriving before the Spring, and about his wife's (if he should have one) not employing a maitre d'hotel who don't speak English. As it is you may count on his going for an 100.^{tt} a month if you should chuse it. Your successor probably would not be the means of your not having the maitre d'hotel you chuse and of course would not employ him. I expected a letter from you long before this on this subject, as you have not written you probably found one to your liking at Philadelphia. I suppose it probable however that I shall hear from you before the answer which you will send to this and will do for the best respecting this matter according to your letters.—The last which I have recieved from you was from

Monticello, except the short one respecting Mr. Donald sent through his hands. It has been a long time also since I have heard from M. de la Motte at Havre but I hope the Champagne wine and your carriages have been long ago sent although I have no express account of it from him. I have not heard either of M. Vernon's having embarked for America. The last account I recieved was of his being at Bordeaux. I hope he has gone long before this. M. Cathalan informs me he has sent the olive trees to America.

My letter of yesterday to the Secretary of the Treasury will inform you of the loan made here, of the desire of the bankers first to extend it to 3,000,000. of guilders and their intimation that it might if I chose to be carried to 4. millions. The zeal increases and they now think if I would make use of the moment it might be extended to five millions. One of them has just been with me to press it. The moment is certainly very favorable and it would be an agreeable circumstance to those to whom we wish to pay what we owe. But I have resolved to follow the instruction I recieved and not to make any other loan until I hear further. It would be a great advantage to American credit if the U.S. were better known here. Intelligence comes so slow and so seldom from thence, except to a few who chuse to keep it for their own purposes, that the U.S. are considered by most of them as out of the world. I have no hopes that our government will ever be sensible of the advantages of giving frequent and early communication on this side of the Atlantic, and of course I say nothing respecting it.—I was never so sensible of this as since I have been here. Whenever I have declared my ignorance of newspaper reports it has been taken for granted that that was impossible and that I had something to conceal. This of course was considered as inauspicious. Adieu my dear Sir and believe most sincerely Your friend & servant,

W: SHORT

RC (DLC); at head of text: *"Private"*; endorsed by TJ as received 23 Apr. 1791 and so recorded in SJL. PrC (PHi).

The President to the Senate

United States, 18th. February. 1791.

GENTLEMEN OF THE SENATE

The aspect of affairs in Europe during the last summer, and especially between Spain and England, gave reason to expect a favorable occasion for pressing to accommodation the unsettled matters between them and us. Mr. Carmichael, our Chargé des affaires at Madrid, having been long absent from his country, great changes having taken place in our circumstances and sentiments during that interval, it was thought expedient to send some person in a private character, fully acquainted with the present State of things here, to be the bearer of written and confidential instructions to him, and at the same time to possess him in full and frequent Conversations, of all those details of facts and tropics of Argument which could not be conveyed in writing, but which would be necessary to enable him to meet the reasonings of that court with Advantage. Colo. David Humphreys was therefore sent for these purposes.

An additional motive for this confidential mission arose in the same quarter. The Court of Lisbon had, on several Occasions, made the most amicable advances for cultivating friendship and intercourse with the United States; the exchange of a diplomatic character had been informally but repeatedly suggested on their part. It was our interest to meet this nation in its friendly dispositions, and to concur with the Exchange proposed; but my wish was, at the same time, that the character to be exchanged, should be of the lowest and most economical grade. To this it was known that certain rules of long standing at that court, would produce obstacles. Colo. Humphreys was charged with dispatches to the prime Minister of Portugal, and with instructions to endeavour to arrange this to our views. It happened, however, that, previous to his arrival at Lisbon, the Queen had appointed a minister *resident* to the United States. This embarrassment seems to have rendered the difficulty completely insurmountable. The Minister of that court, in his conferences with Colo. Humphreys, professing every wish to accommodate, yet expresses his regrets that circumstances do not permit them to concur in the grade of chargé des affaires; a grade of little privilege or respectability by the rules of their court, and held in so low estimation with them, that no proper character would accept it, to go abroad. In a letter to the Secretary of State, he expresses the same Sentiments, and announces the appointment, on their part, of a Minister *resident* to the United States, and the pleasure with which the Queen will receive one from us at her court. A copy of his letter, and also of Colo. Humphreys' giving the details of this transaction, will be delivered to you.

On consideration of all circumstances, I have determined to accede to the desire of the Court of Lisbon, in the Article of grade.

I am aware, that the consequences will not end here, and that this is not the only instance in which a like change may be pressed. But should it be necessary to yield elsewhere also, I shall think it a less evil, than to disgust a government so friendly and so interesting to us, as that of Portugal.

I do not mean, that the change of grade shall render the mission more expensive.

I have therefore nominated Colo. David Humphreys, Minister *resident* from the United States, to her most faithful Majesty the Queen of Portugal.

FC (DLC); in Lambert's hand; unsigned. The characteristically lucid style of summarization, the oblique recognition of the existence of political hostility to diplomatic arrangements not based on utility and economy, and the forehanded effort to prepare the ground for similar consequences in future all reveal TJ as the indubitable author of the draft of this message. This is confirmed by the presence of the file copy in his papers, by the fact that it is in the hand of a departmental clerk, and by the conclusive entry in SJPL, which reads: "[1791. Feb.] 18. Message to Senate on Humphrey's mission to Sp. nominating him Minister resident.— Humphrey's letter on the same subject. Pinto to Th: J. on the same subject."

The heading "United States," characteristic of drafts and copies by Tobias Lear, may have been TJ's way of suggesting to the Senate that the President himself had prepared the message. Enclosures: (1) De Pinto to TJ, 30 Nov. 1791. (2) Humphreys to TJ, 30 Nov. 1791.

In accordance with custom, Tobias Lear delivered the text of this message to the Senate. "The President sends first, and asks our advice and consent afterward," William Maclay noted in his diary on the 18th (Maclay, *Journal*, ed. Maclay, p. 396). But the Senate confirmed the nomination on the 21st (JEP, I, 74, 75).

From Daniel L. Hylton

DEAR SIR   Richmond Virga. Feby 20th. 1791

Your esteem'd favour of 9th instant came to hand late yesterday evening, in consequence thereof, I immediately went to the Warehouse to see what tobacco of yours was down to embrace the first opportunity offers to execute your little commission in shiping the different qualities of tobacco pointed out in your letter; which shall be duly attended too. The day following has been heavy rains and snow to prevent the inspectors coming down to the warehouse, and the books being lock'd up deprives me of ascertaining at present the quantity of tobacco you have down, tho the pickers inform me, there is some but think not so much as you want to have shipt for the present moment. Whatever there is shall be sent you by the first conveyance, which am inform'd will be in a few days and hope will arrive safe to a satisfactory market, the expences in shiping will with pleasure pay, at the same time will transmit you an account thereof. Be assured by friend it will ever give me pleasure to render you any service in my power and in future request youll by no means think it troublesome in the execution of any coming here, as its attended with no inconvenience to me, being now settled in Richmond with my family, for the benifit of my childrens education, being the first object with me whatever inconvenience may arise to myself. I have not heard of your recieving the Vis a Vis which was sent to Hague and Lister at Rocketts before my removal here, to be shipt you which was done the next day. Mrs. H. is perfectly satisfied with the exchange and hope proves agreeable to you. She and family Unites with me in wishing you health and happiness, believe me to be yours with sincerity of heart Your friend &c.   DANL. L. HYLTON

P.S. Mr. Eppes and family were well a few days past. Mrs. Skipwith is in bad health and understand she is to be in Manchester for some months for the convenience of being near Dr. Currie, I wish to say near Dr. McClurg, whom I am confident must possess more skill than the former, such is the attachment my friend to foreigners, in preference to their own countrymen.—I suppose ere this you have heard of Mrs. Randolph having a fine daughter, of which I congratulate you.

RC (MHi); endorsed. Recorded in SJL as received 28 Feb. 1791.

From Robert R. Livingston

DR SIR   New York   20th. Feby 1791

Knowing the value of your time I should not thus early after the receipt of yours have intruded upon it could I have consented that you should one moment longer misapprehend my sentiments with respect to your invaluable report on weights and measures. I am so far from suggesting any other ideas than those you propose that tho I have examined them with minute attention I find nothing to alter or improve. What I alluded to was a passage in yours in which you seem to acquiess in the necessity of a coinage and the admission of an alloy in your money. After the receipt of your favor I hastily put together a few thoughts on these subjects which I had printed here in order to awaken an investigation which appears to me important in our situation having it in view at the same time to afford you such an answer to your Letter as would

leave you perfectly at liberty to take your own time in reading
it and not subject you to the necessity of answering for if there
is anything in which a man is a free agent it certainly is in reading
news papers or leting it alone. It is so miserably printed that
no regard must be paid to the punctuation in reading it.[1] I feel with
you great pain in the dissatisfaction which prevails in the Southern
states. I see upon almost every important question a territorial division of sentiment (if I may use the expression) which must disgust the minority and carry with it the appearance of a combination against their views. This if well or ill founded will be the
source of jealousies which may lead to disagreeable consequences.
This I am fully satisfied might have been avoided by the omission
of one or two measures in which the interest and honor of the
United States was in no sort involved. Our delegates deceive themselves if they believe that their constituents are satisfied with all
the measures of government. The truth is, they see and speak of
many instances in which their interests have been neglected or
misunderstood and I should suppose the removal of Genl. Schuyler by a majority of 16 to 4 in the Senate in some sort evincive
of this. But the fact is, such is the unbounded prosperity of this
State, doubling its population in 12 years, possessing an extensive commerce, fruitful Lands, encreasing in wealth, and feeling
no taxes that they scarce consider as a serious evil any thing so
remote as the measures of the federal government.[2] In this city
hundreds have made fortunes by speculating in the funds and look
forward to a great encrease of them by the establishment of a
bank, and have no idea of a more perfect government than that
which enriches them in six months. It will doubtless be wise in
government to avail themselves of these fortunate circumstances,
but weak to rely upon them as evidences of their own strength.—
I have the honor to be Dr Sir with the highest respect & essteem
Your Most Obt Hum: Sevt,   ROBT R LIVINGSTON

P.S. I have ordered a model to be made which I shall send as soon
as possible.

RC (DLC); endorsed by TJ as received 23 Feb. 1791 and so recorded in
SJL. Dft (NHi); with numerous variations in phraseology and substance,
some of which are noted below. Enclosure: Livingston's "Thoughts on
Coinage, and the establishment of a
Mint, submitted to . . . those Statesmen
only who dare to quit the *beaten path*"
(*Daily Advertiser*, 19 Feb. 1791), argu-

ing that "old modes of thinking" about
coinage and money should be abandoned
in keeping with other "new and liberal
ideas" of the American Revolution. Livingston objected to the debasing of coinage by the use of alloys and advanced
the idea of bank certificates redeemable
in gold and silver.

[1] At this point in Dft there occurs

the following sentence not in RC: "I shall be much pleased if you should find any thing new or interesting in my Ideas on the subject."

2 Dft reads at this point: "In this disposition their ill humour evaporates in a jest or sarcasm at the expence of their government or their representatives and is remembered no more."

To John Rutledge, Jr.

DEAR SIR   Philadelphia Feb. 20. 1791.

Very constant business, since the meeting of Congress, has obliged me to intermit all my private correspondencies for a while. It is now only that I have as much leisure as will permit me to acknowledge the receipt of your favour of Nov. [20]. and of the lamp which accompanied it, and for which be pleased to accept my thanks. The form I think a fine one, and the hydrostatic improvement in the oil vessel was new to me, and is I think a great improvement. We have nothing from Europe later than the beginning of December. I inclose you a letter from Mr. Short, which has been long on it's way to me. Things in France are still going on tolerably well. Here, the newspapers will have kept you informed of what is passing. To their details may be added the necessity of another Indian expedition, in the ensuing season. Congress will rise the 3d. of the next month, and the President will set out about a fortnight after for Charleston where you will doubtless see him. Be so good as to present me affectionately to your father and family and Mr. E. Rutledge, and to accept assurances of the esteem with which I am Dear Sir Your most obedt. humble servt,   TH: JEFFERSON

RC (NcD); addressed: "John Rutledge junr. esq. Charleston"; franked; postmarked "21 FE"; slightly mutilated and date of Rutledge's letter to which this is the response is supplied from PrC (DLC).

From Fulwar Skipwith

Basse terre 20. Feby. 1791

I beg leave again to remind your Excellency that in none of the french colonies have they received from the Court of France (officially) the Convention with the United States respecting Consuls &c.—therefore no one of their Governors or Commandants can grant me the necessary exequateur or receive me in any form. With Respect I have the honour to be Your Excellys Mo Obt.

F. SKIPWITH

RC (DNA: RG 59, CD); endorsed by TJ as received 16 Mch. 1791 and so recorded in SJL.

To John Trumbull

DEAR SIR   Philadelphia Feb. 20. 1791.

Much hurried while you were here, I was the less exact in sending you the inclosed, because I knew I could send it to Charleston before you would have occasion for it. There I hope it will meet you in good health, and resolved to return by the way of the Natural bridge. Remember you will never be so near it again, and take to yourself and your country the honor of presenting to the world this singular landscape, which otherwise some bungling European will misrepresent. On that rout you will surely take my daughters in your way, who as well as my son in law will be very happy to receive you at Monticello, and do the honours of the house instead of grand-papa. I am with great affection Dear Sir Your friend & servt,

TH: JEFFERSON

PrC (DLC). Enclosure: TJ's general letter of introduction, dated at Philadelphia, 20 Feb. 1791, reading as follows: "The bearer hereof, Mr. John Trumbul, son of the late Governor Trumbull of Connecticut, proposing to pass through Virginia in the ensuing spring, and not certain by what particular rout, I take the liberty of introducing him to any of my friends and acquaintances to whose perusal he may be so good as to offer this note. The honour he has done our country in Europe as a painter, his extraordinary merit personally, and my affection for him will I hope procure for him from my friends all the civilities and attentions on his journey which may be useful or agreeable, which will be more considered than if personally shewn to their very humble servt., Th: Jefferson" (PrC in DLC).

TJ's appeal to Trumbull to visit the NATURAL BRIDGE and to honor himself and the nation by portraying the singular landscape reflects his continuing effort over a long period of time to have some competent artist depict the scene. This desire arose from his belief that the phenomenon was "the most sublime of Nature's works" and it reflected his conviction that its ownership was a public trust of such an exacting nature that no considera-tion could bring him to "permit the bridge to be injured, defaced or masked from the public view" (Notes, ed. Peden, p. 24-5; TJ to William Caruthers, 15 Mch. 1815).

TJ himself in 1767 made what appears to be the first detailed description of the Natural Bridge, together with measurements and an accompanying profile, but this remained unpublished (Account Book; 1767; owned by Dr. Robert H. Kean, Richmond, Va., 1945). His life-long fascination with this object of wonder must have begun much earlier. When Andrew Burnaby traveled through Virginia in 1759-1760, he listed among the natural curiosities that he wanted to see, but did not, "a natural arch, or bridge, joining the high mountains, with a considerable river running underneath" (Burnaby, Travels through the Middle Settlements in North-America [New York, 1904], ed. R. R. Wilson, p. 77). This has been considered to be the first public allusion to the Natural Bridge, though it did not appear in print until Burnaby's first edition was issued in 1775 (TJ owned a copy of the 2d edition, published the same year; Sowerby, No. 4017; C. A. Reed, The Natural Bridge of Virginia and its Environs [New York, 1927]). Since Burnaby was in Williamsburg from the fall of 1759 through the spring of

1760, it is possible that TJ may have met him. It is also plausible to imagine that the son of Peter Jefferson, who as a cartographer of Virginia cannot have been ignorant of the existence of the Natural Bridge, may have called it to the attention of the traveler.

But the first description of the Natural Bridge to appear in print, detailed and based on actual observations, was published in American newspapers over two years before Burnaby's *Travels* came out. This interesting account was first published in Philadelphia in the *Pennsylvania Journal* of 25 Nov. 1772 and was written for the express purpose of inducing an artist to portray the phenomenon. The description was prefaced by a communication signed HUMBLE SERVANT—perhaps written by the editor or even by the artist himself—in which the anonymous writer declared that the description was "sent by a Gentleman of Virginia to his Friend in this City with a view of prevailing upon the ingenious Mr. P—LE [Charles Willson Peale] (who is now among us) to come and oblige the Public with a draught" of the Natural Bridge. Because of its possible influence in exciting anew TJ's interest, the text is given in full:

"This Bridge is thrown by the hand of Nature from one precipice of a rock to another over Cedar-creek, which falls into James River in Bottetout County, Virginia. The precipice seems in some violent convulsion of Nature to have been torn asunder to allow a passage to the water, which flows at least 350 feet below the top of the Arch, which at its base is about 60 feet broad, but widens as it rises, so as to appear halfway up to be 120 broad. The top of the Arch is 25 feet wide, and would allow a ready Passage for Carriages of all kinds.—The edge of the precipice is skirted with trees of various kinds, and growths, and makes a most romantic appearance; nor is it without its terrors, for here and there you see huge piles of rocks, that seem lose and tottering, as if they were about to tumble down, and impede the river's future progress. The imagination keeps pace with probability in this expectation, for below you observe fragments of many tons weight, that have in the revolution of ages fallen at various times from the precipice above. The winter before I visited this place, a very large fragment fell, and the noise it made astonished the inhabitants, who sup-

posed it to be thunder, uncommon at that season of the year. To know whether I was not imposed upon in this circumstance, I made my servant throw over some stones, which sounded like a cannon: after this I fired a pocket pistol under the arch, the report of which was louder than a swivel. The swallows skimming through the arch above, appeared not much larger than humming birds. The crows and the ravens, which build in clefts of the rock, strike the ear with their perpetual cawing. The weeping springs that trickle down the sides of the arch; the ivy and wild vines, forming festoons along its sides, with stragling trees shooting in many places from clefts of the naked rock, and intermixing their roots, entertain the eye with an endless variety above, while below a rapid stream ripling over the opposing rocks washes the roots of some tall mulberry and locust trees, which grow almost under the arch itself. Could the eye for a moment be estranged from such a delicious scene, to look either way through the arch, it might catch the view of mountain rising upon mountain, diversified into a thousand shades from the various trees that form their forests. But it is in vain to dwell longer upon a description, which must appear feint to those who have seen, or shall see, with an enthusiastic pleasure, the numberless beauties of this enchanting place, where the eye, far from being satiated, is still discovering new objects to admire. I felt a sort of a veneration under its arch, which in times of paganism would have led me to invoke the genius of the place, and casting many a lingering look behind, I measured back my steps with reluctance, reflecting with pleasure on the toils I had encountered in my travels through so many wildernesses, since they drew me at length to one of nature's most prodigious works." (The Editor is indebted to Professor David F. Hawke of Dartmouth College for discovering this text in the *Pennsylvania Journal* and for calling it to his attention.)

This description, written "in the full enjoyment of a Romantic enthusiasm," was from the pen of William Carmichael, who spoke so feelingly to Charles Willson Peale about the Natural Bridge that the artist asked for a copy of his notes. Carmichael complied with this "very hasty and incorrect copy" that was published soon thereafter, no doubt at Peale's instigation (Carmichael to TJ, 3 Oct. 1786). It is obvious that there are close parallels between Carmichael's description and that written about a decade later by TJ in *Notes on Virginia*. The former states, for example, that the precipice "seems in some violent convulsion of Nature to have been torn asunder." The latter asserts that the hill "seems to have been cloven through its length by some great convulsion"—an opinion to which TJ clung for many years until his young friend Francis William Gilmer postulated another theory that is still generally regarded as valid (Chastellux, *Travels in North America* [Chapel Hill, N.C., 1963], ed. Howard C. Rice, Jr., II, 446-7). Both accounts reflect the feelings of awe and even terror induced by the scene. Carmichael described it as "one of nature's most prodigious works" and TJ called it without qualification "the most sublime of Nature's works." Both accounts declare the scene to be indescribable in words. Most striking of all, both concur in the mistaken opinion that it was possible to view the distant mountains through the arch. TJ, in a later MS note added to his own annotated copy of the Stockdale, 1787, edition of *Notes on Virginia*, declared: "This description was written after a lapse of several years from the time of my visit to the bridge, and under an error of recollection. . . . The statement therefore in the former edition needs the corrections here given to it. Aug. 16. 1817" (ViU). But the error of recollection was not made over the length of time that TJ assumed, for his detailed description of 1767 makes the same error. Presumably both TJ's notes of 1767 and those of Carmichael of 1772 from which the "very hasty and incorrect copy" was made were set down at the time of the visit to the Natural Bridge or very soon thereafter.

This curious duplication of error by two young and impressionable visitors to the Natural Bridge and other parallels in their descriptions might be dismissed as mere coincidence, if it were not for the fact that Carmichael's account, without HUMBLE SERVANT'S prefatory note, but with the caption "Description of a Natural Bridge in Botetourt County, Virginia," appeared in full in Purdie & Dixon's *Virginia Gazette* on 17 Dec. 1772, just as TJ was setting off from the capital for Monticello. It was only six months

later that he paid £2 15s. 4d. at the "S[urveyor General's] O[ffice at Williamsburg for a survey warrant,] returning my own 157. acres for Natural bridge." Shortly thereafter he paid James Tremble £2 1s. 8d. "for making survey of my entry on Natural bridge." And on 5 July 1774 a patent in the name of George III was issued to him for the property that for the remainder of his life he held and cherished as a sort of public trust (Account Book, 10 June and 15 Sep. 1773; plat of survey in MHi; Betts, *Farm Book*, p. 32). It is difficult to believe that, having allowed five years to pass after making his careful description of the Natural Bridge in 1767, TJ was not inspired to this sudden action by the appearance in the *Virginia Gazette* of the sensitive description by William Carmichael. It is equally plausible to assume that Carmichael's account influenced in part at least the description given in *Notes on Virginia*.

It is another coincidence that, when Carmichael revealed his authorship to TJ in 1786 and recounted his effort to persuade Peale to paint the scene, the owner of the Natural Bridge had just witnessed the publication in Paris of its first pictorial representation—a delineation for which he himself was indirectly responsible by having urged the Marquis de Chastellux, during his stay at Monticello in 1782, to visit the Natural Bridge. When Chastellux returned from that visit he regretted that he had failed to take proper measurements and determined to send someone "who was both a draftsman and a surveyor . . . to the Appalachians for this sole purpose." His commanding general, Comte de Rochambeau, readily supported the suggestion with his orders, thinking that it would be another service to America to make this natural wonder known to the world and that "it would even be rather droll for people to see that the French had been the first to describe it with precision and publish a correct plan of it" (Chastellux, *Travels*, ed. Rice, II, 448). The person selected for the task was Baron de Turpin of the Royal Corps of Engineers, who drew both a flat projection of the Natural Bridge with its environs and two perspective views from upstream and downstream vantage points (same, II, at p. 446; see reproduction of the upstream view in Vol. 6: 204). Both of Rochambeau's motives were realized when engravings of these drawings were published in Chastellux' *Voyages*, which appeared in Paris in 1786. Though TJ had been the first to make measurements and the first to set down an exact description of the Natural Bridge, his account in *Notes on Virginia* printed the previous year was not so explicit as that recorded in his notes of 1767 and carried no illustration. The engravings from Baron de Turpin's drawings became the prototypes of many subsequent reproductions (Chastellux, *Travels*, ed. Rice, II, 608). Very shortly after the French thus achieved the distinction of being the first to depict the phenomenon, TJ learned from Carmichael how "the honor of presenting to the world this singular landscape" had almost fallen to an American more than a decade earlier.

John Trumbull had been in Paris and an intimate of TJ's household when Chastellux' *Voyages* appeared. Baron de Turpin's drawings must have become an object of critical discussion at the time between the American artist and the one who not only owned the property but took patriotic pride in it. TJ clearly was not pleased with the perspective views. Chastellux himself acknowledged that an exact idea of the platform of the Natural Bridge could not be gained from them (same, II, 608). Thus there was no need in 1790 for TJ to argue the importance of having Trumbull visit and depict the scene or even to mention the previous engravings from Baron de Turpin's drawings: his somewhat acerb remark that "otherwise some bungling European" would misrepresent the phenomenon could only mean that Trumbull would understand the allusion to a bungling already committed and that, its results being dismissed, the honor was still available to be claimed by an American. But the lines of convergence that came to the Hôtel de Langeac with Carmichael's news in the autumn of 1786 place in clearer perspective the hope expressed by TJ at that time that another artist would visit America and depict the Natural Bridge. That artist was European but one whom TJ never considered as bungling and before whom even the national pride of claiming the honor for an American gave way. She was Maria Cosway (TJ to Mrs. Cosway, 24 Dec. 1786).

Consular Problems

I. JEFFERSON'S DRAFT MEMORANDUM ON CONSULAR VACANCIES, 21 FEBRUARY 1791

II. REPORT OF SECRETARY OF STATE ON THE CASE OF THOMAS AULDJO, 22 FEBRUARY 1791

III. REPORT OF SECRETARY OF STATE ON CONSULAR VACANCIES, 23 FEBRUARY 1791

IV. SECRETARY OF STATE TO THOMAS AULDJO, 24 FEBRUARY 1791

V. SECRETARY OF STATE TO JAMES YARD, 24 FEBRUARY 1791

EDITORIAL NOTE

In the summer of 1790, shortly after Washington sent to the Senate the first group of nominees for consular posts and thus in effect inaugurated the American consular service, Louis Guillaume Otto professed to see in the designation of a larger number of consuls for France than for England proof that the entire Cabinet was deeply impressed with the need of maintaining amicable relations with the nation he represented.[1] He found it remarkable that all of the executive officers of

[1] See group of documents on the consular establishment under 21 July 1790 (Vol. 17: 244-56).

government, including John Adams, were strongly predisposed toward France. This observation was not quite so wide of the mark as Otto's earlier view of the inevitability of the disruption of the union into three or four separate kingdoms, but he did have the discernment to single out the Secretary of State as being unusually friendly to France.[2] "It appears certain at present," he wrote, "that [John Adams] will never be President and that he will have a very formidable competitor in Mr. Jefferson, who with more talent and knowledge than he, has infinitely more the principles and manners of a republican. There is only one voice with regard to this estimable citizen who ought to be particularly dear to us by the affection he never ceases to show for France and by a sort of enthusiasm which he communicates to persons in office for everything which concerns us. Knowing the great influence of the gazettes, he continues to discredit those of England and he even employs a writer to translate and have printed the most authentic news of France, especially that which can contribute to make the nation loved."[3]

But even as the words were being written there appeared fresh confirmation of a fact long since evident—that neither the institution of consuls nor the enthusiasm of the Secretary of State could unite Americans in affection for France. On the contrary, the inauguration of the consular service, far from being an evidence of unity in the administration, afforded only another illustration of the growing cleavage there and in the nation between those whose preferences lay with England and those who wished to encourage attachments to France. The presence of French and British consuls in the United States provided opportunities enough for augmenting such cleavages. "I am endeavoring to break the Neck of some Enemies to the french Consulate" in Boston, James Lovell wrote mockingly to John Adams. "You must know I admire that Institution, because by the Kings ordonances its Chancery has all the Spirit and Essence of our *Jury of Equals*."[4] French consuls in America, De Moustier pointed out in 1788, had been defied by local authorities for a decade: in Norfolk a French captain indubitably guilty of barratry had been protected from the consul by a Virginia sheriff, in Philadelphia another consul had been assaulted in the streets, in New York even a French man-of-war had been deemed subject to local regulation—and yet the pledge made in the Treaty of 1778 to regulate consular powers and functions by a separate convention was still unredeemed.[5] The Convention of 1788 had been negotiated, ratified, and proclaimed, but the deep-seated antipathies and differences of attitude reflected in the contrasting ways by which Thomas Jefferson and John

2 For Otto's prediction of the inevitable dissolution of the union, see "Otto's *Mémoire* to Vergennes, 1785," ed. Paul G. Sifton, WMQ, 3rd. ser., XXII (Oct., 1965), 632.

3 Otto to Montmorin, 13 June 1790, translation in Margaret M. O'Dwyer, "A French Diplomat's view of Congress, 1790," same, XXI (July, 1964), 433.

4 Lovell to Adams, 19 Dec. 1789 (MHi: AM).

5 De Moustier to Montmorin, 4 Aug. 1788, enclosing a précis of his conversation with the Virginia delegates in Congress about Captain Ferrier's crime of barratry and the refusal of the Virginia civil authorities to support Martin Oster, the French consul at Norfolk (Arch. Aff. Etr., Paris, Corr. Pol., E.-U., XXXIII; transcripts in DLC).

Jay had sought to redeem the pledge had not been erased.[6] The newest evidence of this came in 1790 in the petition of the French consul Létombe to the Massachusetts General Court, presenting an embarrassing problem which that body promptly passed on to the federal government.[7]

In general, the question was whether and how to give effect to the terms of the Consular Convention with France. But as framed by Létombe it was nothing less than a request for coercive power in enforcing consular decrees. This was only the latest of a long series of similar requests that had so greatly embarrassed the Continental Congress in its relations externally with France and internally with the several states. The fundamental nature of the issues involved is indicated by the fact that the framers of the Constitution gave to the Supreme Court original jurisdiction in all cases affecting consuls.[8] But the new grant of powers to the national government did not eliminate grave constitutional difficulties or the underlying national differences and contrasts of attitude toward the institution of consuls that existed between France and the United States. For, while France had had long experience with the forms and practices of a consular establishment and, in its highly centralized state, had evolved a consular system governed by professional principles, the United States, limited by a new kind of federalism, was groping toward the establishment of a consular service that it did not particularly desire. Many shared Senator Maclay's view that salaries for consuls were unnecessary.[9] Jefferson himself believed the institution incompatible with republican principles: its history had begun "in times of barbarism and might well have ended with them."[10] The American mercantile community seemed to regard the consular service largely as an extension of its own network of foreign correspondents and factors, often indeed as a device for recovering losses and for gaining advantages in competition without any corresponding cost of commissions. The demand of merchants that consuls be permitted to engage in trade was irresistible. It would take another quarter of a century before the nation would heed the argument that for a consul to "be useful to his country in arts, sciences, and manufactures, [he] must have no commercial engagements," that his salary should be commensurate with his situation, and that his "time and labor are not his own but those of his country, to the government of which . . . he sought to communicate all that is good and useful to know, concerning the laws, customs, manners, arts, commerce, and manufactures of the country of his residence."[11] Under these circumstances, the creation of a salaried and

---

[6] Julian P. Boyd, "Two Diplomats between Revolutions: John Jay and Thomas Jefferson," VMHB, LXVI (Apr., 1958), 132-46; for a different interpretation, see Samuel Flagg Bemis, "John Jay," *American Secretaries of State* (New York, 1927), I, 253-9, and R. L. Jones, "America's First Consular Convention," *Southwestern Soc. Sci. Qu.*, XIII (Dec., 1932), 250-63.
[7] Washington to TJ, 26 July 1790; Washington to Hancock, 28 Aug. 1790.
[8] Article III, section 2.
[9] Maclay, *Journal*, ed. Maclay, p. 257, 297.
[10] TJ to Montmorin, 20 June 1788.
[11] D. B. Warden, *On the origin, nature, progress and influence of consular establishments* (Paris, 1813), p. 20-1.

professional consular service was not within the realm of the possible. Even the necessary task of framing regulatory legislation for that service involved serious political difficulties and attempts to enforce the obligation to France under the Convention of 1788 threatened to bring on formidable constitutional problems as well.

It is not surprising, therefore that Washington had proceeded cautiously, avoiding with evident deliberateness any confrontation on the issues raised by Létombe's appeal. Hancock's letter enclosing that plea had arrived in mid-summer of 1790 and Jefferson had promptly drafted a response for the President, resting its argument on the plea that too little time remained in the session for the necessary legislation to be adopted. But Washington held the letter for almost a month before dispatching it, a delay that seems explicable only on the ground that he wished to give to the professed reason a higher degree of credibility.[12] The issue raised by Létombe, burdened with the old familiar challenges to federal and state relations and with the divisive impact upon the feelings of partisans of England and France that had been felt at every phase of the discussion of consular matters from 1782 onward, was too explosive to be laid before a Congress that had just achieved relative calm after the bitter contests over the assumption and residence questions.[13] Even the bill to regulate the functions and powers of American consuls could not be passed.[14] Jefferson's statement that Congress had "not . . . been able to mature the Act sufficiently" was only a polite concealment of the underlying divisions over the institution of consuls.[15] Both aspects of the problem were merely postponed, if not evaded.

But at the opening of the third session the President laid the issue squarely before Congress. There is little reason to doubt that this course was urged upon him by the Secretary of State and that Jefferson, fully aware of the divisive influence of an institution that he did not think necessary for the United States, did so in terms calling for the application of national authority in its full amplitude. His draft of that part of Washington's annual message to Congress confronted both aspects of the problem by recommending legislation to regulate the functions of American consuls abroad and to give effect to the terms of the Consular Convention.[16] The phraseology of his draft was carefully chosen to place both questions in the context of national power and dignity. As originally framed, the draft rested the argument for a consular establishment and the resultant need for regulation merely on

[12] See note, Washington to Hancock, 28 Aug. 1790. Actually, the Senate decided to postpone consideration of the bill ten days before adjournment and more than three weeks before Washington dispatched the letter to Hancock. See note 14.

[13] The Residence Act was signed on 16 July 1790 and Washington transmitted Hancock's letter to TJ ten days later.

[14] The House passed the bill on 21 July 1790. Three days later the Senate referred it to a committee (Morris, King, and Langdon), but on 2 Aug. 1790 postponed further consideration until the next session (JHR, I, 243, 255, 256, 271, 274, 275; Annals, I, 1698, 1714, 1715-6, 1739-40, 1742; JS, I, 187, 189, 194).

[15] TJ to American consuls, 26 Aug. 1790. In the draft of Washington's letter to Hancock of 28 Aug. 1790, TJ at least alluded to the real cause when he said that the "Subject . . . was new, and might be found difficult."

[16] See draft, 29 Nov. 1790.

the argument that the "interests of our commerce, of our merchants and seamen" required it. But Jefferson made a deliberate and extremely significant alteration by striking out the word "interests" and substituting "patronage" in its place.[17] Always precise in his choice of words, he undoubtedly intended in this instance to add some special significance to the immense authority of the President's recommendation to Congress. For, as originally phrased, the passage implied a relatively restricted view of the power over commerce. As altered, it suggested that there rested upon the national government an obligation to give active countenance, support, and encouragement to trade, thereby investing the regulatory authority granted by the commerce clause of the Constitution with an indefinitely extended meaning. This revealing choice of a single word seems to embody the views of commercial policy that, in the years since the peace, Jefferson had pursued with an unequaled consistency and range of experience at home and abroad. It reflected his recognition of trade as an instrument of policy, his aim to redress the European balance of power in favor of America by diminishing the whale fishery of England while augmenting that of France and the United States, his attempt to arrange a concert of powers to open the Mediterranean to American trade, his endeavor to promote in every way possible the mutual exchange of American and French products, and his unremitting efforts to arrange a system of commercial reciprocity with the nations of Europe so as to induce Great Britain to ameliorate her discriminatory policy if not to negotiate a treaty of commerce. It is not surprising that this significant change of a single word came as Jefferson was considering anew the effects of Sheffield's arguments on British policy and when he was preparing his reports on the state of the fisheries and of trade in the Mediterranean.[18]

The second aspect of the consular problem he met on a similar plane of national responsibility. Jefferson was well aware of the long history of American hesitance, evasion, and even opposition to meeting the pledge given to its ally in 1778. In 1782 Congress, yielding to persistent pressure from France, had authorized Franklin to negotiate a consular convention in accord with the plan it had adopted. But within a year an attempt was made to modify if not rescind this action and James Madison had been obliged to denounce it as an "indecent and dishonorable" proposal.[19] Yet within a few months John Jay called for a similar action even while Franklin was carrying on the authorized negotiations. When the Convention of 1784 finally arrived, Jay defeated its ratification in an opinion that was narrowly legalistic and strongly contrasted to the attitude he assumed later in upholding the national honor in respect to treaty obligations with England.[20] There

17 Same, note 2.
18 Report on fisheries, 1 Feb. 1791; report on Mediterranean trade, 28 Dec. 1790.
19 JCC, XXV, 846.
20 JCC, XXIX, 500-15. Jay's report to Congress on infractions of the Treaty of Peace was an elevated and even eloquent definition of national authority, but that on the Consular Convention was a contrived and narrowly legalistic attempt to defeat the object (JCC, XXX, 781-874). Since the theme in both cases was essentially the same—that of redeeming a treaty obligation—it is difficult to ex-

were many in the nation who shared his doubts and fears, believing that French consuls enjoying extraterritorial rights would form a network of espionage detrimental to American interests. Such fears were most evident in those centers of commerce where affection for Great Britain was strongest—Boston, New York, Philadelphia, Norfolk, and Charleston—where such British consuls as Sir John Temple, Phineas Bond, and John Hamilton not only did not awake corresponding anxiety about alien surveillance but were given access to official information about American policy with considerable freedom.[21] It is not surprising, therefore, that Jefferson, in his draft for the President's message to Congress, should have called for action on a matter so long delayed and not yet effected.

Létombe's petition was thus the latest reminder of an unredeemed pledge and Jefferson placed the issue in the context of the obligation assumed in the Convention ratified in 1789 but not proclaimed until he took office.[22] Here, too, he made a significant change in his draft for Washington's message to Congress. As originally phrased, the text declared that the Convention of 1788 had "stipulated, in certain cases, the aid of the civil power" to French consuls in the United States. This was ambiguous. Congress could have construed it as authorizing a reliance on state and local authorities, in whose hands the problem had lain so long and resulted in such evasions and animosities. Jefferson therefore struck out "civil power" and substituted the words "national authority." Some legislative provision by Congress, he declared, was necessary to give "full effect" to this obligation that had become a part of the supreme law of the land.[23] The national duty was clear but the old cleavage in attitudes remained. Jefferson's insistence upon meeting that duty did not pass unnoticed in the mercantile community of Boston whence had arisen both Lovell's mockery of the French consulate and Létombe's plea for coercive authority. "Observing in the President's Speech, that he introduced the Subject of the Consular Convention to the Consideration of Congress," Samuel Barrett wrote to Henry Knox, "I have now to request of you (in Confidence) to inform me, on whose suggestion the matter came to be introduced; as it will be of Consequence in conducting such memorial, as, under the

_____

plain this remarkable contrast except in terms of Jay's friendly inclinations toward Great Britain and his suspicion if not hostility toward France. See note 21.

21 Jay, for example, refused to tell Otto what the chargé already had learned in private from Virginia delegates in Congress. But he freely informed the British consul, Sir John Temple, of the nature of his secret report to Congress, even going so far beyond the bounds of official propriety as to express the opinion that England was justified in holding the western posts so long as the states continued to impede the collection of private debts (see references, note 6). Later, the problem of desertions from British vessels did cause some friction between British consuls and local authorities (see Newton to TJ, 24 Aug. 1791; TJ to Newton, 8 Sep. 1791). But such clashes never equaled in number or intensity of feeling those resulting from jurisdictional disputes with French consuls.

22 The Convention was ratified on 29 July 1789 and proclaimed on 9 Apr. 1790. Jay acted as Secretary for Foreign Affairs until TJ assumed office on 22 Mch. 1790.

23 Draft for Washington's message, 29 Nov. 1790, note 5.

advice and Patronage of the Trade in this Place I may, if you shall think it eligible, lay before Congress on the subject."[24]

The mere asking of the question seemed to point the finger of suspicion at the Secretary of State, whose role as promoter of improved trade relations with France and as negotiator of the Consular Convention was well known. It also reflected the enduring hostility within the mercantile community to the enforcement of the terms of that obligation. As a result, the bill to regulate consular functions again fell victim to such opposition. Jefferson seems to have anticipated this. Even before Washington's message was delivered to Congress, he advised one consular appointee not to await passage of the bill but to depart for his post "with due dispatch."[25] Having taken a particular interest in the terms of the bill introduced at the previous session, he no doubt followed its course in the third session with equal concern.[26] The Senate took up the subject first. Its bill, drawn by Oliver Ellsworth, was described by Maclay as being so chaotic as to make a new draft desirable, but the author "hung like a bat to every particle of it."[27] The Senate nevertheless passed it promptly.

The House did not act for more than a month and then seemed to concur in Maclay's opinion by offering an amendment to the Senate bill that changed its title and struck out all save the first section. This drastic alteration crystallized the issue in unmistakable terms: it limited the bill to the single object of "carrying into effect the convention between his Most Christian Majesty and the United States." It provided that federal district judges should assist French consuls in arresting deserters and that federal marshals should give aid in all cases in which the assistance of "the competent executive officers of the country" was pledged by the Convention.[28] The Senate refused to

[24] Barrett to Knox, 22 Dec. 1790 (MHi: Knox Papers).

[25] Sylvanus Bourne to James Madison, 1 Dec. 1790 (DLC: Madison Papers), quoting TJ's instructions. Bourne told Madison that he was very anxious to see the consular bill "matured or passed as early as other public interests" would permit. Nevertheless, he said that he would comply with TJ's instructions "in full confidence that Government will be disposed to pass a bill more clearly specifying the Rights and Powers of Consuls and ascertaining the quantum minuit of their services." In urging that an adequate allowance be made, Bourne demonstrated the fact that the only insistence on salaries for consuls came from candidates themselves. Richard Harrison declined appointment as consul at Cadiz because of the absence of any provision for a "decent subsistence" (Harrison to Washington, 6 Jan. 1791, DNA: RG 59, MLR, M/179, acknowledging Lear's peremptory note of 28 Dec. 1790 asking him to accept the consulship or return the commission and stating that he had never received the commission and the only knowledge he had theretofore had of his appointment was "through the public papers.").

[26] When the bill was before the House in the second session, TJ urged that fees be granted consuls to induce them to report entries of American vessels in foreign ports and that a clause be included to recognize consular authentication of documents as legally valid in courts of the United States. Only the second of these provisions was incorporated in the bill and in the Act of 1792. For a general account of TJ's role as principal founder of the consular establishment, see B. E. Powell, "Jefferson and the Consular Service," Pol. Sci. Qu., XXI (1906), 626-38.

[27] Maclay, Journal, ed. Maclay, p. 368.

[28] JS, I, 222, 231, 232; JHR, I, 364, 365, 400, 401, 402; Annals, II, 1933, 1934, 2027, 2028.

concur. The House retaliated by passing its own bill precisely in accord with the terms of its amendment of the Senate bill.[29] The ensuing debate in the Senate exhibited "such a degree of heat not usual" in that body that Secretary Otis later deemed it prudent to submit the journal to John Adams for verification.[30] The House bill was defeated by a small combination of what newspaper writers occasionally referred to as "mercantile Senators."[31] Once more Jefferson was obliged to excuse the failure on the ground that there had not been sufficient time and once again his words left much unexplained.[32] The old divergent attitudes toward the consular obligation to France continued. They were given fresh confirmation by the defiance of local and national authority on the part of consuls acting under the deluded guidance of Genet.[33] They lingered on even after a Federalist Congress finally abrogated the Convention by law in 1798.

But if commercial interests felt no enthusiasm for the engagement with France, their attitude was quite otherwise in respect to the consular service of the United States. One desired object that was lost in the deadlock over the Senate bill would have permitted American consuls or vice-consuls, if citizens, to own ships in their own names or in partnership with other citizens residing in the United States—a loss that no doubt accounted for some of the heat engendered in the debate late in the evening of the last day of the session. The section granting this privilege to consuls did not even survive in the consular act as finally adopted in 1792.[34] But what the law did not prohibit in this and other respects could be achieved in other ways.

The case of John Telles illustrates one way in which some commercial houses sought to achieve their own private objects by means of the consular establishment. Robert Morris, who had been somewhat diffident in making recommendations for consular appointment, was the chief advocate in support of Telles' desire to be made consul at Lisbon, though he remained in the background while others presented the case.[35] Telles, a naturalized citizen and a highly respected merchant in Philadelphia, had important connections with the court and with leading merchants in his native Portugal. He was well acquainted with its laws, language, and customs. Since the Revolution he had

[29] This was in the evening of the final day of the session; William Loughton Smith, James Madison, and John Vining were directed to bring in the bill and Smith reported it (JHR, I, 406, 407; JS, I, 311-12).
[30] Samuel A. Otis to John Adams, 21 Mch. 1791 (MHi: AM).
[31] On motion to permit the second reading of the bill, only Richard Bassett (Dela.), Oliver Ellsworth (Conn.), William Samuel Johnson (Conn.), Rufus King (N.Y.), Robert Morris (Pa.), and Philip Schuyler (N.Y.) voted in the negative. Unanimous consent was required for a bill to be read the second time on the same day and so the motion failed (JS, I, 311-12).
[32] See Document V.
[33] TJ to Madison, 1 Sep. 1793; TJ to French consuls, 7 Sep. 1793; TJ to Genet, 9 and 15 Sep. 1793, 30 Nov. 1793; TJ to Hammond, 9 Sep. 1793. The Treaty of 1778 and the Consular Convention of 1788 were abrogated unilaterally by Act of Congress on 7 July 1798.
[34] JHR, I, 256; JS, I, 299-301 (sect. 8 of bill).
[35] See Morris to TJ, 1 May 1790 (Vol. 17: 254, note). But for other solicitations by Morris, see note 46 below and Willing, Morris & Swanwick to TJ, 8 Sep. 1791.

carried on an extensive trade with that country. In all these respects, his credentials should have impressed a Secretary of State eager to consummate the commercial treaty with Portugal that he and John Adams had negotiated in 1786.[36] Jefferson did in fact recognize Telles' personal merit. But nothing could have more clearly delineated the gulf between his concept of public service and that of some of the leaders in the commercial community than the manner in which they candidly urged upon him as the most persuasive reason for making the appointment what he considered to be an even more conclusive ground for not bestowing it—that is, that the office would enable both Telles and themselves to protect their own private interests. Their arguments naturally identified these interests with the public good.

In the spring of 1790 John Telles had been brought from a position of some affluence to the verge of bankruptcy through the instrumentality of one of the favorites of the Portuguese court, Antonio Ferreira. Under a license from the queen to import 80,000 barrels of flour from the United States, Ferreira ordered half of this amount from John Telles & Company. But the flour arrived a few days late and on the basis of a technicality in the contract Ferreira refused to accept the consignment, caused its forced sale and exportation, and induced the London guarantor of the shipment to protest Telles' bills of exchange amounting to £30,000 sterling. Telles escaped bankruptcy only because of his probity and because other houses, deeply involved, saw a possible means of extrication. He himself explained the situation frankly in making his candidacy known to the Secretary of State.[37] John Swanwick, representing the heaviest creditor (Willing, Morris & Swanwick), made the underlying motive of his testimonial in favor of Telles even more explicit. The mercantile interest of Philadelphia and New York, he informed Jefferson with innocent candor, had been "put in danger of loosing at least 100 to 150,000 Dollars." Further, he believed that the matter was one on which the United States might have remonstrated to Portugal, "and perhaps by doing this strenuously, this whole Sum might yet be saved to the Commercial Interest of our Country." By going to Portugal as a public character, Telles could prosecute his own case at court, injure no one, and of course benefit the commercial interest of the United States.[38]

The mere fact that a prospective benefit to private interests was openly advanced as an argument for appoinment to public office is revealing. Such an argument may have been persuasive enough to those in the Cabinet against whose concept of public administration the Secretary of State was contending. But the use of public office for private ends, no matter how often practiced or how favorably clothed as a means of cultivating ligaments of interest for the ultimate public good, was one of the evils of government that the Revolution had brought to an end as a valid philosophy of government if not as a fact. For Jefferson the controlling principle was clear. But the illumination cast by the application of John Telles on the fundamental contest of

[36] See documents on treaty with Portugal, Mch.-Apr. 1786 (Vol. 9: 410-33); TJ to De Pinto, 7 Aug. 1790 (Vol. 17: 117).
[37] Telles to TJ, 13 Dec. 1790.
[38] John Swanwick to TJ, 14 Dec. 1790.

principles within the Cabinet extends also to the relations between the Secretary of State and the President. For, in giving Washington information about the various applicants for consular vacancies, Jefferson first prepared a report in finished form and then rejected it in favor of another. It is obvious that the case of John Telles caused him to do so, for while the two states of the report vary in a number of minor points, their most conspicuous difference pertains to his candidacy. In the first form of his report Jefferson referred Washington to the testimonial letters, made the brief comment that Telles was well recommended by Morris and Swanwick, and added that the candidate's affairs were deranged if not bankrupt.[39] The only other candidate for the Lisbon vacancy was scarcely to be considered, despite his important Virginia connections, for he was not a native American, he was actually bankrupt, and he was also a drunkard.[40] But Jefferson evidently feared that Telles, having the powerful backing of Robert Morris, might be chosen by the President. He therefore drafted the second report and abandoned his noncommittal position. It would rest with the President, he said, to decide whether to appoint Telles or wait for another candidate. But, withholding the principle, he then advanced a compelling practical argument against the appointment. The "low reputation of our merchants . . . in foreign countries," he declared, "will be confirmed rather than relieved by sending abroad as Consuls those who are under difficulties."[41] Washington, though he had meticulously reviewed Jefferson's correspondence with John Jay when he became President, may not have remembered his even more emphatic warning in 1788 against bankrupts "or young, ephemeral adventurers in commerce without substance or conduct, or other descriptions which might disgrace the consular office, without protecting our commerce."[42] Whether or not he decided on the basis of the principle or the practical argument, or both, the President chose to wait for another candidate.

But this only stirred Telles' influential backers to more zealous effort to obtain the nomination before Congress adjourned. Two days before the session ended, a committee of merchants appointed by the creditors of John Telles & Company appealed to the Secretary of State. The committee was composed of several of the leading commercial houses in Philadelphia and New York—Willing, Morris & Swanwick, Mordecai Lewis & Company, Robert Smith, Edward Tilghman, and John Wilcocks of Philadelphia and Lynch & Stoughton of New York

---

[39] See Document I. The comment on Thomas Thompson represents another important difference between the first and second states of TJ's report. TJ may have made this comment less detailed in the final form of the report on the assumption that Washington was familiar with the Pleasants family and its connections. See note 40.

[40] This was Thomas Thompson (see Documents I and III). Thomas Pleasants had urged James Madison to support Thompson's candidacy (Pleasants to Madison, 8 Mch. 1789, DLC: Washington Papers; same to same, 10 July 1790, 6 Jan. 1791, and 4 Mch. 1791, DLC: Madison Papers). Thompson had also asked Pleasants to intercede with TJ, but on his kinsman's refusal to do so the candidate made the approach directly and also through T. M. Randolph, Jr. (Thompson to TJ, 8 Dec. 1790; Randolph to TJ, 5 Mch. 1791).

[41] See Document III.   [42] TJ to Jay, 14 Nov. 1788.

—and all were involved in the loss of the flour shipment. They repeated the account of Telles' misfortunate as detailed earlier by John Swanwick and then declared:[43]

> In this situation Mr. Telles is desirous of passing over to Lisbon, where he has many and powerful Friends at Court, and where his character as an honest and Worthy Man stands as high, as it does on this side of the Water; he solicits the very honorable appointment of Consul General of the United States at Lisbon, because he conceives that from his having been these 30 Years a Citizen of the United States and from his knowledge of it's Language Commerce and products he may be of use in that Capacity, while he desires from it the additional weight arising from so respectable an office in the suing from the Court that Redress from it's Contractors so essential not only to his own, but to the general Commercial Interests of the Cities of Philadelphia and New York and which may possibly be obtained by this shorter mode of Application while the Suits at London are still depending, the favourable Issue whereof would not only pay fully all Mr. Telles's Creditors, but leave him possessed as he was before these painfull Circumstances took place, of an Ample Fortune.

In recommending Telles for the post, the committee of merchants assured the Secretary of State that they not only would interpose no obstacle to Telles' departure from the country but, on the contrary, would "offer . . . every facility to his going." They believed all of the creditors represented by the committee would take the same position. They concluded in a final effort to identify their particular interest with the public good: "We shall esteem ourselves highly flattered if your General attention to the Interests of the Commerce of America shall point out the Propriety of your assenting to our Sentiments and views on this Occasion." Jefferson apparently did not reply.

Later in the year Telles again asked Robert Morris, as "one of the greatest" holders of his protested bills, to intercede in his behalf with the Secretary of State. He also sought the influence of the Attorney General. Randolph, urged by "many virtuous men" in Philadelphia, talked with Jefferson about the case. Afterward he feared that the Secretary of State had not understood him and he sought to clarify the matter by pointing out that Telles' suit was in England, that he could not sue the court or any individual in Lisbon, and in consequence he could not "be in danger of irritating any man in or out of power in Portugal."[44] But it was Randolph who had misunderstood. The committee of merchants had made it clear in their appeal to Jefferson that the candidate wished the office in order to seek redress from the Portu-

[43] Committee of creditors (signed by all save Lynch & Stoughton, but written in their behalf also) to TJ, 1 Mch. 1791, enclosing their printed circular, undated and unaddressed, giving the facts about the shipment of flour from John Telles & Company and its result, stating their opinion of Telles "as a worthy, honest Man," and expressing the hope that "his former Friends will not forsake him now, in the Hour of his unexpected and unmerited Misfortunes" (DLC: Washington Papers, endorsed by TJ as received 2 Mch. 1791 and so recorded in SJL).

[44] Randolph to TJ, 2 Nov. 1791.

guese court and thus achieve a more immediate relief while the London suits were still pending.[45] Randolph informed Telles that he had "had a conversation with Mr. Jefferson respecting this business, but could not do anything in it, as Mr. Jefferson, or our President, thought it improper to appoint a person that was in debt."

Telles was stung by the implication. He appealed again to Robert Morris, conceding that some men might be capable of doing anything dishonorable but that there were others who "would rather forfeit their Lives than do the least dishonourable Action." He denied that it had been his intent to oblige Ferreira to pay "or to apply to Government to force them to it." Having disavowed this private object, he then innocently confessed others.[46]

> But Sir to be plain and sincere, the reason I have to wish for that Post is this. I think I can do business here more advantageously and with greater safety, by living there than continuing here. In the 2d place I am old and have two children who are heirs to a very good Estate in the Island of Madeira, and if I and they continue here, by the Laws of Portugal they cannot inherit it. Therefore, as a Father I can do no less than do all in my power to leave them settled and Independant. But at the same time I rather will forfeit every thing than live in Portugal as a subject (*vassal*). I have lived too long here, and am [too] much of an American to enslave myself, tho' at the same time No One respects Superiors and Authority more than myself.—If you think Sir that these reasons will have any influence with Mr. Jefferson, I would be glad you would communicate them to him, and Let me know the result, as I am about to depart for England in a few days.

Presumably Robert Morris did think that such reasons would influence Thomas Jefferson, a compassionate and understanding father. But the mere fact that he forwarded the letter betrays his inability to grasp the principles that animated the Secretary of State in the conduct of public office. The candidacy of John Telles for the consulate of Lisbon

[45] Committee of creditors to TJ, 1 Mch. 1791.
[46] Telles to Morris, 29 Oct. 1791 (DLC: Washington Papers, endorsed by TJ: "Telles for Lisbon. By Mr. Morris."). Telles' appeal in 1790 to Morris in connection with the candidacy of John Street for consul in the Azores illuminates one means of seeking to evade the Rule of 1784 against appointing aliens to consular posts. Street had performed services for American prisoners during the war and had been designated to act as consul by "the Portuguese Legislator and Senate of the Western Islands" until one should be appointed by the United States. When Telles pointed out the fact that he was not a native, Street induced his kinsman John D. Street, a naturalized American with the firm of John Telles & Company, to apply for the appointment. Dominick Lynch of the firm of Lynch & Stoughton, who were interested with Morris in Telles' flour contract, asked Tobias Lear to speak to the President on the matter, saying that he made the request to "serve a most respectable friend." Lynch also urged Daniel Carroll to lend his support, adding: "A few words to the President and Mr. Jefferson will undoubtedly insure success" (Lynch to Carroll [ca. June 1790], endorsed by TJ: "Consulate of the Azores. Mr. Carrol & Mr. Lynch propose John D. Street"; undated, unsigned statement about John Street's services to American prisoners; Telles to Morris, 12 May 1790; Lynch to Lear, 4 June 1790, all in DLC: Washington Papers). But Morris supported John Street as vice-consul and his candidacy prevailed (see Vol. 17: 247, 251).

ended with this revealing transmittal of a letter whose disclosures were greater than its author or its conveyor realized, among these being a protestation of American attitudes combined with an equally fervid avowal of what was coming to be a hallmark of Federalist expectations from the citizenry—a due acknowledgment of respect for "Superiors and Authority."

Thus, long before the Revolution in France had inflamed American politics, there appeared in the gropings toward an effective consular service, as in most other matters, indubitable evidences of divergent attitudes between sections, between economic interests, between pro-English and pro-French protagonists, and between two fundamentally opposed principles of administration whose respective advocates sought to guide the ship of state in this critical decade as they had done from the beginning of the struggle for independence. On this occasion the President acted in full accord with the recommendations of the Secretary of State. The decision to meet the obligation to France, the search for able and disinterested candidates for consular appointment, and the resistance to powerful pressures exerted to use public office for private ends were important. But these objects were by no means capable of dividing national opinion with the bitterness that ensued when the opposing principles of administration collided on far more momentous issues and when the President and the Secretary of State found themselves on different sides of the gulf.

I. Jefferson's Draft Memorandum on Consular Vacancies

A note of the vacant consulships and of the candidates.

Gottenburg, in Sweden. No body applies

Amsterdam. Greenleaf was formerly a candidate, but not appointed because from a part of the Continent which has already furnished more than it's proportion of Consuls; and because it was thought that the kind of character for that place could be better decided, after it shall be decided whether any and what diplomatic appointment shall be made for the Hague.

Cadiz. P. R. Randolph [Randall] of N. York, and Richd. Codman of Massachusets were candidates. Also Thomas Thompson, who will be spoken of below. There are no new applications.

Canary islands. viz. Teneriffe, Palma, Ferro, Gomera, Canary, Fortaventura and Lancerota. Sarmento a Portuguese who married in Philadelphia was a candidate. I believe he was named by the President and rejected by the Senate. John Culnan asks it. See the letters of John and Jasper Moylan. There is no other candidate, nor is it important to name a Consul.

Lisbon. Thomas Thompson, I believe an Irishman. He has resided 17 years as a merchant in Madeira. He came over to Virginia, where he married one of the Pleasants on James river, against consent. He resided there seven years. He is strongly recommended by T. Pleasants of Virginia, and S. Pleasants of Philadelphia: but is a bankrupt and addicted to the bottle. See his letter from Madeira, asking Lisbon or Cadiz. Bulkeley. Recommended by the members from Massachusets. He is an American, but of what state they do not say. He has been long settled at Lisbon, and is among the most opulent merchants. They give him a good character. Colo. Humphreys names him in a note to me as a merchant of integrity.

Mr. Palyert says some think him a native of Engld. some of America. He travelled in the U.S. before the war. During the war he was at Lisbon, a tory. He is now a member of the Eng. factory. Is very rich and has great connections with this country.[1]

John Telles, whose papers were laid before the President some time ago, is also a candidate. He is well recommended by Mr. R. Morris and Mr. Swanwick. He is not a native, but has very long resided here. His affairs are deranged, if not bankrupt. See letters.

Lorient. No new nor proper candidate. Vale [Vail], a bankrupt is the only one.

Alicant. Robert Montgomery of America I believe, but I know not of what state. He has a brother in commerce at Boston. He is of old standing in that line at Alicant, has been long a busybody in our affairs, doing more harm than good, and all thro' an excess of zeal. As yet, no appointment has been made in the Mediterranean, except at Marseilles.

Poole in England. That government does not recognise a consul at Cowes, but is willing we should have one at Poole, and will suppose that his residence. A new commission to Thomas Auldjo is requisite for this purpose.

Sta. Cruz. Danish West Indies. James Yard of Philadelphia (but a native of N. Jersey) asks the consulship. He is established there, wealthy, and connected by marriage with the Governor of the island. I should rather think one Consul enough for the Danish islands: and if so, St. Thomas's would be the position. An agent would suffice at Santa Cruz. See Colo. Monroe's letter.

TH: JEFFERSON
Feb. 21. 1791

MS (DLC); entirely in TJ's hand. PrC (DLC). Entry in SJPL reads: "[1791. Feb. 21.] Consuls."

This report—signed, dated, and recorded in SJPL—was ready to be handed in to the President, but TJ then altered it in a number of particulars both in text and substance and employed it as the basic draft for the final version. That this first draft was not submitted is proved by the fact that no file copy was retained in the departmental files. The most significant difference between the two drafts relates to the candidacy of John Telles (see Editorial Note above). But there were other interesting differences: the increased emphasis on the candidacy of John Culnan for Tenerife, the more favorable estimate of Robert Montgomery, the elimination of details about Thomas Thompson, the adverse comment on John Bulkeley, &c.

JAMES GREENLEAF: On 25 May 1789 Thomas Dawes, Jr., informed Washington that he had been approached by friends of James Greenleaf, a native of Boston, a partner in the New York firm of Watson & Greenleaf, and a former resident of Amsterdam, urging his appointment. Greenleaf, he wrote, had "married into a family of rank and influence" at Amsterdam and would "do honor to his country in the character of resident or consul at the Hague" (DLC: Washington Papers).

PAUL RICHARD RANDALL: See Randall to TJ, 11 Mch. 1790, note. Randall had also applied directly to Washington (—May 1789, DLC: Washington Papers). See TJ to Randall, 25 Nov. 1790.

RICHARD CODMAN: John Codman, Jr., applied to John Adams asking support for his brother's candidacy. Adams promised to deliver the recommendation to TJ and Washington and added: "I think it advisable for you to send on to me the best letters . . . that you can readily obtain, and they shall be communicated too" (Adams to Codman, 10 Oct. 1790, MHi: AM).

FRANCISCO SARMENTO: See Vol. 17: 247.

JOHN CULNAN: The recommendations of John and Jasper Moylan were dated 13 and 15 Feb. 1791 and recorded in SJL as received 14 and 18 Feb. 1791, respectively, but have not been found. Robert Morris also interested himself in Culnan's candidacy. On 14 July 1791 John Moylan wrote Morris on the subject and Morris transmitted his letter to Washington or TJ, along with the following, all from Tenerife: (1) Peter de Franchi to Morris, 14 July 1791, recommending his "friend and neighbor" John Culnan to the attention of Morris and his "col-

leagues in Congress"; (2) John Cologan & Sons to Morris, 16 Aug. 1791; (3) Pasley, Barry & Little to Morris, 14 July 1791 (the last two are almost identical to the first in phraseology and all are written in the hand of the same clerk); (4) attested copy of a certificate dated at Philadelphia, 4 Dec. 1782, stating that Culnan, "a Gentleman from Ireland," had taken the oath of allegiance as directed by the Act of Pennsylvania of 13 June 1777 (all in DLC: Washington Papers, the first being endorsed by TJ: "Culnan. For Teneriffe. Given in by Mr. R. Morris."). In 1793 Stephen Moylan recommended Culnan in a letter to TJ: "My knowledge of that gentleman's honor and integrity interests me in his behalf. It will oblige me to let me know whether any Steps have been taken thereon, if not—what mode will be proper to pursue to forward this business which I have very much at heart" (Moylan to TJ, 30 Dec. 1793, DLC: Washington Papers; endorsed by TJ). Culnan had served during the war as Deputy Clothier General under John Moylan. He was appointed consul at Tenerife by Washington a few months after TJ left office (Washington to the Senate, 28 May 1794, JEP, I, 157-8).

JOHN BULKELEY: See Humphreys to TJ, 19 Nov. 1790, TJ to John Bulkeley & Company, 13 July 1791. Part of TJ's information about Bulkeley came from the Portuguese consul general, Ignatius Palyert, who himself involved in the flour transaction that inspired the candidacy of John Telles (see Editorial Note above and Swanwick to TJ, 14 Dec. 1791).

AARON VAIL: See Vail to TJ, 28 Feb. 1791.

ROBERT MONTGOMERY: John Montgomery's letter to TJ of 20 Nov. 1790 may have related to his brother's desire to be consul at Alicante (recorded in SJL as received 22 Nov. 1790, but not found). On 22 Jan. 1793, John Montgomery, "by the request and special orders" of his brother, presented a memorial giving a flattering account of Robert Montgomery's influence with the emperor of Morocco and recommending his brother as consul (John Montgomery to TJ, 22 Jan. 1793, enclosing his own undated memorial in behalf of his brother, DLC: Washington Papers; endorsed by TJ as received 31 Jan. 1793 and so recorded in SJL). Shortly thereafter Robert Montgomery was nominated and confirmed as consul at Alicante (JEP, I, 130-1). A year later Robert Montgomery appointed his brother agent at Barcelona (John Montgomery to TJ, 22 Apr. 1794, forwarded from Boston by William Smith to Edmund Randolph, 23 Dec. 1794, DLC: Washington Papers).

THOMAS AULDJO: See Documents II and IV.

JAMES YARD: Washington nominated Yard as consul at St. Croix on 23 Feb. 1791 and the Senate confirmed him on

the 24th. TJ issued the commission on the same day (JEP, I, 76; PrC of TJ to Yard, 24 Feb. 1791, enclosing commission, DLC; Yard to TJ, 4 Mch. 1791, acknowledging receipt of commission, DNA: RG 59, CD). Yard served as consul at St. Croix from 13 May 1791 to 31 May 1792. COLO. MONROE'S LETTER: See Monroe to TJ, 17 Feb. 1791.

¹ This paragraph written in margin of MS and does not appear in PrC.

II. Report of Secretary of State on the Case of Thomas Auldjo

The Secretary of state having recieved information from Thomas Auldjo, who was appointed Vice consul of the United States at Cowes in Great Britain, that his commission has not been recognised by that government, because it is a port at which no foreign Consul has been yet recieved, and that it has been intimated to him, that his appointment to the port of Poole and parts nearer to that than to the residence of any other Consul of the U.S. would be recognised, and his residence at Cowes not noticed

REPORTS to the President

as his opinion that it would be expedient to nominate Thomas Auldjo to be Vice-consul for the United states at the port of Poole in Great Britain and such parts within the allegiance of his Britannic Majesty as shall be nearer thereto than to the residence of any other Consul or Viceconsul of the United states within the same allegiance.

TH: JEFFERSON
Feb. 22. 1791.

MS (DNA: RG 59, MLR); in TJ's hand; endorsed by Lear. PrC (DLC). FC (DNA: RG 59, SDC). Entry in SJPL reads: "[1791. Feb. 22. Consuls.] Auldjo for Poole."

That part of Washington's message

to the Senate of 23 Feb. 1791 pertaining to Auldjo was a precise adaptation, with two or three appropriate changes in phraseology, of the above report. Auldjo was confirmed by the Senate on the next day (JEP, I, 76). See Document III, note.

III. Report of Secretary of State on Consular Vacancies

Reasons for not Reporting to the President, at this time, consular nominations for the following ports.

Gottenburg.	No candidate
Amsterdam	Greenleaf
Cadiz	P. R. Randolph [Randall] (he has not applied lately), Richd. Codman of Massachusets, and Thomas Thompson.
Lorient	Vale [Vail]

It is desireable there should be a greater choice of candidates; and appointments at those ports are not very pressing.

The Canary islands. The recommendations of John and Jasper Moylan in favour of John Culnan are as pointed as could be desired. But themselves are unknown to me, as well as the circumstances of connection &c. which may exist between them and the candidate. If they are so known to the President as to satisfy him, or if the Candidate be otherwise known to him and approved, the nomination might go in the following form 'John Culnan, citizen of the U.S. late of it's armies, and now a merchant at Teneriffe, to be Vice-consul of the U.S. for the Canary islands.' If the President be not satisfied, there will be no harm in taking time, for enquiry, till another session.

Alicant. Candidate Robert Montgomery.
Malaga. Candidate Wm. Kirkpatrick.
Appointments are not yet made for the Mediterranean.

Whenever they shall be, I know no person for Alicant who stands on better ground than Montgomery. Kirkpatrick would be inadmissible at Malaga, as being a foreigner, and of a nation not in favour in that country.

Lisbon. Thomas Thompson
John Telles
Bulkeley
candidates.

Thompson is a good man: but a drunkard and bankrupt, and not a native.

Telles is a good man and a sober one, but bankrupt and not a native.

Bulkeley is a good man, very opulent, and of long establishment in Lisbon. But the weight of evidence (tho not certain) is that he is an Englishman by birth: he is certainly a member of the English factory at Lisbon, and his sentiments during the war, were those of an Englishman. He travelled in America before the war, and has great commercial connections with it. But his birth and sentiments seem to set him aside.

It rests then with the President to say whether Telles shall be appointed, or let it lie till other candidates may offer. Telles's circumstances are the great objection to him, for that of his not being a native, could I suppose be got over. The low reputation of our merchants, as to their credit, in foreign countries, will be confirmed rather than relieved by sending abroad as Consuls those who are under difficulties. If the President thinks proper to name Telles, it may be as follows 'John Telles, citizen of Pennsylvania, Consul for the United States at the port of Lisbon in Portugal and for such parts within the allegiance of her most faithful Majesty, as shall be nearer thereto than to the residence of any other Consul or Viceconsul of the U.S. within the same allegiance.'[1]

Santa Cruz. I had thought that as St. Thomas's was a free port, and Santa Cruz pretty much restricted, the former would be the proper position for a Consul, and the latter an Agent. But on further enquiry among mercantile men, I find that there do not go above 20. vessels of ours a year to St. Thomas's, while about 200 go to Santa Cruz; as it is from thence we draw a great part of our sugars. I am therefore of opinion that it will be more important to provide a patronage for our vessels at Santa Cruz, because there are more of them, and less protected; those which go to St. Thomas's being protected by the freedom of the port. If this be decided on, I think Mr. Yard an unexceptionable candidate: and therefore propose a nomination for 'James Yard, of Pennsylvania, to be Consul for the U.S. in the island of Santa Cruz and such other parts within the allegiance of his Danish majesty as shall be nearer thereto than to the residence of any other Consul or Vice-consul of the U.S. within the same allegiance.'

TH: JEFFERSON
Feb. 23. 1791.

MS (DNA: RG 59, MLR); entirely in TJ's hand. PrC (DLC). FC (DNA: RG 59, SDC). Entry in SJPL reads: "[1791. Feb. 23. Consuls.] Do."

That part of Washington's message of 23 Feb. 1791 to the Senate pertaining to James Yard is a precise adaptation, with one appropriate addition in phraseology, of the words within quotation marks proposed by TJ (JEP, I, 76). In view of the similar adaptation of TJ's words respecting Auldjo, the whole of the message may therefore be reckoned as drafted by TJ (see Document II, note).
WILLIAM KIRKPATRICK: An English-man living in Malaga and a member of the house of Grivegnie & Company there. George Cabot recommended him to Washington as consul on the solicitation of some of "the *Principals* of the commercial establishment [in Spain] to which Mr. Kirkpatrick belongs" (Cabot to Washington, 29 Jan. 1791, DLC: Washington Papers; Lodge, *George Cabot* [Boston, 1877], p. 43).

[1] At this point, marking the bottom of the second page of the report, TJ signed and dated MS in error, doing so again at end of the document. No signature or date appears at this place in FC.

IV. Secretary of State to Thomas Auldjo

Sir   Philadelphia February 24th. 1791

The President of the United States desirous of accommodating his views to the convenience of the British Government, has determined to change the Port of your nomination as Vice-Consul for the United States, and to substitute Poole instead of Cowes. I have now the Honor of enclosing you the Commission, and of expressing to you the Sentiments of perfect esteem with which I am Sir Your most obedient & most humble Servant

PrC (DLC); in Remsen's hand. Not recorded in SJL.

V. Secretary of State to James Yard

Sir   Philadelphia February 24th. 1791

It is uncertain whether Congress will have time to pass at this Session a Bill which is now before them, prescribing some special Duties and Regulations for the Exercise of the Consular Offices of the United States. In the mean while I beg leave to draw your Attention to some Matters of Information which it is interesting to receive.

I must beg the Favor of you to communicate to me every six months, a report of the Vessels of the United States which enter at the Ports of your District, specifying the Name and Burthen of each Vessel, of what Description she is (to wit, Ship, Snow, Brig, &c.) the names of the Master and Owners, and number of Seamen, the Port of the United States from which she cleared, Places touched at, her Cargo outward and inward, and the Owners thereof, the Port to which she is bound, and Times of arrival and departure, the whole arranged in a Table under different Columns, and the Reports closing on the last days of June and December.

We wish you to use your endeavors that no Vessel enter as an American in the Ports of your District which shall not be truly such, and that none be sold under that name which are not really of the United States.

That you give to me from time to time Information of all military preparations, and other indications of War which may take place in your Ports; and when a War shall appear imminent, that you notify thereof the Merchants and Vessels of the United States within your District, that they may be duly on their guard: and in general that you communicate to me such political and commercial Intelligence, as you may think interesting to the United States.

The Consuls and Vice-Consuls of the United States are free to wear the Uniform of their Navy, if they chuse to do so. This is a deep blue Coat with red facings, lining and cuffs, the cuffs slashed, and a standing collar; a red waistcoat (laced or not at the election of the wearer) and blue breeches; yellow buttons with a foul anchor, and black cockades and small swords.

Be pleased to observe that the Vice-Consul of one District is not at all subordinate to the Consul of another. They are equally independent of each other.

It is understood that Consuls and Vice-Consuls have authority of course to appoint their own Agents in the several Ports of their District; and that it is with themselves alone those Agents are to correspond.

It will be best not to fatigue the Government in which you reside, or those in authority under it, with applications in unimportant cases. Husband their good dispositions for occasions of some moment, and let all representations to them be couched in the most temperate and friendly terms, never indulging in any case whatever a single expression which may irritate.—I have the Honor to be Sir Your most obedient & most humble Servant.

PrC (DLC); in Remsen's hand. Not recorded in SJL. Text is slightly modified version of TJ's circular to consuls, 26 Aug. 1791.

To Luis Pinto de Souza

SIR   Philadelphia February 21st. 1791

I have duly received the Letter of November 30th. which your Excellency did me the honor to write, informing me that her most Faithful Majesty had appointed Mr. Freire her Minister resident with us, and stating the difficulty of meeting us in the exchange of a Chargé des affaires, the Grade proposed on our part. It is foreseen that a departure from our System in this instance will materially affect our arrangements with other Nations, but the President of the United States has resolved to give her Majesty this Proof of his Desire to concur in whatever may best tend to promote that Harmony and perfect Friendship so interesting to both Countries: He has therefore appointed Colonel Humphreys to be Minister resident for the United States at the Court of her Majesty.

This Gentleman has long been of the President's own family, and enjoys his particular Confidence. I make no doubt he will so conduct himself as to give perfect satisfaction to her Majesty and yourself, and I therefore recommend him to your friendly Attentions and respect. Mr. Freire will have every title to the same from us, and will assuredly receive it. It is always with pleasure that I repeat the Homage of those Sentiments of Respect and Esteem with which I have Honor to be Your Excellency's Most obedient and most humble Servt.

PrC (DLC); in clerk's hand, unsigned; at foot of text: "Addressed to Ao Illmo. e Exmo. Snr. Luiz Pinto de Sousa Coutinho Ministro e Secretario de Estado de S. M. F. dos Negocios etrangeiros e de Guerra &c.&c.&c."

The letter of credence that TJ prepared for David Humphreys, addressed "To our great and good Friend Her most Faithful Majesty," Maria I of Portugal, named him as "one of our distinguished Citizens, Minister resident for the United States of America near your Majesty" and requested that he be given "entire Credence to whatever he shall deliver on our Part, and most of all when he shall assure you of the Sincerity of our Friendship" (PrC in DLC, dated 21 Feb. 1791, entirely in Remsen's hand including signatures of Washington and TJ).

From Maxcey Ewell

SIR   Virginia, Albemarle County 21st Feby. 1791.

I received your Letter dated October 16th 1790 wherein you directed me to call on Mr. Hopkins for my Certivicates and forward them by post to Mr. Maddison at Philadelphia where he would put them in the necessary train. I since have made application to Mr. Hopkins for them. He informs me that by dire[c]tions of the late Board of treasury [they] were forwarded to the Treasury of the united States in New York where alone application must be made which you will see by the inclosd from Mr. Hopkins. Now Mr. Jefferson I wish you to be so kind as to Inform me in what Manner I may come at them my circumstance at present will not admit of my going that distance. Could it be in your power to get them drawn from New York to Philadelphia where they may be settled, as I am Now in a distres'd Situation. I have a wife and a Number of Small children to do for. I purchas'd a piece of land with the expectation of paying for it with the Money the united

States were owing me for my services but have not received any of it as yet. I made out a part of it. The person whom I purchas'd of brought suit against me for the ballance and after our april district court will obtain a judgment and then I must Lie in prison and leave my family to Suffer unless I get releived by receiving part of that money. And Mr. Jefferson as you are the only source to whom I can apply for relief I humbly implore your goodness to use your influence with the gentlemen in Congress to do some thing for me before that day comes when I must lie in a dark prison Which I expect will be the case with me unless I am relievd in that way. All other depart[ment]s except ours have drawn some of their pay but when I consider the matter I can but chearfully wait as the Gentlemen who are to settle those Matters have things of greater moment before them which makes me hope that after a while ours will come under their consideration.

I know not what more to say in regard of the matter. I would wish to inform you some thing concerning the Number of My Certivicates. Their is one of 157£. 14s. obtained from Mr. Allen another from Capt. Rice of 54£. 6s. also another from Mr. Robertson for five months and Twenty two days Service as Commisary at the albemarle Barracks. At the time he gave me that Certivicate he knew not what congress had settled our pay at but I suppose that will be settled as the others were. I must conclude most Humble and hearty thanks to you for communicating the matter to Mr. Maddison being with much esteem Sir, Your Most Obt. & Humbl. Servt.,

MAXCEY EWELL

RC (DLC); endorsed as received 12 Apr. 1791 and so recorded in SLJ.

As TJ knew, he was not the only one to whom an appeal was made. On the same day Ewell wrote James Madison setting forth the same facts and in terms that commanded the respect of both men. To Madison he stated: "I am reduc'd to so low an ebb by a long servitude to my Country that its out of my power to get to New York for during the late war I aided in evry place I could when calld on with my Muskett on my shoulder and at the raising of Men I chearfully threw in my mite and so on till I was calld in to the Staff department where I continued three years or nearly so till what little I had was quite exhausted.

I was then turnd loose with a wife and a number of small children without Bread Meat or money. I labourd Night and day for their support very chearfully knowing that from a long teadious war things was not be settled in a day and knowing things of a greater moment were before the Gentlemen in Congress" (Ewell to Madison, 21 Feb. 1791). Madison and TJ not only respected the Maxcey Ewells of the Revolution but they also knew the tendency of "matters of greater moment" occupying the attention of government—tendencies that not merely neglected such soldiers as Ewell but exploited them (see Vol. 18, Appendix). Together they went to the Auditor's office to inquire into his claim (TJ to Ewell, 8 May 1791).

From Thomas Mann Randolph, Jr.

DEAR SIR   Monticello Feb: 21. 1791

Patsy, the little girl Polly and myself have been in good health since you heard last from us. Your silence for the two last weeks, makes us fear that you are not so fortunate. Patsy had just begun to visit the public room, but a very deep snow which fell yesterday and today obliges her to return to her Chamber. During the whole of her confinement, she has scarcely felt the smallest indisposition. —I shall have the pleasure of writing again in a few days at greater length. I am Dear Sir your most aff. Servt.,

THOMAS M. RANDOLPH

RC (MHi); endorsed by TJ as received 5 Mch. 1791 and so recorded in SJL.

To David Rittenhouse

Feb. 22. 1791.

Th: Jefferson will be obliged to Mr. Rittenhouse to inform him who has the best assorted shop of Mathematical instruments in town.

RC (Miss Elizabeth Sergeant Abbot, Philadelphia, 1954). Not recorded in SJL. TJ's inquiry was made in behalf of George Wythe (see Wythe to TJ, 10 Jan. 1791; TJ to Wythe, 14 Mch. 1791).

From William Short

DEAR SIR   Amsterdam Feb. 22. 1791

The last post from Paris which arrived in the evening after my No. 56 was sent off by the way of England brought me intelligence that the national assembly had at length decided the great and embarassing question of the cultivation of tobacco in France. It is evident that the troubles in Alsace accelerated this decision and influenced it.—They had some days before determined that they would postpone this question until some others relative to public revenue were decided. On the report of the troubles of Alsace being made by one of the committees, in which the affair of tobacco was mentioned as one of the causes of them, some members insisted and carried in the house that the order of the next day should be the discussion of that question. It was accordingly brought on and decided that the cultivation should be free for every person in France—the manufacture and sale of it to be subject to such modifications as the assembly shall fix. By which is meant licenses that are to be granted for that purpose and from which the committee count on a revenue of two millions only. These modifications however have not yet been discussed in the assembly: but the foreign and home-made tobacco will probably be put on the same footing as to these modifications. The second article decreed without a division was that the importation of foreign manufactured tobacco should continue to be prohibited. The third which passed after much debate as to the rate of duty is on these terms. "Il sera libre d'importer par les ports qui seront designés du tabac en feuille, moyennant une taxe de 25#. par quintal. Les navires François qui importeront directement du tabac d'Amérique, ne seront soumis qu'aux trois quarts du droit." Nothing further was then decided, and the assembly according to its desultory mode of proceeding took up other business. It is in the sequel of the plan of the committee, which I should suppose the assembly would again soon resume, to form a national regie to purchase, manufacture and sell the article for public profit. Such tobacco as the regie shall import from abroad to be subject to no duty. They are to have no monopoly except such as they may acquire by this exemption from foreign duty, their superior capital and greater skill in the manufacture of this article. It remains still for the assembly to decide with respect to this regie. I shall lose no time in informing you of what shall be further done on this subject.

I mentioned in my last what the assembly had done with respect to whale oil and codfish. They take up from time to time the subject of duties imposed on foreign articles. You will of course be informed of them in proportion as they are fixed.

The commissaries that were sent to Strasburg on account of the disorders already mentioned have re-established tranquillity there. At Colmar they were insulted and exposed to danger by the people and some of the *grade nationale*, but they were supported by others and have the strongest party. It is thought the decree of the assembly respecting tobacco and the troops which are to be sent there will prevent further disorder.

Admiral Cornish has returned with his squadron from the West Indies as I hear, and the French fleet consisting of six ships of the line and frigates has sailed for their islands in order to restore the force of government.

It is thought that England is still negotiating with Denmark relative to the operations of the next spring, but there is no reason as yet for believing that that country will separate its interests from those of its maritime neighbours.

It seems certain that the court of Berlin does not intend to take any further part with respect to Liège. The pretensions of the Imperial minister at the conferences of Szistow are so different from what was expected after the negotiations of Reicheinbach that they have suspended for the present the proceedings of the Congress assembled there. The best understanding certainly prevails between the two Imperial courts.

I enclose a letter to the Secretary of the Treasury and beg you to continue persuaded of the sentiments of the most perfect respect & attachment with which I have the honor to be, Dear Sir, Your most obedient & Most humble servant, W: SHORT

PrC (DLC: Short Papers); at head of text: "*No. 57*"; at foot of text: "Thomas Jefferson Secretary of State." Tr (DNA: RG 59, DD). Recorded in SJL as received 23 Apr. 1791.

From John Jay

DEAR SIR   N York 24 Feb. 1791

I this Day received the enclosed from the Post Office. It is the only Letter that I have received from Mr. Chiappe since I left the Office for foreign Affairs; and as it belongs to that Department I take the earliest Opportunity of transmitting it to you.—I have the Honor to be with great Respect & Esteem Dear Sir your most obt. & hble. servt.

JOHN JAY

RC (DNA: RG 59, MLR); endorsed by TJ as received 2 Mch. 1791 but not recorded in SJL though enclosure is. Enclosure: Francisco Chiappe to Jay, Tangier, 3 Nov. 1790, enclosing copy of his last of 4 Sep. 1790 and continuing the account of the arrival of the Spanish envoy, who fled with the frigates and merchantmen despite the emperor's entreaties. On the 23rd a squadron of five Spanish vessels stood before Larache where the emperor was, took two xebecs, and departed with them for Cadiz: "This action infuriated the Emperor, who regarded it as treachery all the more because the xebecs brought the new passport for the Spanish consul." This caused the emperor to set out for Tangier and Tetuan and to hasten preparations against Ceuta, to which siege had already been laid; he took into custody two Spanish consuls and several priests, who would be given up when the two xebecs were returned and 150,000 piastres paid for grain loaded at Darkida. Chiappe said that European consuls going from Tangier to Tetuan and Larache to meet the emperor incurred expenses of 3,000 piastres each for gifts and travel, to be reimbursed by their courts; he had tried to avoid such expenses but feared that he would have to adopt the customs of representatives of other nations. He therefore appended a note of his expenses amounting to 394 piastres, including the gift of a watch and handkerchief to the emperor. He awaited with impatience answers to his letters of 3 Aug. and 4 Sep. 1790 "because the ministers do not fail to torment me with the question when the ambassador of America is coming. Thanks to God everything goes well and nothing is lacking but the arrival of your ambassador to compliment the new sovereign with the usual gifts and confirm the good peace and harmony" (RC, in Italian, in DNA: RG 59, PCC. No. 98). There was also enclosed in this letter a duplicate of Chiappe's letter of 4 Sep. 1790, recorded in SJL as received on 2 Mch. 1791.

Chiappe's letters of 3 Aug. and 4 Sep. 1790, also addressed to Jay, were received by TJ on 1 Dec. 1790, evidently having been transmitted directly to him by William Short (see Vol. 18: 402-3).

Jefferson's Report on the Petition of a Hessian Deserter

The Secretary of State having had under consideration the Petition of Nicholas Ferdinand Westphal, to him referred by the House of Representatives, and having made such inquiry into the facts alledged as the case admits, makes thereon the following

REPORT

It appears by the affidavit of the Petitioner (the best evidence the nature of the case admits) that he was a Sergeant Major in the British service in the earlier part of the late war: that he was induced by certain handbills, dispersed in their Camp, to desert from Fort Edward and to bring off his whole picquet, consisting of 12 men, which he did on the 8th. of August 1777. that after great hardships and dangers he arrived on the 17th. of the same month at the American Camp at Stillwater, with only 5 of his men whom he presented with himself to the American commanding officer, by whose orders he brought the men on to Philadelphia, where they were permitted to disperse: the facts of his desertion and bringing to the American Camp a part of a picquet being confirmed by the certificate of General St. Clair.

It appears that the Petitioner afterwards retired into the Country, and married; that after the war he sent his wife and two children to Hanover, by the way of Hamburg, to endeavour to recover his property there, from whence they returned without having been able to do it: that he is, by an accident, disabled permanently from labour, and is, with his wife and three children, in a very indigent and helpless condition.

It appears by a Resolution in the printed Journals of August 27th. 1776, that Congress promised to every non commissioned officer who should leave the service of the Enemy and become a Citizen of these States one hundred acres of unappropriated lands: and moreover that where officers should bring with them a number of foreign soldiers they would (besides the lands promised to the said officers and soldiers) give "to such officers further rewards proportioned to the numbers they should bring over, and suited to the nature of their wants"; which Resolution was translated into German, printed in handbills, sent into the Enemy's Camp and there circulated.

The Secretary of State seeking for principles whereon to estimate the further reward promised by the said Resolution of Congress, considering that a Soldier withdrawn from an Enemy saves the necessity and consequently the expences of raising one on our part: that the first expences of raising a soldier were, by the Resolution of June 26th. 1776, 10 dollars of bounty in money, and by that of September 6th. 1777, a bounty of clothes estimated in the Resolution at 47.67 dollars, and worth at the then rate of depreciation 46.14 dollars of silver, the two articles making together 56.14 dollars on each soldier: that the Petitioner having brought 5 others with him, saved these first expences on 6 men, amounting to 336.84 dollars. That in relinquishing this benefit to the officer, there will yet remain to the United States the saving of the subsequent expences of annual pay, clothing and subsistence:

Is of opinion that one hundred acres of unappropriated lands should be granted to the Petitioner free of all charges, and that there be paid to him as a further reward the sum of 336.84 dollars with interest thereon at the rate of 6 per cent per annum from the 17th. of August 1777 until paid.　Th: Jefferson
Feb. 24. 1791.

PrC (DLC); in clerk's hand except for signature; accompanied by unsigned PrC of Tr of TJ's letter of transmittal. FC (DNA: RG 59, Record of Reports of Thomas Jefferson, p. 286-9); with House resolution of 16 Feb. 1791 referring to Secretary of State, with instructions to examine and report upon "A petition of Nicholas Ferdinand Westfall . . . praying a gratuity of lands and other advantages promised by the late Congress to those who would quit the British service, in consideration of his having left that service, and joined the American Army, during the late war." Entry in SJPL reads: "[1791. Feb.] 24. Report Th: J. on Westphal's petition and claim."

The House of Representatives accepted TJ's recommendation as to the grant of lands and the sum of money but did not award interest, whereupon Westphal entered another petition at the next session of Congress asking interest as recommended in the report. That petition was referred to a committee appointed to bring in a bill for compensating widows, orphans, and invalids in certain cases (JHR, I, 380, 391, 394, 446). TJ himself was author of the RESOLUTION . . . OF AUGUST 27TH. 1776 offering lands to Hessian officers who should desert, as he was almost certainly the one who drafted that of a similar purport of 14 Aug. 1776 addressed to Hessian soldiers (see Vol. 1: 509-10, note). As adopted, the resolution of 27 Aug. 1776 applied only to deserters who left the British army before recall of the offer; TJ's draft included the additional precaution of a terminal date, but this was eliminated by Congress (JCC, V, 708).

This highly interesting propaganda effort of 1776, aided by Franklin's ingenious suggestions, was aimed at the Hessian troops then occupying Staten Island. Despite its initial promise, the plan was not successful. Because of this and particularly in view of the fact that Westphal's desertion took place a year later, in another army, and on the northern frontier, some doubt is cast upon his assertion that he was induced to desert by handbills distributed among the mercenaries. It has been estimated that several thousand Hessians did desert before and after Saratoga (A. B. Faust, *German element in the United States*, I, 356; see also A. J.

Wall, "The Story of the Convention Troops," NYHS, *Bull.*, XI [1927], 92, showing that 785 of the Convention Troops deserted from Oct. 1777 to Aug. 1779). If other deserters had rested claims on the ground chosen by Westphal, TJ's report could have established a costly precedent. But the man's indigence, St. Clair's affidavit, and perhaps other circumstances induced him to accept the petitioner's affidavit at face value.

A single copy of the handbill containing the German text of the resolution of 14 Aug. 1776 exists in the German State Archives at Marburg and is reproduced in L. H. Butterfield, "Psychological warfare in 1776: the Jefferson-Franklin plan to cause Hessian desertions," Am. Phil. Soc., *Procs.*, 94 (1950): 233-41. If Westphal's affidavit may be relied on, the handbill that induced him to desert was a comparable German text of the resolution of 27 Aug. 1776, of which no example is known to exist.

To Thomas Mann Randolph, Jr.

DEAR SIR   Philadelphia Feb. 24. 1791.

I received your favor of the 2d. on the 21st. inst. and am happy to be assured that my correspondence with Monticello will be regular hereafter. I wish the post when reestablished, had been put into the hands of some body in or near Charlottesville. Whenever that question shall come on again, I would give liberally to a Charlottesville competitor to enable him to underbid any one so distant as the present man. Will you be so good as to inform me what is the day of his departure from Albemarle for Richmond, and also on what day he leaves Richmond for Albemarle, that I may be enabled to fix the day of my writing from here to greatest advantage?—I congratulate you sincerely, my dear Sir, on the birth of the little daughter. 'Happy the man, in the scripture phrase, who hath his quiver full of them.' I rejoice also to hear that Patsy is doing well, by this time I hope quite well: I sent her by last post a book of Dr. Gregory's very useful to her in her new character. While it guards us against projects which we are too apt to run into, and one of which, obstinately perservered in by myself, was within an ace of costing us her life, at 9 months old, it gives a great deal of useful instruction relative to the care of young children, founded in a combination of theory and experience. I do not know when I can have the happiness to see you at Monticello. The President sets out for S. Carolina about the middle of March. But I am afraid that being on so distant a journey, it will be thought more essential for the executive officers to be on the spot to meet unexpected occurrences. He has intimated to me a wish that I would accompany him as far as George town to assist in fixing the site of the public buildings, plan of the town &c. Should he persevere in this wish, there might be a possibility of my taking a flying trip to Monticello, when within three days journey of it. Tho' upon the whole I hardly think the idea admissible; as I should never forgive myself, nor be forgiven by the public, should any evil arise from my absence, in my department.

I am this day packing up for you the Encyclopedie and Buffon, of which I ask your acceptance. Also your harness, 6. mattrasses, and 7 Venetian blinds, that they may be ready to go by the first vessel bound for Richmond after the river opens. I shall add 2. or 3 doz. green chairs if the vessel will take them, which they will rarely do, on account of the space they occupy. You shall have notice when they sail.—I have ordered 20. hogsheads of my tobacco to be brought here by way of experiment of this market, since which I recieve such encouragement from the tobacconists, who are perfectly intimate with the quality of the Albemarle and Bedford tobaccos that I am now pondering whether I shall not order the whole. The principal objection is that they never begin to manufacture tobacco till the month of September of the year following it's growth: then they call it *old* tobacco and will give generally ⅔ of a dollar more for it than in the spring of the year. Their capitals do not enable them to buy in the spring and let it lye by them, dead, till the fall. I believe I can have 5. dollars, crediting till September, that is to say if the quality is as good as what they have been accustomed to have from Albemarle and Bedford. The expences of bringing here will be 3. Doll. a hhd., to which must be added the state tax on exportation. Still it will leave me 4⅔ Dollars or 28/ our money. The only risk is that the quality may not be what they count on. I have mentioned these details, as you might perhaps be disposed yourself to try this market. Perhaps tho' it may be wiser to wait the result of my experiment.

I wish you would seriously undertake the investigation of the great question relative to the Opossum. The proper season is now coming on, and you can so easily procure them in any number you please. If you can obtain satisfactory evidence of the whole process of gestation and parturition it would be an acceptable thing to the philosophical society here to recieve a paper from you on the subject. Mr. Rittenhouse tells me he is satisfied from the information he has received that the flap of the false pouch is done away entirely during the interval between weaning the young, and a new conception, and that then again it is reproduced. I thought it existed at all times. This therefore is a new doubt to be cleared up.

Mr. Trumbull, well known to my daughters, is now at Charleston, and intends taking Monticello in his return. I recommend him particularly to your civilities and good offices. He is one of the best men as well as greatest artists in the world. I subjoin my meteorological observations of the present year, and if you have a thermometer shall be glad to exchange them with you by every letter. My morning observation is taken before sunrise, that of the afternoon between 3 and 4. in winter and 4. and 5. in summer. Present me affectionately to my daughters and accept assurances of the sincere esteem & attachment of Dear Sir Your friend & servt,

TH: JEFFERSON

	A.M.	P.M.				
Jan. 1.	18. c.	22. c.		20	26 f	36. c.
2.	9. f.	— f		21	31. f	48. f.
3.	15. f.	— f		22	32. f.	30. f.
4.	33. c.	— c		23	19. c.	36. f.
5	— c.	— c		24	25. f.	— f.
6	37 f.	— f		25	28. c.	— car
7	43. c.	53. c.		26	41. c.a.r.	53. f.
8	39. c.	— c.		27	35. f.	43. c.
9	31. r.h.	32 r.		28	32. c.	32 c.
10	35 c.	— c.		29	20. f.	35. f.
11	30. c.	31. f		30	36. c.	— s.
12	22. f.	34. f		31	22. f.	31. f.
13	35. c.	50. f		Feb. 1.	22. c.	31. c
14	38. f.	50. f		2.	30. f.	35. c
15	41. c.	44. r.		3.	17 f	— f
16	39. c.	45. c.		4.	33. cas.	41. c
17	53. s.a.r.	— f.		5.	36. r	38 r
18	32. f.	40. f.		6.	37. c	49. f.
19	25. f.	30. c.		7.	41. c	52. r.

8.	55. c.	50. r.		20.	29. c.	— c.
9.	28. rs.	29. s.		21.	19. f.	28. c.
10.	26. s.	35 f.		22.	15. fas.	— f.
11.	23. c.	33 f.		23.	29. c.	45. f.
12.	28. f.	45 f.		24.	27. f.	
13.	31. f.	41. r.				
14.	37. c.	56 f.		c. cloudy		
15.	25. f.	37 f.		f. fair		
16.	43. r.	37 f.		h. hail		
17.	10. f.	— f.		r. rain		
18.	15. f.	34 f.		s. snow		
19.	27. s.	35 r.		a. after		

Example. cas. means 'cloudy after snow.' That is to say that it is *cloudy* at the time of the observation, but has *snowed* in the interim since the last. Without this notice, an intermediate snow or rain between two observations would escape.

RC (DLC). PrC (DLC). Entry in SJL shows that TJ included his meteorological "diary to this day."

The course obstinately pursued by TJ that almost cost Martha her life was probably that of employing a wet nurse, for this seems the only advice offered in DR. GREGORY's book that is applicable to the circumstances. If TJ really feared a repetition of such a danger, it is strange that he did not allude to it when he first dispatched Gregory's *Comparative view* and still more so that in neither instance did he specify the nature of the danger. The allusion in the present letter, therefore, seems to confirm the conjecture advanced above that he had a hidden motive in sending Gregory's book to Monticello (see note, TJ to Mary Jefferson, 16 Feb. 1791). TJ's inclusion of the meteorological observations must have been another example of such indirect prompting. Almost a year had elapsed since he proposed the keeping of such records, but all he had received in exchange was Randolph's excuses (TJ to Randolph, 18 Apr. 1790; Randolph to TJ, 3 May 1790).

From Alexander Watt

HONOURED SIR   Savannah in Georgia 24th. Feby. 1791

I beg you will pardon me for the freedom I take in troubling you with this at a time when no doubt Matters of great consequence require your Attention.

The Legislature of this State in the beginning of the year 1789, appointed or continued a Health officer for this Port, to go on board of every Vessel, from any foreign Port, and ordered a fee of three Dollars to be paid the said officer by the Captain of such Vessel. The New Government beginning to operate about the same time, he never appeared to act under the State appointment untill, within two or three Months past, and almost all the Masters of Vessels had been in different Ports of the States since the New Constitution took place, and no fee of this name demanded, they and almost every other person think it an imposition and ought not to be suffered; This however triffling it may appear to you has made a great deal of Noise here. He (Doctor Geoghagen) has got warrants from a Justice of the Peace to stop I suppose not less than One hundred Masters of Vessels, two or three among the first of them were Consigned to me. I have become their Security and mean to carry it through the Courts, but that being tedious I give you this information. If it is worth your notice it may be determined sooner. I am sorry to see Strangers so dissatisfied and haunted by the Constables in every corner of the Streets, and for what is generally thought Stretching the power of this State; There being no House of Assembly sitting We can get no redress here just now. There is no Hospital here nor the smallest provision for any seafaring man that may be on shore and without money nor would the Health officer give them any Assistance. I hope you will excuse so much freedom and I remain Sir Your Most Obedient and very humble Servant,   ALEXANDER WATT

RC (DNA: RG 59, MLR); endorsed by TJ as received 12 Apr. 1791 and so recorded in SJL. There is no evidence that TJ responded to this appeal.

From Joshua Johnson

SIR   London 25 February 1791

On the 19 Instant, Charles Calvil, Carpenter, of the Dolphin, Captn. Richard O'brian, belonging to Messrs. Allens of Philadelphia, who was Captured on her Passage from St. Ubes to America on the 30 July 1785, and carried into Algiers on the 16 August in the same Year, call'd on me; He tells me that he was liberated by Subscription obtained by the British Consul in July last, that when he left Algiers, Six of the Dolphin's Crew had fallen Sacrifices to the Plague, to wit

Peter Smith	on the 19 January 1787
Robert McGinnis	on the 27 June
John Doren	on the 30. ditto
Edward O'reily	on the 15 May 1788
William	on the 19. ditto
Zachariah Coffin	on the August

That he left Captn. O'brian, Andrew Montgomery, his Mate, William Patterson, James Hull, Philip Sloan, Patrick Loring, John Robinson, and Jacob Tirionear, Seamen, there, suffering every Hardship, and Inconvenience, particularly since the Allowance made through Mr. Carmichael had been stopt, and which had then been Six Months, owing as he understood to some difference between the Spanish Consul, and Mr. Carmichael. That the Algierenes allowed them only Bread, Olives, and Water, that they employed them in erecting Fortifications, dragging Stone, Timber, and rigging their Cruizers, and frequently compelled them to work in Chains, that when their Days Labour was over, they were with Six or Seven Hundred other Slaves, ordered into a House, and locked up until the next Day, and that this had invariably been the case ever since their being carried in. He likewise assures me that the Dey only allows each man ℞ Year, a Shirt, a pair of Trousers, a Blanket, and one pair of Slippers, and those of no duration, that they suffer in their Feet much more in the Summer from the Heat of the Pavement than from Cold in the Winter. When Calvil left Algiers, he says that the Captain, Mate, and all the Crew of the Schooner Maria, from Boston, vizt Captn. Isaac Stephens, Alexander Forsyth, Mate, James Cathcart, George Smith, and James Harnet, were living, and in the same wretched Situation with that of Captn. O'brian, and the remainder of his Crew, all of them ready to sink under Despair.

Amongst the many Questions I asked him, I put these, "Whether he discovered any more Friendly Disposition in the Algierenes towards them than at first when taken," to which he replied in the negative, tho' he said frequent intimations had been made that was Congress to make any farther Offers for their Ransom, they should considerably lessen their Demands, that when Mr. Lamb was there for the purpose of treating for their liberation, they had no idea that America was so distant from them, and that their hopes was making frequent Captures, and procuring Slaves. I asked him if in his Conversation with his Overseers, or from any other means, he had discovered what would be deemed sufficient to liberate them and what would be the best Steps to pursue. He answered that he understood that the Admiral of their Fleet had exprest a great desire for an American Frigate from 24 to 36 Guns, that the Dey had even given Mr. Logie the British Consul a Commission to purchase one in England, but that he had not succeeded. Such a Ship with some Naval Stores, and a little Money, he thought might secure them, but altho' he had recovered his Liberty through the benevolence of the English Consul, yet he would not advise or recommend Application to be made through him, or any other representing an European Nation, that he was certain of their not being friendly to us. I have been thus particular Sir, in giving you the relation of Mr. Charles Calvil, of the situation of our unfortunate, and suffering fellow Citizens, and as Calvil seems desirous to return to Philadelphia, I will promote it all I can, that he may appear before you, confirm this, and give you further Information.

I have the honor to be with perfect Respect, and Esteem Sir Your most Obedt. Hble. Servant,   JOSHUA JOHNSON

Calvil is a Scotch Man by Birth.

RC (DNA: RG 59, CD); in clerk's hand, except for signature; endorsed by TJ as received 23 Apr. 1791 and so recorded in SJL. Dupl (same); unsigned.

From Madame de Lur-Saluces

Bordeaux le 25 fevrier 1791

Ayant eu le Malheur de Perdre Mr. le Comte de Lur Saluces Monsieur et étant Consequament rentrée en Possession de Mes vins Blancs d'yquem, haut Sauterne, Monsieur fenwick a bien voulu M'envoyer La Lettre que vous avies adressée à feu Mr. Le Cte de Lur-Saluces. J'espere Monsieur que vous serai content de Lenvoi que je vous fais expedier, qui Consiste en 10 Caisses de 50 bouteilles chacune savoir 3 formant 150 Bouteilles Pour vous et 7 formant 350 bouteilles Pour Le general Washingston. Le desir que vous fussies Mieux servi Ma decidé a faire distraire Cette Partie dun envoi destiné a Paris et que Partant d'ici je puis vous envoier a raison de 30 Sols la Bouteille et 4.ª Pour La Caisse. Je vous Prie Monsieur de vouloir bien Madresser toujours directement vos demandes je les ferai remplir avec le Plus grand Soin et La Plus grande exactitude. J'ai Lhonneur detre Monsieur votre tres humble et tres Obeissante Servante

D'YQUEM CSSE DE LUR-SALUCES

RC (ViWC); at foot of text: "A Madame Madame La Csse de Lur-Saluces rue Porte Dijeaux A Bordeaux"; addressed: "A Monsieur Monsieur Th jefferson A Philadelphie"; endorsed by TJ as received 21 June 1791 and so recorded in SJL.

From William Short

I received a few hours after the departure of my last letter an account of the additional articles decreed by the national assembly relative to tobacco. I mentioned to you that the cultivation in France was allowed, that its importation in the manufactured state was prohibited and permitted in leaves subject to a duty of twenty-five livres the quintal, except when in French vessels coming immediately from America, then to pay only three fourths of that duty. Two other articles have since been decreed as follows.

1. Le tabac en feuilles provenant de l'etranger, pourra être mis en entrepôt pendant un an dans les magasins de la regie qui seront destinés à cet usage et re-exporté à l'étranger sans payer aucun droit.

2. Une regie nationale fera fabriquer et vendre du tabac au profit du tresor public et *payera les mêmes droits que les particuliers.*[1]

The committee had proposed that the tobacco imported by the regie should be exempted from duty: but the assembly rejected it by the amendment underlined. The article respecting licenses of manufacture and retail was not decided when my last letters left Paris. It is possible that the post which will arrive this evening after the English mail, in which this letter goes, shall have set off, may bring an account of its decision.

The object which seems most to agitate the minds of the people in Paris at present is the determination of the Kings aunts to go to Rome. The municipality denounced it to the King, who in his answer quoted the declaration of rights which allowing every citizen to go and come as he pleased, permitted his aunts of course to pursue their journey.—Since then every thing has been done to alarm them with respect to the dangers of their journey. Still they seem to persevere and preparations are making for it. It is remarkable that for some time past those who are considered as the greatest enemies to liberty have been obliged most often to invoke the declaration of rights and the principles of the constitution. They in general however invoke them in vain. The acts of tyranny exercised by the people assembled or by their municipal or legislative representatives are considered for the most part as legitimate, by a kind of subversion of all the ideas of true liberty. This will necessarily last until the government becomes organised and the powers of its different branches defined. I confess however I cannot form a conjecture when that will be, as it appears to me, it will require some unforeseen event to dispose the national assembly to disgorge all the powers which they have swallowed. I take it for granted however that will happen, and that the present deplorable state of anarchy will be succeeded, either at a greater or less price, by a free constitution.

It is said that the Russian troops, contrary to general expectation, have gone into winter quarters, and that Prince Potemkin has returned to Petersburg to have a personal interview with the Empress.

The conferences of Szistow for the confirmation of the peace between the Emperor and the Porte after having met with some delay, on account of unexpected pretensions, are said to be now in activity, with a probability of success. Yet there seems no doubt from the present good understanding between the two Imperial Cabinets, that if war continues, and new actors mount the stage on the side of the Porte, Russia will also be aided by Austria.

I hoped to have received the form of the obligations (to be given on behalf of the U.S. for the loan made here) so as to have sent a copy by this post to the Secretary of the Treasury. It is now making out by the notary who has promised it for several days past without keeping his word. As soon as I shall have signed them I shall return to Paris, the term prescribed for my stay here having expired.—I have the honor to be, with sentiments of the most perfect respect and attachment, Dear Sir, Your most obedient and most humble Servant,   W: SHORT

RC (DLC: Washington Papers); at head of text: "No. 58"; endorsed by TJ as received 21 Apr. 1791 and so recorded in SJL. PrC (DLC: Short Papers); lacks signature and complimentary close. FC (DNA: RG 59, DD). Tr (DNA: RG 59, SDC); see note 1 below.

1 In Tr the foregoing decrees are translated as follows: "1. Leaf tobacco of foreign growth may be received during one year in the magazines belonging to a company which shall be appointed for that purpose and may be exported without paying any duty.—2. A national company shall manufacture and sell the tobacco for the benefit of the public Treasury, *who shall pay the same duty as individuals.*"

From John Garland Jefferson

MY DEAR SIR   February 26. 1791.

I have waited for some time with anxious hopes, in expectation of a letter from you; but having not as yet had that satisfaction, induced by the fairness of the occasion, I have resumed my pen to comply with one of his requests whose injunctions shall ever be held sacred by me; for believe me Sir, of the many incidents in life, there are few circumstances which cou'd give me more real, and heart felt satisfaction than your esteem. I hope you will favor me with a line by my uncle Garland: such a testimony of your regard will afford me the highest gratification.

I intend every spring and fall to give you an account of the progress I make in reading, as I imagine it will give you some pleasure to receive such an information. The space has been so short since I saw you, that it is not possible I can have made any great advancement. What I have read however you shall hear. I have finished Cokes, first, second, third, and almost his last institutes: I have perused with attention three or four of Gilberts works, and Millot's antient, and three volumes of his modern history. I shou'd have read something more but I have had very sore eyes.

Gilbert I find highly agreeable, as well as edifying; for as to the matter he contains I think him equal to any thing I ever read: Millot I think also a very good work; and serves to give an idea of the different religions which have prevailed in the world, and the biass of prejudice on the mind, when in a rude, and uncultivated state. Coke I think improving, tho dry, and pedantic.

I have heard from Albemarle not long since, and have the pleasure to inform you that Mrs. Randolph has a fine girl, and was then tolerable well. The rage of the people in that county has much abated, and almost a total calm has succeeded.

The presumption in this case is that time will wear off the remembrance of that fatal libel, and that I may be delivered from the odium incured, by that unfortunate suspicion, which has so much tended to disturb my quiet. But if the fates will be so propitious as to grant me the smiles of your approbation, I will bear it all with fortitude; and perhaps may learn to profit by past misfortunes. To you I look up as to my second father, and will in every thing be guided by you, as if you were my first. Then be it my greatest care to merit your esteem, and confidence, and as far as possible to recompence your generosity.

Sam Carr has made a conditional contract with Mr. John Carr of Albemarle: he has stipulated to give him thirty five pounds to be discounted from a bond to his father, and an hundred payable in two years, for his lease of Mrs. Reddicks dower; and Mr. Carr, has determined to move to Albemarle next winter.

I heard some time since from Peter Carr who is still at Monticello, and who means to return to Goochland in the spring. Will my Benefactor if the request [seems] not unreasonable furnish me with a watch? [It gives] me pain to add to the obligations I am alrea[dy under] by such an act; but I am persuaded you are so well convinced of the convenience, and even the necessity of one that it will plead my excuse for applying to you. If it is convenient to you Mr. Garland will convey it; but if it is not convenient, it is by no means my wish to receive it. I am dear Sir, with cordial, and sincere esteem Your most grateful hbl. servt,   J G JEFFERSON

RC (ViU); at foot of text: "Mr. Thomas Jefferson"; addressed: "Thomas Jefferson Esqr. Secretary of state Philadelphia. Mr. Garland"; MS mutilated when seal was broken, and concluding words of three lines have been conjecturally supplied; endorsed by TJ as received 13 Mch. 1791 and so recorded in SJL.

From Joshua Johnson

SIR   London 26th. February 1790 [i.e., 1791]

My last was on the 1st December by the British Packet; since then, I have deferred writing you for several reasons; the first, I was anxious to have the power to say, whether this Court really meant to send out Mr. Elliott or not; but I am still in the same state of suspense, the Minister, not denying, or confirming the report.

The second reason, was my wish to make trial of the conduct of the Captains Commanding American Vessells, and the Sailors, (Citizens) navigating the same; and after near four Months experience, and great attention I am sorry to tell you that a regulation, *and that strict, and very strong*, must be made by Congress, or my appointment will be of no avail, but rather reduce our Country in the eyes of this Government.

It is too true Sir, that near a third of the Captains, neither make their Report with me, or Clear, and many who do, furnish such an imperfect List of their Cargoes, that it is impossible to render Congress a satisfactory Account; this I however do not think altogether owing to willfullness, or disrespect, on the part of the Captains, but rather that of the designs of the Brokers who do their Ships business, and who wish to overset the Establishment of a Consular Office, as it is an eye-sore to many, and gives them somewhat more trouble.

It is true, I have a remedy, and can compel them to do their duty, by applying to the Commissioners to give orders, to stop their inward, and outward Entries, untill they produced a Certificate of having entered with me; but, it fully accords with my Ideas, and probably will, with those of Congress, that this Government might say, the Subjects of the United States, were not to be governed, without calling in their assistance.

The next regulation, and which is wanted as soon as possible, is between Captains, and Men; during the threatening of War, between England, and Spain, Mens wages rose to a considerable height in America. This induced many landsmen, or half Seamen, to ship for the Voyage, and the Captains were glad to take them; on their arrival here, finding the dispute settled and Numbers of experienced Seamen to be had for half the Money; they, regardless, of Contract, good Faith, and Duty to their Country, too generally, set on devising ways of getting rid of those poor Men and either from bad usage or threats, induce them to take their discharges, then, when the little Money they had received is consumed, and no employ to be had, they are reduced to Poverty, and Distress, and on application to the Lord Mayor of London, or to the Parish Officers for relief, they are rejected, and referred to me, as Consul for America, who, they say, must provide for his poor. The piteous, situation many of them are in, would rouze the feelings, and Compassion of the most hard hearted; indeed I had one brought, and left in my House, and so far exhausted, that I feared he would expire, before I could secure him Lodgings, Refreshment, and Assistance; his Name was Job Henly, belonging to New York, and since I have had to bury him. Others I have got into the Hospitals, and some I have supported at Lodgings, the expense of which I have made as light as possible, but still it is too heavy for me to bear, and I trust Congress, will not reject my reimbursement. In some instances where the Men have come to me, and made their Complaints, I have summoned their Captain, and from threatening to send them home at their Countrys Expence, and representing their Conduct to you, they have been frightened; discharged the Bills, and taken them on board again; tho', had they persevered I have not the power of Compulsion, as no Law has been enacted (as I know of) by Congress, punishing such offences.

By Permission I would propose some such regulation by Congress, as is established in France, that is to say; that at the time of every Ship, or Vessell, taking her Clearance, that it should be the duty of the Officer of the Custom House, to see each Man, that he enter a regular record of their Names, Ages, places of Birth, and residences, and that a duplicate be delivered to the Captain, which, on his arrival in a Foreign Port, he should deposit with the Ships Register, with the Consul, untill he takes his Clearance for sailing; that on his return back, he should produce this at the Office where he enters, and account for each, and every Man, he took out of the Country. This will preserve your Seamen; otherwise, they will be left in Foreign Countries, and become useless to their own when wanted, as those employed in Navigation will be the Seamen of this Country, and taken from you, at the pleasure of the King, and his officers.

The Records of each office, should be made Quarterly, and transmitted to the Marine office, when a set of Books, should be opened for each State, and those Lists entered regularly; this would enable you to make immediate reference on any complaint being exhibited to you, by any Consul, or Subject of the United States, and if the offence was of magnitude, the President might direct the Attorney General to prosecute the Offender; independent of which you would always have the satisfaction of seeing at one look, the state, and progress of your Maritime strength.—Having said so much on the part of the Seamen, may incline you to think, that I'm prejudiced in their favor; I would not have you to infer from which, that I have not the strongest desire, that in the Regulations of Congress, due care should be taken of the Commanders; many years experience has taught me to know what a profligate set seamen are; yet, to every Commercial Country, they are the first Jewel, and good Policy will direct an extension of every encouragement to them.

In your letter of Instructions to me dated 26th. August last, you direct me to prevent any Vessell entering as an American, *who is not such*, if in my power; I discover much abuse, in this particular, but what can I say; the Register is granted to a Person in America, on his Swearing that he is the sole Owner when it is notorious, that the Principal resides here, and that the Person in whose Name the Register is granted, is no more, or less than an Agent, or Junior Partner. Whether it may be wise, to abolish this kind of Property or not, you can best judge; but my own opinion is, that we should not be too Scrupulous, as it gives employment to our Countrymen, and that of the Funds of Foreigners.

Application has been made to me by the Merchants Trading to America, to administer Oaths to them, to prove their Accounts; altho' I find it the custom of Consuls from other Nations, yet I have my doubts, therefore wish your instructions on that head; as to the Administration of oaths, where they relate to maritime, or Public Affairs; I have no doubt but that it is a part of my Official Duty, as well as that of Legalizing the executions of Powers, Notarial Certificates &c. &c.

The Export of Goods from this Port, to the United States has not been so large this Spring, as the last; tho' I understand that of the out-ports is considerably more; the greater part, shipped from this is in Vessells belonging to the United States, and which I find has given cause of Discontent, to the Ship Owners of these Kingdoms. They growl, and say, unless Government retaliates, and levy's either Duty, or Tonnage, that they will be ruined, and the Americans run away with all the carrying Trade. You know how jealous these People are of their Interest, and instantly, they find it any ways affected, they Complain, however, I do not apprehend any inconvenience from it.

I had taken the Liberty in a former letter to you, to mention, that I thought all Captains at clearing in the United States, should be furnished by the Custom House, with a Manifest, or Certificate of his Ships Cargo; under the Officers hand, and seal of Office, and which on his arrival in a Foreign Port, he should produce, and deliver in the Consular Office, who should grant him a certificate of his having done the same, and made due Report. This would prevent frequent Seizures by the Custom House Officers, as well as the pain, and fatigue, of Presenting Memorials to the Commissioners, and Lords of Trade for their liberation.

As I find much of my Time taken up, in legalizing the Authorities of Notaries Public; granting Consular Certificates to the execution of Powers of Attorney, and other Public Instruments of writing; as well as settling Accounts between Captains, and their Men; granting Certificates of such settlements, and discharges; opposing Proctors in the Commons, and Attorneys at Law, granting Passports, and Protections &ca. I beg to know from you, if these services are considered by Congress as duties attached to my office; or, whether individuals reaping benefits therefrom, are not considered as private Matters and should Compensate me for them.

I have heretofore given you a plan, and my Ideas for raising a Fund, for the relief of those, who are unfortunately, Shipwrecked, or meet with other misfortunes; the instance of the Ceres from Baltimore for London, and wrecked on the coast of France, the other day presented Objects, which call for the immediate attention of Government: I have from the benevolence of some American Captains, secured them Passages and employ, back to their own Country, as well, as many others who were impressed in the English service and now turned loose on the World: indeed, when speaking of this denomination of Men, I with pain, tell you, the Number is so great, that I Cannot on any terms procure passages for them to their own Country; in a similar instance, the Prussian Consul tells me, that he represented the situation of his Countrymen, to his King, who directly wrote, and ordered him to ship so many in each Ship returning, and to draw orders on the Magistrates of the Town, where the Ship was bound, for the payment of their passages; in the present instance, these Men must be starved before Congress can adopt any plan for their relief: I must therefore do the best I can for them; but, I hope something will be done against any future emergency. Inclosed I transmit you, an account of the American Vessells which have entered the Port of London, from 1 Nov: to 31 Decr. also an account of those who have cleared, during the same period with remarks at the foot of each account, referring to those Captains who have neglected to pay respect to the office; hereafter I will make up the accounts quarterly, and forward them. Under cover you have my Account of expenditures up to 31 December Balance £13. 15. 1 which I hope will be approved.—I beg reference to what I shall write you in a few days and with assurances of Respect, I am Sir, Your very obedient, & most Humble Servant,   JOSHUA JOHNSON

RC (DNA: RG 59, CD); endorsed by TJ as received 23 Apr. 1791 and so recorded in SJL. Dupl (same); with minor variations.

To Thomas Leiper

SIR   Philadelphia Feb. 26. 1791.

I shipped to a person in London, some time before the war, 4 hhds. of my Albemarle tobacco. No account of sales was ever rendered, and being now in settlement with the representative of that person, we are obliged to find out the worth of that tobacco as we can. Mr. Charles Carrol (who lodges at Mrs. House's) is to settle the price with me. As I can only procure circuitous evidence, I shall prove to him that it was made on the red mountain lands of Albemarle. It will remain to satisfy him of the quality of that kind of tobacco, and finding that your purchases have made you acquainted with it, I am obliged to ask the favour of you to call on Mr. Carrol, and inform him what you have found to be the quality of that tobacco and what was it's worth, before the war, here, and in London as well as you can judge. Mr. Carter's lands and mine join. I am sorry to give you this trouble, but the impossibility of procuring direct evidence obliges me to recur to circuitous. Mr. Carrol said he should be at home and at leisure tomorrow morning. Your taking this trouble will oblige Sir Your very humble servt,   TH: JEFFERSON

PrC (MHi).

From Gouverneur Morris

DEAR SIR,   Paris 26 February 1791

I am to acknowledge your favours of the twenty sixth of November and seventeenth of December which reached me two days ago. The System of Finance did not indeed fully meet my Opinions but I know it is necessary to conform even to the Prejudices of Mankind. I fully believe with you that any Resources dependent on Consumption will greatly encrease. I believe this Encrease will not be meerly in Proportion to that of Population but in the compound Ratio of Numbers and Wealth. This last will be abundantly produced by an industrious People from a luxuriant Soil. Taxation moreover excites Industry and necessitates Oeconomy. It encreases also the commercial Medium inasmuch as it creates a domestic Object for the Application of Money and forces an interior Circulation. Pardon me while on this Chapter for expressing my Apprehension that the Sale of Western Lands will not produce the present Relief expected and consume a valuable future Resource. America has not the needful Money Capital. I put aside Taxation and consider only the three great Objects of Agriculture, Manufactures and Commerce. These in populous and policied Societies present themselves in the Order I have just placed them but this Order is inverted with us. Commerce by more potent Means commands a Preference. To supply her Wants a Bank is useful but its Operations will not produce all that is expected, among many other Reasons because we have not yet a great Center of Commerce, Finance and *Money-Dealing*. The Payment of Interest in the States has a Tendency also to obviate and impede Bank Circulation. The Channels of Commerce are not yet duly filled, those of Manufactures are scarcely moistened, those of Agriculture are absolutely dry. Whenever therefore the Government puts up Lands for Sale it calls Money from those Objects to which I verily believe it might be more advantageously applied. The Purchaser calculates and will not part with his Cash till he sees greater Benefit than in any other Appropriation. Under present Circumstances the Hesitation will be whether to purchase Stocks or Lands. If by lowering the Price of Land you make that the greater Temptation Stocks must fall and then Foreigners will buy them cheap. The Land if sold cannot be cultivated but if not sold it cannot run away as the Stocks do. Besides by throwing more Land on the Market you ruin those who have no Means to pay Debts but by Sale of real Estate &c. &c. &c.—I quit the Discussion and indeed beg your Pardon for entering into it.

My Letters from London of the 24 and 28th. of December will have communicated what passed with the british Administration I am sorry now that I spoke to them because from yours of the 17th. of that Month I find it was the President's Pleasure no other Application should be made, but I flatter myself that the Manner was such as by no Means to compromize the Dignity of our Country.

You very kindly my dear Sir in that Letter communicate the President's Approbation of my Conduct. I cannot tell you the Pleasure which this occasions but you will estimate it by your own Feelings under similar Circumstances. Pardon me for adding that I feel highly gratified in receiving the Communication from you.

In this Letter you enclose an Order for ƒ2475 on the Bankers in Holland. Make for me I pray you the proper Acknowlegements. Pecuniary Considerations never yet weighed with me where the public Service was in Question and therefore immediately on Receipt of the Presidents Orders I proceeded without regarding other Objects as speedily as I could to London. Previous Engagements had indeed rendered it my Duty to go to Amsterdam and on that Route I made those Enquiries which you once desired I would. The Result has since been occasionally communicated to Mr. Short. I embarked at Helvoet Sluys the twenty fourth of March and continued in London till the twenty fourth of September altho I had no Business of my own there but such as I could have transacted by Letter. I would have stayed still longer had I imagined that it could be of any Use. My Expences during that Period were £489..6..6 but I did not intend to ask Compensation nor do I mention them now in that View.

Since I have been in this City a Matter has turned up which is very interesting to America and the Result of which is by no Means pleasing. I mean the Decrees respecting Tobacco. The second Day of this Month I was requested to go to Monsieur de la fayettes and thence with him to speak on that Subject to the Committee of Commerce. I went to his House but declined waiting on the Committee unless they should previously desire it. This was fortunate, for the Arrangements had been so illy made that the Committee did not meet and for little Reasons not worth mentioning some of the Members were predisposed not to receive Information. On the 9th. I dined with him in Consequence of a Note desiring me to confer on American Business. After Dinner Mr. Swan, Colo. Walker and I were introduced into his Closet with a Mr. Raymond and another Man whose Name I forget, but he was I believe Something in the Consulate at New York. Monsieur de la fayette asked our Opinions on the Question then agitated respecting a free Culture of Tobacco in France. Mirabeau had moved to prohibit it (after a certain time) even in the privileged Provinces, but Monsr. de la fayette considered it as standing closely connected with the Disaffection then prevalent in Alsace. Mr. Swan gave it as his Opinion that if the free Culture was allowed the Introduction of that Article from America must speedily cease. Mr. Raymond insisted that the Culture if permitted would not be pursued but it seemed to me that he did not and indeed could not think so. The other Gentleman was silent. Colo. Walker observed that he supposed France would consult her own Interest and therefore it was not worth while to enquire what was the Interest of America and in this I think he judged perfectly well. I refused to give an Opinion but stated Facts to shew that Mr. Swan was right in his Judgment, and then observed that the Question seemed to turn on the single Point whether they could dispense with the Revenue for if they could not they must consider the Means of obtaining it, which were either Duty, Excise, Farm or Regie. That the first would if great be eluded. The second was not now practicable, the third was unfashionable and by the last they would be cheated. If however they could dispense with the Revenue then not only they might allow the free Culture but they ought to allow also the free Commerce. I stated the Advantages which would result from the Latter. He seemed surprized at some things as not having previously presented themselves and pressed for an opinion to which I replied that I would not advise but predict. That they would begin by allowing the free Culture which would annihilate the Revenue and in less than two Years they would prohibit the Culture to recover the Revenue. The Thing has turned out as I expected as far as it went. Colo. Ternant has endeavoured to prevent the Culture and to render the Commerce as free as possible but in Vain. We have held sundry Conferences on the Subject together. He communicated to me what was doing and I gave him all the Information I could. The Assembly have allowed the Culture and laid a Duty of 25^{tt} per Quintal upon the Import one fourth of which is taken off for such as may be brought from America in french Bottoms. This in Addition to the heavy Duty on our Oil bears hard. To the Arguments of such as blame these Decrees it is answered that it will be necessary to form a commercial Treaty with America and then every Thing can be regulated.

I have hitherto you will observe kept as clear as I could from interfering but the Matter had now put on an Appearance which demanded the Exertions of every American Citizen. On the 17th. therefore I called on Monsieur de la fayette. He desired me to give him a Note on the Subject, said that Mirabeau had promised to speak about it and that he expected the diplomatic Committee would take the Matter up. I had been told long before what Part Mirabeau would take and how much he was to receive for his Agency. I asked therefore whether it would not answer for the King to object because the Assembly being much divided a Trifle would turn the Ballance, and it had been said that if he would himself have taken a Part in the Debate the Question would have been otherwise decided. He told me he would rather the United States should be indebted to the Nation than to the King. But if Things go on at the present Rate we shall be indebted to neither. The next Day I called on the Count de Montmorin who assured me he would do all in his Power. By way of a Spur I told him that it was commonly reported in London the british were going to send out a Minister to America; that I had good Reasons to believe it was their Wish to form an offensive and defensive Alliance with us and presumed that he was acquainted with their Intentions. He replied as I supposed he would in the Affirmative. Upon this I asked him whether it would answer any good Purpose for me to write him a Letter on the Subject. He pressed me earnestly to do so the next Day as he was in the Evening of it to meet the diplomatic Committee. In Consequence I wrote on the 19th. that of which a Copy is enclosed. You will observe that I hint at the Views of Great Britain in such Manner that he must take on himself any Communication of that Sort to the Committee. As to the Observations, I stated them as being made by American Citizens in Order to supply the Defect of ministerial Character and also to keep Myself out of Sight, not chusing to be quoted in any of their

Deliberations. I have communicated these Steps to Mr. Short and am now endeavoring to obtain if possible a Duty per Arpent on the Culture equivalent to the import Duty; supposing each Arpent to produce 8 quintals. This which would I sincerely believe be useful to France would also prevent the sudden Decrease in the Consumption of our Tobacco. And altho I am convinced that planting it is bad Husbandry, Yet I wish my Countrymen rather to correct themselves from their own Experience than receive such a Shock from abroad.

As yet there is little Hope of Success to any Proposition for alleviating much less removing the Burthens they have laid upon us. The greater Part have adopted Systematic Reasoning, in Matters of Commerce as in those of Government so that disdaining Attention to Facts and deaf to the Voice of Experience while others deliberate they decide and are the more constant in their Opinions in Proportion as they are less acquainted with the Subject which is natural enough. Stat pro ratione voluntas has you know been the Adage with those who have much of one and little of the other from time immemorial and the Assembly will not I think loose by Non-user that valuable Franchise.

I will do myself the Honor to communicate such farther matter as may occur in this Regard and beg Leave in the mean Time to assure you of the Sincerity with which I am &c.

FC (DLC: Gouverneur Morris Papers). Recorded in SJL as received 21 June 1791.

Morris' good reasons for believing that England wished to FORM AN OFFENSIVE AND DEFENSIVE ALLIANCE were evidently based on nothing more substantial than TJ's letter to him of 12 Aug. 1790.

ENCLOSURE

Some observations of American Citizens on the late Decrees respecting Tobacco

In sofar as these Decrees relate exclusively to France it is not proper for Foreigners to express an Opinion. From the present Consideration therefore, shall be excluded the questions Whether to cultivate Tobacco be useful or pernicious. Whether on the former Supposition Articles of first necessity such as Grain or superior Utility such as Hemp might not be preferred on Ground of public Safety or Advantage. Whether a Consumption dependent on meer Fancy does not present to the Fisc a desirable Object of Revenue. And Whether in the supposable Cases of unfavorable Seasons or calamitous Wars the unavoidable Encrease of Price on imported Articles would be more or less injurious according to the Nature of those Articles.

But in sofar as the Decrees may relate to the Commerce of France, and particularly as they may concern her Connection with the United States they command the Attention of Americans. And first it appears that the Liberty of cultivating Tobacco must alone in a very short Time put an End to the Importation of it from Virginia. The Medium Produce of an Acre of Land cannot be transported from the Place of its growth to a French Port for less than three louis.[1] Wherefore admitting the Price of Labor to be the same (Which it is not) and rejecting the Cost of Transportation from the Ports to the interior Parts of the Kingdom, there remains a Bounty of three louis per Acre on the Cultivation in France whose southern Provinces will doubtless produce Tobacco of the best Quality. Hence it is inferred that the commercial Relations dependent on this Article must speedily cease.

Secondly the general Permission to import Tobacco in Leaves from any Part of the World must give new Vigor to the Commerce of Great Britain. She now enjoys almost a Monopoly of the Trade to Virginia. Of course during the short Period that American Tobacco may be used in France the Vent of French Merchandize in Exchange for it will be precluded.

Thirdly the Preference given to French Ships or rather the Penalty on those of the United States (nugatory in itself) will probably give Rise to a System of commercial Hostility between the two Countries Whose End cannot be foreseen nor its Consequences calculated. That this Preference will be nugatory is clear because many Means of eluding it will occur to mercantile Men and the Congress will doubtless meet it by similar Impositions so as to restore the Equilibrium.

But it is said that this Part of the System has been adopted in Consequence of the Duties laid by the Congress on French Ships. If so, a serious Reflection arises from the very Circumstance which gave Birth to the Decree. Resentment it seems is easily excited even against intimate friends. May not the same Emotion influence those who live on the other Side of the Atlantic Ocean. The American Law laid no particular Duty on French Ships, and the English (not without reason) complained that tho the Expressions were general, yet the Effect was exclusively felt by them, since theirs were the only foreign Ships employed in the American Trade. But waving this Observation, it is proper to examine the Nature of the Burthens laid in America on foreign Ships. These are first an additional Tonnage Duty of forty Sous which is an equitable Tax for the Support of Beacons, Buoys and other aids to navigation of which foreigners stand more in need than Natives being less acquainted with the Coast. Secondly there is a Deduction of ten per Cent from the import Duties in favor of American Ships. This can hardly touch the French Commerce but deeply affects that of Great Britain and is therefore an actual tho not apparent Preference to France. Of the French Articles whose Volume is such that the Preference to American Ships may be felt, the most considerable is Brandy and on that the Difference is not twelve livres per Ton whereas the Difference decreed here respecting Tobacco amounts to at least one hundred livres per Ton, and is therefore a Prohibition.

It must farther be remarked that as the American Productions are of

1767

the breadth of this bridge is about 60 feet at narrowest. the top of
it is very uneven and rocky. many large trees growing
on it. at the bottom by the waterside is a tree
growing which when you are under it appears to be a tall
tree but when on the ridge you find that it scarcely
reaches more than half way. each side of the bridge
is one rock of limestone. the bridge itself and each abut-
ment seems to be solid, but a little above and below
it has large cracks, and there seems to be large
peices quite loose and there may be some danger. just where
the bridge joins to the precipice at f. it hangs over more than
common. here grows a cluster of cedars. the rock has broken away from under them to within a crust of a few feet
in thickness which seems to hold to the precipice by a
small peice and that cracked so that it will probably
fall in in time. the stream is so small in dry weather
that it would pass thro a hole a foot sq. where it runs moderate
and being very rocky it is not rapid. the precipices on
the upper side continue perpendicular a considerable distance
between them you see the N. mountain. at the distance of about 5 miles. one of the precipices
does the same on lower side. the other also a little way, and
from that wears off more gradually and here you descend.
the base you see blue ridge about 5 miles. the same
large rocks below which seem to fallen from sides. water distils
from sides guttatim. spring or head about 2 miles above. large
collections of brush and logs, as also plants a mill on the stream above
shew there are considerable floods. stone suspended in about
s E but at time of the floods. on sides of precipice tho' rather in-
clining wherever a little level of very few feet, perhaps 4 or 5 f. are
cedars growing.

Jefferson's description of the Natural Bridge.
(See p. xxxi.)

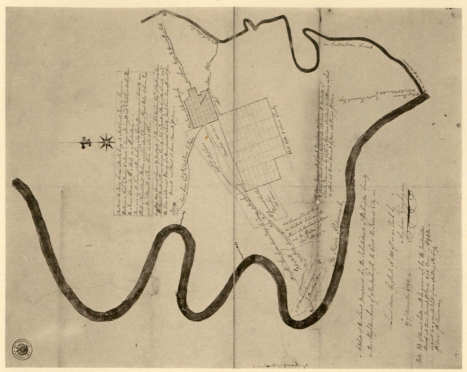

Sharpsburg.

Williamsport.
Proposed Sites for the Federal District on the Upper Potomac.
(See p. xxxi–xxxii.)

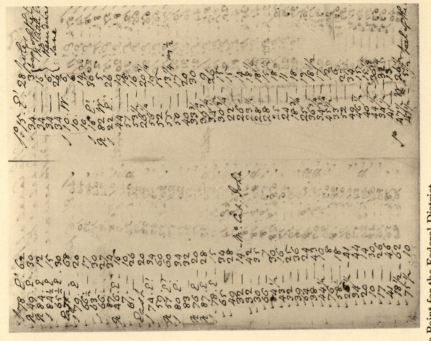

Washington and Jefferson fix the Base Point for the Federal District.
(See p. xxxii.)

2

REPORT

OF THE

SECRETARY OF STATE,

ON THE SUBJECT

OF THE

Cod and Whale Fiſheries,

MADE CONFORMABLY

To an Order of the HOUSE of REPRESENTATIVES of the
UNITED STATES,

Referring to him the Repreſentation of the General Court of the Commonwealth of *Maſſachuſetts* on thoſe Subjects;

February 1ſt, 1791.

PUBLISHED BY ORDER OF THE SENATE
OF THE UNITED STATES.

PHILADELPHIA:

Printed by *JOHN FENNO*, No. 69, in HIGH-STREET.
M.DCC.XCI.

The Breach in the Government becomes Public Knowledge. (See p. xxxii-xxxiii.)

Representative John Brown of Kentucky.
(See p. xxxiii-xxxiv.)

By the Prefident of the United
States of America.

A PROCLAMATION.

WHEREAS it hath been reprefented to me, that *James O'Fallon* is levying an armed force in
that part of the ftate of Virginia which is called Kentucky, difturbs the public peace, and fets
at defiance the treaties of the United States with the Indian tribes, the act of Congrefs, intituled,
" An act to regulate trade and intercourfe with the Indian tribes," and my proclamation of the
fourteenth and twenty-fixth days of Auguft laft, founded thereon : And it is my earneft defire
that thofe who have incautioufly affociated themfelves with the faid *James O'Fallon*, may be warned
of their danger, I have therefore thought fit to publifh this Proclamation, hereby declaring, that
all perfons violating the treaties and act aforefaid, fhall be profecuted with the utmoft rigor of the
law.

And I do moreover require all officers of the United States, whom it may concern, to ufe
their beft exertions to bring to juftice any perfons offending in the premifes.

IN TESTIMONY WHEREOF I have caufed the Seal of the United States to be affixed to thefe
Prefents, and figned the fame with my Hand. DONE at the City of Philadelphia, the
nineteenth Day of March, in the Year of our Lord one thoufand feven hundred and
ninety-one, and of the Independence of the United States the fifteenth.

GEORGE WASHINGTON.

By the PRESIDENT,
THOMAS JEFFERSON.

Proclamation against James O'Fallon.
(See p. xxxiii.)

P R O P O S A L S
For PRINTING by SUBSCRIPTION,

A COLLECTION OF STATE PAPERS,

INTENDED AS MATERIALS FOR

An HISTORY of the UNITED STATES of AMERICA.

By EBENEZER HAZARD, A. M.

IN this Collection will be contained the CHARTERS of the several States which now compose the UNION;—the Records of the UNITED COLONIES of NEW ENGLAND;—Royal Instructions to COLONIAL GOVERNORS;—EXTRACTS from PUBLIC RECORDS;—and other authentic Documents tending to elucidate our History.

The design of this Compilation was intimated to Congress, and honored with their approbation.—On the 20th July, 1778, their Committee, to whom his memorial was referred, reported it as their "Opinion, that Mr. Hazard's undertaking is laudable and deserves the public Patronage and Encouragement, as being productive of public Utility:" Whereupon they "Resolved, That it be recommended to the Governors, Presidents, and Executive Powers of the several States in the Union, to assist Mr. Hazard, and give facility to his Labors; and that for this purpose he be admitted to an inspection of public Records, and be furnished without expence with Copies of such Papers as he may judge will conduce to the valuable End he hath in view.

He was, of consequence, admitted to the inspection and use both of public Records, and the Collections made by individuals, from whence this Compilation (much the largest he has ever met with on the subject, and, he flatters himself, the largest ever made in America) was formed. It has since met the approbation of many eminent Characters, and, even its Manuscript state, has facilitated the settlement of some important controversies.

The Compiler cannot suppress the following Letter from the Honorable the Secretary of State, to whose inspection part of the compilation was submitted, as it contains so flattering and respectable a testimony in favor of the importance of the Work.

"Philadelphia, February 18, 1791.

SIR,
I return you the two volumes of Records, with thanks for the opportunity of looking into them:—they are curious Monuments of the Infancy of our Country. I learn with great satisfaction that you are about committing to the Press the valuable Historical and State Papers you have been so long collecting. Time and accident are committing daily havoc on the originals deposited in our public offices: the late war has done the work of centuries in this business: the lost cannot be recovered; but let us save what remains; not by vaults and locks, which fence them from the public eye and use in consigning them to the waste of time, but by such a multiplication of Copies as shall place them beyond the reach of accident: this being the tendency of your undertaking, be assured there is no one who wishes it a more complete success than,

SIR,
Your most obedient and most humble Servant,
MR. HAZARD.   Thomas Jefferson."

C O N D I T I O N S.

I. The Work to be published in numbers, each containing 160 pages, large quarto:—A number to be delivered every three months.

II. On delivery of the first Number, payment to be made for the first and second, and afterwards for each Number as delivered (except the last) so that the price of one Number will be constantly in advance. The very great expence attending so large a Work, at the same time that it renders this condition absolutely necessary, will be a sufficient apology to the candid, for its insertion.

III. The price to Subscribers will be one Dollar for each Number. It is supposed that the Work will probably be comprised in eight Numbers, forming two handsome Volumes, in large quarto printed on a neat Type and good Paper.

IV. To those who choose to subscribe for the Work in Volumes, the price will be Four Dollars and a Quarter of a Dollar, for each Volume, in boards.

V. The collection will be put to the Press as soon as there shall be a sufficient number of subscriptions to justify an hope that the expences will be defrayed.

☞ Those who receive Subscriptions will please transmit accounts of the numbers obtained to Thomas Dobson, No. 41, Second-street, Philadelphia, by the first of May next.

SUBSCRIPTIONS will be received in Portsmouth, (New-Hampshire) by Jeremiah Libbey; Boston, Thomas & Andrews; Worcester, Isaiah Thomas; Hartford, Thomas Hildrop; New-Haven, Isaac Beers; New-London, Timothy Green; Newport, (R. I.) Jacob Richardson; Providence, John Carter; New-York, Hodge, Allen & Campbell; Albany, Abraham G. Lansing; Philadelphia, Thomas Dobson, and Hazard & Addoms; Wilmington, (Delaware) Frederick Craig; Baltimore, I. Holmes; Alexandria, Joshua Merriman; Norfolk, Mr. Lindsey; Fredericksburgh, Callender & Henderson; Petersburgh, John Grammer; Richmond, Augustine Davis; Newbern, (N. C.) F. X. Martin; Wilmington, John Bradley; Charleston, (S. C.) William P. Young.

SUBSCRIBERS NAMES.   SUBSCRIBERS NAMES.

G. Washington

The Secretary of State Commends the Publication of State Papers.
(See p. xxxv-xxxvi.)

John Adams. In volumes neatly bound

Rufus King   do

Ph. Schuyler   do

Ralph Izard   Do

Benjamin Hawkins   ditto

Sam Johnston   do

Gro. Read   do

John Langdon   do

Oliv. Ellsworth   do

Richard Bassett   do

Theodore Foster   do

Ch. Carroll of Carrollton in volumes neatly bound } do

Tristram Dalton   do

Caleb Strong   do

Rob. Morris   do

Jno. Henry   do

Jas. Monroe   do

Richard Henry Lee   do

Joseph Stanton jr.   do

P. Butler   in vol. neatly bound

James Gunn   do

Paine Wingate.

Samuel Livermore

George Thatcher. in vols. neatly bound

Fredk. A. Muhlenberg. do

P. Sylvester in Vol. neatly bound.

B. Bourn, in Boards.

Ald. Burke.

Tho. Scott, in Vol. neatly bound

Richd. Matt. do do

Wm. Duer do do

Th. Jefferson in volumes neatly bound.

Edm. Randolph in volumes neatly bound

Tench Coxe in Numbers

Jeremiah Smith in vol.

John Laurance in volumes to be neatly bound

Elias Boudinot do do

Egbt. Benson do do

Theodore Sedgwick do do

Samuel Griffin do do

Jona. Trumbull do do

Wm. B. Giles do do

George Gale do do

Lamb. Cadwalader

Tho. Hartley do do

Jere. Wadsworth one in volumes one in numbers

John Vining

John Beckley one in volumes.

Hon. Ted. Tucker

J. Parker

A. Moore

Alex. White

M. J. Stone in volumes bound

J. B. Ashe

Wm. Smith S. C.

Wm. Floyd

P. Muhlenberg

Jer. Van Rensselaer

T. Tucherman in volumes bound

Abr. Baldwin bound

Ben. Contee, in Boards.

John Hathorn, bound.

Nh. Gilman, in Vol. neatly bound.

Henry Wynkoop, in Vol. neatly bound

Andrew G. Fraunces

Daniel Heister

Nathl. Niles

Joseph Sansom's silhouette of Franklin (1789).
(See p. xxxiv.)

State-House Square (1790).
(See p. xxxv.)

great Bulk compared to those of Europe it results from the Nature of Things that a navigation between the two Countries must be supported by Articles brought from the former to the latter,* and therefore as the far greater Number of Ships whether French or American must go home in Ballast no Difference of Duties laid on the Imports in America can materially affect the Navigation whereas a considerable Preference given to vessels of one Kind on the Imports in Europe amounts to a total Prohibition of all others.

It is evident from a due Consideration of Facts, that by the System now adopted the Revenue to arise from Tobacco can no longer be worthy of Consideration and must soon dwindle away entirely. It cannot therefore be doubted that the Assembly in their Wise Consideration have determined to replace it by other Taxes less burthensome and more consistent with the Rights of free Citizens§ and it is therefore to be lamented that this exceptionable System was not at once surrendered and the free Importation from the United States allowed either in French or American Bottoms as well as the free Fabrication in France because thereby not only the present Monopoly of Great Britain would have been destroyed but the greater Part of the Tobacco Trade would have been turned to this Country and eventually a considerable Consumption been thereby occasioned in America of the Productions and Manufactures of France.

It cannot escape the Notice of this enlightened Nation that intimate Connections of Commerce must sooner or later draw after them those of a political Nature. And altho it may be supposed by some that an Alliance with the United States is of no Consequence those who wish well to France cannot but wish that the Value of American Friendship may rather be estimated by sound Reason and preserved by prudent Conduct, than felt by painful Experience and lamented when lost. Those valuable Colonies which the greater mercantile Powers possess in the neighbourhood of and as it were Dependent on the United States excite mutual Cupidity; and a very slight Knowlege of Geography will shew that if in a War between those Powers the Forces be nearly balanced, America can bestow the Colonies on that Party which she may incline to favor even without the actual Commission of Hostilities. But this is a Subject of too delicate Nature to be strongly urged, and therefore the Arguments to be drawn from it with many others apposite to the present question will not here be debated.

* It is a fact well known that if a Vessel be hired to go out to America and take in there a Cargo for Europe no Advance of Price is asked for Articles put on board in Europe unless Delay be thereby occasioned.

§ If the Hypothesis be just that the Revenue drawn from Tobacco can be dispensed with in France it may be safely asserted that the Measure here mentioned would deprive Great Britain of that Resource; and every Body knows that she cannot replace it without serious Inconvenience or even Injury.

FC (DLC: Gouverneur Morris Papers); at head of text: "The following is Copy of the Paper referred to in the two foregoing Letters"—that is, the above letter to TJ and Morris' covering letter to Montmorin of 19 Feb. 1791, which reads: "Permettez Monsieur le Comte que je soumette a votre Consideration quelques reflexions sur les decrets relatif au tabac. Elles ont eté dictées par l'Attachement que vous me connoissez pour les interets de l'alliance entre la France et mon pays. Les principaux de mes compatriotes que se trouvent ici ont desirés que je vous les presentasse. Quoique je ne suis revetu d'aucun caractere public j'ai cependant cru ne pas devoir laisser echapper cette occasion d'etre utile a la France et aux's etats unis. Des circonstances du Moment qui vous sont connues me persuadent que vous appreceriez la force de mes Observations, et que vous vous efforcerz d'obtenir dans les decrets sur le tabac les modifications ou les changemens les plus propres a ecarter tout inconvenient. Je vous supplie surtout de n'attribuer qu'a mon zele la liberté que je prends de vous ecrire cette lettre" (FC in same; at head of text: "Public").

[1] In margin opposite this point Morris inserted the following tabulation of costs:

"Hogshead	6tt
Carriage to Warehouse	3tt
Warehouse Expences and Inspection	3tt
Carriage to Lighter	1tt
Craftage to Ship	6tt
Comn: on Cost and Charges	10tt
Freight &ca. 40 pt.	40tt
Insurance & Comn: on Making it 3%	8tt
Charges of Landing	2tt
Commn: on receiving &ca.	3tt
Average Loss which Insurers do not pay say about 2%	5tt
	87tt"

To Tench Coxe

Monday morn. [ca. 28 Feb. 1791]

Th: Jefferson presents his compliments to Mr. Cox and is much obliged to him for the inclosed pamphlet. He had received a copy the last year soon after it's publication. It was the first acknowlegement publicly made that England was an importing country as to bread. The report was written by Ld. Hawkesbury. The same thing had been satisfactorily proved before by a private hand in 1784. Can Mr. Coxe judge what the privilege of storage will be worth to the British bottom on each bushel of wheat?

RC (Dudley L. Vaill, Jr., Albany, N.Y., 1954). Not recorded in SJL. The letter to which the above was a reply is printed in Vol. 18: 461 at the end of 1790, though it was probably written later. TJ's reply is assigned to the last Monday in February 1791 because it was about this time that he was becoming concerned about British regulations providing free storage for wheat imports intended for other markets, against which he advocated retaliation (see TJ to Carroll, 4 Apr. 1791). The enclosed pamphlet was Hawkesbury's *Representation of the Lords of the Committee of Council . . . upon the present state of the laws for regulating the importation and exportation of corn* (London, 1790). See Sowerby, No. 3591.

TJ's letter to Coxe is revealing. In soliciting a calculation of the sort that made Coxe's mercantile experience useful, TJ seemed at the same time to be suggesting that other and prompter channels of information were available to him. Such a gentle curb on the overly zealous and at times officious services volunteered by Coxe must have appeared necessary at this particular moment (see Editorial Notes to group of documents at end of January and under 15 Mch. 1791). The publication of 1784 to which TJ alluded was probably Bryan Edwards' *Thoughts on the late proceedings of Government respecting the Trade of the West India Islands with the United States* (London, 1784) which TJ had sought to borrow from Coxe at a time his own books were unavailable (TJ to Coxe, 30 Nov. 1790).

To Philip Freneau

SIR   Philadelphia Feb. 28. 1791.

The clerkship for foreign languages in my office is vacant. The salary indeed is very low, being but two hundred and fifty dollars a year: but also it gives so little to do as not to interfere with any other calling the person may chuse, which would not absent him from the seat of government. I was told a few days ago that it might perhaps be convenient to you to accept it. If so it is at your service. It requires no other qualification than a moderate knowledge of the French. Should any thing better turn up within my department, that might suit you, I should be very happy to be able to bestow it so well. Should you conclude to accept the present, you may consider it as engaged to you, only be so good as to drop me a line informing me of your resolution. I am with great esteem Sir Your very humble servt,   TH: JEFFERSON

PrC (DLC).

From Aaron Vail

                                Philadelphia 28 March [i. e. Feb.] 1791
SIR   North Second Street No. 62

With an apology for intruding on your valuable time I beg leave to address you once more on a subject on which I have troubled you already several times.

I have sir, some time past determined on residing some years in France where I have found some commercial, and other connections that, to me are very flattering. The owner of the packets a very respectable merchant at St. Malo, and myself have entered into a copartnership to establish an American house at L'Orient under my direction with a capital sufficient to carry on a considerable commerce between that port and this country.

Under those circumstances I beg leave to submit to you a few hints on the utility of a Consul at that port and the preference that I flatter myself you will think me intitled, in Case you should think me quallified for the trust.

I have sir, at a considerable pains and expence introduced into most parts of Britany, and some parts of Normandy, the article of American flaxseed in which I have had to contend with the prejudices of the peasants and the jalousy of the dealers in that article, but by persiverence have so far succeeded that we may in future find a market for five or six cargoes annually consequently furnish voyages for so many American vessels. I have likewise made myself acquainted with the port, dockyards, and magazines of Brest, where with attention and perseverance we may find a market for large quantities of our ship timber Masts and other lumber, and sometimes provisions. In short, we may vend the above articles, rice tobacco, iron and naval stores, in the various ports in that province and its neighbourhood to which we intend to pay great attention and wherein I hope I shall have it in my power to render a service to my country as well as render the trade profitable to myself. There are many other commercial advantages that might be forwarded by the residence of an industrious merchant in that part of the country, but should I be fortunate enough to enjoy the confidence of the executive so as to have the appointment of Consul at L'Orient I flatter myself that I should have it in my power to render services to my country for which I feel a patriotic zeal, as that place has in its district many places to which American vessels will resort, and moreover L'Orient being the seat of the packets and no Consul appointed that will probably be a constant resident between Bordeaux and Havre de Grace I hope sir that I shall be so fortunate as to find those observations correspond with your opinion in which case I beg the favour of you to propose me for that place to the executive, and I hope by my future conduct you will be convinced that your confidence has not been misplaced.

I have sir mentioned to several Senators of my acquaintance my intention of addressing you on this subject who approve of my plan and promise me their friendship.

I have sir one object wherein I promise myself a material advantage in receiving this appointment before my return to france, which I would relate to you in confidence in case I should be honoured with a personnal interview, and I should almost promise myself your friendship.—I have the honour to be Sir Your Most Obedt Humble Servt,   AARON VAIL

RC (DLC: Washington Papers); endorsed in an unidentified hand: "this is the person recommended by Mr. Laurence of the Senate"; endorsed by TJ as received 28 Feb. 1791 and recorded under that date in SJL, but TJ's entry, which sought to correct Vail's error in dating, made another: "[1791. Feb. 28.] Vail Aaron Phila. Mar. [for April] 28."

There is no evidence that TJ replied or took action on this application. Nor does it appear that he responded to Vail's offer from New York a few months later: "I take the liberty to inform you that I shall sail on sunday next for france, in the packet, and to acquaint you that if you have any packets at [present] or any other time that you would wish to intrust to a private conveyance, or at least not in the mail, I shall request my friend Mr. Lewis Moore with whom I leave the directions of the packets in this place to pay particular attention to your command and you may depend on their being attended to at L'Orient, or should you at any time have oc-casion to procure any article from france that requires particular care you may forward your commands with certainty of their being chear-fully obeyed" (Aaron Vail to TJ, 6 July 1791; RC in DNA: RG 59, MLR; endorsed by TJ as received 8 July 1791 and so recorded in SJL).

To Daniel L. Hylton

DEAR SIR   Philadelphia Mar. 1. 1791.

I recieved yesterday your favor of Feb. 20. and should not so soon have troubled you with an answer, but that you mention that the Vis-a-vis has been long ago shipped for this place. This is the first news I have heard of it, and I imagined it still at your house. I now presume that some accident has happened respecting it, and will therefore thank you for the name of the vessel and captain by which it was to come, and such other circumstances as may serve as a clue to search into the matter.—I thank you for the readiness with which you have been so good as to undertake my little commission about the tobacco. I know that there was among my tobacco from Bedford certain hogsheads injured by having fired in the field. If the inspectors can point them out, be so good as to let only one of the fired hhds. come, as I have reason to believe they will not do here. I have great encouragement to bring this as well as my future crops here. I shall be determined by the sample I have asked you to send, which will be large enough to enable the tobacconists here to decide whether the quality suits them. If it does, I shall have the residue brought. This makes me anxious to recieve the twenty hogsheads. Present my affectionate compliments to Mrs. Hylton, and am Dear Sir Your friend & servt,   TH: JEFFERSON

PrC (MHi).

The vis-à-vis was one that TJ evidently had admired when he stopped with the Hyltons on 4 Oct. 1790 and for which he proposed an exchange with Mrs. Hylton, whom he also admired (see TJ to Hylton, 1 Mch. 1791). Adam Lindsay wrote from Norfolk on 4 Mch. 1791: "About three weeks ago, a box was sent to my house from Williamsburg, directed to you. I suposed some person had instructions to forward it but no one has apply'd. I take the opportunity of the Sloop Netty Capt. Cuningham of sending the box round to you. I shall be happy it arrives safe. Should there be any services in my power to render you here you may at all times command me. I had the pleasure of hearing by Mr. Hylton that Mrs. Randolf was well. I hope your little daughter is likewise so" (RC in MHi; endorsed by TJ as received 12 Mch. 1791 and so recorded in SJL). The vessel on which the vis-à-vis was shipped was evidently lost at sea (Hylton to TJ, 14 Apr. 1791).

From Lucy Ludwell Paradise

DEAR SIR   March ye. 1st. 1791   London

I hope you will pardon My troubling your Excellency with these few lines to make an enquiry after your health, and that of your amiable families: And to know at the same time if you have received a Letter I did Myself the honour to send you by Bishop Maddison. You will greatly oblige Mr. Paradise and Myself if you would let Us know by the return of the Spring Ships whether your Agent has remitted you the Money you were so good as to advance Mr. Paradise during his stay at Paris, as our Merchant Mr. Anderson has paid it to your Agent. Mr. Paradise joines with me in respectful Compliments to You, and your good family. Dear Sir I have the honour to be Your ever Obliged Friend,

                                        LUCY PARADISE

Please to direct your Letter to Mr. Anderson No. 10 Crosbey Squr. Bishopgate St.

RC (DLC); endorsed by TJ as received 26 July 1791 and so recorded in SJL.
Mrs. Paradise's LETTER . . . BY

BISHOP MADDISON was that of 26 Sep. 1790. There is no evidence that TJ replied to this or other letters from Mrs. Paradise until 11 Sep. 1792.

From Daniel Smith

Southwest Territory, 1 Mch. 1791. Enclosing proceedings of Gov. Blount. He has not thought it his duty to notice his proceedings as Superintendent of Indian Affairs.—Must requirement of Act of 13 July 1787 be met by submitting executive proceedings precisely at end of each six months or not exceed that time?—Judge Peery not yet arrived. Distance and danger of going from one district court house to another require that judges reside in territory, otherwise business cannot be done.

RC (DNA: RG 59, SWT); endorsed by TJ as received 21 Apr. 1791 and so recorded in SJL. Enclosure: Journal of Executive Proceedings of the Southwest Territory, 22 Oct. 1790

to 26 Feb. 1791 (same; in Smith's hand and signed by him as "A true Copy . . . March 1st. 1791"; full text in Carter, *Terr. Papers*, IV, 429-43).

From John Vining

SIR   [Philadelphia] March 1st 1791.

The Gentleman (Mr. Feliechy) whom I had the honor to mention to you, as a Candidate for the Consulate of Leghorn, is a Man of the highest reputation as well in this Country where he is known, as in that of which he is a Native. Having married in New York and lived some Years in this Country for the Purpose of establishing the best commercial Connexions, he has acquired every kind of knowledge, as a *Merchant*, which will be of mutual Benefit to our Trade and to himself. Added to this he possesses the highest Attachment imaginable for the United States.—I am sir with every Sentiment of respect your very Hu. Srvt. J. VINING

RC (DLC: Washington Papers); endorsed by TJ: "Felici by J. Vining Consulship of Florence. Recd. Mar. 7." 1791 and so recorded in SJL.

TJ took no action on this appeal, perhaps suspecting that Vining only echoed other sponsors of Feliechy: his letter in fact almost paraphrased that of William Seton to Alexander Hamilton of 3 Feb. 1791 (Syrett, *Hamilton*, VIII, 4-5). In the closing weeks of his term, TJ was again approached on the subject, this time by Seton himself. Again he failed to act. When Seton renewed the solicitation with Edmund Randolph a few months later, he explained that this was because no action had been taken on trade with the Mediterranean. "I am confident," Seton wrote TJ's successor, "that no Person residing in that Country has an equal Claim to his honor with my friend [Feliechy]. He has both before and since the Peace kept up a constant Trade with the United States, his Cargo's have been extremely valuable and the Duties paid on them amount to very considerable Sums, his Returns have always been made in produce from this Country, and by his knowledge and perseverance he has laid the foundation of a most valuable branch of Commerce whenever the Navigation of the Mediterranean will admit of it. He resided here some time, married a Lady of this City, and is from principle every way attached to America, which his unremitted attention to every thing relating to it evinces —and I can say with firmness that no Man will do more credit to the Appointment if he is honored with it. For the want of such a Character at Leghorn (as there are no American merchants residing there) the Trade labours under great difficulties with respect to the Certificates required by our Laws to cancell Bonds at the Custom House or to recover the Drawbacks on goods exported from here, which is the case now with the Cargo my House of Commerce exported in the Brigantine Minerva that was taken on her return home by the Algerines" (William Seton to Edmund Randolph, 29 Mch. 1794; DLC: Washington Papers). In this case Feliechy was at once appointed consul at Leghorn, but under the name of Peter Feliechy—an error that was corrected before the end of the year and a new commission issued under his correct name (JEP, I, 157, 158, 165).

To Pierre Charles L'Enfant

SIR March [2] 1791

You are desired to proceed to George town where you will find Mr. Ellicot employed in making a survey and map of the federal territory. The special object of asking your aid is to have drawings of the particular grounds most likely to be approved for the site of the federal town and buildings. You will therefore be pleased to begin on the Eastern branch, and proceed from thence upwards, laying down the hills, vallies, morasses, and waters between that, the Patowmac, the Tyber, and the road leading from George town to the Eastern branch, and connecting the whole with certain fixed points of the map Mr. Ellicot is preparing. Some idea of the height of the hills above the base on which they stand would be desireable. For necessary assistance and expences be pleased to apply to the Mayor of George town who is written to on this subject. I will beg the favour of you to mark to me your progress about twice a week, by letter, say every Wednesday and Saturday evening, that I may be able in proper time to draw your attention to some other objects which I have not at this moment sufficient information to define. I am with great esteem Sir Your most obedient humble servt.,   TH: JEFFERSON

PrC (DLC); at foot of text: "Major L'Enfant"; day of the month left blank. Entry in SJL is under 28 Feb. 1791, but the (missing) RC evidently bore the date of 2 Mch. 1791. FC (DNA: RG 59, PCC No. 120); day of the month also omitted. Tr (DLC: Digges-L'Enfant-Morgan Papers); at head of text: "Copy of a letter . . . dated March 1791"; signature and complimentary close omitted.

From James Maury

SIR   Liverpool 2nd. March 1791

I was honored on the 4th. past with your letter of 23rd. Decr. covering packets for Joshua Johnston Esqr. of London, and Messrs. Willink, Staphorst & Hubbard of Amsterdam, which were forwarded in the manner you directed.

I am in great hopes of soon receiving the Act you allude to in your letter of 26th. August; untill then I shall remain in doubt as to many things. I am frequently applied to by the Masters of Vessels and Crews to settle and determine their disputes, in such instances I invariably endeavor to accommodate, but have not considered myself warranted in doing more.—I pray your information as to this matter. Your instructions require me to take down the owners of the Cargo, in and out. This in many instances is impracticable; I can give you the Consignee here and the Exporter hence. Be pleased to say if this will do.

Since the approbation of my appointment only one American Vessel has departed hence, particulars whereof I have the honor to inclose you, with those of the Newbern which was wrecked on this coast in December; and supposing it might be acceptable I have procured from the Custom-house the most exact account I could of the departures for the last six months previous to the 1st.

January.—I have the honor to be with much respect Sir your most obt. St.,   JAMES MAURY

RC (DNA: RG 59, CD); endorsed by TJ as received 17 Apr. 1791 and so recorded in SJL. On a separate leaf Maury wrote the following and asked that TJ insert it in the *Gazette of the United States*: "The Captain of the Newbern and two of the crew perished on the wreck. I should consider myself extremely wanting in my duty were I to omit mentioning to you the very humane attentions the remainder of this unfortunate Crew experienced from the Inhabitants of this place. On understanding I was not provided with Funds for relief on such emergencies, a voluntary subscription was opened and more than fifty Guineas given them and their generous deliverers: some boatmen, who, at the risk of their own lives, had saved theirs, by taking them from the wreck. I have the Honor &c. J.M."

To De Moustier

SIR   Philadelphia, March 2d. 1791.

I have received your Favor of November 6th. wherein you inform me that the King has thought proper, by a new Mission to the Court of Berlin, to put an End to your Functions as his Minister Plenipotentiary with the United States. The President, in a Letter to the King, has expressed his Sense of your Merit, and his entire Approbation of your Conduct while here, and has charged me to convey to yourself the same Sentiments on his Part.

Had you returned to your Station with us, you would have received new and continued Marks of the Esteem inspired by the general Worth of your Character, as well as by the particular Dispositions you manifested towards this Country.

Amidst the Regrets excited by so early a Loss of you, it will be a Consolation if your new Situation shall contribute to advance your own Happiness. As a Testimony of these Sentiments we ask your Acceptance of a Medal and chain of Gold with which Mr. Short is instructed to present you on the Part of the U.S.[1]

To this general Tribute, permit me to add my own, with sincere Wishes for your constant Happiness, and Assurances of the Respect and Esteem, with which I have the Honor to be, Sir, Your most obedient and Most humble Servant,   TH: JEFFERSON

FC (The Rosenbach Company, Philadelphia, 1946); in Remsen's hand except for signature. Although in appearance this seems to be the recipient's copy, it is not, as proved by the inserted sentence (see note below) and Remsen's docketing on verso ("To the Count de Moustier March 2d. 1791"). PrC of missing Tr (DLC); at foot of text "(Copy)." FC (DNA: RG 59, PCC).

On the MEDAL AND CHAIN OF GOLD, see Vol. 16: xli-xlii, 356-7; TJ to Short, 8 Mch. 1791. It was TJ himself who first suggested that the KING . . . PUT AN END to De Moustier's mission in the United States (see TJ to Jay, 4 Feb. and 11 May 1789).

[1] This sentence inserted in text interlineally and marginally.

To Martha Jefferson Randolph

MY DEAR DAUGHTER   Philadelphia Mar. 2.

The present will serve just to tell you that I am well, and to keep up my plan of writing once a week whether I have any thing to say or not. Congress rises tomorrow. They have passed no laws remarkeable except the excise law and one establishing a bank. Mrs. Trist and Mrs. Waters always enquire after you and desire me to remember them to you. I hope you are by this time able to be about again and in good health as well as the little one. Kiss it and Maria for me. I have received her letter and will answer it next week. I inclose a letter for M. de Rieux. Present my esteem to Mr. Randolph.—Your's affectionately,   TH: JEFFERSON

RC (NNP). The letter from Mary was evidently that of 22 Jan. 1791 (see Mary Walker Lewis to TJ, 23 Jan. 1791, note).

George Washington to William Deakins, Jr. and Benjamin Stoddert

GENTLEMEN   Philadelphia March 2d. 1791.

Majr. L'enfant comes on to make such a survey of the grounds in your vicinity as may aid in fixing the site of the federal town and buildings. His present instructions express those alone which are within the Eastern branch, the Patowmac, the Tyber, and the road leading from George town to the ferry on the Eastern branch. He is directed to begin at the lower end and work upwards, *and nothing further* is communicated to him. The purpose of this letter is to desire you will not be yourselves misled by this appearance, nor be diverted from the pursuit of the objects I have recommended to you. I expect that your progress in accomplishing them will be facilitated by the presumption which will arise on seeing this operation begun at the Eastern branch, and that the proprietors nearer George town who have hitherto refused to accomodate, will let themselves down to reasonable terms.* I have referred Majr. Lenfant to the Mayor of George town for necessary aids and expences. Should there be any difficulties on this subject, I would hope your aid in having them surmounted tho' I have not named you to him or any body else, that no suspicions may be excited of your acting for the public. I am, gentlemen

* This communication will explain to you the motive to my request in a letter of the 28th. Ulto.—I now authorise the renewal

of the negotiations with Mr. Burns agreeably to former powers,¹ at such time and in such a manner as, in your judgment is likely to produce the desired effect.—I will add however that if the lands described by the enclosed plat, within the red dotted line from **A** to **C** thence by the Tiber to **D**, and along the North line to **A** can be obtained I shall be satisfied although I had rather go to the line **AB**.

Dft (DLC: District of Columbia Papers); in TJ's hand except for the paragraph keyed to text by asterisk, which is in Washington's hand with a few minor alterations, one of which is indicated below; at foot of text in TJ's hand: "Messieurs Stoddart & Dickens"; docketed by Washington: "To Messrs. Stoddart & Deakins 2d March 1791." Enclosure not found.

¹ Washington first wrote "directions," and then deleted it.

From John Joseph de Barth

au Roi Indien market street
ce 3 fevr [i.e., Mch.] 1791

Monsieur Jefferson est supplié d'agreer avec Bonté les homages Respectueux de M. de Barth qui a l'honneur de lui envoyer la Dent de l'Elephant Carnivore, ou plustot de l'animal inconnu dont il a été question à l'audience que Monsieur Jefferson a bien voulu accorder à M. De Barth. Il ajoute une peau Chamoisée Par les Sauvages d'un Jeune Buffalöe qui est un des plus petits de cette espece. Il sera aisé de Juger par la Douceur du poil de l'animal, qui est plus long dans ceux qui sont plus agés, combien il sera aisé d'en faire usage, non seulement pour des matelas et des Couvertures de Chevaux, mais encor pour de la filature, ainsi que M. de Barth en a fait faire l'epreuve avec Succès. Celui cy se propose d'envoyer ces Deux pieces en France d'ici une quinzaine de Jours ou trois Semaines. Monsieur Jefferson est bien le Maître de les garder aussi longtems qu'il Jugera à propos pour les faire voir à qui il lui plaira; et M. de Barth les fera retirer au premier ordre qu'il recevra de Monsieur Jefferson.

RC (MHi); endorsed by TJ as received 3 Mch. 1791; entry in SJL under that date reads: "Feb. 3. [for Mar. 3]."

De Barth's presentation of curiosities from the west may have been prompted by other than scientific motives: he was one of the unfortunate immigrants from France who had been victimized by the speculative venture of William Duer and others for the purchase of about five million acres of land between the Ohio Company purchase and the Scioto River. He and others had presented two addresses to the President in 1790 setting forth their distresses and Washington had assured them "of all that *countenance and protection* from the General Government of the United States, which the Constitution and Laws will enable the Executive to afford under existing circumstances" (Washington to Duchesne, De Barth, Thiebaud, and their Associates, 30 June

1790; *Writings*, ed. Fitzpatrick, XXXI, 64-5; FC in DNA: RG 59, MLR with last three words added by Washington). For contemporary descriptions of the difficulties of French settlers on the Scioto, see N. Y. *Daily Advertiser*, 25 May 1790 and 2 June 1790; see also Playfair to TJ, 20 Mch. 1791.

From Tench Coxe

SIR   March 4th. 1791

A large mail was received yesterday at the Treasury office in which was contained the enclosed letter. Presuming upon the care of the postmaster I did not look at the Superscription of the letter with much attention, and opened it as if to the Secretary of the Treasury. On reaching the 3d. or 4th. line, which has relation to a subject unconnected with the business of this department I was led to look to the signature and then to the superscription of the letter, and discovered with a good deal of pain that I had opened one of your dispatches. I trust, Sir, you will acquit me altogether of improper Intention, and that you will believe me when I assure you that I read no further than the 3d or 4th. line of the letter.

As I have my pen in my hand I beg leave to say that you will find enclosed the rough draughts of some returns of Tonnage made up in the form I had the honor to shew you. I think I can make some valuable additions in the general returns which is to be formed upon these. In their present state they exhibit interesting facts. After you have given them such inspection as you may desire you will be pleased to return them. They will not be wanted for a week or ten days.

I am of opinion on examining the documents in the Treasury that I can exhibit the imports in the same form, before the meeting of Congress.

I beg leave to repeat the offer of my services in collecting for you any materials that may be in my power towards the promotion of the Object refer'd to you by the house of Representatives. I mean the Navigation of the United States. Should any particular points of enquiry occur to you in which my application can be of use I shall deem myself favor'd by a minute of them at some time before your departure for Virga. prior to which I shall take the liberty to wait on you. I have the honor to be with the highest respect, Sir, yr. most obedt. & most hum. Servt.,

TENCH COXE

RC (DLC). Neither the above letter nor its enclosure is recorded in SJL, though possibly a letter from John M. Pintard of 23 Jan. 1791, recorded as received on 7 Mch. 1791, is the one that Coxe mistakenly opened.

The OBJECT for which Coxe pledged his aid was the preparation of the report on the privileges and restrictions on foreign commerce as required by HR 14 Feb. 1791 (see TJ's report, 16 Dec. 1793).

Jefferson's Affidavit Concerning Timothy Pickering, Samuel Hodgdon, and Levi Hollingsworth

Philadelphia Mar. 4. 1791.

Timothy Pickering, Samuel Hodgdon, and Levi Hollingsworth, citizens of the United States of America, having communicated to me their intention of sending agents to Europe to sell certain lands of theirs on Guyandot and Sandy rivers, and desirous that their propositions may stand on fair ground so far as may depend on their personal characters, I have made enquiry into their characters and find them to be men of truth and fair dealing, and I should not hesitate to give credit myself to any fact which they should affirm. But while I recommend the said Pickering, Hodgdon and Hollingsworth, as worthy of being credited for any facts they affirm, I must caution those whom it may concern, not to extend their confidence in this recommendation beyond the persons to whom it is confined by name. Knowing nothing of their agents, nor of what they may state as matters of fact, I must not be understood as vouching in the most distant degree for what such agents may say or do. Given under my hand at the time and place above-mentioned.   TH: JEFFERSON

PrC (DLC).

TJ's caution was no doubt induced by the rising complaints against the Scioto Company, particularly in France and among the French settlers on the Scioto, one of whom had recently called upon TJ (see note, TJ to De Barth, 3 [Mch.] 1791).

From William Short

DEAR SIR   Amsterdam March. 4. 1791.

I inclose you at present a letter for the Secretary of the Treasury which contains a copy of the bonds to be given here on behalf of the United States for the loan they have lately made. I am promised the private copies for the day after to-morrow which I am only waiting to sign, and shall then immediately leave this place for Paris. It will be probably in five days from hence.

On my return there I shall endeavour to obtain those alterations in the decrees respecting oils and tobacco which those who act for me there have been constantly aiming at. I cannot however too often repeat to you that it is impossible to form a conjecture either of what the assembly will do or undo on any subject. Their mode of deliberation and decision renders their being surprized into measures against their intention, unavoidable. Their decree with respect to tobacco may serve as an example. The difference in the duty paid between French and American vessels, suggested probably by some owner of ships, was proposed and passed without its being even suspected that such a proposition would be made. They had no idea certainly that it was a navigation act in a degree of vigor to which it was impossible that any country would submit without attempting to counteract it. You will have seen the debates on that question, which together with the present conveyance prevent my saying more on it. My two last letters sent in the same way gave you simply the decree on tobacco without comments. They will suggest themselves to you of course.

I don't doubt that you are fully sensible that the decrees of the assembly are so essentially the work of accident, of the force of parties and the force of circumstances, that no person in any situation whatever can control them; and of course that no person in my situation could have prevented those which have been passed with respect to the articles of American commerce. Still I feel that it is an unfortunate circumstance for me personally that they should have been passed during my residence. Time and experience will certainly correct them and that probably during the residence of some other person. In the minds of all the people in America, a very few excepted who like yourself search for and know the true causes of things, I shall have all the censure and he all the merit of these decrees and of their alterations, without its being more just in the one case than the other.

The affair of the *droit d'aubaine* remains as when I last mentioned it to you. The daily hope of its being brought on and decided in the assembly of themselves has prevented hitherto any thing being said about it except in the manner of which you have been already informed.

The King's aunts persevered in their determination to leave the Kingdom. An unsuccessful attempt was made to stop them at Moret. Beyond Dijon the same attempt was made with effect at *Arnay le Duc*. The municipality was for allowing them to pass, but the *conseil de la commune* were of a different opinion and prevailed. An express was sent to receive the orders of the national assembly, who determined that there was no law to prevent their going where they pleased, and referred the affair to the executive. This as was foreseen created much tumult, the people and *poissardes* immediately surrounded the Thuilleries in order to force the King to recall his aunts. The guard were obliged to be under arms to prevent their entering the chateau. This was the situation of things when the last letters left Paris. It is not until this evening, after the departure of the English post, that more recent accounts will be received.

There has been a mob also at Brussels, if not excited at least connived at by the present government. Count de Mercy and the States of Brabant have been for some time negotiating and disputing about the intended re-establishment of the council of Brabant. He has siezed the circumstance of these disorders as admitting no longer the suspension of justice, to re-integrate the council, which has been long his wish. At the same time he condemns the excesses of the people, endeavours to exculpate himself from the imputation of connivance, and assures the States he has taken measures for their future safety. In a situation like his however at present, with so much popular confidence and so many troops at his orders, permission and causation seem to be so nearly the same thing, that he will necessarily be considered as not averse to the excesses he condemns.—The same people who idolized the States a few months past, and who assassinated with all the horrors of rage and fanaticism a respectable citizen for having spoken irreverentially of a procession of monks, now forced the doors of the States and dispersed them after ill treating the members most active in the late revolution. They forced also one of the convents and threatened several others. It cannot fail to give the people an high idea of their force when they see themselves thus employed by the most powerful sovereigns. Accept the assurances of sincere attachment with which I am, dear Sir, your most obedient humble servant   W: SHORT

PrC (DLC: Short Papers); at head of text: "*No. 59*"; faded, and a few illegible words supplied from Tr (DNA: RG 59, DD). Recorded in SJL as received 21 June 1791.

To the Supervisors of the Excise

SIR   Philadelphia March 4. 1791.

The President of the United States desiring to avail the public of your services as Supervisor for the District of   I have now the honor of enclosing you the Commission, and of expressing to you the sentiments of perfect esteem with which I am Sir &c.

TH: JEFFERSON

FC (DNA: RG 59, PCC No. 120); at head of text: "(Circular)." Not recorded in SJL or SJPL. A form of the enclosed commission with a list of the supervisors and their districts attached is in DLC: Washington Papers, with a note by Remsen, who drew the form and the list, that commissions were issued 4 Mch. 1791 to the following: Joshua Wentworth for New Hampshire; Nathaniel Gorham for Massachusetts; John S. Dexter for Rhode Island; John Chester for Connecticut; Noah Smith for Vermont; William S. Smith for New York; Aaron Dunham for New Jersey; George Clymer for Pennsylvania; Henry Latimer for Delaware; George Gale for Maryland; Edward Carrington for Virginia; William Polk for North Carolina; Daniel Stevens for South Carolina; and John Mathews for Georgia (Tr also in DNA: ML/179). These nominations were presented at the convened session of the Senate on 4 Mch. 1791 and were confirmed the same day (JEP, I, 80-2).

The Admission of Kentucky and Vermont to the Union

I. REPORT ON THE POWER OF THE PRESIDENT IN NOMINATING OFFICERS FOR VERMONT, 19 FEBRUARY 1791

II. JEREMIAH WADSWORTH TO THE SECRETARY OF STATE 22 FEBRUARY 1791

III. REPORT ON CANDIDATES FOR OFFICE IN VERMONT, [23 FEBRUARY 1791]

IV. SECRETARY OF STATE TO THE GOVERNOR OF VERMONT, 28 FEBRUARY 1791

V. SECRETARY OF STATE TO THE PRESIDENT OF THE KENTUCKY CONVENTION (GEORGE MUTER), 28 FEBRUARY 1791

VI. DRAFT OF A MESSAGE FROM THE PRESIDENT TO THE SENATE, [4 MARCH 1791]

EDITORIAL NOTE

A piece of doggerel in Bache's *General Advertiser* at the opening of Congress voiced the politics of equilibrium underlying this first of a series of compromises for achieving sectional balance within the nation:[1]

> Kentucky to the Union given—
> Vermont will make the ballance even;
> Still Pennsylvania holds the scales,
> And neither South or North prevails.

But Kentucky had not been given to the union. Six years of persistent effort on the part of her people and their leaders lay back of the Virginia-Kentucky compact of 1790 which awaited only the approval

[1] *General Advertiser* (Philadelphia), 13 Dec. 1790.

of Congress to become final.[2] The ill-concealed sectional conflict over the rejection of Kentucky's petition in 1788 had aroused deep animosities and left mutual suspicion as its legacy. The memorial from the Kentucky Convention of 28 July 1790 asking the President and Congress to approve the unprecedented compact therefore took pains to point out what all other evidence seems to confirm—that the people of Kentucky in general were "as warmly attached to the American Union, and . . . to the perfect happy establishment of the Federal Government as any of the citizens of the United States."[3] In recommending that the necessary sanction be given, Washington also was careful to commend the spirit of loyalty that prompted the transaction between the Commonwealth of Virginia and the people of Kentucky: "The liberality and harmony, with which it has been conducted will be found to do great honor to both parties; and the sentiments of warm attachment to the Union and its present Government expressed by our fellow citizens of Kentucky cannot fail to add an affectionate concern for their particular welfare to the great national impressions under which you will decide the case submitted to you."[4]

On this occasion action was prompt. The committee of the Senate to whom this portion of Washington's address was referred reflected in its composition sectional concern as well as attention to the interests of Vermont and Kentucky. Its members were Philip Schuyler of New York, who as a great landlord and as an ardent supporter of Hamilton's measures had ample reason to keep a watchful eye on Vermont and to be equally wary of any increase in the power of the South and its hostility to the funding system; William Samuel Johnson of Connecticut, who had been an investor in lands in Vermont since before the Revolution and had helped keep its people from being coerced into accepting the jurisdiction of New York; and James Monroe of Virginia, who had been one of the most outspoken southerners in defending the interests of Kentuckians at the time of the Jay-Gardoqui negotiations. The committee reported favorably on the Kentucky memorial, and the only debate concerned Maclay's objection to the definition of boundaries in the bill. But, as Maclay himself admitted, the discussion on this point was conducted "entirely in the gentlemanly way."[5] The House of Representatives took even less time and on 4 February 1791 the bill admitting Kentucky to the union became law.[6] The petition from Vermont had not yet been presented to the President.

[2] See group of documents on the new policy toward Spain, Editorial Note, under 10 Mch. 1791.

[3] Memorial of the Kentucky Convention, 28 July 1790, enclosed in George Muter to the President, 4 Oct. 1790 (texts in JHR, I, 411-2; JS, I, 219-20).

[4] Annual Message, 8 Dec. 1790 (Washington, *Writings*, ed. Fitzpatrick, XXXI, 165).

[5] Maclay, *Journal*, ed. Maclay, p. 366. Washington sent the Kentucky memorial to the Senate and House on 9 Dec. 1790. The Senate committee was appointed on the 14th—Schuyler and Johnson having taken their seats the previous day—and reported on 3 Jan. 1791, when it was instructed to bring in a bill. It did so the next day and the bill was passed on 12 Jan. 1791 (JS, I, 219-20, 222, 228-9, 232; *Annals*, II, 1774-5, 1784, 1785, 1788).

[6] The House took up the Senate bill on 12 Jan. 1791 and passed it without amendment on 28 Jan. 1791. In accordance with the terms of the Virginia-Kentucky compact, the statute provided that on 1 June 1792 Kentucky should be

But Senator Schuyler and others in Congress who voted for Kentucky's admission were well aware that in the summer of 1790 New York had finally given up hope of sustaining the eastern limits of the grant of 1664 to the Duke of York and had come to terms with Vermont.[7] This bone of contention involving the titles of farmers and the interests of land speculators, however, had not been the sole reason that kept Vermont out of the union. Like Kentucky, she was growing in population and needed a commercial outlet to the sea. She was also politically divided. But the Allens and Chittendens who led one powerful faction were not the counterparts of James Wilkinson and Benjamin Sebastian of Kentucky. They combined ambition for political power with the aggrandizement of their private interests, to be sure, but they could look back upon an era of autonomous experience that from their point of view had been as successful as Kentucky's isolation had been frustrating. Their negotiations with General Frederick Haldimand in the last years of the war gave them reasonable grounds for hoping for a continuation of political power in an independent Vermont occupying the enviable role of a neutral state and having the advantages of being courted by both neighbors without being burdened by the necessity to support either. Ethan Allen, fresh from his abortive attempt to carve another independent state out of similarly disputed jurisdictions in New York and Pennsylvania, could not have made this dream more explicit than he did in his appeal to Lord Dorchester at the very time that Kentucky's petition for admission to the Confederation had been rejected by the Continental Congress.[8]

The people of Vermont, Allen declared in the summer of 1788, would refuse to join the United States under the proposed new Constitution. They believed that to do so would expose them to debt, ruin their commerce, and evoke the displeasure of Great Britain. Further, the states were divided and confused: "They are spread over different climates, have different religions, prejudices, customs, and interests . . . [and] the licentious notions of liberty taught and imbided in the course of the late revolution, operate strenuously against their uniting in any confederate Government." Even if the new Constitution were to be adopted, the large and influential minority opposing it would cause the government to be so weak as to make it "difficult, precarious, and probably im-

---

"admitted into this union, as a new and entire member of the United States of America" (JHR, I, 353, 366, 367, 368, 377; Annals, I, 1910, 1934; U.S. Statutes at Large, I, 168-9).

[7] By the terms of the settlement, Vermont agreed to pay $30,000 to the state of New York to compensate the "Vermont Sufferers." The proceedings between New York and Vermont are printed in Records of the Governor and Council of the State of Vermont, ed. E. P. Walton, III (Montpelier, 1875), 421-63. One of the sufferers, James Duane, stated that the bargain between the two states "was made by our [New York] politicians to obtain a new state to overbalance Southern influence, and in this paramount object with them compensation to the comparatively few landholders among her citizens was almost entirely overlooked" (same, III, 462, note 1).

[8] For an account of Allen's assistance to John Franklin in attempting to create a new state in northern Pennsylvania, see Julian P. Boyd, "John Franklin," Numismatic and Antiquarian Society of Philadelphia, Procs., XXXIII (Philadelphia, 1946), 35-49; also, "A Rare Broadside by Ethan Allen" by Boyd in festschrift for A.S.W. Rosenbach (Philadelphia, 1946), p. 18-44.

possible for the United States to subjugate Vermont." Small as she was, Vermont had much influence in American politics and might tilt the scales as she wished. She could put 15,000 men in the field in an emergency and count on the sympathetic support of neighboring states, for "besides her own natural population, she has a constant immigration from the United States, and whether whig or tory it alters not the case, as they remove to Vermont to obtain a landed interest, and to rid themselves and their posterity, from exorbitant taxation, very cordially unite in the policy of the state, in rejecting every idea of a confederation with the United States. . . . property not liberty is their main object." Allen spoke as if he were the ambassador of a sovereign state and, in urging a continuation of the favor and friendship of Great Britain, he pointed out the means of sustaining a delicate and mutually advantageous neutralism. He believed the policy followed by Haldimand to be the most prudent course, for "matters were so contrived between the General, and certain men of influence in Vermont, the last three years of the War that it answered all the purposes of an alliance of neutrality, and at the same time prevented the United States from taking any advantage of it." The leading men of Vermont, he assured Dorchester, were not "sentimentally attached to a republican form of government, yet from political principles, are determined to maintain their present mode of it, till they can have a better . . . or till they can in principles of mutual interest and advantage, return to the British government without war or annoyance from the United States."[9]

Clearly, with such assurances being given to the British government by one of the most influential leaders of Vermont at the very moment that a fully authorized representative from Kentucky was urging the Continental Congress in vain to admit his constituents to statehood, the political experiences upon which the people of Kentucky and Vermont could look back were quite dissimilar. Kentucky could count on no similarity of language, customs, and institutions in its neighboring power but upon forms of government, law, and religion that were unfamiliar if not uncongenial. A few of her inhabitants had been favored with bribes or commercial concessions, but Spanish efforts to detach the West from the union by these and other means had failed. The record of Kentucky's long effort to achieve statehood through constitutional means exhibited no genuine or widespread movement for independence or for a manipulated neutralism.[10] Vermont, on the other hand, had declared itself an independent republic in 1777, relying for justification upon legal doctrines that Jefferson found repellent.[11] The party of the Allens and Chittendens not only commanded a wide following at home: their overtures were also listened to with keen interest in Quebec and London. On his journeys between Quebec and New York, the British agent, George Beckwith, was careful to pay particular attention to the leading men of Vermont, finding among them as in the United States

[9] Ethan Allen to Dorchester, Quebec, 16 July 1788, enclosed in Dorchester to Sydney, 16 July 1788 (PRO: CO 42/60, f. 231, 233-9).
[10] See group of documents on New Approaches to Spain, Editorial Note, under 10 Mch. 1791.
[11] TJ to Randolph, 15 Feb. 1783.

government a group sympathetic to Great Britain. Indeed, the Allens' efforts to obtain a naval contract and to foster closer ties of friendship and commerce between Vermont and England were still in progress when their state decided to join the union. Levi Allen had left for England early in 1789 with instructions from the "Principal Men of Governor Chittendens and Allens Party . . . to Assure the British Court, that Vermont was truly from local situation as well as inclination firmly attached to them, and that whenever Vermont should find it necessary to Join Great Britain or Congress, they would positively Join the former."[12] As late as the summer of 1791, Allen—long out of touch with the changing scene of Vermont politics—still believed that, so long as Thomas Chittenden was governor, it was impossible for the state to have joined the United States. But later in the year, landing in Boston as Lewis Alden, and sustained with secret service funds, he hastened to Vermont and found to his mortification that the independent republic had in fact become a state of the union. "I think I may affirm without arrogance," he wrote to Henry Dundas, "that if I had got up the River St. Lawrence last year with the well chosen assortment of Goods; Vermont would not have Joined Congress; in fact a majority of Both houses now confess they are Very sorry, and feel themselves much hurt on hearing many advantages that would have accrue'd to Vermont had they remained Independent."[13] But during his absence Ethan Allen had died, Ira Allen had remained silent because his own lands were involved, and Chittenden had thought it imprudent to oppose the tide, "So that Poor Vermont had not a man of any considerable consequence to say a word for her real interest." Others looked to their own political preferment. "The facts are," Allen concluded his report, "a number wanted to go to Congress and tho' but four can go, yet 44 at least expected to be appointed."[14]

Place in the new government may have been coveted by many, but the commissioners who were authorized to state the case for Vermont, Nathaniel Chipman and Lewis R. Morris, came fully prepared to advance their own claims at the same time. On Saturday, the 5th day of February—the day after the bill to admit Kentucky became law—the two commissioners had their first audience with the President. They

[12] [Grenville] to Dorchester, 5 Sep. 1788 "(Private)"; Dorchester to Sydney, 13 June 1787, enclosing Levi Allen to Dorchester, 22 Nov. 1786; same to same, 18 Aug. 1787, enclosing proposal of Levi Allen of 2 July 1787 to furnish masts "as large as any ever cut in America" from lands on both sides of Lake Champlain; Henry Motz to Evan Nepean, 27 July 1788, enclosing proposal of Ethan, Levi, and Ira Allen of 24 July 1788 to furnish naval timber in accordance with terms published; Henry Motz to Evan Nepean, 29 July 1788 (PRO: CO 42/51, f. 6-8, 9-10, 119-20; 59, f. 271-3; 61, f. 1-7; 63, f. 134).

[13] Levi Allen, Ranelagh, to [Henry Dundas], 9 Aug. 1791 (PRO: CO 42/85, f. 371-2).

[14] Lewis Alden [Levi Allen] to [Henry Dundas], 27 Nov. 1791 (PRO: CO 42/85, f. 383; dated at Onion River, Vt.; entirely in Allen's hand). [Henry Dundas] to [Grenville?], 19 Nov. 1791, enclosing letter from the Rev. Samuel Peters of same date forwarding one from Levi Allen to Peters, dated Boston, 15 Oct. 1791, saying that he had arrived at noon from Halifax, that he had called on Dr. A. A. Peters of Boston who "gave him the signal of *Lewis Alden*" and advanced £100 sterling, and that he was about to set out on horseback for Vermont "to execute the Business I have so much at Heart" (PRO: CO 42/88, f. 159, 161).

came armed with various acts and proceedings of New York and Vermont that reflected in their meticulous choice of phraseology an old issue that had been finally settled but had left emotions still smoldering.[15] The Act of the New York legislature of 6 March 1790 designated commissioners with power to declare its consent that "a certain territory within the jurisdiction thereof should be formed and erected into a new state." But the wording of the actual declaration of consent several months later showed that Vermonters had refused to make such a tacit admission. It declared instead that New York granted its consent "that the community now actually exercising independent jurisdiction as the state of Vermont" should be admitted to the union.[16] Only in the Act of the legislature of Vermont convoking a ratifying convention was there any expression of purpose or of justification for the course taken. This Act merely declared it to be the opinion of the legislature that the "future interest and welfare" of the state required the matter to be placed before a convention of the people.[17] All other proceedings were only records of official action, not arguments of persuasion or protestations of attachment to the union.

Thus up to this point the Vermont proceedings were identical with the position assumed in the negotiation of the compact with New York —that is, that the issue was one to be resolved by compact, convention, or treaty negotiated between two sovereign and independent bodies, not one to be settled on the appeal of a petitioner for a grant or concession. Governor Chittenden's letter to the President transmitting the official Acts and proceedings merely announced that Vermont had "appointed commissioners to apply to the Congress of the United States." It made no request for action by the Chief Executive but only recommended the commissioners to his favorable notice.[18] Indeed, the commission that Chittenden issued to Chipman and Morris authorized and empowered them to "proceed to the Congress of the United States . . . and *negociate* on behalf of this state," as if their mission were only to conclude negotiations begun with New York and not, as in the case of Kentucky, simply to present a memorial for admission.[19] This purpose was made explicit in a document that neither Chittenden nor the commissioners saw fit to disclose to the President—the Act of the Vermont legislature that appointed Chipman and Morris, defined their authority, and gave directions to them in the conduct of their negotiations. This Act required them, first of all, to seek to have any measures of Congress on the subject so framed as to recognize and affirm the terms of the compact with New York respecting land titles, compensation, jurisdiction, and boundaries. It was even more emphatic in declaring it to be their "duty . . . in such act or acts of Congress as shall recognize the sovereignty and independence of this State to en-

[15] See note 7. For a general background of the controversy, see Dixon Ryan Fox, *Yorkers and Yankees* (New York, 1940); Hiland Hall, *History of Vermont* (Albany, 1868); Ira Allen, *History of Vermont* (London, 1798); Chilton Williamson, *Vermont in Quandary: 1763-1825* (Montpelier, 1949); C. M. Thompson, *Independent Vermont* (Boston, 1942).

[16] JS, I, 241-2.
[17] JS, I, 244-5.
[18] JS, I, 245-6.
[19] JS, I, 246. Emphasis supplied.

deavor that the same extend as far back as the first formation of government in this State." It made it their duty also to try to obtain for Vermont the right to have three representatives in Congress.[20] In brief, the commissioners were charged to negotiate terms of admission to the union as emissaries of a republic whose independence had been declared in 1777. Theirs was an embassy governed by instructions like those given to diplomatic envoys, not to be disclosed to those with whom the negotiations were to be conducted. In the light of this Act, Chittenden's communication to Washington takes on the character of a letter of credence from one head of state to another—but with the confused assumption that negotiations were to be carried on not with a minister of foreign affairs but with the legislative branch of government. This was precisely what commissioners from Vermont had done with the Continental Congress a decade earlier, but the adoption of the Constitution had rendered such a posture legally anomalous.[21]

When the commissioners had their first meeting with the President, they had not as yet prepared a petition or formal communication of any kind to the government of the United States. In the absence of Washington's diary for this period, it is not possible to know with certainty what transpired at this first interview. But, considering the terms of the Act appointing the commissioners, it is a plausible inference that the consultation, opening with the delivery of Governor Chittenden's letter to the President, took on something of the character of a presentation of diplomatic credentials. On the same basis, it is equally plausible to suppose that the question of procedure came up. Washington could scarcely have failed to observe the difference between this approach of envoys prepared to negotiate terms and that of the simple petition based on the Virginia-Kentucky compact which he had so warmly endorsed in his Annual Message. Always sensitive to the dignity of the national government and to the danger of establishing ill-founded precedents, he may possibly have pointed to the manner in which the Kentucky petition had been presented to him and laid before Congress. Such a procedure naturally would not have satisfied the categorical instructions set forth in the Act of the Vermont legislature. But the supposition that the President set his face firmly against any departure from the Kentucky precedent seems justified by two facts about this first meeting that are known with certainty—that he had agreed to see the commissioners again on the ensuing Monday at noon and that they were then to present to him an official communication stating the object of their mission.[22] The commissioners must have emerged from the meeting well aware of the fact that the office of the President of the United States would not be lent to anything properly describable as a negotiation on a question so important as that of admitting a new state to

[20] *Records of the Governor and Council of the State of Vermont*, ed. E. P. Walton, III (Montpelier, 1875), 485.

[21] Same, III, 231-65, 266-96, 341-56.

[22] Tobias Lear to Chipman and Morris, 7 Feb. 1791, asking them to make their communication at two o'clock instead of noon. He explained that the President had not been on horseback for several days "and finding it necessary for his health to ride frequently he intends to take a longer ride today than usual, and will not probably be in by twelve o'clock" (DLC: Washington Papers).

the union. For, as the official communication presented at the next interview proves, the posture of the envoys had been wholly transformed. They now approached the government not as negotiators but as petitioners. One feels justified in ascribing this remarkable transformation to the effect of their confrontation with the immense dignity and firmness of the President of the United States.

But there were also other influences that undoubtedly affected the result. Neither the President nor the Secretary of State could have known the full ramifications of the key role played by the Secretary of the Treasury in the settlement of the long controversy between New York and Vermont. This had begun with a letter that Nathaniel Chipman sent by express to Alexander Hamilton in the summer of 1788 stating in urgent and cogent terms the predicament in which Vermont had been placed by the adoption of the new Constitution. The essence of Chipman's plea was that the conflicting land grants acted as a bar to Vermont's admission to the union, since it was generally believed that the federal judiciary would sustain the New York titles. Governor Chittenden and others deeply interested in lands under Vermont grants, he reported, had in consequence "expressed themselves somewhat bitterly against the new federal plan of government." Chipman therefore thought that only confusion would result if Vermont were to be admitted unconditionally into the union. One of the conditions he suggested was that "the fœderal Legislature . . . might, on our accession, be induced on some terms to make a compensation to the New York grantees" out of their western lands.[23] Hamilton, then leading the Poughkeepsie convention to a triumphant ratification of the Constitution, thought that it was not only an opportune moment for Vermont to enter the union but also a matter of great public importance for her to do so. There were also particular circumstances that would expedite a proper accommodation of existing difficulties: "One of the first subjects of deliberation with the new Congress will be the Independence of Kentucky for which the southern states will be anxious. The northern will be glad to find a counterpoise in Vermont. These mutual interests and inclinations will facilitate a proper result." He therefore thought Vermont should ratify the Constitution as soon as possible and on condition that "Congress . . . provide for the extinguishment of all existing claims to land under grants of the State of New York, which may interfere with claims under . . . the State of Vermont."[24]

This was not the course that Vermont chose to follow. But in the negotiations leading to the compact between New York and Vermont two years later Alexander Hamilton was the guiding genius. Now in 1791, Nathaniel Chipman, who had first broached the idea of a conditional adherence to the union, was in Philadelphia confronted by a dilemma. The state he represented, claiming to be sovereign and independent, had made it his duty to negotiate with Congress about the

[23] Chipman to Hamilton, 14 July 1788 (Syrett, *Hamilton*, v, 161-2).
[24] Hamilton to Chipman, 22 July 1788 (Syrett, *Hamilton*, v, 186-7). Hamilton succeeded in dissuading Vermont from attempting to enter the union conditionally by attaching amendments to the Constitution or in any other way embracing the "impolicy of perplexing the main object with any such collateral experiments" (Hamilton to Chipman, Sep.-Dec. 1788; same, v, 218-9).

terms that had prompted his original appeal. The President, on the other hand, had certainly disclosed no inclination to advise Congress how to exercise its constitutional function of admitting new states. Although there is no recorded evidence to support the inference, it would have been remarkable indeed if, under these circumstances, Nathaniel Chipman had not again turned to the Secretary of the Treasury for advice and counsel. It would seem even more remarkable if Hamilton, the principal architect of the compact between New York and Vermont, had not had a hand in determining the tone if not the language of the official communication the commissioners were obliged to present to the President at their next interview.

For that remarkable document disposed of the dilemma by an abrupt departure in language, in procedure, and in substance from all other official proceedings of Vermont on the subject up to the interview on the 7th of February. It set forth no conditional terms of admission. It contained no expression of a desire to negotiate. Its tenor was that of deference and respect, leaving the decision to the wisdom of Congress and accompanied by hitherto unvoiced expressions of attachment to the union. It was exactly in the nature of the Kentucky petition and was addressed to "The President and Congress of the United States of America":[25]

> Nathaniel Chipman and Lewis R. Morris, commissioners, authorised and appointed by the state of Vermont, most respectfully represent, that the citizens of that state, having shared in common with those of the other states, in the hazards and burthens of establishing the American revolution, have long anxiously desired to be united with them, under the same general government. They have seen, with great satisfaction, a new and more perfect union of the people of America, and the unanimity with which they have recently approved the national constitution manifests their attachment to it, and the zeal with which they desire to participate its benefits.
>
> Questions of interfering jurisdiction between them and the state of New York have heretofore delayed this application. These points being now happily adjusted, the memorialists, on behalf of their constituents, most respectfully petition, that the Congress will consent to the admission of the state of Vermont, by that name and style, as a new and entire member of the United States.
>
> They have the honor to accompany the memorial with such papers and documents as have relation to the same, and, with the highest deference for the wisdom of Congress, the memorialists repeat their solicitations that, during their present session, they would be pleased to adopt such measures as will include within the national government a people zealous to support and defend it.

It is difficult not to believe that the character of this document which voiced such respect for the dignity of the national government and which so greatly transformed the role of the emissaries from Vermont was shaped in its essential features by the man who in 1788 had so accurately predicted an equipoise of mutual interests on the part of

[25] JS, I, 246, dated 7 Feb. 1791.

North and South leading to the admission of Kentucky and Vermont and who was now unquestionably in a position to assure the commissioners that adopting the manner and style of petitioners instead of negotiators would "facilitate a proper result."[26]

Even so, this petition and the Acts and proceedings accompanying it presented Washington with a troublesome problem, one that touched the exercise of constitutional powers. The petition was that of the authorized commissioners of "the state of Vermont," an insistence on terminology clearly apparent in the documents relating to the compact with New York and therefore different from the petition that had been presented by a convention of the people of "the District of Kentucky." Vermont had refused to be considered as being, in the terms of the Act of the New York legislature, "a certain territory within the jurisdiction" of that state. For the past fourteen years, as every informed person knew, all of Vermont's executive, legislative, and judicial proceedings had run in the name of a sovereign and independent community. If she was not a community emerging into statehood from territorial status and not one created out of another state with its consent, as in the case of Kentucky, was she then a truly independent republic, a foreign "state"? If so, of what relevance were the documents pertaining to the compact with New York? If not admitted by the consent of that state, should she come into the union by treaty arranged with the President and ratified by the Senate? Every issue that came before Washington in this critical month seemed to turn on constitutional points. In the face of such questions as these the President laid the documents before the Secretary of State and asked for his advice. The commissioners would have to wait another day for an answer to the question of procedure.

Jefferson's solution to the problem was such as to place all of the known proceedings before Congress, to accommodate the pretensions of both New York and Vermont, and to assume for the latter a territorial status that had no foundation in federal law. If his advice was set forth in a written report, it is not known to exist and is not recorded in Jefferson's register of public papers. But on the 8th, Tobias Lear informed the Vermont commissioners that it was the opinion of the President "as well as that of the Secretary of State that copies of all the papers . . . should be laid before Congress," that this would require copies for both the Senate and the House, and that these could not be prepared and submitted until the next day.[27] On the 9th the President, using phraseology that adroitly evaded all constitutional problems implicit in the idea of treating with an independent republic, sent the following communication to the Senate and House:[28]

I have received, from the Governor of Vermont, authentic documents, expressing the consent of the Legislatures of New York and of the territory of Vermont, that the said territory shall be admitted to be a distinct member of our Union: and a memorial of Nathaniel Chip-

26 Hamilton to Chipman, 22 July 1788 (Syrett, *Hamilton*, v, 186-7).
27 Lear to Chipman and Morris, 8 Feb. 1791 (DLC: Washington Papers).
28 Washington to the Senate and House of Representatives, 9 Feb. 1791 (JS, I, 241; Washington, *Writings*, ed. Fitzpatrick, XXXI, 212-3).

man and Lewis R. Morris, commissioners from the said territory, praying the consent of Congress to that admission, by the name and style of the State of Vermont; copies of which I now lay before Congress, with whom the constitution has vested the object of these proceedings.

This message exists only in a text recorded by a clerk, but its authorship and the useful legal fiction of regarding Vermont as possessing territorial status may with confidence be ascribed to the Secretary of State.[29]

But this practical mode of avoiding embarrassing constitutional questions did nothing more than pass the problem to the Congress, where Vermont's claim to statehood triumphed after all. The President's message and accompanying documents were referred in the Senate to a committee composed of Rufus King of New York, Oliver Ellsworth of Connecticut, John Langdon of New Hampshire, and Benjamin Hawkins of North Carolina, carefully chosen with regard to sectional balance. The committee reported a bill the next day which omitted all reference to the compact between New York and Vermont and provided that "The state of Vermont" by virtue of its petition should on the 4th of March and in "the name and style of 'the state of Vermont' . . . be admitted into this Union, as a new and entire member of the United States of America." The House concurred without amendment. Washington signed the bill into law on the 18th of February.[30] Senator Maclay, bitter over the excise bill, did not even deign to notice the undebated and ambiguous admission of Vermont to the union. The ambiguity was emphasized in the fact that federal law had not run in Vermont as it had in Kentucky. A special Act was therefore necessary to cause the laws, except in cases locally inapplicable, "to have . . . the same force and effect within the state of Vermont, as elsewhere within the United States."[31] Both branches of government had chosen ambiguity and evasion in preference to a confrontation of the troublesome question. Vermont had been admitted to the union neither as a territory nor as an independent republic but as an undefined community already possessing *de facto* but incomplete statehood.

On the 18th of February—the same day the President signed the bill admitting Vermont—the commissioners presented another trouble-

[29] The message is not recorded in SJPL, but this fact does not preclude the probability of TJ's authorship: a number of public papers written or received by TJ are not noted therein, including one from Washington to him on this same day (same, XXXI, 213). TJ's not uncommon habit of volunteering drafts of messages when called upon for advice, his training as a lawyer, his experience in diplomacy, and his habitual manner of seeking simple and practicable solutions are among the reasons for ascribing this message to his pen. The dateline "United States, February 9, 1791" is, of course, the touch of Tobias Lear.

[30] JS, I, 246, 247; JHR, I, 373, 377, 378, 381, 382. The members of the House Committee were John Laurance of New York, Elias Boudinot of New Jersey, and Daniel Carroll of Maryland.

[31] This Act created Vermont as a judicial district, annexed to the eastern circuit; provided for a district judge with a salary of $800; extended the census Act of 1790 to the state and directed the enumeration to be completed between 1 Apr. and 1 Sep. 1791; established the compensation of the marshal at $200; designated Alburg as a port of entry; and authorized the appointment of a collector (*U.S. Statutes at Large*, I, 176-7).

some question to him, one affecting their personal as well as public concern. Since Vermont would not be a member of the Union until the 4th of March, could the President nominate officers before that date? If not, could he do so after the Senate had recessed? These were questions for which ambiguous answers would not suffice and the commissioners discussed them with the President's secretary. Washington instructed Lear to request the commissioners to lay the matter before the Attorney General and the Secretary of State for their opinions.[32] This they did by letter and Jefferson submitted his opinion to the President the next day advising a special convening of the Senate.[33] On the 22d both commissioners applied for office. Nathaniel Chipman, who had been "repeatedly elected chief Justice of the Supreme Court of Judicature" of Vermont, sought the post of district judge and presented to Washington a testimonial from Governor Chittenden describing him as "the first Law character in this state" and as "an honest upright candid man."[34] Morris asked Washington to consider him for any office in Vermont for which he might be thought qualified, but bore a letter from Governor Clinton of New York stating that he was "desirous . . . to be Marshall of the District" and that, besides being respectably connected in a family known to the President, he was "a young Gentleman of good character and . . . well qualified to fill that office."[35] Washington asked the Secretary of State to sound out members of Congress and others about proper candidates and Jefferson, who included the commissioners in his canvassing, reported the results the next day.[36] On the 4th of March, in a message drafted by the Secretary of State in which the President set forth the reasons for the special session of the Senate, Washington gratified the desires of both commissioners and sealed the success of their mission both public and private.[37] Under suspended rules the Senate immediately confirmed the nominations and Jefferson dispatched their commissions the same day.[38]

Thus, yoked together in a silent sectional compromise that had its

[32] Tobias Lear to Chipman and Morris, 18 Feb. 1791 (DLC: Washington Papers).

[33] See Document I. The commissioners' letter to TJ is recorded in SJL as written and received on 18 Feb. 1791 but has not been found.

[34] Chipman to Washington, 22 Feb. 1791, enclosing a letter from Governor Chittenden "on the subject of appointing a Judge for the District of Vermont." Chipman added: "I flatter myself the contents of that letter will suggest a sufficient apology for my not delivering it before"; Chittenden to Washington, 25 Jan. 1791 (DLC: Washington Papers). For TJ's interview with the candidates, see Document III.

[35] Morris to Washington, 22 Feb. 1791, enclosing Clinton to Washington, 1 Feb. 1791 (DLC: Washington Papers).

[36] Documents II and III.

[37] Document VI. Washington's message convening the Senate to deliberate on "Certain matters touching the public good" was addressed to the President of the Senate and dated 1 Mch. 1791. Aaron Burr, who had been appointed to replace Philip Schuyler, did not attend, but six of those whose terms had expired and who had been reappointed were present on 4 Mch. 1791 and all save Charles Carroll presented their credentials. In addition to confirming the Vermont nominees, the Senate also confirmed the appointment of Arthur St. Clair as Major General, of the officers of the first and second regiments, and of fourteen supervisors of the excise (JEP, I, 79-84; see TJ to Supervisors, 4 Mch. 1791).

[38] JEP, I, 81. TJ issued commissions to the nominees on the same day (FC in DNA: RG 59, PCC).

origins in the critical summer of 1788, Vermont and Kentucky came into the union as equals, each being allowed two representatives.[39] Jefferson could scarcely have looked upon the past or the promise of these two border states with equally balanced detachment. He was well acquainted with the leaders of Kentucky, with the people who had settled there, with their desperate need for access to the sea, with their fundamental loyalty to the nation, and with their long struggle for admission to the union. Vermont was unknown to him except as a region of tangled and separatist politics, of disruptive jurisdictional disputes with neighboring states, of land speculations and intrigues with the British.[40] But he could not have been unaware of the signs of independence and liberalism in her unicameral legislature, in her abolition of slavery, in her free manhood suffrage, and in her provision for religious tolerance. Such aspects of the character of the newest border state were, in all probability, not absent from his calculations when he and James Madison decided a few weeks later to undertake their northward journey. The search for the answer as to which of these elements was dominant among the people of Vermont may well have been one of the chief objects of that journey.

I. Report on the Power of the President in Nominating Officers for Vermont

The Secretary of State having recieved from the Commissioners for the State of Vermont a letter proposing these Questions 1. Whether, as that state will not be a distinct member of the union till the 4th. day of March next, the President can, before that day,

[39] U.S. Statutes at Large, I, 169.

[40] TJ may have seen Hamilton's reply to Richard Harison in the New York Assembly on 28 Mch. 1787 which appeared in the *Daily Advertiser* (N. Y.), 5 Apr. 1787. Harison, representing the "Vermont Sufferers," had charged that the allegation that "the inhabitants of Vermont (having assumed actual independence) are forming improper connexions with the British in Canada, which at some period may be destructive to America" had no basis in fact and was "a mere phantom" (*Records of the Governor and Council of the State of Vermont*, ed. E. P. Walton, III [Montpelier, 1875], 426). Hamilton replied that during the latter part of the war a variety of circumstances produced a conviction of the existence of such a connection everywhere—"in the army, in the legislature, and in Congress." Furthermore, there were evidences that "Since the peace, this intercourse has been cultivated with reciprocal zeal." Hamilton found no reason to suppose such a connection had been dissolved; he perceived a number of "motives of immoderate interest which would dispose the British government to cultivate Vermont"; and he penetrated the attitude of the ministry as acutely as if he had read Grenville's dispatches to Dorchester or the reports of Major Beckwith: "It will no doubt take care to be in such a situation as to leave itself at liberty to act according to circumstances; but it will, and I have no doubt does, by the intermediation of its officers, keep up a secret intercourse with the leaders of that people, to endeavour gradually to mould them to its interest, and to be ready to convert them to its own purposes upon any favourable conjuncture or future emergency. This policy is so obvious and safe, that it would be presumeable, without any evidence of its existence" (Syrett, *Hamilton*, IV, 137-7).

nominate officers for it? and 2. if he cannot, whether he can nominate them after the recess of the Senate? makes thereon to the President of the U. S. the following Report.

He is of opinion the President cannot, before the 4th. of March, make nominations which will be good in law: because, till that day, it will not be a separate and integral member of the U. S. and it is only to integral members of the union that his right of nomination is given by the Constitution.

But that nomination may be made on the 4th. of March, and, if the Senate will meet on that day, may be reported to them for their approbation. It is true that the two or three new members will be absent, unless they chuse to come on for this purpose, but as the occasion of consulting an imperfect Senate will not be produced by any act of the President's, and as it is in the power of the new Senators to render the body perfect, by coming on if they chuse it, this difficulty appears smaller, than that of making original nominations without the concurrence of the Senate. This therefore is what the Secretary of State thinks best to be done.

TH: JEFFERSON
Feb. 19. 1791.

MS (DNA: RG 59, MLR); endorsed by Lear. PrC (DLC). Tr (DNA: RG 59, SDC). Entry in SJPL reads: "[1791. Feb.] 19. Report Th: J. on nominations on the accession of Vt."

II. Jeremiah Wadsworth to the Secretary of State

SIR   Feb 22 1791

Nathaniel Chipman Esq. is the most proper person in Vermont for District judge. I believe he is without a competitor in the state. Their present Attorney General is Samuel Hitchcock, but I do not believe he would relinquish his State appointment for a federal one as the latter would be less lucrative. Israel Smith Esqr. would be suitable for the office. There are other Lawyers in the State of some eminence—Stephen Jacob Darius Chipman Daniel Farrand Isaac Tichenor. I have placed them as they rank in my opinion. I should have placed at the Head of the list Stephen Rowe Bradly Esq. but I have no doubt he will be a Senator. At Allborough I know no person fit for a Naval officer. Stephen Keyes is a Man of education with little property, who I believe would remove from Burlington Bay for the office and could procure Bonds for the faithfull execution of the office.—I am sir Your H Svt.   JERE WADSWORTH

RC (DLC: Washington Papers); at foot of text: "The Secretary of State." Not recorded in SJL.

On the same day Theodore Sedgwick wrote TJ: "I have been informed this morning of the characters recommended by Mr. Wadsworth to fill offices in Vermont. I very fully, from all the information I have received, concur with him in opinion" (RC in DLC: Washington Papers; addressed: "The Honor-

able Mr. Jefferson"; not recorded in SJL). The next day Sedgwick joined with Fisher Ames in addressing another letter to TJ, perhaps on the same subject (recorded in SJL as received 23 Feb. 1791 but not found).—Wadsworth was correct in thinking that BRADLEY would become a Senator: he took his seat on 4 Nov. 1791 and drew by lot a four-year term (JS, I, 336, 337).

III. Report on Candidates for Office in Vermont

[23 Feb. 1791]

Mr. [Theodore] Sedgewick. There can be no competitor with Chipman for the place of judge. He is by far the most able lawyer in that state, a man of very fair moral character. The strait-laced old people think him not very orthodox in his religion.

Mr. [Jeremiah] Wadsworth. Chipman the first man for a judge. Bradly, a lawyer of eminence, remarkeable for his eloquence; not so steady a character as Chipman.

Mr. [Abraham] Baldwin. He and Chipman were at Yale college together. Chipman was then 23. years of age, a young man of great natural abilities and of as good an education as that place could give. His moral character was unexceptionable: his religious ideas latitudinarian. As far as he has had sight of him since, he has supported a solidly good character.

Mr. L. R. Morris and Mr. Chipman. On being asked, the latter was silent, the former said he had conferred with Colo. Wadsworth and Mr. Sedgewick who would write to me on the subject. I asked them particularly who was proper to be Marshal: he said they had named a person to Colo. Wadsworth who would write of him to me. On going away however, he said he had offered himself to the consideration of Colo. Wadsworth as Marshal. Colo. Wadsworth however has not named him in the preceding letter.

Noah Smith of Vermont (now in Philadelphia) The general expectation is that Chipman will be judge. He is a good lawyer and a good man. Governor Robinson is also a good man, and has been thought of by some. He is not of the law at all. For Attorney Israel Smith (brother of Noah) was spoken of by Colo. Wadsworth and Sedgewick (who conferred with Noah Smith). Isaac Tichinor is also a proper person. L. R. Morris and Stephen Keyes are the only persons thought of for Marshall. Both good and proper men.

Mr. [Caleb] Strong. He thinks it unquestionable that Chipman is the properest person for judge: and Tichinor is preferable to Israel Smith, for Attorney. He observes that in all the instances of persons named by their assembly to bring forward their claims, Tichinor has been one, which is a proof of their confidence in him, and a presumption that he deserves it. L. R. Morris is a very good man, and proper for the marshal. His present appointment shews he is respected.

MS (DLC: Washington Papers); entirely in TJ's hand; at head of text: "Substance of Conversations"; endorsed by Lear: "From the Secy of State relative to Appointments in Vermont. No. 3." PrC (DLC). Date established from entry in SJPL under 23 Feb. 1791, reading: "Vermont characters. Chipman. Bradley. Morris. Smith. Ti[chenor]."

IV. Secretary of State to the Governor of Vermont

SIR   Philadelphia February 28th. 1791.

I have the Honor to transmit to your Excellency an authenticated Copy of the Act of Congress for the admission of the State of Vermont into this Union, and of the Act regulating the Number of Representatives to be chosen by the States of Kentucky and Vermont, also two Copies of the Acts passed at the first and second Sessions of the Congress of the United States.

Permit me at the same time through the Channel of your Excellency, to lay before the Legislature of your State, an authentic Copy of the articles in addition to, and amendment of, the Constitution of the United States, proposed by Congress to the Legislatures of the several States for their Ratification, pursuant to the fifth article of the original Constitution.—I have the Honor to be with great Respect, Your Excellency's Most obedient & most humble servant,   TH: JEFFERSON

RC (VtMS); at foot of text: "His Excellency Thomas Chittenden Esquire"; in clerk's hand except for signature by TJ. FC (DNA: RG 59, PCC No. 120). Not recorded in SJL or SJPL.

In the office of the Secretary of State in Montpelier, Vermont, there is a collection of printed Acts of Congress signed and attested by TJ between 25 Feb. 1791 and 2 Mch. 1793, many in duplicate and one in triplicate. These

Acts, numbering forty-three separate titles, constitute perhaps the largest group of Acts attested by TJ as Secretary of State to be found in any state archives. The second of the Acts mentioned above has the seal affixed to a separate sheet and attached by ribbon to the printed text; the attestation in a clerk's hand and TJ's signature appear below the seal. Another copy of this printed text bears the statement above TJ's signature: "Deposited among the Rolls in the Office of the Secretary of State"; beneath this Henry Remsen wrote: "Mr. Childs will please to ob-serve, that since the words 'Deposited among the rolls &c.' have been substituted for the words 'A true copy,' it will be unnecessary and perhaps improper to continue the use of the latter—from his h'ble Servt. H. R. Junr." (RC in PHC; addressed "Messrs. Childs & Swaine printers New York"; postmarked 27 Feb. [1791] and franked by TJ).

The amendments to the Constitution that TJ enclosed were the twelve proposed to the states on 25 Sep. 1789. Vermont ratified all of them on 3 Nov. 1791.

V. Secretary of State to the President of the Kentucky Convention (George Muter)

SIR   Philadelphia Feby. 28. 1791.

I have the honor to acknowledge the receipt of your letter of October 4. 1790. to the President of the United States, and to enclose you in return, an authenticated copy of the act of Congress declaring the consent of Congress that a new State be formed within the jurisdiction of the Commonwealth of Virginia and admitted into this union by the name of the State of Kentucky, and also of their Act regulating the number of Representatives to be chosen by the States of Kentucky and Vermont, of which I must beg the favor of you, as late President of the Convention of Kentucky, to cause due promulgation to be made. I have the honor to be with great respect Sir &c.   TH: JEFFERSON

FC (DNA: RG 59, PCC No. 120). Not recorded in SJL or SJPL.

VI. Draft of a Message from the President to the Senate

GENTLEMEN OF THE SENATE   [4 March 1791]

The 'Act for the admission of the state of Vermont into this union' having fixed on this, as the day of it's admission, it was thought that this would also be the first day on which any officer of the Union might legally perform any act of authority relating to that state. I therefore required your attendance to recieve nominations of the several officers necessary to put the federal government into motion in that state.

For this purpose I nominate &c. [Nathaniel Chipman to be judge of the district of Vermont; Stephen Jacobs [Jacob] to be attorney for the United States in the district of Vermont; Lewis R. Morris to be marshal of the district of Vermont, and Stephen Keyes to be collector of the port of Allburgh, in the State of Vermont.][1]

Dft (DLC); entirely in TJ's hand. Entry in SJPL reads: "[1791. Mar.] 4. Message to Senate on reasons for calling them, to wit, Verm[ont]." FC (DLC: Washington Papers); see note 1 below.

[1] Brackets and matter enclosed therein supplied from FC.

The Judicial Appointment of Joseph Anderson

EDITORIAL NOTE

Joseph Inslee Anderson's first appointment to civil office initiated a long career on the bench, in the Senate, and in the federal administration.[1] But it brought anxiety and embarrassment to the candidate, disturbed his political sponsors, and, for the first time, obliged the President to confront the question whether he should withhold a commission even after the Senate had confirmed his nominee. The candidacy of Anderson began in the summer of 1790 and culminated in the hectic closing hours of the first Congress. At the last moment the President passed the prickly nettle to the Secretary of State, placing in his view only a part of the information that had been gathered over a tortuous course during the preceding eight months. Under the circumstances, Jefferson's brief and hasty opinion was perhaps the only one permissible and it may stand justified in the event. But it brought injury to another Revolutionary officer whose record was quite as worthy as that of the

[1] Joseph Inslee Anderson (1757-1837)—who seems to have 'ropped his middle name on entering public life—was judge of the Southwest Territory from 1791 to 1797; Senator from Tennessee from 1797 to 1815, being appointed initially to fill out the unexpired term of William Blount who had been expelled; and Comptroller of the United States from 1815 to 1836 (biographical sketch in DAB, but must be used with caution). As Comptroller, Anderson had to face the problem of unsettled accounts with the United States (see White, *The Jeffersonians*, p. 168).

candidate and whose appeals for rectification were coldly ignored by the President. The bungled episode casts some light on the manner in which Washington handled matters of patronage and on his relations with Jefferson in dispensing it.

Two weeks after the Act creating a government for the Southwest Territory was passed, Joseph Anderson announced to the President his wish to be appointed as one of the judges in that jurisdiction. He had previously held no state or federal office, but had risen to a captaincy in the Third New Jersey Regiment and had been breveted major. On leaving the army he had studied law in New Jersey. In his letter of application he asserted that he was licensed to practice "in several of the Supreme Courts of the United States." He also stated that he was obliged to seek office because he had "sustain'd *great Losses* from *ill reposed* Confidence," but he did not elaborate. He submitted written testimonials supporting his good character and in addition referred the President to Senators William Paterson of New Jersey and George Read of Delaware. Washington was impressed enough to confer with both men.[2] Paterson, who knew Anderson only as a military officer, questioned the adequacy of his legal preparation. On learning of this the candidate explained to the President that, after preparing himself for the law in New Jersey, he had gone to Delaware to settle the affairs of his father who had died there intestate. Though licensed to practice in that state, he had not done so. He had instead applied himself to intensive study in order to be admitted to the Pennsylvania bar, whose "rules of admission . . . were more strict than those of any other state in the Union." He had been licensed in 1787 to practice in Pennsylvania, but, being determined to move to the western part of the state, he had not deemed it prudent to begin practice for so temporary a stay. He was prepared, he stated, to take any sort of examination to test his fitness for the post. Doubts raised by so able a lawyer as Paterson must have carried some weight, yet Washington sent word to the Senator that he was satisfied with Anderson's testimonials.[3]

The very next day, however, Paterson interposed an even more effective barrier between the candidate and the realization of his ambition. It now appeared that Anderson's account with the United States as paymaster of the Third New Jersey Regiment had never been settled. Whether the officer had been previously aware of this fact or not, he was given the information shortly before soliciting appointment but did not disclose it. On learning, however, that the delayed settlement might operate to bar him from "any Public appointment . . . *for ever*," as he interpreted the President's position, he reacted to the severe blow with a long and earnest attempt at justification. He explained that, shortly before the dissolution of the army, he had been granted leave

2 Anderson to Washington, 11 June 1790 (DLC: Washington Papers). An endorsement by Lear shows that Anderson's testimonials were returned to him on 21 June 1790. These were later made available to TJ, having been resubmitted by Anderson on 17 Feb. 1791 (see notes 13 and 14). In addition to these testimonials, TJ probably had access to the letters of Anderson and Vining here printed, together with the certificate of Jaquett and the letter of testimonial from an unidentified Philadelphian enclosed in Anderson's letter to Washington of 1 Mch. 1791.

3 Anderson to Washington, 23 June 1790 (DLC: Washington Papers).

of absence until commanded to return. Since he was absent at the time the army was dissolved, the commanding officer of the First New Jersey Regiment (with which his own had been merged) had ordered its paymaster to take Anderson's books and "make a Settlement of the whole accounts." Anderson said he had assumed that such a settlement had been made because the paymaster "detained at that time the *Particular* sum of one hundred and eighty dollars and fifty seven nintieths . . . due from me to the Public on Settlement of my Accounts." He was confirmed in this assumption, he added, because the Paymaster General after first deducting this amount had issued certificates of the balance due him and these certificates revealed on their face "that on the *final Settlement* of Accounts between the United States and *Joseph I. Anderson* there *remains* due to him *so many* hundred Dollars." Anderson stated that he took this acknowledgment to supersede all claims of the United States against himself even though "no entry of Settlement appears on the face of the books." He added that he had always considered the accounts as having been "*fully* and *finally* settled," but that, if the President would postpone the nomination for two or three weeks, he would go in search of his books. He was not even aware whether these had ever been returned to him, but he thought it would be "a *very hard* case" if his misfortunes should have the effect of crimes merely because of "the Omission or Carelessness of Clerks." But Washington had already directed his secretary to inform Senator Paterson that Anderson, as "*Circumstanced at present*," could not be given the nomination even though his testimonials were fully satisfactory. Paterson informed the candidate, and the disappointed office-seeker immediately asked for a personal interview with the President. This was not granted. Anderson dispatched further letters to Washington in an effort to justify himself, but without effect. He thereupon embarked upon a search for his paymaster's records so that he might exculpate himself from the charge of "Voluntary delinquency."[4]

It was unfortunate that these records were not available at the time Anderson attempted to justify himself. For the fact is that his assumption concerning "the *Particular* sum" of $180 $^{57}\!/_{90}$ and his inference drawn from the statement on the face of his certificates of pay were both erroneous. That amount was not, in fact, owed by Anderson to the public but just the reverse. It represented his subsistence allowance as an officer and it had been withheld specifically as a condition and perhaps as a means of compelling settlement of his account. It is puzzling that this fact should have escaped Anderson's recollection. He must have been informed of the reason for retaining the amount owed by the public at the time his certificates for back pay were issued to him. Further, if he was able to ascertain shortly before applying for office

---

[4] Anderson to Washington, 23, 24, and 25 June 1790 (same), the second of which enclosed an unidentified letter (not found). All of Anderson's letters to Washington in 1790 were written from New York, those in 1791 from Philadelphia. All were addressed simply "George Washington Esquire President of the United States"—an outward reflection of the widespread public resentment over the discussion in the Senate concerning titles in 1789 (Maclay, *Journal*, ed. Maclay, 22-9, 31-8; TJ to Madison, 29 July 1789). In his letters, however, Anderson made elaborate use of the honorific "Your Excellency."

that "no entry of Settlement" appeared on the face of the books, it seems likely that he would have learned at the same time the nature and contingency of the balance due him. Yet, puzzling as it seems, he forgot or was unaware of the actual state of the balance until, at the time of renewing his application for the judgeship early in 1791, he came across the following entry at the foot of the summary statement of his account as paymaster of the Third New Jersey Regiment: "By subsistence retained till he settles his Public Accounts—180 57/[90]."[5] When he did make the discovery, he did not trouble to correct his earlier opinion that fixed responsibility on "the Omission or Carelessness of Clerks." It was not the last time that Anderson placed the blame elsewhere.

While Washington had not granted the request for a postponement of the appointment for two or three weeks to permit the applicant to search for his books, he waited longer than that before making an overt move to find a substitute candidate. Evidently committed to the idea of selecting someone from Delaware for the judicial post, he eventually turned for suggestions to the other Federalist Senator from that state, Richard Bassett. Bassett recommended William Peery, one of his constituents. Washington promptly sent his name to the Senate and confirmation followed the next day.[6] But Peery ultimately declined the office on account of age and personal concerns, entrusting delivery of his letter of declination to Delaware's single member of the House of Representatives, John Vining.[7] The fact that Peery had allowed four and a half months to elapse before rejecting the commission, during which time Anderson was busily engaged in an attempt to straighten out his army account, suggests at least the possibility that the eventual result may have been designedly anticipated in order to indulge the candidate with the time for searching and settlement that had been denied him. Certainly there was ample opportunity between Anderson's rejection and the proposal of Peery's name for the Delaware Senator to have discovered whether his nominee wished to be considered as a candidate. Other candidates may also have been advanced in the summer of 1790, as was certainly the case later when Peery's resignation created a vacancy.[8] But whether he learned of it from Vining or someone else, Anderson was among the first to know that a vacancy existed. Within two weeks after the resignation was sent in he renewed his application for the office.

[5] MS summary of account of "Capt. Joseph I. Anderson" from May 1779 to May 1781, evidently copied from the books of the Paymaster General and employed by Henry Knox in preparing his report on Anderson's petition (DLC: Washington Papers). Anderson evidently left the army in 1781. In 1782 he indicated his willingness to resign in an exchange of places with Captain Francis Barber. But, despite Washington's warm approval arising from his esteem for Barber, the arrangement fell through when officers junior to Anderson objected (Washington, *Writings*, ed., Fitzpatrick, XXIV, 62, 80).

[6] Richard Bassett to William Jackson, 30 July 1790 (DLC: Washington Papers); Washington to the Senate, 2 Aug. 1790 (JEP, I, 53, 54); TJ to Peery (Perry, Pery), 3 Aug. 1790, enclosing commission (DNA: RG 59, PCC).

[7] William Peery to the President, 24 Dec. 1790 (DNA: RG 59, MLR, with endorsement showing it was delivered by John Vining; Carter, *Terr. Papers*, IV, 40).

[8] See Sevier to TJ, 17 Jan. 1791.

Immediately after writing the last of his explanatory letters to the President in the summer of 1790, Anderson had set out to find his records and effect a settlement. He found the books but discovered that one of them "(by some fatality) had receipts torn out of it, to the amount of near fifty thousand Dollars," thus making a settlement "impracticable." In view of this misfortune, he had been obliged to petition Congress on the matter. His petition is not known to exist, but in addition to other explanations for the delayed settlement, it may have contained that now advanced by the candidate in a letter to the President:

> By what remains of my receipt books, it appears that I have receiv'd from the General Pay Office (and paid to the Regiment) upwards of twenty thousand dollars, more than I am charg'd with.—To this circumstance I apprehend it may be owing that my accounts . . . remain open, Mr. Pearce[9] probably not being able to satisfy himself respecting it, or to account to the Public, for so great a difference, between the sums charg'd to me as Pay Master, and the sums for which, I *then had receipts*, which I apprehend Mr. Pearce must have noticed when going over my Pay Books, with the Pay Master [of the First New Jersey Regiment] whom I supposed had finally settled my Accounts.

This "mistake of twenty thousand Dollars" Anderson explained by saying that he had commanded a company of light infantry under Lafayette in 1780 and that the nature of the campaign had precluded the filing of abstracts of pay, forcing him to draw the money for the Regiment on account and sometimes through other officers. The sum in which the mistake was made was drawn by Colonel Francis Barber on a warrant from Washington himself under date of 28 August 1780, but not charged to Anderson as paymaster or accounted for by Barber's agent on the settlement of his account with the United States. Anderson offered this explanation as "the *most probable* . . . Cause" of his having been made to appear a delinquent and concluded with a renewed solicitation of the President's favor:[10]

> it has been suggested to me, that the office . . . which I formerly solicited . . . is at present vacant by the *Resignation* of Mr. Perry. If it shou'd remain so, until the Settlement of my Public account is *Effected*, I hope your Excellency will not think me presumptuous, if I again solicit you for that appointment.—My fortune at present is Humble, my *real friends* are *Consequently* few; and I have never yet mov'd in the sunshine of favour.

But apparently there were some real friends who stood ready to lead him into the sunshine. Three days earlier Congress had referred his petition to the Secretary of War.[11] Whether or not Anderson was aware that another candidate for the office he was seeking had just been recommended to the Secretary of State, he was understandably

[9] John Pierce, then Paymaster General.
[10] Anderson to Washington, 7 Jan. 1791 (DLC: Washington Papers).
[11] Anderson's petition was laid before the House on 4 Jan. 1791 (JHR, I, 349).

concerned at any delay on his own petition.[12] He therefore lost no time in pressing his cause at the War Office. He was so insistent or possessed such influential political support that he was able to induce the Secretary of War to make his anticipated recommendation in the case known to the President even before his report to Congress had been drafted. This Knox did for the specific purpose of aiding Anderson in his candidacy:[13]

> Major Anderson [he wrote to Washington's secretary, Tobias Lear] has petitioned Congress that he may be allowed to settle his accounts as pay master in the late army, notwithstanding certain resolves of limiting settlements combined with claims against the United States. His petition has been referred to me, and it has been investigated so far as that a satisfactory judgment is made on his case.—Although he cannot receive anything which may be due him, and there does appear a small balance in his favor, yet I shall report, that his accounts be closed; and I presume on such principles as will be adopted. I mention this circumstance to you as the Major informs me he has some application for an appointment before the President, with which, his not having settled his accounts, would perhaps militate.

The fact that Anderson pressed for and obtained this advance summary of Knox' report and that he immediately forwarded it to the President suggests that he regarded it as conclusive. The House of Representatives, however, had forwarded the petition to the Secretary of War with instructions to examine and report upon it. Knox' letter to Lear shows that he understood this requirement. Yet, in the three weeks that elapsed before he drafted his report, something transpired to alter its nature so as to make its effect depend not on such principles as Knox presumed would be adopted but on his own determination. In the report as finally drawn Knox recited the facts presented in Anderson's memorial, which were substantially the same as those previously set forth in the candidate's letters to Washington, and gave it as his opinion that, as Anderson had relinquished the balance due him and as his only object was "to obtain the settlement of his account, and not any allowance or payment, it would seem reasonable that it should be granted, as much as if it appeared on the public books, that he was a debtor for any Sum, and being compelled to make a payment, the account should then be ballanced." This was indeed a plausible premise. But Knox' conclusion that the "Account of the Memorialist will therefore be settled by the Commissioner of Army Accounts, and any Act of Congress thereon will be unnecessary" was an administrative decision that conflicted both with the intent of the resolution of the House of Representatives and with his own earlier indication to Lear that he would defer the ultimate decision to that body.[14] Nevertheless, this

[12] See Sevier to TJ, 17 Jan. 1791.
[13] Knox to Lear, 20 Jan. 1791 (DLC: Washington Papers); the "certain resolves" were those of 2 Nov. 1785 precluding adjustment or allowance of claims for military service after 1 Aug. 1786 (JCC, XXIX, 866).
[14] Anderson to Lear, 23 Jan. 1790 [i.e., 1791] (DLC: Washington Papers); Report of Knox to HR, 8 Feb. 1791 (DNA: RG 15, Pension Files, J. I. Anderson, N.J., W 23449; Tr attested by John Beckley).

was the controlling determination. On the very day that Congress received and tabled Knox' report, Joseph Howell, Acting Commissioner of Army Accounts, gave effect to the decision. Two days later Anderson assured the President that he had "with some trouble Obtain'd a final settlement." He submitted various papers to support this statement, including Knox' report and Howell's certificate. Assuming that he had at last been cleared, he renewed his application for office:[15]

> Permit me therefore Sir, Once more to Solicit . . . the Office of Judge now vacant by Mr. Perry's resignation.—When I first presum'd to address Your Excellency upon this Subject I presented several Certificates which Your Excellency may possibly recollect. But least through the excess of business, their support shou'd now be forgotten, I again beg leave, to offer the Certificates of my Military Character, and a Certificate of my Admission, as a Councellor at Law, in the Supreme Court of the United States, which I had not before the Honor of presenting to Your Excellency.—The foregoing Testimonials I with great Deference Submit to Your Excellencys *Consideration.* And if Sir, they can give a *Sanction* to my request and Your Excellency shou'd think proper to Honor me with the appointment, I shall *Study* to *deserve* the *Honor*, and *Confidence* thereby Confered.

But once again, just as the eagerly sought prize seemed within grasp, another formidable obstacle arose. Tobias Lear, acting on Washington's instructions, informed Anderson that a report to his disadvantage had come to the President. The exact nature of Lear's information remains in doubt and the manner in which the report came to Washington was as unknown to the candidate as it is to history. But it is clear that the rumor involved a transaction between Anderson and Peter Jaquett of Wilmington, a fellow officer and member of the Society of the Cincinnati.[16] John Vining was familiar with the history of the transaction, but at this time he was friendly to Anderson's candidacy, as were the two Senators from Delaware. Jaquett himself is not likely to have originated such a report since, as subsequent developments proved, his own interest was involved in the appointment. Whatever the source or

---

[15] Certificate of Joseph Howell, 15 Feb. 1791, stating in part: "and whereas the receipts for the expenditure of this money [charged to Anderson on the books of the Paymaster General] only in part appears by reason of many being destroyed by accident, I therefore certify that I have examined the receipts which do appear, and from this examination am of opinion, that the Accounts . . . were regular and kept agreeably to the Acts of Congress, but casualties in the Army of the United States, [dai]lly arising by Deaths, Desertions or otherwise, there were few persons who acted as paymasters to Regiments who had not on settlement of their accounts a balance in their hands. I have therefore (in consequence of part of the Vouchers being destroyed . . . and the evidence before me) commuted the balance . . . which might be in the hands of the said Joseph I. Anderson, with a sum retained from him by the late Commissioner of Army Accounts (untill [his] public accounts were settled) [he] having agreed to this mode of settlement and having relinquished all further demands against the United States, I do certify that the accounts of . . . Anderson are finally settled and closed [on] the Books of this Office" (DNA: RG 15, Revolutionary War Pension Files, *J. I. Anderson*, N.J., W 23449; Anderson to Washington, 17 Feb. 1791, DLC: Washington Papers).

[16] Anderson to Washington, 2 Mch. 1791 (DLC: Washington Papers).

nature of the report, Anderson rallied as quickly as before and pressed
forward. No doubt it appeared natural to seek out his partner in the
transaction and obtain from him the explanation required, and so he
made a swift journey to Wilmington to consult him. Within two or
three days he was back in Philadelphia, bearing with him a certificate
signed by Jaquett and witnessed by George Bush, Collector of the Port
of Wilmington. This certificate is not known to exist. But there is no
doubt that Jaquett obliged Anderson by placing the transaction in a
favorable light. The candidate promptly transmitted this document
to the President.[17] Two days later Washington nominated him for
the vacant judgeship. The Senate confirmed the nomination the next
day.[18] At last the Revolutionary veteran seemed to be warmed by the
sunshine of favor. Nothing remained but for the commission to be
passed under the Great Seal.

Even at this late moment, however, there arose another report so
ominous and so serious as to give the President pause and to bring
agony to the candidate. It was now rumored that something more had
transpired during Anderson's journey to Wilmington than had been
revealed. This time the report originated with Jaquett himself. For
some reason—perhaps because Vining, as a friend of long standing, was
familiar with the history of the transaction—Jaquett informed the
Congressman by letter about Anderson's mission to Wilmington and
commented upon the certificate that he had signed at the request of
the candidate. He later claimed that the letter was "intended *for his*
[Vining's] *Eye alone*."[19] But Vining revealed it to the two Senators
from Delaware just a day or so after Anderson's nomination had been
confirmed. Read, perhaps Bassett also, was sufficiently disturbed by its
contents to advise that it be made known to the President. This Vining
did by showing the letter to William Jackson, who informed Washington that in it Jaquett had "Observ'd that he had told the truth, in
the Certificate, but not the whole truth."[20] Washington at once disclosed the information to Anderson in what, surprisingly enough, was
their first meeting in person. The candidate later declared that in this
interview the President had assured him the commission would issue
notwithstanding Jaquett's letter to Vining. Improbable as such an
assurance seems under the circumstances, Anderson nevertheless appealed to Vining for a copy of the letter. The Congressman, perhaps
having had doubts of his own by this time, replied that it had been
inadvertently destroyed but gave his remembered impression of its
principal fact and of the more favorable interpretation given to that
fact by the witness to the certificate, George Bush.[21] Anderson also
obtained another testimonial from a Philadelphian and added to this a
certificate from Colonel Francis Barber, an officer whom Washington
had greatly admired. All of these he submitted to the President in a
final letter which, in addition to his own reiterated interpretations of
statements made in Vining's letter, rested his candidacy ultimately on

[17] See Document I.
[18] Washington to Senate, 25 Feb. 1791 (JEP, I, 77).
[19] Jaquett to Washington, 14 Mch. 1791 (DLC: Washington Papers).
[20] Document V.
[21] Document III.

a plea for compassion. Rejection in the full light of public knowledge of his nomination and confirmation by the Senate, Anderson declared, would cause him to "grow old in wretchedness, perhaps in poverty and what is worse even Contempt."[22]

Washington himself was obviously uncomfortable in what the candidate had aptly described as a "very *delicate* and *peculiar* Situation." To withdraw or cancel a public action would possibly call for public explanation. To deliver a commission to one about whom serious doubts had been raised might bring on subsequent embarrassment. To withhold it after confirmation might be an injustice to one whose record of service in the Revolution had been meritorious. These patent difficulties were compounded by the fact that the appointment concerned the judiciary in a new and experimental form of territorial government. The incumbent would hold office during good behavior. He would have common law jurisdiction. He would be obliged to confront a maze of conflicting land titles that complicated law, politics, and the whole social fabric. He would exercise his judicial prerogatives in a region of mounting tensions between East and West, where at any moment— as both the President and the Secretary of State would acknowledge in a few days[23]—an explosive situation of unpredictable consequences for the nation might develop. Civil and military appointments of easterners in the Northwest Territory had already caused discontent in the region south of the Ohio, and Anderson had no known connection with the West or its problems. Faced with such a dilemma, the President turned to the Secretary of State. Jefferson, unapprised of all that had taken place in the preceding months, concluded at once that the overwhelming weight of testimony was favorable to the candidate and that that of a contradictory nature originating with Jaquett was to be considered as nothing.[24] Washington, on an admittedly more "complete view of the circumstances," concurred immediately and no doubt with a sense of relief.[25] The commission was delivered to the anxious candidate the same day, just as the first Congress expired.[26] The issue was thus quickly resolved on a note of untroubled confidence that was belied by the President's prior hesitation and unwarranted by the known and discernible facts.

For even a hasty and partial review of the evidence should have exposed substantial grounds for doubt about the fitness of the candidate for judicial office. First of all, Anderson's effort to dispel skepticism about his legal qualifications raised more questions than it answered. Exactly a decade had elapsed since the candidate had left the army. In this same period many other veterans of the Revolution had prepared themselves for the legal profession and had even risen to places of distinction at the bar, as the careers of John Marshall and others proved.

[22] Document v.

[23] See group of documents on the new policy toward Spain, under 10 Mch. 1791.

[24] Document vi. Much of the previous testimony in support of Anderson's candidacy had been returned to him.

[25] Document vii.

[26] TJ to Anderson, 4 Mch. 1791 (DNA: RG 59, PCC No. 120). Anderson evidently acknowledged receipt of the commission in a letter to TJ of 9 Mch. 1791 (recorded in SJL as received the same day, but not found).

Yet Anderson had never tried a case. Moreover, his explanation seriously qualified, if it did not contradict, his original statement to Washington that he had been authorized to practice in "several" states. In fact
he had been admitted to the bar only in Delaware and Pennsylvania.
His explanation for not having followed his profession in either state—
that he was determined to remove to the West and deemed it inexpedient
to engage in practice for so temporary a stay—should have raised some
question in view of the fact that more than three years had elapsed since
he had been admitted to practice in Pennsylvania.[27]

As for the matter of his army account, all that the candidate had
obtained from the various quarters of his solicitation was an administrative decision to consider the matter as closed.[28] But this very fact
raised a more serious question. As he had previously explained to the
President, Anderson could not effect a settlement without appealing
to Congress. This, as he and others in his situation well knew, was
because settlements of claims involving military service had been precluded by the Continental Congress after 1 August 1786. Yet, even
while his petition was pending, he had pressed for and obtained a closing of his account without any action by Congress.[29] The obstacle
that had required such an appeal had not been removed. Its existence
was in fact explicitly acknowledged by Knox both in his letter to Lear
and in his final report. But between the drafting of these two statements
something induced the Secretary of War to adopt a different position
with respect to the basic principle. His first opinion showed, clearly
and properly, due deference to the House of Representatives in deciding
a matter that had been placed before them as of necessity. But his final
report merely announced to that body the reasons for an administrative decision that had been taken. Thus, in abandoning his earlier position of deference to the legislative branch, the Secretary of War in
effect had suspended a legislative regulation in existence since 1786
and had assumed the right to decide whether legislative revocation or
suspension of the rule in this and presumably in all similar cases was or
was not necessary. Some of this contradiction between the words
which acknowledged the existence of the legislative obstacle and the
decision which in effect disavowed it may perhaps be attributed to
simple confusion over principles of administration. But it is difficult
to escape the conclusion that the persistent candidate and his political
supporters in Congress also had some influence in bringing about this
shift of position on the part of the Secretary of War. In the attempt
to remove his paymaster's account for the Third New Jersey Regiment
as an obstacle to his appointment, Anderson himself had obviously been
one of the most aggressive proponents of a solution that, leaving nothing
to legislative chance or delay, denied the premise on which his memorial
to the House of Representatives had been based. The principal fact

27 In his explanation to Washington, Anderson did not see fit to reveal the fact
that, after settling in Wilmington, he had taught school there for a time (John A.
Munroe, *Federalist Delaware 1775-1815*, p. 173-4).

28 Anderson to Washington, 17 Feb. 1791 (DLC: Washington Papers).

29 Knox' report on Anderson's petition was not laid before the House until
15 Feb. 1791, when it was tabled. No further action was taken (JHR, I, 378).
See notes 13 and 15 above.

that emerged from his persistent appeals to various quarters was that, in the beginning, this legally trained candidate had been mistaken in the nature of the unsettled balance in his public account as well as in the inferences he drew from it and that, in the end, both his words and his actions betrayed his confusion respecting the proper boundaries of legislative and administrative authority.

Similarly, the matter of the transaction between Jaquett and Anderson vanished as an obstacle without being resolved, though in its implications it posed the most serious questions that had yet been raised about the fitness of the candidate for judicial office. In the assessment of this problem by the President and the Secretary of State the crucial evidence was missing. But this very fact should have aroused probing questions at the outset. Why, in attempting to dispel the doubts that had been raised, did not Anderson produce at least a copy of the original instrument in the transaction? Why was it necessary to rely instead on a certificate to explain its nature? The questions gain force by the fact that Anderson, who later asserted that the certificate merely recited the facts contained in the original record, nevertheless felt obliged to explain to Washington an otherwise obscure allusion in the certificate. Clearly, explanatory testimony that required elucidation could not have had equal evidential value with the actual terms of the original instrument. Not until later did the candidate see fit to inform Washington that the original was "at too great a distance to Obtain speedily."[30] But this explanation, too, begged the question. Even if Anderson himself had not retained a copy of the original in which his property rights were committed, the other party to the agreement must have done so as proof and protection of his own rights. If so, why had not *he* provided a copy of the document too distant to be obtained speedily? Failure to provide even a text of that agreement was thus compounded by failure to explain why the candidate chose to rely upon an affidavit of secondary authority—a fact and a proceeding that should immediately have raised questions about Anderson's fitness for a judicial post. The doubts and ambiguities had not been dispelled. Washington, without even a personal knowledge of the candidate, had merely accepted the certificate that Anderson had produced and had sent his name forthwith to the Senate.

But after the Senate had acted, there arose other and graver questions about the manner in which the candidate had endeavored to clear the path to his nomination. What actually had transpired between Anderson and Jaquett when the former made his swift journey to Wilmington? The answer to this troublesome question came only in the form of conflicting rumors, explanations, and denials. Here again the President and the Secretary of State did not have access to the original and crucial document—Jaquett's letter to Vining—but were obliged to rely on Vining's summary of its contents and on reiterated interpretations of its meaning by Anderson. Even so, several important and incontrovertible facts should have been discernible through the fog of assertion and contradiction. First, the original agreement between Anderson and Jaquett had been renewed at the time the certificate

<hr/>

[30] See **Document IV.**

that purported to explain its nature had been drafted, thus making the text of the renewal available. Second, this renewed or "additional Contract" was, with one exception, identical with the first. Third, it was in the nature of an agreement or bond of indebtedness with Anderson as debtor and Jaquett as creditor. Fourth, the one exception or addition to the original agreement provided for a diminution of Anderson's obligation through payments to Jaquett from the anticipated salary as judge. These facts went to the heart of the matter and provided the key to an impartial assessment of the evidence. They allowed the inference that this understanding, contingent upon the appointment of Anderson, gave to each perhaps unequal but definite motives of interest in the nomination and in the drafting of the certificate designed to promote it. The statements of both men respecting that document were, therefore, presumably entitled to equal consideration.

But Anderson, by his reiterated emphasis upon the supposed conflict between Jaquett's certificate and his "repugnant letter" to Vining, obviously sought to divert attention from the real issue by the simple device of impugning the credibility of the man to whom he had so recently appealed for assistance. He labeled as contradiction what, according to his own statement, Washington's aide and perhaps Washington himself had regarded merely as partial disclosure—as being "the truth . . . but not the whole truth."[31] Indeed, he succeeded at the end in shifting the issue to a simple contest of veracity between the author of the certificate and the witness to it.[32] In doing so he did not deny that a contingent understanding had taken place but asserted, in ambiguous language and on the basis of the reported testimony of George Bush, that this was "a Consequence rather than a Condition" of his appointment. This distinction had only a technical relevance to the real issue, but it did enable Anderson to swear "upon the *Honor* of a *Soldier*" that he had never empowered Jaquett to receive part of his compensation if appointed. Jaquett himself might have taken the same irrelevant oath: what Anderson was careful to avoid denying was that he had arranged by the renewed agreement to have Jaquett receive payments on the debt out of his anticipated salary.

This diversionary effort, an exercise in special pleading that left the substantive question unanswered, met with success. The obvious contradictions and partial disclosures in the arguments Anderson advanced to support charges of such defects in the testimony of Jaquett were seemingly disregarded. So also, apparently, the "principal Fact" in Jaquett's explanation of the drafting of the certificate was overlooked. But that fact, even as filtered through the imperfect screen of Vining's brief summary, emerged with crystal clarity. Jaquett had *obliged* Anderson to enter into a renewal of the contract and to add to it a new stipulation. He had been able to compel this as a condition precedent to his compliance with the request for a certificate explanatory of the nature of their original understanding. He had, in brief, simply seized the opportunity presented by the candidate's eagerness to obtain

[31] See Document v.   [32] See Document v.

the appointment in order to bind him to a stipulated mode of payment on the indebtedness if and when he was placed on the bench. In other words, Anderson himself had knowingly participated in the partial disclosures of the certificate that told "the truth . . . but not the whole truth."

The instrument for revealing the full extent of this bargaining transaction at Wilmington was at hand but was not employed. Anderson himself had unwittingly revealed its existence in his effort to destroy the credibility of Jaquett. If his object had been to present the facts with candor, all that was necessary for him to do was to exhibit to the President a copy of the renewal of the original bond that had just been signed. By so doing he would have avoided the self-impeachment of his own credibility in the assertion that he could not supply the text of that original agreement because it lay at too great a distance to be obtained speedily. For he himself had assured the President that the renewed bond was the same as the original, with one exception—the exception that was central to the question of his fitness for office.[33] He could have gone further. Instead of relying on the memory of John Vining and the secondhand testimony of George Bush, he could have appealed again to Peter Jaquett. That interesting individual, as the President and the Secretary of State might also have discovered, was still eager and willing to testify at length and in support of Anderson's candidacy. He, too, had a personal interest in the outcome.

Peter Jaquett belonged to a well-known Huguenot family that had settled on the lower Delaware even before the beginning of English rule.[34] His record in the Revolution and his devotion to republican principles were so exemplary as to lead John T. Scharf to characterize him as "one of the ideal patriots of the great struggle for independence."[35] Like Anderson, Jaquett entered the army as an ensign at the beginning of the war, rose to a captaincy, and was breveted major. From the beginning of 1776 to the end of 1781 he fought with the much-eulogized Delaware Continentals in almost every major engagement from New York to Charleston, being twice wounded.[36] At the close of the war, broken in health, he returned to his patrimonial estate at the confluence of the Christiana and the Delaware and found it in ruins. Successive floods over a period of years after the war broke through the dikes, inundated his lands, and baffled his efforts to reestablish the family farm of Long Hook. Early in 1789 he applied

[33] See Document V.

[34] The founder of the Jaquett family in Delaware was made vice-director in that jurisdiction under Peter Stuyvesant exactly a century before Peter Jaquett (1755-1834) was born. For a sketch of Jaquett, see E. J. Sellers, *Genealogy of the Jaquett Family* (Philadelphia, 1907), p. 97-102 (for some corrections, see *Delaware History*, VI [Mch. 1955], 233-7). An obituary published in an 1834 newspaper is printed in Sellers, *Jaquett Family*, p. 138-41; the tomb of Jaquett in Holy Trinity (Old Swedes) Church, Wilmington, recites his Revolutionary services.

[35] J. T. Scharf, *History of Delaware 1609-1888*, I (Philadelphia, 1888), 212.

[36] Christopher L. Ward, *The Delaware Continentals 1776-1783* (Wilmington, 1941); W. G. Whiteley, *The Revolutionary Soldiers of Delaware* (Wilmington, 1875).

to Washington for some civil or military employment in the new government.[37] He had been "narrowed in his private circumstances . . . not by indolence, extravagance or waste, but from inevitable misfortune," wrote Dr. James Tilton, who testified that there was "not a disinterested *whig* or revolutionist in Delaware, but would rejoice at any benefit which Captain Jaquett might derive from government."[38] John Dickinson supported Jaquett's candidacy by pronouncing his "conduct as an officer . . . unquestionably very meritorious" and by condemning as altogether inadequate the provision "made by the publick for the comfortable and reasonable accommodation of such men, after their dangers, sufferings and services in the cause of their Country."[39] The judges of the Supreme Court of Delaware and of the courts of Newcastle county, "from a long acquaintance with the Major's Abilities, integrity, and activity, as a Soldier, from the commencement to the Close of our Glorious Struggle for the Liberties of our Country, and since as a peaceful and useful member of Civil Society," declared that his appointment "would give Great Pleasure to the Virtuous Citizens" of the county.[40] Charles Pope and other officers who had served with Jaquett stated that his "distinguished services in the Army . . . greatly endeared him to his Countrymen, and particularly to his brother officers and soldiers."[41] This was impressive support, and the testimonials carried an unmistakable tone of sincerity and esteem not always discernible in such declarations. Jaquett nevertheless failed to obtain either a civil or military appointment.

He waited two years and then, early in 1791 and still in the same difficult circumstances, he renewed his application in the hope of obtaining one of the additional offices called for under the Excise Act. In doing so he referred the President to the various letters of recommendation that had accompanied his previous appeal, "signed by the Gentlemen of the Legislature of this State, the Judges of the different Courts, the Justices of the Peace, together with all the officers of the late Delaware Regiment and a number of private Gentlemen."[42] The letter came to the President's attention only a few weeks before Jaquett was called upon by Anderson for the certificate about their transaction. Thus, perhaps in part at least because Jaquett's effort to aid Anderson's candidacy had branded him in the eyes of the President as a

[37] Jaquett to Washington, 18 Apr. 1789 (DLC: Washington Papers). Jaquett evidently had met Washington during the war, for he concluded his letter with this comment: "When I recollect how accurately your excellency used to recognize and discriminate each and every officer of your army, I cannot but flatter myself that I am not entirely unknown as a soldier, notwithstanding the three last years of my service I was detached from your excellency" on the southern campaigns.

[38] Tilton to Washington, 12 Mch. 1789 (same).

[39] John Dickinson to Richard Bassett, 24 Mch. 1789 (same).

[40] David Finney and ten others to Washington, 13 Apr. 1789 (same).

[41] Charles Pope and ten other officers to Washington, 13 Apr. 1789 (same). Jaquett had informed Washington that he was the only one among the Delaware officers who would ask to be considered for office—a fact which naturally led him to suppose that his application would thereby be benefited.

[42] Jaquett to Washington, 16 Jan. 1791 (same). It is obvious from this statement that the testimonials that survive do not include all that Jaquett originally submitted.

person of dubious veracity, his own considerable claims to civil or military office went unrecognized. Indeed, the supervisorship of the excise for Delaware went to Dr. Henry Latimer on the very day that Anderson's accusation against Jaquett for having invalidated his own testimony was officially endorsed.[43]

Somehow, in the next few weeks, Jaquett learned that the Secretary of State had written a report that disparaged his testimony. This can only have happened through the instrumentality of someone close to the President who had access to his files. It is plausible to suppose that Lear was the one who disclosed the nature of Jefferson's report and that it was to Jaquett's friend Vining that he made the communication. But, whatever the source or channel through which Jaquett obtained the information, two facts are beyond doubt. First, sole responsibility for the disparagement was placed upon the Secretary of State. The fact that his opinion had received the emphatic concurrence of the President was not revealed. Second, Jaquett experienced such a sense of injury that he immediately appealed to the President—not by urging his own claim to an appointment and not by impeaching the veracity of Anderson, but in order to redeem himself in the eyes of the Commander-in-Chief whom he had followed so loyally during the Revolution.

"I feel myself much hurt by the unfair manner in which I have been represented in Major Anderson's affair," he began, "and exceedingly mortified that it should leave an unfavorable impression of me in the mind of your Excellency." He believed that an interview of a few moments would enable him to convince the President that he had "certified nothing but truth concerning Major Anderson" and that he could reconcile the "apparent contradiction" between the certificate and the letter to Vining. He then proceeded to give the explanation that, had they desired it, either the President or the Secretary of State might have elicited earlier:[44]

I had been long in habits of friendship with Mr. Vining and he was well acquainted with all the circumstances concerning the affair between M. Anderson and myself and I had some reasons to believe that Mr. Vining had interested himself with your Excellency in favor of the Major's appointment; but I never knew that Mr. Vining or Mr. [Gunning] Bedford had represented the Major's affair in a disadvantageous point of view to your Excellency, untill five days after I had wrote the letter to Mr. Vining which was intended *for his Eye alone.*

From the opinion which I always entertained of M. Andersons honor and entegrity I was convinced that he would discharge the debt as soon as he was in a situation to do it. I therefore felt myself obliged to Mr. Vining (who I knew entertained a favorable opinion of M. Andersons abilities and understanding) for the aid

[43] Nomination and confirmation of supervisors on 4 Mch. 1791 (JEP, I, 81, 82). Latimer soon resigned and Gunning Bedford urged Jaquett for the vacancy, but Andrew Barratt was appointed (Washington to Hamilton, 16 Sep. 1791, *Writings*, ed. Fitzpatrick, XXXI, 371-2).

[44] Jaquett to Washington, 14 Mch. 1791 (DNA: RG 59, M 179/5).

which I imagined he had given in recommending him to your Excellency, as I knew it would put the Major in a situation to do what he heartily wished namely to discharge a debt of honor due to me. I call it a debt of honor, because I lent it to him upon his word of honour to return it to me in three months and took no written obligation for that purpose. At the same time the Major told me that he had attatched a large sum of money in the hands of the treasurer of the United States the property of Nathaniel Twining for whom he had been security to a large amount and to his very great injury,[45] that he expected to receive this money in less than three months when he would repay me. For some reasons unknown to me I believe the Major received but about one eighth part of the money he expected, which disappointment put it out of his power to comply with his engagement to me.

I am convinced that the Major was severely mortified at the idea of being unable to pay me, especially as he knew that my situation was by no means a comfortable one. But as he was unable to pay me, he in some measure avoided me, for more than a year, during which time I scarce saw or heard from him.

After the debt had been due upwards of four years, upon my hearing that he was about going to Kentucke,[46] I directed my attorney to institute a suit against him in hopes that his Brother in Law, would become security for part of my demand; giving my Attorney my directions at the same time, to use no rigor and informing him that the Major had certain Land Warrants in his possession which I would take at ⅜ per Acre as a security to his bond which I directed him to take. Major Anderson being in Maryland my order was executed with more rigor than I wished or expected and he was sent to Gaol his bond taken and the Lands as security.

When the Major came to me for the certificate which he obtained, I told him I was very ready to certify anything to his advantage consistent with truth, that I had always viewed the affair as his misfortune not his fault. He then assured me that he would give me any instrument of writing which I should chuse, to convince me that he did not want inclination but ability to pay me. We then called Major Bush the Collector (who was witness to all our transactions) to our assistance, and in his presence I gave him the certificate, when he renewed his bond and gave me an article of agreement approved of and witnessed by Major Bush, by which he bound himself to give me immediately on his appointment a power of attorney to draw from the treasury of the United States such part of his salary as I should demand. I did not think it necessary to state all those circumstances in the certificate, because that I believed that Your Excellency having had some hint of the debt due me (from whom I knew not) un-

45 This, perhaps, is an allusion to the losses that Anderson, in his original application to Washington, attributed to "*ill reposed* Confidence" (see note 2 above).

46 Both the spelling and the rumor of Anderson's intention to go to Kentucky reflect the influence of the Kentucky explorer, James Filson, whose *Kentucke* appeared in Wilmington in 1784. Filson, like Anderson, also taught school in Wilmington (Munroe, *Federalist Delaware*, p. 173).

favorable to the Major, only wished to know from me whether he had acted honorable with me or not in respect to that debt, and I firmly believe that he has done, and would at any time do every thing in his power to comply with his engagements.

But my mentioning some circumstances in my private letter to Mr. Vining which were not in the certificate (and which Mr. Vining well knew before if his memory has not deceived him) have been apprisd as contradictory to the certificate, and I believe it will appear upon a review of the Letter that I have not stated that Mr. Anderson *had given* me a power of attorney but that he *had agreed to give* me one to draw a certain part of his Salary.

I must therefore request your Excellency to believe that when I mentioned in my letter to Mr. Vining, that I *had not certified all the truth* (tho' an unhappy expression) I only intended to convey the Idea that I had not certified all the particulars mentioned in this letter, (which particulars Mr. Vining well knew) because I thought them unnecessary. I am indeed sorry that my letter to Mr. Vining was shewn to the Senators of this State as I did not wish to give persons who were not my friends an opportunity of saying anything more to my disadvantage.

I hope therefore that what I have now said will reconcile this apparent contradiction of which so much has been said and shew that I wrote nothing with a view of deceiving your Excellency, or of injuring an individual.

I should have been much hurt by hearing myself accused by my Equals of a crime of which I hold myself incapable. Your Excellency may then judge of my uneasiness when I found a report from the Secretary of State, certifying that I had contradicted myself. I hope it will be viewed by you Sir in a different light and that Major Andersons virtue will highly justify all that I have said or believed of him as well as your Excellencys confidence in him.

I have now to request if after reading this Letter there should remain in Your Excellency's breast a doubt to my disadvantage, that I may be honored with an interview.—Your Goodness Sir I am convinced will forgive me the trouble I have given you in reading this letter in which I have endeavored to acquit myself of the duplicity of which I have been accused and of which I hope I stand acquitted by Your Excellency.

There was no answer and no interview. Seven months later Jaquett went to Philadelphia and again appealed for an opportunity to justify himself. The answer that Tobias Lear gave in Washington's name was cold and final:[47]

I am commanded by the President to inform you, that he has neither time nor inclination to enter into an investigation of the affair between Major Anderson and yourself. And the President observes, that if your conduct in the matter has been such as was satisfactory to yourself, he has no cause to be dissatisfied with it and further, if

[47] Lear to Jaquett, 25 Oct. 1791 (DLC: Washington Papers), acknowledging Jaquett's of the same date (not found).

the President was inclined to go into the particulars of the affair, his having returned all the papers &c. which were laid before him respecting it, has put it out of his power to form a precise opinion upon it.

How much of the language and tenor of this communication should be attributed to the secretary and how much to the President cannot be known. But, quite aside from its tone of cold finality, the note was both imperceptive and inaccurate. The issue, first of all, was not between Anderson and Jaquett but between Jaquett and his government. The question was whether the plea of a citizen for rectification of an injury should be heard by the Chief Executive who, if an injury had been committed, was ultimately responsible for it. What Jaquett had asked was an opportunity to defend himself against a charge that—with far better grounds than he could have known—he believed and unequivocally declared to be unjust. His sole complaint was that of a citizen who believed that his character had been traduced by a high officer of government. In the second place, as Lear should have known, all of the documents relevant to Jaquett's grievance had not been returned. The documents Anderson had received back were letters of testimony and certificates recommending him for office. These had nothing to do with the immediate issue. All of the evidence on which the adverse opinion had been founded was still available for placing in juxtaposition the statements of accuser and accused. Finally, though the President now chose to stand aloof and to insist that it was "out of his power to form a precise opinion" on the question, the simple fact is that both he and the Secretary of State had already committed themselves to an opinion. That opinion, being altogether *ex parte*, had given the official stamp of approval to Anderson's impugning of Jaquett's veracity. It was that opinion that had committed the government and thus exposed it to the legitimate request of a citizen to be accorded a hearing. All that this officer with an exemplary record in defense of the nation professed to seek by way of indemnification was that, in the eyes of his former Commander-in-Chief, he be permitted to stand acquitted of the charge of duplicity. This, under the circumstances, was not much to ask. But Jaquett was obliged to return to his ancestral farm and live out the days of a long life without ever knowing that the President had fully agreed with the Secretary of State in estimating the nature of his testimony as contradictory and its value as nothing. This was precisely what the successful candidate had sought to achieve, using means that—on the face of the evidence available to both officials —should have been sufficient to raise in their minds grave questions about his fitness for judicial appointment. For, whatever other qualifications Anderson may have possessed, his own letters in seeking the office reveal beyond question that candor, impartiality, and a sense of justice were, in this instance at least, conspicuously absent.

It is understandable that Washington should not have wished to re-open the troublesome issue even to rectify a palpable injury. But the manner of rejecting the plea of an old soldier seemed to reflect a growing sensitiveness to criticism that was to become one of the dominant characteristics of his administration. Political considerations, too, were evidently involved. The two Delaware Senators who had supported Anderson were strong Federalists, and one of the most revealing statements in Jaquett's letter is that George Read and Richard Bassett were not among his friends. His own ardent support of the whiggish doctrines of the Revolution was well known. As an officer of the Delaware Society of the Cincinnati, he doubtless had an influence in causing even that body—unlike its counterpart in most other states— to be "full of Republican spirit."[48] The fact and the manner of Washington's rejection of his appeal can scarcely have diminished the natural tendency of Jaquett to gravitate toward the Jeffersonians. There is no evidence that he ever placed responsibility upon anyone except the Secretary of State for the report that seemed to him so unfair. But, exactly a decade later, it was to Jefferson as President that he appealed because of his "known attach[ment] to the principles of [the] Revolution and to those men who were the firm and active supporters of it." Once again, unsuccessfully, he sought office under the national government. He gave as his references John Dickinson and Joseph Anderson, now Senator from Tennessee. The latter, he stated, had known him "in the respective Characters of Citizen and Soldier."[49] A month earlier, immediately after Jefferson's inauguration, Anderson had in fact written to the President recommending Jaquett for the vacancy caused by the resignation of Allen McLane as Collector of the Port of Wilmington. "He served as an officer in the Delaware Regiment through the whole revolutionary War," wrote Anderson, "supported a fair Character, and has never appostatized from his *former* Principles."[50]

One of the significant facts of a case marked by indecisive administrative action from beginning to end is that the President, on a judicial appointment of some consequence, did not see fit to turn to the Secretary of State for advice until the last moment. In addition to the motives influencing Washington, Jefferson thus had others for not wishing to reopen the issue. Because of his unfamiliarity with the history of the case and under the extraordinary pressures then existing —including preparation for the reconvening of the Senate called to meet on the 4th of March—the mere task of reading and analyzing the partially disclosed evidence was a formidable one. The preponderance of testimony favorable to Anderson coming from political sources that commanded respect, to say nothing of the difficulty of finding another candidate of suitable qualifications at a moment's notice, could have caused Jefferson to seize the only option that seemed to be open and to recommend that the commission be delivered. A contrary course

[48] Munroe, *Federalist Delaware*, p. 202. Jaquett was a charter member of the Society, as was Anderson. He was its vice-president from 1795 to its dissolution (H. H. Bellas, *History of the Delaware State Society of the Cincinnati*, p. 12, 24, 26, 60). Jaquett was also a supporter of Delaware's ratification of the Constitution in 1787.

[49] Jaquett to TJ, 8 Apr. 1801 (DNA: RG 59, M 418/6; endorsed by TJ as received 27 June 1801 and so recorded in SJL).

[50] Anderson to TJ, 6 Mch. 1801 (RC in DLC; endorsed by TJ as received 7 Mch. 1801 and so recorded in SJL). Few letters passed between TJ and Anderson and these were chiefly about patronage; obviously, no close relationship existed between the two men during the eight years of TJ's Presidency.

would also perhaps have brought on unprecedented questions with respect to a candidate already confirmed. All of these factors, however, leave unexplained in any satisfactory manner why, in consummating an appointment against which so many warning flags had been raised over so long a time, it was necessary for the President and the Secretary of State to accept Anderson's indictment of Jaquett's testimony when the interested accuser was so patently guilty in equal measure of the same charge.

Whatever the answer and despite the tone of confident assurance in the opinion submitted by Jefferson, it is nevertheless certain that he at least had penetrated the screen Anderson had erected to obscure the deficiencies in his own testimony. It is equally certain that he had arrived at his recommendation to the President only after experiencing genuine doubt and hesitation about the course to adopt. Two entries in his brief but invaluable register of public letters, opinions, and reports as Secretary of State reveal the existence and the stages of his doubt even if they do not disclose the reasons for it. As shown by interlinear alterations, the first of these entries marked off two separate advances in his deliberations and the second indicated his final conclusion. As originally phrased, the first entry read: "on revocation of a nomination approved by Senate in the case of M[ajor? Anderson]." As altered by interlineation, it read: "draught of a message on revocation of a nomination approved by Senate," &c. This first entry was not canceled but beneath it Jefferson inserted the second and definitive one: "Opinion Th: J. in favor of Anderson." No document has been found to correspond to any save this final stage of Jefferson's wrestling with the dilemma.[51] But these brief and highly significant entries in the register prove that Jefferson originally drafted a report to the President on the case. Its recommendation was almost certainly negative on the question whether to deliver the commission to Anderson and very likely it discussed the alternative courses open to the President. This inference is supported by the conclusive meaning of the first entry as revised, for the revision shows that Jefferson, abandoning the idea of a simple communication of advice, had advanced to the stage of drafting a message for Washington to send to the Senate. This message, of course, could have had no other object than that of announcing the "revocation of a nomination" already approved. It must, therefore, have stated the reasons for such action. It must also have suggested that the Senate concur by revoking its confirmation. These inferences as to procedure are rendered plausible not merely by the fact that the message was drafted and registered but also by Jefferson's known deference to the legislative branch in matters involving its constitutional prerogative.

But this marked the ultimate point in his progress toward an official act of annulment. Having arrived there, Jefferson then backed away—perhaps at the same time destroying his original report to the President and the draft of the message to the Senate. Several foreseeable consequences, actual or potential, may have induced this retreat. Possibly, on reading the testimonials favorable to Anderson, he came to

[51] See Document VI; both entries in SJPL are under 4 Mch. 1791.

doubt the validity of a conclusion based on obviously incomplete information. Perhaps influential support for the candidate from Delaware, New Jersey, and Pennsylvania caused him to give due weight to the political consequences. But these factors appear relatively minor by comparison with another specter that must have disclosed its shadowy outlines in the distance. Suppose the Senate, already sensitive about its right to advise and consent, should refuse to revoke its confirmation even when the President sought to recall his nomination? Suppose that Anderson, urged on by offended political sponsors, should resort to litigation to claim an office for which all constitutional requirements had been met by the two branches of government authorized to participate in the appointment? Suppose, abandoning his plea for compassion, he should support such a legal claim on the not implausible theory that the sealing and delivery of a commission after confirmation was a mere administrative act on the part of the Secretary of State which he could be compelled to perform by a writ of mandamus?

Thus, along the path of his thinking marked out by these brief fragments in his register of state papers, there loomed at least the possibility of a truly formidable conflict over the constitutional powers of all three branches of government. It is, of course, scarcely conceivable that the Supreme Court under Jay could have engaged in such an epic contest with the Presidency under Washington as emerged a dozen years later when this doctrine of compelling by mandamus the issuance of a signed commission found its obiter expression in Marbury v. Madison.[52] Even if judicial construction of the constitutional grants of power to the President in nominating and to the Senate in confirming appointments were not involved, a rancorous debate on the exercise of these powers was still within the realm of possibility, with no assurance that the discussion could be confined to the closed sessions of the Senate. The mere threat of a collision on questions of such moment, coming so soon after the bitter confrontation on the constitutionality of the national bank bill, evoked far graver considerations than any likely to be involved in the consummation of a dubious appointment to office.

In the face of such actual and potential dangers, the Secretary of State retreated from his advanced position. Locking his doubts in his own bosom, he assumed an air of assurance and dispatched the seemingly confident report to the President. But two conclusions emerge inescapably from this clearly delineated route of advance and retreat. First of all, whatever the substance and phraseology of the proposed message to the Senate, it could only indicate Jefferson's belief that Anderson had revealed himself as unfit for judicial office. The mere act of drafting such a message testifies to the strength of his convic-

[52] In Marbury v. Madison, of course, the commission had already been signed by the President. It is not known whether this was so at the time TJ wrote his opinion, but presumably the commission had been prepared immediately after TJ learned that the Senate had confirmed Anderson. The commission to William Murray was actually issued on 26 Feb. 1791, the day before Lear notified TJ of the appointment of both Anderson and Murray (see Document II)—a typical instance of TJ's customary dispatch. See TJ to Hay, 2 June 1807.

tion, even though it was formed upon a hasty reading of only a portion of the one-sided evidence. Second, the Secretary of State had displaced this conclusion with one of a contrary tenor without disclosing the fact to the President. It is impossible to say how far this putative opinion influenced Washington. What we do know is that he received it as being merely corroborative of a verdict he himself had already "formed upon a complete view of the circumstances."[53] This supposed opinion that concurred with his own ran also with "the whole current of evidence . . . produced in favour of Mr. Anderson."[54] But it was flatly contradicted by the concealed opinion that had been formed on a more penetrating analysis of the testimony. The Secretary of State, choosing his words with meticulous care, had confined his report solely to a descriptive summary of the tendency of the evidence, avoiding by the slightest hint any disclosure of his own view of the merits of the case. In this very uncharacteristic action he had submitted a report but not an opinion, the truth but not the whole truth.

Perhaps, therefore, the real significance of the episode lies in the light it casts on the manner in which the President had sought the advice of the Secretary of State. The distant and reserved posture that Washington had adopted seems characteristic and in this instance it undoubtedly caused Jefferson to be confronted with such a belated and admittedly incomplete view of the circumstances as to foreclose all other alternatives. Jefferson had not been in office more than a few months before he learned that to press an argument too far with the President was to nullify its effect, particularly in matters of appointment to office.[55] In this respect and in others involving relationships with Cabinet officers, Jefferson may have benefited during his own Presidency from such a mismanaged case as Joseph Anderson's eager search for office. Perhaps experience thus fortified inclination in prompting the adoption of a contrary style of administration and a less distant relationship with Cabinet advisers.

I. Joseph Anderson to the President

SIR   Philadelphia 23rd Feby. 1791

When I last did myself the Honor of waiting upon your Excellency, on the Subject of my application, now before you, Mr. Lear inform'd me, that something had been Suggested, to my disadvantage, respecting a transaction between Major Jaquet and myself, relative to some Certificates.

In Order to set that business in a proper point of View, I have

[53] See Document VII.
[54] See Document VI.
[55] TJ to Short, 16 Mch. 1791, makes the point explicitly, but TJ's earlier letters to Short on the subject show clearly that he discerned the relationship almost from the beginning (TJ to Short, 6 and 27 Apr. 1790, 26 July 1790, 30 Sep. 1790).

for your Excellency's satisfaction Obtain'd from Major Jaquet, a Certificate, Containing a Statement of the facts attending it, By which Your Excellency will perceive whether I deserve censure on the Subject.

Your Excellency will please to Observe, that Major Jaquet acknowledges, to have Receiv'd from me, Miami Land Warrants, to the amount of the Certificates I have Receiv'd from him, at a price fixed by himself. On his seting the price on the Warrants, I thought it considerably Less than their Real Value. He therefore agreed to allow me the *equity* of *Redemption* at any period within three years, Upon the Terms, Contain'd in the Certificate. I have thought it adviseable to explain this part of the Certificate, in order that Your Excellency might clearly understand, the Real principles of Our Settlement.

It gives me Very Sensible pain to have caus'd your Excellency so much trouble. But sundry circumstances having interven'd (since I first made application to Your Excellency,) which I cou'd not possibly foresee, I must crave your Excellencys forgiveness for my Obtrusions. And Permit me to assure you Sir, that I hold *your approbation* of my Character *more Dear*, than any Emoluments I might derive from the Office I Solicit.

Not having the Honor of being personally known to your Excellency, I feel myself imbarrass'd, in requesting the *Special indulgence*, of waiting on your Excellency in person.

To your Excellency I *look up* as to a *Common Parent*, and have no doubt Sir, but what you will do me all the Justice, to which my Small claims to merit may entitle me. I am Sir, with every Sentiment of the highest Respect your Excellencys most Obedt. Servt.

JOS ANDERSON

RC (DLC: Washington Papers); addressed: "George Washington Esquire President of the United States"; endorsed by Lear. Enclosure: Certificate from Peter Jaquett concerning the facts in the transaction between himself and Joseph Anderson (not found).

II. Tobias Lear to the Secretary of State

United States February 27th 1791.

By the President's command T. Lear has the honor respectfully to transmit to the Secretary of State a Resolution of the Senate upon the President's Message of the 19th of January last. T. Lear has, moreover, the honor to inform the Secretary of State that on the 26th of this month the Senate did, in pursuance of the

President's nominations, advise and consent to the following appointments viz.

JOSEPH ANDERSON, of the State of Delaware, to be one of the Judges in the Territory of the U. S. south of the Ohio, in place of *William Peery* who has declined his appointment, and

WILLIAM MURRY, of Kentucky, to be Attorney for the U. S. in the District of Kentucky, in place of *James Brown*, who has declined his appointment.

TOBIAS LEAR
Secretary to the President
of the United States

PrC (DNA: RG 59, MLR); docketed by Lear. Tr (DNA: RG 59, SDC). Not recorded in SJL. Enclosure: Resolution of the Senate on 26 Feb. 1791 concerning complaint by France against tonnage Acts of 1789 and 1790 (JEP, I, 77; see group of documents on that subject).

III. John Vining to Joseph Anderson

SIR   March 1st 1791

Not being able to lay my hands upon the Letter you have requested, and **fearing very much that I** inadvertently, together with some other loose papers, threw it into the Fire in changing Papers from one coat Pockett to another, I have nothing now left in my Power but to state to you the principal Fact which it appeared to contain.

As I mean however to be perfectly explicit with you, I think it my Duty in Justice both to you and to myself to relate all that I have since heard concerning the Transaction at Wilmington. Major Jaquett as well as I remember impressed me with the Idea that he had given the Certificate which was delivered to the President in Consequence of your having empowered him to recieve a certain part of that Compensation which was to go in gradual diminution of a Bond of £1200 which he represented to have recieved from you together with other Securities. This I believe as it related to you was the Substantial part of his Letter. Major Bush with whom I have conversed since I saw the President, I confess stated it differently, and to my mind more favourably. He appeared rather to consider the additional Contract as a Consequence, than a Condition of your Appointment. I requested him if he saw the President as he then informed me he expected to do, to mention the Circumstance to him, which he promised to do. Bush also mentioned to me that you had not given to Jaquett any Power of Attorney to recieve part of your Compensation, which was also I

believe mentioned in Jaquetts Letter (as far as I can recollect) to
have been the case.

Conceiving it a confidential and a responsible Duty in me to
make the Communications I did to the President, you will not, I
trust, suppose that I have been actuated either by an unfriendly
motive to you or a desire to change the good Opinion the President
had previously entertained of you.—I am your very Hle. Sert,

J VINING

RC (DLC: Washington Papers). Enclosed in Anderson to Washington, 1 Mch.
1791 (see Doc. IV).

IV. Joseph Anderson to the President

SIR   Pha. 1st March 1791

I take the liberty of inclosing to Your Excellency, a letter I
receiv'd from Mr. Vining, in answer to One, I adress'd to him,
on the Subject of a letter he a few days since Receivd from Mr.
Jaquet. By which Your Excellency will see that Mr. Jaquet is
Contradicted in what he has said in his letter to Mr. Vining, and
that by a person who wrote the Certificate, and attested it. The
Certificate had for its basis, an Original Receipt, and Contains
only a State of facts, Contained in that Receipt. The Receipt being at too great a distance to Obtain speedily, the Certificate was
ask'd. With Respect to what Major Bush Says, Concerning his
Considering the additional Contract, as a Consequence Rather than
a Condition of my appointment, I wou'd beg leave to Observe That
I agreed with Mr. Jaquet, as I had rather have the Land Warrants he Receiv'd of me, at the prices he receiv'd them, than the
money, that if he wou'd Keep them, I wou'd impower my friend
Major Bush, to purchase them of him, for my use, and that to
Enable him to do it, I wou'd impower Major Bush to Receive
Money to my use for that purpose. Your Excellency will please
to Observe, that Mr. Vining says, in his letter, that Major Bush
mention'd, I had not given Jaquet any Power of Attorney to receive part of my Sallary in Case I Shou'd recieve the appointment,
which he says he believes Jaquet had mentiond in his letter—
meaning that I had given him such power.

Upon the whole, Your Excellency will I trust, see this business,
in its true point of View, and that in the Circumstance of my
agreeing to purchase the land Warrants of Major Jaquet, at the
price he Receivd them of me, was neither a Deviation from Prin-

cipal nor integrity, But Compatible with duty to myself, the War-rants being worth more to me at this period, than what he al-lowed me for them. In further Support of my Private Character, I beg leave to present a letter, to your Excellency, from a Gentle-man now of this City, who has Known me and my family from an early period of my life. His Character is well know[n] to Both Mr. Read and Mr. Vining.—I am Sir with Very great Respect your very Obedt. Servt.   Jos Anderson

RC (DLC: Washington Papers); addressed: "George Washington Esquire President of the United States"; endorsed by Lear. Enclosure: Vining to Ander-son, 1 Mch. 1791 (see Doc. III).

V. Joseph Anderson to the President

Sir   Phila. 2nd March 1791

I inclose your Excellency the Certificate of Colonel Barber, and beg your indulgence, for again, offering to trouble you by letter. But trust that your Excellencys benevolence, will suffer my very *delicate* and *peculiar* Situation, to plead my Appology.

Your Excellency yesterday Observ'd to me, that Major Jackson inform'd you, that Mr. Jaquet, in his letter to Mr. Vining, Ob-serv'd that he had told the truth, in the Certificate, but not the whole truth. If he told the truth, it must then appear that he was amply compensated, by receiving the land warrants, for he says that he receiv'd them at a price *affixed* by *himself*, and to the Amount of the Certificates I had of him; it is a maxim in Law, and *founded* on *Reason*, that every Mans words, shall be taken most Strongly against himself. Here then *he* wou'd Stand Con-victed, and in a Court of Law or equity the Certificate and the repugnant letter, if produced, wou'd totally invalidate Mr. Jaquets Testimony as an evidence. Mr. Vining in his letter to me men-tions, that Jaquet in his letter to him said, that I had impowered him to receive a part of my Sallary. But Mr. Vining also says that Major Bush told him, that I had not given Mr. Jaquet any Such power. Here then Sir, is an Issue Joined. Mr. Jaquet *asserts*, on his own account, and Major Bush, who as a man of reputation Stands, uncensured, was present the whole time, wrote and At-tested the Certificate, (as your Excellency may *see*) not even his own account, but for another, possitively denies, which Mr. Jaquet asserts. To whom then Sir Ought Credence to be given. Your Excellency will I trust, Readily agree to the impartial person. To this Sir, I will add, upon the *Honor* of a *Soldier*, that I never gave him any Such power. The Contract or Agreement as Mention'd in my papers to you of yesterday, was a Renewal of the Original Agreement, when he receiv'd the Land Warrants of me, respecting which Your Excellency may possibly Recollect that in a former letter *previous* to my being Nominated, I mention'd that in the transaction between Mr. Jaquet and myself, I had reserv'd, the equity of redemption, at any time within three Years, upon the terms and for the reasons, in that letter mention'd. The principles of this last Contract, was a mere renewal of the former, with this addition, That I wou'd impower Major Bush to act as my Attorney in Case I went to the Westward, and that I impower to Receive Money to my Use, to repurchase those Warrants at the same price Mr. Jaquet had them of me. But Mr. Jaquet was not prevented, by this Contract, from Seling the Warrants to any Other person, or from locating them whenever he pleas'd.

Your Excellency, I think told me, that when Mr. Vining, presented you Mr. Jaquets letter, you did not mean to take any notice of it, but intended that I shou'd notwithstanding have my Commission. Your Excellency Judgment being then form'd, even after recieving the letter, There are Strong Circumstances to Confirm it namely Those Contain'd in Mr. Vinings letter to me, in which Major Bush positively Contradicts the assertions of Jaquet. Your Excellencys nomination of me, being founded, I believe, principally upon my Military and professional Certificates. A View of those Certificates by the Senate, wou'd I Judge, have induced their accession, without the interference of any individual member. But respect, and Politeness induced me to apply to Mr. Read, Whose dissatisfaction appeard, founded on a belief, that What Jaquet said respecting my having impowerd him to receive my Sallary was true. This your Excellency will Observe, is positively contradicted by Major Bush.—The business now rests entirely with Your Excellency. It is now generally Known in the City that The Senate have approved your nomination of me to the Office of a Judge. And if under those Circumstances, it shou'd be Your Excellencys Opinion that I ought not to be Commission'd, my Reputation is for ever blasted, an eternal Mark will be fix'd on me, and then may I indeed (to use borrowed Language) grow old in wretchedness, perhaps poverty and what is worse even Contempt. To use your Excellencys own Language to Congress, it will embitter every moment of my future days. But Sir, shou'd you determine against me, I pledge you my sacred Honor it will not lessen my affection for you, for I am confident that you will do every thing for me, that to Justice can appertain.—I am Sir with every Sentiment of Respectful Regard Your Excellencys most Obedt Servt,

JOS: ANDERSON

RC (DLC: Washington Papers); endorsed by Lear. Enclosure: An "original Certificate of Colo. [Francis] Barber" of the Third New Jersey Regiment, probably testifying to Anderson's service in that regiment and certainly dated before 11 Feb. 1783, when Barber was accidentally killed (not found).

VI. Opinion of the Secretary of State

On view and consideration of the testimonies in favour of Mr. Anderson's character, they appear to me to place it on high ground. Against this there is no testimony but that of Mr. Jaquet, which being contradicted by his own former testimony and by the person who committed it to writing, and who seems to have been made acquainted by the subject of it, I should estimate it at nothing, and certainly as not sufficient to oppose the whole current of evidence which has been produced in favour of Mr. Anderson.

TH: JEFFERSON
Mar. 4. 1791.

RC (DNA: RG 59, MLR); endorsed by Lear: "The Secy of State on the Case of Majr. Anderson March 4th. 1791." PrC (DLC). Tr (DNA: RG 59, SDC). For comment on entries in SJPL, see Editorial Note.

VII. Tobias Lear to the Secretary of State

United States, 4th. March 1791

By the President's command T. Lear has the honor to inform the Secretary of State, that the opinion given by the Secretary in the case of Mr. Anderson agrees fully with that which the President has formed upon a complete view of the circumstances.—And it is the President's wish that Mr. Anderson's Commission should issue accordingly.

TOBIAS LEAR
Secretary to the President
of the United States

RC (DLC: Washington Papers). PrC (DNA: RG 59, MLR); docketed by Lear. Tr (DNA: RG 59, SDC). Not recorded in SJL.

From Robert Coram

SIR   Wilmington March 5. 1791

In conformity to an act of Congress for the encouragement of
Learning I herewith send you a Copy of a Pamphlet which I have
lately published. You will perceive from the 76 page that I had
not read your notes when I wrote it, as your plan is more liberal
and extensive than the one I have proposed; but as the pamphlet
bids fair to run a second edition, I will endeavour to make amends
for the error I have committed by not having your book in my
posse[ss]ion when I finished my pamphlet.—I am Sir with Respect
&c.
                                          R. CORAM

RC (DNA: RG 59, MLR); endorsed as received 9 Mch. 1791 and so recorded in SJL.

Robert Coram (ca. 1761-1796) was born in England and brought as an infant to Charleston, S.C. His father, a merchant, became a Loyalist during the Revolution, but Coram enlisted in the state navy and served with Alexander Gillon on the *South Carolina* and, for a brief time, with John Paul Jones on *Bon Homme Richard*, being cited for "gallant behavior" in the engagement with *Serapis*. He was captured by the British in 1782 and, on being discharged from prison ship, he went to Delaware, married, kept school, served as librarian for the Wilmington Library Company, was elected to the Delaware Constitutional Convention in 1792, and, for six months before his death on 9 Mch. 1796, edited *The Delaware Gazette*. He was an ardent republican and a founding member in 1794 of the Patriotic Society of Newcastle County (John A. Munroe, "The Philadelawareans," PMHB, LXIX [Apr. 1945], 138).

The enclosed pamphlet was Coram's *Political inquiries: to which is added, a plan for the general establishment of schools throughout the United States* (Wilmington, 1791). The author sent a copy to Washington on the same day, stating that he "wrote it Chiefly with a design of being useful to my Country" (Coram to Washington, 5 Mch. 1791, DLC: Washington Papers). If TJ did look up the page indicated, he found this statement: "Mr. Noah Webster is the only American author, indeed the only author of any nation, if we except perhaps Montesquieu, who

has taken up the subject of education upon that liberal and equitable scale which it justly deserves. I had the present work in idea, some time before Mr. Webster's essays made their appearance; and was not a little pleased to think he had anticipated my idea" (*Political inquiries*, p. 76). Coram's statement that he had not read *Notes on Virginia* when he wrote his own pamphlet collides with another observation about the aborigines: "Excepting Clavigero's history of Mexico, the short account given by Mr. Jefferson, Carver's travels, the history of the five nations, and Bancroft's history of Guiana, I do not recollect an account of the American, which deserves the name of history" (same, p. 12).

Coram's pamphlet did not run to a second edition. It had little influence in its own day and its chief interest lies in the fact that it exemplified the widespread feeling arising out of the ferment of the Revolution that laws and institutions in the United States, particularly systems of education, should be framed in accordance with republican principles of equality. His *Political inquiries* was indeed less coherent than the speculations on the subject by such contemporaries as Noah Webster, Benjamin Rush, James Sullivan, Nathaniel Chipman, Samuel Knox, and Samuel Harrison Smith—the two last being winners of the award of the American Philosophical Society, itself exemplifying the republican impulse, that had been created to encourage the development of plans of liberal education "adapted to the genius of the Government of the United States . . . on principles of the most extensive utility" (Knox, *An essay on the best system of* education adapted to the . . . United States [Baltimore, 1799]; Smith, Remarks on education [Philadelphia, 1798]). Coram's admittedly undigested plan, his heavy dependence on Webster, his idealization of the American Indians, his extravagant language, his emphasis on class differences, and his obvious utopianism made his diffuse observations on education quite impracticable and unrealistic for the society to which he addressed himself. His treatise was, in fact, an emotional response to revolutionary ideals by a man of some talent who was genuinely interested in education but who lacked both formal instruction and intellectual discipline. Civilized man, Coram declared, "has neither habitation nor food; but forlorn and out cast, he perishes for want, and starves in the midst of universal plenty" (p. viii). Man had been miserable at every stage of civilization and, in spite of all his science and philosophy, had made only "a retrograde advance to happiness" (p. v). These were astonishing words to address to Americans in 1791 who were far from starving and who believed themselves to be opening a new era in history. But this was the premise that Coram set forth.

The essence of his political view was that the unequal distribution of property was the parent of almost all disorders in government and society. He saw the remedy for this in a system of equal education so that all might be sufficiently trained in the sciences and the arts to gain a subsistence. Pointing to the widely accepted doctrine of equality in America and indeed postulating an equality of mental powers as well as an equality of rights, Coram then incongruously grounded his plea for education on the assumption of deep inequalities existing in the American economy and society. His thesis—it was scarcely more than that and certainly lacked the qualities required for a truly systematic and coherent plan—was obstensibly addressed to the United States, but his proofs of decadence and degrading inequality were drawn from Europe. This air of unreality in the context of his own society perhaps explains why the pamphlet received no attention until modern historical investigation brought it to light and the wars and depressions of the twentieth century seemed to give some relevance to its assertion that man in civilized society "starves in the midst of universal plenty" (Charles A. and Mary R. Beard, The rise of American civilization, IV [New York, 1942], p. 126-37; A. O. Hansen, Liberalism and American education, p. 63-79; H. G. Good, A history of American education [New York, 1956], p. 81-2, 93-4—the last a perceptive comment on the unrealistic and ill-timed proposals of Coram and others). But in his own day the irrelevancy of Coram's premise provided the most distinguishing feature of an otherwise unoriginal essay.

From Tench Coxe

March 5th. 1791

Mr. Coxe has the honor to enclose to Mr. Jefferson some notes upon navigation marked [A] which he prepared at the request of the Chairman on the Navigation Committee. That subject being now refer'd to Mr. Jefferson by the house of representatives Mr. Coxe takes the liberty of depositing these papers with him in the hope that they may be of some use. Mr. C. also has the honor to enclose a little pamphlet of his written about four years ago on American commerce and another on American Manufactures, which, tho not a part of the subject, has a near relation to it.

RC (DLC); endorsed by TJ: "Navigation." Not recorded in SJL. Enclosures: (1) Coxe's MS on navigation, printed below. (2) An enquiry into the principles on which a commercial system for the United States of America should be founded. (3) *An address to an assembly of the friends of American manufactures*. These two pamphlets by Coxe, both printed in Philadelphia in 1787, had long since been sent to TJ by John Browne Cutting (Cutting to TJ, 11 July 1788, note; Sowerby, Nos. 3622-3).

Thoughts on the Navigation of the United States, and concerning further means of encouraging it.

The following propositions are freely hazarded by way of opening the subject. None of them should be tenaciously insisted on, nor will they it is hoped be hastily rejected. If on reflexion they shall appear reasonable and safe, they may serve to guide us in this interesting and difficult enquiry. It is affirmed then—

1. That there is no branch of business in which the people of the United States are more skilful and expert than in the building and navigating of ships.

2. That no people excel the citizens of the United States in building and navigating of ships.

3. That the territories of the United States contain greater quantities of the materials for building and equipping ships than any other country bordering on an ocean.

4. That there are few or no manufactures essentially necessary to the building and out fit of ships, but which are either well established in the United States or of which the establishment is rendered certain by satisfactory experiments.

5. That we have derived and shall continue to acquire many and very valuable citizens and much capital from foreign nations by the temptations which have been and may be presented to them in a prosperous navigation resulting from an highly productive Agriculture and carried on in excellent and cheap ships, remarkably well supplied with cheap necessaries and refreshments.

6. That there is no object in the affairs of the United States to which the aid of men and capital are more frequently or more easily derived from Europe than that of navigation.

7. That such measures for the encouragement of our national shipping as will not injure our agriculture, by closing some vent for our produce or some inlet of supply may generally be deemed safe and expedient.

8. That such measures as will favor our navigation, without encreasing the burdens upon foreign ships, will be less offensive to them and less likely to produce what are termed retaliating measures on their part, than those which while they operate only the same degree of benefit to our shipping, encrease the actual burden upon theirs.

9. That it is better for our landed interest that we promote our navigation by decreasing the actual burdens on our own ships, than by laying equivalent additional burdens upon those of foreigners: because a duty on the vehicle, which transports our produce to market, whether that vehicle be *a vessel* or *a waggon*, or whether it be the property of *a citizen* or *a foreigner* is manifestly an *equal deduction* from the gross value of our productions.

10. That for the last reason also it is as bad policy for an agricultural country to aim at drawing revenue from vessels as from farming waggons. This position however is not intended in the least degree to influence the question concerning the expediency of reasonable duties on foreign tonnage expressly to favor our own ships and without a view to revenue.

11. That if the fund produced by this impost on foreign vessels (in the laying of which it is conceived no view to revenue should be had) is adequate to defraying the cost and charges of improvements and establishments for the promotion and accomodation of navigation, 'tis not consistent with the landholders interest to oblige the American shipping to contribute to it, more than it would be to make their waggons contribute to the ordinary expence of repairing the highways.

12. That by encouraging our navigation *in general* by exempting it from every avoidable charge and burden, we lessen or remove the necessity and inducements to expensive and (often) deceptive bounties and premiums to encourage particular branches, from mere naval policy, and other measures of doubtful propriety.

13. It is generally to be presumed that a branch of commerce, which has been known and pursued by a nation for several years and which still requires the aid of bounties is not worth following, *as a trade*, though considerations of *policy* may sometimes, yet very seldom, render it expedient to give it that assistance.

14. That no foreign nation can be reasonably displeased with or consider itself as improperly treated by a *general regulation* the tendency of which is to produce the same effects upon their navigation or commerce, which their *general* or *particular* laws produce and are avowedly intended to produce upon ours.

15. That the shipping of the United States (which is two thirds of the whole Tonnage employed by them) is, in co-operation with the shipping of any foreign nation adequate to the importation of many times the quantity of goods with which that nation supplies us.[1]

16. That if no prohibition to export, nor no new duty on tonnage is laid on foreign vessels they will be as well able *to export our produce* as now, and consequently no present vent or foreign market for it can be lost or diminished.

If the members of the legislature from the several parts of the union should not on examination dissent from the foregoing propositions, they may contribute to a concordance in accepting or rejecting the following

MEASURES FOR ENCOURAGING THE NAVIGATION OF THE UNITED STATES.

I. To exempt American coasting vessels from the tonnage of six cents.*

II. To exempt American fishermen from the same. This class of traders are aided by heavy bounties by all our rivals. To relieve them

---

* The public faith will require an adequate fund in lieu of that arising from these three sources, to be provided.

from unnecessary charges appears therefore to be expedient on our part and seems to be safe and inoffensive.*

III. To exempt American ships in the foreign trade from the tonnage of 6 cents.*

IV. To give such further aid to the fisheries as on consideration of the expected report of the Secretary of State shall be found expedient.§

V. To prohibit the interference of foreigners in our coasting trade, with an exception in favor of the cargoes they may have last brought in until they shall have sold and delivered them to a purchaser.†

VI. To confine the importation of goods to the ships of the nation making or producing them and our own.

VII. To apply the surplus of the tonnage in building Lighthouses, Beacons, Buoys, public piers, dock yards, naval fortifications to be occupied also as naval hospitals, nautical schools and other measures that will give aid, and permanency to our navigation. If this idea were to be adopted by law the Tonnage of six cents would be less exceptionable, but its expediency would still be doubtful.

VIII. The encouragement of the manufacture of ships, cordage, sail cloth, anchors, paints, brass and iron cannon, sheathing paper, sheet copper, composition metal to be used with copper in lieu of iron work, small arms of all kinds, gunpowder, &c.

IX. The free importation of hemp, iron, wood and timber for the promotion of those manufactures and for the preservation of our magazines of timber. The attaining of the right to cut and import mahogany, cedar and logwood from Honduras, Campeachy and the Musquito Shore is of consequence to our Shipbuilding in this view, and to our carrying trade; also the right to import Mahogany and Logwood from French St. Domingo. `Treaty`

X. The encouragement of Manufactures in general will aid our Navigation, if we admit raw articles free of duty, such as cotton, copper, iron, hemp, &c. because our exports being much more bulky than our imports our Ships return often two thirds or half empty. By making raw articles free we could obtain a freight home out of those bulky commodities. New England would take iron always and hemp now from Russia; the middle and northern towns would take cotton from Bombay and Surat; and so of wool and other articles.

XI. The junction of Chesapeake bay and Albemarle sound and that of Chesapeak and Delaware bays by canals and other improvements of the same nature, by substituting *boats* for *waggons* would add greatly to our nursery for seamen and consequently encourage navigation. Of the same nature will be the effect of the canal from the Virginia collieries to James River, as it will exceedingly promote the coasting trade in coal. This is found the most certain source of mariners on any sudden emergency in England.

XII. A reduction of the Admiralty fees which are oppressive in private suits, and particularly in the little but frequent business of disputes about Seamen's wages.

XIII. The abolition of the discrimination of 20 cents in favor of

§ Enlarging on this head here, is deemed improper.
† The coasters above 20 Tons appear to be 113,000 Tons.

"recorded vessels" or vessels built in the United States but belonging to foreigners. This is a sacrifice of *Navigation* which wants aid, to the *manufactory of ships* which does not want it.

XIV. Regulating the business of pilots throughout the United States.

XV. The regulation of harbors throughout the United States.

XVI. To guard against frauds in the ownership of vessels, by penalties on persons who shall have collusively held or shall have collusively transferred an American ship or without notice in a limited time after, by providing a power to call in registers occasionally, by the form of the oath of the Master, by the form of the oath of the owner, by obliging all the owners to swear to the register, by the forfeiture of the vessel, collusively held, to the use of the informer.

XVII. The establishment of health offices in all our principal ports to avoid as far as may be prudent, the injurious and expensive delays of quarantines.

XVIII. The exemption of professed mariners from militia duty, whether officers or common sailors.

The exemption of our own ships from the Tonnage of six cents will be favorable to our Agriculture, because, as hath been remarked it will be *a diminution of the charges on carrying our productions to foreign markets*. It is the more advisable *in the foreign trade* because the freight of a bushel of wheat, for example, to Europe is more than from most of the great corn countries of Europe to their principal foreign markets. Sicily for instance can supply all the ports in the South of France, and most of those in the South of Spain without going out of the Mediterranean, and can export to Cadiz, Lisbon, Bilboa, &c. at much less than an American freight. *In the fisheries* an exemption from the duty of six cents appears to be a small and very reasonable encouragement when compared with the great bounties extended to this branch of commerce by foreigners. *The coasting trade* appears plainly to be our principal nursery for Seamen. The licensed coasters being 113,000 Tons, will be found, with those under 20 Tons, to be more than our foreign traders; for if the American traders to foreign parts make on a medium three entries per annum then the duty on 363,000 Tons will appear to be paid by 121,000 Tons of vessels. As we have no foreign colonies, a very extensive sea coast, and an unexampled variety of productions, and as our wood boats will be gradually exchanged for colliers, it is plain that the coasting trade will be more important to us than any other branch of navigation and more valuable to the United States than to any other country in the world.

Before closing these remarks upon the abolition of the Tonnage of six cents it may be observed that the *foreign* Tonnage in one year preceding 30th. September 1790 was about 135,000 Dollars, and the light houses and other nautical establishments through the year 1790 have only required appropriations of 44,442 Dollars including the grant for building one of the best lighthouses that will exist, which grant is larger by one third than what proves requisite, and the finishing of that at Portland head.

The proposed regulation for confining importations to our own ships and those of the nation making or producing the commodities, must prove a very efficient measure. Let us examine its effects on any particular Nation, taken in combination with another regulation, viz. the addition of 10 per cent to the quantum of the duties on goods in foreign bottoms. Let the British shipping be the example. The *confining clause* will cut off from those vessels the importation of all China goods, all East India goods, all melasses, coffee, cocoa and other articles from the French West Indies, all coarse salts from all the world except the trifle from their West Indies, all goods from Amsterdam or Rotterdam, that is all goods from Holland, all french brandies, wines, fruits, &c. In short it will deprive them of all participation in the freight of our importations, except from their own dominions. The *additional 10 per cent* will operate against them upon all our importations from their dominions, except in one particular, viz. those from their insular and other colonies. The course of the business then, exhibited by figures, will be as follows.

	Dollars
Let the new duties under the present impost act be taken at	3,000,000
It is proved by the late return that near three fourths of the goods imported have received the allowance of the 10 per cent deduction, that is to say, there are imported in American bottoms—¾ of 3,000,000 which deduct is 2,250,000, say only	2,200,000
There will be imported then in foreign bottoms goods that pay duty to the amount of	800,000
Of these the English vessels would lose the following by the *confining clause* — Teas, and other China and East India goods, wines, brandies, gin, arrack, foreign rum except their own, Dutch, Russian, French, German, and other dry or bale goods, coarse salt from *Europe*, melasses, foreign iron, cordage, hemp, and other articles of which the duties will probably be one half of the above remainder; which deduct, say	400,000
	400,000

There will remain Rum, coffee, sugar, fish &c. from the British colonies, and goods from Cuba, S. America and other foreign ports into which our vessels are not admitted, being less than one seventh of our imports.

Should Great Britain complain of it, she may be told *it is not aimed at her*, for the terms of the act should be general—that *it is taken from her own existing laws*—and that we are ready *to repeal our clause as it regards all our dominions*, if *they will repeal as generally.*

Foreigners at present do but little in our coasting trade, but the encouragement of this branch of our navigation, that will arise from a prohibition, is still desirable. Whatever interference by foreigners does take place will be prevented. A safe principle of legislation will be adopted in our navigation system. The merchants and mariners of the United States will consider this branch as secured to them exclusively, and will have more confidence to extend in it. Our coasting vessels being a moiety of our shipping and encreasing, those seamen whom we employ that are subjects of any foreign power with whom we may be at war, *will be able to find a safer employment there, without leaving our service, than if they should go into our ships in foreign trades*. This it will be perceived, must be *a great advantage* to us considering how many of our seamen are or have been *subjects of Great Britain*, the legal doctrines of that nation with regard to a *subjects allegiance* and the compulsion on and temptation to British sailors *to enter on board their ships after capture*. By emplying our own seamen in the foreign trade, these hazards will be so avoided, and a vacancy will be created into which the foreigners in our employ may be introduced.

The XVI article wants attention: There is no doubt but that many frauds are committed. Penalties might be inflicted, if a merchant, owning a vessel, and *assuming to be a citizen of the United States*, should be found exercising functions or pursuing objects or callings in a foreign country, which require or are accompanied with acknowledgment of a foreign allegiance. In such case or any other case of fraud in regard to the ownership of a vessel the person might be rendered liable to an action (or his property to Attachment) for reimbursement of the public dues, of which the pretended ownership had occasioned the United States to be deprived, and the vessel might be forefeited to the informer.

Should the above two regulations [*the 10 ⅌ Cent additional* and *the confining clause*] have the expected effect upon the *inward* voyage of foreign vessels, tis plain it must also affect us favorably in the competition for the carrying of our produce to foreign countries. It would decrease the sum of their benefits in the American voyage and thus prevent their being found here in the same numbers to interfere with our vessels in the transportation of our produce.

Were France, Spain and Portugal to adopt the *confining regulation* the carrying trade of the world would sustain a considerable revolution, and, consequently, considerable effects would be produced upon the balance of *naval* power.[2]

MS (DLC); entirely in Coxe's hand; 25 numbered pages, plus a leaf bearing the following: "Notes upon the Navigation of the United States. **A**." MS is undated, but Coxe evidently began it before TJ handed in his "expected report" on the fisheries, that is, before 1 Feb. 1791.

[1] In margin opposite the two preceding paragraphs are two vertical lines, possibly made by TJ for emphasis.

[2] The handwriting of the two preceding paragraphs suggests that they were added after the main body of the notes had been composed (see Editorial Note to group of documents under 15 Mch. 1791).

From Philip Freneau

SIR   New York March 5th. 1791

I did not receive the Letter you did me the honour to write till this day, and cannot sufficiently express my acknowledgements for the offer you make me of occupying the place you mention, in your office.

Having been for sometime past engaged in endeavouring to establish a Weekly Gazette in Monmouth County, East Jersey, and having at present a prospect of succeeding in a tolerable Subscription, I find myself under the necessity of declining the acceptance of your generous unsollicited proposal, in Justice to my engagements with the people in the quarter of New Jersey above mentioned, and other patrons of my plan.—I have the honour to be, Sir, with the highest respect, Your most obedient humble Servant,   PHILIP FRENEAU

RC (DLC). Recorded in SJL as received 9 Mch. 1791.

From Lewis Littlepage

DEAR SIR   Paris 5th: March. 1791.

I take the liberty of writing to you to request that you would inform me, by the earliest opportunity, whether the President has ever recieved a letter which I wrote to him from Madrid, of the 25th: February 1790. I inclosed it by a private opportunity to the Marquis De La Fayette, who assures me it was forwarded in due time, but the reception has never been intimated to either him, or me, which, I own, occasions me great uneasiness, as the contents were of a most private and delicate nature, and (should the letter have fallen into other hands) might be infinitely prejudicial to me.

You may also have been informed by Mr. Carmichael that he had obtained a promise from me to make some political communications of a secret nature to the President, respecting the late contestations between the Courts of Madrid and London, in which, from very peculiar circumstances, I was personally, and deeply involved. I had even obtained an eventual permission from the King of Poland for that purpose, but as those communications could only be considered as a continuation of my letter of the date before mentioned to the President, to which no answer has been recieved, and as he may have motives for that silence which it would be presumptuous in me to attempt to penetrate, I conclude that it might be deemed equally so to intrude myself further upon his notice. All that I intreat to know, is whether the letter in question has been recieved, or not: in the first case I shall be easy as to future consequences; in the second I must make enquiries as to it's fate.

The political horizon in the North is still gloomy. Russia has corrupted the Divan, but the Sultan is still obstinate for prosecuting the war, and has lately been very pressing to know what are the final intentions of the King of Prussia, and even *"in what month* he means to commence hostilities against Russia." The answer is defered until the British Cabinet can be consulted.

You know, I presume, that the Guarantee of Prussia, and the Maritime powers, her allies, is still the great obstacle to peace: Russia offers it upon the *Statu Quo*, but rejects all mediation or guarantee: the King of Prussia persuades Selim (and not without reason) that the existence of his Empire can never be secure, unless it makes part of the *General System*; and that if he concludes a *separate* peace, he may be again attacked upon the slightest occasion, or indeed, no occasion at all, without being entitled to the support of any European power.

Upon the same principle the Court of Berlin presses the conclusion of the Alliance between Poland and the Porte, and even holds out the idea (which circumstances may realize) of a Confederation for preserving the peace and equilibrium of Europe, between England, Prussia, Holland, the Germanic League, Poland, the Ottoman Empire, and, *perhaps*, Sweden. The first preparatory step toward that system, was fixing the succession of Poland upon the Duke of Brunswic:—that has failed:—the second is an official ouverture lately made by the English Minister at Warsaw, for some commercial arrangements between Great Britain and Poland, in which Prussia is to be comprehended. I have besides reason to believe that, by this time, orders are really sent to the Polish Envoy at Constantinople to conclude the Treaty which has been so long in negociation.

The grand point in Polish politics, is the system of *Hereditary* Succession, and there still exists a strong party for establishing it, but so far with little prospect of success. The *Elective* Succession you know, is already settled upon the Elector of Saxony: the King of Sweden however is yet Quixote enough to aspire to it secretly, or rather is gulled by Russia, with the idea.

You are doubtless in need of no information upon the affairs of this country; I shall therefore only observe (as it is not yet public) that some uneasiness is excited both here and in Spain, by the suspicion that England means to send a fleet to the Mediterranean, not so much in the view of supporting the Turks as of forming an establishment for herself in the Archipellago.

The fact is, that it has been for some time very seriously

agitated in the British Cabinet, whether, in case of a rupture with Russia, it would not be more adviseable to assist the Turks directly by a fleet upon the Black Sea, than by sending one to the Baltic, where it can only cruise a few months, and, if the Russians chuse to remain in port, must return, like Caligula, with cockle-shells, by way of trophy;—as you know Russia has no Convoys to intercept.

Reports of foreign invasion, and projects for a counter-Revolution, are daily circulated here. You may easily concieve that both parties occasionally make use of these political Bug-Bears:—the Aristocrats, to keep up the spirit of their disponding party:—the Democratical Cheifs, from the principle that public confidence is never so implicitly bestowed as in times of real, or supposed, danger.

My private affairs begin to assume a more promising aspect than they have done since the opening of the present Diet. The King has recalled me once more to Poland, and I shall set out in a few days by the way of Berlin, where I may continue some time. The Deputation for Foreign affairs in Poland have sanctioned all my ostensible transactions with the Court of Spain, and at the same time refuse to acknowledge the legality of my Mission. If obscurity may pass for depth in politics, you must allow that combination to be profound.

I hope you will find a moment of leisure to write to me: if so be pleased to inclose your letter to Mr. Short, as by means of Mazzei, or the Polish Minister (who is now on his way here). He will always be able to convey it to me safely. In the mean time beleive me ever, with great respect, and the most sincere attachment, Dear Sir, your most obedient & most humble Servant,

LEWIS LITTLEPAGE

RC (DLC); at foot of text: "T. Jefferson Esqr. Minister and Secretary of State of the United States." Recorded in SJL as received 21 June 1791.

On 16 Feb. 1791 David Humphreys also informed the President that Carmichael said Littlepage had sent "a clear, interesting and intelligent view of affairs in the North, in a letter written from Madrid last Summer, and sent at the same time with one written . . . by the King of Poland in his own hand" (RC in DLC: Washington Papers).

Washington replied that he had "never received any letter from Mr. Littlepage, or from the King of Poland, which you say Mr. Carmichael informed you were sent to me last summer" (Washington to Humphreys, 20 July 1791, *Writings*, ed. Fitzpatrick, XXXI, 321). TJ gave him the same assurance, couched in the kind of information on American affairs that he knew would find its way into the Polish court and diplomatic circles through the medium of this American adventurer (TJ to Littlepage, 29 July 1791).

From Thomas Mann Randolph, Jr.

DEAR SIR   Monticello March 5 1791.

Mr. Thompson the gentleman whom I mentioned last summer to you as a Candidate for a Consulship has applied to me again on the same subject by a letter which I inclose to you now. I will not repeat my desire that my representation may not have the least weight, as I know that it ought not, and of course am fully convinced that it will not. However as in this case perhaps the inquiry into the character of a candidate will aim principally to ascertain his Integrity and Industry of which every man ought to be a judge, it may not be improper for me to say something of Mr. Thompson. The reception he met with on his return to Madeira shews that he could not have been looked on unfavorably before he left that Island. He had resided there a considerable time and was concerned during the whole of it in a Mercantile house. His behaviour during his stay in Virginia was such as to gain the esteem of a great many genteel people who are very much interested in his success. From my Intercourse with him I am fully convinced that he is worthy of confidence and sincerely wish that he may not be disappointed.

My Father continues to press the purchase of Edgehill on me and shews so much eagerness to have the affair resumed, that I have not as yet given him a decisive answer, which must have been in the negative. If my circumstances admitted of it with the greatest ease, still my aversion to increase the number of my negroes would be an insurmountable objection. My desire to gratify my Father would induce me to attempt it if there was a prospect of my making myself whole, without employing slaves in the cultivation of the lands. It will be better I believe to confine my views to a small tract, just sufficient to supply me with provisions. Patsy agrees with me, but we both wish to be guided by you.—I am Dear Sir your most obedt. & aff. Servt.,

THOMAS M. RANDOLPH junr.

RC (DLC); addressed: "Thomas Jefferson Sec: of State Philadelphia"; postmarked "FREE" and "Richmond March 17"; endorsed by TJ as received 24 Mch. 1791 and so recorded in SJL. Enclosures: (1) Thomas Thompson to Randolph, not found (but see Thompson to TJ, 8 Dec. 1790). (2) Mary Jefferson to TJ, 6 Mch. 1791, a letter bearing obvious marks of promptings from her sister and brother-in-law.

From David Humphreys

Sir   Lisbon March 6th. 1791.

I do not wait to become fully acquainted with the commercial intercourse which subsists between the United States and Portugal, before I resume the subject mentioned in my letter of the 19th of Novr. last, so far as relates to the manner in which our trade has been managed here, since the year 1783.

Immediately after the war, upon the arrival of the first vessels from America, there appeared to be no Person whose business it was to assist the Captains in the different transactions of entering and clearing the vessels at the Custom House. The English Consul applied to the Portuguese Government for authority to perform the duties and receive the same fees as on British vessels. This would have been granted, had not Mr. Henry Arnold Dorhman (who interested himself so much in favor of American Seamen during the war, and to whom Congress have since made so honorable a compensation) heard of the matter; and produced an authenticated Copy of the Resolution of Congress appointing him Agent of the U.S. in Portugal. In consequence of which it was directed that he should be allowed to act also as Consul for the protection of their Trade. Soon afterwards, when he went to America, he left annexed to his original Appointment a written Instrument, with his brother Jacob Dorhman, deputing, as far as he was able, all the Powers with which he was himself invested, to the said Jacob Dorhman. Under cover of this, the business has hitherto been conducted. And I know of no complaints but that it has been well done. Although Mr. Dorhman, and Mr. Harrison (who acts as a kind of Assistant to him) had no reason to suppose I was any thing more than a private American traveller, they have both been extremely attentive, and in some measure useful to me. Particularly in getting my Baggage through the Custom House, and in saving me the trouble of applying for the Portuguese and Spanish Passports which were necessary in my Journey to Madrid.

I believe that Mr. Jacob Dorhman has been embarrassed by his Connection in a Mercantile House some years ago; but that he is now liberated from his embarrassments and doing business in a creditable manner. He was called upon last summer, by an Edict of the Court, as the Person charged with the Consulate of the U.S. of America, to be present and assist in the litigated affair of the flour which was refused to be received, because it was shipped after the date limited by the Order for exportation.—I

[421]

know little of him. His appearance, manners and conversation are in his favor. Mr. Harrison is also a decent, well-behaved man, who appears to be acquainted with business. When any number of American vessels are here, the whole time and attention of one man, at least, is employed in making applications for them at the various Offices.

Thus every thing has been managed by Courtesy until now; and our vessels have been treated generally on the footing of those belonging to the most favored Nations.

The Court has been at Salvaterra, a Royal Residence on the Tagus, at about 14 leagues distance from Lisbon, ever since I returned from Spain. This is, at present, no Theatre for Politics.

In France the national Assembly are wisely using some precautions to guard against the effects of the interference of foreign Powers in their domestic Affairs. Upon the Motion of Mirabeau and Charles Lameth, provisional arrangements are taken for raising 100,000 Men, somewhat on the plan of our Minute Men at the commencement of the war. The Post Masters have offered the use of 5000 Horses for transporting military supplies where they may be needed. And 10 Men are to be selected from each Company in Paris (which will make a force of 10,000 Men) in order to march towards the frontiers, under the orders of Gouvion. Estates continue to sell for nearly double the sums at which they were estimated.

As I am lodged here in an English Hotel, where nothing is spoken but English or French, I find no proficiency is to be made in the Portuguese language. Not knowing when I may hear from America, and desirous of profitting of this interval, I have determined to remove tomorrow to Mafra, a small pleasant Village, a few Leagues distant, where is a Palace, a Convent, and a very considerable College. As I shall carry letters of introduction to the principal Professors, from the Secretary of the Academy of Sciences, the Pope's Nuncio and others, I hope to pass my time not altogether disagreeably or unprofitably. Directions will be left with Mr. Bulkeley to send a Messenger to me, as soon as any letters shall arrive for me. In the mean time, it is uncertain whether I may have opportunity of writing again to you for three or four weeks, unless something of importance should intervene, in which I shall not be wanting in endeavours to make the earliest communications.—I have the honor to be, With every sentiment of esteem & respect, Sir Your Most obedient & Very humble Servant,   D. HUMPHREYS

RC (DNA: RG 59, DD); at head of text: "(No. 13)," altered by overwriting to correct number; endorsed by TJ as received 25 Apr. 1791, with number similarly corrected; corresponding entry in SJL reads in part: "No. 13 for 14." Tr (same).

From Mary Jefferson

march 6

According to my dear Papa's request I now set down to write. We were very uneasy for not having had a letter from you since six weeks till yesterday I received yours which I now answer. The marble Pedestal and a dressing table are come. Jenny is gone down with Mrs. Fleming who came here to see sister while she was sick. I suppose you have not received the letter in which Mr. Randolph desires you to name the child. We hope you will come to see us this summer therefore you must not disapoint us and I expect you want to see my little neice as much as you do any of us. We are all well and hope you are so too. Adieu dear Papa I am your affectionate daughter   MARY JEFFERSON

P.S. My sister says I must tell you the child grows very fast.

RC (ViU); punctuation supplied; endorsed by TJ as received 24 Mch. 1791 and so recorded in SJL.

TJ would not receive for another week Randolph's letter of 8 Feb. 1791 asking him to name the child. His letter to Mary was that of 16 Feb. 1791. Delay of the mails on the cross-posts and in particular the situation in Albemarle county added to TJ's long-felt concern for efficiency in the postal service (see TJ to Randolph, 11 Jan. and 24 Feb. 1791). Since his arrival in Philadelphia TJ had kept up his methodical posting of letters to Monticello in rotation, usually on Wednesdays in time to catch the south-bound post, and evidently had missed his schedule only in the last days of January, a period of extraordinary pressure. In that interval in which he wrote to the Monticello family a total of 13 letters, young Randolph wrote 4, Mary 3, and Martha 2. Already it was being reported that the President was dissatisfied with the administration of Postmaster-General Samuel Osgood (Samuel Hodgdon to Timothy Pickering, 15 Feb. 1791; RC in MHi), and it may well be that the Secretary of State who was so deeply interested in the postal service on personal and public grounds helped contribute to that feeling.

From George Washington

Sunday 6th. Mar: 1791

The P. would thank Mr. Jefferson for placing all, or such of the enclosed Papers (after he has perused them) in the hands of the Attorney General as he shall deem necessary for the purpose of drawing the several conveyances of the ceded Lands, or the form of one.

For the former, it is conceived farther information than the enclosures contain, is wanting.—For the latter, the agreement, and perhaps the Plat to which it refers, is all that is necessary; but the plat referred to, does not apply to the subsequent purchases.

Dft (DLC: Washington Papers); docketed by Washington. FC (DLC: Washington Papers). Not recorded in SJL or SJPL.

To Edmund Randolph

[6? March 1791]

The inclosed papers will shew you that cessions are to be made by landholders near George town, to the President for carrying into effect the establishment of the federal government there. In all cases where it is permitted, the lands are to be paid for, and the private title cleared off. I am not certain whether some of the cessions are not with a reservation of a portion of the land, without any other alternative. In these cases the condition must be submitted to.—The President wishes you to prepare a form of conveyance to be executed by each landholder separately, the lands to be conveyed to him in fee, to be disposed of to such persons, on such estates and conditions, or to be retained and so applied, as he in his discretion shall think most promotive of the objects of accomodating the federal government there, erecting and appropriating buildings, reserving grounds for public use of pleasure, annexing such conditions to his reconveyances of the lots and grounds as may secure a submission to such regulations as may be expedient till there be a corporation authorised to enact byelaws &c. &c. &c.—I rather believe the President would wish to have this as soon as you can.

Dft (DLC: Washington Papers); undated; at head of text: "Th: J. to E. R. inviolable secrecy"; docketed by Washington: "From Mr. Jefferson to the Attorney-General." Not recorded in SJL or SJPL.

To William Short

DEAR SIR   Philadelphia Mar. 8. 1791.

A conveyance offering by which we can send large packets you will recieve herewith the following articles.

1. The newspapers.
2. The acts of the 2d. session of Congress.

3. A report on the fisheries of the U.S. It is thought that this contains matter which may be usefully communicated. I am persuaded the better this subject is understood in France, the more they will see their interest in favouring our fisheries.

4. A letter from the President to the King, of which an open copy is inclosed for your information.

5. A letter from myself to the Count de Moustier in answer to his to the President and myself taking leave.

6. A letter from myself to the President of the National assembly of France in answer to his to Congress on the death of Dr. Franklin. Let it be understood that Congress can only correspond through the Executive, whose organ in the case of foreign nations is the Secretary of state. The President of the U.S. being co-ordinate with Congress, cannot personally be their scribe.

7. Some papers in a case interesting to Dr. McHenry of Baltimore. He at first sent them to me with a desire to commit the subject of them wholly to you. I informed him we could not consent that you should be used as the agent of private individuals, but that if he would provide an agent on the spot who would undertake the details of sollicitation, management, correspondence, &c. I would desire you to patronize the measure so far as you should find it prudent and just. It is put on this footing as you will see by his answer to me.

8. A correction of the Report on weights and measures.

You are desired to have a medal of gold struck from the diplomatic die formerly ordered and present it with a chain of gold to the Count de Moustier who is notified that this will be done by you. I formerly informed you that we proposed to vary the worth of the present by varying the size of the links of the chain, which are fixed at 365 in number. Let each link in the present instance contain 6. livres worth of gold, and let it be made of plain wire, so that the value may be in the metal and not at all in the workmanship. I shall hope to recieve the dies themselves when a safe conveyance presents itself.[1]—I am with great esteem, Dear Sir Your friend & servant,* TH: JEFFERSON

RC (DLC: Short Papers); partly in code, with interlinear decoding by Short; endorsed as received 28 May 1791. PrC (DLC); text *en clair* of passage to be encoded is on verso of first page. FC (DNA: RG 59, DCI); entirely *en clair*. Enclosures: (1) The newspapers included Fenno's *Gazette* of the United States and Davis' *Virginia Gazette* (TJ to Short, 23 Jan. 1791). (2) The President to the King of France, 2 Mch. 1791, reading: "Very Great and good Friend and Ally.—I have received the Letter wherein you inform me that you have thought proper to give a new Mission to the Sieur de Moustier, and thereby to put an end to his Functions as Minister plenipotentiary here. His Conduct during the Time of his Residence in this Country, has been such as to meet my entire Approbation and Esteem; and it is with great Pleasure I render him the Justice of this Testimony. He carries with him my Wishes, that in continuing to serve your Majesty faithfully, he may continue to enjoy your Favor and Protection. I renew sincere Assurances of the Friendship and Affection which I bear to your Majesty and your Nation, and I pray God to have you, Very great and good Friend and Ally, in his holy keeping.—Written at Philadelphia the second Day of March 1791.—Your good Friend and Ally. George Washington"

(Tr. in DLC: Short Papers; entirely in Remsen's hand, including attestation by TJ; at foot of text: "To our Very great and good Friend and Ally—His Most Christian Majesty"; Entry in SJPL under 2 Mch. 1791 reads: "G. W. to K. of France on [De Moustier's taking leave]"). (3) TJ to De Moustier, 2 Mch. 1791. (4) TJ to the President of the National Assembly, 8 Mch. 1791. (5) James McHenry to TJ, 9 Feb. 1791, recorded in SJL as received 14 Feb. 1791.

1 Preceding words in italic are written in cipher. Short's interlinear decoding has been collated with the texts *en clair* and verified by the Editors, employing Code No. 10.

From Nathaniel Colley

DEAR SIR   Norfolk March 9th. 1791

I have Received your favour of the 9th. Feby with an Enclosd note of 70 Dollars which is Considerable above the Amount of the Account I sent to you as I never meant to Charge freight or Commission: and I Earnestly Entreat youll never think you give any trouble in Collecting any thing of the sort that you may want at any future time as I shall be always happy to be honourd with your Commands in that Respect or any other. I am a little surprisd to find that Captn. Anderson had not Arrivd when you Wrote me as he was to sail in a day or two after the Date of my Letter. I dont Recollect Whether I sent you a bill of Loading in the letter you have Received or by the Captain. But I have one with me Which I can send if any Accident has happend to the Vessel or the Captain Neglected to Call on you. I expect to sail tomorrow for Falmouth and orders if the Wether permits. I shall Esteem it a favour if youll please to Drop me a few lines at my Return to inform me Wheather you have Received the Tables and how they will answer. I am Dear Sir with Esteem your Most Obdt Hb St.,   NATHL COLLEY

RC (MHi); endorsed by TJ as received 22 Mch. 1791 and so recorded in SJL.

When TJ did not respond to the above, Colley wrote again from City Point, just after his arrival from Nantes, saying that he had not yet heard whether the tables had arrived, that he had one of the triplicate bills of lading given him by Captain Atcheson Anderson, and that he would like TJ to send him "a few Lines . . . to the care of John Grayson at Petersburg or Thos. Ritson at Norfolk" (Colley to TJ, 21 July 1791; RC in MHi, endorsed by TJ as received 28 July 1791 and so recorded in SJL). TJ immediately responded: "Dear Captain—I received three days ago your favor of the 21st. The tables had come to hand in due time and in good order. I congratulate you on your safe return to Virginia and hope your returns will ever be safe. Having nothing new worth communication, I have only to add assurances of the esteem of Dr. Sir Your very humble servt, Th: Jefferson" (TJ to Colley, 31 July 1791; PrC in MHi).

To Mary Jefferson

My dear Maria   Philadelphia March 9. 1791.

I am happy to have at length a letter of yours to answer, for that which you wrote to me Feb. 13. came to hand Feb. 28. I hope our correspondence will now be more regular, that you will be no more lazy, and I no more in the growls on that account. On the 27th. of February I saw blackbirds and Robinredbreasts and on the 7th. of this month I heard frogs for the first time this year. Have you noted the first appearance of these things at Monticello? I hope you have, and will continue to note every appearance animal and vegetable which indicates the approach of Spring, and will communicate them to me. By these means we shall be able to compare the climates of Philadelphia and Monticello. Tell me when you shall have peas &c. up, when every thing comes to table, when you shall have the first chickens hatched, when every kind of tree blossoms, or puts forth leaves, when each kind of flower blooms. Kiss your sister and niece for me, and present me affectionately to Mr. Randolph and Miss Jenny.—Yours tenderly, my dear Maria.   Th: J.

PrC (MHi).

From Richard Potts

Sir   Maryland Frederick Town 9 March 1791

Agreeably to your request, I took the earliest opportunity of procuring for you a complete collection of all the Laws of this State, and forwarded them to you by Mr. Jeremiah Warder of Philadelphia, who was so obliging as to take charge of them at Annapolis and to assure me of his safely delivering them to you. Inclosed is the printers Account for them and receipt for the Price which may be reimbursed by an order, on the Collector at Baltimore.[1]

[I know of but one judicial decision that hath taken place in this State which was influenced by the treaty of peace, or to which that applied, and in that Case the Judgment of the Court was in favour of the British Creditor. By a Law passed in this State in October session 1780, Chapter 5 Sect. 11, the debtors of british creditors under certain Circumstances were authorized to pay their debts into the State treasury, and such Payments were declared to be Payments of their Creditors. Very large Sums were paid into the treasury under that Law, and at the last General Court in Annapolis October Term 1790, in a Suit by Mr. Mildred against Mr. Edward Dorsey who in every particular had complied with that Law, and paid a considerable Sum into the Treasury in discharge of his Debt, the Court gave judgment in favour of the Creditor, for his debt and interest, except that Part of the interest that accrued during the War, for which period they decided that no Interest was recoverable. This determination was in the Case of a debt due by Bond executed before the War,]² and took place so short a time before I left Annapolis that I had not an Opportunity of obtaining an official transcript of the Case.—I know of no Laws or Acts of Government that have passed in this State which may certainly be considered as infractions of the treaty of peace. By a law passed at October Session 1780 Chap 45 all property in this State (debts only excepted) belonging to British subjects, was seised and confiscated to the use of this State. Some of this property remained unsold at the time of the treaty and several Laws have since passed for discovering british property, and directing Sales thereof, and under those Laws Some Sales have been made. To the confiscation Law and those passed since the treaty on the subject I refer you, the Latter are I believe the only Laws of this State that have in any manner been objected to as inconsistent with the Treaty, and will be found in November Session 1785. Chap 88 Sect 3, November 1788 Chap 49 Sect 2 and November 1789 Chap 47 Sect 19.—I have the honour to be with great respect Sir Your most obedt & very humble Servt,   RICHARD POTTS³

RC (DNA: RG 59, MLR); addressed: "Thomas Jefferson Esqr."; endorsed by TJ as received 23 Mch. 1791 and so recorded in SJL; with interlinear notes in pencil in TJ's hand (see notes below). FC of Extract (DLC); in clerk's hand, with caption reading: "Extract of a letter from Richard Potts Esquire Attorney of the United States for the District of Maryland, to the Secretary of State"; consisting of that portion of the text indicated in notes below. PrC of Extract (DLC).

It is obvious that TJ originally intended to employ a part of this letter in the Appendix to his reply to Hammond of 29 May 1792, having carefully omitted from the Extract that part which seemed to be at variance with his principal argument (see notes below). Subsequently, however, he chose instead to obtain statements from Maryland's Senators and Representatives as well as from others, and he employed these in substitution for the Extract (see TJ to Senators and Representatives of Maryland, 11 Apr. 1792, and their response, 23 Apr. 1792; Tilghman to TJ, 26 Apr. 1792; Gwinn to TJ, 23 Apr. 1792; Appendixes Nos. 49, 50, and 51 of TJ's reply to Hammond, 29 May 1792). TJ's REQUEST was that of 8 Aug. 1790.

1 At this point in RC TJ interlined in pencil the wording of caption as it appears above on Extract and then bracketed two parts of the text.

2 That part of text enclosed in brackets, inserted in RC by TJ, comprises all of Extract save caption and complimentary close (see notes 1 and 3). Immediately following this point TJ added in pencil interlineally: "add conclusion."

3 TJ bracketed complimentary close and signature to indicate its inclusion in Extract.

Threat of Disunion in the West

Confrontation with Spain on the Mississippi Question

I. SECRETARY OF STATE TO JUAN NEPOMUCENO DE QUESADA, 10 MARCH 1791

II. SECRETARY OF STATE TO EDWARD TELFAIR, 26 MARCH 1791

III. THE PRESIDENT TO JAMES SEAGROVE, 20 MAY 1791

IV. THOMAS JEFFERSON TO HARRY INNES, 7 MARCH 1791

V. THE PRESIDENT TO THE SECRETARY OF STATE, 10 MARCH 1791

VI. SECRETARY OF STATE TO WILLIAM CARMICHAEL, 12 MARCH 1791

VII. SECRETARY OF STATE TO WILLIAM SHORT, 12 MARCH 1791

VIII. SECRETARY OF STATE TO THE PRESIDENT, 18 MARCH 1791

IX. THE PRESIDENT TO THE SECRETARY OF STATE, 19 MARCH 1791

X. SECRETARY OF STATE TO WILLIAM SHORT, 19 MARCH 1791

EDITORIAL NOTE

The Western Country is indubitably the one which will give the first signal of defection, and the power which is in possession of New Orleans will be able to reap the first fruits or to become the first victim of a rising people. This opinion is that of Americans the least biassed about the permanence of the Government they have established. It will be that of all men who reflect dispassionately on the posture of interests and the character of the American people.

—*Otto to Montmorin, 18 Nov. 1790*

Early in 1791 there arose an urgent demand by Georgia planters for the return of slaves that had escaped into the Floridas. Simultaneously, Kentucky leaders, already angry over fumbling measures of frontier defense taken by the federal government and long embittered by its inattention to their need for access to the sea, intensified their old threats of separation in warnings as candid as they were unmistakable. Jefferson's response to these inescapable problems reveals two quite different facets of his diplomacy. To the slaveowners he urged

[429]

an expedient policy of restraint. To the westerners he gave a pledge of bold and decisive action, grounded ultimately upon the conviction he had long held that "the act which abandons the navigation of the Mississippi is an act of separation between the Eastern and Western country."[1] It was such a fateful possibility as this that, through almost two decades, enabled him to anticipate and to be prepared for whatever realistic diplomacy the shifting currents of European politics might require, until at last in 1803 he was able to set the issue forever at rest through an embassy on which depended, in his view, "the future destinies of this republic."[2] Compared with such a challenge to statesmanship the complaint of the Georgia planters was trivial, yet capable like any triviality of endangering affairs of great moment.

The opposed strategies employed by Jefferson cannot, therefore, be dissociated. Both were initiated immediately after the close of the first Congress, both involved relations with Spain, and both were indubitably associated in the mind of their author. It is also important to emphasize their connection because, in each case, the President and the Secretary of State held somewhat different views. It is even more significant to note that it was Jefferson who forced the issue on the American claim to free navigation of the Mississippi, that his policy was ultimately successful, and that the accepted explanation of its origins cannot be sustained by the facts.

I

When Governor Quesada of Florida informed the Secretary of State in 1790 that his instructions forbade the entry and liberation of slaves fleeing from the United States, Jefferson at once made the information available to Governor Telfair of Georgia and to the northern press as well.[3] But this hope of more amicable neighborhood only provided further stimulus to Georgia slaveowners, whose complaints had already caused remonstrances to be made to Spain, or at least to be sent to the ineffectual chargé at Madrid, William Carmichael.[4] The emboldened planters now determined to seek recovery of those slaves that had entered Spanish territory since 1783. They induced the legislature to

[1] TJ to Madison, 30 Jan. 1787.
[2] TJ to Monroe, 13 Jan. 1803.
[3] TJ to Quesada, 12 Aug. 1790, note; TJ to Governor of Georgia, 27 Oct. 1790. George Beckwith, noting Quesada's proclamation in the newspapers, concluded that this "marks an improving disposition" on the part of Spain toward the United States (Beckwith's memorandum of conversations [17 Oct. 1790], enclosed in Dorchester to Grenville, 20 Nov. 1790, PRO: CO 42/72).
[4] Telfair to TJ, 12 Jan. 1791; TJ to Carmichael, 11 Apr. and 29 Aug. 1790. It may have been on this same subject that Telfair wrote TJ on 5 and 30 Aug. 1790; these letters are recorded in SJL as received on 14 Sep. and 22 Nov. 1790 respectively, but have not been found.
    The refugee problem entered into the Jay-Gardoqui treaty negotiations in 1788. When Georgia appealed to Congress, perhaps in response to Gardoqui's protest in 1785 against Georgians' encroachments on territory claimed by Spain, Jay reported that "these and similar matters cannot be conveniently regulated" except by treaty. But in the meantime he recommended that a representation be made to Spain urging a reciprocal agreement for return of slaves and that Gardoqui's interposition be asked (Report, 14 Aug. 1788, JCC, XXXIV, 430-1). Acting on resolu-

ask the Governor and the Georgia delegation in Congress to use "the utmost influence with the President" to achieve this object. Telfair's letter transmitting the request arrived in time for Jefferson to discuss the subject with Washington prior to the latter's departure on his tour to the Southward.[5] Presumably he did so, but Washington's diary for this period is missing and thus a possible explanation for an otherwise puzzling sequence of events is unavailable.

On the 10th of March Jefferson drafted a mild letter from the President to Quesada designating an agent, whose name was left blank, to agree with the Spanish governor concerning the recovery of slaves.[6] The discussions on the Mississippi question had already begun and Jefferson had already decided how that issue should be met.[7] Yet he did not dispatch the letter to Quesada until more than two weeks later. Even then he sent it by post under cover of one to Washington, with the space for the agent's name still blank. Under the same cover he also enclosed a copy of his letter to Governor Telfair, drawn up on the 16th before Washington's departure and presumably submitted to him at that time as indicated by Jefferson's register of official letters and reports. But the original of that letter was not mailed until five days after the President had left Philadelphia. Two months later Washington stated to the agent sent on the mission to Florida that the response to Telfair had been written at his own direction. Perhaps this was said only to extend his authority to a communication obviously dispatched after he had departed from the seat of government.[8]

But there can be little doubt that Jefferson's response to Telfair urging restraint and his device of postponing its dispatch so as to place squarely upon the Georgia governor full responsibility for pressing the matter further were calculated to discourage the attempt. Always reluctant to saddle diplomacy with repetitive, ineffectual, or hopeless tasks and preferring instead to husband another government's "good dispositions for occasions of some moment,"[9] Jefferson was obviously disinclined to make a representation going so far beyond the claims about which he had remonstrated the previous autumn, especially as this might interfere with the matter of much greater moment on which his whole attention was then focused. This is made

tions drawn by Hamilton, Congress approved the resolution, thus leading ultimately to Quesada's proclamation (same, p. 458-60; Syrett, *Hamilton*, v, 205).

The Georgians were also extremely angry at this time over the treaty negotiated in 1790 with the Creek Indians, the secret article of which—drawn by Alexander Hamilton, supported in an unusual opinion by TJ, and approved by the Senate —granted to McGillivray a continuance of the trade monopoly he enjoyed through Panton, Leslie & Company (undated draft in Hamilton's hand in MHi: Pickering Papers, LV, 181; TJ's opinion, Vol. 17: 288-9; JEP, I, 55-6). The secret article was becoming known at this time. McGillivray was also an object of hatred by Georgia planters because he had received, and retained, many runaway slaves from Georgia (De Moustier to Montmorin, 5 June 1788; Arch. Aff. Etr., Paris, Corr. Pol., E.-U., xxx).

[5] Telfair to TJ, 12 Jan. 1791, which arrived in Philadelphia on 4 Mch. 1791.
[6] See Document I.
[7] See Document IV.
[8] See Document III.
[9] TJ to Consuls, 26 Aug. 1790.

clear both by Jefferson's strong intimation to Telfair against making "a demand of such doubtful and dilatory effect" and by a note appended to the copy of the letter that Jefferson forwarded to the President. In this note he stated that the original had been sent by post and then added: "This letter leaves it to Govr. Telfair to explain to the President, (if he chuses) the number of negroes fled from Georgia into Florida, and which may probably be there now. If the value be so considerable, and the recovery so probable, as to induce the President to make the demand from the Governor of Florida, he will only have to fill up the blank in the letter . . . to Don Quesada, with the name of the person he may think proper to send."[10] Since the letter itself made these facts clear enough without explanation, Jefferson's repetitive summary of its real intent can only be taken to be an additional appeal to the President to resist the pressures being brought by southern slaveowners through their governor.

It is very probable that Washington, in conversations with the Georgians, did reinforce the position of his Secretary of State. But in the end he yielded to the pressures. Arriving in Augusta on the 18th of May, he endured two and a half days of salutes, addresses, dinners, and assemblies.[11] Governor Telfair delivered one of the polite and laudatory addresses of welcome to which the President was obliged to respond. But neither the festivities nor Jefferson's plain intimations deterred him from bringing "the utmost influence" to bear. Washington dined privately with Telfair on the 20th and by then he had decided to yield and had chosen the emissary. This is proved by the fact that he then handed to Telfair the "dispatches for the Spanish Govr. respecting the Countenance given . . . to the fugitive Slaves of the Union, which dispatches were to be forwarded to Mr. Seagrove, Collector of St. Mary's who was requested to be the bearer of them, and instructed to make arrangements for the prevention of these evils and, if possible, for the restoration of the property."[12]

Washington's own feelings as a slaveowner and his proximity to Spanish territory when the decision was made may have caused him to see these evils much as the Georgians did. Resentment in that state over the treaty with the Creek nation, the secret article of which had long since been rumored and condemned, may also have affected the decision. This is perhaps reflected in the decision to choose as emissary James Seagrove, who was also United States agent for the Creek. Seagrove, a Savannah merchant who had served in the war and was aide-de-camp to Benjamin Lincoln at the siege of Charleston, had hoped to be made collector at the port of Savannah but instead had been given the unremunerative post at St. Mary's, despite his powerful political support and his record as "a zealous supporter of the Libertyes of this Country."[13] In 1790 he had applied for another

10 TJ's note to Washington, in his hand, was appended to the copy of Document II that he transmitted to the President (PrC in DLC).

11 Freeman, *Washington*, VI, 315-6.

12 Washington, *Diaries*, ed. Fitzpatrick, IV, 180-1, under 20 May 1791.

13 Otho H. Williams to Washington, 14 July 1789; Seagrove to Washington, 24 July 1789 and 16 Apr. 1790 (DLC: Washington Papers). In the former letter

office and this, too, perhaps influenced Washington's choice. He seems to have been reliable and discreet and he did succeed in negotiating an agreement with Quesada.[14] But even though the President yielded to the pressures, his emphatic instructions to Seagrove show that Jefferson's desire for a conciliatory policy had had some effect.[15] This was further reinforced by Washington's sending Seagrove in confidence a copy of Jefferson's letter to Telfair and stamping it with his own authority.

In using the "utmost influence" to obtain these results, the Georgia authorities at least recognized that appeals to an official of a foreign government should be channeled through the office of the President, a requirement not always observed in this formative period when habits initiated under the Articles of Confederation sometimes continued beyond the point at which the Constitution had rendered them obsolete. Indeed, at the very moment that Seagrove was negotiating the agreement with Quesada, the Governor of South Carolina took it upon himself to make a brusque demand of the Governor of Florida for the extradition of two counterfeiters. Charles Pinckney, who as a framer of the Constitution should have known better, not only requested return of the persons indicted for counterfeiting but also proceeded to elucidate Quesada's obligations under the law of nations and even to make pronouncements about American policy as if he were the head of state:[16]

On the occasion permit me to remark that although no example I believe has yet occurred of a similar application in the United States, yet that the Usages of Nations &c. the interest they must have in guarding against such flagrant instances of fraud and injustice will well warrant you in acceding to the present demand.

I apprehend it to be a fixed principle that in the intercourse between nations *in amity* they are strictly obliged to cultivate justice with respect to each other, to observe it scrupulously, and carefully abstain from every thing that may violate it. By this I mean that all civilised nations being essentially concerned in the strict execution of those Laws which are calculated to promote the happiness of the citizen or subject and to ensure protection of the public as well as private rights of the community, it is their interest not to countenance much less to afford an asylum to men who have been obliged to fly from the justice of the country they have resided in, whose

Seagrove referred Washington to such Congressmen as Pierce Butler, Robert Morris, William Samuel Johnson, Jeremiah Wadsworth, Aedanus Burke, George Mathews, James Jackson, and Abraham Baldwin, as well as to General Lincoln. In the latter he said he had received "not one shilling from the office" at St. Mary's and solicited some other post.

[14] See TJ to Governors of Georgia and South Carolina, 15 Dec. 1791, for text of agreement made between Seagrove and Quesada; Washington to Seagrove, 14 Sep. 1791, *Writings*, ed. Fitzpatrick, XXXI, 370-1. On Seagrove's mission, see Randolph C. Downes, "Creek American Relations 1790-1795," JSH, VIII (Aug. 1942), 350-4; Dale Van Every, *Ark of Empire*, 64-74, 212-14. See also TJ to Washington, 3 July 1792.

[15] See Document III.

[16] Pinckney to Quesada, 18 Aug. 1791 (DNA: RG 59, MLR).

Laws they have violated. It is the policy of the United States not even to afford protection to Debtors of other countries their courts being as equally open to foreigners as their own citizens, and it appears to me that it would very much promote the intercourse and good offices necessary between different nations if a precedent was established by which it was understood that no protection could be afforded to fugitive offenders against the Laws, but that in every instance where legal proof could be obtained of the probability of Guilt that upon a demand of the Executive their persons should be delivered up.

The Spanish governor who received this astonishing appeal from an emissary of one state at the same time that an agent of the President delivered a request on behalf of another state might well be forgiven for wondering if the Americans had yet become accustomed to their new form of government. But Pinckney not only demanded extradition of the fugitives: he also informed Washington that he had done so, reminding him that during the President's stay in Charleston he had mentioned "the great inconvenience the people of this and the neighboring State labour under in having so near a receptacle for their fugitive public offenders, debtors, and even Slaves as St. Augustine." He even went on to say that the expected arrival of a Spanish minister in Philadelphia made it probable that some arrangements between the United States and Spain would take place and he therefore "thought this the proper time to make the communication." He did not believe Quesada would consider himself authorized to deliver up the fugitives, but he thought that the request "may in its event be useful by leading to the Establishment of instructions . . . in future to do so and may hold out an idea to offenders that the justice of their Country will pursue them as far as it possibly can."[17]

On receiving Pinckney's letter and the copy of the one he had sent to Quesada, Washington turned both over to Jefferson for comment. Normally the practice long since adopted of having the Secretary of State handle correspondence with the governors would have been followed. But Pinckney's blundering intrusion into relations with other countries called for an exception. Jefferson emphasized this by drafting an answer for the President to sign and by suggesting that it would be proper for Washington "on fit occasions" to make a direct response to letters received from governors, leaving correspondence on ordinary business in its accustomed channel. The reply that he drafted was characteristically laconic and lent the authority of the Chief Executive to its indirect comment on the intermeddling in foreign affairs by the governor of a state: "Your favor of the 18th of August has been communicated to the Secretary of State within whose department foreign affairs are, and I enclose you a copy of his observations to me on that subject."[18]

17 Pinckney to Washington, 18 Aug. 1791 (DNA: RG 59, MLR).
18 TJ to Washington, 6 Nov. 1791; Washington to Pinckney, 8 Nov. 1791 (DLC: Washington Papers; *Writings*, ed. Fitzpatrick, XXXI, 412-3). Pinckney's

Jefferson's observations to the President on that subject—the law, the practice, and the implications of extradition—were both learned and detached. Nevertheless his report was a forceful and calculated rebuke to one who had overstepped the bounds of his authority if not those of international comity. Perhaps to soften its effect upon the feelings of a man whose pride was an outstanding trait, Jefferson chose to assume that Pinckney had only proposed to make a request for extradition. This, of course, was a fiction: Pinckney had simply announced to Washington an action already taken. He had stated that he had already transmitted to the Attorney General of the state "a copy of the . . . Letter [to Quesada] for the purpose of being sent to St. Augustine."[19] But the fiction could not have blunted the point that Jefferson drove home with such force. Even his phraseology added to the emphasis by echoing that of Pinckney, who in justification of his demand had said that it might "in its event be useful" through its effect on fugitives and on the Spanish court. On the contrary, Jefferson declared, such a demand might "commit us disagreeably, perhaps dishonorably in event." This was strong language, but he went further: "I do not think we can take for granted, that the legislature of the United States will establish a convention for the mutual delivery of fugitives; and without a reasonable certainty that they will, I think we ought not to give Governor Quesada any grounds to expect, that in a similar case, we would re-deliver fugitives from his Government."[20] The rebuke was inescapable. Pinckney had both invaded the prerogative of the Chief Executive and presumed upon the treaty power of the Senate.

Thus did the acquiescence of the President in the demands of Georgia and the behavior of the Governor of South Carolina complicate Jefferson's effort to preserve good neighborhood with the Floridas at the moment he was planning a bold stroke on a far more significant sector. Spanish officials in America, acting under a recent change in policy, added to these complications by attempts to lure American settlers into their territory. Against that policy Jefferson wished to protest only enough to induce the Spaniards to think "this seduction of our inhabitants . . . very wise policy for them," thus in time enabling the United States to acquire by peaceful penetration what might otherwise cost a war.[21] He certainly had no desire to see either this strategy

---

action in the case of the counterfeiters was duplicated by his officiousness in corresponding with the government of St. Domingo. In both instances his zeal may have been prompted by his ambition to obtain a diplomatic post. See note, TJ to Washington, 7 Nov. 1791. Pinckney finally realized his ambition when, following his important role in placing South Carolina in the Republican column in 1800, he was appointed minister to Spain by TJ (M. R. Zahniser, *Charles Cotesworth Pinckney*, p. 227).

[19] Pinckney to Washington, 18 Aug. 1791 (DLC: Washington Papers).

[20] TJ to Washington, 7 Nov. 1791. For TJ's draft of a proposed convention with Spain for the extradition of fugitives, see TJ to Washington, 22 Mch. 1792; Washington to TJ, 25 Mch. 1792; TJ to Short and Carmichael, 24 Apr. 1792 and enclosure.

[21] TJ to Washington, 2 Apr. 1791, note. Pinckney had pointed out to Wash-

or the object of his other policy nullified by matters of merely local importance. Once the Floridas had been acquired through American infiltration, the problem of fugitive slaves would disappear with the disappearance of the Spanish boundary. The issue of transcendent importance was the cause of the men on the western waters. That issue involved the future of the union.

II

"The Western Country is daily growing into greater importance, and many members of Congress are not sensible of its Consequences to the United States," Adam Stephen wrote to James Madison soon after the new government was set in motion. "Proper attention to that Country is Absolutely Necessary. In time it will give law to America. . . . The strength and vigor of the United States lie in the mountains and to the westward."[22] The furore in the West over the Jay-Gardoqui negotiations, the bitterly partisan divisions in Kentucky, the long series of frustrations encountered in the struggle of the state for admission to the union, the intensified hostilities of the Indians, the activities of emissaries from England, the overtures of Governor Miró to such men as George Morgan—all had produced clamors that could scarcely

ington that "the great number of people" fleeing to Florida included not only slaves and criminals but also "some . . . of large fortunes who have secretly removed themselves to that place with their properties" (Pinckney to Washington, 18 Aug. 1791).

[22] Adam Stephen to James Madison, 12 Sep. 1789 (DLC: Madison Papers). Like George Nicholas, Stephen spoke as a westerner yet an ardent nationalist. While he hailed Hamilton's Assumption Act as "a masterly Stroke of Policy," he believed it possible that the "N E and S W parts of our Empire are not like to assimilate" and that a dissolution of the union was possible (Stephen to Madison, 3 Mch. and 25 Apr. 1790; DLC: Madison Papers). He also spoke with the experience of a formidable Indian fighter. He had been with Washington at Great Meadows, succeeded to the command of the Virginia forces in 1754 when Washington resigned, and was seriously wounded at Braddock's defeat but recovered and served throughout the French and Indian War. He commanded the Virginia regiment during Pontiac's uprising and was second in command to the governor in Dunmore's War (R. G. Thwaites and L. P. Kellogg, eds., *Dunmore's War*, 191, 236-8; VMHB, XVI [1908]. 136-7; his autobiography down to 1775 is in PMHB, XVIII [1894], 43-50). He and Washington were friends and comrades in arms, but conflicting personalities, politics, and land interests drove them apart. Washington's harsh comments on Stephen's character and behavior were evidently not reciprocated by Stephen. Historians' estimates of him have been equally one-sided and lacking in full justice. For an account consistently partial to Washington, see Freeman, *Washington*, II, 145-6; III, 55-6, 61-2, 98, 119-20; IV, 311-3, 417-8, 475-7, 479-82, 511-3, 535-6. An illuminating example of the way Washington's towering figure affected one scholar's judgment of Stephen is to be found in the attribution of an unsigned and undated plan for mounting a campaign against Fort Duquesne in 1758. Authorship of this plan was ascribed to Washington for several reasons, one of the more important being that his subordinates—Adam Stephen, George Mercer, and Andrew Lewis—"gave no evidence in their careers of such creative generalship." Immediately after publication the document was proved conclusively to have come from the pen of Adam Stephen (E. Douglas Branch, "An Unpublished Washington Document from the Bouquet Papers," PMHB, LXI [1937], 204-13; LXII, 120).

be disregarded. The opening of the Northwest Territory under strikingly different methods of organized settlement, with provisions for schools and churches, contributed to the feelings of the older inhabitants south of the Ohio that they were neglected by the national government. A new generation and a new breed of emigrants, farmers rather than woodsmen, added their inexperienced numbers and their considerable goods to the temptations held out to the Indians. In the brief but epochal period from the Annapolis Convention of 1786 to the inauguration of the new government, no less than 1,019 boats carrying 18,761 persons, 8,487 horses, 2,199 cattle, 1,833 sheep, 33 hogs, and 598 wagons passed by Fort Harmar on their way down the Ohio.[23] John Brown, reporting to Madison about the settlement at New Madrid, thought emigrants would be enticed into Spanish territory as rapidly as they arrived from the Atlantic states. "All these circumstances," Madison wrote to Washington, "point out the conduct which the New Government ought to pursue with regard to the Western Country and Spain."[24]

But the precise nature of the conduct to be pursued was less obvious than the danger looming in the West. No one in the government was more acutely aware of that danger than Washington. Indeed, no one in America had had a longer, more direct, more varied, or more deeply interested connection with the West, whether in a civil or military capacity, than he. This fact and the confidence that the entire nation placed in his leadership provided a cohesive force of incalculable value.[25] Yet, for all of his experience, Washington always felt some uneasiness about the men on the western frontier. He could not look upon squatters as anything but lawless banditti. He could not forget that the West generally had opposed the Constitution and that the Kentucky delegates in the Virginia Convention had voted overwhelmingly against ratification. He could never share "the peculiar confidence in the men from the Western side of the mountains" so deeply felt by Jefferson, who had never been fifty miles westward of his own home or

[23] Knox to Washington, 12 June 1789 (DLC: Washington Papers).
[24] Madison to Washington, 8 Mch. 1789 (DLC: Washington Papers).
[25] An instance of this confidence came from Kentucky in the critical year 1788 when Harry Innes discovered that John Connolly, British agent, had "touched the Key to Fomentation and offered assistance to enable the Inhabitants of the Western Country to seize on the City of New Orleans and secure thereby the Navigation of the Mississippi." Innes knew it to be hopeless to appeal to the expiring Congress and he doubted the integrity—that is, feared the presence of British sympathizers—among the Council of Virginia. "Never," he wrote, "was a person more perplexed than I am at the present moment. I have it in my power to communicate important intelligence, which not only affects the happiness of the Western Country but the prosperity of the Union. To what power then shall I make the communication?" He turned to Washington in full confidence that "whatever tends to disturb the peace of United America would distress and injure your tranquility and repose, and that your aiding hand would not be withheld when your Country's cause required it" (Innes to Washington, 18 Dec. 1788; DLC: Washington Papers). Washington did not receive the letter for over two months, but in a hasty acknowledgment expressed implicit confidence in Innes' "very patriotic sentiments" and efforts (Washington to Innes, 2 Mch. 1789; *Writings*, ed., Fitzpatrick, xxx, 214-5).

endured frontier dangers and discomforts as Washington had.[26] He believed westerners required the restraining force of law and order, while Jefferson valued the spirit of independence fostered by the wilderness and was not disturbed even when it seemed defiance. Both were humanitarian in their attitudes toward the Indians and both were cognizant of the dangers, domestic and foreign, that threatened to separate the West from the union. Equally determined to prevent such a disaster, the President and the Secretary of State nevertheless exhibited their fundamental differences of attitude toward the West as the first Congress came to its close.

In thanking Harry Innes for the gift of an Indian artifact, Jefferson voiced a characteristic interest in the natural history of the West. But his letter was no ordinary item in the proposed "exchange of epistolary communications."[27] Its purpose in fact was to make a political statement of the first importance. It sought to allay fears and to multiply ties binding the West to the nation. It appealed for support against the prevailing military strategy of the administration. Most important of all, it announced a bold new advance in policy concerning the issue that had disturbed the politics of Kentucky so bitterly for the past few years that its consequences would remain for generations. That issue pivoted on the means to be employed in securing the free use of the Mississippi.

In assuring Innes that there was some good news from Congress—an allusion to the admission of Kentucky to statehood—Jefferson embraced the pleasing form while evading the disagreeable substance. This was characteristic, too, but what he sought to include under the unconvincing rubric "so so" was the Excise Act, the National Bank, and other evidences of fiscalism about which the West felt much as the South did. "A spirit of jealousy which may become dangerous to the union, towards the Eastern states, seems to be growing fast among us," Washington's friend David Stuart had written a year earlier. "It is represented that the northern phalanx is so firmly united, as to bear down all opposition, while Virginia is unsupported, even by those whose interests are similar with hers."[28] Not all in the South or the West disapproved of the tendency of federal measures, but in the months that had elapsed since Stuart reported these sentiments the legislation enacted by Congress had done little to soothe and much to exacerbate the feelings of both regions about the aims of the northern phalanx. Kentuckians in particular, remembering and still deeply em-

[26] TJ to Muhlenberg, 31 Jan. 1781; TJ to D. A. Leonard, 20 Jan. 1814.
[27] See Document IV.
[28] Stuart to Washington, 15 Mch. 1790 (DLC: Washington Papers). Stuart added that many who had been warm supporters of the government, were "changing their sentiments, from a conviction of the impracticality of Union with States, whose interests are so dissimilar from those of Virginia." Shortly after the new government was organized, Tench Coxe told Madison that "a phalanx [had] been forming for two years by the states east of Jersey" and had so clearly manifested itself in the debates on all the leading subjects before Congress as to cause one to tremble for the safety of the union (Coxe to Madison, 9 Sep. 1789, DLC: Madison Papers).

bittered by the Jay-Gardoqui negotiations, were disposed to see in the acts of the national administration an almost exclusive preoccupation with fiscal concerns that had no relation to their urgent need of access to the sea and to the immense national interests contingent upon meeting that need. Their reasons for feeling so had a cogency and found an expression that could not be disregarded.

For to the fears and resentments engendered by the failure to confront this paramount issue of the right to navigate the Mississippi, Kentuckians added a mounting sense of anger and frustration over the failure of the government to provide protection against the Indians —a failure attributable in their view to a stubborn disregard of the lessons of experience and the realities of Indian warfare. Long before Harmar's defeat a Kentuckian had sounded a warning so emphatic that Washington paid it the tribute of recording it at length in his diary. If the government thought the West could be defended by a few posts along the Ohio, this candid westerner admonished, it had embraced an idea "most erroneous . . . for an army would scarcely supply the chain that would be necessary." But coupled with this was a proposal. If lack of finances prevented the government from doing what was necessary and if Kentuckians were given official sanction, they could raise "any number of men and furnish any quantity of provisions." Moreover, they would wait for reimbursement until finances became available. Washington's lengthy abstract closed with this warning from the Kentuckian: "the most serious consequences will follow from persisting in the measures which have [been] pursued for some time past."[29] This was only one of a number of similar warnings and petitions coming from field officers, legislators, and indignant individuals testifying in urgent tones to the same lesson of frontier experience—that the system of employing seasoned woodsmen and hunters as scouts to watch the passes, supported on the outer fringes of settlement by small bodies of rangers equipped with rifles and experienced in Indian warfare, was the only effective defense against marauding bands that could slip so easily between army posts to steal livestock and slaughter settlers.[30]

These pressures from the West were so powerful as to induce the administration early in 1790 to make a fleeting concession to frontier ideas of defense. But such ideas, the Secretary of War made clear, were "uncertain, opposed to the principles of regularity, and to be adopted only in cases of exigence, and to cease the moment the . . . exigencies shall cease."[31] Even this carefully circumscribed indulgence to western sentiment was soon withdrawn and the administration placed its reliance upon conventional campaigns. Principles of regularity could scarcely have been more detached from western reality than in the

[29] George Nicholas to James Madison, 2 Nov. 1789 (DLC: Madison Papers). Madison, whose advice Washington was depending upon heavily at the time, handed the letter to the President "for information of the sentiments of the people" of Kentucky (Washington, *Diaries*, ed., Fitzpatrick, IV, 74-7).

[30] ASP, *Indian Affairs*, I, 84-91, 101-2, 109-11.

[31] Knox to St. Clair, 3 Mch. 1790, same, I, 101.

directions given by Knox in the hastily organized expedition of 1790
urging that the frontier militia be persuaded, if possible, to give up
their rifles—weapons that were uniquely suited to the particular
demands of the frontiersman in war and peace—and to use army
muskets instead.[32] Harmar's defeat only produced still angrier out-

[32] Knox to Harmar, 24 Aug. 1790, same, I, 99. Knox argued logically enough
that rifles were "certainly not good arms in a close fight." But this begged the
question. Frontier methods of fighting imitated the Indians' reliance upon stealth,
surprise, use of cover, precision of individual aim, strategic withdrawal when
necessary, and other actions intended to inflict the greatest damage upon the
enemy while avoiding every preventable loss. The folly of attempting by a bayonet
charge to fight at close quarters in the woods had been proved by King's Mountain in 1780: the riflemen simply gave way, took to trees in the Indian manner,
and exacted their deadly toll as the enemy wave receded.

The chasm between the administration's conventional military thought and the
frontiersman's method of fighting was nowhere more clearly exhibited than in the
commentary of one of the ablest and most experienced Indian fighters of the day,
James Smith (1737-1812). Smith's *Remarkable Occurrences* (Lexington, 1799) is
the most cogent and informed analysis of the Indian style of fighting by any
American of the eighteenth century. Dismissing as "a capital mistake" the idea
that Indians were undisciplined fighters, Smith analyzed twenty-two expeditions
that had been mounted against them from 1755 to 1791 and pointed out that
this very considerable outpouring of blood and treasure had inflicted only slight
losses upon the Indians, owing to their disciplined command, their ability to communicate orders, their punctual obedience, their competence in executing slowly
or swiftly in scattered order difficult maneuvers of encirclement or of retreat, and
their prudence in avoiding engagements except when the odds in favor of success were great. Smith estimated that from 1755 through 1758 the Indians
"killed, or took, fifty of our people, for one that they lost." But this ratio he
thought was reduced to about ten to one by 1763 because "the frontiers (especially the Virginians) had learned something of their method of war." He pointed
out that in producing "marksmen, and in cutting . . . rifles, and in keeping them
in good order," Americans had the advantage over Indians, yet he considered them
"far behind in their manoeuvres, or in being able to surprise, or prevent a sur-
prize." Confessing his astonishment "that no one has wrote upon this important
subject," Smith attributed the failure to learn from experience to a disinclination
to pay the requisite price: "no important acquisition is to be obtained but by
attention and diligence; and as it is easier to learn to move and act in concert,
in close order, in the open plain, than to act in concert in scattered order, in the
woods; so it is easier to learn our discipline, than the Indian manoeuvres" (Smith,
Remarkable Occurrences, p. 156, 158-9, 160).

The explanation was far more complex in origin than Smith indicated in his
cogent analysis, but the very obliqueness of his commentary reveals his awareness of a puzzling and important fact. The capital mistake about Indian military
discipline, he was careful to say, was a British mistake. So, too, did he characterize the system that failed to engage Indians on their own terms: "Is it not the
best discipline," he asked, "that has the greatest tendency to annoy the enemy
and save their own men? I apprehend that the Indian discipline is as well
calculated to answer the purpose in the woods of America, as the British discipline
in Flanders: and British discipline in the woods, is the way to have men slaughtered, with scarcely any chance of defending themselves" (Smith, *Remarkable Occurrences*, p. 157-8). Here and elsewhere in his criticism of modes of fighting that
would get men slaughtered, Smith affixed the British label to orthodox military
tactics.

But his analysis included the two costly campaigns of 1790 and 1791, the
ultimate responsibility for which rested not upon British discipline in the woods
but upon the Commander-in-Chief who, like Smith and other Virginians, had
experienced the disaster on Braddock's field. Such lessons from the past were
now being disregarded at a cost in casualties in the St. Clair expedition alone,
Smith estimated, greater than those suffered by the Americans in any engagement

bursts from the West. One of the bitterest reactions was provoked by Knox' emphasis on economy and his argument that scouts received exorbitant pay, "greatly disproportioned to any known compensation for military services."[33] The challenge to administration policy was accompanied by a plea for the "old experienced mode of keeping out scouts and rangers."[34]

Such was the context of Jefferson's astonishing assertion, made so casually in this letter about a carved Indian image, that "the federal council has yet to learn by experience, what experience has long ago taught us in Virginia, that rank and file fighting will not do against Indians."[35] The revealing comment was much more than a tacit

---

of the Revolution. When, during the next war, he thought the warnings of experience were still being ignored, the aged Indian fighter brought forth another edition of his shrewd commentary on forest warfare, with enlarged contents that defined the manner in which an army of two thousand men could march in scattered order over a great area, with directions for manning frontier stations, conducting scouting parties, and utilizing spies, and with a revised title that more explicitly emphasized his original intent: *A Treatise on the Mode and Manner of Indian War, Their Tactics, Discipline and Encampments, the Various Methods They Practise, in Order to Obtain the Advantage, by Ambush, Surprise, Surrounding, &c.* (Paris, Kentucky, 1812). The frontiersman and the Secretary of State were agreed about the realities of frontier warfare, but in their oblique allusions neither fixed responsibility upon the great leader of the Revolution who, in giving approval to conventional military measures developed by the Secretary of War and the Secretary of the Treasury, seemed to have forgotten his own lessons of experience as an Indian fighter.

[33] Knox to Washington, 5 Jan. 1791, ASP, *Indian Affairs*, I, 107.

[34] Delegates from eight counties of western Virginia to Beverley Randolph [10 Dec. 1790], transmitted in Randolph to Washington, 10 Dec. 1791, same, I, 107-8, 110-11.

[35] Document IV. The Rev. James Maury may also have taught TJ at an early age an understanding of both the political importance of the West and the inappropriateness of conventional military campaigning in the woods. Just before TJ entered Maury's classical school at the age of fourteen, Maury argued for intercolonial union and expressed the opinion that, within a few years, the power controlling the Ohio, the Great Lakes, and the Mississippi would be the "sole and absolute Master of North America" (James Maury to Moses Fontaine, 10 June 1756; Maury's letterbook, Sol Feinstone Collection, microfilm, PPAP). Feeling both shame and indignation because a brave but imprudent Braddock had been defeated "by a contemptible band of naked French and Indians," Maury also urged a method of frontier defense employing Indian scouts and expert woodsmen ranging along a chain of 10 or 12 stockades stretched across the Virginia frontier at intervals of about thirty miles. He proposed that each garrison have six groups of rangers, two in regular rotation constantly out scouring the woods, each made up of woodsmen and Indians and employing—as Franklin also recommended in Pennsylvania—some "well tutored and mettlesome dogs." "The diligence and activity that may be expected in officers thus cautiously chosen [by county courts for their expertise in the woods and their ability as leaders], and the garrisons under their command having a proper mixture of Indians, no less subtil than the enemy, as bold, and equally well versed in all the barbarian arts and stratagems of war," Maury argued, "would be much more formidable to those brutal ravagers, and embarras them much more than many thousands of the best disciplined troops: would either keep them at due distance, or, should they adventure within the barrier, severely chastise their insolence and temerity." In addition, he thought such a measure would be less expensive than any other, not requiring supply trains, quartermasters, paymasters, commissioned officers, or, for the most part, bounties (James Maury to Philip Ludwell, 10 Feb. 1756, and to Moses Fontaine, 9 Aug. 1755; same).

acknowledgment of divergent views in the cabinet over military policy. Intentionally or not, it pointed toward the ultimate repository of power. Was not the head of the national councils a Virginian? Had he not begun his extraordinary career with first-hand knowledge of the sort of disaster likely to attend rank-and-file fighting in the woods? Had not the campaign of 1790 taught the same lesson? Jefferson's appeal to Innes for George Rogers Clark to be brought forward was, as he must have known, hopeless. But the guarded criticism of the administration's military policy could scarcely have been comforting to Kentuckians who for well over a year had been angrily challenging that policy.

Jefferson, like the inhabitants of the western waters, must have sensed the fact that higher pay for scouts and the state of federal finances did not in themselves foreclose the choice of frontier methods of defense. But neither he nor the Kentuckians could have penetrated at this time the full implications of conventional military ideas as embraced by the federal council. These involved, among other considerations, large contracts for supplies and costly logistics that were by no means to be dissociated from fiscalism and prevailing concepts of energetic government. As the manner in which these were handled became imperfectly unfolded to view, Jefferson may have recalled his own instructions to George Rogers Clark years earlier, at a time when Kentucky was sparsely settled, urging him to obtain provisions on the frontier so far as possible, even to the use of skins for clothing.[36] But he now witnessed the outward manifestations if not the inner operations of a quite different system of frontier defense. A central feature of this system was that, through privileged favors and hidden collaboration, the Secretary of War, the Secretary of the Treasury, and William Duer, whom Madison aptly described as "the Prince of the tribe of speculators" of the day, permitted private interests to intrude so greatly upon public objects as to bring disaster to the military efforts for the defense of the West.[37] So concealed were these operations that a full disclosure has never been made and perhaps, in all of the extended ramifications, never can be. Yet much more is known than has been supposed and it is essential to note at least the salient features. For these operations, echoing the kind of abuse and corruption Americans of the revolutionary era had believed characteristic of the British administrative system against which they had rebelled, contributed greatly to the increasing alienation of the West.

III

Henry Knox and William Duer were friends and associates of long standing. Both had speculated in public securities. Both, together with

---

[36] TJ to George Rogers Clark, 29 Jan. 1780; Clark, it should be noted, had taken precautions to store up provisions in advance of need and TJ had congratulated him on doing so—a practice in marked contrast to that of the expeditions of 1790 and 1791. These later disasters, however, led ultimately to reforms in the matter of military supplies. In instituting these reforms Alexander Hamilton played a vigorous role (White, *The Federalists*, p. 360-3).

[37] Madison to Pendleton, 23 Mch. 1792 (DLC: Madison Papers).

the Secretary of the Treasury, were involved in the notorious Scioto affair that was now causing such a clamor in France and among the disillusioned French settlers on the Ohio as to embarrass the government in its foreign relations.[38] Both affected a costly scale of living and both were usually in financial straits. Indeed, some of Knox' holdings in the Waldo Patent in Maine were at this time in danger of being sold for taxes.[39] Hamilton and Duer were also friends, having been associated in politics, in society, and in the founding of the Bank of New York. Although Duer was well known as a speculator in government securities and public lands—activities forbidden by statute to anyone holding office in the Treasury—and was in debt to the government under contracts going back several years, he was appointed by Hamilton to the second highest office in the department. During his six months as Assistant Secretary, Duer continued his speculative activities and so compromised his public trust as to lay himself open to serious charges of malfeasance.[40] Knox, Hamilton, and Duer had gained an intimate knowledge of each other during their years in New York. The warning signals about the last, a now discredited official, were fully displayed—and blandly ignored.

"It is essential to the minister of a great department," Alexander Hamilton wrote years later to the successor of Knox as Secretary of War, "that he subdivide the objects, distribute them among competent assistants, and content himself with a general but vigilant superintendence."[41] This precept, expressed when its author was in a position to appreciate the effect of administrative mismanagement on a commander in the field, was violated in almost every particular in the spring of 1791 by the Secretary of the Treasury and by the Secretary of War. Both had official responsibility in greater or lesser degree for the campaign of 1791, just as both had participated in planning that of the previous year. Both also shared obligations in the crucial task of obtaining and transporting supplies for the army. This last, an open invitation to confusion if not disaster, was a direct result of the propensity of the Secretary of the Treasury for extending the powers and jurisdiction of his department. As early as July, 1790, Hamilton took it upon himself to advertise for bids for supplying army rations for the year 1791, though no statute authorized the Treasury to concern itself with pro-

[38] See De Barth to TJ, 3 Mch. 1791; Playfair to TJ, 20 Mch. 1791; Playfair to Hamilton, 30 Mch. 1791 (Syrett, *Hamilton*, VIII, 227-33).

[39] It is regrettable that there is no adequate biography of either Duer or Knox. The best account of the speculations of the former is J. S. Davis, "William Duer, Entrepreneur," *Essays in the Earlier History of American Corporations*, I, 111-345. The best account of Knox' speculations is Frederick S. Allis, Jr., ed., "William Bingham's Maine Lands 1790-1820," *Colls.*, CSM, XXXVI-XXXVII.

[40] Mitchell, *Hamilton*, II, 146, states flatly that "William Duer, while Assistant Secretary of the Treasury, was guilty of the gravest malfeasance"; J. R. Jacobs, *The Beginning of the U. S. Army* (Princeton, 1947), p. 120, describes him, inaccurately and unjustly, as "a felon at large." Duer is said to have accepted appointment with the understanding that he would continue his private business affairs (Davis, *Essays*, II, 176). Hamilton and Duer were not only intimate friends, but their wives were first cousins.

[41] Alexander Hamilton to James McHenry, 30 July 1798 (White, *The Federalists*, p. 154).

curement of stores for military purposes. He also handled contracts for army clothing. On 28 Oct. 1790 he negotiated the contract for rations not as Secretary but as "Alexander Hamilton for and in behalf of the . . . United States of America."[42] Under this engagement one Theodosius Fowler was the nominal public contractor, but the actual principal soon turned out to be the recent officer of the Treasury, William Duer.[43] Knox, to whom fell the duty of supervising their friend's

[42] Hamilton advertised for bids for flour, beef, pork, spirits, &c. without specifying that the supplies were intended for the western posts or even for the army (*Gazette of the United States*, 17 July 1791; Syrett, *Hamilton*, VIII, 127, 226, 334; White, *The Federalists*, p. 145-55, 359-60).

[43] Syrett, *Hamilton*, VIII, 127. This contract, the original of which disappeared from the Treasury files some time before 1802, became the subject of litigation in 1800 when Fowler was sued for a balance of $10,199.20 claimed by the Treasury. Fowler petitioned Congress on 3 Feb. 1801 asking relief and claiming that he was only the nominal contractor; that the contract was made "on account of William Duer, and . . . was so understood at the Treasury when he made the contract"; that he was in no way personally interested in the agency or profits; that he never furnished any supplies or drew any moneys from the Treasury under it; that Duer "supplied the army, and drew all the advances made by the Treasury"; that Duer "negotiated the whole . . . exclusively and independently of him"; and that he knew nothing about it save what information he had "lately obtained . . . from the public accounts and documents." The committee to which Fowler's petition was referred corroborated these assertions, urged that the claim against him be extinguished, and found a balance "of about $10,000" due to William Duer instead of the larger amount claimed against him. An Act for the relief of Fowler was passed (ASP, *Claims*, I, 259-62).

This contract, though well known, requires elucidation. On the basis of information supplied by the Treasury and War Departments, the committee appointed to inquire into the causes of St. Clair's defeat had drawn in its report of 8 May 1792 a damaging contrast between the "Fowler" contract and a later one with Duer for furnishing supplies to the troops on the way to Pittsburgh. The report pointed out that the former carried a bond of $100,000, with Walter Livingston and John Cochran as securities, whereas the latter had a bond of only $4,000, "without any security whatsoever." On the same authority the committee found that the first contract had been *wholly transferred* from . . . Fowler to Duer" (emphasis supplied) on 3 Jan. 1791 and a copy of this transfer lodged in the office of the Secretary of the Treasury; that Knox had written to Duer in such terms as to show that he considered him to be the *de facto* contractor; and that no further correspondence between Fowler and the War or Treasury Departments under this contract had taken place (ASP, *Military Affairs*, I, 36). The report did not explore the implications of these facts but permitted the obvious inference to be drawn: Duer, then in debtors' prison, had been favored and the public not adequately protected by securities for performance of obligation. But this raised another question. If, as originally claimed, the contract had been wholly assigned by Fowler to Duer at the time stated, had its bond been similarly transferred?

It is improbable that the Secretary of the Treasury could have anticipated the embarrassing and perhaps politically-inspired inference, but he met it boldly. After the report was published, he or someone acting in his behalf informed the committee that the transfer of Fowler's contract had not in fact been submitted to the Treasury on 3 Jan. 1791 but had been known to the department only on 7 Apr. 1791, when Duer had asked for advances and Hamilton, on the same day, had authorized such to Duer "as Agent to Mr Fowler" (Syrett, *Hamilton*, VIII, 246). At the same time Hamilton answered the implied question by submitting to the committee various opinions of the Attorney General and "several other lawyers of eminence," all concurring in the view that the securities given by Fowler were "now responsible for all damages . . . upon any breach of that contract." The committee were also informed that all Treasury warrants under the contract had been issued to Duer as agent. In its subsequent report on 15 Feb. 1793 the committee merely pointed out that the Secretary of War had always corresponded with Duer as the contractor (ASP, *Military Affairs*, I, 42; *Annals*, III, 602,877). The committee of 1802 contributed some light by noting that on 12 Aug. 1793 a debit balance against Duer under his own contract had been "carried to the credit of Theodosius Fowler, on account of his contract with the Secretary of the Treasury of the 28th of October 1790, for draughts of I. Ludlow, agent of William Duer, assignee of . . . Fowler." The committee added: "had not William Duer been considered by the agents of the government as the actual contractor responsible for the advances under both contracts, such transfer of a balance from an account of one contract made with the War Department could not with any propriety or justice have been placed to another account, under a contract of T. Fowler with the Secretary of the Treasury; it being an absurdity too gross and palpable to be attached to the conduct of the accounting officers of the Government, who made this transposition, under any other circumstances" (ASP, *Claims*, I, 262).

This was sound logic, but the observation and the facts of the case subject the actions of the Secretary of the Treasury to these alternative interpretations: (1) that the accounting officers made the transfer of balance in 1793 of their own volition and without the knowledge or authorization of the Secretary, the Controller, or the Auditor; (2) that the assignment of Fowler's contract had in fact been made "wholly" on 3 Jan. 1791, with a copy thereof lodged in the office of the Secretary as he informed the committee some time before 8 May 1792; or (3) that Hamilton's letter recognizing Duer as Fowler's agent and authorizing advances to him was, at least in its essential point, a contrived document prepared after publication of the report of 1792 in order to show that Fowler's securities could be considered as having a continuing legal liability. The first of these alternatives is scarcely conceivable. The second was contradicted by Hamilton himself in information handed in to the committee after its initial report. The third seems the only plausible and acceptable explanation. Hamilton's letter to Duer, at least in respect to Duer's contractual relationship, cannot for this reason be accepted as an altogether genuine document written on its assigned date of 7 Apr. 1791.

Even if it were, this would still leave Hamilton exposed to the grave charge of intentionally misleading a committee of Congress with the assurance that Duer was merely an agent and the public was therefore protected under Fowler's bond of $100,000, while at the same time both the Treasury and War Departments were officially treating him as the principal. The committee itself in its 1793 report seemed to call attention to the contradiction by the emphasis it gave to the words *"as the agent of Theodosius Fowler"* and by its taking note of the fact that the Secretary of War had written to Duer not as agent but as principal (ASP, *Military Affairs*, I, 42).

While Fowler's contract called for a settlement at least every six months (ASP, *Claims*, I, 260), none was ever made and nine years elapsed before the Treasury endeavored to recover balances due to the public, though early in 1792 the Comptroller initiated a suit against Duer for debts to the government going back several years—an action which hastened Duer's collapse and imprisonment (Mitchell, *Hamilton*, II, 174). During the years Duer was in prison, proceedings against Fowler or against the securities who allegedly had a continuing liability could not have been instituted without demonstrating beyond question what the committee reports of 1792 and 1793 had so strongly intimated—that in this case administrative theory was flatly contradicted by administrative actions. Not until after Duer's death did the Treasury take steps to protect the public interest. Even then it proceeded against the nominal contractor, not against the securities. Walter Livingston, the principal security, had also been the chief victim of Duer's financial distress. When the panic of 1792 began, he was signer or endorser of a total of 28 notes in favor of Duer aggregating $203,875.80 (Mitchell, *Hamilton*, II, 174). Since Livingston had no hesitancy in endorsing Duer's notes of hand and presumably would have had none in acting as security for him on a government contract, it follows that the act of the Secretary of the Treasury in making the award to Fowler in the first place must have been a mere subterfuge to conceal from public view Hamilton's intimate friend, kinsman by marriage, and recently malfeasant assistant. This interpretation accords not only with Fowler's own testimony but also with the facts of the case. It

performance, seems from the beginning to have regarded him as the real contractor and to have treated him as such. In January he wrote Duer privately and confidentially:[44]

> I have written you twice in my private capacity relatively to the supply of rations upon the frontier to which you have not particularly replied. It is true you have written a public letter to the secretary of the treasury respecting the necessity of anything further. I am really concerned upon your account as well as the public that the supplies should be adequate to the demand. I sincerely hope the means you have taken will answer the end.[45] . . . Every appearance indicates an extensive Indian war. Great preparations must be made and probably great quantities of provisions will be required. I give you this hint *in confidence* as the measures are not yet decided upon by Congress. But as soon as they shall be it will be necessary to proceed with great vigor.

In fact, the Secretary of War had only a few days earlier submitted to the President his plans and estimates for an expedition that he hoped would be superior to all opposition. But the repetitive private promptings suggest that Knox had no great confidence in the adequacy of Duer's arrangements to meet his public responsibility.

In his proposal for a larger expedition Knox recognized that if protection to western settlers were not afforded, "seeds of disgust will be sown; sentiments of separate interests will arise out of their local situation, which will be cherished either by insidious domestic, or foreign emissaries." The tense was wrong but the implication was clear. The

---

seems equally clear that Fowler and Knox were both privy to the true facts of the situation from the beginning and lent themselves to the concealment, from what motives of interest or influence one can only guess. Ironically, the disaster to which this act of favoritism so greatly contributed made it impossible to keep the *de facto* principal of the contract under cover. The collaborators thus exposed themselves.

The only known text of the letter from Hamilton to Duer recognizing him "as Agent to Mr Fowler" (NHi) bears the date "April 7th 1792." It is difficult to escape the conclusion that its essential passage if not its entire text was in fact drafted in that year after the committee's report was handed in and that this was done as a contrivance to meet the damaging implications of that report. See also notes 44 and 49 below.

44 Knox to Duer, 27 Jan. 1791 (MHi: Knox Papers). According to information from the War and Treasury Departments, the date of the formal transfer of the contract from Fowler to Duer was 3 Jan. 1792 (ASP, *Military Affairs*, I, 36; but see preceding note). Knox' two earlier letters are missing, but it is scarcely conceivable that the first of these was written in the little more than three weeks that had elapsed since the supposed transference. Knox' letter of the 27th crossed one in the mails from Duer in reply to his previous letters, saying only this in respect to the contract: "Morris will shew you my Letter to Col. Hamilton and the Enclosure on the Subject of Supplies" (Duer to Knox, 25 Jan. 1791, MHi: Knox Papers; Duer's letter to Hamilton has not been found). In his own defense against the committee report of 1792, Duer spoke of "my contract" and signed himself as "late Contractor for the Western Army," but said nothing about the date of transfer (*National Gazette*, 21 May 1792).

45 At this point Knox first wrote and then deleted: "But really from the best information it appears that the business in the western country requires *mighty exertions*."

frontiers had to be defended not only for the sake of the inhabitants, but also to demonstrate to lawless and dissident elements the power of the government to preserve peace and good order. "It is true economy," Knox concluded, "to regulate events instead of being regulated by them."[46] Had the Secretary of State known all of the ramifications of this belief that Indians could be subdued, foreign emissaries thwarted, separatism quieted, and ties of loyalty to the union strengthened by a show of force, his allusion to the failure of the administration to learn from experience in its conduct of Indian warfare might have been less muted. For at the time Knox reported to Washington the probable need of "another and more effectual expedition against the Wabash Indians" and simultaneously condemned the Virginia plan of frontier defense as being "destitute of those principles of unity and responsibility, essentially necessary to guard the public from abuse,"[47] he himself set an illuminating example of the manner in which orthodox military methods could provide a convenient nexus between public responsibility and private interest.

Since the chief contractor for supplies was not only a debtor to the government of long standing but was also embarrassed by debts to private individuals, the Secretary of War found himself handicapped from the start in the effort to proceed with great vigor. On the day after the necessary legislation was passed, Knox, obviously with Hamilton's approval, wrote the following remarkable letter to John Holker, prominent Philadelphia merchant:[48]

> I have the honor to inform you, that the interests of the public, require that the secretary of the treasury and myself should make some arrangements with William Duer Esq of New York, who is interested in the contract for supplying the troops on the Frontiers with provisions.
>
> The duties of our station forbid our going to New York, and I understand that some unsettled business between Mr. Duer and you may render it inexpedient for him without some previous explanations with you to repair to this city.
>
> The object therefore of this information to you, is to request, (if it be not incompatible with your interests,) an assurance, that Mr. Duer may repair to this City, on the public business herein mentioned and that you will not directly or indirectly, take any measures on his journey to, during his stay in this City, or on his return to New York, arrest or in any other way molest him on account of the points in dispute between you and him.

Holker must have given the assurance not to impede the public and private debtor on whom the government placed its reliance, for Duer arrived in Philadelphia early in April and remained at least until the end of the month. While there he received an advance of $30,000 on the Fowler contract.[49] On the 26th Knox awarded him another con-

[46] Knox to Washington, 22 Jan. 1791 (ASP, *Military Affairs*, I, 112-3).
[47] Knox to Washington, 15 Jan. 1791 (same, I, 109).
[48] Knox to John Holker, 5 Mch. 1791 (MHi: Knox Papers).
[49] A further reason for doubting that Hamilton's letter to Duer was written

tract for supplying the troops on their way to Pittsburgh, on which an advance was also made.[50] Two days later Knox personally borrowed $10,000 from Duer, half in specie and half in promissory notes signed by Duer and later discounted, through Knox' friend Thomas Randall of Shaw & Randall, at the Bank of New York.[51]

Thus with the aid of capital made available from the largest sum to be appropriated for Indian warfare in any single year since the Revolution,[52] the two men allowed the urgent spring months to slip away while they concentrated their energies upon a vast scheme to purchase from one to four million acres of land in Maine. Early in June they met in New Brunswick and signed a partnership agreement which in its salient aspects—particularly in the plan to sell large tracts of land to French émigrés—was copied almost exactly from the Scioto speculation. But experience in that failing venture had at least taught the two partners that absolute control in this one should rest in their hands and not be shared by any associates who might be admitted.[53] They also acted in secrecy. The Secretary of War and the

exactly as claimed on 7 Apr. 1791 (see notes 43 and 44 above) is that its figures for advances made and promised do not agree with the actual record of dates and amounts. Written in response to a request made in conversation the same day (if Hamilton's later testimony is accepted), that letter allowed Duer an immediate advance of $30,000 and promised a further sum of $20,000 in 45 days. But according to the report of the committee, the following sums were advanced on the Fowler contract: 22 Mch., $10,000; 7 Apr., $15,000; 25 Apr., $15,000; 7 May, $20,000; and 20 July 1791, $10,000 (ASP, *Military Affairs*, I, 36). The dates and figures given by the committee are confirmed by the record of Treasury warrants issued under the Fowler contract. This record also reveals that the first payment was made to "Joseph Howell [Acting Paymaster General] his [Fowler's] Assignee," the next two were made to Duer as "his Agent," the fourth to Laban Bronson as Duer's attorney, and the last to Duer himself (Account No. 6139, Theodosius Fowler "under Contract with the Secretary of the Treasury," 25 Apr. 1800, DNA: RG 217, M-235/20; a note by a departmental clerk, Henry Kuhl, states that a copy of this account was sent to Fowler on 9 Dec. 1794). This account included the debit against Fowler of $13,453.29 for eleven payments down to 9 May 1792 for the bills of exchange drawn by Israel Ludlow, protested by Duer, and discharged as authorized by the Secretary of War. Advances and payments totaled $83,708.32, against which credits for rations supplied amount to $71,267.38. The latter figure included many estimates which seem quite unrealistic—for example beef, flour, and salt valued at $4,323 "either taken or destroyed by the Enemy" on 4 Nov. 1791. The adjusted balance against Fowler of $10,799.29 was liquidated by a credit for that sum on 7 Aug. 1802 "for the purpose of closing his Contract" in accordance with the Act of Congress (Account No. 13691, Theodosius Fowler, DNA: RG 217, M-235/53).

[50] The committee report of 1792 gave the date of this contract as 6 Mch. 1791 and stated that $15,000 had been advanced under it on 23 Mch. 1791. The report of 1793 corrected the date to 26 Apr. 1791 and stated that on this contract only $4,000 had been advanced to Duer on 26 Mch. [Apr.?] 1791 (ASP, *Military Affairs*, I, 36, 42).

[51] Receipt given by Duer to Knox, 28 Apr. 1791, for 6% and 3% securities of the United States amounting to $14,787, to be returned on reimbursement of $10,000 advanced on loan with interest from date (Knox to Duer, undated but Apr.-May 1791; Randall to Knox, 13 Apr. 1791; Knox to Randall, 22 and 25 Apr. 1791; MHi: Knox Papers).

[52] Knox' estimates called for $320,942.20 and Washington transmitted these to Congress without comment (ASP, *Military Affairs*, 103-4, 107, 112-3). Congress appropriated $321,686.20 (*U.S. Statutes at Large*, I, 224).

[53] Duer to Knox, 24 May 1791, stating that he had a plan to "make the specula-

public contractor were to be carefully screened from view while the delicate negotiations were carried on by trusted agents—General Henry Jackson, an old friend and comrade-in-arms of Knox, and Royal Flint, a merchant and associate of Duer who had long been engaged in various speculative activities and procurement operations for the government.

The principals in this scheme laid down revealing guidelines for their agents. If the committee of the General Court of Massachusetts balked at conditions to permit aliens to buy from the partners but were otherwise amenable, Jackson and Flint were directed to close with them rather "than hazard a Legislative Decision." Reports had come to Knox and Duer that the committee were hostile to sales of immense tracts "from a Jealousy of Monopoly, and perhaps other Causes." But this, they told the agents, need present no difficulty. Different companies could be formed under different names, provided the agents took care to vary the amounts of land asked for "in order to avoid suspicion of Combination." If, however, an application to the General Court should prove to be necessary, "no Time should be lost in securing an Interest favorable to our object"—that is, by permitting members to share in the speculation. The agents were to seek lands contiguous to navigation, since it was probable that four million acres well located would cover all "Considerable Tracts of Cultivable Land, in which Case the Purchase of half would operate as a Monopoly of the whole, and Enable us to fix the price." Above all, they directed as they themselves set the example, "It is of great Importance that no Time should be lost in carrying our Plan into Execution."[54] The following day Knox sent Duer's two notes to Shaw & Randall to be discounted.[55] In the next few days he took it upon himself to obtain the necessary relinquishment of Samuel Ogden's claim to Maine lands, a task at which he succeeded at the cost of future disagreements.[56]

---

tion solid and productive: but then all arrangements must be within our own Controul" (MHi: Knox Papers); text of the agreement between Knox and Duer, dated at New Brunswick, 2 June 1791, signed by Knox and Duer and witnessed by Henry Jackson and John Lane (same; printed in Allis, *Maine Lands*, CSM, XXXVI, 40-3, where the confused numbering of the articles to the agreement is set straight).

[54] Knox and Duer to Jackson and Flint, New Brunswick, 2 June 1791 (same, XXXVI, 44-5).

[55] Knox to Thomas Randall of Shaw & Randall, 3 June 1791. On 17 June 1791 Knox wrote the firm: "[Duer] has agreed to accept my drafts for the Cash sum of 5000 Dollars for my eastern expences and I wrote him that I shall draw in your favor, which I now do. These drafts are for 2500 dollars," one at 33 days after date and the other at 60 days. They were to be discounted and Duer agreed to pay them when due. Knox added: "I am responsible to you for the result which in case of failure on the part of Mr. Duer shall be reimbursed to you without any delay" (Dfts of two drafts enclosed and letters in MHi: Knox Papers). The acceptances were discounted at the Bank of New York by Shaw & Randall (Randall to Knox, 18 June 1791, same). Before they fell due Knox gave notes of hand to Duer at 30 and 45 days, each for $2,500, presumably to provide for their payment (Duer to Knox, 29 July 1791, same). It is impossible to know the exact state of the transactions between the two men at this period, but on 17 Dec. 1791 Duer gave Knox a demand note for $1,000 and on 13 Feb. 1792, just before the panic broke, he gave Knox another for $3,000 (same).

[56] Allis, *Maine Lands*, CSM, XXXVI, p. 45-6, 56; Knox to Duer, 8 June 1791,

The secrecy, the object, the close collaboration between a public officer and a private individual, and the deceptive methods to be practiced upon a state legislature were in the classic pattern of the great land speculations of the day. Knox was the guiding spirit, Duer the willing accomplice.

Jackson proved to be an adept negotiator and the committee of the General Court was amenable. In just a month and a half from the time the partnership was formed, the agents signed a contract in Boston to purchase 2,000,000 acres of Maine lands at ten cents an acre, tax free for ten years and payable in eight annual installments.[57] The partners were so jubilant that they at once included their agents in another agreement to purchase an additional million acres, with no one else to be admitted to this partnership save by consent of all four.[58] To add to Knox' satisfaction, his long negotiations as agent of the Commonwealth for the sale of about 70,000 acres of other Maine lands of a confiscated estate left in insolvency by his Loyalist father-in-law, Thomas Flucker, against which creditors' claims of more than £17,865 were filed, had been brought to a happy climax just at this time. These negotiations, begun in 1790, had paralleled the speculation with Duer and, like that, had engrossed the attention of Knox during the critical months of spring and early summer. Knox stipulated that the sale of Flucker lands at auction should comply with the law in every respect and there is no reason to doubt that this was done. But when the auction was held at the Bunch of Grapes Tavern in Boston, the estate was knocked down to Dr. Oliver Smith at a figure much lower than Knox had anticipated—lower even than the appraised value—and Smith, in accord with a previous understanding arranged by Jackson, promptly reconveyed the lands to Knox for $3,000. Everything, the agent assured the Secretary of War, "was perfectly agreeable *to Law*—so, you may rest satisfied that no difficulties can arise on that head."[59]

"(Secret)," stating that he had not revealed to Ogden the names of those concerned in the venture except himself and Jackson, but had promised for relinquishment of his claim a "handsome quantity of lands without any advance." Ogden gave Knox credit for trying to persuade his associates to "perform what they certainly were bound in honor and equity to have done," but then added: "I can but detest the Men, who so unjustly have availed themselves of an advantage, that as far as I can judge would disgrace an Israelite" (Ogden to Knox, 2 Aug. 1791; see also Knox to Duer, 19 June 1791; Ogden to Knox, 19 June 1791; certificate of Duer 5 Nov. 1791, saying that Knox, Duer, Flint, and Constable met in New York in July 1791 and Knox proposed to offer Ogden an option on "the residuing profits of 100,000 Acres of Land, or 5000 Dollars in money at the expiration of nine months," but that the others thought an option limited to 50,000 acres and $3,000 would be ample; MHi: Knox Papers).

[57] Jackson to Knox, 12, 23, 30 June and 3 July 1791, in the third of which Jackson wrote: "I have neither slumbered nor slept"; Knox to Jackson, 19 June 1791 (MHi: Knox Papers); Articles of Agreement for sale by Massachusetts to Jackson and Flint, 1 July 1791 (MHi: Knox Papers, printed in Allis, *Maine Lands*, CSM, XXXVI, 47-53).

[58] Agreement signed by Duer, Knox, Flint, and Jackson, New York, 25 July 1791; Knox and Duer to Jackson, 30 July 1791 (MHi: Knox Papers). This particular agreement was later cancelled, but ultimately another million acres was added to the original purchase.

[59] Knox to Joseph Peirce, 9 Oct. 1790, 21 Mch. 1791, the latter enclosing

Late in June, only a few days before St. Clair's army was supposed to move against the Indians, Knox wrote to Duer: "If [Jackson and Flint] can execute the advice I have given them *they will do well*." He chided his partner for being "a terrible correspondent." Then, as if startled by a sudden realization that other matters of great urgency also required advice and direction—matters to which he had given only perfunctory attention since issuing orders to St. Clair in March —he added: "For Gods sake put the matter of provisions on the frontiers *in perfect train*. All our troops are in motion forwards, 2500 besides the old troops before on the Ohio."[60] Knox had just reported to the President that all was tranquil in the West. To the Vice-President he had stated that 2,800 troops would have marched by the end of June— a detachment he asserted would "be adequate in addition to the force already on the frontier."[61] But early in July he wrote to Duer privately and more urgently: "I am much alarmed by the information just received from Mr. Walker that you are yet to make arrangements for the pack horses for the expedition. I hope in God you have made other and more effectual arrangements or you will suffer excessively in your interests besides greatly retarding the public service." He asked to be informed by return of post what steps had been taken with respect to both supplies and transportation.[62]

The next post brought Jackson's gratifying news about the speculation but no word from the contractor. Knox at once congratulated Duer on their "capital acquisition." Creditors evidently were still keeping the latter under restrictions in his travels, and so the Secretary of War promised to come at once to New York to settle plans for realizing the rich promise of the Maine venture. Then, as usual relegating public matters to second place in his letters, he echoed in almost identical

---

text of advertisement for newspapers and handbills and urging him to consult judges Hichborn and Sullivan . . . so that the sale shall be valid and legal in every respect"; printed copy of handbill, 21 Mch. 1791, setting date of sale as 17 June 1791; Knox to Thomas Dawes, 13 Oct. 1790; Jackson to Knox, 19 and 26 June 1791; Knox to Alexander Stewart, 12 Aug. 1791; Joseph Peirce to Knox, 19 June 1791; Knox to Smith, 26 June 1791; Knox to Mrs. Smith, 27 July 1791 (MHi: Knox Papers). The lands, containing some improvements, lay along the sea-coast just below the river and bay of Penobscot (Cyrus Eaton, *History of Thomaston* [Hallowell, 1865]. I. 206-9).

60 Knox to Duer, 26 June 1791; Knox said he had received "not a line . . . public or private" since he and Duer met in New Brunswick the first of the month (MHi: Knox Papers).

61 Knox to Washington, 30 May, 6, 8, and 16 June 1791 (DLC: Washington Papers); Knox to Adams, 10 June 1791 (MHi: Knox Papers).

62 Knox to Duer, 7 July 1791 (MHi: Knox Papers). It was at this time that Knox, repeating his instructions of 31 May 1791, told the quartermaster general that he was responsible only for obtaining horses needed to move baggage, artillery, and hospital stores and that packhorses to carry provisions were not to be acquired unless the contractor failed to supply them as required by contract (Knox to Samuel Hodgdon, 30 June 1791, DNA: RG 75, M-15/1). Thus at this late date and on this crucial matter, the Secretary, despite previous experience and Duer's failure to communicate, had blandly assumed that his partner was meeting his public duty. Walker's alarming information proved how groundless the assumption was, yet Knox continued to the end to put the responsibility where it did not belong—on the commander in the field (see note 103 below).

words the repetitive warnings given so long ago as January: "I have written repeatedly upon the subject of the provisions on the frontiers. I pray you most earnestly as you value yourself and friends that you have every preparation made to the extent of the probable demand— indeed every thing to be done after this month may be too late for the expedition. I should have little doubt that all would go well were you present with your stock of resources. But I am greatly anxious!"[63] The anxiety was understandable and the appeal was urgent, but it was already too late. These words were in fact written on the very day —postponed by Knox from the first of July as originally planned— that the expedition was supposed to move against the Indians.[64] The un-trained and poorly equipped troops had been slow in moving forward, but provisions and packhorses to transport them had been even more laggard. While Knox had been so zealously guiding the private speculation, more than a month had elapsed with not a word from the contractor. Public duty had been subordinated to personal con-cerns as the Secretary of War, screened alike from public view and from associates within the administration, sought a vast monopoly of Maine lands through manipulation and avoidance of legislative scrutiny. Washington, as dubious about land speculators as he was about frontiersmen, was convinced that peace with the Indians could not last "while land jobbing and the disorderly conduct of our borderers is suffered with impunity."[65] But he could not have known any more than Jefferson did how seriously landjobbing had penetrated his cabinet and interfered with the western campaign.

IV

While William Duer had many reasons for being a poor correspond-ent, these had nothing to do with his responsibility as a public con-tractor. His first interest at this time was an increasing speculation in public securities.[66] Secondary to that, not even excepting the venture with Knox, was his collaboration with the Secretary of the Treasury on a quite different kind of monopoly. Hamilton, besides shielding Duer as the real principal in the contract for supplying the western posts, had in other ways acted for ostensible public ends in such a way as to benefit his friend. Before learning of Harmar's defeat and as the entire West recoiled from the blow, he had directed the extension of public surveys in the Northwest Territory at a time when such an activity could only have been carried out under protection of troops sorely needed for other purposes.[67] This, of course, would have in-

63 Knox to Duer, 10 July 1791 (MHi: Knox Papers).
64 St. Clair, *Narrative*, p. 95, 96.
65 Washington to Hamilton, 4 Apr. 1791 (Washington, *Writings*, ed., Fitz-patrick, XXXI, 273). Washington spoke out of the experience of many years as a speculator in western lands (see Bernard Knollenberg, *George Washington The Virginia Period, 1732-1775* [Durham, N.C., 1964], p. 91-100).
66 Davis, *Essays*, I, 260-2, 371-2, 394-5. For an account of Duer's inability to restrain his "projecting spirit . . . to a single object however important" see Rem-sen to TJ, 23 Apr. 1792.
67 Hamilton to Israel Ludlow, 30 Nov. 1790; St. Clair to Hamilton, 25 May 1791 (Syrett, *Hamilton*, VIII, 360-2). St. Clair's complaint about the instructions was referred to TJ (TJ to St. Clair, 6 Aug. 1791; TJ to John Cleves Symmes,

directly benefited the Scioto purchase and those interested in it. Now, at the very time that Knox and Duer were planning another Scioto in Maine, the Secretary of the Treasury unfolded his plan for the Society for Establishing Useful Manufactures and enlisted the collaboration of Duer as its chief promoter. The idea for such an institution may have originated with Tench Coxe, but Hamilton at once made it his own and during the spring and summer, with Duer's enthusiastic assistance, brought it into being.[68] Early in August the two men met in New Brunswick with Governor William Paterson and others to organize what was to become—through the useful offices of the governor and interested members of the New Jersey legislature—one of the most comprehensive private monopolies ever chartered by a state legislature. Aiming at perpetual control of water power of the Passaic at the Great Falls, this grandiose scheme for a national manufactory of textiles and other goods was the largest capital venture yet to be launched in the United States. The franchise included lottery privileges and the use of public securities as collateral for the purchase of shares, two features that made it easy for Duer to connect the operation with his primary speculative interests. Though the Secretary of State had advised the President against lending his office to the enticement of textile workmen from England because it was contrary to British law, the Secretary of the Treasury himself assumed responsibility in this venture for procuring British artisans, machines, and managers and for engaging them under contract.[69] All of this naturally created much concern on the part of the British agent George Beckwith, who had been assured by Hamilton that the United States would remain an agricultural nation and a market for British manufactures, offering no field for a clash of interests.[70]

6 Aug. 1791), who had already acted upon it when Hamilton transmitted a later representation of 8 Aug. 1791 (not found) to Washington (Hamilton to Washington, 24 Sep. 1791; Washington to Hamilton, 2 Oct. 1791, Syrett, *Hamilton*, IX, 237, 269).

[68] Tench Coxe to TJ, 15 Apr. 1791, and enclosure; Davis, *Essays*, II, 349-518; Mitchell, *Hamilton*, II, 181-98. Henry Knox was also brought into the enterprise as a subscriber, along with some of Hamilton's other friends.

[69] See TJ's opinions of 3 Dec. 1790 and 13 Jan. 1791; Mitchell, *Hamilton*, II, 186-8; power of attorney from Low, Duer, and others on behalf of the Society, 9 Aug. 1790, authorizing Hamilton "to procure and Engage . . . such Artists and and Workmen, as you shall deem necessary" (Syrett, *Hamilton*, IX, 24-5); Hamilton's report of his actions under this authority, 7 Dec. 1791, quoted in Davis, *Essays*, II, 399-400; receipts of William Pearce for funds advanced by Hamilton for procuring machines, contracts with Thomas Marshall and Joseph Mort, Syrett, *Hamilton*, IX, 73-4, 85-6, 90-1, 184, 214, 490, 509-10; see also Washington to TJ, 12 July 1791. "Toutes ces dispositions," Cazenove reported, "requierent le sécret. Cette importante partie ne Sauroit étre confiée á plus de prudence et d'habilité que n'en á Mr. Hamilton." He also stated that Governor Paterson was present at the organization meeting in New Brunswick on 7 and 8 Aug. 1791; that, as a result, there was no doubt the New Jersey legislature at its next session would "accorde les faveurs qui sont indiquées dans le prospectus commes des préliminaires nécessaires"; and that Hamilton had taken upon himself responsibility for preparing the petition to the legislature (Cazenove to Stadnitski, &c., 23 Aug. 1791, Cazenove letterbook, Holland Land Company Papers, City Archives, Amsterdam).

[70] On Hamilton's assurances to Beckwith, see Beckwith's report of conversations, ca. 25-30 Sep. 1790 (PRO: CO 42/72, f. 69-72); Syrett, *Hamilton*, VII, 73. Beck-

The enterprise further impinged on foreign relations by its effect on the negotiation of American loans in Europe. Even before the plan for the Society was drawn up, Hamilton brought his considerable powers of persuasion to bear upon Théophile Cazenove in the hope of obtaining financial support for the scheme in Holland. Cazenove was agent in America of four financial houses of Amsterdam, one of which was actively involved in loans on behalf of the United States and all of which, as heavy investors in American securities, were naturally aware of the importance of having close and friendly access to the fountainhead of fiscal policy.[71] Cazenove was by nature disposed to be optimistic about American economic enterprise and he was an ardent admirer of the Secretary of the Treasury, whom he considered resourceful, brilliant, and profound—"cet homme veritablement Supérieur." Hamilton made the agent his confidant, gave him "the most secret details" about his interconnected program of public finance, promised to lay before him in a few days the plan for the manufacturing establishment, and informed him that he depended upon the concurrence of the Amsterdam financiers "for the success of all prudent measures that will promote the prosperity of the United States and thus enable them to maintain their engagements faithfully." Hamilton also dropped a hint that, the moment public revenues made it possible, the deferred annuities would become "un fond actif" at least to the extent

with considered Hamilton's plan for a competitive manufacturing establishment "so important in itself, and so essentially so, in its ultimate effect upon the interest of The Empire in this country" that he informed the British government of it within two days after the Society was organized. He pointed out that models of different textile machines were exhibited at the meeting in New Brunswick, identified Hamilton as the author of the plan, and stated that the following was "the language and spirit" of the meeting: "that if The States were permitted to barter their raw materials, their flour and their Oil, with the manufacturing Countries in Europe on fair and equal terms, it might be a question whether it was their real interest to make great exertions in anticipating those causes which usually produced a Manufacturing spirit; but that this was not the case; that they were admitted or excluded, as it suited local policy and local interest; that cramped and restricted in foreign markets, it became essential for them to create a consumption at home, for those Articles which they could not dispose of to advantage abroad, and that in the progress of an object so essential to the interests of this Country, all reasonable and proper countenance might be expected from the National Government" (Beckwith to Grenville, 10 Aug. 1791, PRO: FO 4/12, II, f. 164-8). Thus in effect the argument for meeting British restrictions with a policy of commercial discrimination, but without the element of reciprocity, was appropriated by those who had rejected that argument on the ground that it would lead to economic warfare. Such a justification, of course, was not employed in the public prospectus issued by the Society and published in various newspapers (Syrett, *Hamilton*, IX, 144-53). The British agent, like TJ, also pointed out the intimate connection between fiscalism and the mania for speculation in bank scrip that broke out simultaneously with the formation of the Society (Beckwith to Grenville, 25 Aug. 1791, same, f. 169-70; TJ to Monroe, 10 July 1791).

71 Nicholas & Jacob van Staphorst participated in the loans of 1790 and 1791 as partners in the firm of Wilhem & Jan Willink, N. & J. van Staphorst, and Nicolas Hubbard; the four houses were Pieter Stadnitski, N. & J. van Staphorst, P. & C. van Eeghen, and Ten Cate & Vollenhoven (Hamilton to Willink, Van Staphorst, & Hubbard, 28 Aug. 1790; Hamilton to Short, 1 Sep. 1790; Short to Hamilton, 2 Dec. 1790; Syrett, *Hamilton*, VI, 580-5; VII, 8, 175-87).

of being exchangeable under a new loan for other securities bearing a yield of 4%. In reporting these facts to his principals, Cazenove emphasized the confidential nature of the information but urged them to bear it in mind when forming plans for the deferred annuities. "A genius such as Mr. Hamilton," he added, "can neither remain idle nor avoid useful and grand objects, hence one may expect each year to see good plans hatched and a vigorous thrust made to reduce the legal rate of interest." As a further mark of confidence, Hamilton informed Cazenove that a firm of Paris and Geneva bankers had offered to purchase the American debt to France.[72] Cazenove duly reported the fact, mistakenly assuming that the proposals had been sent by William Short to the Secretary of State, but he promised additional information.[73] Hamilton also assured Cazenove, some eight months before making his official report to Congress, that he had prepared and hoped to have enacted into law "An act for the encouragement of Manufactures under which the Government will promise a fixed and guaranteed interest on funds subscribed by shareholders in all companies of this sort"—all, that is, that were organized on the principles of this first venture and capitalized at not less than half a million dollars. Cazenove was so impressed by the unusual marks of confidence displayed in these disclosures that he did not wait for authorization but at once subscribed for $25,000 of the Society's stock to be equally divided among his four principals. Independently of the pleasure this would give the Secretary of the Treasury, he informed the financiers, the probability of success was great and, in any case, "the risks were not to be compared to the advantages." Whatever these cautious capitalists may have thought of the grandiose scheme, they promptly ratified Cazenove's action and even authorized him to increase the subscription. But the agent, restraining his usual optimism, declined. "This enterprise being more for the public interest than for profit of the Shareholders," he explained, "I did not venture to commit you beyond your desire to contribute to the success of a plan that Mr. Hamilton has so much at heart."[74] There was no need to risk more for the public good when "les chances avantageuses" for the shareholders were already secured by a modest investment in what the Secretary of the Treasury had so much at heart.

[72] Cazenove to Pieter Stadnitski, &c., 29 Mch. 1791 (Cazenove letterbook, Holland Land Company Papers, City Archives, Amsterdam). Henry Knox had been urged by James Swan to persuade Hamilton to give his approval to this proposal of Schweizer, Jeanneret, & Cie.: perhaps, Swan suggested, "Duer . . . might work H[amilton]" (Swan to Knox, 27 Dec. 1790, MHi: Knox Papers). At the time of the hint to Cazenove, Hamilton had not yet received from Short the documents on the subject (Short to TJ, 29 Dec. 1790, enclosing Short to Hamilton, 18 Dec. 1790, both received on 14 Apr. 1791; Hamilton to TJ, 15 Apr. 1791). Nor had he received those transmitted by TJ from Otto (TJ to Hamilton, 10 Apr. 1791; Hamilton to TJ, 12 Apr. 1791). It therefore seems probable that it was Knox who enabled Hamilton to inform Cazenove and to assure him, almost a fortnight before the Secretary of State himself learned of the matter from the French chargé, that more exact details would be forthcoming.
[73] Cazenove to Stadnitski, &c., 27 Apr. 1791 (Cazenove letterbook, Holland Land Company Papers, City Archives, Amsterdam).
[74] Cazenove to Stadnitski, &c., 28 Aug. 1791 (same).

The benefits that Cazenove had in mind were already apparent in the confidential disclosures thus freely made to a private representative of foreign capitalists. They are also apparent in the fact that, at this moment, Cazenove was urgently pressing the army contractor, William Duer, to purchase large sums of public securities for the houses that he represented. He had already contracted with Duer for future delivery of $130,000 in United States six per cents and now he was pressing for an additional purchase of $120,000. The sum of these purchases was the amount needed to acquire the 400 shares in the Bank of the United States that the financiers had directed their agent to purchase. Late in April, Duer, in an unwonted moment of prudence, declared to Cazenove that he dared not commit himself for more than half of the securities desired. But two days later—immediately after Duer had received from the Treasury an advance of $15,000 on the Fowler contract—he changed his mind and obligated himself for the entire sum.[75] It is difficult to believe that, in an operation having for its object the procurement of a large block of shares in the Bank of the United States and involving both a privileged friend and the agent of financiers whose aid was being solicited in behalf of his favorite project, the Secretary of the Treasury did not have some connection with this sudden change of mind on the part of William Duer.

It is certain that Hamilton, Duer, and Cazenove acted in unison and mutual understanding in reporting the plan of the Society to the Amsterdam houses. For even after Cazenove had informed his principals of the Secretary's conversation in which he expressed his hope of support, Hamilton chose to repeat the appeal through Duer as if he had not already discussed the subject with Cazenove. This contrived indirection enabled him to voice words of praise for the agent while extolling the interrelationship of his public and private objects. Though addressed to Duer for transmittal to Cazenove, the message was aimed at the Amsterdam capitalists:[76]

I send you herewith a plan for a manufacturing Society in conformity to the Ideas we have several times conversed about. It has occurred to me that Mr. Cazenove might be willing to adventure in the project. The good sense and discernment, which he possesses, assure me that he will readily appreciate whatever of good there may be in the plan, and there has appeared to me in him a disposition very liberal and very favourable to whatever tends to advance the prosperity of the country. Besides the merit to which he is intitled on this score . . . he Seems to have adopted the solid position that those things which tend to promote the developpement and amelioration of the means of this country tend also to render his speculations on its affairs more beneficial and to enlarge the sphere for future operations. He will not improbably regard the projected undertaking in this light and could he be induced to engage in it, it would have an encouraging effect. . . . The more I have considered the thing, the more I feel persuaded that it will equally promote the

75 Cazenove to Stadnitski, &c., 27 and 30 Apr. 1791 (same).
76 Hamilton to Duer, 20 Apr. 1791 (Syrett, *Hamilton*, VIII, 300).

Interest of the adventurers and of the public and will have an excellent effect on the Debt.

In brief, by joining in efforts to promote the public good the bankers would benefit themselves, protect their interest in the national debt, and enlarge their own sphere of operations. Having just gratified Cazenove by the contract for purchasing federal securities, Duer added his own appeal to that of Hamilton. The agent transmitted both letters to his superiors and enclosed with them the Secretary's acknowledgment of the subscription that had been made in behalf of the bankers:[77]

> I learn with Satisfaction the light in which you view the plan for a manufacturing Society communicated to you by Mr. Duer, in consequence of my suggest[ion]; and feel myself indebted for the dispositions towards me, on the part of the Dutch Capitalists, which you so politely assure me of. These dispositions are not merely flattering—I regard them as a real resource towards the success of my public views. And shall cherish a Sincere wish to preserve them.
> The readiness with which You, Sir, enter into the Plan proposed by me is a new proof of that liberal and enlightened judgment which has led you, on every occasion that has occurred since your arrival in this Country, to discern the perfect harmony that subsists between the interests you represent and measures tending to give solidity to the affairs of the United States.

William Short, fiscal agent of the United States in Europe, knew no more about these arrangements by which the Secretary of the Treasury used the weight of his office to benefit a private monopoly than Arthur St. Clair knew about the land speculations of the Secretary of War. Like the field commander, he only felt the frustrating results without penetrating the underlying cause. Not all of the frustrations, to be sure, emanated from this source. Some arose from restrictions that Jefferson himself had originated as a safeguard against the artifices of the Amsterdam bankers and, when Short pointed out their restrictive effect, Hamilton promptly obtained Washington's concurrence in having them removed.[78] But these limitations were known and ephemeral. Those arising from the private relationship between the Secretary of the Treasury and some of the financiers from whom his agent was seeking loans for the nation were hidden and lasting.

In negotiating the first loan some months before Hamilton solicited an investment from Cazenove, Short was able to force the Amsterdam bankers to reduce their commission by stating, politely but with stubborn

77 Hamilton to Cazenove, undated but received on 26 Apr. 1791 (Cazenove letterbook, Holland Land Company Papers, City Archives, Amsterdam; caption indicates that Cazenove forwarded the original in his letter to Stadnitski, &c., 27 Apr. 1791).
78 TJ's opinion on fiscal policy, 26 Aug. 1790, and note; Short to Hamilton, 2 Dec. 1790, 17 Feb. 1791, 9 Apr. 1791; Hamilton to Washington, 10 and 14 Apr. 1791; Hamilton to Short, 13 Apr. 1791; Washington to Hamilton, 7 May 1791 (Syrett, *Hamilton*, VII, 175-87; VIII, 53-4, 263, 270-1, 280-1, 288-9, 330).

insistence, that otherwise he would be obliged to look elsewhere.[79]
But in the months that followed the bankers who had so long directed
American loans were confirmed in their desire to retain the business
and only prevented from dictating its terms by the skill and monu-
mental intransigence of the fiscal agent. Short, well aware that European
capital was becoming increasingly available to the United States, could
recommend that the Amsterdam financiers be placed in competition
with those of Geneva, Genoa, Antwerp, Paris, and even London.[80]
He could urge the importance of giving all European financial centers such full and authentic information about the United States and
its fiscal affairs as Willink, Van Staphorst, & Hubbard received
regularly by virtue of their established connection—information it was
far "from their interest to render . . . Public."[81] He could even hint that
the bankers had access to his own reports to the Secretary of the Treasury.[82] He could point to the manner in which some of these houses
floated loans on the American liquidated debt at a higher rate of interest than that offered on loans of the United States and were thus
competitive.[83] He could reiterate his belief that the opportunity of

[79] That Short's insistence compelled the reduction is proved by the bankers'
own testimony to Hamilton of 23 Dec. 1790, quoted in theirs to Short of 25
Aug. 1791 (same, IX, 137; see also Short to Hamilton, 2 Dec. 1790 and 15 Jan.
1791, same, VII, 183-5, 428-9).

[80] Short to Hamilton, 15 Jan. 1791, 17 Feb. 1791, 9 Apr. 1791, 4 May 1791,
3 and 10 June 1791, 8, 19, and 24 July 1791 (same, VII, 433; VIII, 53-6, 261-3,
324, 459, 534-5, 560-1, 573-5). Washington was informed confidentially by a
Philadelphia merchant that, in response to inquiries made in Italy and Holland, he
had received responses giving him "the fullest conviction that Loans may be obtained for the United States on more advantageous terms than are proposed by the
commissioners in Holland to Mr. Short" (Matthew Clarkson to Washington, 30
May 1791, DNA: RG 59, MLR, M/179; endorsed: "Not answered").

[81] Short drew on his experience as TJ's secretary by suggesting to Hamilton
that authentic American documents be published regularly in Dutch: "This
might be done by some of your clerks and an arrangement made here with a
gazetteer. . . . This would contribute more than any thing else to emancipate your
foreign operations from a dependence on the agents employed here" (Short to
Hamilton, 11 Mch. 1791, 9 Apr. 1791, Syrett, *Hamilton*, VIII, 172-3, 263-4).
Hamilton's own silence over many months was another reason for Short's insistence on regular communication, a silence which not only brought acute embarrassment to Short, but even surprised the bankers in whose hands "large sums
of money [were left] lying idle at the same time that a double interest is
paid . . . when it might have been so easily foreseen and prevented" (Short
to TJ, 30 Mch. 1791, 2 May 1791; Short to Hamilton, 3 June 1791, Syrett, *Hamilton*, VIII, 415-7). When Hamilton finally broke silence, his letter conveyed no
information about the United States save the market price of public securities,
its chief object being to convey the hastily-arranged removal of restrictions on
Short so that a new loan might be arranged at once (see note 78). Months
later Short wrote: "I cannot too often repeat the propriety of exposing the U.S.
(particularly in whatever relates to their finances) to the public eye in Europe.
The more they are known the more they will be independent of those few whose
business it has been hitherto to make themselves acquainted with them" (Short
to Hamilton, 10 Oct. 1791, same, IX, 315-6). The simple fact is that the Amsterdam bankers were much better informed of Hamilton's plans and policies through
his relations with Cazenove than was the fiscal agent of the United States who
labored, with remarkable success under the circumstances, to keep the public
interest "independent of those few."

[82] Short to Hamilton, 9 Apr. 1791 (same, VIII, 264).

[83] Short to Hamilton, 15 Jan. 1791 (same, VII, 429-31). Both Adams and TJ

obtaining reduced interest rates depended on resources the United States might find outside of Holland.[84]

But in fact Short's position as an independent negotiator had been seriously compromised by the superior to whom these cogent observations were made. On the negotiation for the next loan when Short agreed to double the amount borrowed on condition that a reduction in commission take place, the bankers blandly ignored him, announced a new loan of six instead of three million florins, demanded a higher commission on the larger sum, and thus sought to deprive him of his sole weapon at the same time that they charged him with attempting "to recede from a Bargain" already agreed upon and approved by the Secretary of the Treasury.[85] The charge was groundless, the enlargement of the loan unauthorized, and Short stood adamant in the conviction that the United States should not be required to "make a sacrifice of a right so clearly ascertained."[86] But when the bankers appealed to the Secretary of the Treasury, they were sustained by him, with the concurrence of the President. Hamilton conceded that Short was right, but he nevertheless thought it "more interesting to the United States to keep the commissioners in good humor, in order to a more cheerful co-operation in the more important point of a reduction of interest, than to make so small a saving in charges." To the bankers he gave the assurance that their difference with his agent would not impede cordial relations in future and coupled this with what appeared to be a strong threat to look elsewhere if the bankers could not contract for loans at 4% interest. The price of the public securities, he wrote, would satisfy them that it was "ceasing to be the interest of the United States to borrow abroad at a higher rate. . . ." Hamilton sent a copy of this letter to Short. "You will easily comprehend the motives which directed the turn of it," he added. But only the Amsterdam bankers could have grasped the meaning of this remarkable communication in the full extent of its ambiguous aim to "conciliate in a satisfactory degree all interests, public and private."[87]

For the fact is that Hamilton's failure to sustain his agent came on the heels of Short's signal success in proving that competition was far more effective in negotiation than attempts to keep the bankers in good

---

had pointed out the effect of such speculations on American efforts to borrow abroad (see TJ's proposal for funding the foreign debt, Oct. 1788, Vol. 14: 190-2).

[84] Short to Hamilton, 4 May 1791, 23 Aug. 1791 (Syrett, *Hamilton*, VIII, 324; IX, 97-101).

[85] Short to Hamilton, 23 and 31 Aug. 1791; Willink, Van Staphorst, & Hubbard to Short, 24 Aug. 1791 (same, IX, 98, 132-42).

[86] Short to Hamilton, 10 Oct. 1791 (same, IX, 311-2). Earlier, in transmitting the bankers' letter which set forth the so-called bargain, Short had informed Hamilton of a discrepancy between their written words and their assurances to him, but added that no harm could result since the United States would always "be at liberty at the end of each loan to change the agents themselves" (Short to Hamilton, 15 Jan. 1791, same, VII, 428-9).

[87] Hamilton conceded that Short "had a right to insist on the point . . . made with the commissioners, and did right to insist upon it till there was a concession of the principle" (Hamilton to Short, 14 Feb. 1792; Hamilton to Willink, &c., 14 Feb. 1792; Syrett, *Hamilton*, XI, 32-3).

humor. Late in 1791 when he negotiated a loan in Antwerp at 4.5% interest—a rate the commissioners of American loans had theretofore declared to be unobtainable in Amsterdam—their cries of mortification and charges of impropriety on the part of Short did not prevent them from offering to meet this competitive rate and even to declare their willingness to open the next loan in Holland at 4% interest. Short immediately gave his authorization and at the same time bluntly informed the bankers that no other loans would be negotiated at a rate higher than that.[88] This offer by the bankers and authorization by Short were fully known to the Secretary of the Treasury when he expressed to the former his apparent threat to seek resources elsewhere unless they agreed to a 4% interest rate. In consequence, Hamilton's words take on a quite different meaning. What he had actually said was that, if the bankers agreed to an interest rate of 4%, this would "effectually obviate the *possibility* of any future recourse elsewhere, and . . . secure to all parties the important advantage of *permanently* concentrating the loans of the United States in one great money market, upon terms which [would] conciliate in a satisfactory degree all interests, public and private."[89] In other words, if the bankers did what Hamilton knew they had already offered to do and what he also knew Short had authorized them to do, the business would remain in their hands beyond the possibility of any future competition elsewhere. Thus translated, the contingent threat vanishes, an unequivocal promise takes its place, and the fiscal agent stands bereft by his superior of even the possibility of using the one weapon that had proved so successful.

Such a contingent pledge of permanent relations with one group of financiers or even with one financial market was at variance both with prudence and with the spirit of the Acts of Congress authorizing negotiation of loans anywhere in Europe. The Amsterdam bankers were naturally overjoyed with a settlement in their favor that simultaneously removed the threat of competition and exacted of them in return only the performance of what they had promised—and what, in fact, they had already done. For on Christmas Eve of 1791, more than six weeks before Hamilton repudiated his agent's position and made his pledge to the bankers, Short had signed the contract for a loan of 3,000,000 florins at 4% interest.[90] The victory was his alone. Hamilton was gener-

[88] Willink, &c., to Short, 8 and 22 Sep. 1791; Short to Willink, &c., 11 Nov. 1791, 1 Dec. 1791 (DLC: Short Papers). Short to Hamilton, 1 Dec. 1791 (Syrett, *Hamilton*, IX, 554-6).

[89] Hamilton to Willink, &c., 14 Feb. 1792 (Hamilton, *Works*, ed. J. C. Hamilton, IX, 187; emphasis supplied). In his letter to Short of the same day, Hamilton acknowledged receipt of his letter of 1 Dec. 1791 (see foregoing note) and thus was well aware of the outcome of the Antwerp loan and of the Amsterdam bankers' counter-offer. The letters of Willink, &c., to Hamilton of 25 Aug. 1791, 21 and 24 Nov. 1791, and 2 Dec. 1791, giving their view of the dispute with Short and the Antwerp loan negotiations, have not been found. It is to be doubted whether these could alter in any substantive manner the facts as presented in the full accounts given by Short. Short's letter to Willink, &c. of 1 Dec. 1791 (DLC: Short Papers) is fully as candid as the summary of its contents given in his letter to Hamilton of the same day and bears out his claim that he had "found no difficulty in obviating the several objections" the bankers had made (Syrett, *Hamilton*, IX, 555-6).

[90] Agreement to make the loan had been reached within a few days after Short

ous in his congratulations. "The event," he wrote, "is a confirmation of the good policy of opening to the United States more than one market."[91] This could scarcely be denied. But it was a policy exactly the opposite of that to which the Secretary of the Treasury had committed himself. No word of either censure or praise of Alexander Hamilton seems to have escaped Short in all of his voluminous correspondence.[92] But even at the moment of his most conspicuous success, when he still had reason to hope that he would be sustained by his superior in the dispute with Willink, Van Staphorst, & Hubbard, he confided to Gouverneur Morris his wish that he had "never been employed in this most disagreeable of all kinds of business."[93]

William Duer was the common link in these land and manufacturing speculations that had such ramified effects for the military commander in the West and for the fiscal agent of the United States in Europe. But these enterprises were only ancillary to the great object that diverted Duer's attention from the conduct of his public business. The stock market was his natural element. There, Cazenove reported, he speculated with "une grande ardeur" at a time when two-thirds of the promissory notes discounted by the Bank of New York were estimated to be for purchase of public securities and when the financial centers of Boston, New York, and Philadelphia "reciprocally electrified themselves" and "Expresses galloped between the three great markets more swiftly than between London and Amsterdam in a crisis of war or peace." All that had happened in the past twelvemonth, the Dutch agent concluded, grew from such small seeds that the best eyes had not perceived them "and Mr. Hamilton, although possessing the eyes of a Lynx, has confessed to me more than once, in intimacy, that he still seemed to be under illusions of a dream."[94] Equally in private and just as the ambitious manufacturing scheme was being launched, the Secretary of the Treasury felt obliged to give Duer a stern warning.[95] But the foundations of the pyramid of paper had been laid long since and had not escaped the eyes of men who faced the realities of existence on

arrived in Amsterdam (Short to De Wolf, 16 Dec. 1791; Tr of English text of contract, 24 Dec. 1791; Short to Hamilton, 30 Dec. 1791, DLC: Short Papers).

[91] Hamilton to Short, 2 Apr. 1792 (Hamilton, *Works*, ed. J. C. Hamilton, IV, 194).

[92] George Green Shackelford, *William Short* (Ann Arbor, University Microfilms, 1956), p. 320. On the national debt, on the National Bank, and even on the idea of democracy Short ultimately revealed himself to be closer to Hamilton than to Jefferson (Shackelford, "William Short: Diplomat in Revolutionary France, 1785-1793," *Procs.*, Am. Phil. Soc., CII [Dec. 1958], 612, citing Short to J. H. Cocke, 12 Aug. 1826, 13 Nov. 1827, 27 Feb. 1833, 9 Aug. 1841, ViU: Cocke Papers).

[93] Short to Morris, 3 Dec. 1791 (DLC: Short Papers).

[94] Cazenove to Stadnitski, &c., 28 Aug. 1791 (Cazenove letterbook, Holland Land Company Papers, City Archives, Amsterdam). Cazenove stated that the estimate of uses of funds received on promissory notes was made by some of the best informed directors of the Bank of New York. For another and more exact description of the speculative mania, see Henry Remsen, Jr., to TJ, 23 Apr. 1792; see also TJ's conversation with Washington, 29 Feb. 1792. The Amsterdam financiers were more disturbed over the resultant panic than over St. Clair's defeat (Mitchell, *Hamilton*, II, 133).

[95] Hamilton to Duer, 17 Aug. 1791 (Syrett, *Hamilton*, IX, 74-5).

the western waters. The contractor of supplies for St. Clair's expedition was merely one of the chief builders among those who utilized materials lying ready at hand as a result of fiscal and banking policies of which the Secretary of the Treasury was the architect.[96] Within a few months the panic broke in full force, Duer was sent to jail on the suit of private creditors, and the Society for Establishing Manufactures suffered disastrous consequences along with others. But the basic cause of its failure lay elsewhere. Hamilton, well persuaded that both the public interest and his own policies were involved in the fate of the company, had the misfortune to choose as the chief instruments of its doom two of the most sanguine visionaries of the day—first, William Duer to head the enterprise and, second, Pierre L'Enfant to try to salvage the wreck. Both choices were ill-advised, made in each case after the individual had been obliged to leave government service under discreditable circumstances. But the fundamental mistake was Hamilton's own and, whatever his lynx-eyed gifts, was equally visionary. This was the attempt to usher in the industrial age at least a generation ahead of its time. The collapse and wreckage of the Society for Establishing Useful Manufactures served chiefly as a warning against the dangers of a fiscalism not grounded in the realities confronting a nation predominantly agrarian and commercial and having in its rear vast undeveloped territories for expansion.[97]

Thus did the Secretary of War and the Secretary of the Treasury divert from his public duty the army contractor to whom they had awarded the trust, tempting him with the sort of speculations to which he was notoriously addicted. There were, of course, ample precedents

[96] "The reports of Hamilton in 1790 and 1791, taken together, constitute a theoretical plan which is just beginning to be appreciated. . . . A fully negotiable funded debt, drained originally from the small-property classes and met by taxes paid by the masses, was to be used by an emerging moneyed class to create profitable speculative enterprises in lands, industry, and finance" (R. G. Tugwell and Joseph Dorfman, "Alexander Hamilton: Nation-maker," *Columbia University Quarterly*, xxx [1938]. 63-4, cited by Joseph Charles, "Hamilton and Washington: The Origins of the American Party System," wmq, 3rd ser., xii [Apr. 1955], 244). Even New England contemporaries expressed fears of a resultant speculative mania long before it occurred. One, disapproving of the bill for a National Bank as reported, thought it would "in operation . . . have become a refined System of Paper Money and would more or less have had the same Effects as that worst of Evils a paper medium has had" (Cotton Tufts to Abigail Adams, 23 Feb. 1791, MHi: AM). John Trumbull, an admirer of Hamilton, feared that the "Millions of Paper-securities so rapidly appreciating, and the circulation of Bank-notes [might] injure those general habits of Industry and Oeconomy, introduced by former years of Penury and Distress" (John Trumbull to John Adams, 20 Mch. 1791, same).

[97] Davis, *Essays*, ii, 497-503, and Mitchell, *Hamilton*, ii, 191-2, 197-8, provide cogent analyses of causes of failure. But contemporary comment on the failure of this and other manufacturing ventures, giving due respect to such factors as the high cost of labor and the quality of the emigrant artisans employed, took note of the central point: "it may reasonably be questioned, whether manufactures of the kind mentioned, can succeed in this country for many years to come. . . . There is a time in every country where manufactures will spring out of necessity and favorable circumstances" (*Newark Gazette*, 1 June 1796, quoted in Davis, *Essays*, ii, 497-8). The unrealistic vision in the 1790's of a great manufacturing center at Paterson rested neither on necessity nor on favorable circumstances.

for such intermingling of public and private interests. From the earliest days of the Revolution, to look no further, officials of such probity as Robert Morris and Nathanael Greene saw no conflict of interest in bestowing procurement contracts upon themselves and their partners in business. But it is misleading to attribute this to the supposedly unrefined mores of the age.[98] It is equally so to place responsibility upon the mere absence of a clear administrative distinction between public obligation and private advantage.[99] Corruption, collusion, and favoritism in office, whether in the age of Walpole or earlier, had always had its denouncers and disinterested performance of duty its champions. But the essential fact is that a distinction long recognizable in ethics had been given a new clarity and an immensely greater binding power by the revolutionary proclamation that the people were the sole repository of sovereignty. Thenceforth private interest could not properly be the touchstone of official conduct, much less take precedence over public responsibility. Some, like Jefferson, grasped the fact immediately and fully, though none followed him in this so far as to make it an explicit matter of principle to avoid land speculation and other forms of aggrandizement lest this affect his decisions as legislator and public officer.[100] Others required administrative and statutory regulations that lay chiefly, though not altogether, in the future. The generality of the people in this revolutionary age, however, perceived the line of demarcation so instinctively that Jefferson thought the first requirement for a public official to retain their confidence was to convince them of his personal disinterestedness. Yet in this critical and divisive decade when disunion was threatened so often from the West and elsewhere, there was a growing conviction of favoritism in government and a diminishing confidence in the will of the federal administration to insure that "the bond of union . . . be the equal measure of justice to all its parts."[101] These were among the most conspicous results of Hamiltonian principles of administration that deliberately, if covertly, rejected this ethical distinction of the new order. They were also at the root of western disaffection.

However secretly the Secretary of War and the favored contractor carried on their speculations, the effect on measures for the defense of the West could not long be concealed. Exactly mid-way between the signing of Knox' contract for the Maine lands and the organization of Hamilton's manufacturing enterprise, Arthur St. Clair wrote in desperation to

[98] Mitchell, *Hamilton*, II, 155-7.
[99] E. James Ferguson, "Business, Government, and Congressional Investigation in the Revolution," WMQ, 3rd ser., XVI (July, 1959), 318.
[100] TJ to Abner Nash, 11 Mch. 1783. A decade later when a Vermont supporter offered TJ the opportunity to join a small group in purchasing two million acres in Canada, he declined in these words: "When I first entered on the stage of public life (now 24. years ago) I came to a resolution never to engage while in public office in any kind of enterprize for the improvement of my fortune, nor to wear any other character than that of a farmer. I have never departed from it in a single instance" (Joseph Fay to TJ, 26 Feb. 1793; TJ to Fay, 18 Mch. 1793).
[101] James Monroe to Archibald Stuart, 14 Mch. 1792 (ViHi; in the hand of Monroe, with signature clipped; text printed in Ford, V, 452-5, with authorship erroneously attributed to TJ).

the Secretary of the Treasury: "General Butler (nor any of the levies) has not yet arrived, and three companies only of the recruits. I am at my Wits end about it, for much will be to be done after they do arrive and the Season is passing—from every appearance it will be September at Soonest before it will be possible to move, and then there is not much time left for the operations of the Campaign.—Mr. Duer has not put the affairs of his department in that Certain State they ought to be with respect to the transportation."[102] A fortnight later Duer's agent still had not received instructions "from the contractor . . . directing the means for transporting the supplies of the army on the intended expedition."[103] Late in August, Knox, obviously reflecting the President's deep concern over the failure of the army to get under way, informed St. Clair that he had repeatedly directed him to make good any deficiency in supplies or transportation by giving his own orders, holding the contractor answerable.[104] But this, besides being too late to remedy matters, only threw upon the commander in the field a responsibility properly belonging to the contractor and the quartermaster who were under the immediate supervision of the Secretary of War. The failure of performance was not only in transportation. In May and June, the period of most active attention by Knox and Duer to their speculations in land, General Richard Butler's letters to Knox made repeated complaints "of fatal mismanagements and neglects, in the quartermaster's and military stores department, particularly as to tents, knapsacks, camp kettles, cartridge boxes, packsaddles, &c. all of which articles were deficient in quantity and bad in quality."[105] Supplies were so deficient indeed that the troops were almost constantly suffering from hunger. The expedition was delayed so long from lack of transportation and other causes that forage for artillery and packhorses was almost non-existent. Desertions multiplied to such an extent toward the close of the expedition that St. Clair was obliged to send some of his best troops back to guard the line of supply against pillaging. The disastrous end came on a snow-covered clearing at dawn on 4 Nov. 1791 when the hungry and dispirited army, reduced by want to almost half its original strength and exhausted by the labor of building forts and hacking an artillery road through hard-

[102] St. Clair to Hamilton, 21 July 1791 (Syrett, *Hamilton*, VIII, 562-3).

[103] Israel Ludlow to St. Clair, [6 Aug. 1791], in response to St. Clair's inquiry of the same date, both in *St. Clair Papers*, ed. Smith, II, 230-1.

[104] Knox to St. Clair, 25 Aug. 1791, *St. Clair Papers*, ed. Smith, II, 232. One letter granting such authority was written by Knox to St. Clair shortly before Walker informed him of Duer's delinquency in providing packhorses (see note 62 above). But neither then nor later did Knox give St. Clair the slightest indication of the alarm he felt and expressed privately to Duer that the contractor might fail to meet his obligation. His silence on this important point in the face of his own experience and Walker's report, his being satisfied merely to grant contingent authority without providing St. Clair with any guidance to its use save reiteration, his failure to give a formal and official warning to the contractor of the fact and implications of such instructions, his reliance instead upon urgent and repeated private appeals as from one friend to another—all of these evidences of partiality and confusion in administration provide a marked contrast to the close supervision and efficiency of Knox' guidance of Jackson and Flint in the private speculation.

[105] Report of the committee of inquiry, 8 May 1792 (ASP, *Military Affairs*, I, 36).

wood forests, suffered the most crippling blow ever given by Indians to an American military force, the casualties being greater even than those at Braddock's defeat almost four decades earlier.[106]

This unhappy fate of the expedition that Knox hoped would protect the frontier, "curb the licentious, and prevent the evils of anarchy, and prevent the usurpations of the public lands," helped confirm western antipathy to federal measures because of its stark contrast with what Jefferson called "this years experiment."[107] That experiment was in effect an unleashing of the Kentuckians to permit them to fight Indians in the frontier manner. The Secretary of War had embraced the plan only under pressure and with extreme reluctance. He was in fact so opposed to anything like local initiative in such matters that he gave a private and blunt rebuke to offers of cooperative action coming from western Pennsylvania. "In Answer to your Request on the subject of the Frontier Defense," he wrote Richard Peters as the campaign of 1791 was being planned, "I can explicity inform you that the Measures taken for the Purpose will be immediate and must take Effect as soon as any State Arrangements can possibly get into Operation."[108] But Kentuckians were in no mood to be put off with such illusory promises. The President was so aware of their feelings that he not only championed them in his message to Congress but also authorized the experiment that proved such a contrast to the "principles of regularity" advocated by the Secretary of War.

Thus when John Brown left Philadelphia for Kentucky early in March, he was followed by an express carrying orders from Knox authorizing Charles Scott, Harry Innes, Benjamin Logan, Isaac Shelby, and Brown himself to raise a force of militia and volunteers and to undertake expeditions when authorized by the commanding general. St. Clair followed soon thereafter on a special mission of conciliation to the Kentuckians, whom he found enthusiastic over the plan for a cooperative action. "I do not believe," he reported to Knox, "there is more

[106] J. R. Jacobs, *Beginning of the U. S. Army* (Princeton, 1947), p. 115, gives total casualties of 918, plus about 30 women, but suggests that the actual numbers were much larger, since these represented only persons officially authorized to accompany the army. Braddock's casualties numbered 714.

[107] Knox to Washington, 22 Jan. 1791 (ASP, *Indian Affairs*, I, 113; Document IV). Butler, *Kentucky*, p. 196, states that when Alexander Hamilton mentioned St. Clair's appointment to John Brown, the latter opposed it but withdrew his opposition after "considerable consultation and compromise"—a compromise due to Brown's insistence on having "a local power . . . deposited in the district, to organize mounted expeditions against the Indians in the old way." Butler's work was based on the papers of Clark, Shelby, Innes, and others, as well as interviews with prominent Kentuckians, including John and James Brown, one of whom must have supplied the information about this compromise.

[108] Knox to Richard Peters, 10 Mch. 1791 (Dft, "Private," MHi: Knox Papers). This letter was evidently contrived by Knox and Peters in order that the latter could communicate its substance to the heads of militia in Westmoreland, Washington, and Allegheny counties, for its draft is in Peters' hand and its correction, date, and the names of the militia commanders are in the hand of Knox. In the draft Peters had stated that both the duty and inclination of the administration would "render such Interference unnecessary." Knox altered the expression so as to invoke the immense prestige of the name of Washington: "The Honor and inclinations of the President of the United States will prompt him to give instant orders upon this subject."

affection, among all ranks, for the General Government in any part of the United States."[109] Raising a force in Kentucky was not without difficulties, but the western leaders with astonishing rapidity organized, equipped, and set in motion a small army of eight hundred mounted volunteers. Late in the afternoon of the 23rd of May General Scott led his men northward of the Ohio and in the next ten days destroyed several Indian towns, killed a score or so of warriors, captured fifty-eight others, and lost no man in action. The swift expedition was over before the Secretary of War finally got around to giving positive orders to St. Clair to let it begin.[110] There was no organized opposition and therefore no triumphant victory. Yet surprise had been achieved and one prominent Kentuckian was quick to point out to Madison and to anyone in government who would listen that frontier methods of warfare offered useful contrasts to conventional strategy:[111]

more real injury was effected than . . . by the expedition last fall which cost so much blood and treasure. The taking of so many prisoners, the undeniable proof that the Indians have received that they may be attacked at any time without their having any previous notice of the design, the appearance of such a body of men on horseback, the return of the army without the loss of a single man, and the knowledge that the whole army comes from a country which ten years before was their hunting ground must all tend to strike a great terror into the Indians. . . . Will not this expedition prove unquestionably what is the most proper mode to attack Indians? If this does not satisfy government they will be one day convinced that the greater the expence and preparation for an attack on them and the greater the parade and form which is used in the business, the smaller will be the chance of success.

[109] Knox to Scott, 9 Mch. 1791 (ASP, *Indian Affairs*, I, 129-30); St. Clair to Knox, 26 May 1791 (*St. Clair Papers*, ed. Smith, II, 214).

[110] The rapidity of this achievement is all the more remarkable in view of the fact that St. Clair, awaiting the outcome of John Proctor's mission to the Iroquois, felt obliged to delay the expedition for two weeks. On 18 May 1791 he wrote Scott to urge that "a few days should be whiled away, provided it could be done without its being discovered that the delay was an affected one" (ASP, *Indian Affairs*, I, 132). St. Clair later pointed out that Knox did not issue express orders until 9 July 1791 and that the Secretary seemed to have expected Scott to be detained until these orders arrived, "which would have brought it to some time in August" (St. Clair, *Narrative*, p. 3).

[111] Nicholas to Madison, 20 June 1791 (DLC: Madison Papers). Nicholas wrote a similar letter to Edmund Randolph, who showed it to the President. Washington sent it to Knox "to shew the uniform sentiment of that district; and how little confidence the people of it will place in the plan which is proposed by your statement." He also suggested that Knox draw up "for the purpose of comparison only" an estimate of the cost "of a plan upon their principles" (Washington to Knox, private, 26 Dec. 1791, *Writings*, ed. Fitzpatrick, XXXI, 450-1). Long before the expedition John Brown had reported that Kentuckians were determined to wipe away the stain of Harmar's defeat and to "prove to the general government that expeditions can be conducted with less expense and greater success" (Brown to ——, 29 Nov. 1790, quoted in R. M. McElroy, *Kentucky* [New York, 1909], p. 157). Such motives, added to feelings of hostility to the Indians, help explain the zeal and enthusiasm of Scott's volunteers commented on by Nicholas, Innes, and others (see Innes to TJ, 30 May 1791 and 27 Aug. 1791).

Another mounted force of seven hundred men had been organized to move against the Cherokee at the same time Scott's force crossed the Ohio, but had been restrained because of reports that these Indians were in treaty with Governor Blount. In July James Wilkinson did lead five hundred mounted volunteers still farther northward and killed or captured a larger number of Indians. A third expedition might have been launched, such was the zeal of the Kentuckians, but St. Clair withheld his permission.[112] In October the President, praising the "enterprise, intripidity, and good conduct" of the Kentucky militia, reported to Congress that these offensive operations had "been crowned with full success."[113] Late in November Jefferson informed Short and others that "our Indian expeditions have proved successful."[114] Then, early in December, the shattering news of St. Clair's defeat arrived in Philadelphia, stunning the nation. As if to make the grim contrast between the frontier method of quick forays and the lumbering pace of conventional measures all the more conspicuous, Scott, Wilkinson, Logan, and other Kentucky leaders had remained south of the Ohio when St. Clair, in desperate need of able subordinates, started northward on his fateful march.

It is understandable that, as St. Clair later declared, the disaster should have agitated "the public mind . . . in an extraordinary manner."[115] The response of the administration was to disregard the lesson that Jefferson thought experience had suggested long ago and that the remarkable contrasts of 1791 had freshly demonstrated. It called for greatly augmented military estimates and for increasing the regular establishment to about 5,000 men. "To this," wrote a Virginia Senator, "I was opposed from a conviction that they were useless and that 12, or 1500 woods men would soon end the war, and at a trifling expense."[116] The response of the House of Representatives was to appoint a committee of inquiry. That committee found, on the basis of overwhelming evidence, that the chief cause of the disaster was the failure of the public contractors to meet their responsibility, compounded by the mismanagements and inefficiency of the quartermaster, Samuel Hodgdon. Duer, in prison, considered himself to be an innocent victim,

112 St. Clair, *Narrative*, p. 19.

113 Message to Congress, 25 Oct. 1791 (*Writings*, ed. Fitzpatrick, XXXI, 397-8). The draft that Knox prepared for this passage lacked such a tribute to the Kentuckians and made no distinction between the main expedition and those from Kentucky: "a respectable force consisting of the regular troops, and of the yeomanry of Kentucky, have been marched into the Indian country. So far as advices have been received success has hitherto attended our arms" (MHi: Knox Papers, undated, XLVII, 3).

114 TJ to Short, 28 July 1791, 24 Nov. 1791; TJ to Morris, 26 July 1791; TJ to Donald, 23 Nov. 1791, in which he expressed the opinion that the mounted volunteers of Kentucky had "proved the superiority of militia for Indian expeditions." Washington reported St. Clair's defeat to Congress on 12 Dec. 1791 (*Writings*, ed. Fitzpatrick, XXXI, 442).

115 St. Clair, *Narrative*, p. vii.

116 James Monroe to Archibald Stuart, 14 Mch. 1792; Monroe stated that a proposition to this effect was carried in the Senate by one vote, "but one of the members in favor of it afterwards shifted his ground and established the regular force" (ViHi; see note 101).

"stretched on the rack of public investigation." On the crucial charge
that there had been a total failure in the procurement of horses and that
St. Clair had been obliged to purchase between six and seven hundred,
paying for them with bills later protested by Duer, he could only say
that this was "as void of foundation" as the other accusations and that
he had engaged a special sub-contractor for obtaining horses, had given
him orders, and had supplied him with funds. Such, in general, were his
responses to all of the charges.[117] At the ensuing session of Congress
Knox and Hodgdon vigorously defended themselves.[118] The Secretary of
War tried to shift the major burden of responsibility to St. Clair. He
even went so far as to argue that the general had discretionary power
to suspend the expedition if increasing obstacles seemed to make its
prosecution imprudent, though the Secretary's own repeated orders at
the end of summer, expressed with increasing emphasis on behalf of
the President, left St. Clair no alternative short of direct insubordina-
tion. Knox' extended reply rested on essentially the same ground Duer

[117] Report of Committee, 8 May 1792 (*National Gazette*, 14 May 1792); Duer's
"Strictures on the Report of a Committee of Congress" (same, 21 May 1792),
accompanied by receipts, returns of provisions, and Duer's instructions to Laban
Bronson, undated, appointing him principal agent "for managing all purchases . . .
in the western country, not only on account of the contract, but on account of the
French emigrants" on the Scioto. "In managing the former," Duer directed, "you
will act according to your own discretion, and for my best interest; in the latter,
you will from time to time, govern yourself by such special instructions as you
shall receive from me. . . . In short, sir, in executing the business entrusted to
you, you will consider yourself unfettered by any other considerations than a
regard to my interest *which is inseparable from an honorable fulfilment of my
contract*: and you will use every exertion to retrieve any loss of credit, or reputation which I may have suffered from the fate of Mr. M'Farland [agent of
Theodosius Fowler, deceased], or from the scandalous insinuations of such persons as wish my contract to fail" (emphasis in original). In brief, the agent
would be supervised in the matter of the private Scioto speculation; on the
public obligation, he would use his own discretion.
[118] Knox' voluminous rebuttal, consisting principally of affidavits and certificates
of interested persons, has never been published (Tr in DNA: RG 75, M-15/1;
fragmentary portions of PrC in MHi: Knox Papers). St. Clair's restrained and
effective comment upon it convicts the Secretary of indecision, confusion, and
neglect—a verdict generally sustained by the committee of inquiry as well as by
historians (Tr, undated, in DNA: RG 75, M-15/1, attested by John Beckley,
15 Apr. 1793; Tr of Hodgdon's report to the committee and St. Clair's comment thereon [same]; St. Clair's *Narrative*, p. vii-xiii, 89-96, 100-5; ASP, *Miltary
Affairs*, I, 36-9, 41-4; Davis, *Essays*, I, 260-1; Smith, *St. Clair Papers*, II, 230-62;
White, *The Federalists*, p. 147-9, 360-1). But Jacobs, *Beginning of the U.S. Army*,
p. 119-20, while praising St. Clair's justice, his dignity in defeat, and his high
sense of responsibility, states: "As experienced soldiers, Knox and St. Clair
must have realized how slim were the chances of success with so little time
for preparation. Once they had accepted the responsibility for performing their
mission, however, the utmost haste was mandatory. When every moment was
precious, they both dawdled inexcusably." This conclusion is scarcely just to
St. Clair. Once the expedition had been authorized, Knox hastened to his speculations but St. Clair hastened to Kentucky with a celerity equalling that of
his remarkable journey of 1790 (see Vol. 17: 131-4 n.), resulting in such injury
to his health as to affect his conduct of the campaign. The ensuing months of
delay were due primarily to lack of support from the Secretary of War and
the public contractor in respect to troops, supplies, and transportation, not to
St. Clair's dawdling. For cabinet discussions of the campaign and Washington's
criticism of St. Clair for not keeping his army in such a position as "always to

had chosen—that the superior, having issued and even repeated the necessary orders, could not be held responsible for the manner of their execution by the subordinate. St. Clair always believed that the Secretary of War had contrived to delay his voluminous reply so that, in the closing days of the session, the committee would be unable to report and thus a veil would be drawn over the whole matter. He himself was permitted only three days in which to answer documents that rested on extensive use of official files and "had been many months upon the anvil." But the committee of inquiry, while amending its report in a few minor particulars, stood firm on its original conclusion as to the chief cause of failure. That conclusion—that the breakdown of army supply services had been almost complete—is amply supported by the evidence.

V

The combined impact of federal measures and the manner of their administration not only contributed to the rising spirit of discontent in Kentucky but also influenced political rivalries that had developed there and had been aggravated by the imperative need of westerners for access to the sea. These rivalries, in part mirroring divisions in national politics that had long since become evident, were exemplified in two very different letters written from Kentucky late in 1790. Both communications, coming from men of standing and intelligence in the West, arrived in Philadelphia at the right moment to add force to their meaning.

The first of these letters was written by Thomas Marshall, friend of Washington and father of the future Chief Justice. It was addressed to the President and voiced the belief that "a great Majority of the people" of Kentucky were well disposed to the government.[119] But its real aim was to confirm Marshall's prior allegation that "a violent seperation from the United States had been intended by James Wilkinson, John Brown, and others in order to form a commercial or other connection with Spain or, if amicable measures failed, to obtain free use of the Mississippi by force with the aid of England.[120] In this prior communication Marshall had been particular in pointing

---

be able to display them in a line behind trees in the Indian manner," see TJ's memorandum of 9 Mch. 1792.

[119] Marshall to Washington, 11 Sep. 1790 (DLC: Washington Papers, enclosing *Kentucky Gazette*, 23 Aug. 1790).

[120] Marshall to Washington, 12 Feb. 1789 (DLC: Washington Papers). It is clear from this letter that Marshall already had access to Brown's letter to Muter of 10 July 1788 and was using it in the same manner in which it was employed in the campaign of 1790 and subsequently (see notes 122 and 124). Early in 1790 the charge of a Spanish conspiracy was made in the Senate by Rufus King. William Maclay challenged him for proof, declaring that he could not "tamely sit and hear the characters of the people on the Western waters traduced by the lump" (Maclay, *Journal*, ed. Maclay, p. 240). Maclay saw this as a phantom conjured up to bolster the demand for larger regular forces, especially when King thought it dangerous to arm the westerners lest the weapons be turned against the United States. Thus charges originated in Kentucky had their repercussions in government.

suspicions of treason toward John Brown, former law student of George Wythe, friend of Madison and Jefferson, and for the past six years a principal architect of measures leading to the admission of Kentucky to statehood.[121] Subsequently Marshall's son, James Markham Marshall, had been defeated by Brown in the bitter campaign of 1790 in which the losing candidate charged his opponent with having "entered into treaty with the Spanish Minister [Don Diego de Gardoqui] for the purpose of separating the district of Kentucky from the United States and forming an alliance with Spain." In an effort to sustain this charge Marshall, after the election, revealed in the *Kentucky Gazette* some pertinent passages from a letter written by Brown in 1788 transmitting in confidence the news of overtures made by Gardoqui when the Continental Congress failed to admit Kentucky to the union.[122] It was the issue of the *Kentucky Gazette* containing

[121] The oft-repeated supposition that Brown read law under TJ (Brown, *Political Beginnings of Kentucky*, p. 111; E. M. Coulter, sketch of Brown in DAB; Patricia Watlington, *The partisan spirit*, p. 80) is without foundation. He began the study of law in Williamsburg in 1779 under Edmund Randolph but, on Randolph's removal to Richmond, enrolled in Wythe's law class and became an eager participant in the two famous institutions founded by Wythe for instruction in law and legislation—the moot court and the moot legislature (John Brown to William Preston, 20 Oct. and 9 Dec. 1779, 26 Jan. and 6 July 1780, WMQ, IX [July and Oct. 1900], 21, 22, 75, 80).

[122] *Kentucky Gazette*, 23 Aug. 1790, quoting that part of Brown's letter to George Muter of 10 July 1788 in which he discussed the action of Congress on Kentucky's petition, expressed the belief that the eastern states would never consent unless Vermont or Maine were admitted at the same time, and transmitted information about Gardoqui's overtures. Burnett, *Letters of Members*, does not include the text, perhaps because no manscript copy is known to exist (full text in Humphrey Marshall, *History of Kentucky* [Frankfort, Ky., 1824], 304-6, but with italicized passages—those concerning the conversations with Gardoqui—not present in the parts published in *Kentucky Gazette* of 23 Aug. 1790 and almost certainly not in the original, though accepted even by some who repudiated Marshall's extreme interpretations, e.g., Mann Butler, *History of Kentucky* [Louisville, Ky., 1834], p. 171). Brown sent a similar letter to Samuel McDowell, but in that was an "enclosed paper" by Brown reporting Gardoqui's suggestion in conversation that, "if the people of Kentucky would erect themselves into an independent state, and appoint a proper person to negociate with him, he had authority for that purpose, and would enter into an arrangement with them for the exportation of their produce to New-Orleans on terms of mutual advantage" (affidavit of Samuel McDowell, 7 Aug. 1806, Frankfort *Palladium*, reprinted in *Littell's Political Transactions*, ed. Bodley, p. 97-8).

In 1806, testifying on oath in the impeachment proceedings against Benjamin Sebastian on the well-founded charges of having been a pensioner of Spain, Brown stated: "The proposition of Mr. Gardoqui originated with himself, and was suggested by him in conversation on the subject of his negotiation with Mr. Jay, and was communicated by me to Col. Muter and Col. McDowell, Judges of the Supreme Court, in reply to letters from them requesting whatever information I might obtain relative to that negotiation. At the date of my letter to Muter I intended to write letters of the same import to other friends who corresponded with me, but upon further reflection, and more especially after an interesting conversation with a highly distinguished statesman of Virginia relative to Gardoqui's project, I deemed it inexpedient to make any further communication on the subject, the public mind of Kentucky being in a high state of excitement in consequence of the rejection by Congress of the application to be admitted into the Union as an independent State" (*Report of the Select Committee* [Frankfort, Ky., 1806],

this letter that the defeated candidate's father sent to Washington as supposed proof of Brown's perfidy. Thomas Marshall also offered it as evidence that, though well disposed, the majority of the people had been beguiled into placing their confidence in such a person as Brown "through the influence and industry of his confidential friends" —that is to say, those friends who were supposedly interested in separating from the union and in forming a connection with Spain. But he closed his letter by assuring Washington that there was no danger —"our officers and influential characters having taken the Oath to support the general Government together with the position the continental troops have taken . . . leaves us little to fear from the Machinations of any Spanish party."[123] On the insubstantial foundation thus laid by Marshall was erected the legend of a treasonable conspiracy that embittered the politics of Kentucky for more than a generation and provoked a historical controversy lasting from that day to the present.[124]

---

quoted in Brown, *Political Beginnings of Kentucky*, p. 159). The Virginia statesman in whom Brown confided was James Madison, who immediately reported to TJ, in strictest confidence and as an established fact, the Spanish emissary's attempt to take "advantage of . . . disgust in Kentucky and . . . to seduce them from the union" (Madison to TJ, 23 Aug. 1788, 29 Mch. 1789). No documentary evidence has ever been produced to show that Brown had any other motive in view than that expressed by him in 1806 and supported by Madison's attestation many years later (Madison to Mann Butler, 11 Oct. 1834, *Writings*, ed. Hunt, IX, 544-6). On the contrary, the testimony of Brown's public career before and after the event, the indisputable fact of his confiding to Madison the news of Gardoqui's approach at the time, his acceptance of Madison's advice to limit the transmittal of the information to the letters to Muter and McDowell, and the fact that the theory of a conspiratorial and treasonable motive originated in bitter partisan politics combine with other evidences and plausibilities to forbid acceptance of such a hypothesis. See note 124 and Patricia Watlington, *The partisan spirit*, p. 160-5.

[123] Marshall to Washington, 11 Sep. 1790 (DLC: Washington Papers).
[124] Actually, Thomas Marshall and George Muter had made use of Brown's confidential letter to Muter in their campaign as candidates for the Kentucky convention of Nov. 1788 (Marshall, *Kentucky*, I, 297-8). Immediately thereafter the charge of treasonable negotiations on the part of Brown became public in eastern newspapers. Early in 1789 an Alexandria paper stated: "By information received from Kentucky we learn, that many of the principal people of that district, are warmly in favor of a separation from the union, and contend that it is injurious to the interests of that country, to be connected with the Atlantic states. This idea, so pregnant with mischief to America, is said to be much cherished by the intelligence carried there by Mr. Brown . . . to the effect—that he had the strongest assurance from the Spanish ambassador that, on such a declaration by the people of Kentucky, Spain would cede to them the free navigation of the Mississippi, and give them every support and encouragement in her power. Tho' this does not correspond with the opinion that had commonly been entertained of that minister, as to prudence, it is so serious in its consequences, to the peace and existence of the Atlantic states, as to deserve the immediate attention of Congress. If it be authentic, Mr. Brown has incurred high penalties for holding such a correspondence; and it is to be hoped, the executive of this state will consider it as a part of their duty to enquire into it" (*New-York Daily Advertiser*, 23 Feb. 1789, as from an unidentified Alexandria paper of 22 Jan. 1789).
The source of this serious charge is unmistakable. Of the two letters Brown wrote to Kentucky about Gardoqui's overtures, only that to George Muter was revealed. It was divulged to Muter's political ally, Thomas Marshall

Washington, now dependent more on Marshall than on those of the opposite political persuasion for confidential communications from Kentucky, was highly pleased with this evidence of the good disposition of the people of the district. "I never doubted," he replied early in 1791, "that the operations of this government if not perverted by

---

(Marshall, *Kentucky*, I, 297-8, 301-6). Soon after the first public imputations of treasonable intent by Brown appeared in a newspaper immediately under the eye of the President-elect, Marshall wrote his famous letter to Washington, an old friend, and repeated the substance of the charge (Marshall to Washington, 12 Feb. 1789, DLC: Washington Papers). In the ensuing months repetitions of the story in other eastern newspapers led to political repercussions in Kentucky (George Nicholas to James Madison, 8 May 1789, DLC: Madison Papers, giving a cogent analysis of the position of John Brown and others in advocating separate statehood before admission to the union and in denying an intent to separate from it). In the campaign of 1790 James Markham Marshall, defending himself for having made similar allegations against Brown, alluded in justification to the Alexandria newspaper squib. Thomas Marshall, in turn, transmitted his son's printed defense to Washington as proof of Brown's guilt (Marshall to Washington, 11 Sep. 1790, enclosing *Kentucky Gazette*, 23 Aug. 1790, DLC: Washington Papers). All of these circuitous reiterations and imputations of motive thus had a single point of origin in partisan politics and rested without exception on the mere fact that Brown had informed two high judicial officers of Kentucky, without comment or recommendation, of overtures made and initiated by the Spanish emissary.

This solitary fact is the basis also of all subsequent elaboration of the hypothesis of conspiracy and treason on the part of Brown. In the next quarter of a century duels, libel suits, and recriminations marked the development of this seed of political bitterness. By 1807 "Democrats and Spanish Conspirators" was a phrase in common usage by partisan opponents (Samuel McDowell to Andrew Reid, 10 Aug. 1807, quoted in T. M. Green, *Historic families of Kentucky*, p. 74). In 1812 Humphrey Marshall's *Kentucky*, animated with all of the rancor of Federalism defeated, made the most extreme charges of traitorous conduct by Brown, identified his aims with those of Wilkinson, compared him with Guy Fawkes, described his reporting of Gardoqui's overture as "a new hatched, and growing treason," and flatly declared that Brown, *"while a member of Congress, entered into a clandestine intrigue with the Minister to Spain, to separate Kentucky from Virginia, and the Union, and attach her to the Spanish monarchy"* (Marshall, *Kentucky*, p. 307-9; emphasis in original). While Marshall's animus was obvious, his method and style caused him to be widely read, influencing among others C. E. A. Gayarré, whose *Histoire de la Louisiane* (New Orleans, 1846) gave wide circulation to the belief that John Brown was merely the tool of James Wilkinson. The impeachment of Benjamin Sebastian and the libel suit of Harry Innes against Humphrey Marshall added little information and much fuel to the flames of controversy, while William Littell's *Political transactions in . . . Kentucky* (Frankfort, Ky., 1806) refuted the old calumnies effectively but with biasses of its own. Mann Butler's *History of the Commonwealth of Kentucky* (Louisville, 1834), made wide and conscientious use of original sources, appealed to a new generation to remit the "sentence of conspiracy, and every dishonorable treachery" pronounced in Marshall's *Kentucky* against John Brown and others, but extended its roster of innocents too far by including James Wilkinson.

Just a century after the origin of the charges of treason against Brown, his grandson, John Mason Brown, arose to defend his ancestor's memory. His *Political beginnings of Kentucky* (Louisville, 1889) utilized documents from the Spanish archives but cautiously evaded the partisan origins of the controversy. Even though Brown was generous in his interpretations of the acts and motives of members of the Marshall family, his work inspired an embittered revival of the controversy. Thomas Marshall Green, editor of the *Maysville Eagle*, grand-

prejudice or evil designs, would inspire the Citizens of America with such confidence in it as effectually to do away with those apprehensions, which, under the former confederation our best men entertained of divisions among ourselves or allurements from other nations; I am therefore happy to find that such a disposition prevails

son of Humphrey Marshall, and a man of deep biasses mirroring those of his ancestor, retaliated with charges of Brown's wilfull evasions, distortions, and suppressions. His *The Spanish conspiracy* (Cincinnati, 1891) purported to give "proofs of the intrigues of James Wilkinson and John Brown" and of the complicity therein of Sebastian, Wallace, Innes, and others, but its main effort to identify John Brown with the intrigues of Wilkinson rested only on a repetition of hypotheses originating in Thomas Marshall's letters to Washington. Thus far the controversy, bitter and long-lived as it was, had been local and familial in character. But in 1926 Bemis' investigations in the diplomatic archives of Europe and his assessment of the effect of western politics on foreign affairs lifted the Marshall-Gayarré-Green hypothesis about Brown's relation to the so-called Spanish conspiracy to another level of discussion. Bemis' *Pinckney's Treaty* (New Haven, 1926) based its account of the Kentucky moves toward statehood entirely upon the accounts of Gayarré and Green, whose *The Spanish Conspiracy* he considered an able and shrewd analysis (p. 108-17). Having thus committed himself to one side of the controversy, Bemis found no difficulty in asserting that Brown's real purpose was to spy on Congress rather than to represent the people of Kentucky faithfully, that it was he who initiated negotiations with Gardoqui, that he wrote artfully and with variant reports to Jefferson, Madison, and others, that Jefferson was unaware of Brown's "real connection with the 'Spanish conspiracy,'" and that, as Kentucky's representative in the Continental Congress, "Brown was a hand-picked man, elected through Wilkinson's influence" (p. 132, citing Gayarré, who gave no authority but obviously relied on Marshall's *Kentucky* in this and other respects; see also, p. 150, 156). Bemis' work, unpublished at the time, was used by Arthur P. Whitaker in his *The Spanish-American frontier* (Boston, 1927) though some of its interpretations were modified or rejected. But, while demonstrating that westerners such as White, Wilkinson, and Sebastian initiated approaches to Spanish officials, Whitaker accepted the theory of a "dangerous intrigue" and concurred without qualification in the view that Brown was a participant (p. vii, 115-9, 121, 129, 144-6). Almost simultaneously, Temple Bodley brought forth a new edition of Littell's *Political Transactions* of 1806 and *A letter from George Nicholas . . . to his friend in Virginia* of 1798 (Filson Club Publications, No. 31, Louisville, 1926), a work almost unnoticed in the critical literature. Bodley's avowed purpose was to present the side of the controversy that had been least explored and his competent, thorough, and relatively dispassionate analysis succeeded in its aim. He discussed the Spanish intrigues of Wilkinson and Sebastian, denied that their self-seeking ambitions fostered anything like an organized plot or conspiracy, and demonstrated the partisan origins of the charges of treason against Brown. His work was unavailable to Bemis and noticed only bibliographically by Whitaker. Unfortunately, the second edition of Bemis' *Pinckney's Treaty* (New Haven, 1960) and the 1962 reprinting of Whitaker's *The Spanish-American frontier* take no notice of the correctives provided by this serious and, on the whole, successful effort to redress the balance in the ancient controversy that began with Thomas Marshall's partisan accusations. See also F. S. Philbrick, *The rise of the West*, p. 174-6. Patricia Watlington has shown that John Brown did in fact write several letters in 1788 in addition to those to Muter and McDowell. On the basis of these she identifies him with the conspiracy and finds Green's charge of treason technically correct (*The partisan spirit*, p. 253-60).

In respect to the acts, motives, and public character of John Brown—perhaps also in respect to the existence of anything properly describable as a "Spanish party" in Kentucky—these accusations rest on no other proofs than Marshall's own inferences and their elaboration by his descendants and others, among these being the argument that even Brown's silence in the face of the gravest of political aspersions was tantamount to an admission of guilt (Green, *The Spanish*

in your part of the Country, as to remove any idea of that evil which a few years ago you so much dreaded."[125] Though Marshall had touched upon foreign affairs by raising suspicions about a member of Congress and his supposed involvement in Spanish intrigues, Washington did not deposit his letter among the records of the Department of State. Jefferson probably never saw it.

The second of these letters from Kentucky late in 1790 was from George Nicholas and was altogether different in nature. It impugned the loyalty of no one. Instead of repeating partisan accusations, it was concerned with western realities. While affirming that the bulk of the inhabitants were attached to the union, it held forth no comforting assurances. It was, on the contrary, a warning so blunt as to be almost an unofficial ultimatum from a respected Kentuckian who felt that westerners had been neglected too long by the national government. In effect this letter was a continuation of the previous communication from Nicholas that had so greatly impressed Washington.[126] Like that, it was addressed to Madison. But Madison no longer enjoyed the role of principal adviser to the President and Nicholas' letter was so candid, so exigent, and so peremptory in its challenge to the national administration that it would have been obviously impolitic to reveal it to one whom no man could press too far. It arrived, too, in the midst of the debate over the National Bank and it assailed the bargain over the Assumption and Residence Acts in such a way as to implicate all participants, including the President who had signed the measures. Despite Nicholas' characteristic authorization to Madison to make such use of the letter as he saw fit, it is virtually certain that the President never read it. It is equally certain that the Secretary of State did and that, toward the close of the session, Jefferson, Madison, and John Brown conferred about the response to be made by the administration to its central argument. For the fact is that this letter affords an essential key to the decision to commit the government to a new policy toward Spain. It is therefore necessary to take some note of its author, its background, and its substance.

George Nicholas, connected by birth and marriage with distinguished families of Virginia and Maryland, was a former Revolutionary officer, a lawyer, a man of wealth and enterprise, a considerable land specula-

---

conspiracy, p. 280). No other state of the revolutionary era left a legacy so bitter, so enduring, and so blinding. For, among its other unfortunate fruits, the controversy consigned to obscurity the central fact of Kentucky's long, unequalled, and often frustrated struggle to achieve admission to the union by constitutional means, during the course of which the people repeatedly chose as the single representative of their interests, their cause, and their loyalty to the nation the man whose character his defeated political opponents so unconvincingly traduced.

[125] Washington to Marshall, 6 Feb. 1791 (Washington, *Writings*, ed. Fitzpatrick, XXXI, 211-2), stating that such little intelligence as the administration received from Kentucky often came "through such channels, as in a great measure to prevent confidence from being placed in it." This has been interpreted, no doubt correctly, as an allusion to Washington's lack of confidence in John Brown. There is evidence that such distrust existed (Washington to Lear, 20 Sep. 1790, same, XXXI, 123).

[126] Nicholas to Madison, 2 Nov. 1789 (see above, note 29).

tor, an acute political observer, and an ardent champion of republican principles. He had once been led to serve Patrick Henry's purposes so as to inflict a grievous wound on Jefferson, but when challenged he stood firm as "a freeman and the representative of free Men," believing that elected officials not only could but should be called to account.[127] In the Virginia ratifying convention of 1788 he was such a strong advocate of the Constitution that Hugh Blair Grigsby thought him Henry's most formidable opponent, being so cogent and sustained in argument that posterity might even "hesitate in awarding the palm of superiority to Madison."[128] Nicholas was a zealous suporter of Madison in the ensuing campaign and believed it to be a crucial test of strength, for he thought that Henry and his followers advocated a second convention not so much to amend the Constitution as to destroy it.[129] Early in 1789 he moved from Albemarle to Kentucky, being immediately captivated by its climate, its promise, and its enterprising people. Late in 1791 Washington referred to him as "an influential character in Kentucky."[130] During his remaining years in the state, Nicholas became an ardent Republican, an opponent of such Federalist measures as the Jay Treaty, and a bitter enemy of the Alien and Sedition Acts. Like his college-mate Harry Innes and other leading Kentuckians, he took advantage of James Wilkinson's concession from Governor Miró to trade with New Orleans—a quite public and legitimate enterprise, however much it may have been conceived for the enrichment of the concessionaire. But it is scarcely credible to suppose that the man who dared to call Jefferson to account, to oppose Henry, and to admonish Madison and even Washington could have become a mere follower of Wilkinson on his removal to Kentucky. Indeed the two men were not intimate. Nicholas, however, was a friend and supporter of John Brown. His contemporaries regarded him as an unusually independent spirit, devoted alike to the principles of republicanism and to the union. "There never was a man of a character less equivocal," wrote one who knew Nicholas well. "Ardent in his temper, highminded and sincere, he was above and incapable of disguise."[131]

[127] Nicholas to TJ, 31 July 1781.
[128] Grigsby, *History of the Virginia Federal Convention of 1788*, ed. R. A. Brock, I (Richmond, 1890), 79, 99, 140, 281-98.
[129] Nicholas to Madison, 2 and 24 Jan. 1789 (DLC: Madison Papers).
[130] Washington to Knox, private, 26 Dec. 1791 (*Writings*, ed. Fitzpatrick, XXXI, 450-1).
[131] Biographical sketch by his brother, Wilson Cary Nicholas (MS unsigned and undated but ca. 1799, MHi: TJ Papers). This sketch amplifies and corrects the account of George Nicholas in DAB: it establishes Nicholas' birth as 31 Jan. 1755, his beginning the study of law and appointment to a customs house office in his 17th year, and, after the war, "his fixed determination never to accept any appointment or employment in the government except as a representative of the people." Thus, declared his brother, "He had no disappointment to sour him, he had no ambition to gratify. . . . Disinterested, Devoted to his country, ardently and enthusiastically attached to republican government, he was always ready to make any sacrifice to the public good. As a man generous, just, and of habits not only irreproachable but exemplary, as a husband father or friend preeminent, as a lawyer faithful, able and indefatigable, as a citizen spotless. It is no more than justice to G. N. to give this portrait of him. The

All of Nicholas' letters to Madison in the years following his emigration to the West testify to the accuracy of this characterization. These letters are in fact the most acute political commentary available concerning the situation of Kentucky and its relation to the union, the major theme to which Nicholas addressed himself. Their value for Madison was augmented by the fact that he knew the man who wrote them was not ambitious for office. Before leaving Virginia, Nicholas had asked Madison to keep him informed about the probable attitude of the national government, as well as "the present views and future conduct of Great Britain and Spain," toward Kentucky. "I make these inquiries," he said, "not as a politician but as a private citizen of that country for I go there with a determined resolution never to engage in a public business of any kind."[132] In his first communication to Madison after emigrating, Nicholas declared that, though the situation of Kentucky was critical and though the desire to separate from Virginia was general, a majority of the people wished to remain a part of the union. A few proper steps taken by the national government would "make it more popular [there] than in any part of America." The first step was "to assert the right and procure the enjoyment of a free navigation." The second was to provide defense. If these reasonable demands were neglected, the westerners would all unite in demanding them and they would "live under any Government to obtain them." "You know my attachment to the union," he concluded,[133]

> but I declare freely to you if I am disappointed in my expectations from the justice and policy of the new Government that I shall be ready to join in any other Mode for obtaining our rights. That government which with-holds from us the necessary defence and suffers our most valuable rights to be taken from us by another nation has no right to expect our support.—These points are so essential to our

sincere grief of a whole state at the death of a man is the best evidence of his worth. It is believed that no man was ever more respected than G. N. was by the people of Kentucky." This sketch, obviously written during the political crisis of 1799-1800, was evidently inspired by charges that Nicholas had changed from a strong advocate of the Constitution to an equally strong opponent of Federalist measures—a phenomenon that characterized many others and began with the Assumption Act (Joseph Charles, "Hamilton and Washington: The Origins of the American Party System," WMQ, 3rd ser., XII [Apr. 1955], p. 235). These posthumous attacks were, in fact, a tribute to Nicholas' lasting influence, for *A letter from George Nicholas of Kentucky to his friend, in Virginia* (Lexington, 1798) was so powerful a defense of Kentucky's strictures on national measures that TJ himself distributed copies by the dozen in Virginia "to such as have been misled, are candid and will be open to the conviction of truth" (TJ to Archibald Stuart, 13 Feb. 1799; TJ to Monroe, 11 Feb. 1799; Malone, *Jefferson*, III, 412-3).—TJ said that Nicholas became insolvent under immense debts, implying that this was the cause of his going to Kentucky (TJ to Mazzei, 2 Aug. 1791). Patricia Watlington, *The partisan spirit*, p. 200-1, states that Nicholas quickly became "the best lawyer in the district" and a prosperous planter.

[132] Nicholas to Madison, 24 Jan. 1789 (DLC: Madison Papers). Madison obviously had received this letter when he wrote TJ on 29 Mch. 1789: "Some of the leaders in Kentucky are known to favor the idea of connection with Spain. The people are as yet inimical to it. Their future disposition will depend on the measures of the new government."

[133] Nicholas to Madison, 8 May 1789 (DLC: Madison Papers).

well-being that delays in establishing them will be dangerous. Recollect how willingly Great Britain would have acceded to the terms first demanded by America after she had in vain attempted to subjugate her. Reasonable terms when once rejected will not give satisfaction. . . . If the general government consider us as enemies or aliens at least let us be treated as men and told what we have to expect from her. She may fix in her interest this people as one man who will always be ready to oppose any improper attempts that may be made by any other states. I may be too sanguine but I do not think any part of America can boast so large a proportion of independent men who will be desirous of giving up to their government all necessary power and will ask at their hands nothing but what freemen and fellow-citizens have a right to demand.

Given the situation of Kentucky and the state of parties there, Nicholas thought it sufficient to let Madison know "that *danger* may arise." A wise government would forestall the danger: "timely applications may prevent, but none will be effectual enough to cure the disorder." Such was the beginning of these candid reports from the western country. Nicholas' warnings became steadily more solemn, his belief in the justice of the Kentuckians' cause more profound, his criticism of the national government more blunt.

"I shall never write any thing to you," he told Madison late in 1789, "the truth of which I am not well assured of. You make any use of what comes from me that you may judge proper." He believed no late attempts had been made by Spain or England to detach Kentucky from the union. But Spain was playing a game that might depopulate the region if not counteracted, offering to those who would settle within her jurisdiction lands, protection, freedom of religion, a choice of government, and a market for tobacco open only to Spanish subjects, the last equal to a differential of seven dollars a hundredweight in 1789:[134]

If Spain perseveres steadily in this conduct for only two years no man can say how far the emigrations to that country may be carried. . . . These considerations I should suppose would make the new government take the most decisive steps as to our right of navigation and also induce them to pay particular attention to the gaining the affection of the people. So far have the steps that have been taken hitherto . . . been from having a tendency that way that they must necessarily have produced a contrary effect. No support has been given us by the general government and the regulation of Indian matters has been placed in hands who were interested in a continuation of their depredations on us. It is known to every person that if a trade is not established with them on such a footing as to supply their real wants that they will supply themselves by plunder. The management of Indian affairs being placed in the hands of persons living on, and interested in the welfare of, the other side of the Ohio, and no adequate provision being made to

[134] Nicholas to Madison, 2 Nov. 1789 (DLC: Madison Papers); this is the letter that Washington summarized at length in his diary (see note 29 above).

supply the Indians with those articles they cannot subsist without it became their policy to hold out to the Indians that we were a separate and distinct people from them, and that they might be at peace with them and at war with us, by this means giving them security at our expence. Besides as long as this difference subsists between the different sides of the river in the opinion of the Indians it gives their settlement a much better chance of being inhabited. Thus our interests are placed in the hands of men who have a contrary one to pursue and who have already given sufficient proofs that they will follow their own interests when they clash with ours.

As an extensive holder of Kentucky lands, Nicholas could not have been a wholly unbiassed witness to the drain of population to the southward or to the apparent advantages given to federal officers, civil and military, on the north side of the river. But, disinterested or not, he reported on the prevalent attitudes of Kentuckians with candor and realism: "Surely this district the inhabitants of which are twenty times as numerous as the people on the other side of the river ought to have as great a share in the management of Indian affairs as the people on the other side. I am well convinced the bulk of the people here are strongly attached to the union and that characters might be found in the district better qualified to manage this business than those in whose hands it is now placed. If it is not the desire of the new government to lose *all* its friends in this quarter a change must be made in this business. Let them take such steps as will convince the Indians that the Americans are all one people, that they shall never attack any of them with impunity, and that in future their real wants will be supplied in time of peace." Kentucky could not only raise all the men and provisions necessary for defense, but the failure to make use of her resources and the mistaken reliance upon a few army posts had produced a general belief that the purpose was less to protect Kentuckians than to hold them in check. "I can only say," Nicholas concluded this second warning, "if we are treated as fellow citizens any check will be unnecessary, but that if it is intended to withhold from us all the benefits of good government, a little time will shew that as heretofore we have found the troops useless and faithless as friends, hereafter we shall disperse them as enemies. Upon the whole I shall close this subject with assuring you that government has been deceived in the accounts they have had from this country, and that it is my opinion that the most serious consequences will follow from their persisting in the measures which have been pursued for some time past." Nicholas could not have meant that the deceptive accounts came from Kentucky's representative in Congress, John Brown, in whom he had full confidence and to whom he regularly referred Madison for confirmation and elaboration of his own information. They came from interested officials and individuals north of the Ohio.

This was made clear in his next letter to Madison, written late in the spring of 1790. Nicholas reported that Indian depredations "have been of a more striking nature this spring than formerly, but not to a greater amount. They have taken several boats, *attacked a few of*

the troops, and stolen the officers horses. These last have opened their
eyes which have remained so long shut. They no longer consider them
as brethren and declare them the aggressors. Their conduct has been
the same for ten years, and the only change that has taken place
is in their attacking the property and persons of these men who I
suppose are the servants of government and not the objects they wished
to protect. If these Gentlemen now change their language to government
it will prove very sufficiently that what I suggested in my former
letter was true: that they disregarded the interest of Kentucky entirely
and only thought of that of the other side of the river." Should offensive
actions be contemplated, such regulars as could be spared and the militia would be sufficient: "The people would go with pleasure and we
could furnish every thing necessary but the military stores." The
command, he thought, should be given to some Kentuckian skilled in
Indian warfare. His own choice was Isaac Shelby. Such prospects
seemed to give Nicholas a glimmer of hope and so also did the choice of
persons for the chief administrative offices in the national government:
"The Western country consider their interests as safe in the hands of
Mr. Jefferson." But federal measures filled him with new anxiety.
Assumption was too much like consolidation. The funding system was
dangerous: its prototype "was introduced into England when the government doubted it's own strength and popularity. I hope that is not
the case here. A government that relies for support on it's creditors
and not on the affections of the people cannot be durable. And yet I find
this one of the arguments relied on in favor of this system. . . . I
wish success to all the attempts that have been made in favor of liberty.
It will be a greater honor to this age to have it hereafter said that it
best understood and asserted the rights of man, than to have repeated
of them ten times as much as ever was said of the age of Lewis 14th.
or Augustus."[135]

In a single sentence Nicholas had set the problem of Kentucky in
perspective and defined the essential nature of the contest that racked
the administration for years to come. But the mere observation that
the durability of the union was to be found in the affections of the
people rather than in the ligaments of interest, like all of Nicholas' reports from the troubled region, only reflected the many tensions and
divisions within the nation—the claims of agriculture against the
objects of fiscalism, the demands of local interests as opposed to those
of the nation, the preference for frontier ways of fighting over the
conventions of traditional warfare, and above all the deep-rooted
cleavages between the North and South, brought into sharp relief here
along the river that might have unified but only served to accentuate
the boundaries of two great streams of migration having such variant
systems of land settlement, education, religion, manners, and ways of
looking to the national government. No officer of that government to
the northward of the Ohio could have uttered what this private citizen
had been expressing with such force for the past two years. Now, on
the last day of 1790, Nicholas looked back upon the events of the

[135] Nicholas to Madison, 3 May 1790 (DLC: Madison Papers).

preceding months and found Kentuckians' loyalty tried to the utmost, their patience at the limit of endurance. His letter to Madison on that day assessed the cost of federal measures and equated it with the future of the union.

"All the real friends of the Union and the General Government must have been very much hurt by the proceedings of your last session," he began. Assumption was both unjust and beyond the powers of Congress. Yet the measure was not so bad as the method of its enactment by representatives who decided issues not "according to the dictates of reason and justice, but [made] their voting for one measure the price of another." Nicholas could not have known how uncomfortably applicable this observation was to both Madison and Jefferson, but he went on to suggest that the Residence Act was based on a delusion, that the eastern states would support Pennsylvanians in its repeal, and that the only hope of preventing this lay in a presidential veto, which he would regret because it would defeat the will of "so great a proportion of the Continent." Kentuckians were willing to assume that these two questions had "called forth more of the spirit of party and intrigue" than would ever again be exercised in Congress. But, he added, "if you go on so hereafter we must suppose either that a general government composed of many independent states cannot be kept long together; or that all attempts of men to govern themselves will end in confusion and factions. If either of these facts should be established would not prudence dictate to us to look out for a master in time and by agreeing to terms of submission prevent the more rigid ones which would be imposed on us after a revolution?"

With this opening, Nicholas turned to the central issue:[136]

I am happy that the contest between Great-Britain and Spain has turned the serious attention of Government to the Western country. Every thinking man who is acquainted with the extent and fertility of our soil must be satisfied that the U:S: will have every thing to hope or fear from us at a period not now very distant. It must also be obvious that it will depend on Government whether the event will be favorable or unfavorable to them. We have every wish to continue united to you, and that built on the surest foundation a belief that it will be to our interest: but this opinion is formed on a supposition that we shall receive from Government that protection as well of our persons and property as of our just right that we have an unquestionable claim to. Would you be contented to the Eastward with a government which left you exposed to the ravages of a merciless enemy and which permitted another power to prevent you from enjoying the fruits of your labour; would you not disgrace the name of free and rational beings if you did? And if this conduct could not be expected from you why should it from us?

I agree with you in opinion that if G: B: was possessed of the key to the Western country that it would be a vital blow to the independence, trade and power of the U:S: but I differ with you as to the effect it would have on the Western Country itself. Consider-

136 Nicholas to Madison, 31 Dec. 1790 (DLC: Madison Papers).

ing us a part of the U: S. we should certainly be affected with whatever lessened their power and importance. But as after such an event it would be impossible that we should continue united to you, we ought to consider what would be our situation if seperated from you and remaining unconnected with any power, or subject to Great-Britain. In either of the last cases, it would be manifestly the interest of G: B: to give us every encouragement that she possibly could, for as what we made would all pass through her hands it would manifestly tend to increase her resources, besides acting as such a drain to you as would prevent your being able to enter into any competition with them. There is nothing which their colonies or commerce would want from America but what the Western country could supply them with. Making N. Orleans a free port only subject to the navigation laws of Great Britain would answer all their purposes of ambition and commerce and our's of interest. Figure to yourself what effect it would have on your population if [we] were clear of taxes, protected against the Indians, with a free trade down the river, with the highest prices for our commodities that the price for them in any part of the world would justify and you labouring under all the inconveniences which would attend a war with such a maratime power. But you say after having made us answer her purpose she would oppress us. To this I answer that at first she would readily give us advantageous terms; that as long as any contest continued between you and her she would rather add to than diminish those terms, and that after having been so long fostered by her, we should be able to set her at defiance, and if not arrived at that degree of strength, we would again unite with you upon those principles of mutual benefit and advantage which altho' you do not fully comprehend at present, a connexion of a few years between G: B. and the Western country would fully explain to you.

These are the thoughts of the most enlightened men amongst us, but such thoughts as they only give utterance to in whispers; because it is yet hoped and believed that you will do us justice. But let it once be established that this hope is vain, they will be immediately published and with what effect you must judge.

I am so zealous a friend to the Union upon proper principles, that it is not believed here that I entertain a thought of this kind; but I am only a friend to that Union as I think it may be serviceable to my country, and if I find that the powers of government are either withheld from us, or perverted to our destruction, then I should be compelled with my countrymen, however reluctantly, to look out for other anchoring ground. The critical situation in which we are placed has drawn forth this chain of thinking; for the particulars of which I refer you to Mr. Brown. If you think that any thing I say upon this subject deserves attention use it as you please; let what will happen I have no objections to my sentiments being known, and in case of any future necessity it will give me pleasure to reflect that I did not join in any measures which may prove destructive to my old country without having first given them timely warning of their danger. We have risked and sacraficed every thing to try our fortunes here, and childish fears and scruples will not make us lose all chances of benefit from our change of situation.

This astonishing communication, unequivocal in its warning that a people who had migrated to the wilderness to seek their fortunes would neither be submissive nor restrained by childish fears, must have echoed with strange familiarity in the consciousness of the Secretary of State. Composed in a different era and under other circumstances, it was indeed nothing less than a refrain from his own powerful arguments set forth in 1774 in *A Summary View of the Rights of British America*, an unequivocal restatement of his own warning in a private letter of 1775 that was also accompanied by protestations of a desire to remain united. The rhetoric of the Revolution, multiplied with immense force many times by the public consciousness of that epochal experience, was now being turned upon the administration. Petitions, addresses, and private letters had poured in from the West for the past six years beseeching both Virginia and the national government for protection against the Indians and for aid in gaining free use of the Mississippi as a natural right. Year after year conventions had been held and duly elected representatives had called for admission of Kentucky to the union in order that the westerners might meet their local problems under their own political institutions.[137] Yet these parallels to proceedings before the Revolution had thus far been unavailing. Significantly, Nicholas made no appeal for statehood. His silence on the point only underscored the ominous warning that the time for appeals was running out. The essential reality was not statehood in itself but the nature of the problems to be faced, within the union if possible but without it if necessary.

This, as Jefferson and Madison well knew, was far blunter than the warnings that had come from John Brown and others during the crisis of 1788. At that period Virginia and Kentucky, by "Compact solemnly entered into," had declared their assent to statehood. Brown as a delegate to Congress had introduced the petition and worked assiduously to gain its object.[138] Congress, by almost unanimous

[137] TJ to John Randolph, 25 Aug. 1775.
[138] Motion by Brown, 29 Feb. 1788 (JCC, XXXIV, 72). All delegates seemed to sense the delicacy and complexity of the problem and one declared, at the time of the crucial vote, "this day is big with the fate of Kentucky and the world" (Otis to Thatcher, 18 [May] 1788; Mass. delegates to Hancock, 27 May 1788; Read to Irvine, 30 May 1788; Paine Wingate to Samuel Lane, 2 June 1788; Rhode Island delegates to John Collins, 5 June 1788; Sedgwick to Dane, 3 July 1788, S. C. delegates to Pinckney, 16 Aug. 1788 (Burnett, *Letters of Members*, VIII, 733, 736, 741, 742, 745, 749, 759, 780). Brown correctly assessed the sectional cleavages and consistently reported his fear that, denied a constitutional mode, Kentucky would assume independence. For a contrary interpretation by political opponents and by historians, see note 124, above. In the ensuing months when Thomas Marshall's charges of treasonable conspiracy were reported in eastern newspapers, Brown and others denied the charge and stated that "all they wished was that as Congress and [the Virginia legislature] had both declared that it was proper and necessary to indulge the district with a seperate government that the district should set their government in motion without waiting for the formal assent of Congress. They supposed that the district would be more likely to

vote, had approved the idea but deferred action to the new government. Brown could not have known that one New England delegate had foreseen that Congress would find "some very decent excuse . . . for deferring the determination at present," but he easily penetrated the fact that arguments of inadequate powers under the Confederation conveniently covered a general opposition among New England delegates "lest another Vote should be added to the Southern States."[139] In this he had not been alone and his prediction that Vermont would be coupled with Kentucky as a balancing weight—the first of a long sequence of sectional compromises—was borne out. The near unanimity of the vote on that occasion, reflecting an understandable desire not to embarrass the new government, could not conceal the sectional issue or prevent a bitter disappointment to Kentuckians who remembered that seven northern states only recently had indicated their willingness to yield the right of navigation of the Mississippi for a period of years.

Now in 1791, having been vindicated at the polls against the allegations of Thomas Marshall and others, Brown was again in Congress, again pressing for admission of Kentucky to statehood, and again a confidant of Jefferson and Madison in matters concerning the West. Three years had passed since he had warned that the "Jay-Gardoqui negotiations had laid the foundation for the dismemberment of the American Empire by distroying the confidence of the people in the Western Country in the Justice of the Union and by inducing them to Dispair of obtaining possession of that Right by means of any other exertions than their own."[140] During the long years of petitioning, the Kentuckians, confident of their growing strength and fully aware of the weakness of Spanish defenses on the lower reaches of the river, had left as the most conspicuous evidence of their attachment to the union a massive record of their restraint, their patience, and above all their aim to achieve their purposes through constitutional proceedings. But now the old issue suddenly assumed a more ominous gravity, as if only a Thomas Paine were needed to touch the combustibles into flame. It could no longer be postponed or even confronted by the mere formality of admitting Kentucky to statehood.

When George Nicholas drafted his blunt warning he did not know that the threat of war in Europe had been averted, thereby nullifying Jefferson's hope of using the crisis to open the Mississippi. But John Brown in Congress knew it and both he and the Secretary of State could not have been unaware that the fact only added urgency to

---

be received into the Union after such a step than on an application from her as a part of the State of Virginia and that they would have less to fear in that situation than in their present one from Northern Politicks. These are the sentiments sent to the district by Mr. Brown after Congress had referred the matter to the new Government and such as he now avows" (Nicholas to Madison, 8 May 1789; DLC: Madison Papers).

[139] Paine Wingate to James Sullivan, 23 Apr. 1788; John Brown to Archibald Stuart, 25 June 1788 (Burnett, *Letters of Members*, VIII, 724, 725, 757). Brown used a similar expression in his letter to George Muter of 10 July 1788 (*Kentucky Gazette*, 23 Aug. 1790).

[140] Brown to TJ, 10 Aug. 1788.

Nicholas' candid words. Both men also understood that the removal of the danger of war would not in itself deter such an adventurer as James O'Fallon from setting in motion plans for an expedition of conquest down the river.[141] Jefferson had long ago urged the Kentuckians to avoid such aggressions and to await the outbreak of war in Europe as a means of attaining their goal.[142] Now the arrival of Nicholas' letter, the possibility of a collision between rash westerners and Spanish troops, the news of fresh Indian incursions following Harmar's defeat, and the general tendency of federal measures all conspired to make inadvisable if not dangerous any further reliance on a diplomacy of opportunistic waiting for the outbreak of a European conflict. Six years earlier Washington had thought the western settlers stood "as it were upon a pivot: the touch of a feather would turn them any way."[143] As Nicholas' reports proved, the words were far more applicable in this new crisis than at the time they were uttered. It was now imperative for the government to give Kentuckians unmistakable evidence of its determination to hazard everything up to the point of actual rupture with Spain.

VI

But even as the chorus of warnings from the West grew in volume and intensity, those delegates from the middle and eastern states who had voted with unbroken solidarity to achieve a treaty Brown and others thought would dismember the empire were validating the suspicions of the men on the western waters. The unanimous northern majority—led by a Massachusetts delegation that Monroe considered "the most illiberal" he had ever known[144]—had been powerful enough not to yield a single vote even in the face of southern efforts at a compromise arrangement.[145] Their essential aims had not been deflected by the change in government that had taken place. On the contrary, their hopes for a successful resumption of negotiations on the terms proposed had been strengthened by the augmented powers of the government. Whether Jay and his supporters discounted or disregarded the threats of disunion, whether they failed to grasp the gravity of the sectional crisis, or

141 TJ to Murray, 22 Mch. 1791.
142 TJ to Brown, 28 May 1788.
143 Washington to Benjamin Harrison, 10 Oct. 1784 (*Writings*, ed. Fitzpatrick, XXVII, 475).
144 Monroe to TJ, 16 July 1786. When Gorham of Massachusetts declared in Congress on 23 Apr. 1787 that closing the Mississippi would be advantageous to the Atlantic States and that he "wished to see it shut," Madison rebuked him for "the illiberality of his doctrine," contrasting it with the "principles of the Revolution, and the language of American patriots" (Madison's notes of debates, JCC, XXXIII, 736).
145 The principal Virginia compromise, prepared by Monroe and Grayson in consultation with Madison, would have permitted westerners to export produce down the Mississippi but their imports could be received only through Atlantic ports (Monroe to Madison, 14 Aug. 1786, Burnett, *Letters of Members*, VIII, 427, 440-2; Monroe to TJ, 19 Aug. 1786). Madison based his attack on the constitutionality of the seven-state repeal of Jay's instructions chiefly on the "settled disinclination in some of the delegations to concur in *any* conciliatory expedient for defending the Mississippi" (Madison's notes of debates, 25 Apr. 1787, JCC, XXXIII, 736; emphasis supplied).

whether they conceived the national interest in terms of commerce and navigation that transcended western concerns, they did in fact attempt to resume the negotiations shortly after the new government was established.

This revealing episode has never entered into accounts of American foreign relations because the documents pertaining to it are incomplete, some of the principal ones are undated or have had erroneous dates assigned to them, and no proper ordering of those that have survived has been made. Two of the key documents, both by Washington, have been misconstrued.[146] This attempt was both audacious and ill-timed. But the fatal miscalculation its leaders made was to misgauge the character of the President, hence the carefully laid plan came to wreck upon the solid rock of his prudence and understanding of western political realities. This effort to project the suspended policy toward Spain as if nothing had happened since it was first proposed—as abortive as that of the mission of Gouverneur Morris which originated in the same quarters and was inspired by similar political and sectional interests—requires attention despite its failure. For Washington's response in 1791 to Jefferson's decisive departure from that policy can best be understood by comparison with his response to Jay on the same issue in the summer of 1789. The origins of the scheme extended back to the political contests of more than four years earlier.

Indeed, the roots go deeper. When Jay was in Madrid during the war and Gardoqui, acting for Florida Blanca, suggested that the navigation of the Mississippi be given up as a consideration for the Spanish loan being sought, the American minister, knowing full well the feeling back of his instructions, replied: "The Americans, almost to a man, believe that God Almighty had made that river a highway for the people of the upper country to go to sea by."[147] After independence had been obtained, Congress' instructions to the American minister to Spain, drafted by James Monroe, made this attitude explicit: unless the boundaries set forth in the Treaty of Paris and the right of navigation of the Mississippi from its source to the ocean were expressly stipulated, he was directed to "enter into no treaty." This categorical limitation was not approved or sent to Carmichael, having been rendered unnecessary by the arrival of Gardoqui a few months after Jay became Secretary for Foreign Affairs.[148] Gardoqui's commission gave him full powers to fix the boundaries and "other points on which . . . it is always convenient and necessary to have established regulations," to which the King pledged his royal word

[146] These documents are discussed below in notes 202, 203, 204, 206, 207, 208, 209, 210, and 211. Bemis, *Pinckney's Treaty*, p. 148, states that nothing was done toward resuming the negotiations from their suspense in 1788 until the arrival of TJ as Secretary of State.

[147] Quoted in Richard B. Morris, *The Peacemakers*, p. 232-3. For the struggle in Congress over the instructions given Jay, drawn by Madison, see Brant, *Madison*, II, 70-88.

[148] Report, in Monroe's hand, submitted 23 Dec. 1784 (DNA: RG 360, PCC No. 25, II, f. 369; JCC, XXVII, 705-6). A note in the committee book states that this report was recorded as "filed being rendered unnecessary by arrival of Gardoqui and appointment of Mr. Jay to negotiate with him" (JCC, XXVIII, 706n.).

to ratify and execute "whatsoever shall be . . . stipulated and signed."[149] Congress, approving a report by Elbridge Gerry, William Samuel Johnson, and James Monroe, similarly gave Jay full powers to treat and sign whatever articles might be necessary for fixing the boundaries "and for promoting the general harmony and mutual interest of the two nations." The next day a commission, drawn by Charles Thomson, echoed the royal pledge by committing Congress to ratify "whatsoever shall be by him . . . stipulated and signed."[150] But Jay was instructed by Congress to report to it any proposals that he offered to or received from Gardoqui prior to the making of any commitment. Understandably, Jay thought the commission "well drawn" and the instructions a handicap. He therefore requested that the requirement to report every proposition be removed, otherwise Gardoqui would discover the fact and thus become more cautious in negotiating.[151] This was a valid argument, but it was also one that worked both ways. For if the absolute restriction set forth in Monroe's instructions of December 1784 were not made a part of Jay's instructions, Gardoqui would discover that also. Congress acceded to Jay's request but restated in explicit language the requirement that any articles arranged with Gardoqui should particularly stipulate the boundaries and the right of navigation as confirmed by the Treaty of Peace.[152] Since Gardoqui's own instructions forbade him to yield on the latter point, there could of course be no treaty as long as the stipulation remained in Jay's instructions and he respected it.

By October Richard Henry Lee thought that this obstacle had caused the negotiations to become stalled and that the troublesome issue of navigation had been "postponed to a distant day."[153] But behind the curtain Jay and Gardoqui had no difficulty in coming to a prompt understanding about the essential features of such a treaty of commerce and alliance as both desired, the most far-reaching provision of which would have committed the United States to a guarantee of the possessions of Spain in North and South America. Another article provided full reciprocity, by which merchants in either country would have their ships and merchandise treated as those of nationals in the other, thus eliminating duties levied on fish, flour, lumber, and other northern produce in the already flourishing trade with Spain. This was the principal object of the treaty and to achieve it Jay sought to avoid the obstacle posed in his instructions. Without yielding the right of navigation, Jay conceived the idea of stipulating a "forbearance" in the use of the river for the duration of the treaty. Such an accommodation

[149] The commission is dated 27 Sep. 1784. Gardoqui was received as *encargado de negocios* plenipotentiary on 28 June 1785 (JCC, XXVIII, 484; XXIX, 562-4).

[150] Report of Gerry, Johnson, and Monroe, 20 July 1785 (JCC, XXIX, 562). Thomson was directed to draft a commission similar in substance to that of Gardoqui; the commission was dated 21 July 1785 (JCC, XXIX, 567-8).

[151] Jay to the President of Congress, 15 Aug. 1785 (DNA: RG 360, PCC No. 80, I, f. 337; JCC, XXIX, 627-9). Jay's letter was referred to a committee consisting of Monroe, Pettit, Gerry, McHenry, and King.

[152] The report, in Monroe's hand, was submitted on 17 Aug. 1785 and agreed to on the 25th (DNA: RG 360, PCC No. 25, II, f. 441; JCC, XXIX, 657-8).

[153] Lee to Washington, 11 Oct. 1785 (Burnett, *Letters of Members*, VIII, 233).

through postponement of the issue naturally made Gardoqui's task easier and he readily agreed to this proposal as an equivalent for the grant of full commercial reciprocity. Late in November he reported to Florida Blanca that he and Jay were at work on the draft articles and that, when they saw a favorable moment, Jay would present the result to Congress to determine whether or not Jay's proposal to forbear use of the Mississippi would be acceptable. Unless it were, Gardoqui added, "I have declared I can proceed no farther."[154]

This revealing assertion affords the key to an understanding of the true character of the ensuing four years of "negotiations" between Jay and Gardoqui. For the fact is that, from the moment the two diplomats arrived at their private understanding in the autumn of 1785 until Jay made his final effort in the summer of 1789, the American plenipotentiary was not so much engaged in diplomatic bargaining with the Spanish *encargado* as he was negotiating with Congress, seeking to gain acceptance of the compromise proposal without which Gardoqui had said he could not proceed. Jay's role thenceforth was less diplomatic than political, less that of an envoy for the nation than that of an advocate for the interests of a particular section which he identified with the national good. In filling that role Jay engaged in political connivance, in partisan intrigue, and in concealment from Congress of the full extent of his agreement with Gardoqui. His first exercise in the use of such tactics was unfortunate and all were unsuccessful.

[154] Bemis, *Pinckney's Treaty*, p. 77-9, presented the first account of the substance of the articles agreed upon early in the negotiations. After these had been drafted and initialled by the two diplomats, Gardoqui submitted them to his government for approval early in 1786.

While the Spanish *encargado* was not a penetrating judge of men or of the character of the American people, he and Jay, who had known each other in Spain, were always harmonious in their social as well as their diplomatic relations. Before coming to the United States and on the basis of their fairly limited acquaintance, Gardoqui described Jay as vain, self-centered, acquisitive, dominated by his wife, and so influential politically that he could control the votes of six or seven northern states. He therefore urged that "a few timely gifts" to the Jays, as well as good dinners with fine wines for members of Congress, would be useful in the negotiations—suggestions which seem more calculated to elevate Gardoqui's own style of living than to advance the negotiations. At the very outset Gardoqui caused a fine stallion to be presented to Jay by the King, a gift Jay was permitted by Congress to accept. Gardoqui also urged that a Spanish jackass be given to Washington—which had already been done by the King. He claimed he had made loans amounting to about $5,000 to Henry Lee, a member of Congress (Bemis, *Pinckney's Treaty*, p. 62, 75-6, 94, 95, 99). Bemis characterizes Lee's acceptance of the loans as "unpardonable." But since the only evidence of their existence lies in Gardoqui's account of his expenses—a document that seems to have been prominent in his calculations before, during, and after the four years of "negotiations"—the allegation must be viewed with some skepticism. In any event, Gardoqui's lavishness in entertainment and in the bestowal of gifts was noteworthy in being directed principally toward those already persuaded—at Jay, with whom he had had no difficulty at all in coming to terms; at Rufus King and other northern delegates who were as eager as Jay for a commercial treaty; at the Lees who in general supported their objectives; and at Washington who at that time desired the Mississippi issue to be postponed. Such actions may have indicated zeal, but not astuteness. Actually, Gardoqui's diplomacy amounted only to a quick and uncomplicated arrangement of terms with Jay, followed by several years of waiting in elegance while Jay and his supporters sought to secure politically what the two diplomats had so easily agreed upon at the start.

Late in 1785, perhaps because he was aware that the Lees of Virginia did not share the views of most southern delegates on the Mississippi question, Jay decided to sound out the author of the restrictive instructions, James Monroe. Somewhat freely, he disclosed that his primary object was a commercial treaty with Spain, that Gardoqui would negotiate one on condition that the United States forbear the use of the river for twenty-five or thirty years, and that Jay "was desirous of occluding the Mississippi" to achieve this object. Monroe was reserved. Jay then went on to suggest that, if the matter were "brought to the view of Congress they wo'd most probably disagree to it, or if they sho'd approve the project, conduct themselves so indiscreetly as to suffer it to become known to the French and Engl'h residents . . . and thus defeat it." To avoid these embarrassments, he then hinted at the expediency of asking Congress to appoint a committee "to controul him in the negotiation." Monroe reminded him of the instructions with which Virginia had bound her delegates and warned him of "the impossibility of their concurring in any measures of the kind."[155] This ended their personal communications on the subject. But in the following months, while Jay awaited whatever turn of events might be favorable for presenting his compromise proposal, Monroe became fully convinced that the Secretary for Foreign Affairs was intriguing with members to carry his point. When William Grayson joined the Virginia delegation the following March, Monroe briefed him about Jay's disclosures. But this information and the apparent lull in the negotiations persuaded Grayson that, as he informed Washington in confidence, there did not appear to be "the most distant prospect of forming a treaty . . . with Spain."[156]

It is not surprising that he should have felt so. Rufus King was not the only member of Congress who was gloomily predicting the inevitable dissolution of the government unless the states soon exerted themselves to support it.[157] Attendance had fluctuated so that, late in May, only six to nine states were in attendance, thus requiring unanimity to enact any legislation and making it impossible to act on important matters such as the ratification of a treaty. Yet this was the moment Jay chose to bring forward one of the most disruptive issues that could be laid before Congress. He did this by asking Congress to appoint a committee "to instruct and direct [him] on every point and subject relative to the proposed treaty." He made this request because the negotiations had encountered "certain difficulties which . . . should be so managed as that even the existence of them should remain a secret for the present." He desired even the appointment of such a committee to be kept secret.[158] Of course the real difficulty lay with his own instruc-

---

[155] Monroe to Patrick Henry, 12 Aug. 1786 (Burnett, *Letters of Members*, VIII, 422-4).

[156] Grayson to Washington, 27 May 1786 (Burnett, *Letters of Members*, VIII, 372).

[157] King to Elbridge Gerry, 30 Apr. 1786; King to John Adams, 5 May 1786; Charles Pettit to Jeremiah Wadsworth, 27 May 1786; Grayson to Madison, 28 May 1786 (same, VIII, 345-7, 354-6; 369-71; 372). See notes 171 and 172.

[158] Jay to the President of Congress, 29 May 1786 (DNA: RG 360, PCC No. 80, II, f. 185; read in Congress on 31 May 1786, JCC, XXX, 323).

tions, not with Gardoqui. Most members of Congress and some outside
knew it was this that had prolonged the discussions for almost a year.
Later, when called upon by Congress to explain, Jay produced a letter
from Gardoqui, dated four days before his request for the appointment of the committee, which asserted that the American claim to
navigate the Mississippi was ill-founded and that the King would never
permit such navigation between "the two banks belonging" to Spain.
But this letter, coinciding with Jay's own arguments about improving
Spanish-American commercial relations, was clearly contrived for the
eyes of Congress. Jay had known since his first conference with
Gardoqui in the summer of 1785 that the King would not yield on this
point. That the letter was concerted between the two diplomats is also
indicated in Gardoqui's opening statement: "The period is arrived that
we have wished for many months when there would be a full meeting
of Congress, that you might refer to them the difficulty which you have
manifested to me respecting the claim to navigate the river Mississippi.
. . . I request the favour of you to do it as soon as possible."[159] This
assigned the correct cause but asserted a fact which also proved the
letter of the *encargado* to have been arranged. For on the date borne
by that letter only six states were in attendance. At that time, too, Jay
had merely requested the appointment of the committee without disclosing the nature of the difficulties. But, after being requested to appear
before Congress early in August when twelve states were represented,
Jay handed in the letter from Gardoqui describing a non-existent situation in May as the reason for *his* request for immediate attention to
the matter. This was an inept and unimportant contrivance, for Jay
had long since revealed his real object to Monroe. It was he who was
waiting for the opportune moment, and he was forced to accept August
as such when Monroe defeated his move in May.[160]

[159] Gardoqui to Jay, 25 May 1786 (translation by Jay in DNA: RG 360,
PCC No. 97, f. 166). Gardoqui's original letter, according to Bemis, *Pinckney's
Treaty*, p. 82, was written on 23 May 1786 because the opportune moment had
come "when Congress had finally . . . assembled in full." (The page of Gardoqui's
letter bearing the date is no longer with the remainder of this RC in Spanish
[same], but the Editors have accepted Bemis' reading.) On the 23rd only six
states were present. On the 25th and 26th there were nine. On the latter date the
Connecticut delegates departed immediately after approval of that state's cession
with its western reservation. "It is a practice with many States," Grayson wrote
Washington on 28 May 1786, ". . . to come forward and be very assiduous till
they have carried some State jobb and then decamp with precipitation leaving the
public business to shift for itself" (Burnett, *Letters of Members*, VIII, 372). On the
29th when Jay wrote his letter requesting the appointment of a committee, there
were again only six states present.

[160] Jay presented Gardoqui's letter of 23 May 1786 to Congress on 3 Aug.
1786. At the same time, he transmitted an "unofficial and unsigned" paper from
Gardoqui which argued not only that Spain was a very important consumer of
American produce but also that she and the United States were "the almost only
Masters of this vast Continent, who if well join'd may defy the other powers or at
least keep them in eternal peace." This argument for a treaty of commerce and
alliance was probably presented to Jay early in the negotiations (DNA: RG 360,
PCC No. 97, f. 170; in the hand of James Gardoqui and in somewhat awkward
English). Since Jay concealed from Congress the article he and Gardoqui had
agreed upon calling for a defensive alliance guaranteeing the American possessions

Having been forewarned, Monroe immediately saw that the plan was merely to obtain a committee to cover the proposed forbearance of the use of the Mississippi. He knew that Rufus King was associated in the move and he accurately described the terms of the proposed treaty long before Jay disclosed them to Congress. In support of Jay's request, King made a long speech which Monroe interpreted as "a tryal of the pulse of the house."[161] The result was that Jay's letter was referred to King, Pettit, and Monroe, a committee well-balanced sectionally but with the supporters of Jay dominating.[162] Monroe, believing that no advantages equivalent to the commitment involved in the guarantee of Spanish possessions in America had been or could be made and agreeing with Jefferson that any engagements closing the Mississippi would "separate . . . all those westward of the mountains from the federal Government and perhaps throw them into the hands eventually of a foreign power," proved to be an intransigent minority of the committee.[163] When it met on the 1st of June, Jay was present. But King, Pettit, and Jay could make no headway against Monroe's stubborn insistence upon the express stipulation of the right of navigation that, for over a year and a half, he had made the *sine qua non* of any treaty with Spain. The committee adjourned, unable to agree on a report. Rufus King then expressed deep regret that only Massachusetts of all the New England states was represented, being convinced that the subject more vitally affected eastern interests than any question since the peace. At first, he hesitated to put his views in writing.[164] But after the fruitless meeting of the committee he unburdened himself to Elbridge Gerry. Writing urgently and in confidence, King revealed Jay's article forbearing use of the river for a period of years and concluded that if an uninterrupted navigation should take place at that time, as he conceded was the desire of the public generally, every emigrant to the western country could be regarded "as forever lost to the Confederacy." His arguments for a commercial treaty "formed . . . upon principles of exact reciprocity" anticipated those later employed by Jay before Congress. He saw this as beneficial for the western inhabitants and declared that, if they were not attached by interest to the union, he could discover no principle

---

of the two countries, this document may have been presented to Congress to test its views on such a far-reaching commitment.

[161] Monroe to Madison, 31 May 1786 (DLC: Madison Papers). Monroe was so well aware of the intentions of Jay and his maneuvers that he knew at this time about the "reciprocal guaranty of their respective possessions in America." This may explain why, after Jay appeared before Congress and failed to mention this commitment, Monroe thought he had "come forward fully" in disclosing the terms (Monroe to Patrick Henry, 12 Aug. 1786, Burnett, *Letters of Members*, VIII, 423).

[162] Charles Pettit (1736-1806) was a Philadelphia merchant and speculator in government securities. Monroe thought him "entirely eastern" in his views. Of King, married to a wealthy New York lady, Monroe wrote: "if he secures a market for fish and turns the commerce of the Western country down this river [the Hudson], he obtains his object" (Monroe to Madison, 31 May 1786, Burnett, *Letters of Members*, VIII, 377; JCC, XXXI, 323).

[163] Monroe to TJ, 16 June 1786; Monroe to Madison, 31 May 1786 (Burnett, *Letters of Members*, VIII, 377).

[164] King to Gerry, 1 June 1786 (same, VIII, 379).

that would bind them.[165] A few weeks later he had reached the conclusion that nature had "severed the two countries by a vast and extensive chain of mountains," that interest and convenience would keep them separate, and that the feeble policy of a disjointed government would not be able to unite them.[166]

Monroe, already forewarned, declared that Jay had told the committee nothing not already known. Within two weeks he had come to the conclusion that the scheme to obviate the restrictive instructions had failed.[167] But once again Jay's political moves were only held in abeyance, undoubtedly because of meager attendance in Congress. Six weeks after the committee held its inconclusive meeting, however, delegates from New Hampshire, Connecticut, and Rhode Island had appeared, so that for the first time since Jay presented his request twelve states were present, with those of the North in the majority. Rufus King, convinced that Monroe would not yield, then decided to put the question to a decisive test—a decision which would scarcely have been made without prior consultation with Jay and the northern delegates. Late in July King informed Monroe that he and Pettit had concluded the committee could do nothing better than to ask to be discharged and to recommend that the matter be referred to a committee of the whole, with Jay being directed to attend and explain his request.[168] Monroe concurred and on the 3rd of August Jay appeared before Congress, presented the letter that Gardoqui supposedly wrote to him on the 23rd of May, and supported its principal arguments with a speech he had reduced to writing for the sake of accuracy and precision. While urging full reciprocity in trade, by which codfish, flour, masts, and timber would be exchanged for Spanish gold and silver, Jay did not even suggest that the prohibition against the vending of tobacco in Spain be made a matter for negotiation. This prohibition, he thought, would probably continue whether or not a treaty were concluded. Most important of all, despite his declared purpose to present his "sentiments on the subject . . . with precision, and authentick evidence of them," he concealed the most fateful of all of the articles that he and Gardoqui had initialled—that which would have converted the treaty into one of alliance mutually guaranteeing possessions along a boundary of more than two thousand miles. In effect, he gave Congress the alternative of accepting a treaty that stipulated closure of the Mississippi or of facing war with Spain.[169]

Monroe anticipated that seven northern states would sustain Jay and that, repealing the mandate in his instructions, they would thus "risque the preservation of the confederacy on it."[170] This, he reported to Governor Henry, "is one of the most extraordinary transactions I have ever known, a minister negotiating expressly for the purpose of defeat-

[165] King to Gerry, 4 June 1785 (same, VIII, 380-2).
[166] King to Jonathan Jackson, 3 Sep. 1786 (same, VIII, 458-60).
[167] Monroe to TJ, 16 June 1786.
[168] King to Monroe, 30 July 1786 (Burnett, *Letters of Members*, VIII, 407).
[169] JCC, XXXI, 457; 467-84; Bemis, *Pinckney's Treaty*, p. 86-90; Monaghan, *John Jay*, p. 257-61.
[170] Monroe to Madison, [11] and 14 Aug. 1786 (Burnett, *Letters of Members*, VIII, 419, 426-7).

ing the object of his instructions, and by a long train of intrigue and management seducing the representatives of the states to concur in it." He was certain that northern delegates were planning a separate confederacy of those states eastward of the Hudson and, if possible, of those north of the Potomac. Hence he concluded that the Massachusetts delegation under King's leadership had brought Jay's proposal to issue as a means of preparing the public mind for such a dismemberment. He feared that Jay had fixed his supporters so firmly that there was no "possibility of their forsaking him."[171]

In this as in other essential points Monroe's estimate of these political maneuvers proved to be well founded. In the bitter debates in committee of the whole following King's motion to repeal the restrictive instructions, not a single delegate north of Maryland failed to sustain the proposition which, in Grayson's phrase, "Decides the Existence of the Confederation."[172] Southern attempts at compromise failed by the same unyielding majority. Monroe was so disturbed that he appealed to Washington in unusually frank terms, seeking his counsel on the desirability of having the negotiations transferred to Madrid and placed in Jefferson's hands. He asserted, and offered to make proofs available at any time, that for months Jay had been "negotiating with Congress to repeal his instructions (or rather with particular members) so as to occlude the Mississippi, and not with Spain to open it."[173] Washington did not respond.[174] Monroe was certain that Jay would not proceed with the negotiations but he felt that the eastern delegates had gone

[171] Monroe to Patrick Henry, 12 Aug. 1786 (same, VIII, 424). Theodore Sedgwick declared that it was time for "the eastern and middle states, who are in interest one, seriously to consider what advantages result to them from their connection with the Southern States. They can give us nothing, as an equivalent for the protection which they derive from us but a participation in their commerce. This they deny to us. Should their conduct continue the same, and I think there is not any prospect of an alteration, an attempt to perpetuate our connection with them . . . will sacrafice everything to a meer chimera. . . . No other substitute can be devised than that of contracting the limits of the confederacy to such as are natural and reasonable, and within those limits instead of a nominal to institute a real, and an efficient government" (Elbridge Gerry to Caleb Strong, 6 Aug. 1786; same, VIII, 415-16).

[172] King's motion was on the 10th of Aug. The debates in the committee of the whole took place between the 16th and the 23rd and the final vote authorizing Jay to proceed without the restrictions took place on the 29th (JCC, XXXI, 509, 510, 524, 527, 535, 554, 575-93, 595). It was in the debates on the 18th that Grayson charged the proponents of repeal with endangering the existence of the union. Henry Lee regretted hearing delegates "talk so lightly of a separation and dissolution of the Confederacy" (notes of debates by Johnson and Thomson; Burnett, Letters of Members, VIII, 437, 438).

[173] Monroe to Washington, 20 Aug. 1786 (DLC: Washington Papers).

[174] This was doubtless because Washington did not view the closure of the Mississippi as a pressing issue. Like TJ, he thought no power could deprive westerners of the use of the Mississippi when they became populous enough. But, at this time, more apprehensive of the "restless and impetuous spirit of Kentucke" than of anything the Spaniards could do, he thought it best "to let it sleep" (Washington to Henry Lee, 18 June and 26 July 1786; Writings, ed. Fitzpatrick, XXVIII, 460-1, 480-5; see Lee to Washington, 3 July and 7 Aug. 1786; Burnett, Letters of Members, VIII, 400, 417). A copy of Washington's letter of 18 June 1786 was made available to Gardoqui, who quoted it to his government both in 1786 and in 1791 (Bemis, Pinckney's Treaty, p. 92, 159).

too far to retreat and would wreck the union if not supported by Pennsylvania and New Jersey. He therefore thought the Pennsylvania leaders should be urged to keep their state from being thrown into the eastern scale in case the northern states should form a separate confederacy. The gravity of the situation at this juncture is revealed in his belligerent suggestion to Madison: "It were as well to use force to prevent it, as to defend ourselves afterward."[175]

But even though King and his supporters had forced the issue and had prevailed, the negotiations with Gardoqui were once again held in suspense. Early in 1787 Madison reported to Jefferson that the "Spanish project" was sleeping. A month later he made a direct attack on the constitutionality of the repeal and moved that the negotiations be transferred to Madrid.[176] King successfully blocked the former and Jay the latter. Thus by May when Madison departed for the Federal Convention, he considered "the project of shutting the Mississippi . . . at an end"—a point deemed of great importance lest the jealousies aroused by it should jeopardize the movement for strengthening the powers of the federal government.[177] Within a week after his departure, Jay asked Congress for express instructions on the points of difference between the United States and Spain. The response, drawn by Benjamin Hawkins, declared that any departure from the instructions originally given in 1785 "would be obviously disagreeable to a large majority of the Citizens of the United States"; that, while desirous of conciliating Spain, the Congress should so conduct itself as to merit the confidence of their constituents and also to convince Spain "by a fixed and stable plan of policy of their determination to preserve inviolate the rights of their citizens, and in no case whatever to enter into engagements which should be violated"; and that Jay be directed to state to Gardoqui "in a decent but firm decided and candid manner . . . their indispensable obligation" to preserve the boundaries and the right of navigation as established in the Treaty of Paris.[178] Only seven states were present, those from the South being in the majority, and thus the fixed and stable policy could not be acted upon. But so great had been the change since the confrontation of 1786 that even King in the spring of 1787 could move that the proceedings of Congress did not authorize Jay to enter into any stipulations with Gardoqui.[179] During the next twelve months the transcendent public debate on the form of the American government—at bottom a question of whether an enduring union could be formed—absorbed and to some degree was influenced by the Missis-

[175] Monroe to Madison, 3 and 29 Sep., 7 Oct. 1786 (same, VIII, 460-1, 473, 476).

[176] Madison to TJ, 19 Mch. and 23 Apr. 1787; Madison to Edmund Randolph, 15 Apr. 1787; Madison to Washington, 16 Apr. 1787 (Burnett, *Letters of Members*, VIII, 578, 579).

[177] Notes of debates, Apr. 1787 (DLC: Madison Papers; JCC, XXXIII, 739).

[178] Jay to the President of Congress, 9 May 1787; the committee reported on 4 July 1787 (JCC, XXXII, 277, 299-300).

[179] King's motion was made on 19 May 1787 as an amendment to one offered by Few declaring that the proceedings of 29 Aug. 1786 did not authorize Jay to stipulate that the right of navigation should be "relinquished or impaired" (JCC, XXXII, 289-90).

sippi question and other divisive issues. The principal author of *The Federalist* ranked the navigation of the Mississippi along with the fisheries as among those "rights of great moment to the trade of America" whose future existence might be impaired by a dissolution of the Confederation.[180]

But as soon as that great issue had been decided, western suspicions aroused by the Jay-Gardoqui negotiations once again made their appearance. John Brown, greatly disturbed over the refusal of Congress to admit Kentucky into the union, thought that Jay's proposed treaty had destroyed the confidence of westerners in the justice of the federal government and now feared that they would declare their independence.[181] Madison informed Jefferson that the eastern states had been "rendered extremely . . . obnoxious by the Mississippi project" and that Spain was taking advantage of this disgust to detach the westerners from the union.[182] It was at this critical moment in the summer of 1788 that southerners moved to reaffirm the policy set forth in Congress' instructions to Jay in 1785. Hugh Williamson of North Carolina offered a resolution declaring that the United States had "a clear absolute and unalienable Claim" to the free navigation of the Mississippi founded both on treaties and on "the great Law of Nature." The resolution specifically declared that its purpose was to quiet the minds of westerners who had manifested their uneasiness at the report that Congress was disposed to surrender the claim.[183] The gesture could scarcely have been unconnected with the refusal to admit Kentucky as a state, for Williamson was by no means sympathetic to westerners' opposition to the Constitution arising in part from their fear that the augmented powers of the government would be used to put Jay's proposed treaty into effect.[184]

The resolution was referred to Jay, who did not report for six weeks. During this interval, marked also by crucial debates over the place of meeting of the new government, Jay and his supporters obviously sought to allay sectional fears and suspicions. In his report on the resolution he categorically denied the allegation that Congress was disposed to surrender the right of navigation and urged that the injunction of secrecy be rescinded so that it could be contradicted in the most explicit terms. He recommended that, since the new government would "speedily . . . be established, it would be prudent to suspend all further progress [in the negotiation], and refer the same *with all the papers and documents respecting it* to the new Government." Jay saw no objection to declaring the right of navigation clear and absolute. But, going further in his effort to conciliate, he confessed that "circumstances and discontents" had made his former suggestion to forbear the use of that right "more questionable than it then appeared to be." Nevertheless, he candidly declared that any resolution calculated to

180 Hamilton, *The Federalist*, No. 11 (Syrett, *Hamilton*, IV, 343).
181 Brown to TJ, 10 Aug. 1788.
182 Madison to TJ, 23 Aug. 1788.
183 The motion was made on 14 July 1788 and referred on the 15th to Jay, who reported on 2 Sep. 1788 (JCC, XXXIV, 319, 328n., 493).
184 See Williamson to Madison, 2 June 1788 (Burnett, *Letters of Members*, VIII, 746).

exclude such modifications as would not impair the right would not in his opinion be wise. He thought the new government would "undoubtedly be tenacious of the public rights, and [might] be enabled by *circumstances not yet developed*, to terminate these negociations with Spain in a manner perfectly consistent with the right in question, and with the Interests and wishes of their constituents."[185] The conciliatory tone of the report, the readiness to concede the questionable nature of his earlier proposal, and the confidence expressed in the new government's justice and firmness were enough to gain the approval of both Williamson and Madison.[186] Jay's posture in 1788 seemed on the whole to exhibit a spirit of accommodation that had been wholly lacking in 1786. But the carefully chosen words of his report closed off no alternatives the new government might choose to adopt, including of course his earlier suggestion of an appropriate policy respecting the Mississippi.

The recommendations of the Secretary for Foreign Affairs were referred to Alexander Hamilton, James Madison, Hugh Williamson, Nathan Dane, and Pierpont Edwards. Hamilton presumably deferred initially to Madison, who drafted the committee report. This was submitted as drawn, but all three of its resolutions as ultimately adopted by Congress were altered. These amendments have been regarded as minor changes in Madison's phraseology.[187] But in fact they reveal the persistence of the old sectional cleavages and place the new spirit of accommodation in its true light. After being reported for the committee, the three resolutions offered by Madison and based on Jay's recommendations were redrafted by Hamilton. On the first point, Madison accepted Jay's position but urged it in more inclusive terms: "That the Report mentioned in the said motion, being not founded in fact, the Delegates in Congress be authorized to contradict the same and to communicate all such circumstances as may be necessary to correct misconceptions on this subject." Hamilton's version, instead of authorizing the delegates gave them liberty to make such a communication and contradiction and to "remove misconceptions." This was indeed a minor alteration, but on the second and central point, Madison's draft was an implicit and unequivocal reaffirmation of the policy stated in 1785: "That the United States have a clear and absolute right to the free navigation of the river Mississippi; and that the same ought in no manner whatsoever to be invalidated." This emphatic language would seem to have closed the door upon such a modification of the right as Jay had proposed. Hamilton's substitute removed the implied restriction: "That the free navigation of the River Mississippi is a clear and essential right of the United States, and that the same ought to be considered and supported as such."

On the third point Madison's draft was general and inclusive: "That no negociation for Treaties with foreign powers be prosecuted by virtue of any authority heretofore granted by Congress for that pur-

[185] Jay's report, 2 Sep. 1788 (JCC, XXXIV, 493, 530-4; first emphasis supplied, second in original).
[186] Williamson to Samuel Johnston, 17 Sep. 1788 (Burnett, *Letters of Members*, VIII, 797-9); Madison to TJ, 21 Sep. 1788.
[187] JCC, XXXIV, 493n.

pose, and that the requisite provision for such cases be referred to the federal Govt. about to be organized." Jay's recommendation, however, had been more specific: "That no further progress be made in the . . . negociations [with Gardoqui] by the Secretary for foreign Affairs; but that the same *in the state they now are*, be referred to the federal Government about to be established and organized."[188] Hamilton, discarding Madison's text for one closer to Jay's, proposed that "the subject . . . be referred to the Fœderal Government, which is to assemble in March next." Jay's version seemed to call for a resumption of discussions on the basis of his adjustment of the crucial article with Gardoqui, Hamilton's to point to resumption at the first session of Congress. Only Madison's preamble survived the final adoption of the resolutions, and the direction in which Hamilton's substitutions pointed was unmistakable.[189]

The first two resolutions were made available to the delegates of any state who applied for copies, but the third was a secret instruction to Jay.[190] The manner in which he communicated the decision to Gardoqui, like the alterations of the resolutions by Hamilton, casts new light on his confession that events and circumstances had made his earlier proposal inadvisable:[191]

> The dissolution of one Government and the establishment of another, form a period little adapted to negociations, especially in a popular Government. The inconveniences which thence arise are obvious, and need not be enumerated . . . I am persuaded you will so represent and explain it to his Catholic Majesty, as that it may be ascribed to the peculiar situation of our national Government and not to any desire or disposition to postpone a business which it is the interest of both parties to have speedily and satisfactorily settled.

Gardoqui had good reason to interpret this language as meaning that the negotiations would be resumed soon after the new government came into being. As before, the Spanish project was only sleeping. The new spirit of accommodation had persuaded Williamson that Jay, Hamilton, and others were now convinced that the policy proposed in 1786 was neither "*prudent* nor *practicable*." He believed that the vote of all of the northern states for his resolution meant that their delegations now understood the question much better than they had.[192]

[188] JCC, XXXIV, 532; emphasis supplied.
[189] The committee was appointed on 8 Sep. 1788 and Madison's report was submitted on the 15th (JCC, XXXIV, 502n., 527; Madison's draft is in DNA: RG 360, PCC No. 25, II, f. 503; the first and third resolutions were crossed out and the substitutions in Hamilton's hand were attached on separate slips; the second resolution was deleted and Hamilton's version interlined).
The resolutions as adopted on the 16th were Hamilton's substitutions, which of course were made in Congress after his committee had reported Madison's version (JCC, XXXIV, 527, 534).
[190] In the *Secret Journal, Foreign*, Thomson made the following entry: "N.B. The two first may be given to the delegates of any state applying for the same, but the latter is considered as a private instruction" (DNA: RG 360, PCC No. 6, III, f. 432; JCC, XXXIV, 534n.).
[191] Jay to Gardoqui, 17 Oct. 1788 (DNA: RG 59, PCC No. 120).
[192] Williamson to Samuel Johnston, 17 Sep. 1788 (Burnett, *Letters of Members*, VIII, 797-8).

Madison was equally persuaded that the negotiations had been effectively stopped and that Congress at last had been "brought into the true policy which is demanded by the situation of the Western Country."[193]

Westerners were not so easily convinced. Their fear that under the new government "the Navigation of the Mississippi would infallibly be given up" may have been unduly manipulated by Anti-federalists and the effect of the negotiations on the constitutional requirement that treaties receive a two-thirds vote of the Senate for ratification may have comforted few save easterners.[194] But all of the evidence suggests that, from the time Jay began the discussions with Gardoqui in 1785 to the establishment of the new government four years later, the various suspensions of negotiations and the adroit shift of northern delegates from intransigency in 1786 to conciliation in 1788 could not eradicate westerners' belief that the original project had never been abandoned. This conviction was soon proved to be well founded, for Jay and his supporters immediately perceived that the new structure of government seemed more likely to bring the long-sought goal within reach. The Senate was now the only part of the legislature whose consent was required to make treaties the law of the land. Its proceedings were secret. Its votes were cast by individuals, not by states. Moreover, the two most formidable opponents Jay had had to contend with were now safely out of the way—Madison in the House of Representatives and Monroe not yet in the Senate. Even southern Senators —Grayson, Izard, and Butler, for example—could at times be depended upon to cooperate with the close-knit group of members from the middle states and New England. Richard Henry Lee, now a Senator from Virginia, had indeed been allied with northern delegates in the earlier contests.[195] Jay's supporters in the Senate had also been greatly strengthened by the addition of such men as Robert Morris and Charles Carroll, both active in commerce and both having special interest in Spain. The leading proponent of the Spanish treaty, Rufus King, was now a Senator from New York and another, William Samuel Johnson, was a Senator from Connecticut. Northern commercial and financial interests could now tip the scales decisively in the Senate.

But, most important of all, the determination of foreign policy now rested with the President, with whom Jay was then on such terms of confidence that he had been offered his choice of posts in the new government. Jay was also acting as Secretary for Foreign Affairs. He knew that Jefferson was returning from France and he may have known that Washington desired to make him Secretary of State. He certainly knew that, from the very beginning of the negotiations with Spain, Washington's attitude on the Mississippi question had been closer to that of Rufus King than to that of Madison, Monroe, and

[193] Madison to TJ, 21 Sep. 1788. Madison, highly gratified that the negotiations had been brought to an end, offered no comment about the changes Hamilton had made in his draft of the committee report (see note 189).

[194] Williamson to Madison, 2 June 1788 (same, VIII, 746-7).

[195] Monroe to Madison, 29 Sep. 1786 (same, VIII, 473).

other leaders in the South and West. At the outset Washington had predicted that Gardoqui would cause "a good deal of trouble respecting the Navigation of the Mississippi" because of Spanish pride, jealousy, and limited views of their own interest in matters of trade.[196] He also thought that, while the right should not be surrendered, neither should it be insisted upon at that particular juncture. Instead, he believed that the "true line of policy" for the United States would be to improve the navigation of the Potomac, to establish trade connections with the western settlements, and to depend upon such economic bonds to bind them to the union.[197] Washington therefore had viewed with equanimity the possibility that the Spanish closure of the river would remain in effect for some time. He was well aware that for a southerner this was a "singular" position to take, but he made his attitude very clear in 1785 in a manner that could not have been unknown to Jay, King, and other advocates of the Spanish treaty.[198] Even during the bitter debates and political maneuvers of 1786 his position remained unchanged. Indeed, he could then envisage no considerations that would cause him to change it, a fact which provides explanation enough for his ignoring of Monroe's urgent appeal for support against the northern majority.[199] Western opposition to the Constitution, based in part on fear that the new government would surrender the right of navigation, must have persuaded Jay and others that nothing had occurred to cause Washington to alter the view he had so consistently held.

Thus all of the auguries must have seemed to indicate to the proponents of the Spanish treaty that this was a propitious time to resume the negotiations. Acting on his suggestion to Gardoqui that this should be done speedily, Jay did in fact initiate the move within little more than two months after Washington's inauguration. He did not even wait until the executive departments had been created, but acted immediately after the debates over the first revenue bill were concluded. It is scarcely conceivable that he did so without prior consultation with—perhaps even prompting by—King, Hamilton, and others with whom he had concerted his plans during the preceding four years. In any event, Jay called on Washington early in July 1789 and left with him a paper on the subject of the Spanish negotiations. This paper has not been identified and may not have survived. Its object, however, is clear. As *pro tem* Secretary for Foreign Affairs and of course acting under the resolution of Congress of the preceding September, Jay sought the President's authorization to reopen the "negotiations" with Gardoqui. Also, as Washington's response makes clear, he wished to do this without prior official consultation with

[196] Washington to the President of Congress, 15 Mch. 1785; Washington to Marbois, 21 June 1785; Washington to Rochambeau, 7 Sep. 1785 (*Writings*, ed. Fitzpatrick, XXVIII, 109, 169-70, 256).

[197] Washington to David Humphreys, 25 July 1785 (same, XXVIII, 204-5).

[198] Washington's position was made explicit in his letter to the President of Congress, 22 Aug. 1785 (same, XXVIII, 231).

[199] Washington to Henry Lee, 18 June and 26 July 1786 (same, XXVIII, 460, 484). The former letter was made available to Gardoqui and the opinions expressed in it must also have been known to Jay (see note 174).

the Senate. This was both understandable and prudent: unless diplomatic secrecy were to be preserved, opposition might be needlessly aroused and obstacles to success might be interposed just as had been done in 1786.

But in this difficult formative period, Washington was acutely aware that almost every executive act could establish a precedent for good or ill. He had already, by written message, sent the French Consular Convention to the Senate for its consideration and advice.[200] But his extraordinary personal appearance before the Senate to consult with it on the policy to be adopted with respect to southern Indian tribes—to have it function, as some thought it should, as an executive council—was yet in the future.[201] Also, at this time, Washington was taking unusual pains to familiarize himself with all aspects of American foreign relations, having just examined and abstracted Jefferson's dispatches from France for the preceding year. He knew what deep divisions had been created in the country by the Jay-Gardoqui negotiations, but this was all the more reason for him to desire to see the documents bearing on the subject that Jay had not supplied. He therefore wrote to Jay, formally though privately, that he felt "incompetent to form any decided opinion upon the paper . . . received from you the other day without having a view of the transactions which have been had with the Spanish Minister." But that was not all:[202]

> I wish to know whether, if the negotiations are renewed, it can be made to appear from anything that that Gentleman has said, as the result of an advance towards it from him, in his official character?—Unless this is the case, and prima facie the reverse, will it not convey to him and his Court an idea that a change of sentiment has taken place in the governing powers of the Country? —will it be expedient and proper (at this moment) for the President to encourage such an idea?—at any rate without previously advising the Senate?

Washington not only perceived that Gardoqui had not made such an advance officially—he knew of course that Jay and the Spanish *encargado* were intimate socially—but he feared that the government was about to be committed to a step showing *prima facie* the reverse.

Only a few months earlier, Jay had recommended the referral of the negotiations to the new government, together "with all the papers and documents" bearing on the subject. Yet he had brought to Washington's attention only one paper—perhaps his matured plan of a treaty, perhaps his written proposals of 1786, perhaps only Con-

[200] Washington to the Senate, 11 June 1789 (JEP, I, 5); Washington had just gone over and abstracted TJ's dispatches of the previous year and had made a detailed summary of the terms of the Convention (Notes, June 1789, DLC: Washington Papers).
[201] This memorable encounter is best described in Maclay, *Journal*, ed. Maclay, p. 128-33; see JEP, I, 20-4.
[202] Washington to Jay, 14 July 1789 (Tr in DNA: RG 59, DL, signed "I am, Dear Sir, Your Affectionate George Washington"; Trs with variant complimentary close in DLC: Washington Papers, as in *Writings*, ed. Fitzpatrick, XXX, 355).

gress' resolution of referral—but certainly not such information as the President needed concerning an issue that had produced very genuine dangers of disunion. Washington's delicately phrased response carried an implication that could not be ignored and Jay promptly supplied the correspondence, reports, and resolutions of Congress bearing upon the subject. The extent of Washington's concern is reflected in the care with which he reviewed and then set down a résumé of the entire record.[203] Nor could Jay ignore Washington's query about prior consultation with the Senate. He therefore presented the draft of a message from the President to the Senate which explained that the "advantages expected from a commercial Treaty with Spain, and from a Satisfactory settlement of all Points in difference" had led to the negotiations; that some progress had been made to achieve this object; and that the matter had been "suspended and referred to the Management of the present government." The draft message then presented two questions for the Senate to consider and advise upon: "1st. Whether it is expedient now to renew those negotiations?" and, if so, "2dly. what Terms ought, on the part of the United States, to be insisted on." The draft concluded: "The delicate state of our affairs with his Catholic Majesty lead me to wish that this Subject may be considered and decided upon with as little Delay, as the Nature of it, and other circumstances may admit.—Mr. Jay has my Directions to lay the necessary Papers before you, and to give you whatever information he may possess, and you may find it necessary to require of him."[204]

"It is much to be wished that all these matters had lain dormant for years yet to come," John Jay had once declared to the old Congress, "but such wishes are vain; these disputes are agitating; they press themselves upon us, and must terminate in accommodation, or War, or disgrace."[205] Even in 1786, as the event proved, there had been no inescapable need to make the hard choice that Jay offered—Washington indeed had held firmly to the view that the true policy for the United States required it to postpone the issue. In 1789, with the new government not fully organized and with the western inhabitants apprehensive that its powers might be used to bargain with Spain at their expense, there was no such pressing need to bring the question forward as the draft message indicated. But the call for prompt action and the directions for a full disclosure of all necessary papers —the latter providing a striking contrast with Jay's attitude toward the former Congress—afford grounds for believing that this moment was deliberately chosen by Jay and his supporters because they were convinced the negotiations could be brought to a speedy conclusion on the terms outlined by him in 1786. Two facts strongly support the inference. The first is that Washington set the draft message aside, as he probably would not have done if its directions had originated

203 Washington's undated abstract of "Negotiation with Spain," 1785-1789, concluding with Jay's letter to Gardoqui of 17 Oct. 1788, occupies 13 pages and is filed at the end of 1789 in DLC: Washington Papers, vol. 245, 37-38.
204 Draft message in Jay's hand, undated but obviously drawn between 14 and 24 July 1789 (DLC: Washington Papers, ser. 4, vol. 243, f. 104; filed at end of July 1789).
205 Jay's address to Congress, 3 Aug. 1786 (JCC, XXXI, 483).

with him. The second is that, within a week, Gardoqui cooperated by supplying a timely message just as he had done in 1786. This time he sent an official notice to the President, through the Secretary for Foreign Affairs, that he had been given leave to return to Spain to attend to his domestic affairs, that he proposed to take advantage of "the present leisure of his station" to depart by the first available vessel, and that his secretary would be in charge of the legation during his absence.[206] Jay communicated the message to Washington on the same day. At the same time, presumably, he submitted a draft reply to the Spanish minister that apparently has not survived. Its tenor, however, gave Washington some concern.

Up to this point, so far as the record discloses, Jay's effort to obtain Washington's authorization for resuming the negotiations had not brought into view the great obstacle that had caused their suspension. But Washington then focused attention on the central difficulty. He did this by submitting three important queries for Jay to ponder. First, if a majority or even a strong minority of the Senate were of opinion that, on the whole, the terms proposed were such as should be accepted, despite the difficulty posed by the Mississippi problem, could he be justified in allowing the Spanish minister to depart without bringing the matter in some form to the attention of the Senate, "notwithstanding . . . the opinion of the President that the claim of the U. S. to this Navigation ought not to be weakened by any negotiation whatsoever"? Second, was there any danger that Gardoqui could misconstrue as a softening of this position Jay's allusion to the time "when the present derangements are done away, and we shall be in a condition to renew the Negotiations under the new Government"? Third, besides withholding or qualifying this expression, would it be "improper to . . . convey verbally (a memorandum of which to be taken) but delicately to Mr. Gardoqui that from the very nature of things, and our peculiar situation we can never loose sight of the use of that Navigation however it might be restrained, and that by a just and liberal policy both Countries might derive reciprocal advantages"? Having posed the queries, Washington then stated his own view: Gardoqui "had better . . . return with our ideas to this effect, delicately and tenderly expressed, than with any hope or expectation of our yielding the navigation of a River which is so tenaciously contended for by a large part of the Union, and the relinquishment of which, *or the fear of which, founded on appearances, would occasion, certainly, the seperation of the Western territory.*"[207] Clearly,

[206] Gardoqui to Jay, 24 July 1789, enclosing his letter of the same date to Washington (Tr in DLC: Washington Papers; *Dipl. Corr.*, VI, 268-9). This was the first official communication between Gardoqui and Jay since the latter announced on 17 Oct. 1788 the referral of the negotiations to the new government. The secretary of legation was José Ignacio de Viar.

[207] Emphasis supplied. Washington's "Quaeries" are undated but were clearly drafted between 24 and 27 July 1789 (MS in Washington's hand, DLC: Washington Papers, ser. 4, vol. 245, f. 38, filed at end of 1789). It has been conjectured that these queries were submitted to Madison or TJ (*Writings*, ed. Fitzpatrick, xxx, 486n.; see also Freeman, *Washington*, VI, 238). They were certainly submitted to Jay and may have been revealed to Madison, but could not have been presented to TJ, who arrived after Gardoqui had departed.

Washington's position had not changed since he first declared it in 1785, though he was now acutely aware that even the appearance of a relaxation on the central point would bring on a dismemberment of the union.

Jay knew very well how the majority of the Senate felt about the terms of the proposed treaty, despite the difficulty posed by the Mississippi problem. He therefore readily seized the opening afforded by Washington's first query and laid before the President the draft of another message. This one informed the Senate that Gardoqui was about to depart for Spain. It also was intended to convey documents pertaining to the negotiations, together with the resolution of Congress referring the matter to the new government. In view of this referral, the draft pointed out, Spain would naturally expect that the suspension of negotiations would continue only "until the present government shall be in a Situation to take the proper measures for resuming them." The draft then concluded:[208]

> If it should be deemed advisable for the United States to conclude a Treaty with Spain, on the Terms to which she seems willing to accede, it may probably be done before the Departure of Mr. Gardoqui.
>
> I wish that no Delays in public affairs, which may be judged inconvenient to the united States, and which may be in my Power to avoid, should take place. The Policy of concluding a Treaty on those Terms, involves Questions of great magnitude and Difficulty. I submit it to your Consideration and request your advice. In my opinion it is expedient, that nothing which may pass on this Subject in your Body, should at least for the present transpire; that in Case the Negociations should not proceed, the public Mind may not be unnecessarily agitated.

Obviously, "those Terms" that were acceptable to Spain and on which a treaty might be concluded before Gardoqui departed were substantially such as Jay had proposed in 1786, for the *encargado* was still bound to reject American claims to the right of navigation. The draft message, being prepared in response to Washington's first query, thus inescapably carried the implication that Rufus King and others in the Senate had given Jay reason to believe a treaty embracing these terms would be promptly ratified. But no one knew better than Jay the danger of having "the public Mind . . . unnecessarily agitated" on the subject. As if to underscore the point, he queried the final sentence of his draft and added this marginal note: "This latter Hint however proper is capable of being improperly used, tho' I do not think it probable." John Jay, the last Secretary for Foreign Affairs, obviously enjoyed a confidential relationship with the dominant party in the Senate that the first Secretary of State would never attain.

It is possible that the President turned to Madison for advice at this point. But since Washington was already sensitively aware of the

[208] Draft message in Jay's hand, undated but drawn between 24 and 27 July 1789 (DLC: Washington Papers, ser. 4, vol. 243, f. 102).

hostility with which westerners would view any resumption of negotiations on the terms originally proposed by Jay, it is more likely that he kept his own counsel. It is also possible that he used the occasion primarily to transmit to the Senate, through the queries he put to Jay, his firm conviction that the right of navigation "ought not to be weakened by any negotiation whatever." For the fact is that Washington also set aside Jay's second draft message, thereby producing what must have been a bitter disappointment to the proponents of a Spanish treaty that might otherwise have been speedily achieved. But, under a government of checks and balances, the northern majority in the Senate could not overpower the opposition as its counterpart had done in 1786. The bitter pill had to be swallowed. Hence, in response to Washington's suggestion that Gardoqui not be allowed to entertain false hopes that the United States might yield on the central point, Jay drafted a memorandum of instructions from Washington to himself. His draft did not allude to the thorny Mississippi problem, but it did pledge the President in a manner that had met his objection when Jay first opened up the subject:[209]

> Ordered, that Mr. Jay assure the Encargado de Negocios . . . in the name of the President that the suspension of the negociations . . . is to be ascribed to those derangements and Causes of Delay which such a change in the national Government as has taken place in this Country must naturally produce; that the President is desirous that these negociations should be recommenced and brought to a speedy Conclusion and that he will as soon as possible take the necessary measures for the putting that Business in proper Train on the part of the united States. That he is sincerely desirous of seeing the two Nations connected by a Treaty satisfactory to both, and that nothing on his part shall be wanting to promote that object, and to manifest those Sentiments of Respect and attachment which the united States, as well as the President individually, entertain for his Catholic Majesty and the Spanish nation.

Washington later supposed that the views expressed in this memorandum were communicated at his request to Gardoqui.[210] In this he was evidently mistaken. For Jay's official response to Gardoqui's notice of his departure contained no assurance from the President that he would take steps to see that the negotiations were resumed and no expressed hope for a speedy conclusion:[211]

> Considering how long the negotiations depending between our Countries have unavoidably been suspended by the derangements

[209] Draft in Jay's hand, undated but before 27 July 1789 (DLC: Washington Papers, ser. 4, vol. 243, f. 103; designated as "A" by Washington. For Washington's comment on this document, see following note).

[210] Washington docketed Jay's three drafts of messages and instructions (see notes 204, 208, and 209) as follows: "Note. The enclosed Papers were never acted upon, unless the sentiments in that marked A were communicated by Mr. Jay at the Presidents request to the Encargado of Spain Mr. Gardoqui" (see note 209).

[211] Jay to Gardoqui, 27 July 1789 (DNA: RG 59, PCC No. 120; DLC: Washington Papers; *Dipl. Corr.*, VI, 269-70).

which such a change as has taken place in this Government will always occasion [Jay wrote for the President], it is much to be regretted that your departure should be so near the period when those derangements will cease, I am authorized to assure you that the President is exceedingly desirous to see the most cordial friendship established between the Spanish monarchy and the United States, and on the most permanent principles of liberal policy—That he will omit no opportunity of promoting and confirming it.

There was much more about the general esteem Gardoqui had acquired in the prosecution of a mission necessarily retarded by "national events and questions of great difficulty and magnitude." There was also a tribute to Gardoqui's candor which had inspired the confident belief that he would ascribe the delays to their true cause and so represent them to the king. But the question of resuming the suspended "negotiations" was itself left in suspense and there was not a word about the matter of great difficulty and magnitude that had been—and still was—the true cause of delay. Jay's expression of regret that Gardoqui was departing just as the derangements were thought to be ending, however, seemed to offer another gleam of hope. Whether this was intended or not, the Spanish minister did delay his departure for almost three months. But the derangements—or, as Jay had first expressed it, the "embarrassments"—had by no means ended. While Gardoqui delayed his departure, Congress was deeply involved in such questions as the creation of a judicial department and the fixing of a permanent seat of government, subjects both important and divisive. Soon after the session came to an end—and with it the end of all hope entertained by Jay that the Spanish policy he had consistently advocated since 1786 could become the law of the land before Jefferson took office as Secretary of State—Gardoqui took formal leave of the President, intending to depart for Spain the next day.[212] No doubt he went away with the President's assurances of good will and with expressions of his desire for amicable arrangements with Spain "on the most permanent principles of liberal policy." He may have been given other views privately which, added to these vague politenesses, led the Spanish ministry to misconceive Washington's firmness.[213]

[212] Washington, *Diaries*, ed. Fitzpatrick, IV, 17, entry for 8 Oct. 1789.
[213] On arriving in Spain, Humphreys was informed on good authority that "all the representations of Gardoqui . . . tended to excite a belief that the most respectable and influential people throughout the United States did not wish to have the navigation of the Mississippi opened for years to come, from an apprehension such an event would weaken the government, and impoverish the Atlantic States by emigrations" (Humphreys to TJ, 15 Jan. 1791). Gardoqui in fact declared that the language employed by TJ in 1791 was very different from that he had heard on his departure in 1789 (Bemis, *Pinckney's Treaty*, p. 157). In 1786 Monroe was convinced that even the agitation of the Mississippi question had weakened the American position and "given Spain hopes she had no reason to calculate on" (Monroe to TJ, 19 Aug. 1786). Certainly the "mild, vague" tone of Jay's official letter to the *encargado* on his departure (Freeman, *Washington*, VI, 238n.) had had much the same effect—as indeed had Washington's letter to Henry Lee of 18 June 1786, of which Gardoqui had a copy (Bemis, *Pinckney's Treaty*, p. 92, 159).

But, whatever misconceptions and false hopes Gardoqui may have received from soft diplomatic language, Jay and his supporters in the Senate knew that their audacious attempt had failed. They knew, too, that the President, in order to avoid what he regarded as a certain disruption of the nation into East and West, would never allow the right of navigation to be weakened by any negotiation whatever. They had reason to believe—as westerners already did—that the new Secretary of State stood on the same ground, differing with the President chiefly as to the time and manner in which this great national question should be faced finally and with resolution. It was Jefferson's task to persuade Washington to do this with language so firm and explicit as to leave no room for doubt about its meaning either in Madrid or in the Senate. His most powerful instrument for achieving this end was the one that Jay most feared—the agitation of the public mind on the subject. By the close of Jefferson's first year as Secretary of State, such agitation had become so pronounced in the West that it could no longer be ignored. In the face of George Nicholas' blunt warnings that arrived in Philadelphia in the spring of 1791, the question was no longer whether Kentuckians could be placated but whether the union could be preserved.

VII

Fortunately, there was ready at hand an incident that exactly suited Jefferson's purpose, one involving a violation by Spanish soldiers of the rights of an American citizen engaged in his lawful pursuits within the jurisdiction of the United States. The general question would no doubt have been brought forward at this time in any event, as Jefferson declared, but he described the fortuitous provocation with some diplomatic license when he said that it had presented itself "in the moment" of decision.[214] The incident in fact had occurred in 1787 and had been brought to the attention of the government in two separate appeals. In that year merchandise on the left bank of the Mississippi belonging to Joseph St. Marie, a well established and respected Indian trader, had been seized by Spanish troops. In 1788 St. Marie went to New Orleans to seek restitution from Governor Miró. Failing in this, he testified to the facts and sent his affidavit to General Harmar, who forwarded it to the Secretary of War. Knox was absent when the communication arrived in New York but his brother transmitted it to Congress. There it lay neglected in the interim between the end of the old and the beginning of the new government. In the summer of 1790 St. Marie again presented his claim, not only for compensation but also for the resolution of the "grand national Question" posed by this violation of American sovereignty. His memorial was addressed to Winthrop Sargent, Secretary of the Northwest Territory, who at once forwarded it to the President.[215] In December Washington

[214] Document VII.
[215] Joseph St. Marie to J. F. Hamtramck, 26 Aug. 1788, enclosed in Hamtramck to Harmar, 31 Aug. 1788 (MiU-C: Harmar Papers); William Knox to the President of Congress, 6 Oct. 1788, enclosing St. Clair's letter of 14 Sep. 1788 and its enclosures (JCC, XXXIV, 597-8); Sargent to Washington, 29 July 1790 (Carter, *Terr. Papers*, II, 294-5; III, 323).

turned it over to Jefferson, together with Sargent's report on proceedings in the Northwest Territory. A month later he also directed that the Secretary of War give his attention to St. Marie's "memorial lodged in the office of the Secretary of State."[216] This would seem to suggest that, at the time Jefferson first became aware of the incident, Washington sought to have the complaint investigated by Henry Knox, whose department had responsibility for matters involving trade with the Indians. By Washington's particular request, Knox did in fact report at a cabinet meeting in the middle of January, but the nature of his report is not known. Since there is no text of a report at this time by Jefferson and no reference to the subject in his register of official papers, it is clear that St. Marie's claim was not then regarded by the administration as a pressing problem in foreign affairs.

During the two months that elapsed after the cabinet discussions in January, however, George Nicholas' emphatic warning was received by Madison, who unquestionably made it known to Jefferson. This, together with other unmistakable evidences of westerners' discontent with federal measures, was enough to produce prompt and decisive action, despite the assurances of peace in Europe. The administration's choice of alternatives was neither to ask Governor Miró to disavow the actions of his subordinates nor to make its commitment dependent upon the intercession of France. Instead, its decision was to bring on the question of navigation of the Mississippi in a direct representation to the Spanish court, expressed in language so exigent that the issue could no longer be evaded. Whatever neglect may have attended St. Marie's first appeal, his second, having been in the hands of the government for three months without effect, was now seized upon with alacrity. His memorial not only fell into Jefferson's official care at an opportune moment: it also breathed the spirit of a "Freeman and Citizen of the United States of America," whose right to trade within its territory had been trampled upon "by an armed Force, in Pursuance of the Orders of a foreign Prince."[217] Even St. Marie's words seemed fashioned for the occasion.

When John Brown departed for Kentucky on the 9th of March, he bore Jefferson's private letter to Harry Innes announcing the government's unequivocal commitment and assuring him, with something less than full justification, of the President's "determined zeal . . . in this business."[218] The next day, having read the draft of Jefferson's instructions to Carmichael, Washington defined the limit of his zeal. He approved the policy but urged a significant—indeed a drastic—softening of the language. His rather imperative directive to Jefferson to reconsider the phrasing was impossible to ignore. In the absence of even the kind of written exchange that took place with Jay in 1789, when Washington also insisted on delicate and tender language, one can only guess at the nature of the discussions that followed. What is

[216] Lear to Secretary of State, 16 Dec. 1790 (DNA: RG 59, MLR); Lear to Secretary of War, 15 Jan. 1791 (DLC: Washington Papers). See also Knox to TJ, 16 Jan. 1791.

[217] St. Marie's memorial, 22 July 1790 (Document VI, enclosure).

[218] TJ to Innes, 7 Mch. 1791 (Document IV).

known with certainty is that Jefferson, who himself believed that civility and candor were both essential to diplomatic discourse, was convinced the time had come to declare American policy in terms that would remove all possibility of misconception. He therefore opposed, with success, Washington's first suggestion that Carmichael be cautioned to use such prudence and circumspection as to avoid committing the government "to the necessity of proceeding to extremity."[219] To have yielded on this point would have been to nullify Jefferson's argument that at any instant an accident could irrevocably commit the United States. Although comparative texts are not available as proof, it is no less certain that Jefferson overcame the President's second suggestion as well, for the expression on the final page that Washington thought too bold under the circumstances and in light of the national interests could scarcely have been put in firmer language than that finally seen by the court of Madrid. This was indeed the heart of the new policy: "Should any spark kindle . . . our borderers into a flame, we are involved beyond recall by the eternal principles of justice to our citizens, which we will never abandon. In such an event, Spain cannot possibly gain, and what may she not lose?"[220] The irrevocable commitment and the confident determination involved the gravest of risks. But the chance was one that Jefferson felt it urgently necessary to take in a situation in which a cautious or equivocal posture might, by lulling Spanish fears, avoid war but split the union into East and West. As between these two fateful choices, he did not hesitate. The essential fact about the decision to embark on the new American policy toward Spain, therefore, is that Jefferson was ready to commit the government without equivocation, that the President wished to avoid doing so, and that the purpose of the Secretary of State—through whatever efforts of persuasion one can only imagine—ultimately prevailed. Even without the advantage afforded by a European conflict, Jefferson at this time believed himself compelled by events and by the temper of westerners to drive the nail "as far as it will go peaceably, and farther the moment that circumstances become favorable."[221] As if to underscore the unequivocal language of the instructions to Carmichael, he made no use of cipher at all, being no doubt convinced that Florida Blanca would be the first to read and understand the significance of the message.

Late in May, in accordance with Jefferson's instructions, William Short announced the decision to Montmorin and Lafayette and asked French support for the representation that would be made at Madrid by William Carmichael. Lafayette urged a course of aggression. Montmorin feared the Kentuckians might place the United States in the position of being the aggressors and thought the best thing to do would be to let the westerners take New Orleans without trying to support them or to legitimatize their act. He said that he had long ago warned Madrid the westerners could neither be restrained nor abandoned by their nation, that the navigation of the Mississippi

[219] Document V.
[220] Document VI.
[221] Document IV.

was a matter of necessity to the United States, that "it was always useless to struggle against *necessity*," and that, since the Spanish had at that time rejected all suggestions of an accommodation, he had no hope they would do so then. Moreover, he felt "the influence of France would at all times have been ineffectual against their prejudices in maters of this kind, but at present would be entirely vain." Nevertheless, he asked Short to write him and promised to forward the letter with instructions to the French chargé at Madrid to support Carmichael's representation. Short complied, Montmorin went over the draft closely, and the letter was transmitted exactly as written.[222] During the summer the disposition of the Spanish court, as reflected in Montmorin's conversations with Short, went through several changes. At first its mood was conciliatory. By mid-summer, it was against negotiation, and rumors of impending war between the United States and Spain appeared in English newspapers. But early in August when Carmichael made his representation, the ministry changed its attitude again and acted with surprising swiftness. Within two weeks Montmorin in Paris was able to inform Short that Spain had revealed "a propensity to listen to terms."[223] The bold words of the Secretary of State had had their effect. French support had been given but the result, so the evidence indicates, would have been the same without it.[224]

[222] Short to TJ, 6 June 1791.
[223] Short to TJ, 20 July and 24 Aug. 1791.
[224] Bemis states that Short's communication to Montmorin "made a great stir when transmitted by Montmorin to the Spanish Government and actually supported by the French chargé at Madrid. Carmichael already had opened as portentously as was possible, without support of any kind, discussion of the claims of the United States. He had met with no ready response. The new American note from Montmorin was referred immediately to Gardoqui" (Bemis, *Pinckney's Treaty*, p. 157). But this conclusion, which attributes the decisive change in attitude to French influence, is supported neither by Montmorin's own estimate of that influence nor by the evidence of chronology. Having demonstrated in the Nootka incident her weakness as Spain's family ally—a fact of which Gardoqui took note (as does Bemis himself, same, p. 154, 156)—France was scarcely in a position to create concern. In any case, the Spanish court acted with remarkable speed after Carmichael's representation was made on 8 Aug. 1791. Short's letter to Montmorin was presumably presented by the French chargé at the same time or soon thereafter. Gardoqui's memorandum was drafted 22 Aug. 1791. Florida Blanca's instructions to Jaudenes and Viar bore the date 6 Sep. 1791 (AHN, Est., leg. 3384, 3889, 3890, 3894; AME/AL, Washington, Caja 5, leg. 198, photocopies in DLC). A lapse of just two weeks from the date of Carmichael's representation to that of Gardoqui's response seems to render implausible the assumption that the ministry attached a special importance to the Short-Montmorin communication that was not bestowed on that by Carmichael. Both reflected the substance of Jefferson's instructions and, as Florida Blanca made clear, it was the emphatic, grave tone of these that created both surprise and displeasure.
    Whitaker, *Spanish-American Frontier*, p. 146-52, agrees with Bemis about the effect of French influence, but identifies Short's memorial with the Nootka crisis of the preceding year. He also interprets the Spanish response as an "invitation" to negotiate and concludes that, being insincere in making proposals for an accommodation and unable to ignore Spain's "advances" openly, the American government, trying to keep up appearances and to persuade westerners it was defending their essential interests, betrayed its insincerity by appointing unwelcome and undistinguished persons to conduct the negotiations and by adopting dilatory tactics once they had been appointed. But this interpretation of

The Spanish ministry had at once consulted Diego de Gardoqui as the one most intimately informed about American affairs. He, too, was greatly impressed by the firm language of the United States: "when I left that country," he observed, "it was very far from setting forth in writing the pretenses it now makes." He ascribed the unexpected firmness as being due to the weakened situation of France and to the likelihood of a combination between the United States and England against Spain.[225] The assumptions were mistaken but, within a month after Carmichael had presented his note, Florida Blanca gave instructions to the Spanish agents in the United States to inform the Secretary of State that discussions "to settle everything on the most friendly footing" would be welcomed. He expressed surprise at the tone of the representation, but offered to open negotiations either in Spain or in America. Before the year was out, Jaudenes told Jefferson at a dinner at the City Tavern that the new instructions had been received. The Secretary of State thereupon reported to the President this promising ray of hope along the path leading ultimately to the Treaty of San Lorenzo. The route was to prove tortuous and often frustrating, but the first decisive step had been taken. The Spanish court now knew beyond all possibility of mistake that the American government was unalterably committed to a right it would never relinquish and that the choice lay between friendly accommodation and a force as inexorable as the Mississippi itself that might, at any moment, foreclose even that option. The reversal of the policy advocated by the Secretary for Foreign Affairs since 1786 was complete and lasting. Where Jay and his supporters had placed a commercial treaty foremost in their calculations and were willing to bargain over the navigation of the Mississippi, Jefferson took exactly the opposite position. He was prepared to negotiate on matters of trade but only on the separate merits of the case and under a treaty of severely limited duration. As for the questions of boundary and navigation, which in his view transcended other considerations so greatly that he desired them to be treated under a separate instrument, his instructions to the American negotiators made the new policy irrevocable. The settlement of these issues,

TJ's confrontation of the issue as being devoid of serious intent to negotiate collides with the facts and with the character of TJ's diplomacy.

On the contrary, it was Gardoqui who, surprised and shocked by the firmness of the American position, urged the Spanish court to "get as much as we can out of a bad business" and to employ temporizing expedients in the negotiations. This advice was accepted. During the next five years Gardoqui was "the monarchy's chief adviser and negotiator in questions pertaining to the United States" (Bemis, *Pinckney's Treaty*, p. 61, 158-9, 160). It is to this fact that much of the dilatory and temporizing nature of the negotiations from 1792 to 1795 must be ascribed. As a realistic diplomat, TJ anticipated that this would be the case (TJ to Short, 18 Mch. 1792, private; TJ to Washington, 9 Sep. 1792). He was indeed dubious about the effect of the intercession of France in persuading Spain to open negotiations in 1791 and in his instructions to Short and Carmichael in 1792 he specifically directed them not to communicate with the French ministers because their interposition might not be agreeable to Spain (TJ's report to the President, 19 Mch. 1792).

[225] Quoted in Bemis, *Pinckney's Treaty*, p. 157. Gardoqui's memorandum, dated 22 Aug. 1791, is in AHN, Est., leg. 3889, photocopy in DLC.

he declared with the President's approval, "must be perpetual and final."[226]

VIII

Such, in brief, was the immediate context and such the first consequences of Jefferson's determined effort to reach an accommodation with Spain. From this it is clear that the generally accepted view of the origin of the new policy cannot be reconciled with the known facts. That view derives ultimately from the thesis that the distant and detached position of the United States enabled it to become great and powerful by taking advantage of European turmoils.[227] It holds in particular that Jefferson rested his entire foreign policy on his readiness to profit from the inevitable quarrels of Europe, as in the war crisis of 1790; that the essence of his diplomacy was to wait patiently until "another opportunity should chance to fall . . . out of the unquiet European sky"; that in this case he raked up an incident of 1787 in order to bring French influence to bear on the Spanish ministry; and that when Gardoqui mistakenly attributed the new language of firmness to a possible rapprochement with England and to the weakness of Spain's family ally, he overlooked the change of sentiment that had taken place in the northern states on the question of the navigation of the Mississippi, besides failing to discern the source of increased resolution in the greatly augmented powers of the American government and in the effect this had had in commanding the respect of foreign powers.[228]

As applied generally to American history this thesis may have some cogency, despite its serious weakness in the fact that it tends to depreciate the value and uses of diplomacy, it overlooks the general prevalence of peace in Europe throughout most of the nineteenth century, it disregards the countervailing disadvantages for the United States in the danger that it might be pulled asunder by the contentions of European powers and their consequent efforts to influence its policies, and, most important of all, it fails to take account of the

[226] TJ to Washington, 22 Dec. 1791; Jaudenes and Viar to TJ, 25 Jan. 1792; TJ to Viar, 25 Jan. 1792; TJ to Jaudenes and Viar, 26 Jan. 1792. See also TJ's report on negotiations with Spain, 18 Mch. 1792. TJ informed John Brown of the disposition of the Spanish court to negotiate (John Brown to Harry Innes, 20 Jan. 1792, DLC: Innes Papers).

[227] Bemis' *Jay's Treaty* and his *Pinckney's Treaty*, two path-breaking works in the field of diplomatic history, are, as the author states in the preface to the revised (1960) edition of the latter, essentially case histories documenting the thesis that American success in diplomacy arose out of "a fortuitous and nonrecurring geopolitical situation in the world, to which we owe not only our independence itself and the liberation of our western territories after the Revolutionary War, but also the preservation of our nation and its expanded territory of 1812, and its further expansion through to the Pacific Ocean" (p. vii-viii). The thesis is also expounded in J. Fred Rippy's *America and the Strife of Europe* (Chicago, 1938). C. Vann Woodward's "The Age of Reinterpretation," AHR, LXVI (Oct. 1960), 1-19, recognizes limiting factors but insists that the United States during most of its history enjoyed relatively free security and that the sudden end of this favored position came in the 20th century.

[228] Bemis, *Pinckney's Treaty*, p. 154-62. Malone, *Jefferson*, II, 406-9, recognizes the boldness of TJ's decision but accepts Bemis' explanation of it.

immense force generated by an enterprising people who, in a new land and under the spell of the most potent concept of modern history, thought of themselves as forming a new kind of society under a new kind of federal republic. But, as applied to Jefferson's bold choice in the spring of 1791, the thesis and the accepted view deriving from it are overwhelmingly contradicted by the facts. The first and most obvious contradiction is that the decision was made not during one of the recurrent crises of Europe but just after the latest danger of war had subsided. The instrument employed to announce the policy was an old one, to be sure, but it was not deliberately sought out: it fell to hand at a time of exigent need when the general question, as Jefferson pointed out, would have been brought forward for other reasons. Moreover, the intercession of France was not at all determinative. Unlike the decision arrived at during the crisis of 1790 which was largely contingent upon French support, this was a quite independent commitment, made without regard to what France might or might not do. It was a decision to declare to Spain in direct confrontation, with such simultaneous solicitation of the good offices of France as friendship suggested or as a prudent regard for the national interest required, that the United States considered the peace to be so imminently in danger that it could no longer acquiesce in a suspension of the right of navigation of the Mississippi.[229] This was a decision, in brief, to settle the issue with unequivocal finality, regardless of the contingencies of European distress or of French support.

Nor did this determination arise from a presumed change of sentiment in New England respecting the navigation of the Mississippi or from the increased authority and prestige of the federal government. There not only had been no demonstrable change in northern attitudes toward the continued Spanish closure of the river, but such interest in western affairs as had been awakened there was stimulated in large degree by land speculations in the national domain that served to intensify feelings of resentment and neglect in Kentucky, especially when accompanied by military efforts both ineffectual and costly.[230] When Jefferson alluded to "the impatience of our citizens" and declared that Carmichael's representation to the Spanish court could not be "more pressing than the present situation and temper of this country requires," he was not alluding to New England impatience or to north-

[229] Document VI.
[230] Innes to TJ, 30 Sep. 1791; Rufus King to Hamilton, 24 Mch. 1791 (Syrett, *Hamilton*, VIII, 212-3). Whether or not Madison knew about Jay's effort to conclude the treaty with Gardoqui in the summer of 1789, he soon declared that he was "extremely alarmed for the Western country," fearing that those in the northeastern states were already beginning "to speculate on the event of a separation of that part of the Union." His fears were augmented by northern inattention to western claims in the matter of locating the Federal District, as well as by information received in the autumn of 1789 from Nicholas, Innes, and other Kentuckians (Madison to Henry Lee, 4 Oct. 1789, DLC: Madison Papers; Madison to Washington, 20 Nov. 1789, DLC: Washington Papers).

After St. Clair's defeat, an article entitled *Braddock* appeared in the *Independent Chronicle* for 22 Dec. 1791 calling for an end to efforts "to acquire territory by war. . . . The ill policy of the measure must be evident, for us to depopulate our own territory, to settle a country which must for centuries remain entirely useless to us."

ern temper.[231] The demand for a final determination of the Mississippi question not only was not pressed with urgency in that section of the country: it was at this time simply non-existent. There had been no discernible change in attitude since northern Congressmen voted as a phalanx to acquiesce in the closure of the Mississippi in hope of gaining commercial benefits from Spain.

It is true that the powers of the national government had been greatly augmented. But Jefferson's acceptance of the grave risk at this particular time can scarcely be explained by the mere existence of those powers. It was with some reluctance that Washington committed the government in the full amplitude that Jefferson insisted upon, but neither his reluctance nor Jefferson's boldness provides an adequate explanation for the acceptance of the risk. What had changed since the Jay-Gardoqui negotiations was an attitude toward the use of the powers available. For at the very time that Jay as Secretary for Foreign Affairs was arousing false hopes in the Spanish government by offering to "forbear" the right of navigation for twenty-five or thirty years in return for commercial concessions, Jefferson perceived American interest in other and more fundamental terms: "It would be to deceive them and ourselves to suppose that an amity can be preserved while this right is withheld. . . . [O]ur true interest will be best promoted by making all the just claims of our fellow citizens, wherever situated, our own, by urging and *enforcing them with the weight of our whole influence*, and by exercising in this as in every other instance a just government in their concerns and making common cause even where our separate interest would seem opposed to theirs. No other conduct can attach us together; and on this attachment depends our happiness."[232] Even under the Articles of Confederation,

[231] Document VI.

[232] TJ to Monroe, 11 Aug. 1786. In 1792 TJ stated that three Senators were still opposed to opening the Mississippi (TJ to Short, 29 Jan. 1792). As the old government was expiring, John Dawson received the address of the Kentucky convention on the subject and reported to Madison: "You are well aware of the difficulties which will attend this business, especially as there will not be more than nine states represented, some of which are in favour of the surrender of the river to Spain, in which number I am sorry to include South Carolina" (Dawson to Madison, 29 Jan. 1789, DLC: Madison Papers).

That the old sectional differences still existed was clearly recognized by British officials, as shown by Dorchester's secret instructions to Beckwith urging him to use caution in making specific proposals and instead to "lead them to explain the different lines of policy each party may have in view" (Dorchester to Beckwith, 27 June 1790, enclosed in Dorchester to Grenville, 7 July 1790, PRO: CO 42/68). From his intimate discussions with leading members of Congress from New England and especially with the Secretary of the Treasury, Beckwith soon confirmed the existence of such divisions: "The Atlantic people in general wish the navigation to remain closed, from their dread of a rivalship, especially in the West India market.—The Executive Government are anxious to possess it themselves, in order to connect and consolidate both sides of the Alleghany Mountains, knowing that although the western exports must issue from the Mississippi, their imports will to a certainty be conveyed through the Atlantic States" (Beckwith's report of conversations, enclosed in Dorchester to Grenville, 10 Nov. 1790, PRO: CO 42/72). The possibility that Great Britain might control New Orleans, thus threatening a separation of the West and its emergence as a competitor with the East as Nicholas had warned, was viewed by the government with great concern, so Beckwith reported, being "con-

Jefferson believed that the nation possessed weight and influence and that, above all, it had a common cause. On this issue he was the nationalist, Jay the sectionalist.

Thus, quite aside from being unsupported by the facts, the accepted view obscures the realistic nature of Jefferson's diplomacy and the true springs of his action. The preservation of the union, not the support of a sectional interest, guided him in this as in other potentially disruptive issues. The decision of 1791 clearly involved the risk of war, especially if by inaction the mistaken impressions that the Spanish government had received earlier were not effaced. While Jefferson was prudent, flexible, realistic, and always prepared to seize opportunities arising in Europe or elsewhere, his style of diplomacy was never rash or impulsive. In this instance, his decision to bring on the issue in a time of relative tranquillity and with a degree of firmness that encountered and prevailed over the President's counsel of moderation must, therefore, have arisen from some cause of compelling urgency. It seems obvious that he was moved to embrace the risk by the insistent clamors of the men on the western waters and by what this portended for their attachment to the union.

There were some adventurers in that region such as O'Fallon who, by an act of rashness, might have forced a confrontation with Spain. There were others, men of venality and avarice ready to be influenced by Spanish gold such as Wilkinson and Sebastian, whose grandiose schemes might have embroiled the nation. But lawless and scheming men, flirting with independence and holding secret discussions with both Spanish and British officials, had made their presence manifest for some years and yet had not been able to gain ascendancy in western affairs. Indeed, James Wilkinson himself had warned Governor Miró that the westerners would not subject themselves to the Spanish mon-

---

templated as forming a competition with the Atlantic States, as having a direct tendency to accelerate the population and wealth of the former at the expense of the latter, and as the laying an immediate foundation for a rivalship" (Beckwith's report of conversations, enclosed in Dorchester to Grenville, 25 Sep. 1790, PRO: CO 42/69).

The possibility that Great Britain might control westerners' access to the sea had the effect of uniting the administration on this issue as on no other leading object. Thus Hamilton regarded the navigation of the Mississippi as being "of the first moment to our Territories to the Westward. They must have that outlet. Without it they will be lost to us" (Beckwith's report of conversations, enclosed in Dorchester to Grenville, 25 Oct. 1789, PRO: CO 42/66). Before the threat of war between England and Spain Hamilton thought the issue could not be an immediate concern, but later, before the crisis had subsided, he informed Beckwith: "The rapid increase of our Western country is such, that we must possess this outlet, in a very short space of time, whatever individual interests may be opposed to it. The general advantage of the States points it out more evidently" (Beckwith's "Conversations with Seven" [Hamilton], 7 Apr. 1790, enclosed in Dorchester to Grenville, 27 May 1790, PRO: CO 42/68; Beckwith's conversations with "the gentleman high in office," [17 Oct. 1790], enclosed in Beckwith to Grenville, 3 Nov. 1790, PRO: CO 42/72; shorter versions, one of them dated, appear in CO 42/21 and FO 4/12; Syrett, *Hamilton*, VIII, 111).

Though they approached this important question from opposing points of view that in themselves reflected the continuity and the exacerbation of the old sectional divisions, the Secretary of the Treasury and the Secretary of State for once stood together on this issue.

arch and that the most his nation could hope for would be an alliance with an independent Kentucky. The governor had duly reported to Madrid the failure of the effort to detach them from the union.[233] Even the schemes of O'Fallon, like those of Burr later, called forth nothing more drastic than a presidential proclamation.[234] Whatever the future might hold, in the spring of 1791 there was no urgent threat arising among these elements to stir the Secretary of State to act. But the ominous warning of George Nicholas, echoing and magnifying the fears of disunion John Brown had expressed three years earlier, could scarcely be ignored. This solemn utterance by a responsible citizen, once an ardent advocate of the new government but now deeply distressed by the tendency of its measures, epitomized the general sense of frustration and neglect felt by westerners. It also voiced the moral force of republican aspirations, intangible yet unmistakable and running deep and strong among the people of Kentucky. Its indictment of the national administration was both representative and prophetic.

For long before the close of the first Congress an observer less acute than Jefferson could easily discern that the manner in which the augmented powers of government were being employed had exacerbated rather than alleviated the old sectional animosities. "The Eastern and Western Interests are in my view irreconcilable," Harry Innes had written in 1788, "and I know of no such doctrine in Politicks as Justice —of course there can be no such thing as an Equi Librium kept between the Eastern and Western parts of the Union. We have had a most glaring instance of their selfish contracted Policy—remember the [debates over the] navigation of the Mississippi. I am authorised to say the same principles still continue and what can we expect from the new System? There may be a change of Men but their ideas will be the same, and when you reflect that the promoting of the Interest of the western Country will tend to almost a depopulation of the Eastern, we cannot even hope that our Interests will be considered."[235] Innes' prediction, echoing in its assumption of a fundamental incompatibility of interests the contemporary views of such eastern leaders as John Jay, Gouverneur Morris, and Rufus King, now seemed confirmed by the tone and tendency of the federal administration. Derivative fiscal policies not grounded in the actualities of the national economy, orthodox military measures that fostered collusion and speculation while ignoring the promptings of frontier experience, administrative actions multiplying links of interest with centers of

[233] Wilkinson to Miró, 12 Feb. 1789 (Whitaker, *Spanish-American Frontier*, p. 117, 146).
[234] Though O'Fallon's plan to conquer New Orleans by force was known to the administration some weeks before Congress adjourned, the President's proclamation was not issued until 19 Mch. 1791. It seems plausible to assume that, if that scheme had caused any genuine uneasiness, the official denunciation of it would have taken place at least ten days earlier when John Brown left for Kentucky (Lear to Knox, 15 Jan. 1791, DLC: Washington Papers; proclamation, 19 Mch. 1791, *Writings*, ed. Fitzpatrick, XXXI, 250; Whitaker, *Spanish-American Frontier*, p. 132; J. C. Parish, "The Intrigues of Doctor James O'Fallon," MVHR, XVII [Sep. 1930], 230-63).
[235] Innes to Arthur Campbell, 19 Sep. 1788 (WHi: Draper MSS).

finance but neglecting those of loyalty in distant regions, commercial views subordinating the needs of American trade and the fisheries to British mercantilist claims—these and other manifestations of national policy profoundly intensified the old feelings of distrust and resentment in the South and West. By 1791 even a New England Federalist could voice his fear of the clearly widening sectional cleavages.[236] So, too, the formality of admitting Kentucky to the union, balanced as this was by the simultaneous admission of Vermont, was itself a tacit acknowledgment of the growing spirit of sectional jealousy. Until the spring of 1791 the government had done nothing to alter the conviction among Kentuckians that federal policies, as Nicholas declared in confirmation of Innes' prediction, were still selfish, contracted, and neglectful of western interests. From their point of view the glowing promises of the new political system had not been fulfilled. Worse, the grant of augmented powers to the national government had resulted in increased disequilibrium between the financial and commercial East and the agricultural South and West.

The ominous cloud in the West, like other signs of gathering opposition, also heralded at the start of this divisive decade the differing ways in which Americans conceived themselves and their national character. In 1789, just as the new government was being organized, one Kentuckian secretly advised British officials that the politics of the West were fast verging to a crisis; that natural barriers and irreconcilable interests made its separation from the East inevitable; and that, since the two regions could not be united "on principles of reciprocal interest . . . the flimsy texture of republican government [would be] insufficient to hold in the same bonds a people detached and scattered over such an expanse of territory, whose views, and interests are [so] discordant."[237] The skepticism about the strength of republican institutions was one that many felt and some expressed—covertly, of course—even in the Senate of the United States.[238] But Jefferson, recognizing the obvious gravity of the sectional crisis, based his policy on the conviction that the generality of Americans remained "as firm as a rock in their republicanism" and that the preservation of the union depended more upon their adherence to the revolutionary postulates than upon their form of government.[239] In his view the real danger of a separation of the West arose not from the efforts of British and Spanish officials to detach Kentuckians from the union, nor from clashing sectional interests, but from the seat of government itself. There the tendency of national measures—combined with "heresies preached now, to be practised hereafter," as in Adams' *Dis-*

[236] Paine Wingate to Josiah Bartlett, 26 Jan. 1791 (C. E. L. Wingate, *Paine Wingate*, II, 385).

[237] [James Wilkinson], "Desultory Reflections by a Gentleman of Kentucky" (Grenville Papers, Boconnoc [now in the British Museum]; enclosed in Dorchester to Sydney, 11 Apr. 1789, PRO: CO 42/64, f. 157-60). For other evidences of interest in western separatism on the part of both French and English officials, see Dorchester to Sydney, 6 June, 27 Aug., and 20 Oct. 1789; PRO: CO 42/65, f. 10, 11-24, 88, 193.

[238] See, for example, the remarks of Senators William Samuel Johnson and William Paterson to George Beckwith in 1789 and 1790 quoted in Vol. 17: 52-4.

[239] TJ to Short, 28 July 1791; TJ to Paine, 29 July 1791 and 19 June 1792.

courses on Davila[240]—seemed increasingly to qualify the national commitment to the moral propositions of self-government that Jefferson regarded as the most cohesive bond of union. Being well aware that the decision to force the Mississippi issue involved the risk of war with Spain, he was prepared to accept that risk rather than the greater one that Kentuckians would be driven to the irrevocable step of separation by the government's continued indifference to their views and interests. Disunion was to him the worst of all evils to be dreaded.[241]

This choice of risks, therefore, involved much more than an end to American acquiescence in the Spanish closure of the Mississippi. Jefferson had long been convinced that, soon or late, that issue would be resolved in favor of the United States because its claim was grounded on natural right and supported by an enterprising people who would achieve a settlement either by mutual accommodation, by peaceful penetration, or by armed force. The transcendent question was whether the nation would remain united. The decision to drive the nail as far as it would go peaceably and farther when possible was thus less a defense of sectional interests than it was a blow for national unity—less a warning to Spain than a pledge of support to the West. It was also, at least in related private messages, an invitation for closer political understandings between the South and West. When John Brown returned to Kentucky soon after Congress adjourned, he carried not only Jefferson's announcement of the new policy but also Madison's reply to Nicholas. The latter communication seems lost to history, but we may safely assume that it, too, gave assurances that the right of free navigation of the Mississippi could no longer be denied by a foreign power. We know with certainty that it expressed a desire for Nicholas to become a Representative from the new state of Kentucky.[242] A few days later Jefferson also urged James Innes to come into Congress and lend his "zeal and talents . . . to the republican scale."[243] These particular overtures failed, but they symbolized the beginnings of organized opposition. Federal measures that had so greatly intensified old sectional suspicions and animosities had also prompted these and other efforts to multiply bonds linking southern and western leaders —bonds that would result in potent alliances in 1800 and beyond.[244]

---

240 TJ to James Innes, 13 Mch. 1791; see also TJ to George Mason, 4 Feb. 1791 and note to TJ to Jonathan B. Smith, 26 Apr. 1791. TJ made it clear that he had Adams' *Discourses* in mind when he alluded to "heresies."

241 In 1792, in a desperate effort to persuade Washington to save the union by accepting a second term, TJ pointed out that "whenever Northern and Southern prejudices have come into conflict, the latter have been sacrificed and the former soothed." It was this increasing sectional cleavage that caused him to declare: "I can scarcely contemplate a more incalculable evil than the breaking of the union into two or more parts" (TJ to Washington, 23 May 1792). Washington himself had recently expressed the fear "that there would ere long be a separation of the union" (TJ's memorandum of conversation with Washington, 9 Apr. 1792).

242 Nicholas to Madison, 20 June 1791 (DLC: Madison Papers).

243 TJ to Innes, 13 Mch. 1791.

244 For some of TJ's later comments on the relations of the South and West, see TJ to Middleton, 8 Jan. 1813; TJ to Breckinridge, 9 Apr. 1822; TJ to Rush, 13 Oct. 1824; TJ to Gordon, 1 Jan. 1826; TJ to Gooch, 9 Jan. 1826.

The confrontation with Spain had such internal political consequences largely because, so it seemed to Kentuckians, it stood conspicuously alone as an example of the government's concern for their particular views and interests. When Jefferson's announcement arrived in the West, the men on the western waters knew that at last, after all their years of pleas and threats, the nation would not again equivocate or barter over their right to navigate the Mississippi. Where the Jay-Gardoqui negotiations had "given the western Country an universal shock, and struck its Inhabitants with an amazement," Jefferson's unequivocal declaration united them in gratitude.[245] In the full flush of patriotic fervor that swept over Kentucky in the late spring and summer of 1791, Harry Innes informed Jefferson that the "active measures adopted against the Indians and to obtain the Navigation of the Mississippi have in a great measure silenced our complaints."[246]

But this was said after the success of the Kentuckians' own expeditions and before the disaster that befell St. Clair a few months later. Despite these earlier demonstrations of what could be achieved at little expense by frontier methods of warfare, the federal council continued to place its reliance upon costly military campaigns so favored by eastern contractors and speculators. For a time in 1792, even in the Senate, the challenge to methods of fighting in the woods that belonged in the tradition of Braddock almost succeeded.[247] But if Kentuckians were outraged by the continued disregard of their counsels of defense based on long experience, they at least knew that one champion of their interests in the cabinet had given them the utmost support in his power. Jefferson had made this clear enough in his letters from France. In 1790, during the threat of war in Europe, he restated his policy in terms so explicit that none could have misunderstod it. Even if an accommodation should take place between Spain and England, he declared, the same resolute course would be pursued unalterably—except that negotiations would be pressed more softly, until patience and persuasion prevailed or some other circumstance turned up for achieving an object the United States was thenceforth "determined in the end to obtain at every risk."[248] The Spanish seizure of St. Marie's goods was a fortuitous occurrence, but not the determinative cause of Jefferson's abandonment of soft language. His defining the object with unequivocal finality in the spring of 1791 rested instead upon the exigent warnings from the West.

[245] Letter from a man at the Falls of the Ohio, 4 Dec. 1786, quoted in Patricia Watlington, *The partisan spirit*, p. 119.

[246] Innes to TJ, 30 May 1791.

[247] James Monroe to Archibald Stuart, 14 Mch. 1792, ViHi; see notes 101 and 116. Henry Lee, highly critical of the army contractors, the lack of discipline of St. Clair's troops, and the ineffectual military measures of the government, also urged at this time that cavalry and expert riflemen be employed (Lee to Madison, 17 Jan. 1792, DLC: Madison Papers). Just before St. Clair marched in 1791, Wilkinson gave him this advice: "Believe me, 400 Mounted Infantry would render you more service, than 2000 drafts on foot. It is the display of force made by a body of Horse, and their Capacity for rapid movements, which terrify the Savages and Keep them at a distance" (Wilkinson to St. Clair, 26 Aug. 1791, MHi: Sargent Papers).

[248] TJ to Carmichael, 2 Aug. 1790.

The Treaty of San Lorenzo bears the name of Thomas Pinckney. But just as Alexander Hamilton was the architect of the treaty that bears the name of John Jay, so Thomas Jefferson was the one who planted the seed of that negotiated by Picnkney. In 1800 when the political tide shifted, men in the West joined others in the South—and in the North as well—in supporting one whose aim was to embrace all sectional interests in the overarching common cause. His commitment to the West, prompted by the same concern for the primacy of the national interest that made him a champion of New England commerce and fisheries, was his most important achievement as Secretary of State, both in its immediate political impact and in its far-reaching consequences for the union. For this action, like that of 1803 which permanently settled the question of access to the Mississippi, also involved "the future destinies of this republic."[249]

[249] TJ to Monroe, 13 Jan. 1803.

I. Secretary of State to Juan Nepomuceno de Quesada

SIR   Philadelphia, March 10th. 1791.

We have received with great Satisfaction, Notification of the Orders of his Catholic Majesty,[1] not to permit that Persons held in Slavery within the United States, introduce themselves as free Persons into the Province of Florida. The known Justice of his Majesty and of his Government was a certain Dependence to us, that such would be his Will. The Assurances your Excellency has been pleased to give us of your friendly Dispositions, leave us no Doubt you will have faithfully executed a Regulation so essential to Harmony and Good neighborhood. As a Consequence of the same Principles of Justice and Friendship, we trust that your Excellency will permit, and aid the Recovery of Persons of the same Description, who have heretofore taken Refuge within your Government. The Bearer hereof *James Seagrove Esqr.* is authorized to wait on your Excellency to confer on this Subject, and to concur in such Arrangements as you shall approve for the Recovery of such Fugitives.

I beg you to be assured that no Occasion shall be neglected of proving our Dispositions to reciprocate these Principles of Justice and Friendship, with the Subjects of his Catholic Majesty, and that you will be pleased to accept the Homage of those Sentiments of Respect and Esteem with which I have the Honor to be, Sir, Your most obedient & Most humble Servant

TH: JEFFERSON

PrC (DLC); in Remsen's hand; signature and name of bearer are lacking and are supplied from FC (DNA: RG 59, DCI). Dft (Lloyd W. Smith, Madison, N. J., 1946); lacks signature and name of bearer; numerous interlineations and deletions, one of which is indicated below; date and docketing in Remsen's hand.

1 At this point in Dft TJ first wrote and then deleted: "that no asylum be given within his dominions to."

II. Secretary of State to Edward Telfair

SIR   Philadelphia Mar. 26.[1] 1791.

Your favour of the 2d.[2] of January was received the 4th. instant. The dispositions expressed by the Governour of Florida give reason to hope he will execute with good faith the orders of his sovereign to prevent the future reception within his province of slaves flying from the United States. How far he may think himself authorised to give up those who have taken refuge there heretofore is another question. I observe that the orders he announces to have recieved say nothing of the past. It is probable therefore that an application from us to give them retrospective effect, may require his asking new orders from his court. The delay which will necessarily attend the answer, the doubts what that answer may be, and, if what we wish, the facility of evading the execution if there be a disposition to evade it, are circumstances to be weighed beforehand, as well as the probable amount of the interest which it would be possible to recover. If this last be small, it may be questionable how far the government ought in prudence to commit itself by a demand of such dilatory and doubtful effect. As the President will be at Augusta in the course of the tour in which he is now engaged, you will have an opportunity of explaining to him the extent of the losses complained of, and how far they could probably be recovered, even were the dispositions of your neighbors favourable to the recovery, and what those dispositions may actually be. I have the honour to be with the most perfect respect your Excellency's most obedt. & most hble. servt,

TH: JEFFERSON

RC (NNP); addressed: "His Excellency Governor Telfair at Augusta in Georgia"; franked and postmarked: "FREE" and "MR 26"; originally dated 16 Mch. 1791 (see note 1); endorsed in part: "Ordered to be filed." PrC of RC (DLC). FC (DNA: RG 59, PCC). PrC of Tr (DLC); in Remsen's hand, dated 16 Mch. 1791; with note added by TJ to Washington (see Editorial Note, above). Entry in SJPL reads: "[1791. Mar.] 16. Th: J. to Govr. Telfair. On refugees to Florida."

1 Date changed from 16 to 26 Mch. by overwriting. For explanation of this change, see Editorial Note above.

2 Thus in all texts, an error for 12 Jan. 1791.

III. The President to James Seagrove

Sir,   Augusta May 20th. 1791.

The confidence, which your character inclines me to place in you, has induced me to commit the enclosed letter, from the Secretary of State to Governor Quesada, and the negotiation which will be consequent thereon to your care and management. The letter which is under a flying seal, to be closed before it is delivered, will inform you of the import, and serve to instruct you in the mode of conducting the object of your mission—delicate in its nature, it will require the greatest address and temper in its treatment —nor must any proposition or declaration be made, which in its consequence might commit the government of the United States.

The enclosed copy of a letter, written by my direction, from the Secretary of State to the Governor of Georgia, which is now confidentially communicated to you, is another source, whence some information may be drawn—but, as my ideas of your personal acquaintance with this business combined with my opinion of your character and talents to transact it, have determined me to appoint you, it is from your own knowledge, and the circumstances, which may arise, that you must decide on the best means to accomplish the negotiation.—Your first care will be to arrest the farther reception of fugitive slaves, your next to obtain restitution of those slaves, who have fled to Florida, since the date of Governor Quesada's letter to Mr. Jefferson, notifying the orders of his catholic Majesty. And your last object, which may demand the greatest address, will be to give a retrospective force to the orders of the Court of Spain, beyond the date of that letter, and to procure the Governor's order for a general relinquishment of all fugitive slaves, who were the property of citizens of the United States. This last instruction will require peculiar delicacy, and must be entered on with caution and circumspection, or not be taken up at all, as appearances of compliance may justify the one or the other.

If your collectorate cannot furnish money to defray your Expences, in which you will observe due economy, and of which you will transmit an account to the Secretary of State, you will supply yourself from the Collector of Savannah. I am Sir, Your most obedient Servant   G Washington

FC (DLC: Washington Papers).

IV. Thomas Jefferson to Harry Innes

Dear Sir   Philadelphia Mar. 7. 1791.

Your favor of July 8. came to my hands Nov. 30. The infrequency of conveyances is an apology for this late answer. I receive with pleasure this recognition and renewal of our former acquaintance, and shall be happy to continue it by an exchange of epistolary communications. Your's to me will be always welcome; your first gives me information in the line of Natural history, and the second (not yet recieved) promises political news. The first is my passion, the last my duty, and therefore both desireable. I believe entirely with you that the remains of fortifications found in the Western country have been the works of the natives. Nothing I have ever yet heard of proves the existence of a nation here who knew the use of iron. I have never heard even of *burnt* bricks, tho they might be made without iron. The statue you have been so kind as to send me, and for which I beg you to accept my thanks, would, because of the hardness of the stone, be a better proof of the use of iron than I ever yet saw. But as it is a solitary fact, and possible to have been made with implements of stone and great patience, for which the Indians are remarkable, I consider it to have been so made. It is certainly the best piece of workmanship I ever saw from their hands. If the artist did not intend it, he has very happily hit on the representation of a woman in the first moments of parturition.

Mr. Brown, the bearer of this, will give you the Congressional news, some good, some so so, like every thing else in this world. Our endeavors the last year to punish your enemies have had an unfortunate issue. The federal council has yet to learn by experience, what experience has long ago taught us in Virginia, that rank and file fighting will not do against Indians. I hope this years experiment will be made in a more auspicious form. Will it not be possible for you to bring Genl. Clarke forward? I know the greatness of his mind, and am the more mortified at the cause which obscures it. Had not this unhappily taken place there was nothing he might not have hoped: could it be surmounted, his lost ground might yet be recovered. No man alive rated him higher than I did, and would again were he to become again what I knew him. We are made to hope he is engaged in writing the account of his expeditions North of Ohio. They will be valuable morsels of history, and will justify to the world those who have told them how great he was.—Mr. Brown will tell you also that we are not

[521]

inattentive to the interests of your navigation. Nothing short of actual rupture is omitted. What it's effect will be we cannot yet foretell; but we should not stop even here, were a favourable conjuncture to arise. The move we have now made must bring the matter to issue. I can assure you of the most determined zeal of our chief magistrate in this business, and I trust mine will not be doubted so far as it can be of any avail. The nail will be driven as far as it will go peaceably, and farther the moment that circumstances become favorable. I am with great esteem Dear Sir Your friend & servt,   TH: JEFFERSON

PrC (DLC). Extract (WHi); in hand of Lyman C. Draper, who docketed it in part as follows: "Gen. Clark, but for his intemperance could succeed Gen. Harmar &c."

V. The President to the Secretary of State

Thursday 3 Oclock [10 March 1791]

The P. has given the enclosed letters an attentive reading and consideration, and has found nothing in them but what is *just*, and in the hands of a prudent user *proper*; but at the end of the words of the letter to Mr. C "this wrong" 2d. page 10th. line may it not be well to add—"yet with that prudence and circumspection which will not commit the Government to the necessity of proceeding to extremity"—And may not the expression of the last page be too strong for events and the interest of this Country?—reconsider them.   GW.

RC (DLC); addressed: "Mr. Jefferson"; date established by TJ's endorsement and entry in SJPL: "[Mar.] 10. G. W. to Th: J. on letter to Carmichael. St. Marie's case."

TJ was able to persuade Washington to let the expression on the second page of his letter to Carmichael stand without the serious qualification that is here suggested. It is virtually certain that the passage on the last page also stood unchanged (see notes to Document VI for identification of these passages). See Editorial Note above. TJ, who had every reason to believe that the Spanish ministry would see these instructions before Carmichael did, very probably used this as a persuasive argument against any weakening of the passages. While TJ was minister to France his letters to Carmichael often seemed fashioned less for him than for the Spanish government.

VI. Secretary of State to William Carmichael

SIR   Philadelphia March 12th. 1791

I enclose you a statement of the case of Joseph Ste. Marie a citizen of the United States of America, whose clerk Mr. Swimmer was, in the latter part of the year 1787, seized on the Eastern side of the Mississippi, in latitude 34°-40', together with his goods, of the value of 1980 dollars, by a party of Spanish soldiers. —They justified themselves under the order of a Mr. Valliere their officer, who avowed authority from the Governor of New Orleans, requiring him to seize and confiscate all property found on *either side of the Missisippi below the mouth of the Ohio.*—The matter being then carried by Ste. Marie before the Governor of New Orleans, instead of correcting the injury, he avowed the Act and it's principle, and pretended orders from his Court for this and more. We have so much confidence however in the moderation and friendship of the Court of Madrid, that we are more ready to ascribe this outrage to Officers acting at a distance, than to orders from a just sovereign. We have hitherto considered the delivery of the post of the Natchez on the part of Spain, as only awaiting the result of those arrangements which have been under amicable discussion between us; but the remaining in possession of a post, which is so near our limit of 31.° as to admit some colour of doubt whether it be on our side or theirs, is one thing, while it is a very different one to launch 250 miles further, and seize the persons and property of our citizens; and that too in the very moment that a friendly accommodation of all differences is under discussion. Our respect for their candour and good faith does not permit us to doubt that proper notice will be taken of the presumption of their Officer, who has thus put to hazard the peace of both Nations; and we particularly expect that indemnification will be made to the individual injured. On this you are desired to insist in the most friendly terms, but with that earnestness and perseverance which the complexion of this wrong requires.[1] The papers enclosed will explain the reasons of the delay which has intervened. It is but lately they have been put into the hands of our Government.

We cannot omit this occasion of urging on the Court of Madrid the necessity of hastening a final acknowledgment of our right to navigate the Missisippi: a right which has been long suspended in exercise, with extreme inconvenience on our part, merely with a desire of reconciling Spain to what it is impossible for us to relinquish. An accident at this day, like that now complained of, would put further parley beyond our power; yet to such accidents we are every day exposed by the irregularities of their officers, and the impatience of our citizens. Should any spark kindle these dispositions of our borderers into a flame, we are involved beyond recall by the eternal principles of justice to our citizens, which we will never abandon. In such an event, Spain cannot possibly gain, and what may she not lose?[2]

The boldness of this act of the Governor of New Orleans and of his avowal of it, renders it essential to us to understand the Court of Spain on this subject. You will therefore avail yourself of the earliest occasions of obtaining their sentiments, and of communicating them to us.

I have the honor to be with great Esteem, Sir Your most obedient & most humble Servant,   TH: JEFFERSON

PrC (DLC); in Remsen's hand; lacks signature, which has been supplied from FC (DNA: RG 59, DCI). Enclosure: Memorial of Joseph St. Marie to Winthrop Sargent, 22 July 1790 (printed below).

Although the draft of this letter that TJ submitted to the President appears not to have survived, the passages on the second and third pages of that draft to which Washington objected (see Document v) are easily identifiable. That TJ's original expression was allowed to stand unchanged is certain as to the first modification Washington proposed and virtually so as to the second (see textual notes below). See Editorial Note, above.

[1] This is the passage in the second page of TJ's draft that Washington wished to soften so as not to "commit the Government to the necessity of proceeding to extremity" (see Document v).

[2] These two sentences in the third page of TJ's draft evidently constitute the passage that Washington considered perhaps "too strong for events and the interest of this Country" (see Document v).

E N C L O S U R E

Memorial of Joseph St. Marie

St. Vincennes 22d. July 1790.

Joseph St. Marie of St. Vincennes in the County of Knox in the said Territory, begs Leave to acquaint your Honor that on the 23rd. Day of August 1788 he took the Liberty of addressing a Letter to John Francis Hamtramck Esquire, Major in the First United States Regiment, and commandant at Post Vincennes, of which the following is a Copy.

'Sir,

In Pursuance to the ancient Usage and Custom of this Country, I, in the Month of November last applied for and obtained Leave of Absence on a trading Voyage: in Consequence of which, and of my Right as a Freeman and Citizen of the United States of America, I loaded a Pettiauger with several Goods and Merchandizes to the Amount of five thousand nine hundred and forty one Livres and fifteen Sols in Peltry, Currency of this

Place, equal to one thousand nine hundred and eighty Dollars and forty two ninetieths of a Dollar, and sent them under the Care and Management of my Clerk, Mr. Swimmer, with Directions to proceed down the Missisippi River, and trade them off with the Indian Nations living within the Bounds of the United States of America. Mr. Swimmer accordingly set out and went down that River to a Place called the Chicasaw Lake, which is situate about Ninety Leagues down from the River Ohio, about twenty Leagues higher than where the English Fort of the Arquanças formerly stood, and in about 34° 40′ of North Latitude, according to Hutchins's Map, where he pitched his Camp, on the East, or American side of the Missisippi, in the the neighborhood of some friendly Indians, who were there hunting. Here, after a few Days stay, he was taken up by an Order from Mr. Valliere, the spanish Commandant at the Post of the Arquanças, by a Party of Spanish Soldiers, sent from that Fort, who, at the same Time seized the Pettiauger, and the Goods, and carried them, together with my Clerk, and the other Hands in the Boat, to the Spanish Fort, where Mr. Valliere, the Commandant seized and confiscated the Property, for the Use of the Spanish King, at the same Time informing the men, that his Orders from the Governor of Louisiana, at New Orleans, were express, to seize and confiscate all the Property which might be found on the Missisippi, or on either of it's Shores, any where below the Mouth of the Ohio, and to send the Persons of those with such Goods, Prisoners to him at New Orleans. Being very soon after informed of this Transaction, I went to the Arquanças, and applied to the Spanish Commandant for a Restoration of my Property, who, in very peremptory Terms, refused giving them up, alledging his beforementioned orders, and adding that I might take it as a great Favor that my Clerk, and Hands, as well as myself were not confined and sent in Irons to Orleans as Prisoners. When I reasoned on my Right, as an American Subject, to traffic in the American Dominions, and that my Property was seized in the Territory, to which I conceived America had an undoubted Right, he stopped me short by informing me that the Country on both Sides of the River Missisippi; as high up, as the mouth of the River Ohio belonged to Spain, and that the whole of the Country on the East Side of the Missisippi from the Mouth of Ohio downwards was then under the Spanish Government. Surprised at this Information, and not being satisfied that the Governor had really given such Orders, I went to New

Orleans, and about the Eleventh Day of May last obtained an Audience of the Governor Don Mero who, as soon as informed of my Name, asked me in very haughty Terms, how I could have the Audacity to appear before him on the Subject of the Seizure of my Property; that although I was a Frenchman born, yet that I then was an American Subject, and that if he the Governor was to follow his Orders from the Court of Spain, he would send me Prisoner to the mines of Brazil, and then concluded in a threatening manner, with bidding me depart from thence, and be no more seen, which last Orders I was glad to obey, and withdraw myself as soon and as far as possible from such Despots, without receiving any Satisfaction. Thus circumstanced, my only and last Resource is to the honorable the Congress of the United States of America, as Guardians of the Rights and Liberties of her Subjects, whose Persons have been seized and Properties confiscated on her acknowledged Territory, by an armed Force, in Pursuance to the Orders of a foreign Prince. From the Time that the name of an American has been known in this Country I have been a Subject of the United States; I have fought in Defence of that Country whose Subjects a Spanish Commandant is hardy enough to oppress, and I am now, unless Government interferes, without any Remedy for a Loss which will reduce me with a Wife and a numerous Family to the utmost Distress.

I must beg of you, Sir, to make known my Case to Congress in such Manner as you shall think proper, and as speedily as possible, as in me the Right of Sovereignty of America as well to a very extensive Territory as to the Navigation of the Missisippi, any where below the Mouth of the Ohio, has been invaded: My Cause is become a public Cause, and will, in it's Consequences, determine a grand national Question. I dare hope and Trust, that, as an ancient Inhabitant of this Country, and, as one of the first Subjects of America in it, I shall be thought worthy the Protection of Congress, and that they will adopt some Means to give Satisfaction and Recompence for my Losses. To convince you, and the World of the Justice of my Cause, I propose to make oath before a Megistrate, of the Truth of the whole of the Case, as before stated, and shall, whenever called upon, produce proper vouchers, and Proofs to authenticate the same. I am, Sir, &c, &c.

This Letter was accompanied with the Oath proposed, and with the Invoice hereto-annexed; and also with an affidavit of Mr. William McIntosh, who is now on a voyage, testifying that he had seen and had read to him, by Mr. Valliere, the Spanish Commandant at the Post of the Arquanças the original Letter or Orders from Don Mero, Governor of Louisiana, at New Orleans, directing the said Mr. Valliere to seize and confiscate the Property of all those who should be found on the Missisippi, or on either Shore thereof, from the Mouth of the Ohio downwards as the whole of that Country belonged to Spain. These Letters and Papers Major Hamtramck forwarded to General Harmar, who sent them to Congress. But as they were delivered that honorable Body when their Dissolution was about taking place, and as the many public Affairs, since the Adoption of the New Constitution, have, in a Manner, entirely engaged the Attention of the new Congress, he begs Leave to address himself to your Honor, as vested with the Governor and Commander in Chief's Power in this Country, begging you to lay his Case before Congress and to procure him such Redress, as his distressed Situation as well as that of his Family requires. He also begs Permission to testify the Truth of what is herein before set forth, by his own Oath and he also profers to adduce other sufficient and satisfactory Proofs thereof whenever thereto requested. He begs Leave to subscribe himself, Your Honor's Most obedient and very humble Servant,

JOSEPH ST. MARIE.

PrC (DLC); in Taylor's hand; at head of text: "To the Honorable Winthrop Sargent, Esquire, Secretary in and for the Territory of the United States Northwest of the River Ohio, and vested with all the Powers of Governor and Commander in Chief, &c."; at foot of text is copy of St. Marie's oath taken before Paul and Antoine Gamelin, notaries public, dated 22 July 1790. MS (DNA: RG 59, NWT); text printed in Carter, *Terr. Papers*, II, 288-91). FC (DNA: RG 59, American Letters); with oath taken by St. Marie 23 Aug. 1788. Tr (MHi); containing only St. Marie's letter to Hamtramck. St. Marie's cargo was not one of peltry (Carter, *Terr. Papers*, II, 290, note 67), except in terms of currency, as proved by the "Invoice of the Merchandize &c. that were seized by Orders of Mr. Valliere Commandant at the Arquanças," dated 6 Feb. 1788, covering items used in the Indian trade—6 pieces of stroud, 71 blankets, 2 dozen calico shirts, 1 dozen ruffled shirts, 36 lbs. powder, 130 lbs. ball, 17 dozen large knives, 6 spring clasp knives, 10 looking glasses, lace, ribbon, scarlet cloth, 11 lbs. vermillion, beads, rings, combs, needles, scissors, thimbles, kettles, tobacco, 3200 large silver brooches, "120 pairs small [silver] Ear-bobs," silver bracelets, hair bands, arm bracelets, gorgets, "Ear Wheels," together with articles of use for MR. SWIMMER and the hands —1 pot, 1 axe, 1 tomahawk, 1 tent, 5 bearskins, and "1 Peroque," the whole valued at 5,941.15 livres, "Equal to 1980 Dollrs. 42/90ths." (PrC in DLC).

VII. Secretary of State to William Short

DEAR SIR   Philadelphia March 12th. 1791

The enclosed papers will explain to you a Case which imminently endangers the peace of the United States with Spain. It is not indeed of recent date, but it is recently laid before Government and is of so bold a feature as to render dangerous to our Rights a further acquiescence in their Suspension. The middle ground held by France between us and Spain, both in friendship and interest, requires that we should communicate with her with the fullest confidence on this occasion. I therefore enclose you a copy of my letter to Mr. Carmichael and of the papers it refers to, to be communicated to Monsieur de Montmorin, whose efficacious interference with the Court of Madrid you are desired to ask.—We rely with great confidence on his friendship, justice and influence. A cession of the navigation of the Missisippi and with such privileges as to make it useful and free from future chicane, can be no longer dispensed with on our part: and perhaps while I am writing, something may have already happened to cut off this appeal to friendly accommodation.[1] To what consequences such an event would lead, cannot be calculated. To such very possibly as we should lament without being able to controul. Your earnestness with Monsieur de Montmorin, and his with the Court of Spain, cannot be more pressing than the present situation and temper of this country requires. The case of St. Marie happens to be the incident presenting itself in the moment when the general question must otherwise have been brought forward. We rely on this occasion on the good Offices of the M. de la Fayette, whom you are desired to interest in it.

I am with sincere and great esteem Dear Sir Your most obedient and most humble Servt.   TH: JEFFERSON

RC (DLC: Short Papers); in Remsen's hand except for signature; endorsed as received 28 May 1791. PrC (DLC); lacks signature. FC (DNA: RG 59, DCI). Dft (IHi); in TJ's hand except for date, complimentary close, and docketing, which are in the hand of Remsen. Enclosure: TJ to Carmichael, 12 Mch. 1791 (Document VI and its enclosure), not received by Short when the above letter arrived (Short to TJ, 6 June and 20 July 1791).

Just a week after TJ had given instructions to Short and Carmichael on St. Marie's case, Short's letter of 6 Nov. 1790 arrived with its suggestion that the time was auspicious for determining the attitude of the Spanish court and "that without the U.S. committing themselves at all." TJ immediately seized this opportunity to persuade the President to place the issue not alone on the case of St. Marie but on the "broad bottom of general necessity" (see Documents VIII, IX, and X). It is important to note that TJ had already committed the government on the St. Marie incident and that he did not alter that position at all. Instead, he took advantage of Short's information to try to strengthen the representation of the government through the influence of Montmorin, Lafayette, and the Spanish minister to France, Conde de Fernan-Nuñez.

[1] In Dft TJ first wrote " . . . to cut off the resource of friendly intercourse" and then altered the passage to read as above.

VIII. Secretary of State to the President

Mar. 18. 1791.

Th: Jefferson is sorry to present a long letter to the President to be read at so busy a moment: but the view which it presents of our commercial matters in France is too interesting to be unknown to the President.—The circumstances presented to view in the 2d. page of the letter induce Th: J. to think it may be well to commit to Mr. Short and the M. de la Fayette to press our settlement with Spain on a broader bottom than merely that of the case of Ste. Marie.

RC (DNA: RG 59, MLR); addressed: "The President of the United States"; endorsed by Washington "18th. Mar. 1791 Respecting Commercial Matters in France." FC (DNA: RG 59, SDC). Not recorded in SJL or SJPL. Enclosure: Short to TJ, 6 Nov. 1790, note 1, where the matter "presented to view in the 2d. page of the letter" is identified.

IX. The President to the Secretary of State

March 19th. 1791.

The President concurs with the Secretary of State in opinion that, circumstances make[1] it advisable to commit Mr. Short and the Marqs. de la Fayette to press in a discreet manner our Settlement with the Court of Spain on a broader bottom than merely that of the case of Ste. Marie, and authorises him to take measures[2] accordingly.   Go: WASHINGTON

RC (DLC); addressed: "The Secretary of State"; endorsed by TJ as received 19 Mch. 1791. Entry in SJPL for that day reads: "G. W. to Th: J. on a settlement with Spain." Dft (DNA: RG 59, MLR); containing two differences as noted below; docketed by Lear. FC (DNA: RG 59, SDC); text agrees with RC.

[1] Dft reads "render."
[2] Washington first wrote "write to him" in Dft and then altered the passage to read as above.

X. Secretary of State to William Short

DEAR SIR   Philadelphia Mar. 19. 1791.

Your letter of Nov. 6. No. 46 by Mr. Osmont came to hand yesterday and I have just time before the departure of Mr. Terrasson the bearer of my letter of the 15th. inst. and dispatches accompanying it, to acknowlege the receipt, and inform you that it has been laid before the President. On consideration of the circumstances stated in the 2d. page of your letter, he is of opinion that it is expedient to press at this moment our difference with Spain to a settlement. You are therefore desired, instead of confining your application for the interference of the court of France to the simple case of Ste. Marie, mentioned in my letter of the 15th. to ask it on the broad bottom of general necessity that our right of navigating the Miss[issip]i be at length ceded[1] by the court of Madrid, and be ceded in such form as to render the exercise of it efficacious and free from chicane. This cannot be without an entrepot in some convenient port[2] of the river where the river and sea craft may meet and exchange loads without any controul from the laws of the Spanish government. This subject was so fully developed to you in my letter of   [3] that I shall at present only refer to that. We wish you to communicate this matter fully to the M. de la Fayette, to ask his influence and assistance, assuring him that a settlement of this matter is become indispensable to us,[4] any further delay exposing our peace both at home and abroad to accidents the result of which are incalculable and must no longer be hazarded. His friendly interposition on this occasion, as well as that of his nation will be most sensibly felt by us. To his discretion therefore and yours we confide this matter, trusting that you will so conduct it as to obtain our right in an efficacious form, and at the same time to preserve to us the friendship of France and Spain the latter of which we value much, and the former infinitely. Mr. Carmichael is instructed to press this matter at Madrid, yet if the Marquis and yourself think it could be better effected at Paris with the count de Nuñnez it is left to you to endeavor to draw it there. Indeed we believe it would be more likely to be settled there than at Madrid, or here. Observe always that to accept the navigation of the river without an entrepot would be perfectly useless, and that an entrepot, if trammeled, would be a certain instrument for bringing on war instead of preventing it.—I am with sincere and great esteem Dear Sir &c.   TH: JEFFERSON

Dft (DLC); consisting of text *en clair* of entire dispatch, except for complimentary close and signature, which are supplied from FC; in margin in Remsen's hand: "(This letter was put in Cyphers)"; containing a number of deletions and interlineations, some of which are noted below. RC (DLC: Short Papers); salutation, dateline, and signature in TJ's hand; complimentary close lacking; body of dispatch in code in Remsen's hand, with interlinear decoding in Short's hand. PrC of RC (DLC). FC (DNA: RG 59, DCI). For the identification of the passage in the 2d page of Short's letter, see note 1, Short to TJ, 6 Nov. 1790.

[1] TJ first wrote "acknowledged" in Dft and then substituted "ceded," an alteration perhaps accounted for by the

haste in which TJ wrote. When he developed the case more fully for the United States' position, he was careful to make it a *sine qua non* of the treaty that no phrase be admitted in it "which would express or imply that we take the navigation of the Missisipi as a *grant* from Spain" (TJ to American commissioners, 18 Mch. 1792).

2 TJ first wrote "spot" in Dft and then altered it to "port."

3 Date left blank in all texts, owing perhaps to haste and TJ's habit of keeping his foreign dispatches under lock in his own residence. Remsen thus did not have TJ's letter available as he encoded TJ's text. The allusion is to the letter to Short of 10 Aug. 1790 (Document VI in group of documents on war crisis of 1790).

4 Preceding two words interlined in Dft in substitution for "to our citizens," deleted.

From C. W. F. Dumas

The Hague, *11 Mch. 1791.* Nothing decisive has taken place since his last. The return of spring will tell whether there will be war between Russia and Prussia. The enemies of the latter desire it out of resentment; and the enemies of despotism in general desire it also, in the hope of seeing the two powers weaken themselves. He speaks of the public voice, not that of diplomacy which, especially today, one cannot know what it says, much less what it will say.

"O fortunés les Citoyens des Etats-Unis, qui n'ont ni oligarchie, ni hiérarchie à combattre, ni obéissance passive, ni fanatisme, ni esprit de corps, ni d'autres funestes principes à déraciner, ni d'autre politique à employer que celle de l'équité naturelle et de l'honnêteté mutuelle! Dieu les conserve, avec ceux que leur coeur a choisi et choisira pour être les pères de la patrie!"

The populace and the great, magistrates and others, coaches, horses, and footmen celebrated the 8th of March, each according to his fashion. On the 30th the temples, by supreme command, will withhold acts of grace for the State blessed as a republic. The Bank of Amsterdam has with difficulty kept itself above par. Commerce languishes there. Loans to Russia amount to 30 millions and are well credited because she pays precisely at the time stipulated. And this causes visible pain to the partisans of her rival here.

[P. S.][1] A childish fad has just arrived from England and fascinates the young males and females of a certain class, called "*Joujou de Normandie*" and consisting of two small discs joined with a peg at the center around which a cord rolls and unrolls as the performer in the streets, in coaches, &c., causes it to extend itself and return "en tout sens le *joujou*." The Prince of Wales, they say, is the coryphaeus, being able to keep three *joujous* going at once with his two hands and his mouth, even on horseback. They are sold here at every price according to the value of the materials from which they are made. He concedes that this silliness is unworthy TJ's attention.

P. S. of the 16th. Some informed and trustworthy people have assured him in great confidence that the disaffection among the bourgeoisie at Bois-le-Duc, sustained by a party of the Regency and by all of lowland Brabant, is at its peak and only awaits a spark to explode. The same flame is brooding under the cinders in Friesland and

Overyssel.—The court of Vienna continues to make strong complaints against the government's conduct respecting the Belgian troubles. This causes much embarrassment here and they carefully hide it from the public.—The probability of the pacification of Chistovo descends from one Ordinary to another.—Those of Strasbourg have just elected a professor of their university as bishop.

FC (Dumas Letter Book, Rijksarchief, The Hague; photostats in DLC); at head of text: "No. 75"; with numerous deletions and interlineations. Not recorded in SJL.

The *JOUJOU DE NORMANDIE* was what the English knew at the time as a bandalore (OED) and what is now called by Americans a yo-yo. Dumas' reference to the name of the toy suggests that the *Dictionary of Americanisms* errs in attributing an American

origin to the word and in supposing that it derived from " '*you-you*,' often used by children at play" (*yo-yo* is not included in DAE). The form *yo-yo*, therefore, probably originated in the pronunciation of *joujou* by children of Dutch or German origin in the United States.

[1] This passage was clearly intended as a postscript to the dispatch of the 11th, hence was written after that date and before the 16th.

From William Short

DEAR SIR   Amsterdam, March 11. 1791

A letter which I received by the last post from my Secretary in Paris informs me that the national assembly have changed their decree with respect to the American oils imported into France. On the representation of the committees they have reduced the duty from 12.^{tt} to 6.^{tt} the quintal. I do not find this circumstance mentioned in the journals of the assembly, but he gives it to me as having that moment received it from the member of the diplomatic committee who was most instrumental in obtaining the reduction and who desired him to communicate it to me. The committee were for some time determined to propose the reduction to 8.^{tt} only. The secretary whom I left at Paris urged the reduction to 6.^{tt} with so much force that he at length prevailed on them to risk it. Their greatest objection was the fear of its not passing in the assembly, and that the aversion of the members to change any of their decrees together with so considerable a reduction would defeat the plan altogether. I can have no doubt that this reduction has been decreed, from the manner in which it is communicated to me, still I should have been better satisfied if it had not been omitted in the journal.—The committees calculate that the internal duties hitherto paid on oils and to which the American were subject (independent of the duty of 11.^{tt}5. the barrel on entering the kingdom) were upwards of 5.^{tt} the quintal. By the *arret du conseil*, the duty would have been at present only 7.ᵗ10. the barrel of 500℔. Still the 6ᵗ being in lieu of all other duties is considered as giving greater facilities to the importation of the American oils than they would have had under the former Government.

I received also by the last post an account of some alterations made by the assembly in their decree concerning the importation of tobacco. It is confined to French vessels and those of the country where it is made, except that from the Levant which can be imported in French vessels only. With respect to that made in the United States it must be brought immediately from thence to France. The difference of duty on the article imported in French or foreign vessels remains as when I last wrote to you viz. 6.ᵗ5s. the quintal. The ports at which foreign tobacco is allowed to be entered are very numerous as well in the Atlantic as the Mediterranean and indeed are all where any American vessel would wish to go.

I am making use of the same means to get changed that part of the decree that makes so great a difference between French and American vessels, which I did with respect to the oils. I have long ceased however even attempting to conjecture what the assembly will do in any case. There are many arguments to be used for inducing them to put the vessels of the two nations on the same footing. The objection however which will be constantly made will be the foreign tonnage to which their vessels are subjected with us. They will insist probably on making a similar difference in their ports, but as I am sure that they were surprized into the fixing a difference which exceeds the value of the freight I have some hopes of inducing them to lower it.

Scenes of disorder and riot are exhibited from time to time in Paris of the most alarming kind. The departure of the King's aunts is one of the pretexts. It is not yet known here whether they have been allowed to quit the kingdom. The repairing of the chateau de Vincennes in order to transport there some of those confined in the different prisons of Paris, gave rise lately to a mob which threatened bloodshed between the rioters and the garde nationale. At the same time a number of persons either totally unknown or known as enemies to the present order of things entered in crowds into the King's appartments. It being found that they had arms concealed under their clothes, they were disarmed, and some of them arrested. The reason they give for their conduct is a desire to defend the King whom they supposed in danger in that moment of disorder. It is probable that was the true cause, but many suspect an intention in them to make use of that moment for carrying off the King to some other part of the Kingdom or perhaps out of it.—Such scenes must be expected so long as the present anarchy continues; and it is certain that the assembly either from inability or design do nothing to prevent it.

The Bishop of Spire, one of those foreign princes who suffers by the decrees of the national assembly has refused absolutely to enter into negotiation for an indemnity. The manner in which he has answered the propositions of the minister of France would induce a belief that he counts on being well supported. This however will probably depend on circumstances. The disorders of France may in time beget so much internal discontent as to invite foreign interference, but I cannot think that they would have any thing of that sort to fear if their government were properly organised or order restored. Even the greatest enemies of the revolution wish now for peace and personal security at the expence of the sacrifices they have been obliged to make.

The preparations for defense which the court of Petersburg are now making with much activity, shew that they expect an attack in the north both by land and sea. As yet the scene is not sufficiently unfolded to give a perfect idea of who will be the principal actors. It is said that Denmark insists on being allowed to observe a perfect neutrality and that the urgent applications of England and Prussia have not been sufficient to change their system.

An object of serious negotiation at present is to induce Poland to yield Dantzick to Prussia. There are many difficulties in the way, but they will probably be removed by the influence of England. The inducement held out to Poland is to obtain by this means such a reduction of the transit duties paid to Prussia as to enable them to rivalize Russia in the exportation of naval stores.

I am now signing the obligations as fast as I receive them from the notary who is slow beyond all idea. As soon as they are finished which will be the day after to morrow I shall set out for Paris. I beg you to be persuaded of the sentiments of attachment and respect with which I have the honor to be Dear Sir, Your most obedient & Most humble servant,   W: SHORT

PrC (DLC: Short Papers); at head of text: *"No. 60"*; lacks part of complimentary close and signature, which have been supplied from Tr (DNA: RG 59, DD). Recorded in SJL as received 22 June 1791.

From Thomas Barclay

[*Philadelphia*], *Saturday, 12 Mch. 1791.* Only his inability to sit up kept TJ from hearing from him sooner. He has reflected a good deal on what TJ said about "a Voyage to Africa, which I have concluded to undertake on such Conditions as the President or yourself shall think adequate to my services and expences."—The House some time ago passed a bill granting $2,000 for making the Treaty with Morocco; the Senate doubled this sum, both being exclusive of expenses, but the Senate "made such other alterations in the bill that it was lost."—He will not pretend to say what the allowance should be, but will cheerfully submit to the President's determination in the hope that his temporary absence would not be prejudicial "should he have occasion to make any appointments of greater emolument and duration which I may be thought deserving of."

RC (DNA: RG 59, CD); endorsed by TJ as received 12 Mch. 1791 and so recorded in SJL.

Barclay wrote TJ again on Sunday the 20th, saying that he was improving and could go to town any day after the 21st. He asked TJ to inform him whether his mission to Morocco had been finally determined, how soon it would be necessary for him to embark, and whether TJ desired to see him (RC in DNA: RG 59, CD; endorsed by TJ as received 21 Mch. 1791 and so recorded in SJL). An entry in SJPL shows that TJ had drafted Barclay's instructions on 10 Mch. 1791. These were approved by Washington before he departed on his southern tour, but were not officially transmitted to Barclay for some weeks (TJ to Barclay, 13 May 1791).

To William Blount

Sir   Philadelphia Mar. 12. 1791.

I am honoured with your favour of Feb. 17. as I had been before with that of Nov. 26. both of which have been laid before the President.

Within a few days the printing the laws of the 3d. session of Congress will be compleated, and they shall be forwarded to you the moment they are so.

As the census of all the rest of the union will be taken in the course of this summer, and will not be taken again under ten years, it is thought extremely desireable that that of your government should be taken also, and arranged under the same classes as prescribed by the act of Congress for the general census. Yet that act has not required it in your territory, nor provided for any expence which might attend it. As, however, you have sheriffs who will be traversing their districts for other purposes, it is referred to you to consider whether the taking the census on the general plan, could not be added to their other duties, and, as it would give scarcely any additional trouble, whether it would require any additional reward, or more than some incidental accomodation or advantage, which perhaps it might be in your power to throw in their way. The returns by the sheriffs should be regularly authenticated, first by themselves, and then by you, and the whole sent here as early in the course of the summer as practicable. I have the honour to be with very great esteem & respect, Sir Your most obedt. & most humble servt, TH: JEFFERSON

PrC (DLC); at foot of text: "Governor Blount." FC (DNA: RG 59, PCC No. 120). Blount's letter of 26 Nov. 1790, recorded in SJL as received 23 Dec. 1790, has not been found.

To Alexander Hamilton

DEAR SIR   Philadelphia Mar. 12. 1791.

The President has thought proper to appoint Colo. David Humphreys, minister Resident for the U.S. at the court of Lisbon, with a salary of 4500. dollars a year, and an outfit equal to a year's salary. Besides this, by a standing regulation, he will be allowed his disbursements for gazettes transmitted here, translating and printing papers where that shall be necessary, postage, couriers, and necessary aids to *poor* American sailors. An opportunity occurring, by a vessel sailing for Lisbon within a few days, to send him his commission, I shall be obliged to you to enable me to convey to him at the same time the means of recieving his outfit in the first instance, and his salary and disbursements above described in quarterly paiments, afterwards.

An act of Congress having authorised the President to take measures for procuring a recognition of our treaty from the new Emperor of Marocco, arrangements for that purpose have been decided. The act allows 20,000 Dollars for this object, but not more than 13,000 Dollars will be called for in the first instance, if at all, and these, or the means of drawing for them not till six weeks hence. I thought it proper however to apprise you of the call at the earliest day possible, and while the President is here, and to ask your attention to it. I have the honor to be with sentiments of the most perfect respect & esteem Dear Sir Your most obedt. & most humble servt.,   TH: JEFFERSON

PrC (DLC); at foot of text: "The Secretary of the Treasury." FC (DNA: RG 59, PCC No. 120). See TJ's estimate of expenses on the foreign fund, 18 Mch. 1791.

From Daniel L. Hylton

Richmond, Virginia, 12 Mch. 1791. TJ's of the 1st received three days ago. Has inquired name of vessel and captain carrying vis-à-vis and finds she was forced to go to New York because the Delaware was closed. Bill of lading for vis-à-vis is enclosed; he hopes it has arrived safe and in good order. Not till three days ago could he ship TJ's tobacco, the merchants having generally engaged the vessels to carry wheat before they got to Richmond. Encloses receipt and invoice for 13 hhds. shipped on *Union*, Captain Toulson; he hopes these "arrive safe and to a good Market." The whole of TJ's order would have been shipped had the tobacco been down. Inspectors could not provide information TJ wished about quality and origin of tobacco, but private marks given by government for each hogshead will presumably enable TJ to identify its plantation. He appends note of shipping costs, which TJ can pay by bank note or any other convenient way. Remainder of 20 hhds. will be shipped when it comes down unless TJ advises otherwise. "Mrs. Hylton Unites with me in wishing you every happiness." P.S. *Union* left Rockett's yesterday; did not write by her as this will arrive before she does. Bill of lading for vis-à-vis not sent by this post, the person who shipped it being "out of the way"; he thinks that person said the captain's name was Towles.

RC (MHi); endorsed by TJ as received 22 Mch. 1791 and so recorded in SJL. At foot of text Hylton listed the 13 hhds., each marked "TI," and gave their respective weights. To this TJ added a calculation showing the total weight as 16,744 lbs. He then added: "Warehouse and shipping expenses on 16,744℔. tobacco 22.75 D. Freight @ 3. D. per hhd. 39 [D]."

From William Short

DEAR SIR   Amsterdam March 12. 1791.

I mentioned to you in my letter of yesterday sent by the way of England, the reduction made by the assembly in the duty on oils. The post which arrived last night, after the departure of that letter, brought a journal which contained the decree. It is so concise as to oils that it would appear to me obscure if I did not find that the secretary whom I left at Paris considers it as a substitution for the duty of 12.ᵗ formerly fixed by the assembly. The decree is as follows, copied literally from the journal.

"Sur le rapport fait par M. Vernier le decret suivant est rendu.

Les toiles de chanvre et de lin, importees de l'etranger, seront assujetties au droit de 70.ᵗ le quintal.

Celles importées par terre de la Flandre Autrichienne, et de l'Allemagne seront assujetties au droit de 36.ᵗ le quintal. Et les toiles blanches à 45.ᵗ *Le droit sur les huiles et savons sera de 6.*ᵗ"

The report probably explains this decree so as to shew that the 6.ᵗ are meant to be the only duty paid by American oils and on entering the Kingdom, and that the American are the only foreign oils permitted, agreeably to the late decree which excluded the others.

With respect to tobacco, as the decree stands at present it is permitted to be imported by sea only from the U.S., the Spanish colonies, the Ukraine, and the Levant. From the three first in either French Ships, or those of the U.S. Spain, or Russia respectively according to the place of its growth. From the Levant in French ships alone. The difference of the duty paid on tobacco imported in national or foreign vessels 6.ᵗ5. the quintal. I am endeavoring as I have mentioned in my late letters to get the American vessels put on the same footing with the French as to this article. As I am sure it was not their intention to make this difference greater than the original price of the freight I have hopes of getting them at least to reduce it, perhaps to abolish it (the difference) altogether. This will be the more difficult however on account of the foreign tonnage to which their vessels are subjected in our ports.

I find that the assembly have decreed (upon the proposition of their committee of commerce to whom they had referred the question for deciding what vessels should be deemed French) "qu'à l'avenir les vaisseaux de construction etrangere seront prohibés." They referred at the same time to their committees of commerce and marine some exceptions in favour of merchants who under late laws had purchased vessels of foreign construction, and of foreign fishermen who should come to settle in France.—This is with a view to the Nantucket men.

The Dutch are much alarmed by these proceedings. They had already considered themselves particularly injured by the decree which excluded their tobacco and of course their shipping *quoad hoc*. I find that the article of tobacco grown in this country is much more considerable both as to quantity and value than I had supposed it. It was used principally in the French manufactures.— The Prussian tobacco is excluded also by the late decree. Its quantity and value exported to France was inconsiderable; but the exclusion going to Holland and Prussia shews that the present system of politics adopted by those two countries, had an influence in it.

The reporter of the committee of domains sent me a note by the last post to tell me that the several committees to whom had been referred his former report for the abolition of the *droit d'aubaine* in the French foreign possessions, had all agreed in it, and that he should make their joint report as soon as an opportunity presented itself. As long as there are hopes of this abolition taking place of themselves, I shall withold any application. In this I conform to your idea, which is rendered the more proper by the present jealousy with which the assembly view our access to their islands, and their desire to embarass it as much as possible.

In my letter, private, of Dec. 29. I sent you my several accounts. Among the copies which I kept I do not find that as chargé des affaires. It is possible therefore that the original may have been omitted also. For greater certainty I have made it out again and send it inclosed. It is settled up to July 1, 1790, agreeably to your desire. I find the copy of the account in detail of the two articles making 537.^{tt}9. Of course the original was sent with my private of Dec. 29. to which also I beg leave again to refer you for the article which follows of ƒ.665.12.

This letter will be sent by an American ship which is here and will contain one for the Secretary of the Treasury. The bonds are signed and I leave this place to-morrow for Paris. When there I shall be better able to judge of the real situation of the affairs of that country. At present I can not do better than to send you the following extract of a letter received from the Secretary whom I left at Paris. I have already told you that he is a man much to be relied on and enjoying fully the confidence of M. de la fayette. I must add also that he is in general subject to be easily alarmed and of course that some allowance must be made for that disposition in the writer. The letter is dated March 7. 91.

"Les journées sont orageuses. Jamais les partis n'ont eu un développement si violent. Depuis leur derniere avanture (the entering armed into the King's appartments as mentioned in my last) les aristocrates sont dans une fureur qu'ils ne cherchent point à dissimuler. L'interieur des Thuilleries est en combustion. Les Jacobins et 89 (two clubs composed of the popular part of the assembly) se livrent un combat à mort. Pendant ce tems là on a de justes allarmes sur les rives du Rhin. Un courier arrivé hier m'apprend qu'il y a un corps de 5000 hommes rassemblé en Souabe près Basle, que l'on recrute à force chez le Margrave de Bade, qu'à Carlsruhe et Worms on ne parle que d'invasion, que Cobourg annonce ouvertement qu'il va commander une armée, que toute l'Alsace se defie de plusieurs des commandants militaires, et que l'ennemi entretient des correspondances allarmantes et presque à découvert avec les factieux de l'interieur. Les insurrections les plus violentes menacent ici, nous ne pourrons éviter une explosion ces jours-ci et elle pourra être terrible. S'il se fait une invasion, on ne peut prevoir combien de têtes tomberont. M. de la fayette est maintenant en bonne posture, mais l'assassinat le menace de tous les côtés. Jacobins et Aristocrates dechainent contre lui tous leurs coupes-jarrets. Dans l'affaire de Vincennes (mentioned in my last) il a pensé deux fois être tué."

Two persons have been arrested in Alsace recruiting troops for what they call l'armée des Princes. It becomes every day more probable that the discontented joined by whatever troops they can collect, will enter France and seize on some frontier place. The object will be probably merely to feel the pulse of the people and to retire if they find it unsafe to advance. In such a case much is to be apprehended for the Queen's life. After such a calamitous scene, should it take place, it is impossible to say what would be the denouement, but certainly terrible.

I recieved advice a few days past only of the exequatur on the consular commissions for Bordeaux, Marseilles and Havre being at length obtained. The difficulty proceeded from the suppression of the place of Grand Admiral.

Mr. Skipwith wrote to me from Martinique in Sep. last to desire I would take measures for procuring an exequatur also for him. His letter came lately to my hands. He says the consular convention is unknown to the public officers there and that they can give him no information of the steps he should take to be properly recognized. I mentioned to you in my letters from Paris, the conversations which I had had with M. de Montmorin and Rayneval on this subject. I hope I shall ere long hear from you in consequence of what I then said. It would have been useless to have forced a decision at that moment. The whole turns on the explanation of the word *Etats du Roi*. I wish to know how far you desire the interpretation you mention to be insisted on, and when. I am persuaded that the assembly in their present disposition with respect to our access to their islands, would not hesitate by a decree to abolish the convention if the word *Colonies* had been inserted. When their government becomes organised so as to subject them to some kind of responsability to public opinion it will be otherwise.

I find here that some merchants of Baltimore in conjunction with an house here have sent vessels to the French islands with cargoes which they intend to vest in sugars to be sent immediately here. One, or more, of these vessels is expected here daily. It will increase the jealousy and ill humour which already exist in the national assembly towards us on this subject.

I inclose you a letter from one of the American captives at Algiers. I know nothing further on their subject and have no information with respect to the ransom mentioned therein. I observe by the newspapers, that the bankers have received here that you have made a report to Congress on this subject, but as they did not recieve the report with their other papers I know nothing respecting it.

The last letter which I have had the honor of recieving from you, except a short one by Mr. Donald, was dated Sep. 30. As it answered one which accompanied my No. 33. I take it for granted it was recieved also. From that number I am as yet without knowlege of any written since being recieved. This circumstance makes me fear that many of them must have miscarried. I beg you to be persuaded of the sentiments of attachment & respect with which I have the honor to be Dear Sir, your most obedient humble servant   W: SHORT

PrC (DLC: Short Papers). Tr (DNA: RG 59, DD). Recorded in SJL as received 21 June 1791.

Short's letter to the Secretary of the Treasury, with various enclosures, is that of 11 Mch. 1791 (Syrett, *Hamilton*, VIII, 170-9).

To James Brown

DEAR SIR   Philadelphia Mar. 13. 1791.

A former letter to Mr. Andrew Donald having miscarried, perhaps from a wrong address, as I know not his residence, I take the liberty of putting the inclosed under cover to you and asking the favor of your care of it as it is of some importance.—My information from Marseilles is that wheat finds a good market there, and will do so till harvest. I am Dear Sir Your most obedt. servt,

TH: JEFFERSON

PrC (MHi). Enclosure: TJ to Donald, 13 Mch. 1791, printed below. TJ's former letter to Donald was that of 7 Nov. 1790.

To Andrew Donald

SIR   Philadelphia Mar. 13. 1791.

I have recieved your favour of Feb. 15. 1791. Of the many others you say you have written, none have ever come to hand but that of   1790.¹ which finding me at New York, it was impossible for me to answer it till I could return to Virginia where all my papers were. On my return there, I wrote you an answer dated [7 Nov. 1790]² and, as you had not informed me where to address the letter to you, I governed myself by a newspaper advertisement and addressed it to you at Osborne's. Not knowing what else to do with the present, I shall inclose it to Mr. Brown of Richmond, presuming he will know where you are to be found. I inclose you a copy of my former letter, which contains an answer to so much of yours of Feb. 15. as relates to my own account. As to Mr. Wayles's, Mr. Eppes of Chesterfeild is the only acting executor, my absence and avocations putting it out of my power to interfere in the affairs of the estate, otherwise than by paying my quota of any debts acknowleged and assumed by Mr. Eppes. I am Sir Your very humble servt,   TH: JEFFERSON

PrC (DLC); not recorded in SJL. Enclosure: Copy of TJ to Donald, 7 Nov. 1790.

Donald's letter of 15 Feb. 1791 is recorded in SJL as received on 4 Mch. 1791, but has not been found. None of Donald's letters has been found and only two were recorded in SJL: that of 15 Feb. 1791 and another of 10 May 1794, the latter being recorded in SJL as received on 27 May 1794. See TJ to Donald, 7 Oct. 1791 and 28 May 1794.

¹ Blank in MS; the date of Donald's letter was prior to 1 Sep. 1790, when TJ left New York.
² Blank in MS.

To James Innes

DEAR SIR   Philadelphia Mar. 13. 1791.

Your favour of Feb. 20. came to my hands only four days ago, and I have taken the first moment in my power to prepare my answer, which I now inclose. It is in fact a copy of what I had prepared while in Virginia, when I had the subject under contemplation, except that some useless asperities are rubbed off. I am in hopes either Mr. G. Carr, or Mr. Anderson of Richmond has given you a copy of my opinions of June 20. 1783. and Sep. 28. 1790. wherein I have cited the cases upon which I ground my defence for my nephew. I consider that of Powis & Corbet 3 Tr[acy] Atk[yns] 556. as establishing a rule of construction peculiarly applicable to our case and decisive of it.

What is said with you of the most prominent proceedings of the last Congress? The disapprobation of the assumption with you leads us naturally to attend to your reception of laws for carrying it into effect, which have been thought to present themselves in an unfavourable view.—What will be thought of measures taken for forcing Gr. Britain, by a navigation act, to come forward in fair treaty, and let us substantially into her islands, as a price for the advantages in navigation and commerce which she now derives from us? This is interesting to our agriculture provided the means adopted be sufficiently gradual. I wish you would come forward to the federal legislature and give your assistance on a larger scale than that on which you are acting at present. I am satisfied you could render essential service, and I have such confidence in the purity of your republicanism, that I know your efforts would go in a right direction. Zeal and talents added to the republican scale will do no harm in Congress. It is fortunate that our first executive magistrate is purely and zealously republican. We cannot expect all his successors to be so, and therefore should avail ourselves of the present day to establish principles and examples which may fence us against future heresies preached now, to be practised hereafter. I repeat my wish that I could see you come into the federal councils; no man living joining more confidence in your principles and talents to higher personal esteem than Dear Sir Your most obedt. humble servt,

TH: JEFFERSON

PrC (DLC); at foot of text: "Colo. Innes." Enclosure: TJ's copy of his opinion prepared while in Virginia—presumably that of 28 Sep. 1790—has not been found.

The nephew involved in this case, for which TJ prepared opinions on 20 June 1783 and 28 Sep. 1790, may have been Dr. Philip Turpin, who spent the war years in England and was assisted by TJ in regaining his rights as a citizen (see note, TJ to Turpin, 29 July 1783). Innes' FAVOUR OF FEB. 20. is recorded as received 9 Mch. 1791 but has not been found. The case of Powis v. Corbet was argued before Lord Chancellor Hardwicke on 6 Aug. 1747. The court, acknowledging it to be law that a mortgagee who was also a bond creditor could attach the bond to the mortgage as against an heir since, assets being descended, neither obligation could be discharged without paying off the other, declined to apply the rule in this instance because there were "intervening incumbrancers of a superior nature between his mortgage and the bond" (James Tracy Atkyns, *Reports of cases . . . in the High Court of Chancery*, III [Dublin, 1779], 556; see Sowerby, No. 1754).

For some of the factors leading TJ to desire westerners to add their weight to the republican side of the scale in Congress, see Editorial Note, group of documents on the new policy toward Spain, 10 Mch. 1791.

The Great Collaborators

I. THOMAS JEFFERSON TO JAMES MADISON, 13 MARCH 1791

II. JAMES MADISON TO THOMAS JEFFERSON, 13 MARCH 1791

EDITORIAL NOTE

I shall see you at dinner, and be glad to exchange further
thoughts on the subject, which is an important one.
—*Jefferson to Madison, 1 Jan. 1791*

The subject of that day's dinner conversation—the French protest
against the tonnage acts of 1789 and 1790 and its impact on the political contests that were dividing the government[1]—was indeed important. But not a word exchanged between the Virginia Congressman and the Secretary of State on that winter day has been preserved.
What Madison—and of course Jefferson—gained then and later in their
"hour[s] of unbent conversation" at the dinner table was a loss of incalculable proportions to the historical record.[2] When the two men were
separated by the Atlantic Ocean, as they were during the five creative
years from 1784 to 1789, their exchange of letters constituted one of
the most luminous commentaries on the American political scene that
would be vouchsafed to posterity. Madison's remarkable letter apprais-
ing the work of the Federal Convention of 1787, written at a time when
his labors in that body had left him physically exhausted, and Jefferson's examination of the concept that the earth belongs in usufruct
to the living, written less as a letter to Madison than as advice to
moderate revolutionists in France, are only two examples of the sort
of enlightenment their separation would provide for later generations.[3]
But in the periods when they saw each other almost daily, as at Philadelphia during the crucial years when Jefferson was Secretary of State
and he and Madison were engaged in constant, confidential, and unalterable opposition to the drift of Hamiltonian policies, their exchange
of views was generally unrecorded. Such few notes as passed between
them during this critical period when they were emerging—Madison
in the House of Representatives and Jefferson in the Cabinet—as the
recognized spokesmen for the mounting opposition to Federal measures contained, for the most part, comments about such matters as payment for a horse or attempts to settle a debt owed to their friend
Philip Mazzei.[4]

Yet nothing is clearer than that their collaboration, based on uniquely
complementary traits of personality, intellectual discipline, and talent
for leadership, was as harmonious as it was enduring, whatever the
shifting crises of affairs or whatever the accidents that brought them
together or kept them apart. No other political relationship in American
history can be compared with theirs, either in the qualities of mind

[1] See Editorial Note, French protest on tonnage acts, 18 Jan. 1791.
[2] Document II.
[3] Madison to TJ, 24 Oct. 1787; TJ to Madison, 6 Sep. 1789.
[4] TJ to Madison, 20 and 23 Sep. 1790; 15 Dec. 1790; 10 and 12 Jan. 1791;
Madison to TJ, 24 Sep. 1790.

and character brought to it, the uninterrupted harmony of purpose, the elevation of discourse, or the profundity of commitment to fundamental republican principles. After the departure of Franklin and with the single exception of John Adams, no other American of this enlightened generation could rightfully claim to be their peer in general intellectual attainments and in their knowledge of the history and practice of government. Both, in a sense that Adams and Hamilton never could be, were political realists. Being disciplined both in mind and purpose, neither could engage in such acts of caprice or vanity as made Adams so politically vulnerable or in the romantic delusions and misconceptions of the character of the American people that wrecked Hamilton's ambitions. Jefferson, usually regarded as less pragmatic than Madison, was most effective in diplomacy and administration, where patience and persuasion—two of his most pronounced qualities—could be brought to bear with success. Madison, through the power of his intellect and his skill in debate, was most effective as legislator. At this particular juncture, ironically finding themselves situated in two branches of government that were supposed to operate as a check on each other, they were able to unite their variant and complementary talents in a manner that makes the absence of a recorded collaboration all the more unfortunate. But despite this hiatus in the record, it is beyond question that on every important aspect of domestic and foreign policy Jefferson's reports to Congress and to the President were the administrative counterpart of Madison's legislative maneuvers, all aimed at validating the propositions of self-government that had been declared at the outset and that, as both men believed, were now being challenged by heresies or abandonment on the part of some high in government.[5]

It was just at this moment that, as many feared, the policies advocated by Madison and Jefferson seemed about to succeed. Just a week after the Secretary of State invited Madison to share his household—an invitation that Madison prudently declined for political as well as other reasons[6]—a writer in the *Maryland Journal* pointed to the two statesmen as exemplars of youth:[7]

> Keep always before your eyes the steps by which a Jefferson and Madison have gradually ascended to their present pre-eminence of fame. Like them you must devote your whole leisure to the most useful reading. Like them you must dive into the depths of philosophy and government . . . keeping and holding fast, as to the rock of your political salvation, their unshaken integrity and scorn of party.

But at this moment, too, Hamilton and the supporters of the British interest in the United States provided the essential counterpoint by viewing their two chief opponents as dangerous threats rather than exemplary leaders. The British agent Beckwith, as much influenced by the

[5] For their collaboration on such questions as the constitutionality of the residence and bank bills, diplomatic and commercial relations with Great Britain, trade with the Mediterranean, the fisheries, and the French protest on the tonnage acts, see Editorial Notes and documents under 15 July 1790, 29 Aug. 1790, 15 and 28 Dec. 1790; 18 and 24 Jan. 1791; and 1 Feb. 1791.
[6] Document II.
[7] 22 Mch. 1791, quoted in Brant, *Madison*, II, 336.

opinions of those with whom he was privately consulting as was the French chargé,[8] reflected such views when he reported to his government that the talents of George Washington were much overrated, that his administration was divided by two parties led by Hamilton and Jefferson, that the President usually cast his influence first to one side and then to the other in order to maintain harmony, and that, in the spring of 1791, the influence of the Secretary of State seemed to be in the ascendant.[9] Almost at the same moment Quaker merchants of Philadelphia, perhaps not knowing that Hamilton and his supporters had already sent urgent messages to the British ministry, were voicing similar warnings. Hawkesbury's corn bill with its provision for free warehousing of grain for export, which aroused the hostility of Lord Sheffield as much as it did the American Secretary of State, produced this reaction from an American merchant:[10]

> We are very busy on this side framing new Commercial regulations and Laws, in which we Copy after 'our old Stepmother.' The new Congress meets the last week in October, when it is expected the Navigation Act will be thoroughly discussed and settled, the leading features are, to prevent all intercourse with those West Indian Islands, that do not admit American bottoms—To prevent Foreign Vessels from [carr]ying hither the produce of countries to which said vessels do not belong, &ca.—In short *it is seriously determined in our Cabinet* to prohibit [as] much as possible all trade with England, and to encourage that with [Fr]ance, notwithstanding the difficult Task of altering the Channel in [whic]h we have run for a Century. Therefore beware of provoking us by your too rigorous Laws and let us . . . have half a loaf if you cannot have a whole one.

Such concerns as these may have led Beckwith to take lodgings in Mrs. House's boarding establishment occupied by Madison and other members of the Virginia delegation. He may indeed have been prompted to make such a move. Beckwith apparently had been disinclined to go to Philadelphia when the government moved there, hoping instead to keep in touch with the Secretary of the Treasury through correspondence. But Hamilton had advised against this because of the danger of exposure of his confidential relationship with the agent. In any event Madison, who knew how to keep his counsel even when approached by such an opponent of Hamilton as Senator Maclay, did not leave when

[8] See Editorial Note, French protest on the tonnage acts, 18 Jan. 1791.
[9] Beckwith to Grenville, 11 Mch. 1791 (PRO: FO 4/12, f. 76-81).
[10] "Extract of a Letter from Philadelphia March 18th 1791," emphasis supplied; accompanied by another extract of a letter from New York, 15 Mch. 1791, warning that the adoption of the corn bill would produce similar restraints in the United States (Liverpool Papers, XXXVII, f. 85, British Museum, Add. MSS 38,227). See also Edgar Corrie to Hawkesbury, 18 Oct. 1791, enclosing an extract of a letter from James & Shoemaker of Philadelphia, 10 Oct. 1791, which warned: "We regret that partial local motives should lay general commerce in fetters. The numerous general regulations made by the different European powers it is expected will induce Congress to meet them with others for the benefit of our own trade" (same, f. 98). See Editorial Note, at 15 Mch. 1791.

Beckwith moved in.[11] Aside from the impropriety of an abrupt departure at his arrival, Madison explained to Jefferson, he was surrounded by his books and papers and desired to complete the "little task" which he had allotted himself. That comment, expressed in what Beckwith repeatedly described as a critical moment for the British interest in the United States, reflects the confidence with which Madison and Jefferson viewed their situation. They knew how the South and the West felt about the assumption, the bank, and the excise and they were on the point of departing for New England to learn more about the attitude of the people in that region.[12] They were well aware of the formidable nature of the obstacles they had to contend with, but confident enough to occupy themselves with private concerns.

In declining the invitation because of the "little task," Madison was naturally aware that the allusion would be understood. He also knew, as did Jefferson, that this task was very far from being inconsequential. For there can be little doubt that Madison was now turning his attention to one of the most important documents of modern history—his meticulous record of the debates of the Federal Convention, set down in the midst of the epochal proceedings in which Madison established his right to be regarded as the foremost framer of the fundamental law. These notes, compiled in Jefferson's view "with a labor and exactness beyond comprehension," also established Madison's unrivalled primacy as reporter of the Convention.[13] His unparalleled achievement in reporting was not disclosed to the world until 1840, but, immediately on its publication, "all other records [of the Convention debates] paled into insignificance."[14] However, after Farrand published his *The Records of the Federal Convention* in 1911 and expressed the opinion that Madison had revised and corrected his notes after the publication of John Quincy Adams' *Journal . . . of the Convention* in 1820 and was misled both by the inaccuracies of that official document and by an aging memory, the general reliability of Madison's notes came under question.[15] The indiscriminate doubts should have been set at rest two decades later when Charles R. Keller and George W. Pierson published their revision of the accepted view. For in this excellent example of editorial scholarship, the authors demonstrated that in the autumn of 1789 Madison had borrowed from Washington the manuscript journal of the Convention kept by its secretary, William Jackson; that in September and October of that year he had copied the whole in a meticulously exact transcription; and that his purpose in doing so was to supplement his own far superior notes of debates and, most important of all, to compare and correct the latter whenever the opportunity occurred.[16] Keller and Pierson also proved that the intended comparison was indeed carried out within a few years after Washington had permitted Madison

[11] Maclay, *Journal*, ed. Maclay, p. 199-200.
[12] See Editorial Note, group of documents on northern tour, May 1791.
[13] TJ to John Adams, 10 Aug. 1815. Madison's *Debates* first appeared in *The Papers of James Madison*, ed. H. D. Gilpin (Washington, 1840).
[14] Farrand, *The Records of the Federal Convention*, I (New Haven, 1911), xv.
[15] Same, I, xv-xviii, especially note 20.
[16] Charles R. Keller and George W. Pierson, "A New Madison Manuscript relating to the Federal Convention, 1787," AHR, XXXVI (Oct. 1930), 17-30.

to transcribe Jackson's manuscript journal that had been left in his custody "to be kept sacred until called for by some competent authority."[17] For, as they indicated, among the mass of corrections, interlineations, and insertions in the text made by Madison in the course of revising his own notes, there were some twenty-two slips pasted over his original text and containing alterations made in the light of his collation of that document with Jackson's journal. Their conclusion that many of these and other revisions were made by Madison "at a very early date, either during the winter of 1789 or within a few years thereafter" when his memory was still fresh and selective was fully justified by the evidence.[18]

On the basis of this important revisionist study and in the light of other evidence not then available, it is now virtually certain that such a comparison and revision, involving the pasted slips with their corrections of his own notes, constituted the "little task" Madison had set himself. This was almost the first time since he copied Jackson's manuscript journal that he had been free enough of exacting legislative and other duties to face such an undertaking. The debates on the bank bill had elicited a reference to arguments in the Federal Convention over the power to charter corporations, a fact which may have influenced Madison to take up the deferred task. Also, in view of the general tendency of federal measures, colliding in so many respects with positions taken by Hamilton, Jay and himself in *The Federalist*, it is quite understandable that Madison should have desired no longer to postpone the comparison and corrections of his notes that had caused him to transcribe Jackson's journal in the first place. It is natural, too, that he should have informed Jefferson of the existence of his manuscript record of debates and that, exhibiting toward him the same implicit confidence that had caused Washington to entrust to his care Jackson's official journal, he should have made these notes available to him. Keller and Pierson, knowing that Madison had allowed Jefferson to make a copy of his notes but not having that text available, assumed that it was executed after Jefferson had resigned as Secretary of State and retired to Monticello.[19] The assumption was mistaken, but the inference derived from it—that, if Jefferson's copy ever came to view,

17 Madison to TJ, 4 Apr. 1796.
18 Keller and Pierson, AHR, XXXVI (Oct. 1930), 27, 28.
19 Same, p. 24-5. The authors based their assumption upon an exchange of letters between Madison and TJ in 1795-1796 (Madison to TJ, 8 Nov. 1795; 4 and 18 Apr. 1796; and 1 May 1796; TJ to Madison, 19 Apr. 1796). The letters cited prove (1) that Madison lent TJ some unidentified "papers"; (2) that he did not then have his notes of debates with him in Philadelphia; (3) that TJ did have his copy at that time; (4) and that Madison desired him to verify a particular point by reference to "my notes." This exchange indicates that the unidentified papers did in fact include Madison's manuscript that TJ referred to as "the Conventional history." It is possible that TJ had borrowed it in order to complete his copy, for, as Keller and Pierson state on the authority of Madison's marginal comment in his notes, Eppes did not transcribe the proceedings in Convention from 21 June to 18 July inclusive (same, p. 25, note 27). But as indicated below—and indeed in Eppes' letter to Madison, 1 Nov. 1810, which referred to the "papers . . . I possessed in Philadelphia" (Farrand, *Records*, III, 417)—TJ's copy was made by Eppes while he was studying in Philadelphia from May 1791 to Apr. 1793.

it would be found to include the texts of many of Madison's revisions on the pasted slips, together with other insertions—is well founded.

For the fact is that Jefferson's copy has subsequently appeared and it does indeed include many of Madison's revisions made after he had transcribed Jackson's journal.[20] This copy, transcribed by John Wayles Eppes and corrected by Jefferson, was evidently made soon after Madison finished his "little task" in the spring of 1791. Within a month after the present exchange of letters, young Eppes arrived in Philadelphia to begin his studies. He remained there for two years before returning to Virginia, but it was probably during the summer of 1791 that Jefferson charged him with the task of transcribing Madison's revised notes of debates in the Federal Convention. In mid-May, just as Jefferson was on the point of departing with Madison on their journey up the Hudson, he reported to Eppes' parents that the young man was engaged in his studies and that, besides two to four hours of regular courses and four hours spent reading law, he would "write an hour or two [each day] to learn the stile of business and acquire a habit of writing, and . . . read something in history and government."[21] Among the copying assignments that Jefferson gave his nephew were some of his own letters as governor of Virginia and such contemporary documents as the speech of the Seneca chieftain Cornplanter "To the great Councillor of the thirteen fires," George Washington.[22] But the most important of all tasks of transcribing and the most privileged reading in history and government that could have been given to this youngster on the threshold of manhood was that of copying a document so important in the political development of the nation that, despite urging, Madison steadfastly refused to allow it to be published until after his death.

In bestowing this high privilege, Jefferson left young Eppes in no doubt about the sacredness of the trust. "When the papers relating to the proceedings of the convention were put into my hands for the purpose of being copied," Eppes wrote almost two decades after the event, "Mr. Jefferson was very particular in his charge. I understood from him perfectly that it was a trust entirely confidential. The particular and confidential manner in which he entrusted them to me prevented my making the smallest extract from any part of them—and so careful was I of preserving sacred a document the importance of which to posterity I could not but feel, that I never suffered the papers to mix either with my own or any others entrusted to my care. They were kept in a Trunk in which whenever I ceased writing they were replaced and each original as copied was returned with the copy of Mr. Jefferson. . . . I did not even consider myself at liberty to mention that a copy of the debates of the convention existed."[23]

[20] The MS of Eppes' transcript, with corrections in TJ's hand, is in MHi: Edward Everett Papers; PrC in NN. The Editors are indebted to Ralph Ketcham, Stephen T. Riley, and the late William W. Crosskey for calling this long unidentified transcript to their attention.

[21] TJ to Francis Eppes, 15 Apr. 1793.

[22] Eppes' transcript of the speech delivered by Cornplanter on 1 Dec. 1790 is in DLC.

[23] John Wayles Eppes to James Madison, 1 Nov. 1810 (Farrand, *Records*, III, 417-18).

The trust was indeed a great one, but Jefferson's confidence in his nephew was fully merited. Having himself as a youthful lawyer transcribed and preserved many of the manuscript laws of Virginia and having devoted most of his adult life to collecting books, manuscripts, and paintings pertaining to the history of America, Jefferson may indeed have persuaded Madison to permit him to take a copy of this extraordinarily important manuscript. He had just publicly acclaimed Ebenezer Hazard's publication of the first collection of American state papers, warning that time and accident were daily committing havoc on the original records in the public offices and advising that, instead of consigning the remainder to the waste of time, these should be preserved "by such a multiplication of copies, as shall place them beyond the reach of accident."[24] One may easily imagine how, in their hours of unbent conversation at table, Jefferson could have urged such a precaution upon Madison with respect to this record of such transcendent importance. But Madison also had a sense of obligation to history and could have needed little prompting to provide for the safety of his manuscript. This was in fact the reason that Jefferson was allowed to take a copy. The papers were communicated to Jefferson, so Madison later reminded him, in order that "copies in your hands might double the security against destructive casualties."[25] It is not surprising that Madison should have taken such precautions, for it was his profound respect for the claims of history that had made him decide at the outset to record the debates. Toward the close of his life, he explained that his study of the deficiencies of ancient and modern confederacies had led him to try to preserve "an exact account of what might pass in the Convention, with the magnitude of which I was duly impressed." Nor, he added, "was I unaware of the value of such a contribution to the fund of materials for the History of a Constitution on which would be staked the happiness of a young people great even in its infancy, and possibly the cause of Liberty throughout the world."[26]

The confidences expressed at table where the two great collaborators planned their administrative and legislative opposition to any departure from such high purposes were also important, but these were lost to history. Ironically, it was the disappearance for over a century of Jefferson's copy of the notes that, in some measure, contributed to the ill reward bestowed upon Madison by the posterity whose claims he defended in such acts of devotion and self-sacrifice. The principal argument invalidating the doubts later erected on the supposition that Madison's alterations in his manuscript were the product of an aged memory was provided by Madison himself when, having just discharged his duties as a legislative leader engaged in transforming a plan of government into a reality, he imposed upon himself the exacting task of making his record of the debates of 1787 as complete and as accurate as possible. But it was the fortuitous arrival of young Eppes in the capital, coupled with the desire of his

[24] TJ to Hazard, 18 Feb. 1791.
[25] Madison to TJ, 17 July 1810.
[26] Madison's preface to his notes of debates (Farrand, *Records*, III, 550).

uncle to instruct him in history and in affairs by assigning him important documents to copy, that produced the transcript which amplifies Madison's argument and renders it conclusive. When the original manuscript compiled in 1787 and the incomplete copy executed between 1791 and 1793 eventually receive the careful editorial analysis that their importance merits, Madison's preeminence as the most complete and most reliable recorder of the proceedings of the Federal Convention should be as undisputed as his role of principal architect of that landmark in the history of government.[27]

[27] Such a study, in connection with the preparation of a revised edition of Farrand's *The Records of the Federal Convention*, is now in progress by Leonard Rapport, who first called the Editors' attention to the important article by Keller and Pierson (AHR, XXXVI [Oct. 1930], 17-30).

I. Thomas Jefferson to James Madison

TH: J. TO J. M.   Mar. 13. 1791.

What say you to taking a wade into the country at noon? It will be pleasant above head at least. The party to finish by dining here. Information that Colo. Beckwith is coming to be an inmate with you, and I presume not a desireable one, encourages me to make a proposition, which I did not venture as long as you had your agreeable Congressional society about you, that is, to come and take a bed and plate with me. I have 4. rooms of which any one is at your service. Three of them are up two pair of stairs, the other on the ground floor, and can be in readiness to recieve you in 24 hours. Let me intreat you, my dear Sir, to do it, if it be not disagreeable to you. To me it will be a relief from a solitude of which I have too much: and it may lessen your repugnance to be assured it will not increase my expences an atom. When I get my library open you will often find a convenience in being close at hand to it. The approaching season will render this situation more agreeable than 5th. street, and even in the winter you will find it not disagreeable. Let me have I beseech you a favorable answer to both propositions.

PrC (DLC).

Madison was living at this time at Mrs. House's boarding house, which was the center for the members of the Virginia delegation in Congress. Beckwith had been in Philadelphia at least since the beginning of the year and, after most of the members of Congress had departed, he may have chosen Mrs. House's establishment in order to be near Madison as the leading opponent of Hamiltonian policies in the House of Representatives. Both TJ and Madison had kept the British agent at a distance but, with Washington's approval, TJ would soon transmit a private message to Beckwith through Madison. See TJ to Washington, 27 Mch. 1791.—In referring to the opening of MY LIBRARY, TJ did not allude to the unpacking of his books brought from France, but to the book room then under construction (see TJ to Leiper, 19 May 1791).

II. James Madison to Thomas Jefferson

MY DEAR SIR   [Philadelphia, 13 March 1791]

Your first proposition having been arranged, I have only in answer to your last to acknowledge that I feel all the inducements you suggest and many more to be in a situation where your society would make a part of my hourly enjoyments. In making the sacrifice therefore you will be assured that the circumstances which determine me are unaffected. My stay here is so uncertain and limited that a removal would scarcely be justified by it. I am just settled in my harness for compleating the little task I have allotted myself. My papers and books are all assorted around me. A change of position would necessarily give some interruption— and some trouble on my side whatever it might do on yours. Add that my leaving the house at the moment it is entered by the new member might appear more pointed than may be necessary or proper. As the weather grows better I shall however avail myself of it, to make some amends to myself for what I lose by yielding to these circumstances by seeing you more and using oftener one of your plates. Being never more happy than in partaking that hour of unbent conversation and never more sincere than in assuring you of the affection with which I am Yrs

J. MADISON JR

RC (DLC: Madison Papers); addressed: "Mr. Jefferson"; late in life when Madison received his letters back from TJ, he assigned this one the erroneous date "1790." Its correct date is established by TJ's letter of this date to which it is a reply and by entry in SJL recording its receipt on 13 Mch. 1791.

From Robert Montgomery

Alicante, 13 Mch. 1791. Refers to his of 21 Aug. 1790 and encloses letter from Algiers received yesterday. All is quiet in this quarter. Situation of Turks becomes daily more critical, according to best accounts from Constantinople. A very large Turkish vessel bound from Algiers to Constantinople captured lately by Russian cruiser. She was loaded with military stores and very large sum of money to pay troops. The few corsairs not in Turkish service are not able to keep at sea in winter, but as soon as weather is mild three or four may be generally expected on coast from Alicante to Genoa.

RC (DNA: RG 59, CD); endorsed by TJ as received 2 July 1791 and so recorded in SJL.

From Tench Coxe

[*Philadelphia*, *14 Mch. 1791*]. As result of conversation with Attorney General this morning, he submits to the Patent Board an advertisement George Parkinson is willing to publish. It places before all affected by his patent "the several objects, and the most minute information can be obtained from the drawings, model and descriptions which remain in the office of State."—He was again so unfortunate as to receive among the Treasury letters one for TJ and did not notice address until first part of contents showed it was not intended for that office. He will hereafter take precaution of going over all addresses before opening letters and asks TJ's indulgence for "this inadvertence."

He has seen letters of 1 and 3 Jan. by British packet and learns that "they are reforming their laws relative to the corn trade. A measure which has occasioned opposition is likely to be adopted. The priviledge of storing foreign Grain imported in British bottoms is likely to be given free of expence in the King's warehouses. The tendency of this measure is to deprive our Ships of the Carriage. This is verified by the writer requesting his correspondent here to prefer British Ships. The duty on foreign flour is to be 1/ per bble; it was lately less than 3d. All the ports of the Kingdom to be open and shut according to the Medium price *of the island* not of the *counties* as heretofore."

RC (DLC); endorsed by TJ as received 14 Mch. 1791, but inadvertently recorded in SJL under 13 Mch. 1791.

From James Currie

Richmond, *14 Mch. 1791*. Introducing his particular friend Col. [John] Hamilton, British consul in Virginia, "who with his Lady and pleasing female friend Miss Coxe are on their way to Philadelphia."

Relying on TJ's friendship, he takes liberty of enclosing two bills of exchange of John Tayloe Griffin drawn on Richard Potter of Philadelphia. "After they have been presented by you or under your Auspices (for which I have a very particular reason and which shall be afterwards properly explained to you) I shall be glad and particularly obliged to you to be informed immediately of the result." He has paid and cancelled TJ's note to Colo. Braxton. P.S. The letter of advice from Griffin to Potter promised for tonight will come by next post "as the Gentleman has sailed to Night."

RC (DLC); addressed in part: "Hond. by Jno. Hamilton, Esqr."; at foot of text in TJ's hand is the following: "at 3 mo. 2372. D. [at] 6 mo. 2400. D."; endorsed by TJ as received 20 Mch. 1791 and so recorded in SJL.

On the next day Currie wrote TJ to explain that the above was written in such haste that he forgot to endorse Griffin's bills. He enclosed the second of exchange properly endorsed and asked that TJ return the two first by Hamilton if not already presented. He explained and hoped TJ would "pass over" this liberty: Potter's situation was so distressed that he feared this long overdue debt would be lost, hence "it struck me the Bills being presented under your Auspices would give them a fairer chance for acceptance and ultimate payment as the Gentleman R. P. has effects (papers) of Griffin's in his hands." The promised letter of advice is enclosed. It was accompanied by "one to me to this purpose. 'Extract. As my friend in Philadelphia seems extremely unwilling to part with my property there without my being present and as I wish this business to be upon a certainty shall be oblidgd to you to request the person to whom they are sent, not to present them till I get to Philadelphia which will be about the middle of april when I expect they may be taken up at sight. It will make no difference, as they are not drawn at so many days sight but after date.'" Currie thought this would be hazardous and begged TJ as a particular favor to act as speedily and decisively as he thought proper to secure the debt. He thought the fewer who knew of the bills the better, as there were numerous demands on Potter. He added: "Your note to Braxton I took in when I paid Rickett the Bank Bill and likewise took his receipt. All your friends here are well" (Currie to TJ, 15 Mch. 1791; RC in DLC; addressed and postmarked; endorsed by TJ as received 23 Mch. 1791 and so recorded in SJL).

To Francis Eppes

DEAR SIR   Philadelphia Mar. 14. 1791.

Your favor of the 6th. came to hand two days ago. I heartily congratulate you on the success of your sale. It will determine me to make a decisive stroke in the same way next winter. I will banish the idea of making two bites *at a cherry*. I had desired Mr. Lewis to give Dobson an order on Wilson for about £160 of the money in his hands, which with Bannister's debt I supposed would pay off Dobson. As the balance, over and above the £100 received, of Bannister's will much about replace what you have advanced of Mr. Wayles's money to Dobson, is that balance likely to come in time to answer the purposes of Mr. Wayles's administration? If it is, it will be a convenience to me to continue the appropriation I had made: if not, I will write to Mr. Lewis to make provision for reimbursement in another way.—I have ordered a specimen of my tobo. to be brought here, and have hopes of a very advantageous sale, if the quality suits, as seems probable. In that case I shall order the whole here, and it will completely cover Hanson's and Lyles's demands of this year.—I am now in readiness to receive Jack, and should have written to you sooner, but that the President had asked me to go with him as far as Georgetown to assist in what he has to do there. In that case I should have proposed to Jack either to meet me there, or at Monticello, to which I had a thought of making a flying trip. Other business however, supervening, detains me here: so that the sooner Jack can now come the better. He had better not bring a servant from Virginia, as he will be sure to leave him immediately. I am in hopes you will signify to me your general views and wishes with respect to his future destination, that I may guide his studies accordingly. He will come I presume in the stage, and land at the tavern where that stops. There he will be directed to find me in Market street No. 274. Present me most affectionately to Mrs. Eppes. How or when I am to see her next, god knows. She seems to consider herself as immoveable; and my visits to Virginia being annual, my horses fatigued by the time I get there, and needing rest for their return, and my time short, stand much in the way of seeing her at Eppington. However I must hope that the one side or the other will be able to step aside from their system. I love to persuade myself she will retain dispositions to do it. My love to all the young people, and to those of Horsdumonde when you have an opportunity. The President will return probably through that neighborhood in May or June. Perhaps he may beat up their quarters. I am Dear Sir with great & sincere esteem Your affectionate friend & servt,   TH: JEFFERSON

PrC (DLC). Eppes' FAVOR OF THE 6TH., dated at Richmond, is recorded in SJL as received on 12 Mch. 1791 but has not been found.

From Thomas Mann Randolph, Jr.

DEAR SIR   Monticello March 14. 1791.

Altho the letter carrier between Charlottesville and Richmond is continued in his employment, the conveyance is extremely irregular. He has no fixed day of departure from his own habitation which is about 15 miles from Charlotteslle. but sets out as it suits him on Wednesday, Thursday or Friday, and keeps the letters in his hands frequently 3 days after his return. When the Weather is bad he sometimes misses a week and even 2 or 3 as in December last, if it should be inconvenient to him to perform the journey. I am afraid it will be difficult to establish it on a better footing as there are few of those by whose contribution the expence must be defrayed, who ever think of the advantages of a ready and certain communication.—I am extremely anxious to attempt a determination of the question concerning the Opossum and have begun to make preparations for it. I have had the Wolf which you saw, at Monticello sometime and have just sent it down the country to a gentleman who promises to exert himself in endeavoring to procure the Hybrid animal between it and the common Dog. It is by no means untractable, is extremely fond of being caressed and provokes attention by the same arts as a Spaniel. It is maintained allmost entirely on vegetable food and from its feeding readily and heartily on Persimons, appears not to be entirely carnivorous in its wild state. It wants alltogether the *Bark* of the Dog and has much less command over its tail which points out a difference in the muscles of those parts. It was extremely shy of approaching cows or horses, paid no attention to calves or hogs but was very eager and alert in the pursuit of fowls, which places it in point of boldness and rapacity much below the European Wolf. As soon as we have procured a litter of Mongrels, I shall attempt to investigate the anatomical distinctions between it and the dog, if I should not be able to get another before.

I have begun to keep a Diary and endeavor to render it more complete by inserting Zoological and Botanical observations.

The satisfaction I feel at a new instance of your kindness is heightened by the anticipation of the pleasure I shall receive from the perusal of Buffon and the *Encyclopédie*.

Patsy and Polly are in very good health, and the little one increases rapidly in size and strength. Patsy's plan of nurture, when not opposed by Mrs. Flemings prejudices, has corresponded nearly with Dr. Gregories from the first. Now it is brought as near as possible.

We are in hopes that a flying trip from Georgetown will give us the pleasure of your company at least for a few days. I am Dear Sir your aff. & obedt. Servt.,

THOMAS MANN RANDOLPH

RC (ViU); addressed: "Thomas Jefferson Sec: of State Philadelphia"; postmarked: "FREE" and "RICHMOND March 26"; endorsed by TJ as received 1 Apr. 1791 and so recorded in SJL.

To George Wythe

DEAR SIR   Philadelphia Mar. 14. 1791.

I am really ashamed to be so late in acknowleging the reciept of your favor of Jan. 10. which came to hand the 2d. of February. But during the session of Congress the throng of business was such as to oblige me to suspend all my private correspondence. Their recess now enables me to resume them.

I think the allusion to the story of Sisamnes in Mr. West's design is a happy one: and, were it not presumption for me to judge him, I should suppose that parties pleading before a judge must animate the scene greatly. Usage seems to justify the naming the state on the exergon, tho the emblems are, as they should be, so peculiar as to explain the country to which the design belongs, to those acquainted with it. But your seal may go to those who know nothing but the *name* of the country. The term 'commonwealth' distinguishing the stile of the three great members of our union (Massachusets, Pennsylvania, and Virginia) from that of the smaller ones, which call themselves 'states,' it may not be amiss to change the word 'state' into 'commonwealth' in the exergon.—I have enquired into the shops of mathematical instruments here: they are but two, very illy furnished, and very dear. They ask a clear profit of 50. percent on their articles purchased in London. And as you may get them thence within two months as soon as from hence, I presume you will prefer it. Should you think otherwise I offer my services to execute your commission which it will give me pleasure to do.

Supposing that a glance of the eye over some of the tables of the inclosed report may give you a moment's amusement, I inclose you one, together with a corrected sheet of that on weights and measures. I am with the most cordial esteem & respect Dear Sir Your friend & servt,   TH: JEFFERSON

PrC (DLC). Enclosures: (1) TJ's report on fisheries, 1 Feb. 1791. (2) Printed copy of "Postscript" to TJ's report on weights and measures, 10 Jan. 1791 (see Vol. 16: 674-5; TJ had previously sent a printed copy of the report itself, acknowledged in Wythe to TJ, 31 Aug. 1790).

For the STORY OF SISAMNES, see note to Wythe to TJ, 10 Jan. 1791. The Virginia legislature on 27 Dec. 1790 authorized Wythe, judge of the High Court of Chancery, to have a seal executed for the court "according to a design laid by him before" the General Assembly and appropriated £25 for the purpose (Hening, XIII, 147; on 3 Nov. 1792 the legislature made a further appropriation of £20 for this purpose; same, p. 542). Neither the dies nor any impressions of the seal appear to have survived.

Search for a European Concert on Navigation Law

The Appeal to France, Spain, and Portugal

I. THE SECRETARY OF STATE TO WILLIAM SHORT, 15 MARCH 1791
II. THE SECRETARY OF STATE TO DAVID HUMPHREYS, 15 MARCH 1791
III. THE SECRETARY OF STATE TO WILLIAM CARMICHAEL, MARCH 17 1791

EDITORIAL NOTE

I have ever wished that all nations would adopt a navigation law against those who have one, which perhaps would be better than against all indiscriminately, and while in France I proposed it there.
—Thomas Jefferson to Tench Coxe, 21 Sep. 1807

In March 1791 the anxiety that Hamilton and his supporters felt about the threatened enactment of a navigation bill at the next Congress was matched by Jefferson's fear that the sheet anchor of the commercial connection with France was about to give way.[1] On both sides the apprehensions were fully warranted. Also on both sides preparations for the coming contest were under way. For his part, Jefferson took the unusual step of transmitting, through Otto, a confidential message to the French ministry to the effect that the bill would probably be adopted, but that this would be difficult to accomplish if France engaged in commercial reprisals.[2] Also, undoubtedly with the approval of the President, he prepared the dispatches to Short, Humphreys, and Carmichael that are here presented. These represented an extraordinary effort to redress the European balance of power by a concerted challenge to Great Britain's dominion of the seas. Offering nothing more than the proposed American example, Jefferson pledged no commitment and sought no joint agreements. His ultimate goal was universal reciprocity, but the weapon that he now recommended to France, Spain, and Portugal was one copied from the English model.

In arguing that the commercial interests of these nations coincided with those of the United States and that the proposed bill was worthy of adoption by all, Jefferson characteristically shaped each letter of instructions in accordance with his estimate of the recipient. To Short, in whose ability and discretion he had full confidence, he went so far as to suggest a means of influencing the internal legislation of another country—an act whose diplomatic impropriety Jefferson tacitly

[1] TJ to Short, 15 Mch. 1791 (Document I). For a discussion of the conflict over Madison's navigation bill, see Editorial Note, commercial and diplomatic relations with Great Britain, at 15 Dec. 1790.
[2] See Editorial Note, French protest against the tonnage acts, at 18 Dec. 1790.

admitted in his injunction to Short to conceal its origin. Nevertheless, such was his confidence in the American chargé, Jefferson then authorized him to employ any better means of achieving the desired end. To Humphreys, whose talents he valued less than Washington did, Jefferson merely stated the objective and advised him to consult and be guided by the Chevalier de Pinto, whom he knew and respected. To Carmichael, in whom he placed little if any trust, he wrote so fully, explicitly, and candidly that there can be little doubt he did so in the belief that the Spanish court would see the contents of the dispatch before the American agent did.[3] These dispatches were a calculated extension of the domestic political strategy that Madison and Jefferson had concerted. But within a week after they had been drafted, a fortuitous occurrence enabled Jefferson to utilize the public press in advancing this idea of a European concert. This opportunity came with the timely appearance of Tench Coxe's refutation of Lord Sheffield's *Observations on the commerce of the American states*. Coxe's first number was published in Mathew Carey's *American Museum* and the author transmitted a copy to the Secretary of State.[4] Jefferson at once seized the opportunity and gave counsel to Coxe that is obvious even though unrecorded. The fact that he did not acknowledge this first essay—especially at a time when Jefferson was relying upon the Assistant Secretary of the Treasury for information of all sorts[5]—itself indicates that a personal and private conversation about it must have taken place.

Indeed, it is possible that Jefferson himself had inadvertently stimulated Coxe to undertake such a rebuttal when, shortly before Congress convened, he sought to borrow from him the latest edition of Sheffield's treatise, together with Bryan Edwards' reply to it.[6] A more compelling stimulus may have been provided when Madison's navigation bill was referred to Jefferson by the House of Representatives, a narrow but serious defeat for Hamilton's supporters in Congress. When this happened, Coxe immediately volunteered his services in collecting any materials that might be useful in the investigation of foreign restrictions on American commerce. He was also bold enough to ask what "points of enquiry" Jefferson intended to develop. The very next day, without pausing for a reply, he forwarded some notes on the subject that he said had been "prepared at the request of the Chairman of the Navigation Committee."[7] Two such committees had been designated at the final session of the First Congress. The first, headed by Elias Boudinot, was directed early in the session to bring in legislation on navigation and commerce, but it had reported no bill and was finally discharged. The second, of which the chairman was Benjamin Goodhue, promptly reported Madison's navigation bill after Washington had reported the failure of the mission of Gouverneur

[3] Documents I, II, and III.
[4] Coxe to TJ, 20 Mch. 1791.
[5] See Editorial Note on TJ's relations with Coxe at this time, at end of Jan. 1791.
[6] TJ to Coxe, 30 Nov. 1790.
[7] Coxe to TJ, 4 and 5 Mch. 1791.

Morris.[8] Coxe obviously referred to Boudinot's committee, for the undated manuscript of his "Thoughts on the Navigation of the United States" that he sent to Jefferson was composed, at least in part, before the second committee had been appointed.[9] It is plausible to suppose, however, that, instead of acceding to a request as he claimed, Coxe had voluntarily submitted his paper to Boudinot, as he certainly did in sending it to Jefferson.

His proposals repeated much that he had already advocated in his publications. They were also broadly inclusive, calling for aid to shipping, support for manufactures, encouragement of the fisheries, and the inauguration of such improvements as canals, lighthouses, fortifications, naval hospitals, and even "nautical schools." Some of Coxe's suggestions were advanced for the time, but the very comprehensiveness of his proposals robbed them of the kind of direct, concentrated thrust that characterized the efforts of Madison and Jefferson to counter British restrictions on American trade. Such a broadly encompassing approach to this major problem of foreign policy was typical of Coxe's style.

Yet, buried in his diffuse catalogue of remedies, was the essential element of Madison's navigation bill. This is not surprising, for the precise terms of the bill had been published and its principle had long been the subject of public discussion. Indeed, the Annapolis Convention which Coxe had attended as a delegate from Pennsylvania was the direct result of a demand for some such countervailing legislation. But the closing passage of Coxe's paper, which bears clear evidence of having been added to the manuscript as it stood when submitted to Boudinot's committee, seems shaped particularly for Jefferson's attention. While the principle of Madison's navigation bill had been almost casually included in the main body of Coxe's proposals, the addendum advanced to new and bolder ground. Describing that principle as the confining clause or regulation by which imports would be restricted to American bottoms or those of the nation producing the goods, Coxe applied it directly to Great Britain in a manner that he had been careful to avoid in that part of the paper intended for Boudinot's committee. There he had emphasized the kind of aids to American navigation that would not be offensive to other nations. But in the addendum, in words that could scarcely have enlightened Jefferson and Madison about the consequences of the navigation bill that Hamilton and his supporters now feared would become law, he elaborated the obvious. The proposed regulation, he pointed out, would deprive British shipping of the right to import "all China goods, all East India goods, all melasses, coffee, cocoa and other articles from the French West Indies, all goods from Amsterdam or Rotterdam, that is all goods from Holland, all french brandies, wines, fruits, &c." Then, after calling attention to the probable effect on British shipping of one important provision already enacted into law—the surcharge of 10% on duties levied on goods imported in foreign bottoms

8 JHR, I, 73, 338, 354, 376, 379, 385, 388; see Editorial Note, commercial and diplomatic relations with Great Britain, at 15 Dec. 1790.
9 Printed above as enclosure to Coxe to TJ, 5 Mch. 1791.

—Coxe added this astonishing suggestion as the final paragraph of his manuscript: "Were France, Spain and Portugal to adopt the *confining regulation*, the carrying trade of the world would sustain a considerable revolution, and, consequently, considerable effects would be produced upon the balance of *naval* power."[10]

It is difficult to believe that Coxe could have submitted this final suggestion to a legislative committee made up largely of Hamilton's supporters and so much under his influence that it had refused to report a navigation bill even when directed to do so.[11] It is important to note that this idea—an unequivocal challenge to Great Britain's naval supremacy—was one that Coxe had never advanced in any of his previous publications. Since the suggestion concerned the internal arrangements of other nations, it was not immediately germane to his subject, the defining of a commercial policy for the United States. Coxe did not elucidate, but with these few words pointing to a possible revolution in world trade he closed the paper originally framed for a Congressional committee and to which he placed an addendum shaped especially for Jefferson's attention. This brief, climactic paragraph, unheralded by anything that preceded it, is all the more noteworthy because it was an epitome of the instructions that, within a fortnight, Jefferson sent to American representatives abroad.

This immediately raises the question whether Coxe's hint prompted Jefferson's bold move. In the absence of any written comment by Jefferson, the answer must remain in the realm of conjecture. But it is extremely unlikely that Coxe, whose commercial views derived largely from his experience as a merchant, could have brought a new and unanticipated possibility to the attention of the Secretary of State, whose long years as legislator and diplomat had schooled him to think of commerce in terms of national policy. Through his natural cast of mind and temperament, aided by close study, Jefferson habitually sought to anticipate the course of events and to hold himself in readiness for the auspicious moment, having learned from Solon that a prudent statesman should attempt no more than the nation would bear.[12] As early as 1785 he had expressed the hope that France, Spain, and Portugal would repeal "their navigation clauses except as against Great Britain"—a hope based on his conviction that navigation laws should be specifically directed against those having them, not against all indiscriminately.[13] Whether or not he shared at that time John Adams' optimistic belief that other nations would follow the example if the United States retaliated against the British navigation act, Jefferson had gone as far as possible in trying to achieve reciprocity in trade relations with France and other countries.[14] He had even proposed a treaty providing for reciprocal exchange of the rights of citizens, regarding this as an advance over the customary most-favored-nation provisions and therefore as an indirect countervailing measure against

10 This paragraph is identified in textual note 2, Coxe to TJ, 5 Mch. 1791.
11 See Vol. 18: 232-3.
12 TJ to Walter Jones, 31 Mch. 1801.
13 TJ to Coxe, 21 Sep. 1807.
14 John Adams to TJ, 5 Nov. 1785.

Great Britain.[15] Indeed, on every aspect of liberal commercial policy Jefferson's views had been formed and consistently supported for years before he became Secretary of State. It is therefore implausible to suppose that, given his fixed commercial system and Coxe's rather variable political principles, the suggestion in the somewhat incongruous closing paragraph of Coxe's paper was something Jefferson had not theretofore considered. On the contrary, it is probable that Coxe made the suggestion because he knew it to be an idea Jefferson already had in contemplation. Such a supposition is compatible with Coxe's well-recognized artfulness in cultivating the favor of those in authority. It is also supported by the circumstances surrounding the publication of his reply to Sheffield's *Observations*.

The first number of Coxe's *Brief examination* appeared, as its opening statement declared, at a "season . . . interesting and critical" when the future commercial policy of the United States was about to be discussed. The opponents of an American navigation bill aimed at Great Britain, fearing that the Secretary of State was gaining a dominant influence in the administration, were agreed about the critical nature of the situation. They were in fact at this moment in such a state of anxiety that they urged the British agent, George Beckwith, to return to England immediately in order to convey to the ministry their sense of urgency and their need for support against Jefferson's policies.[16] It was at this juncture, two weeks after Congress adjourned, that Jefferson received the first number of Coxe's reply to Sheffield. In his accompanying letter, Coxe made some revealing disclosures. He first indicated that his plan was limited in scope: he would add only "a couple of numbers more" and not even these, he implied, unless the duties of his office permitted. He also explained that he had adopted "a dispassionate Manner . . . as it might become known that the papers were written by a person in a public Situation." Perhaps for the same reason he was disinclined, he said, to appear in "the Gazette," having chosen instead the *American Museum*. His calling attention to this avoidance of Fenno's *Gazette of the United States*, a paper zealously committed to Hamiltonian policies, may have been intended to create a favorable impression upon the Secretary of State, as perhaps it did. Jefferson must certainly have approved the dispassionate manner, the appeal to ascertained facts, and the reasoned effort to show that the British government had "exceedingly miscalculated with regard to the United States in some essential particulars."[17] There is no evidence that he acknowledged receipt of the essay, but it can scarcely be doubted that he regarded it as a far more timely and useful document than the discursive "Thoughts on the Navigation of the United States" that Coxe had sent him two weeks earlier. Despite the absence of any written response, it seems clear that Jefferson consulted

[15] See TJ's plan of such a treaty, enclosed in TJ to Adams, 28 July 1785; see also, TJ to Vergennes, 20 Nov. 1785; TJ's report of conversations with Vergennes, enclosed in TJ to Jay, 2 Jan. 1786.
[16] Beckwith to Grenville, 11 Mch. 1791 (PRO: FO 4/12, f. 76-81).
[17] Coxe to TJ, 20 Mch. 1791, enclosing the first number of his *Brief examination*, as published in *American Museum*, IX (Mch. 1791), 121-6.

Coxe, encouraged him to proceed, and indeed guided him in his approach to this central question of foreign policy.

This is indicated first of all in the abrupt change that Coxe made in his plan of publication. Though he had said that he intended to give "any future numbers" to the *American Museum*, his first essay, with a few slight modifications, was soon reprinted in Andrew Brown's *Federal Gazette*. Brown, who had benefited from Jefferson's recent report and whose paper was becoming more and more hostile to Hamiltonian measures, introduced Coxe's first number with this statement: "The importance of the following essay will, we presume, be a justification of our conduct in appropriating to it a considerable part of this day's Gazette."[18] The concluding part of the essay appeared on the following day, the 5th of April. On the 6th Brown devoted two full pages of his paper to the second number, which had not yet been printed in the April issue of Carey's *American Museum*. In an explanatory note in that issue, Carey said that "a circumstance of importance, which rendered it unadvisable to wait for the appearance of the Museum, induced the writer to publish that number in a newspaper."[19] So far as is known, neither he nor Coxe gave any hint as to the cause of this sudden change in publishing plans. The sense of urgency that this implied had been wholly lacking in Coxe's letter of two weeks earlier transmitting the first number of Jefferson. Also, his disinclination to patronize Fenno's *Gazette* now became all the more pointed because he had turned to Brown's newspaper. What, then, was the circumstance of importance that prompted this change? The answer is suggested by the obvious difference between Coxe's first and second instalments, another and more important departure that pointed to Jefferson's influence.

Coxe's first number had assumed no position with respect to American commercial policy, being devoted instead to the argument that the British government had been misled by the doctrines of Lord Sheffield. It made no reference to the navigation bill that had been referred to Jefferson and of course it did not comment on the subject broached in the remarkable closing paragraph of Coxe's "Thoughts on the Navigation of the United States." But the second number, which was obviously written late in March after Jefferson had seen the first, presented a remarkable contrast. As if to emphasize the change, the editor of the *Federal Gazette* prefaced that number with another comment: "*The length of the following Essay has obliged us to omit various articles of intelligence, advertisements, &c. But its importance will, we conceive, be considered by our readers as a sufficient apology.*"[20] Coxe began this essay as dispassionately as the first, avoiding suggestions about American policy and limiting himself to observa-

[18] *Federal Gazette*, 4 and 5 Apr. 1791.
[19] Both the second and the third numbrs of *Brief examination* were published in *American Museum*, IX (Apr. 1791), but with the third preceding at p. 177-83 and the second following at p. 217-26; Carey's explanatory remark is at p. 177. The reversed order may have been caused by this shift in publication of the second number to the *Federal Gazette*.
[20] *Federal Gazette*, 6 Apr. 1791.

tions on the increasing productions of such articles as lumber, coaches and carriages, and various iron and steel manufactures. But he then challenged Sheffield's assumption that the British navigation laws would cripple the American carrying trade, declaring bluntly that the private shipping of the United States did not depend on British laws. As for the fisheries, he asserted that the tables accompanying the report of the Secretary of State clearly proved that America was "not dependent on Great Britain for that branch of commerce." So also British laws could have no operation on the coasting trade, already employing over a hundred thousand tons of shipping and certain to increase. The same was true of American "commerce with the Baltic and the North, with the Netherlands, the Hanse Towns, France, Spain, Portugal, the streights, most parts of Africa and India and the colonies of the European nations." Moreover, American imports from Great Britain would decline not only because of her expanding trade with other countries and her development of new manufactures and resources: they would suffer also because of "further commercial acquisitions from liberal foreign nations." If British exports should be reduced to an amount equivalent to the rice, tobacco, and other articles needed for English consumption, then those articles would "not be shipped indirectly to foreign countries thro British ports, as is now the case." Other causes of the existing preponderance of imports from Great Britain—private debts owed by Americans to British merchants and lack of equivalent credits extended by merchants of other countries—would be removed. The arguments were such as Jefferson had repeatedly made while minister to France.

In addition to these reasons for anticipating a decline in British shipping employed in American trade, Coxe then pointed to a still greater threat. This, he said, had not sufficiently engaged the attention of the British government and he warned that it was a force capable of producing "considerable effects."[21]

The regulations of the British navigation act do not appear to have been duly examined by other powers with a view to the adoption of such of them, as will apply beneficially to their own affairs. If they have had effects so favourable to the shipping and naval power of Britain, it is possible they may be in a greater or less degree beneficial to other countries. The present appears a fit season for such an examination, and *we cannot suffer, if we enter on it with temper and discretion.* That it would diminish the number of British vessels, for example, if the United States and all other maritime countries should deem it expedient to enact into a law of their respective nations the clause of the British statute, by which the importation of all foreign goods is confined to native bottoms, and to those of the nation producing the articles, cannot be doubted. Whether this regulation will be convenient to the United States—to France—to Spain—to Portugal—to Russia—to Prussia who, exporting twenty or thirty times the bulk of goods that Great-Britain ships, do not enjoy a part of the carriage for foreign nations equal to what she

21 Emphasis in original.

possesses, is a question those nations are severally to consider and determine. Facts in the meantime are interesting.

The facts that Coxe presented were all calculated to drive home a single point. In 1772, he pointed out, the Baltic trade had employed 6,680 vessels. Of these 1,894 were of British registry and only 45, or about 1.5% of the whole, were French, Spanish, Portuguese, and Russian. "The commodities carried thither (in addition to their own manufactures)," he added, "were the produce and fabrics of all the countries of Europe and of the East and West-Indies, which by their navigation act could not have been imported into Great-Britain in like manner." So also with the cargoes brought away. Elsewhere the statistics revealed similar results. In 1788 there were 351 British vessels trading in Lisbon, but only 283 belonging to Portugal, a maritime nation thus subordinated to Great Britain "in her own metropolis and emporeum." In 1787 a total of 252 British vessels entered Cronstadt, the port of St. Petersburg, while "those of Russia, tho' in her own capital, were only 12, of Spain six, of Portugal two, of Hamburg and Bremen five." As for the United States, Coxe concluded, "We have recently seen that the British have supplied themselves and the other nations of Europe with cargoes of our commodities amounting to 225,000 tons, while those Europeans carried for themselves no more than one sixth of the quantity." This final statistic summarized what Jefferson had recently made public in detailed form in his report on the fisheries.[22]

Coxe disavowed any intention of discussing "the policy of adopting so momentous a regulation as that alluded to, observations on which are rendered peculiarly delicate by the situation in which it is placed by the national legislature." He did not say what the situation was or indicate its most obvious fact, the referral of Madison's navigation bill to the Secretary of State. Instead, he gave this oblique hint: "The instance, it is conceived . . . will forcibly inculcate the utility of the examination [by other powers of the advantages of applying British regulations to their own situation] . . . and will lead to useful reflexions on the consequences, which such an examination may induce." No informed reader of the *Federal Gazette*, least of all Alexander Hamilton and George Beckwith, could have failed to grasp the meaning of these words—that, as Jefferson had confidentially informed the French chargé only two days earlier, a navigation bill would be proposed and almost certainly adopted at the next session of Congress, and that European powers, with a view to their own national interests, might well consider the principle of the British navigation act which that bill would embrace.[23] This was plain enough, considering the situation in which the matter had been left by Congress. But Coxe stressed the point: "The facts . . . appeared too serious, and important to Americans, and to foreigners not to be adduced." He closed on a conciliatory note, pointing out that it would be equally the interest of Englishmen "to consider the effects of such an examination of the British trade

[22] See TJ's report on the fisheries, 1 Feb. 1791, Appendix 17.
[23] Otto to Montmorin, 4 Apr. 1791 (DLC: Henry Adams Transcripts).

laws, and of those who are not. The convictions, which such an enquiry, made with judgment, would create in the minds of candid men, would probably be, that Great-Britain cannot make her ships the carriers for the United States, and that rather than make the attempt, it would be better far to commence the formation of liberal arrangements solidly founded on the mutual interests of the two nations."

What Coxe's second number thus so unexpectedly introduced at this critical juncture was, in effect, a veiled but clearly discernible outline of Jefferson's policy. This was a far cry from the position that Coxe had assumed in his *Enquiry* of 1787 which largely foreshadowed the kind of commercial system of which Hamilton was now the chief protagonist.[24] But just as that essay had disclosed ambiguities, so did his reply to Sheffield. The remaining numbers of Coxe's *Brief examination*, which concluded with the sixth that appeared in the *American Museum* in July, pursued in general the arguments advanced in the first—that, contrary to Sheffield's predictions, the situation of the United States had become vastly altered since 1784: she had remained united, her republican form of government had undergone a successful reformation, her manufactures were prospering, her native resources were being developed, and her trade with other countries was rapidly expanding. In his third number Coxe even developed, in fairly specific terms, plans for a textile manufactory on a large scale such as Hamilton, Duer, and their associates soon translated into reality.

Thus, characteristically, Coxe's reply to Sheffield seemed to place him first on one side and then on the other of the two views of policy which divided the government. In the closing paragraphs of his final number he sought to bridge the chasm, perhaps as a result of that kind of expostulation that he said took place in the Treasury when Hamilton thought his actions indicated "a preference of a person whom he called his Enemy."[25] He did so first by turning his earlier charge against a British government misled by Sheffield into a general one against most of the European powers, and then, simultaneously, by pointing to the possibility of retaliation by the United States. Warning that "a conduct on the part of foreigners which might have been deemed prudent when our political horizon was darkly clouded, would be unwise now, and might be dangerous to some of their interests hereafter," he declared that the United States was disposed to promote freedom of commerce; that she probably would have made no commercial regulations save for revenue had she not "met from almost every nation, duties and restrictions in their home trade, and charges, prohibitions, and exclusions, in their colonial trade"; and that her impost and tonnage levies could not be compared "with the injuries our agriculture, manufactures, and commerce sustain from several of the principal

---

[24] Setser, *Reciprocity*, p. 102, thought the ideas expressed in Coxe's *An enquiry into the principles on which a commercial system for the United States of America should be founded* (Philadelphia, 1787) were judicious and that the system recommended bore a remarkable resemblance to that advocated by Hamilton.

[25] Coxe to TJ, undated but ca. 1801 (DNA: RG 59, LAR); see Editorial Note on TJ's relations with Coxe, at end of Jan. 1791.

European powers." Coxe's final paragraph offered an olive branch in
one hand and a weapon in the other: [26]

> To obtain relief by arrangements as beneficial to foreign states as
> to ourselves, will probably be the liberal aim of our government.
> It is confidently expected, that mutual benefits will create and cement
> a strong and lasting friendship in the case of those nations with
> whom such arrangements shall be formed; and with regard to others,
> the wisdom of the legislature, no doubt will be sedulously exercised
> either temperately to meet them with the requisite policy and firm-
> ness, or to transfer from their hands, to those of more equitable
> nations, the unrequited benefits they receive from us, or to derive
> from our own skill, capital, credit, and industry, the accommodations
> and supplies which they have heretofore furnished upon terms of
> great advantage to themselves, but which have been inadequately
> reciprocated to the united states.

This approximated the view set forth in the eleventh *Federalist*, which
in general was still the position of Jefferson but which Hamilton had
long since abandoned. As so often before and afterwards, Coxe thus
found himself exposed on both sides. Clearly, though to an indeterminate
degree, his important and timely pamphlet revealed the influence of
both leaders in the divided cabinet.

But the hand that influenced the significant second number of the
Brief examination, at least in the shaping of its most important point,
was unmistakably that of the Secretary of State. This is placed beyond
doubt because the only "circumstance of importance" that can plausibly
be supposed to have induced Coxe to print that number in a newspaper
without waiting for the April issue of the *American Museum* was the
very one whose policy it echoed. No other political event, certainly none
touching the very important question of American trade with the world,
had occurred since the appearance of the first number in the March issue
of the magazine. Congress had adjourned, the President had begun
his southern tour, and since his departure Hamilton reported that
nothing new had occurred in his department worth mentioning.[27] Jefferson found that the "little intermission of public business on the
separation of Congress and departure of the President" enabled him to
catch up on long-deferred correspondence and to turn his attention to
his own affairs.[28] The timing of Coxe's transfer of his first three numbers to the *Federal Gazette* is also significant. These appeared just as
the *Molly*, a "new fast sailing Brig," was about to clear for Le Havre.[29]
That vessel conveyed the report of Jefferson's confidential message to
Otto informing him that, as news from all parts of the country seemed
to indicate, Congress would adopt the navigation bill at the next session

[26] *American Museum*, x (July, 1791), 16.
[27] Hamilton to Washington, 27 Mch. 1791 (Syrett, *Hamilton*, VII, 217).
[28] TJ to Lewis, 4 Apr. 1791; see also TJ's letters to various persons on
29 and 31 Mch. 1791.
[29] The advertisements of the departure of *Molly* appeared in *Federal
Gazette*, 24 Mch. 1791 and following.

and that it was the plan of the President and himself to give French subjects the rights of American citizens in matters of commerce.[30] It is plausible to suppose that the same vessel carried Jefferson's instructions to Short, Humphreys, and Carmichael, as well as the issues of the *Federal Gazette* containing Coxe's first three numbers.

The invitation Jefferson extended to the governments of France, Spain, and Portugal was so explicit and forceful that it scarcely needed reinforcement by Coxe's muted echo of the same arguments, even as an apparently independent expression in the public press. But since he considered the proposed concert of retaliatory measures to be founded in a desire for universal reciprocity and "perfectly innocent as to all nations except . . . that, which has a navigation act," the problem he now faced was that of conveying his message with equal force to Great Britain. Jefferson had long since concluded, and the President had agreed, that the next move toward a negotiation of differences would have to be made by Great Britain. "The impossibility of bringing the court of London to an adjustment of any difference whatever," he wrote at this juncture, "renders our situation perplexing." Clashes had been reported on the borders of Maine and New York and he saw "no other safe way of forcing the British government to come forward themselves and demand an amicable settlement" than by repelling force by force. He proposed that, if Washington concurred, this determination be "suggested in a proper manner to Colo. Beckwith" in order to prevent a miscalculation on the part of the British.[31] It seems likely that, on this matter of far greater importance about which, as Coxe's *Brief examination* sought to prove, the government of Great Britain had been led into serious miscalculations through the doctrines of Sheffield, Jefferson at this time made a similar indirect approach to the British agent.

For on the 17th of April Coxe called on Colonel Beckwith, who a fortnight earlier had sent Grenville the first number of the reply to Sheffield without deeming it worthy of mention. On this visit Coxe not only presented to the British agent his second and third numbers: he also revealed that he was the author. The significance of this revelation was not lost upon Beckwith. In reporting to Grenville he did not identify the author of the *Brief examination* as the Assistant Secretary of the Treasury, but he did convey the essential message: the publication, he observed, was "not considered here as a private production." Beckwith thought Coxe's visit, together with the presentation of the second and third numbers, important enough to make it the sole object of a communication written about the "present state of affairs in this country."[32] He had already sent a copy of Madison's navigation bill

[30] Otto to Montmorin, 4 Apr. 1791 (DLC: Henry Adams Transcripts). Otto said that the vessel was on the point of departure; the last advertisement of the sailing of *Molly* appeared on the date of this letter.

[31] TJ to Washington, 27 Mch. 1791.

[32] Beckwith to Grenville, 17 Apr. 1791 (PRO: FO 4/12, f. 121-2). Beckwith said that he had enclosed the first number in his dispatch of 6 Apr. 1791, which does not mention Coxe's essay as an enclosure (same, f. 86-7). He forwarded the fourth number on 14 June and the fifth and sixth, which closed the *Brief examination*, on 31 July 1791 (same, f. 134, 154). In his dispatch of 17 Apr. 1791 Beckwith did not mention Coxe by name but said only that "the author" had that day given him the second and third

to Grenville, accompanying it with a long, detailed report of conversations with Hamilton and others which betrayed their fear that Jefferson's influence in the administration was in the ascendant. Both in transmitting Coxe's second and third numbers, and in another letter written soon afterward, Beckwith left the ministry in no doubt about what he considered the existing state of affairs to be: a situation which placed in "critical condition . . . the interests of the Empire in this country."[33]

Such a sense of anxiety about the threat of retaliation must have been precisely what Jefferson sought to create, hoping that this would induce the ministry to come forward in an amicable effort to adjust differences. If this is why he helped shape Coxe's second number and induced him to place it in the *Federal Gazette*, as all of the circumstances suggest, then it follows that he may have prompted Coxe to hint in this indirect manner that the publication had the blessing of government. The fact that Coxe was a subordinate of the official who was the chief defender of the British interest in the United States made the revelation all the more pointed. Such a use of indirect means, characteristic of Jefferson's style of diplomacy, placed him in this instance in the position of encouraging the Assistant Secretary of the Treasury to give open support to a policy exactly opposite to that advocated by the head of his own department. Ironically this manipulation of Coxe's *Brief examination*, reflecting Jefferson's own deep concern for amicable negotiations between England and the United States, was needless. For the British ministry, almost at this moment, were being moved to action through fears already aroused by the referral of Madison's navigation bill to the Secretary of State.[34] But, as if to confirm beyond question his awareness that Jefferson's hand was detected in the pointed paragraphs of Coxe's second number, Alexander Hamilton two weeks later prompted Coxe to seek Jefferson's patronage for higher office in the Treasury. He then succeeded in persuading some contemporaries and all who have commented on the incident since that it was the Secretary of State who was guilty of intrusion into his own department, seeking to implant there a confidant and informer.[35] The allegation was unwarranted, but concealed behind it lay Jefferson's actual manipulation of the Assistant Secretary of the Treasury on an

numbers. Sir John Temple later reported that *Brief examination* was said to have been "written by a gentleman of the first abilities in these states, Mr. Hamilton of the Treasury" (Temple to Leeds, 20 June 1791, PRO: FO 4/10, f. 145).

[33] Beckwith to Grenville, to 14 June 1791 (PRO: FO 4/12, f. 132-3). The earlier dispatches alluded to are those of 3 and 11 Mch. 1791 (same, f. 31-7, 76-81). In the latter Beckwith also referred to this as a "critical period," describing the "two great parties" that pivoted on the question of an English or a French connection and portraying TJ as being "blindly devoted to a French influence, which he does not take common pains to conceal and there are no lengths in his power to which he will not go to favor the interests of that kingdom."

[34] See Editorial Note, diplomatic and commercial relations with Great Britain, at 15 Dec. 1790.

[35] See note, Coxe to TJ, 16 Apr. 1791; TJ to Washington, 17 Apr. 1791.

issue about which, at this time, Hamilton prudently preferred to be silent.

By the time Congress was about to reassemble—the period at which some have supposed Jefferson had all but given up hope of succeeding with the proposed navigation bill—the anxieties created in Treasury circles by Coxe's reply to Sheffield had by no means diminished. "The Assistant Secretary of the Treasury has been employed during the recess of that Body," wrote a Philadelphia merchant to his correspondent in Liverpool, "in publishing a series of papers . . . which have been circulated thro' the medium of the Public prints; they are intended to shew that these States are not so dependent on Foreign States with respect to Commerce as has been heretofore supposed. They are wrote with much candour and moderation, and are esteemed a preparation for a Bill intended to be brought forward for the purpose."[36] The fact that the bill would be brought forward was well understood. For, as one of Beckwith's informants had observed, Jefferson took no pains to conceal his views of policy. In this instance, however, his concealed use of Coxe had the effect of compromising the position of Hamilton, thus unintentionally giving to the administration an appearance of unity that had no basis in fact.

[36] Extract of a letter from James & Shoemaker of Philadelphia, 10 Sep. 1791, to Edgar Corrie; enclosed in Corrie to Hawkesbury, 18 Oct. 1791 (Liverpool Papers, XXXVIII, f. 98, British Museum, Add. MSS. 38,227). . . . James Madison also sent a copy of Coxe's reply to Sheffield by "a gentleman . . . on his way to England" (Madison to TJ, 24, 29, and 31 July 1791; TJ to Madison, 27 July and 3 Aug. 1791). TJ sent a copy to Sir John Sinclair, describing it as "written by a very judicious hand" (TJ to Sinclair, 24 Aug. 1791).

I. The Secretary of State to William Short

DEAR SIR   Philadelphia Mar. 15. 1791.

In mine of Jan. 23. I acknoleged the receipt of your letters from No. 29. to 48. inclusive except 31. 44. 45. 46. Since that I have recieved No. 45. and 50. The former in 3. months, 7 days the latter 2 mo. 17 days by the English packet which had an uncommonly long passage. Nos. 31. 44. 46. 47. 48. 49. are still missing. They have probably come through merchant vessels and merchants who will let them lie on their counters two or three months before they will forward them. I wrote you on the 8th. and 12th. instant by a private hand on particular subjects. I am not certain whether this will be in time to go by the same conveyance. In your's of Dec. 23. you suppose we recieve regularly the journals of the national assembly from your Secretary at Paris, but we have never recieved any thing from him. Nothing has been addressed to him, his name being unknown to us.

It gives great satisfaction that the Arret du Conseil of Dec. 1787. stands a chance of being saved. It is in truth the sheet anchor of our connection with France, which will be much loosened when that is lost. This arret saved, a free importation of salted meats into France and of provisions of all kinds into her colonies, will bind our interests to that country more than to all the world besides. It has been proposed in Congress to pass a navigation act, which will deeply strike at that of Gr. Britain. I send you a copy of it. It is probable the same proposition will be made at the next congress as a first step, and for one more extensive at a later period. It is thought the first will be carried: the latter will be more doubtful. Would it not be worth while to have the bill now inclosed, translated, printed, and circulated among the members of the National assembly? If you think so, have it done at the public expence, with any little comment you may think necessary, concealing the quarter from whence it is distributed: or take any other method you think better to see whether that assembly will not pass a similar act. I shall send copies of it to Mr. Carmichael at Madrid, and to Colo. Humphreys appointed Resident at Lisbon, with a desire for them to suggest similar acts there. The measure is just, perfectly innocent as to all other nations, and will effectually defeat the navigation act of Great Britain, and reduce her power on the ocean within safer limits.

The time of the late Congress having expired on the 3d. instant they then separated of necessity. Much important matter was necessarily laid over: this navigation act among others. The land-law was put off, and nothing further done with the mint than to direct workmen to be engaged. The new Congress will meet on the 4th. Monday in October. Their laws shall be sent you by the first opportunity after they shall be printed. You recieve herewith those of their second session.—We know that Massachusets has agreed to the amendments to the constitution, except (as is said) the 1st. 2d. and 12th. articles. The others therefore are now in force. The articles excepted will depend on the other legislatures. The late expedition against the Northern Indians having been ineffectual, more serious operations against them will be undertaken as soon as the season admits. The President is just now setting out on a tour to the Southern states, from whence he will not return till June. The British packet being the quickest mode of conveyance I shall avail myself of that as well as of the French packet to write to you. Are the letters which now pass through the French post office, opened, as they were under the former government? This is important for me to know. I am with great & sincere esteem Dear Sir Your most obedient & most humble servt,   TH: JEFFERSON

P.S. I omitted to draw your attention to an additional duty of one cent per gallon on *rum* by name. This was intended as some discrimination between England and France. It would have been higher but for the fear of affecting the revenues in a contrary direction.

RC (DLC: Short Papers); endorsed as received 28 May 1791. FC (DNA: RG 59, DCI). Enclosure: Navigation bill, as reported by Goodhue on 21 Feb. 1791 (JHR, I, 385; text of bill in ASP, *Foreign Relations*, I, 28).

II. The Secretary of State to David Humphreys

DEAR SIR   Philadelphia Mar. 15. 1791.

Your letters No. 1. to 6. from England, No. 7. 8. from Lisbon and No. 9. from Madrid are all recieved.

The President has nominated you minister Resident for the U. S. of America at the court of Lisbon, which was approved by the Senate. You will consequently recieve herewith your Commission, a letter of credence to the Queen, sealed, and an open copy of it for your own information, and a letter to Monsr. de Pinto her Secretary for foreign affairs. Your salary is fixed at four thousand five hundred dollars a year, and an Outfit equal to a year's salary. Besides this you will be allowed your disbursements for any gazettes you think proper to be transmitted here, translating and printing papers where that shall be necessary, postage, couriers, and necessary aids to *poor* American sailors, unless the latter article should be provided for by the consulage fees allowed by the laws of Portugal as has been said. I state these things particularly that you may be under no doubts as to what you may charge and what you may not charge to the public. I expect from the Secretary of the treasury, in time to go with this letter, information how you are to be furnished with these sums of money. You will be pleased annually to state your account on the 1st. day of July, to the end of the preceding day, and to send it to me by the first conveyance afterwards, to enable me to make up a general account of the foreign fund in time to be laid before Congress at their meeting. We shall name a Consul for the port of Lisbon as soon as a proper native shall occur.

The title of the book you desired is 'the Privileges of an Englishman in the kingdoms and dominions of Portugal contained in the treaty of Oliver Cromwell &c. in Portuguese and English. Sold at the Portugal Coffee house in Swithin's alley 1736. 8vo.'

I inclose you the copy of a navigation act proposed in the late Congress, but which lies over to the next, as their time being up on the 3d. of March they were obliged to postpone every thing which would admit of it. It will be taken up at the meeting of the next which will be on the 4th. Monday of October. This act is perfectly innocent as to other nations, is strictly just as to the English, cannot be parried by them, and if adopted by other nations would inevitably defeat their navigation act and reduce their powers on the sea within safer limits. It is indeed extremely to be desired that other nations would adopt it. I send copies of it to Mr. Short and Mr. Carmichael. Could those three countries agree to concur in such a measure it would soon be fatally felt by the navy of England. No body can better judge of it's effect than Mr. Pinto, to whom I would wish you to communicate it, and see whether he would not think it expedient for Portugal.

I inclose you a letter for Mr. Carmichael, which being of importance, I wish you could find a safe private conveyance for it. We have no letter from him since you left this. You will also recieve by this conveyance the newspapers to the present date.—The President sets out within a day or two for the Southern states, and will probably not return till June.—We are in hourly hope of recieving another letter from you dated from Madrid. I am with great & sincere esteem Dear Sir Your most obedt. & most humble servt.   TH: JEFFERSON

P. S. Mar. 18. It is just now arranged with the Treasury that they shall give the department of state a credit with their bankers at Amsterdam of the whole sum allowed to that department annually, which therefore will be subject, in their hands, to my orders. I will consequently write by the first vessel to Amsterdam, to Messrs. Willinks, Van Staphorsts and Hubard to answer your draughts for any balance due on your agency, counted from Aug. 11. to Feb. 21. @ 2250. D. pr. ann. Also your outfit 4500. Dol. and your salary as Resident from Feb. 21. quarterly or monthly as you please. As there is not at this moment a vessel bound for Amsterdam, and your draughts might arrive before my order, you had better draw at a longer sight.

P. P. S. Mar. 19. I have this day remitted bills to Willinks,

V. Staphorsts & Hubard, and informed them you will draw on them at first for between 5. and 6000. Doll. and afterwards for your salary as it accrues, which they are instructed to pay.

RC (NjP); endorsed. PrC (DLC). FC (DNA: RG 59, DCI). Enclosures: (1) Letter of credence from the President to Maria I, Queen of Portugal, 21 Feb. 1791 (Washington, *Writings*, ed. Fitzpatrick, XXXI, 222-3; see note, TJ to De Pinto, 21 Feb. 1791). (2) TJ to De Pinto, 21 Feb. 1791. (3) TJ to Carmichael, 12 Mch. 1791 (Document VI in group of documents on new policy toward Spain, at 10 Mch. 1791). (4) Commission of Humphreys as minister resident at Lisbon, 21 Feb. 1791 (NjP; engrossed text, with seal attached; signed by Washington and countersigned by TJ). (5) Navigation bill as reported by Goodhue, 21 Feb. 1791 (JHR, I, 385; text of bill in ASP, *Foreign Relations*, I, 28).

III. The Secretary of State to William Carmichael

SIR   Philadelphia. Mar. 17. 1791.

The term of the first Congress having expired on the 3d. inst. they separated on that day, much important business being necessarily postponed. New elections have taken place for the most part, and very few changes made. This is one of many proofs that the proceedings of the new government have given general satisfaction. Some acts indeed have produced local discontents; but these can never be avoided. The new Congress will meet on the 4th. Monday of October. Inclosed is the copy of an act reported by a committee to the late Congress, who not having time to go through the subject, referred it to me, to be examined and reported to the next Congress. This measure therefore will be proposed to them as a first and immediate step, and perhaps something further at a more distant day. I have sent copies of this act to Mr. Short and Colo. Humphreys and I inclose this to you, that you may communicate it to the court of Madrid as a measure in contemplation with us. How far such an one may be politic to be adopted by Spain, France and Portugal, is for them to consider. The measure is perfectly innocent as to all nations except those, or rather that, which has a navigation act; and to that it retorts only it's own principles. Being founded in universal reciprocity, it is impossible it should excite a single complaint. It's consequences on that nation are such as they cannot avoid; for either they must repeal their navigation act, in order to be let in to a share of foreign carriage, or the shipping they now employ in foreign carriage will be out of employ, and this act frustrated on which their naval power is built.

Consequently that power will be reduced within safer limits, and the freedom of the ocean be better secured to all the world. The more extensive the adoption of this measure is, the more irresistable will be it's effect. We would not wish to be declared the exciters of such a concert of measures, but we have thought it expedient to suggest informally to the courts of France Spain and Portugal the measure we propose to take, and to leave with them to decide, on the motives of their own interest, how far it may be expedient for them to adopt a similar measure. Their concurrence will more compleatly ensure the object of our act, and therefore I leave it to yourself to insinuate it with all the discretion and effect you can.

Your letter of May 6. 1789. is still the last we have recieved, and that is now near two years old. A letter from Colo. Humphreys written within 24. hours after his arrival at Madrid reached us within two months and 10. days after it's date. A full explanation of the causes of this suspension of all information from you, is expected in answer to my letter of Aug. 6. It will be waited for yet a reasonable time, and in the mean while a final opinion suspended. By the first vessel to Cadiz the laws and gazettes shall be forwarded. I have the honour to be with great esteem Sir Your most obedient & most humble servt,   TH: JEFFERSON

PrC (DLC). FC (DNA: RG 59, DCI). Enclosure: Navigation bill as reported by Goodhue, 21 Feb. 1791 (JHR, I, 385; text of bill in ASP, *Foreign Relations*, I, 28).

From James Swan

Paris, 16 Mch. 1791. Requested by Littlepage to forward enclosed letter "by a safe opportunity," he has delivered it to a passenger in a Philadelphia ship and hopes it arrives "in Season."

RC (DNA: RG 59, MLR); endorsed by TJ as received 21 June 1791 and so recorded in SJL. Enclosure: Littlepage to TJ, 5 Mch. 1791.

From Gouverneur Morris

Paris, 16 Mch. 1791. Since his of the 26th "the Assembly have taken another Step in the same disagreable Road" described there, depriving all ships other than those built in France of the privilege of French bottoms. This, added to the other decrees already noticed, produces much sensation among the few Americans settled in French ports.—He encloses copy of the note he gave to Lafayette. "He told me in conversation when I urged his Interference that by so doing he should injure us because his Enemies had already voted against us contrary to their general Opinions meerly to vex and injure him."

FC (DLC: Gouverneur Morris Papers); at head of text: "public." Recorded in SJL as received 21 June 1791. Enclosure: Printed below.

ENCLOSURE

Notes respecting Tobacco

I. The Culture is pernicious
    (a) This Plant greatly exhausts the Soil, of Course it requires much Manure; therefore other Productions are deprived of Manure yielding no Nourishment for Cattle there is no Return for the Manure expended.
    (b) The Produce is not of equivalent Value. In Virginia it is calculated that Wheat at 4/ is a better Article than Tobacco at 20/. In that Country the Land yields better Tobacco and less Wheat than the Land of France. There is besides a considerable Land Carriage and five Bushels of Wheat weigh three Times as much as a hundred of Tobacco being also of more than five Times the Bulk consequently the Cost of Transportation is much greater. But waving these it would follow that if Wheat be at 5^{tt} for 60℔. in France Tobacco should sell for 25^{tt} at least; but it is presumed that the free Culture admitted, that Price will not be obtained.
II. It is impolitic
    (a) A Fact well established in the System of Agriculture is that the best Hemp and the best Tobacco grow on the same Kind of Soil. The former Article is of first Necessity to the Commerce and Marine in other Words to the Wealth and Protection of the Country. The latter never useful and sometimes pernicious derives its Estimation from Caprice, and its Value from the Taxes to which it was formerly exposed. The Preference to be given will result from a Comparison of them.
    (b) Hemp employs in it's rudest State more Labor than Tobacco, but being a Material for Manufactures of various Sorts becomes afterwards the Means of Support to Numbers of People hence it is to be preferred in a populous Country.
    (c) America imports Hemp and will continue to do so and also sundry Articles made of Hemp, such as Cordage Sail Cloth Drilling Linnen and Stockings: supposing therefore that France had more of it than is needful for her own Consumption, she might find an useful Commerce of Exchange for the Tobacco she consumes.
III. It is dangerous
    (a) The Calculation is not exact that because a given Surface will produce a certain Quantity of this Article, therefore

no more than such given Surface is deducted from the Culture of Grain. It requires ten Times as much Manure to produce good Tobacco as it does to produce good Wheat. The Straw of Wheat supports Cattle in the Winter hence it follows that the Subsistence both in Bread and in Flesh must be greatly dimin[ished].

(b) Supposing that in general there should be no Want of Subsistence yet in one unfavorable Season this Want might be very great And if as we have seen there should be a considerable Deficit of Grain even without that Cause of Scarcity, what might it not be when the Subsistence of a Million or even Half a Million should be habitually deducted from the Mass. At least one Weeks Subsistence for all France.

(c) Supposing that an unfavorable Season should happen in a Time of War when a Necessity of vast Magazines on the Frontiers should be felt on the one Side, and the Impractacability of introducing Grain from abroad on the other.

IV. The Revenue cannot safely be dispensed with

(a) The Expectation that the Duty can yield any Thing when the Culture is permitted is visionary, and the Emolument to be expected from a Regie is equally vain. Hence a Deficit in the Sum on which the Calculations of Finance have been formed.

(b) A Revenue which in the new Order of Things might be carried to 48.000.000^{tt} and which is now anihilated, must necessarily fall on the Land, because if replaced by any other indirect Tax, it is clear that such indirect Tax might (with it) be brought to the Releif of the *Impot fonciere*.

(c) With all due Submission to Messieurs les œconomistes, the Land Tax is that which however wise in Theory must in Practice be either illusory or oppressive. If the Peasant either cannot provide Money before Hand, or has not the prudence to keep it, when the Tax Gatherer comes he cannot pay. If his Excuse is accepted once he will for the next Time provide another Excuse which is of easier Coinage than Money. Of Course no Collection. If his Excuse be not accepted the forced Sale of his Property makes the Tax fall much more heavily than any indirect Tax ever did. The Peasant is ruined.

(d) Admitting the exact Collection of the Impot fonciere it must necessarily either ruin the Farmer or encrease the Price of his Productions, that is the Price of Subsistence, that is the Price of Labor, that is the Price of Manufactures, that is the Object of commercial Competetion with other Countries. Hereby the rich, as in Poland, may be cheaply luxurious but the poor will be miserable and the Land be depopulated.

(e) In a Comparison of their future and former Situation (a Comparison which will be made by the People of France) the Greivance of direct Taxation will go a great Way to disgust them with the Revolution. *Les visites domiciliares* however disagreable to Men of *fine* Feelings are Nothing in the Peasant Mind when compared to the Sale of the Family Cow. The Cry of Starving Infants is more piercing than the rudest Insult of a Commis.

MS (DLC: Gouverneur Morris Papers); at head of text: "Copy of the Paper referred to in the above letter."

Morris' cogent observations about tobacco culture were obviously framed to impress Lafayette, being far more explicit than the generalized statement he presented to Montmorin on 19 Feb. 1791 on behalf of Americans then in France (see note, Morris to TJ, 26 Feb. 1791, and enclosure). For very different reasons, Morris and TJ were both disturbed by the French decrees respecting tobacco.

To William Short

DEAR SIR   Philadelphia Mar. 16. 1791.

Your private letter of June 5. by Dr. Bancroft came to hand Feb. 12. that of Oct. 25. was received Jan. 27. and that of Dec. 23. four days ago. If in consequence of my former letters Petit cannot be prevailed on to come, I will beg the favour of you to enquire about Mde. de Corny's Maitre d'Hotel, who I know understood his business well, and if she considers his character as an honest one, and reasonably frugal in his management, I can rely on her judgment and her friendship to me. In that case if he will come for moderate wages, say three or four Louis a month I to feed him, lodge him, and pay his passage, I shall be glad to recieve him. But he must come immediately. Should he propose and make a sine qua non of my paying his passage back again to Havre, if he chuses to return, *immediately on leaving my service*, it is to be agreed to, provided he stays with me two or three years at least. If he will not come and you can send another of whose skill and honesty you can be satisfied, you will oblige me. If they are not tied up to *Diligence money* only to the port of embarcation, and *passage money across* the sea, they may by sea-stores, sea-clothes and the lord knows what make that part of the business very heavy. I leave the whole to your discretion and friendship, as to person, character and terms, assured you will do better governing yourself according to circumstances.—Pray get me by some means or other a compleat set of Piranesi's drawings of the Pantheon, and especially the correct design for it's restoration as proposed by I forget whom, which was not executed, and of which I have heard you speak. I wish to render them useful in the public buildings now to be begun at Georgetown. To this I wish Frouillé would add Desgodetz's antient buildings of Rome. I must on another occasion open a correspondence with him to send me the books I may want, and have their amount remitted to him once a year. I mention this book now as immediately wanting and as a good opportunity may occur for sending it.

No decision is taken yet with respect to the *missions* either *of France or Holland. The less they are pressed, the better for your wishes as the President will know you more and more himself. To overdo a thing with him is to undo it. I am steering the best I can for you. The excessive unpopularity of the excise and bank bills in the south* [will] *I apprehend produce a stand against the federal government. In this case the public paper will tumble precipitately. I wish there was someone here authorized to take[1] out yours because if the danger does not take place or passes easily he could buy in again to advantage. Indeed you could not do better than subscribe it into the bank where you cannot recieve less than 6 per cent and may perhaps recieve ten. Very particular reasons prohibit me from acting for you in this way. By no means appoint anybody of the Treasury.[2]* I am my dear Sir Your sincere friend & servt.   TH: JEFFERSON

RC (ViW); partly in code, with interlinear decoding by Short (see notes 1 and 2 below); at head of text: "Private"; endorsed as received 28 May 1791. PrC (DLC); second page misfiled at Vol. 60: 10271.

[1] TJ erred in encoding this word, employing symbol *425* for *need*, as Short correctly decoded it. He may have intended to use *629* for *take* and this reading has been conjecturally substituted for the obviously erroneous one.

[2] The italicized words in this paragraph are in code. Short's interlinear decoding has been verified and corrected by the Editors, employing partially reconstructed Code No. 10.

To William Brown

SIR   Philadelphia Mar. 17. 1791.

Your favor of Mar. 11. was received yesterday. You will pardon me if I adhere to the price of my tobacco, because I know that I am justified in it's quality established for at least fifty years back. You will have observed that Capt. Woodford had ensured @ £11. sterl. the hhd. so that[1] I could have had £12. sterl. for it at the time had I sold it in Virginia; less than I could have sold it for in the country then, I cannot consent to take nor do I believe it ever sold for so little in London. The account will stand thus:

Thos. Adams in account[2] with Th: Jefferson

			Dr.	Cr.
1771. July 19.	By goods as stated by			
	Mr. Brown	£25-16-4		£. s. d.
Aug. 9.	By do. do.	4- 6-0		30-2-4
1772. Jan. 28.	By do. sent by			
	Capt. Woodford			36-1-7
July.	To 4. hhds. tobo.			
	shipped by			
	Woodford @ £12		48- 0-0	
1773.	To pd. W. T. Lewis by your			
	order £4-8-6 currency		3-10-10	
	Balance		14-13-1	
	sterl.		66-3-11	66-3-11

Balance as above   £14-13-1

8. year's interest as proposed by Mr. B.   5-17-4

                                      20-10-5

If you think proper to settle the matter thus I will, by return of the post which brings me your letter, send you post notes for 91. Dol. 20 cents the equivalent in our money. It is as unexpected to me that I owe a copper on this account, as to you that I do not owe the whole debt; and it is my firm expectation that the tobacco, if sold by itself, must have paid the whole debt because of it's quality, and because no demand, after a lapse of 18. or 19. years has ever come from Mr. Adams, Perkins Buchanan & Brown, or any person in possession of the books. If the price for the tobo. before stated does not meet your approbation, I can get from Richmond a certificate from the books of the merchant who bought the residue of my crop the same year, of the rate at which he paid me for it. This method of proving the value never occurred to me before, and will produce but a short delay. I am with great esteem Sir Your most obedt. humble servt., TH: JEFFERSON

Tr (ViU); in a 19th century hand. Brown's letter of 11 Mch. 1791, recorded in SJL as received on the 16th, has not been found. An earlier one of 14 Feb. 1791, recorded as re- ceived on the 23rd, is also missing.

[1] Tr reads "as," an obvious error.
[2] Tr reads "Adamson," another error.

To John Lamb

SIR   Philadelphia Mar. 17. 1791.

Since the reciept of your favor of Feb. 17. two paper packages from New York have been left here, containing newspaper and pamphlets. I was not at home and therefore do not know whether they were those committed to Capt. Bayley, and which were the subject of your letter. Should any others come, containing dutiable articles you may be assured of information of it from Sir Your very humble servt.,   TH: JEFFERSON

PrC (MHi); at foot of text: "Mr. John Lamb Collector for New York."

Lamb's letter of 17 Feb. 1791 enclosed receipt of Captain Benjamin Bayley, master of the sloop *Betsy*, for "four paper parcels Directed to Thomas Jefferson Esqr . . . and One paper parcel Directed to Genl. Knox to be delivered to them . . . in Philadelphia." These, Lamb said, had arrived in the *Three Brothers* from London and as he could not ascertain whether the contents were dutiable he requested TJ to inform him whether the shipment was dutiable and in what amount (Lamb to TJ, 17 Feb. 1791, DNA: RG 59, MLR, together with Bayley's receipt dated 16 Feb. 1791; endorsed by TJ as received 21 Feb. 1791 and so recorded in SJL).

To Adam Lindsay

SIR   Philadelphia Mar. 17. 1791.

Your favor of the 4th. inst. has been duly recieved, as also the box you were so kind as to take care of and send hither. It was from Mr. W. Nelson and contain books for public use. Accept my thanks for your attention to it.

Your friendly offer of service at Norfolk induces me to trespass on you by asking the favor of you to procure for me about 100 ℔ of *myrtle wax* candles, which I understood were made in quantities in your neighborhood. Could they be had of about 4. or 5. to the pound it would be preferable; however, provided they be *moulded*, the size will not be essentially regarded. I think they have a method of improving the green colour by putting a bit of brass into the wax when melted. The post which brings me your letter informing me that you have been able to procure this article for me, and stating the amount, shall carry you post-bills on the collector for repaiment: the candles to be forwarded by sea to this place. Your favor herein will much oblige Sir Your most obedt. humble servt,   TH: JEFFERSON

PrC (MHi).

To Thomas Mann Randolph, Jr.

DEAR SIR   Philadelphia Mar. 17.

Your favours of Feb. 8. and 21. have both come to hand. The former not till 4. or 5. days ago. I am made happy by learning that my daughter is so well as also the little stranger. According to your desire expressed in the letter first mentioned, tho' last recieved, I take the liberty of proposing for her the name of *Anne*, a name which must be very dear to you, and belongs also to Patsy's family of both sides.—The President had desired I should go with him as far as George town, to assist in what he has to do there. In that case I should have taken a flying trip to Monticello. Some matters however have supervened which require my remaining here. I have no hope therefore of seeing you till autumn.—I am in hopes my tobacco is getting down from Bedford to Richmond. I expect every day to recieve the 20. ~~hhds.~~ ordered some time ago from the latter place, and have every reason to expect a great price. The moment it's quality is examined and approved, I shall write to Richmond to have the whole sent on except that part which was burnt, the injured or inferior tobacco not answering here. The President sets out on the 21st. to the Southward, to wit, Richmd. Charlestown, Savannah, Augusta. Present my best affections to the girls. I am with great & sincere esteem Dear Sir Your friend & servt,   TH: JEFFERSON

RC (DLC); addressed: "Thomas Mann Randolph junr. esq. Monticello. By the Richmond mail"; franked; postmarked: "FREE" and "17 MR." PrC (MHi).

The LITTLE STRANGER whom TJ named Anne was his first grandchild, Anne Cary Randolph, born on 23 Jan. 1791.

Estimate of Expenses on the Foreign Fund, 1790-1791

			Mar. 18. 1791.	
			Doll.	
France.	Chargé des affaires. His salary		4500	
	His Secretary during his absence in Holland. about 4. months.	About	243	
	His expences on that journey	About	675	
				Dol.
	Gazettes, postage & other Extras.	About	350	5768.
Spain.	Chargé des affaires. His salary		4500	
	Extras.		350.	4850.
Portugal.	Special agent from Aug. 11. 1790. to Feb. 21. 1791. @ Dol. 2250 per ann.		1187.5	
	Extras.	About	185.	
	Resident. His Outfit		4500.	
	Salary from Feb. 21. to July 1.		1625.	
	Extras.	About	126.	7623.5
Hague.	Agent. His salary		1300.	
	Extras.	About	100	[1400.][1]
London.	Mr. Morris's agency		1000.	
	Mr. Cutting's disbursements		233.33	1233.33
Foreign ministers taking leave. Medals. to wit				
	Luzerne	About	1062.5	
	Van Berkel	About	697.	
	Du Moustier.	About	555.5	2315.
Consuls.	Reimbursements to them.	About		100
				23,289.83

Probable demands on the Marocco fund.

	Dol.	
Presents on recognition of the treaty limited to	10,000	
Agent. A year's salary	2,000	
Sea expences going & coming	About 600	12,600

MS (DLC); in TJ's hand; at head of text: "Estimate of the expences on the foreign fund from July 1. 1790. to July 1. 1791."

[1] TJ failed to include this figure in the column of sub-totals, but he did include the amount in the total.

From John Harvie, Jr.

Richmond, 19 Mch. 1791. Forwards enclosed letter under cover to TJ "as the most favorable opportunity of procuring it the quickest Conveyance to the Gentleman to whom it is addess'd. It is my answer to many Enquirys he has made as to his Civil and Religious Rights if he comes amongst us, but more particularly the Situation of some Western Lands that he has purchas'd of an English Merchant at the price of more than twenty thousand pounds sterling, in which purchase he has been most Grossly Impos'd on. He mentions his Intention of coming over this Spring with his family and a number of Tenants to Settle those Lands. It may probably be a happy Circumstance to him if my Letter reaches his hands before he leaves France. I have also thought it my Duty to Warn others through him of the danger they run of great Imposition in becomeing the purchasers of those American Lands that are now offering for sale at most parts of Europe. About a week past I had the pleasure of spending a day at Monticello. Your daughters were both well. Miss Polly much Grown since I before saw her, and Mrs. Randolph much delighted with the Sweet little Stranger that she show'd me."

RC (MHi); endorsed by TJ as received 26 Mch. 1791 and so recorded in SJL. Enclosure not identified.

To David Rittenhouse

DEAR SIR   Saturday. Mar.[1] 19. 1791.

I have to regret that having rode into the country yesterday afternoon, I did not return till it was too late either to take tea with you, or to go to the society, where I should have been pleased to hear Mr. Barton's paper read. Will you be so good as to express to him my regrets?

I send for your acceptance some sheets of drawing-paper, which being laid off in squares representing feet, or what you please, saves the necessity of using the rule and dividers in all rectangular draughts and those whose angles have their sines and co-sines in the proportion of any integral numbers. Using a black lead pencil the lines are very visible, and easily effaced with Indian rubber to be used for any other draught. I am Dear Sir Yours affectionately,   TH: JEFFERSON

RC (Miss Elizabeth Sergeant Abbot, Philadelphia, 1954); addressed: "Mr. Rittenhouse." Not recorded in SJL.

The paper that William Barton read before the American Philosophical Society on the 18th was in the form of a letter to David Rittenhouse, dated 17 Mch. 1791, and published in the Society's *Transactions*, III (1793), 25-62, under the title "Observations on the probabilities of the Duration of Human Life and the Progress of Population in the United States." See TJ to Ritten-house, 21 Mch. 1791.

¹ TJ first wrote "evening" and then altered it to read as above.

From Arthur St. Clair

SIR   Phila. March 19th. 1791

By the Treaty of Fort McIntosh the Lands contained within the following Boundary were allotted to the Wyandots and Delawares, and the Ottowas who were in actual Occupation; viz beginning at the mouth of Cuyahoga River and running up the same to the portage between that and the Tuscarawas Branch of Muskingham; then down that Branch to the Forks at the crossing Place above Fort Lawrence; thence westerly to the portage on that Branch of the big Miami which runs into the Ohio, at the mouth of which branch the Fort stood which was taken by the french in 1752; thence along the said Portage to the great Miami or Omie River, and down the south east side of the same to its mouth; thence along the south shore of lake Erie to the mouth of Cuyahoga.—It seems to have been asumed as a principle that the whole of the Country was the property of the united States, and, by that Treaty, they gave to the Indians the Lands therein contained and the Lands lying east west and south were relinquished to the united States. There were also certain reservations within those boundaries, which are declared to be to the Use and under the Government of the united States—but by the 7th. Article the general principle seems to have been departed from and the Country west and north west of the Miami of the Lakes considered as the property of the Indians. By the Treaty at Muskingham the same Boundaries were confirmed with a small variation, which, as I have not the Treaty by me, I cannot point out, and certain Lands laying without the Boundaries were sold and confirmed to the united States; at the same time an express declaration was made by the Wyandots that the Country to the westward of the Miami, from its Source to the Lake, excepting the reservations, was the property of that Nation. By the Treaty of the Miami a Tract of Country was ass[igned] to the Shawanese by certain Boundaries, and joining to that of the Wyandots and Delawares on one side.—A west line to t[he] River de la Panse, and with that River to the Ouabash is the boun[dary] on another side, and the Lands lying east west and south of the east west and south Lines are relinquished to the united States. The lands then from the mouth of the River de la panse to the Ouabash, and from thence to the Ohio, and between that River and the Shawanese and Wyandot Boundaries, have been considered as the property of the united [States] so far at least as those Nations were interested in them. But between the ouabash and the Ohio are the Ouiatanons, the Piankishaws, and the Miamies; with whom no Treaties have been held, and whose claims are not known with any degree of precision.—Sales have been made to individuals, before the Revolution, of very considerable Tracts of Country, but without the approbation of the british Government. The whole of the Country between the Ouabash, the Illinois the Missisippi and the Ohio seems to have been conside[red] by the French Government as the Domaine of the King. No Vestige of purchase or Cession from the Natives is to be found in the records of the Country.—The Officers of that Government either as the Agents of the Royal Company of the Indies, or immediatly of the King, granted Lands at their pleasure, and the Officers of great Britain followed the example. I wish Sir I could have given you more explicit information, but explicit information I suspect cannot be obtained. I have the honor to be Sir

Dft (O: St. Clair Papers); docketed by St. Clair. Recorded in SJL as received 19 Mch. 1791. Carter, *Terr. Papers*, II, 230-1, publishes this text as having been written from Boston on 19 Mch. 1790, having been misled by St. Clair's mistake in the date as given in his docketing of this letter. St. Clair was in Philadelphia on 19 Mch. 1791 and TJ probably requested this information in person, since no letter of inquiry from him to St. Clair has been found and none is recorded in SJL. See TJ to Blount, 26 Mch. 1791, and TJ to Martin, 26 Mch. 1791, for inquiries similar to that to which the above is a response.

To Willink, Van Staphorst & Hubbard

GENTLEMEN   Philadelphia Mar. 19. 1791.

Congress having appropriated the sum of 40,000 Dollars annually to the department of state in the transaction of it's foreign business, I inclose you the Treasurer's bill on you for 90,000[1] florins supposed equivalent to the beforementioned sum of dollars. You will be pleased to open an account therefore with 'the Secretary of state for the United states of America' wherein you will credit him this draught. This arrangment being taken only this day, and the vessel by which this goes, sailing early tomorrow morning I have only time to observe to you that the allowance to Mr. Short, Mr. Carmichael, Colo. Humphreys, and Mr. Dumas, with some special expences from the 1st. day of July 1790. to July 1. 1791. are to be debited to this account, as I will more particularly explain to you by the first conveyance which shall occur: and that, till I send you such explanation, you are desired to answer any draughts of theirs for the above purposes. Colo. Humphreys will have to draw on you immediately for 4500. dollars his outfit, and about a thousand dollars salary, and it is principally to advise you of his draught and to authorise you to answer it that I hasten to forward the bill on you before I have time to direct specially what demands you are to answer from it. But this shall soon follow. I am with great esteem Gentlemen Your most obedt. humble servt,

TH: JEFFERSON

PrC (DLC); at foot of text: Messrs. W. & J. Willink Nichs. & Jacb. Van Staphorst & Hubbard of Amsterdam." FC (DNA: RG 59, DCI).

1 An error: the figure should have been 99,000 (see TJ to Willink, Van Staphorst & Hubbard, 11 May 1791).

From Tench Coxe

SIR   March 20th. 1791

I have for some time entertained an opinion that it would be an useful Service to the United States to demonstrate to every man of Candor in the British Nation the very great errors and deviations from fact, which are to be found in Lord Sheffields pamphlet. I have also believed that it would inspire confidence in the minds of our countrymen, and of the foreign nations, who are in alliance with us, if it could be shewn that the British nation have not that Monopoly *de facto* in our Trade which is too generally supposed. I have commenced a small attempt of that nature, a copy of which I do myself the honor to inclose you, and if the duties of my office permit it, I mean to add a couple of numbers more. I trust that the truths, which will be contained in these papers, will create some serious reflexions in the mind of every American, who wants confidence in the independent resources of this Country and I hope it will evince to Englishmen themselves that they have exceedingly miscalculated with regard to the United States in some essential particulars. You will perceive, Sir, that there is a studious attention to a dispassionate Manner, which I deemed the more necessary as it might become known that the papers were written by a person in a public Situation.

From a disinclination to avoid the Gazette I have given this, as I shall any future numbers, to the Editor of the Museum who has sent me a few copies. In troubling you with one of them I am influenced as well by a Sense of duty as by the perfect respect with which I have the honor to be, Sir, Your most obedient & most humble Servant,   TENCH COXE

RC (DLC); endorsed as received 20 Mch. 1791 and so recorded in SJL. Enclosure: Copy of the *American Museum* for March, 1791, which contained the first number of Coxe's *A* *brief examination of Lord Sheffield's Observations* (p. 121-6). For comment on TJ's influence on subsequent numbers, see Editorial Notes at end of Jan. 1791 and at 15 Mch. 1791.

From John Paul Jones

DEAR SIR   Paris March 20. 1791.

On my return from Russia to Amsterdam in December 1789. I wrote to several Gentlemen in America, particularly to the *Vice-President* and to Mr. Secy. Thomson, enclosing some evidence of the treatment I met with in Russia. I wrote at the same time to the *President* enclosing a Letter from the Count de Segur. Messrs. Staphorsts & Hubbard undertook to forward my Packets by a Ship then ready to sail for Philadelphia, called the Pennsylvania Packet John Earl master; but though that Ship arrived safe, I have not to this hour received a single line in answer.

I need not express to you the pleasure I receive from your Acceptance of the honorable and high Station of Secretary of State for Domestic and Foreign Affairs. I felicitate our Country on having wisely confided her interests to such worthy and Able Hands; but it gives me Pain that so unadequate a provision has been made for doing the Honors incumbent on a first Minister of a Nation of such resources as America, and I wish that matter may soon be changed to your satisfaction.

As it has been and still is my first wish and my highest ambition to shew myself worthy of the flattering marks of esteem with which I have been honored by my Country, I think it my duty to lay before you, both as my particular Friend and as a Public Minister, the Papers I now enclose relative to my connexion with Russia, viz.—Three Pieces dated at St. Petersburg and signed by the Count de Segur—A Letter from me dated at Paris last Summer and sent to the Prince de Potemkin—and a Letter from me to the Empress dated a few Days ago, enclosing eleven Pieces as numbered in Margin. I have selected those testimonies from a great variety of perhaps still stronger Proofs in my Hands; but though the Baron de Grimm has undertaken to transmit, to her Imperial

Majesty's own Hands, my last Packet, I shall not be surprised if I should find myself constrained to withdraw from the Russian Service and to publish my Journal of the Campaign I commanded: in that Case I hope to prove to the World that *my Operations* not only saved Cherson and Crimea, but decided the Fate of the War.

Chevalier Littlepage, now here on his way from Spain to the North, has promised me a Letter to you on my subject; which I presume will shew you the meanness and absurdity of the intrigues that were practiced for my persecution at St. Petersburg. I did not myself comprehend all the blackness of that Business before he came here and related to me the information he received from a Gentleman of high Rank in the Diplomatic, with whom he travelled in company from Madrid to Paris. That Gentleman had long resided in a public character at the Court of St. Petersburg, and was there all the time of the pitiful complot against me; which was conducted by a little Great Man behind the Curtin. The unequalled reception with which I had, at first, been honored by the Empress had been extremely mortifying and painful to the English at St. Petersburg; and the Courtier just mentioned (finding that Politics had taken a turn far more allarming than he had expected at the beginning of the War) wishing to sooth the Court of London into a Pacific humour, found no first step so expedient as that of sacrificing me!—But, instead of producing the effect he wished, this base conduct, on which he pretended to ground a conciliation, rather widened the Political breech, and made him dispised by the English Minister, by the English Cabinet and by the Gentleman who related the Secret to Chevr. Littlepage.

I have the honor to enclose Copys of my three last Official Letters to the Count de Bernstorff, with that Minister's Answer, dated before I left Copenhagen; and a Letter I received last Year in Holland from the Baron de la Houze, Minister of France at Copenhagen. These may be useful in taking your Ultimate determination on the Danish Business. But I must further inform you, that a few days after my arrival from Denmark at St. Petersburg, I received from the Danish Minister at that Court, a Letter under the Seal of the Count de Bernstorff; which having opened I found to be a Patent from the King of Denmark in the following terms: "Ayant des raisons pour vouloir donnez des preuves de notre bienveuillance au Chevalier Paul-Jones Chef d'Escadre de la Marine des Etats-Unis de l'Amerique, et desirant Surtout lui prouver notre estime à cause des justes egards qu'il a temoignes pour le Pavillon Danois pendant qu'il a commandé dans les Mers du Nord: Nous lui assurons dès à present et pour sa Vie durant annuellement la Somme de Quenze Cent Ecûs argent de Dannemarc, a toucher ici à Copenhague sans retenue quelconque." The day before I left the Court of Copenhagen, the Prince Royal had desired to speak with me in his Appartment. His Royal Highness was extremely Polite and after saying many civil things he said he hoped I was satisfyed with the attentions that had been shewn to me since my Arrival and that the King would wish to give me some mark of his esteem. "Il n'ai jamais eu l'honneur de rendre quelque Service à sa Majesté.["]—["] Cela ne fait rien. Un Homme comme vous doit faire exception aux regles ordinaires: vous vous etes montrez on ne peut pas plus delicat a l'egard de notre Pavillon, et toute le monde vous aiment ici." I took leave without further explaination. —I have felt myself in an embarrassing Situation on Account of the King's Patent, and I have as yet made no Use of it, though three years are nearly elapsed since I received it. I wished to consult you, but when I understood that you would not return to Europe I consulted Mr. Short and Mr. G. Morris; who both gave me as their opinion that I might with propriety accept the advantage offered. I have in consequence determined to draw for the Sum due; and I think you will not disapprove of this step, as it can by no means weaken the Claim of the United-States, *but rather the contrary.*

You will observe that the Empress of Russia has decorated me with the great Order of St. Ann; and as I have appeared with that Order ever since I must beg the favor of you to obtain and transmit to me as soon as possible the proper authority of the United-States for my retaining that Honor. You are sensible that I did not accept the Offer of her Imperial Majesty with a view to detach myself from the Service of America, but that I have done my utmost to fulfil the intention of Congress in sending me last to Europe to "acquire that degree of Knowledge which may hereafter render me more extensively useful." I have in some measure, by my experience and observation, effected the object of my pursuit; though I confess I have still much to learn, and wish to embrace the first occasion to embark in the French Fleet of Evolution.

I have not yet, since my return here, appeared at this Court; but the Marquis de la Fayette will shortly conduct me to the King, when I shall present my Journal of the American War, with the Letter of which I am bearer, from the United-States.

I reserve for my return to America, to produce to the United-States a full and unquestionable evidence, signed by the grand Pensioner, that *my conduct* in 1779 drew the United-Netherlands into the War. This is saying enough to a Man of your information; for it would be superfluous to enumerate the Advantages that thence resulted to America—particularly the great event which took place under your own Eyes, and which could not have happened if Holland had remained a neutral Power.

I am much obliged to you for the trouble you took in forwarding, before you left Europe, the Busts I had promised to different Gentlemen in America. Having lately received a Letter from Mr. Burton a former member of Congress with whom I had the honor of being acquainted at New York, requesting my Bust *in behalf of the State of North-Carolina* I have ordered Mr. Houdan to prepare and forward it by the first Ship from Havre de Grace for Philadelphia; and as that Bust will be decorated with the Order of St. Ann on the American Uniform, this is one Reason for my wishing to be authorized by the United-States to wear that Order. Mr. Burton desires me to forward the Bust to the care of Colo. Ashe; but as that Gentleman may perhaps have left Congress before the Bust arrives I shall take the liberty to address it to you, requesting you to deliver it to the North-Carolina delegates, who will be so good as to forward it to the Governor of that State.

I continue to be sensibly affected by the situation of our poor Country men at Algiers: the more so as I learn indirectly from the Pyrate, now here, who took the greatest part of them, that if they are not very soon redeemed they will be treated with no more lenity than is shewn to other Slaves. He told this to Chevalier Littlepage, who repeated it to me.—I have the honor to be, with great esteem & respect Dear Sir Your affectionate & very humble Servant,

J PAUL JONES

My address is under cover to Monsieur Grand.

RC (DNA: RG 59, PCC No. 168); at foot of text: "His Excellency Thomas Jefferson Secretary of State for Domestic and Foreign Affairs"; endorsed by TJ as received 21 June 1791 and so recorded in SJL (but given the erroneous date 28 Mch. 1791). Dupl (same); at head of text: "*Copy.* The original by Colo. Walker. NB. As there is no doubt but that the Original has reached or will safely reach its destination—Admiral Paul Jones only thinks it necessary to enclose herewith a copy of the grand Pensioner Van Borckel's Attestation, and of Sir Lewis Littlepage's Letter." Endorsed (in an unidentified hand) as received 28 Aug. 1791, but recorded in SJL under 10 Aug. 1791. Enclosures: (1) Statement of E. P. van Berckel, The Hague, 10 Mch. 1784, attested by C. W. F. Dumas (*Dipl. Corr.*, III, 748-51). (2) Littlepage to TJ, 23 Mch. 1791.

To James Maxwell

Dear Sir　　　　　　　　　Philadelphia Mar. 20. 1791.

I took the liberty of asking you to send me at the proper season 3. or 4. casks of the best Hughes's crab cyder, either in casks or bottles as you should think best. As I presume we are now in the proper season for removing it, I shall be in hopes of recieving it soon. Having been disappointed in getting some cyder of a very good kind from Jersey, if you should have found any that is very good, I should be glad to have the quantity made up to half a dozen casks, either in casks or bottles, as you shall judge best. On knowing the amount, the return of the same post shall carry you a post bill for it.

Having heard nothing of the arrival of the half a dozen boxes of furniture which I had desired to be forwarded to Mr. James Brown merchant at Richmond, I will beg the favour of you to inform me whether they are gone forward.—I am with great esteem Dr. Sir Your most obedt. humble servt.,　　Th: Jefferson

PrC (MHi); at foot of text: "Captn. Maxwell."

From William Playfair

Paris, 20 Mch. 1791. Introducing the bearer, M. de Collaney, who goes to America to take possession of Scioto lands he has just acquired. He bears a letter in English and a statement in French which will explain the liberty taken in introducing him to TJ. As no letter arrives from Scioto and as the families of those who have parents there are given great anxiety because they suspect letters are stopped, M. de Collaney wishes to find a house in Philadelphia to which letters back and forth may be confided with confidence. Since he has never been to America and the persons to whom he has written about the Scioto affair do not answer, he begs TJ point out to him some mercantile houses which may be depended upon. This would be the greatest possible service he could render to himself and to "une multitude de français."—To avoid imposing on TJ's precious time, he refers him to the letter in English.

RC (DLC). Not recorded in SJL.

From William Playfair

Sir　　　　　　　　　Paris 20th March 1791

I hope that you will pardon the liberty which I am about to take in writing to you on a subject with which you have not any immediate concern but the Unacountableness of the situation in which I find myself and the Peace of so many individuals is involved in the affair will I hope be my Excuse.

Since I had the honour of waiting on you in France the Sale of the Sioto lands and a considerable emigrating were Set on foot. To avoid long details it was my Plan and I furnished the money necessary to begin in the Month of November 1789. In less than 4 months the affair was in Great Credit and tho' Nobody in France had ever been upon these lands they purchased with a considerable share of Confidence. I considdered that the Great affair was to begin the colony well and with such people as would set an Example to others and there are amongst the list of Purchasers at least 30 people of distinction. The account which I have the honour to send will explain pretty nearly the Finance Part of the affair and the Memoire along with it will explain in a general manner the Best so that Particulars here are unnecessary only there are a few things which I do not wish to put in a memoire which may one day be public and which I shall here say. Mr. Barlow who charged himself with the Correspondence with Mr. Dewer [Duer] and the others concerned would never shew me his letters and it seems now that he had sent over Reports too favourable. It was immagined in America that above 1 million of acres were sold when there was not above ⅛th. of the quantity and they of consequence drew large bills on Mr. Barlow which were Returned for the sale has been totally at an End ever since the first Emigrants were disappointed on their Arrival at Alexandria. It is now 14 months since the First Emigrants sailed and there is not yet one single letter from the Sioto as 2 months might bring a letter after their Arrival and as Mr. Dewer writes to Nobody here we are more likely to be sacrificed by the mob than to sell any more lands as the People think their Parents and Friends are dead or destroyed. To Complete this matter Mr. Barlow has gone off Privately in debt without telling any one and a Mr. Walker from New York who says he had powers to act in the matter but who would not shew his powers (tho' I summoned him to do it) is gone off likewise.

Now Sir what I think absolutely necessary in this Matter for the honour of all concerned and Even of the United States is that as Messrs. Dewer and Company have not paid Congress the values received should be paid into the hands of Congress and possession given legally to the Purchasers at the same time some arrangement made with Mr. Dewer or other persons to Enable the matter to go on for it is certain that the Desolation of France is prodigious and is still encreasing it will not be surprizing if before 10 years a Million of People pass over to America therefore it is very Essential not to let any Mistakes in this affair thro a discredit on Emigration to America in General.

Mr. Walker who began on his Coming here to connect himself with People who have been all along the declared Enemies of the hole affair has acted in the strangest Manner that Ever any man did among other things he declared in cool Blood and serious earnestness that he did not concern himself about the General success of the affair whether it fell or not was alike to him. He only wanted to do what Mr. Dewer had desired him but he would not shew his Powers as I have before said.

Tho' I know Sir that as a Minister of State you cannot honour me with an answer neither can you do it as a Private individual not being connected in the affair let me conjure you for the sake of all the Persons who have Employed their whole fortunes in that affair to Endeavour to make them take such arrangements as will not stop the affair where it is which will Ruin everybody. I am ready to deliver up what remains in my hands My own comission paid in which case the Balance will be in my favour for the future $9/10$ths of the Price was intended to lay in depot here (at a Notaires) untill the Purchasers got Possession in America and certainly neither the treasury of the United States nor any Company that may have treated for the lands will Expect more than $9/10$ths of the Price which by the Mode of selling announced here to the Public they will be certain to have as in the act of sale the deposing of that Portion of the Price is one of the Conditions.

The Probability is that if Good news arrive and no Embarra on the Part of the Company at New York that then the Greater Part of the Lands may be sold in 5 or 6 months in which case all that is past will be considdered as a very fortunate well combined speculation whereas if there are any Embarras to stop the Matter it will be Blamed that I expect as it is the Common lot of all things.

I once more request you will excuse the liberty which I Presume to take and which I shall beg leave to repeat once more if the affaires are not likely to go as they should do and I have the honour to be Sir with Respect Your Most obedient & most humble Servant,

WILLIAM PLAYFAIR

RC (DLC); at foot of text: "To the Right Honorable Thomas Jefferson"; endorsed by TJ as received 12 July 1791 and so recorded in SJL. Enclosures (actually brought by bearer of Playfair's other letter of this date):

(1) Account of sales, expenditures, and receipts of moneys for Scioto lands, entitled "Situation entre Joel Barlow Ecuyer, et Wm. Playfair, pour 148,376 acres de terres vendues 22 Juillet 1790," showing (in livres tournois) "Valeurs qui existente 696,541. Valeurs payées pour la Compagnie 66,036. Valeurs qui paroissent être reçues, mais qui ne le sont pas 93,606," totalling 856,183 (MS, undated, in DLC: TJ Papers, 56: 9634). (2) Statement by Playfair about Scioto affairs, 20 Mch. 1791, in which he undertook to place the blame for the situation upon the American company and its failure to give instructions or detailed information, either general or particular. Playfair stated that, since 15 Feb. 1790, he had written long letters to Duer begging him to send instructions, but "Le manque total de réponse a ruiné cette affaire, quant à présent du moins, et il impossible de décider si jamais Elle reprendra vigueur.—Je Soutiens et Soutiendrai toujours, que tout ce qui a été fait en Europe jusqu'à ce que l'affaire s'est arrêtée a été fait avec profit et avantage, et qui si nous avions été secondés de l'Amerique, les dépenses qu'on a été obligé de faire, et les embarras qui sont survenus, et la suspension de l'affaire n'auraient pas eu lieu, de maniere qu'on ne peut pas m'imputer tout ce qui arrive. Quiconque est doué de l'ombre du bon sens avoüera qu'une affaire de cette importance ne pouvait jamais réussir sans une correspondance exacte et bien suivie." Playfair did not deny that some mistakes had been made in France. Nevertheless, "un Américain" in France had said that the second payments would not be required in one year but in seven or eight, when the proprietors had cleared their lands. "Si le fait est vrai, à qui faut-il imputer l'erreur dans laquelle on est tombé à cet egard, si non à l'agent Américain, qui a entretenû les Européens de ces fausses espérances?" Nor, he added, should it be overlooked that an American, claiming to represent the company, had declared that it could not pay Congress because it had not received enough funds to pay the first instalment: "Quoi donc, cette compagnie a mis en vente des terres qu'elle n'était pas en Etat de payer! Quelle était donc son intention lorsqu'elle a envoyé M. Barlow en Europe pour vendre ou pour emprunter de l'argent sur la totalité ou sur une partie des terres qu'il savait qu'elle ne pourroit payer? Cette conduite peut-elle s'expliquer ... une conduite aussi extraordinaire, et si difficile à accorder avec les principes de l'honneur et de prudence." Playfair claimed that he was the only one in France who placed himself between those interested in the affair and the public in order to prevent the company's being completely discredited, an action proving the purity of his intentions and his concern for the general interest of the enterprise (MS in DLC; in clerk's hand except for signature; undated, but written on 20 Mch. 1791 as proved by internal evidence).

A few days after writing the above, Playfair addressed a letter to Alexander Hamilton on the same subject, enclosing a copy of the first of the documents sent to TJ (Playfair to Hamilton, 30 Mch. 1791, Syrett, *Hamilton*, VIII, 227-33). The striking difference between the letters to TJ and Hamilton sufficiently testifies to the author's awareness of their different attitudes on such speculative ventures. Playfair had known TJ in Paris and the letter to him recognized the impropriety of asking an official of government to intercede in a private affair, while at the same time he took pains to point out that the interest as well as the honor of the United States was involved. In the letter to Hamilton, he was less harsh in his animadversions upon Duer, seemed indeed somewhat solicitous lest he suffer loss in the affair, and placed the burden of responsibility upon the two agents, Joel Barlow and Benjamin Walker, rather than upon the principals. He was also somewhat exigent in calling upon Hamilton to exercise his influence, a fact suggesting that someone—perhaps Barlow—had made known to him Hamilton's close relationship with Duer if not his status as a shareholder in the Ohio Company. In neither letter, however, did Playfair see fit to reveal that litigation had already produced judgments against Barlow and himself, though in the appeal to Hamilton he argued that, if forced to defend himself in the courts, the ensuing notoriety would adversely affect the Scioto prospects (Gouverneur Morris, *Diary*, ed. Davenport, II, 111). In a subsequent letter to Hamilton, Playfair, on hearing what he took to be good news from the French settlement at Gallipolis, allowed himself to be carried away once more by visions of wealth in the Scioto plains, declared that the distressed situation of France would bring about a mass migration of nobles, clergy, and artisans to America, and eagerly advanced new proposals for the consideration of Duer and Hamilton (Playfair to Hamilton, 1791, Syrett, *Hamilton*, IX, 253-5).

But it was too late. The speculation had collapsed in America and in France long before the above letter was drafted. It had in fact been doomed from the very outset, given the lack of confidence, communication, and effective management existing among all of the leaders in the speculation on both sides of the Atlantic. See Editorial Note to group of documents on the Northwest Territory, under 14 Dec. 1790.

There is no evidence that TJ responded to Playfair's appeal.

To David Rittenhouse

Monday morng. [21 Mch. 1791]

Th: Jefferson sends to Mr. Rittenhouse Bp. Watson's essay on the subjects of chemistry, which is too philosophical not to merit a half an hour of his time, which is all it will occupy. He returns him Mr. Barton's papers which he has perused with great pleasure. He is glad the subject has been taken up and by so good a hand. He has certainly done all which the scantiness of his materials would admit.—If Mr. Rittenhouse has done with the last Numero of the Journal de physique sent him by Th: J he will be glad to recieve it, in order to forward it on to Mr. Randolph. If not done with it there is no hurry.

RC (PPAP); addressed: "Mr. Rittenhouse"; not recorded in SJL. Date established conjecturally on the assumption that, in response to TJ's letter of 19 Mch. 1791, Rittenhouse may have sent him the text of Barton's paper before the American Philosophical Society which he had missed (TJ to Rittenhouse, 19 Mch. 1791).

The particular essay by Richard Watson (1737-1816), bishop of Llandaff, that TJ sent with this note has not been identified. TJ possessed Watson's *Chemical essays*, having the 3rd. edn. of volumes I-III and the 1st edn. of volumes IV and V (London, 1784-7; see Sowerby, No. 838).

From Thomas Delaire

La Rochelle, 22 Mch. 1791. He reminds TJ of his promise that he would be appointed agent of the United States in that Department. The free trade in tobacco and the suppression of duties on leather being favorable to use of whale oil are reasons to expect increased commerce and thus to make agents more necessary.

RC (DNA: RG 59, MLR); endorsed by TJ as received 19 July 1791 and so recorded in SJL. Dupl (same); endorsed by TJ as received 27 Dec. 1791. Tripl (DLC: Washington Papers); endorsed by TJ as received 21 June 1791 and so recorded in SJL.

TJ's response to Delaire on 25 Jan. 1789, the only letter he wrote him, had promised to present his name for consideration. Delaire's persistence in interpreting this as a promise to confer the agency evidently brought the correspondence to a close (see Delaire to TJ, 1 Jan., 12 Mch., and 17 Nov. 1789).

From Joseph Fenwick

Bordeaux, 22 Mch. 1791. Encloses list of American vessels entering there between June and January. This, especially with regard to outward cargoes, is not perfectly exact but he will try to provide more precise accounts in future.—The National Assembly since his last have adopted commercial regulations affecting trade with United States, imposing duties of 20^{tt} per cwt. on all foreign salt fish, 12^{tt} per cwt. on American whale and fish oil imported in French or American vessels, and prohibiting all other foreign fish oils except as introduced through the former provinces of Alsace and Lorraine, under same duty. The bounty on French vessels in whaling is continued and, with the duty, "will tend in a short time to preclude American oil, and engage her fishermen to settle in France."

The free culture, manufacture, and sale of tobacco are admitted throughout the kingdom, and a duty of 25^{tt} per quintal levied on all foreign tobacco, with a deduction of one-fourth on that imported in French vessels. "The American, Spanish, Russian and Levant Tobaccos, en feul et en boucauds, are admitted only, and they must be imported direct from the country of their growth in french vessels or those of the nation where grown—except the Levant Tobacco, admitted in french vessels only. An entrepot is granted to the Importer for one year and if exported, free from Duty." Manufactured tobacco prohibited. Duty on natural silk, 10 sous per lb.; in hanks, 20 sous; if dyed, 30.

The regulation that no foreign-built vessels be admitted as French will deprive Americans of a market in France for their vessels. The difference in the duty on tobacco imported in French vessels, being more than the whole freight, will also deprive them "of even a share in the carrying of that article, unless some restriction is made on the french vessels by the United States nearly equivalent, or a modification of the Decree, which Mr. Short writes me he is with some hope of success occupyed in endeavoring to obtain."

Present situation in France "wears an intire peaceful aspect." Credit of assignats is supported, though the exchange with neighboring countries is 12 to 15% against France and conversion into specie is at a discount of 5 to 7% on large bills and 3 to 5% on small ones. But this is due to other causes, not to depreciation. This is attested "by the nominal, and selling price, of real property, all the necessaries of life, house rent and Labour, remaining without the least visible augmentation. The real causes of the low exchange and high value of specie are the late unfavorable balance of trade France has experienced, the emigration and want of confidence in the Malcontents."

RC (DNA: RG 59, CD); endorsed by TJ as received 21 June 1791 and so recorded in SJL.

To William Murray

SIR   Philadelphia Mar. 22. 1791.

A certain James O'Fallon is, as we are informed, undertaking to raise, organize and commission an army, of his own authority, and independant of that of the government, the object of which is to go and possess themselves of lands which have never yet been granted by any authority which the government admits to be legal, and with an avowed design to hold them by force against any power foreign or domestic. As this will inevitably commit our whole nation in war with the Indian nations and perhaps others, it cannot be permitted that all the inhabitants of the U. S. shall be involved in the calamities of war, and the blood of thousands of them be poured out, merely that a few adventurers may possess themselves of lands: nor can a well ordered government tolerate such an assumption of it's sovereignty by unauthorised individuals. I send you herein the attorney general's opinion of what may legally be done, with a desire that you proceed against the said O'Fallon according to law. It is not the wish to extend the prosecution to other individuals who may have given thoughtlessly into this unlawful proceeding. I inclose you a proclamation to this effect. But they may be assured that if this undertaking be prosecuted, the whole force of the U. S. will be displayed to punish the transgression. I inclose you one of O Fallon's commissions signed, as is said, by himself. I have the honour to be with great esteem Sir Your most obedt. humble servt,   TH: JEFFERSON

PrC (DLC); at foot of text: "Attorney of the District of Kentucky." FC (DNA: RG 59, PCC No. 120); at head of text: "To William Murry Esqr. Attorney of Kentucky." Enclosures: (1) Opinion of Attorney General on O'Fallon, 14 Feb. 1791 (printed above). (2) Commission signed by O'Fallon (not found). (3) Proclamation by the President, counter-signed by TJ, 19 Mch. 1791, as published in *Federal Gazette*, 23 Mch. 1791 and other newspapers (see illustration in this volume).

From Martha Jefferson Randolph

MY DEAR PAPA   Monticello March 22. 1791

You gave us reason to hope in your last to Mr. Randolph that there was a probability of our seeing you this summer. Your little grand daughter thinks herself entitled to a visit. I hope you will not disapoint us. My house keeping and Polly's spanish have equally suffered from my confinement. She is beginning again to go on tolerably for so great a habit of idleness had she contracted in one month that it has taken [her almost?] another to get the better of it. I have at last seriously [begun?] writing to my European friends tho I fear it will be a difficult [ma]tter to forward my letters to you as the post has ceased to go. Doctor Gilmer's eldest son is arrived from Scotland in a very deep consumption. His father and mother are gone down to Shirley in all probability to take their last farewell of him, if he is still alive which they almost dispaired of when they set off. A cousin of ours Randolph Lewis is lately married to Miss Lewis of the *bird*. The bridegroom was 18 and she 15. Young Mr. Monroe and a Miss Elisabeth Carr[1] daughter of old Jemmy Carr[1] have followed their example. Polly and My self have planted the cypress vine in boxes in the window as also date seeds and some other flowers. I hope you have not forgot the colection of garden seed you promised me for Bruni. I am under some obligation to her for several things which she has sent me and for which tho not yet come to hand I am not the less grateful. Flower seeds and fruit stones would no doubt be also very acceptable tho *grain de jardinage* was the expression she made use of. I will send you a letter to go with the seeds or be burnt if you cannot get them. I should be extremely obliged to you My Dearest Papa for a green silk calash lined with green also, as a hat is by no means proper for such a climate as ours. The little girl grows astonishingly and has been uncommonly healthy. Adieu My dear Papa. I have read gregory and am happy to tell you it was precisely the plan which we had followed with her for [from?] her birth by Mrs. Lewis's advice. We continue very great friends. She allways calls the child (who till you send her one will go by no other name) her grand daughter. Once more adieu my Dearest Papa your affectionate child,   M. RANDOLPH

RC (MHi); first page mutilated on breaking of seal and some words conjecturally supplied; endorsed by TJ as received 5 Apr. 1791 and so recorded in SJL.

On TJ's advice about GREGORY, see note to TJ to Mary Jefferson, 16 Feb. 1791.

[1] Thus in MS. On the marriage of Elizabeth Kerr to James Monroe's brother, see Monroe to TJ, 29 Mch. 1791.

From Lewis Littlepage

Paris, 23 Mch. 1791. TJ will no doubt share his regret in recalling that "we were the principal means of engaging" John Paul

Jones to accept Russian proposals in 1788. "Never were more brilliant prospects held forth to an individual, and never individual better calculated to attain them." Campaign on the Liman in 1788 added luster to Russian arms and ought to have fixed forever the fame and fortune of the gallant officer who achieved these successes: "but unfortunately in Russia, more perhaps than elsewhere, every thing is governed by *intrigue*. Some political motives, *I have reason to think*, concurred in depriving Admiral Paul-Jones of the fruits of his services: He was thought to be particularly obnoxious to the English Nation, and the Idea of paying a servil compliment to a Power whose enmity occasions all the present embarrassments of Russia induced some leading persons to ruin him in the opinion of the Empress, by an accusation too ridiculous." It is needless to give details: TJ has too much confidence in Jones to doubt the veracity of what he will communicate.

Tr (DNA: RG 59, PCC No. 168); in Jones' hand; at foot of text: "T. Jefferson Esquire Minister and Secretary of State of the United States of America" and "The foregoing is a true Copy from the Original in my Hands. J Paul Jones"; endorsed by TJ as received 10 Aug. 1790 and so recorded (under Jones' name) in SJL.

To James Currie

DEAR SIR   Philadelphia Mar. 24. 1791.

Your favor of the 14th. was delivered to me on Sunday the 20th. I sent on the 21st. (by a person who possesses my confidence) your two notes to Mr. Potter. The intention was merely to prepare him for my calling on him myself, as we were not personally known to each other. His answer was 'no effects at this time.' On the 22d. (the day before yesterday) yours of the 15th. came to hand with the letter of advice and duplicate bills indorsed. I called on him yesterday, the 23d. He was out. I went again this morning and am just now returned. He has given me so candid a statement of his transactions with the drawer, as to leave not a shade of doubt in my mind of it's truth. It was thus. He and the drawer became acquainted in a boarding house here, and attached to one another. He observed him one day very much agitated, and suspecting it was a money matter, asked an explanation. The drawer told him he had 11 pipes of wine in the hands of a broker, in pledge; that he had allowed R. M. £75. a pipe for them, and that they were now about to be sacrificed at vendue, to raise 1000. Dollars. Potter advanced him the thousand dollars and took the wine as a security. Afterwards the drawer sold one pipe to a Mr. Russel of Virga. and received the money with Potter's consent. He then sold a 2d. which Potter would not let go but on the purchaser's paying him 100. Dollars of the money. After this he drew on Potter at different times so as now to owe him about £434. Pennsylva. money, and the 9. remaining pipes are reduced to 8. by ullage and are the only effects the drawer has in Potter's hands. The utmost he expects to get for these 8. pipes is £50. a piece, consequently the effects in his hands fall short of the sum they are pledged for; so that the answer finally given to me was 'no effects in his hands at this time.' All I could do then was to engage him, if he should be put in cash, to secure these bills; and he has promised, the moment he is so, that he will give me notice: and he supposes it rather probable that if the drawer has any thing to recieve or pay here, he will make use of him as his banker. I now inclose you the first bills, unindorsed, *by post*, because it is the safest of all conveyances. The indorsed duplicates I retain for your further orders, and I confess to you that I do not think it probable any thing can be done with them. It is said that R[obert] M[orris] has lately made such a sale of Western lands in France, as will certainly stop all his gaps and overflow him again with wealth. I know not how true it is, but if true, perhaps he may set your debtor afloat. I have been unlucky as to the ladies mentioned to me in your letter, my labours having been so constant as not to leave me a moment to wait on them. I intend doing it this evening. Tomorrow they leave this place. Colo. Hamilton had to call on me three times before he found me at home. He was a witness to the reality of the obstacles to my enjoying more of his company. I shall await your orders & am with great sincerity Dear Sir Your affectionate friend & servant,   TH: JEFFERSON

PrC (MHi); at foot of text: "Doctr. Currie."

COLO. HAMILTON: John Hamilton, British consul in Virginia, who on his return to Norfolk reported that in Philadelphia he had "met with a very polite reception from the President and other officers of state," and that he had been immediately recognized as consul (Hamilton to Leeds, 10 Apr. 1791, PRO: FO 4/9, f. 224-5). See Currie to TJ, 14 Mch. 1791.

To J. P. P. Derieux

DEAR SIR   Philadelphia Mar. 24. 1791.

Intensity of employment will I hope be with you a sufficient, as it is a very real, excuse for my tardiness in acknowleging the reciept of your favors of Nov. 15. and Feb. 5. The letter to M.

Le Roy I put under cover to Mr. Fenwick, our Consul at Bordeaux, to whom I wrote very full details of all those circumstances which I thought might tend to interest your uncle, and I desired Mr. Fenwick to press them on his mind with all the force which might consist with the necessary delicacy and discretion. The letters to Made. Bellanger have been duly forwarded through Mr. Short. The last accounts from France give a favourable view of their affairs. The taxes begin now to be collected with success, insomuch that there comes in enough to answer the current demands. The church lands sell from 50. to 100. per cent more than estimated. Assignats are above par. Their judiciary is getting under way in the administration of justice, which was extremely wanting. Three or four instances have already happened of bishops chosen by the people. They have chosen Curés in every instance. It is thought the National assembly will separate soon. In the islands, the confusion is great. A fleet and army from France are probably arrived there by this time, and will settle every thing.

Wheat has fallen in price here. There is no market for it in Europe except in the Southern parts of France. With great respect for Made. De Rieux, & esteem for yourself I am Dear Sir Your most obedt. humble servt,   TH: JEFFERSON

PrC (MHi).

To Joseph Fenwick

DEAR SIR   Philadelphia Mar. 24. 1791.

I take the liberty of inclosing you a letter for a Monsieur le Roy, of Bordeaux, on the subject of which I must enter into some details. It is from a Monsieur De Rieux, a nephew of M. le Roy's who is my nearest neighbor in Virginia. Being totally without fortune, and married to a young lady, whom he had become acquainted with in France, but who had lived some time in Virginia, he determined to come over to Virginia, depending somewhat on a little property possessed adjoining to me by the lady's father in law, who gave him leave to occupy it till it should be sold. Immediately on his arrival, he saw that lands in Virginia yield nothing unless the occupier can cultivate them, and he had no body to do that. He had resolution enough to determine at once to labour them with his own hands, and by this means maintained his wife and growing family. At the same time he displayed to our neighbors such a fund of solid merit as to endear himself to them all in a high degree. In fact I have never seen a foreigner as much beloved. I was then in France, and received this information in letters from my neighbors. I was well acquainted with an aunt of his, Madame Bellanger, at Paris, and stated to her his situation and his merit. She very generously gave him 12,000 livres, part of which he laid out in a negro or two to assist his wife in the house, part he laid out in the purchase of a house, the rest in an adventure of flour to Cape Francois, in hopes of augmenting it. This adventure happened unfortunately about the height of the troubles there, and I fear the whole is lost. He is now therefore about to sell his house again (which was in Charlottes-ville, where he carried on a little traffic successfully enough for a little while) to purchase with the money a small bit of land, and to labour it again with his own hands. The lands of the father in law are now under sale. Madame Bellanger promised me she would leave him something clever at her death. It is a pity that in the mean time he could not be relieved from labour, so that he might apply his own personal exertions to the education of his children, of which he has four now, and adds one every year or two. Ten negroes, workers, would maintain him genteely, on a footing with his neighbors. They would cost 15,000.^{tt} tournois. I have understood that the uncle to whom the inclosed is addressed, is very wealthy, without a family, and of a generous, friendly disposi-tion, and that he has hitherto been prevented from aiding my neighbor by some improper conduct of the mother. I take the liberty of asking you to deliver the inclosed letter yourself, and to take occasion to state to him these details. It is impossible he should ever help a worthier man than Derieux, or find one who needs his help more, for to lessen the resource of personal labour he is now subject to the rheumatism which sometimes confines him for weeks in his bed. His extreme merit, testified to me by my neighbors while I was in France, and now proved by a personal acquaintance, interest me much in his behalf and I think I should be made as happy, as De Rieux would himself, by any effectual aid which might happen to him from any quarter. You will oblige me infinitely therefore by taking the trouble of communicating these details to Mr. le Roy in such way as to interest him in behalf of his nephew. If I can be made an useful channel of conveying to him either letters or aids, I shall think no time nor trouble lost in doing it. I am with great esteem Dear Sir Your most obedt. humble servt,   TH: JEFFERSON

PrC (MHi).

TJ prudently refrained from mentioning that the YOUNG LADY whom Derieux had met in France was the daughter of Philip Mazzei, whose lands at Colle near Monticello were then under sale.

To Martha Jefferson Randolph

MY DEAR DAUGHTER   Philadelphia Mar. 24. 1791.

The badness of the roads retards the post, so that I have recieved no letter this week from Monticello. I shall hope soon to have one from yourself to know from that that you are perfectly reestablished, that the little Anne is becoming a big one, that you have received Dr. Gregory's book and are daily profiting from it.—This will hardly reach you in time to put you on the watch for the annular eclipse of the sun which is to happen on Sunday sennight to begin about sun-rise. It will be such a one as is rarely to be seen twice in one life. I have lately recieved a letter from Fulwar Skipwith who is consul for us in Martinique and Guadaloupe. He fixed himself first in the former, but has removed to the latter. Are any of your acquaintances in either of those islands? If they are, I wish you would write to them and recommend him to their acquaintance. He will be a sure medium thro which you may exchange *souvenirs* with your friends, of a more useful kind than those of the convent. He sent me half a dozen pots of very fine sweet-meats. Apples and cyder are the greatest presents which can be sent to those islands. I can make those presents for you whenever you chuse to write a letter to accompany them, only observing the season for apples. They had better deliver their letters for you to F. Skipwith. Things are going on well in France, the revolution being past all danger. The national assembly being to separate soon, that event will seal the whole with security. Their islands, but most particularly St. Domingue and Martinique are involved in a horrid civil war. Nothing can be more distressing than the situation of the inhabitants, as their slaves have been called into action, and are a terrible engine, absolutely ungovernable. It is worst in Martinique, which was the reason Mr. Skipwith left it. An army and fleet from France are expected every hour to quell the disorders.—I suppose you are busily engaged in your garden. I expect full details from you on that subject, as well as from Poll, that I may judge what sort of a gardener you make. Present me affectionately to all around you and be assured of the tender & unalterable love of Your's,

TH: JEFFERSON

RC (NNP). PrC (CSmH).

From Delamotte

Le Havre, 25 Mch. 1791. Encloses duplicate of his of the 9th ult. by *Le Vendangeur*, bound for Charleston, in which he erred in saying that several of TJ's cases remained there. He was thinking of some "Caisses de Marbres" sent last summer shortly after the main shipment. There remain here only "une voiture à quatre Roües; un Cabriolet, quatre paniers vin de Champagne; une Caisse emballée contenant un Tableau; une petite Caisse contenant deux cilindres; une autre contenant un vétement de Tafetas, enfin deux paquets de Gazettes," all just shipped by the *Henrietta*, Captain Weeks, for Philadelphia, as shown by enclosed bill of lading. He is expecting later papers from Paris, but if they are delayed they will be shipped by the *Pennsylvania*, also for Philadelphia in two weeks. He encloses invoice of disbursements for these various objects amounting to £282-8-0 which he will settle with Mr. Short.—Political affairs afford nothing interesting for TJ. He corrects his former advice about the decree concerning tobacco: since Dutch tobaccoes were not named, they cannot be admitted. American tobaccoes will only be admitted when brought from America in French or American vessels.

RC (ViW). Recorded in SJL as received 21 June 1791.

To William Blount

Sir   Philadelphia Mar. 26. 1791.

Having in charge to lay before Congress a general statement of all the lands subject to their disposal, it becomes necessary for me, so far as respects the proceedings of North-Carolina, to draw on a map the line which forms the Eastern boundary of the cession of that state to Congress, and then to specify all the private claims within the cession which form exceptions to the general right of Congress to grant the lands ceded. Three classes of these exceptions have been stated to me. 1. The returns from Armstrong's office. 2. The claims of the officers of the N. Carolina line to the lands reserved for them on the Cumberland. 3. a grant of 25,000 acres to Genl. Greene. Your knowlege of this dividing line, and of the three classes of exceptions before stated, and perhaps of other exceptions quite unknown to me, together with a conviction that you will readily lend your aid towards furnishing any information which may prevent the citizens of your territory or of N. Carolina from being involved in litigations by having their lands sold over their heads, which would not be done if their claims can be known, induce me to ask the favor of you to procure me the most exact information possible of these several matters. As I mean to set about the work immediately, it will be a particular obligation to me if the measures which you shall be so good as to take for assisting me, can be immediately executed, and the result communicated without delay. I have the honor to be with great esteem Sir Your most obedient & most humble servt.,

TH: JEFFERSON

PrC (DLC). FC (DNA: RG 59, PCC No. 120).

On the same day TJ addressed similar inquiries to the governor of North Carolina. The first part of his letter was expressed in identical phraseology, but the latter part contained significant variations: "I find myself under the necessity of troubling your Excellency to enable me to lay down with precision this dividing line, and then a precise specification and location of the three classes of exceptions before mentioned, and also any other exceptions which you may know of. Besides that these things can be known only from your offices, I am induced to ask you to take this trouble from an assurance that you will be glad to assist in furnishing any information which may prevent the citizens of your state from being involved in litigations by a sale to others of lands to which they may have a just claim, and which would not be so sold, if their claims could be previously known. As I propose to set about this statement immediately, I shall consider it as a great personal obligation, if the measures which your Excellency may be pleased to take for my assistance, can be immediately executed and the result communicated to me" (TJ to Alexander Martin, 26 Mch. 1791; PrC in DLC; FC in DNA: RG 59, PCC No. 120). Significantly, TJ did not inform either official that he was addressing these inquiries to the other. He had long since anticipated a clash over titles to lands involving the federal government, a state, and individuals and had thought it "very desirable to draw all the claims of preemption within a certain limit, by commuting for those out of it, and then to a purchase of the Cherokees the right of occupation" (TJ to Knox, 26 Aug. 1790; see Martin to TJ, 10 May 1791; Blount to TJ, 17 and 27 July 1791).

To Mathew Carey

Mar. 26. 1791

Th: Jefferson's compliments to Mr. Carey and incloses him a N Caroli[na] newspaper containing a convention between the two states of Virginia and N Carolina and submitting to Mr. Carey whether it be not worth a place in his Museum.

Th: Jefferson has been told that the same convention is complete in the ac[t] of Virginia of about 1786, but he does not possess the act.

RC not found but sold at Story-Reeves auction by Wm. D. Morley, Inc. in Philadelphia on 28 May 1956. Text from 19th century Tr (PHi) in unknown hand written on verso of printed form of Lea & Febiger for acknowledging subscriptions to *Cyclopedia of Practical Surgery and Medicine*; bearing date "1853" and indicating that RC was "Given to Nathl. Levin." Not recorded in SJL.

From Mary Jefferson

[Monticello] March the 26

It is three weeks my Dear Papa since I have had a letter from you. However as it is now my turn I shall not be ceremonious. We are all waiting with great impatience to know the name of the child. Mrs. Lewis was so kind as to give me a Calico habit. Adieu my Dear Papa. I am your effectionate daughter,

MARY JEFFERSON

RC (ViU); endorsed by TJ as received 14 Apr. 1791 and so recorded in SJL.

From Joshua Johnson

London, 26 Mch. 1791. His of 26 ult. sent by *Pigou,* Capt. Collett.—Preparations here indicate immediate rupture between England and Russia. Upwards of 30 sail of the line lie ready at Spithead and many others have been commissioned in last few days. The King this day issued proclamation offering bounty for seamen. Fearing press warrants will be issued in the evening, he gave warning to all "American commanders to be on their guard, and to call on me for Protections for that part of the Crew, who are Americans." He will oppose every measure of the ministry affecting prejudicially American citizens or the honor of Congress. Yesterday he had interview with one of principal secretaries of Duke of Leeds about public report "that Mr. Elliott was nominated to go to America. I asked him whether he would officially say to me if it was, or was not, so; he replied, that such had been the Report, that I might assure you that this Court had serious intentions of sending out some one, but that they had not determined whom; he repeated to me, assurance of the good intentions, and friendly dispositions of Government towards the United States." In a few days he will send TJ accounts of the fisheries and also reply to his of 17 and 23 Dec.

RC (DNA: RG 59, CD). Recorded in SJL as received 21 June 1791. Dupl (same); in margin: "℞ the Changeable Cap. Boway via Geo. Town."

Experiments in Desalination of Sea Water

To Test the Claims of Jacob Isaacks

EDITORIAL NOTE

Mr. Jacob Isaacs, of Newport, has made such an improvement in the art of distilling salt water into fresh, by a secret method he has discovered, that he can now in a few minutes extract eight pints of fresh water out of ten pints of the saltest ocean water. He asserts he can, with his machinery, make with ease one hundred gallons a day, equal to any spring or rain water, and as light as either. Without some consideration, it cannot be expected Mr. Isaacs will discover his secret to the world; this, however, we are sure of, that excepting a tin tube, his discovery is nothing more than what is put on board of all vessels for the purpose of cookery.

—*The* (N.Y.) *Daily Advertiser*, 12 July 1790

There can be little doubt that Jacob Isaacks—an aged, infirm, and poor resident of Newport, but one who enjoyed the esteem of some of the leading citizens of Rhode Island—was convinced that he had made an original discovery for desalinating sea water by quick and inexpensive means, including a secret mixture as well as a tin tube attached to a ship's caboose.[1] He was indeed so persistent in maintaining this belief in the face of overwhelming proofs to the contrary as to cause one of his early supporters to declare later that "in this business he

---

[1] An oven in a ship's galley, also for use on land (OED). The term, of uncertain origin, came into use in the middle of the 18th century. TJ's spelling was *cabouse* (see his report of the experiments of 14, 21, 22, 24, and 25 Mch. 1791, enclosed in Document v, and his report to Congress, 21 Nov. 1791).

could not be brought to acknowledge that *two* and *two*, made four."[2] Isaacks' experiments were evidently made early in 1790 when he was about 71 years of age. In April of that year, Caleb Gardner and several other citizens of Newport witnessed his process and issued a certificate testifying "that notwithstanding the apparatus . . . was of a bad construction, yet in the Course of one and an half Hours, he extracted from Ten pints of Salt water, Eight pints of fresh water."[3] Two months later Isaacks sent this certificate to James Bowdoin, president of the American Academy of Arts and Sciences, seeking the patronage of that learned society, an attestation of the validity of the claim, and advice about means by which he could profit from the discovery.[4] Bowdoin exhibited caution in his reply. Isaac Senter, a physician of Newport, later claimed that he had investigated Isaacks' process at the request of a committee of the Academy and had submitted a true state of the matter which demonstrated that Isaacks' discovery had long been anticipated by others.[5]

But this was remembered testimony. The fact is that in the summer of 1790 Isaac Senter and Nicholas P. Tillinghast testified that they had "seen Mr. Jacob Isaacks . . . distill by a very simple apparatus, nine pints and half of fresh water from ten pints of Ocean water, and that it was freed from the ill taste and disagreeable marine Qualities of sea water so as to answer either at Sea or on the land for all the Common and Culinary purposes of fountain or River water."[6] This, to be sure, said nothing about the claim to originality, but Senter's failure to challenge a pretension he knew could not be sustained could have had no other effect than to bolster Isaacks' false hopes. Despite his later testimony, Senter therefore must be regarded as belonging with those members of the Academy whom he criticized for having incautiously raised Isaacks' expectations. This was unfortunate. For the aging Isaacks, hoping to make a useful contribution and also to provide for his family, needed most of all to have his enthusiasm restrained by such a "true state of his proceedings" as Senter later declared he had provided to the Committee of the Academy.

Instead, within another month, Isaacks' friends led him to embrace still higher hopes. When the President of the United States came to Newport in August, Isaacks addressed a letter to Washington informing him of his recent discovery and predicting that it would be "highly beneficial to Mankind . . . particularly to those concerned in navigation" because it could be performed on board any vessel at a trifling expense.[7]

---

2 Document VIII.

3 Certificate signed by Caleb Gardner, Moses Seixas, William Ellery, George Sears, and Samuel Vernon, Jr. (Tr in an unidentified hand—not that of Isaacks —dated at Newport, 8 Apr. 1790, in DNA: RG 59, MLR, enclosed in Isaacks to Washington, 17 Aug. 1790; see note 7).

4 Isaacks to Bowdoin, 8 June 1790 (printed in Jacob R. Marcus, *American Jewry Documents* [Cincinnati, 1959], 303-4).

5 Document VIII.

6 Certificate of Senter and Tillinghast (Tr in same hand as that described in note 3, dated at Newport 22 July 1790; also enclosed in Isaacks to Washington, 17 Aug. 1790, DNA: RG 59, MLR).

7 Isaacks to Washington, 1790 (same, enclosing the certificates described in notes 3 and 6 and being entirely in the same unidentified hand). Isaacks' letters

Isaacks may have been presented to the President by Moses Seixas, warden of the Hebrew Congregation of Newport and also master of King David's Lodge of Free Masons on the day that he delivered addresses of welcome to Washington on behalf of those bodies.[8] Whether Seixas introduced him or not, the signatures of this and other prominent citizens attached to the certificates that Isaacks enclosed in his letter to the President must have commanded his respect. It is therefore understandable that, when Isaacks presented a bottle of desalinated sea water along with his letter, "the President of the United States . . . was pleased to express himself satisfied therewith."[9] Whatever the nature of Washington's comment, he could scarcely have done less on this occasion of successive public ceremonies than to make some such polite comment. Jefferson must have witnessed the episode, and he certainly read Isaacks' letters and the enclosed certificates when, at that time or subsequently, Washington turned them over to him for deposit in the departmental files. The widespread notice of Washington's comment in the public press could have done nothing to dampen Isaacks' soaring hopes.[10]

The fact is that, shortly afterward, Isaacks began to dream of goals far beyond what he had anticipated when he first appealed to the American Academy of Arts and Sciences. Despite age and infirmity, he set out early in 1791 for Philadelphia to press his claim before Congress. He stopped off in New York to demonstrate his process and one of those who witnessed the proceedings was Henry Remsen, father of Jefferson's chief clerk in the Department of State. Remsen, a merchant who may also have begun to see visions of future possibilities, enlarged Isaacks' confident hopes still further by appealing in his behalf to mercantile correspondents in England. He declared that Isaacks was about to appeal to the American government for encouragement, but would

evidently were drafted for him. The letters that he wrote TJ on 1 Nov. 1791 and 19 Mch. 1792 (Documents X and XII) both have signatures in the hand of Moses Seixas and the text of the latter is in the same hand that drafted, and signed, Isaacks' letter to Washington.

[8] Both addresses are dated 17 Aug. 1790 (DLC: Washington Papers). The response of Washington to that delivered on behalf of the Hebrew Congregation has a passage pointing out the difference between religious toleration and religious freedom which suggests that TJ may have drafted it for the President: "It is now no more that toleration is spoken of, as if it was by the indulgence of one class of people, that another enjoyed the exercise of their inherent natural rights. For happily the government of the United States, which gives to bigotry no sanction, to persecution no assistance, requires only that they who live under its protection should demean themselves as good citizens, in giving it on all occasions their effectual support" (quoted in Freeman, *Washington*, VI, 275-6). Seixas (1744-1809) was a leading merchant and banker of Newport (N. Taylor Phillips, "The Levy and Seixas Families of Newport and New York," Am. Jewish Hist. Soc., *Publications*, IV [1896], 200-4). His younger brother, Gershom M. Seixas (1746-1816) was the well known rabbi and patriot (DAB).

[9] *Providence Gazette*, 21 Aug. 1790; reprinted in many other newspapers, e.g.: *Independent Chronicle*, 25 Aug. 1790; *Gazette of the United States*, 1 Sep. 1790; *Daily Advertiser*, 30 Aug. 1790.

[10] This is another point on which Isaac Senter's remembered testimony must be accepted with caution (see above, at note 6), for he stated that, after his report to the American Academy of Arts and Sciences, "the matter was very little noticed in this part of the Continent" (Document VIII).

not divulge his secret until after he had applied to the great maritime powers of Europe. If France, Holland, Spain, and Portugal "should unite with Great Britain and this country, in deeming the discovery a matter of importance," Remsen suggested, "a moderate encouragement from each would, I believe, satisfy him, for he does not appear grasping at any very great reward." He informed his correspondents that he had witnessed Isaacks' process from beginning to end, watching attentively for any attempt at fraud, but had been fully convinced that none had been practised and that Isaacks was indeed "in full possession of an Art or Mistery of extracting all the Salts from Sea Water and rendering nearly an equal quantity of fresh and good, fit for every purpose and use, equal to Spring or River Water and perhaps in some particulars preferable thereto, on account of its not being liable to ferment for many months." The parallels between the phraseology of this endorsement and that of the testimonials of the previous summer suggest that Isaacks did not hesitate to reveal the latter to any subsequent witnesses who showed signs of scepticism. But Remsen's recommendation was so unreserved and enthusiastic that his English correspondents did it the compliment of bringing it to the attention of Lord Hawkesbury.[11] Having thus inspired an appeal for European encouragement, Isaacks proceeded on to Philadelphia, his hopes augmented by an apparently uninterrupted succession of approving witnesses.

He arrived there during the final crowded days before the adjournment of Congress and presented his petition just two days after the House of Representatives had directed the Secretary of State to report on the privileges and restrictions on the commercial intercourse of the United States with other nations.[12] Jefferson was then at the climax of two months' extremely exacting labors on domestic and foreign policies. With his mind fixed on matters of paramount concern for the commerce of the nation, to say nothing of documents and reports on Barclay's mission to Morocco, the Mississippi question and the grave threat of disunion that it provoked, the preparations for the planning and location of the national capital, and the drafting of dispatches to Carmichael, Humphreys, and Short inviting Spain, Portugal, and France to join the United States in aiming navigation laws at Great Britain—all of which had to be prepared and submitted to the President before he departed on his southern tour—Jefferson could have had little time to consider Isaacks' petition. He could not in any case present his

[11] Henry Remsen to Sargent, Chambers & Company, 8 Feb. 1791 (Liverpool Papers, XXXVIII, British Museum, Add. MSS. 38,227).

[12] Isaacks' petition has not been found, but it stated that, at considerable labor and expense, he had "discovered a method of converting salt water into fresh, in the proportion of 8 parts out of 10, by a process so simple, that it may be performed on board of vessels at sea, by the common iron cabouse, with small alterations, by the same fire, and in the same time which is used for cooking the ship's provisions"; and that he offered "to convey to the Government of the United States, a faithful account of his Art or Secret . . . on their giving him a reward suitable to the importance of the discovery, and . . . adequate to his expences, and the time he has devoted to the bringing it into effect" (TJ's report, 21 Nov. 1791; JHR, I, 389, 23 Feb. 1791; a copy of the resolution referring the matter to TJ, attested by John Beckley, is in DNA: RG 59, Record of Reports).

report to Congress until it met in the autumn. But Isaacks was poor as well as pressing and, in the midst of an extraordinary spate of official labors of the first importance that had kept him on the stretch since early December, Jefferson gave prompt attention to his claim. The result of this considerate action—reflecting Jefferson's innate compassion rather than official obligation—should have accomplished what Isaacks' supporters in Newport had failed to do, but it produced only a sense of injury in the petitioner.

Characteristically, Jefferson's approach was both empirical and historical. He called, first of all, upon David Rittenhouse, James Hutchinson, and Caspar Wistar, Jr. to witness a demonstration by Isaacks in the offices of the Department of State. All were members and Rittenhouse was president of the American Philosophical Society. Hutchinson and Wistar were professors of chemistry and medicine at the University of Pennsylvania. Jefferson had procured sea water from three miles beyond the Delaware capes at flood tide. From 24 pints of this, in four hours of distillation in his special caboose and with the use of a mixture whose composition he did not explain, Isaacks extracted on the 14th of March 22 pints of fresh water.[13] This proved nothing more than had been proved by the demonstrations made before uncritical and sympathetic supporters of Isaacks in Newport and New York. But now, for the first time, the supposed discoverer was confronted with controlled experiments for testing his claim. These experiments, each aimed at an exact reproduction of the method employed in the other, tested Isaacks' claim both with and without his mixture. Altogether, in four days of experimentation, Jefferson and his advisers spent over 20 hours at the task.[14] It is evidence of his desire to give a fair test to the claim of a poor and distressed man—or, as he must have known was an unrealistic hope, to place "another flower in the American wreath"[15]—that he should have been willing to place the hour of the first experiment on the 21st at any time convenient to the others between five in the morning and midnight. This was on the day that Washington departed southward and Jefferson had last minute drafting to perform.[16]

The day after the experiments were concluded, Jefferson made an affidavit of the result. This statement, intended for Isaacks and perhaps executed at his request since Jefferson was not yet prepared to draft his report to Congress, concluded that Isaacks' mixture did "not facilitate the separation of sea-water from its salt."[17] This judgment was somewhat restrained, for in a letter to Washington the next day Jefferson reported that the experiments were "rather in favour of the distillation without any mixture."[18] The unexplained observation, the accuracy of

[13] TJ's record of experiments, enclosed in TJ to Hutchinson, 25 Mch. 1791 (Document V), and his report of 21 Nov. 1791.

[14] This was in addition to the 4 hours required by Isaacks' demonstration on the 14th.

[15] Document III.

[16] Washington departed from Philadelphia shortly before noon on the 21st, with TJ and Knox escorting him as far as Gray's Ferry on the Schuylkill. The experiment was scheduled for that day at noon.

[17] Document VI.

[18] TJ to Washington, 27 Mch. 1791.

which is well supported by the evidence, proves that the President and the Secretary of State had discussed plans for the tests before Washington left Philadelphia. Jefferson transmitted the affidavit to Isaacks in a letter that has not been found.[19] At the same time, knowing that Dr. Isaac Senter was one of those who had given an encouraging certificate to Isaacks, he wrote him asking for the loan of a pamphlet he had been unable to obtain in Philadelphia, deliberately avoiding mention of the experiments or their result. It seems obvious from this omission that, given the resources of the Library Company of Philadelphia that supplemented his own, Jefferson's appeal to Senter was intended less as a request for assistance than as a means of hinting to one of Isaacks' early supporters that he should not be given further encouragement.[20] Senter seemed to confirm this intent by volunteering the assertion that he had sought to put Isaacks' achievement in its true light as being neither a new discovery nor an improvement.[21]

But Isaacks had been too firmly convinced otherwise, both by his own hopes and by his friends' failure to advise him in a way that Senter and others could have done. Six months after departing from Philadelphia, he asked Jefferson to delay making his report because he was still pursuing his efforts to gain European support.[22] But this appeal arrived only a few hours after the Speaker had presented Jefferson's report to the House of Representatives.[23] The request could not have been granted in any case. But for performing a public duty assigned to him by Congress, Jefferson was charged by Isaacks with an action that he claimed had done him personal injury.

Even so, at the very beginning of the experiments, Jefferson saw that the episode could serve a useful public purpose by drawing to the attention of seamen the long established fact that fresh water could be "obtained from salt water by a common distillation and in abundance."[24] To this task he now turned his attention and, after investigating the literature back to Francis Bacon, he contributed to his report the only potentially useful result of Isaacks' innocent intrusion into unfamiliar areas. This, a characteristic example of Jefferson's ingenuity in seeking to disseminate information useful to the public, consisted in printing the results of his inquiries in distillation on the verso of ships' clearance papers.[25] It was on such documents as these that Isaacks' efforts achieved their small modicum of usefulness. It could not have been more

[19] Recorded in SJL under 26 Mch. 1791.

[20] What Senter sent to TJ was the 1774 edition of Lind's *Essay on the most effectual means of preserving the health of seamen in the Royal Navy* (London, 1762). Actually, TJ already had access to the 1774 and 1788 editions (Document IX) and the fact is that, in April 1791, he borrowed from the Library Company of Philadelphia the 1762 edition, together with the London, 1689, edition of John Rudolph Glauber's *Works* (communication to the Editors). This fact makes it virtually certain that the real object of TJ's letter was to suggest to Senter, a well known physician, that Isaacks should no longer be misled about the nature of his supposed discovery.

[21] Documents VIII and IX.

[22] Document X.

[23] Document XI.

[24] Document III.

[25] See TJ's report, 21 Nov. 1791.

than this because seamen for centuries had known what the intransigent optimist of Newport thought he had discovered.[26]

[26] An interesting example of this is cited by David Syrett, "American Provincials and the Havana Campaign of 1762," *New York History*, XLIX (Oct. 1968), 385. The *Juno*, transporting Connecticut provincial troops, was lost and the seamen were marooned on two small cays off Cayo Romano. Their greatest danger was the lack of water and, with Connecticut ingenuity, the sailors managed to construct a still that was capable of producing about 60 gallons of fresh water per day. For general references to efforts at such distillation, see TJ's report, 21 Nov. 1791.

I. Secretary of State to James Hutchinson

SIR   Philadelphia Mar. 12. 1791.

Congress having referred to me a petition from a person of the name of Isaacs, setting forth that he has discovered an easy method of rendering sea-water potable, I have had a cask of sea-water procured, and the petitioner has erected a small apparatus in my office, in order to exhibit his process. Monday morning 10. aclock is fixed on as the time for doing it. It would give me great satisfaction to be assisted on the occasion by your chemical knowlege, and the object of the letter I now take the liberty of writing is to ask whether it would be convenient for you to be present at the time and place beforementioned; which, besides contributing to a public good, will much oblige Sir Your most obedt. & most humble servt,

TH: JEFFERSON

PrC (DLC); at foot of text: "Dr. Hutchinson." FC (DNA: RG 59, PCC No. 120).

Although no texts have been found and none is recorded in SJL, it is virtually certain that similar requests were made of Caspar Wistar, Jr. and David Rittenhouse (see TJ's report, 21 Nov. 1791).

II. Caspar Wistar, Jr. to the Secretary of State

SIR   Saturday Eveng [19 March 1791]

In consequence of your request, I have made several experiments with a view of ascertaining the best method of proceeding in Mr. Isaacks' business. It was our wish that the same precise degree of heat might be applied in both distillations, and therefore we agreed to place the Retorts in a water Bath, and the Receivers in Water and Ice. But I have found it very difficult to make the water in a Retort boil when it is in a water-bath, and altho I saturated the water of the bath with Salt, in order to make its boiling point higher, still the water in the retort boiled so slowly, as [to] require many hours to distill a small quantity. On this account, Dr. Hutchinson and myself have agreed that we will perform the distillation with two Retorts placed in the same Sand Bath at one time, and altho we Cannot be Certain that the degree of heat applied to each will be exactly the same, yet we expect to be sufficiently accurate. I regret the delay which has unavoidably taken place, but we will now perform the distillation at any time you will be pleased to appoint, and if it shall be thought necessary for Mr Isaacks' satisfaction, that the Distillation be made in a common still, we will do it a second time with one that is in the College, and will answer very well.—With sentiments of the most profound & sincere respect I am your humble serv,

CASPAR WISTAR JUNR

RC (MHi); at foot of text: "Honble. Mr. Jefferson"; endorsed by TJ: "⟨Wistar Caspar⟩ Sea-water. Materials for the report. Rough dft. Wistar Caspar recd. Mar. 19." So recorded in SJL.

III. Secretary of State to Caspar Wistar, Jr.

SIR.   Philadelphia Mar. 20. 1791.

I am thankful for the trouble which yourself and Doctr. Hutchinson have taken and are still willing to take on the subject of Mr. Isaacs' discovery. However his method may turn out, this advantage will certainly result from it, that having drawn the public attention to the subject, it may be made the occasion of disseminating among the masters of vessels a knowlege of the fact that fresh water may be obtained from salt water by a common distillation and in abundance. Tho' Lind's, Irvine's and Mc.queer's experiments should suffice to satisfy them of this, yet it may fix their faith more firmly if we can say to them that we have tried these experiments ourselves and can vouch for their effect. If Mr. Isaacs' mixtures can increase that effect, so much the better; it will be a new flower in the American wreath. He is poor, and complains that his delay here is very distressing to him. Therefore I propose tomorrow for the experiment, and will ask the favor of you to fix any hour that may best suit the convenience of Doctr. Hutchinson and yourself, from 5. in the morning to 12 at night, all being equal to me. Only be so good as to notify it in time for me to give notice to Mr. Isaacs. Will it not save time if the great still can be set a going at the same time with the small ones? He protests against any unfavorable conclusions from a small experiment, because never having tried his method in a small way, he does not know how to proportion his mixture. I am with great esteem, Sir, your most obedt. humble servt,   TH: JEFFERSON

I send the Journal de Phisique of October, just received, for your perusal.

PrC (DLC); at foot of text: "Doctr. Wistar."

IV. Caspar Wistar, Jr. to the Secretary of State

[Philadelphia, 20 March 1791]

Dr. Wistar's respectful compliments and informs Mr. Jefferson that twelve oclock to morrow will suit Dr. Hutchinson and himself, if it be convenient to Mr. Jefferson. They purpose to make the Distillation at the College in fourth Street, as the Apparatus is there.—C. W. is much obliged to Mr. Jefferson for the Book.

RC (MHi); endorsed as received 20 Mch. 1791 and so recorded in SJL.

V. Secretary of State to James Hutchinson

[Philadelphia,] March 25th. 1791

Th: Jefferson presents his compliments to Dr. [Hutchinson][1] and sends him the result of the five Experiments which have been made on the sea water.

Tr (DLC); in clerk's hand. Although not recorded in SJL, this was obviously a circular report addressed to Hutchinson, Rittenhouse, and Wistar. Enclosure: Tabular statement of the experiments conducted on 14, 21, 22, 24, and 25 Mch. 1791, showing amounts of sea water used, distilled water derived, and fuel consumed, as well as duration of each experiment. Since the figures given and the descriptions of the methods employed are identical with those set forth in TJ's affidavit of 26 Mch. 1791, this document is not presented here (MS in clerk's hand, DLC; at head of text: "Experiments on Sea Water taken up March 1791. Miles out of the Capes of Delaware, at Flood tide").

[1] Blank in MS (another indication that this was intended as a circular) and name in brackets supplied.

VI. Affidavit of the Secretary of State on the Result of the Experiments

DEPARTMENT OF STATE   Philadelphia March 26. 1791.

Congress having referred to me the Petition of Jacob Isaccks praying a reward for a secret he possesses of converting Salt-water into fresh, I procured a Cask of sea-water to be taken up without the Capes of Delaware at flood-tide, and brought to Philadelphia, and asked the favour of Mr. Rittenhouse, President of the American Philosophical Society, of Dr. Caspar Wistar, Professor of Chemistry and the Institutions of Medecine in the College of Philadelphia, and Dr. James Hutchinson, Professor of Chemistry and Materia Medica in the University of Pennsylvania, to assist at the experiments which were to be made on it for determining the merit of Mr. Isaacks secret. They were so kind as to attend accordingly. The result of the experiments was as follows.

On the 14th. of March from 24 pints of Sea-water, with Mr. Isaack's mixture, 22 pints of potable distilled water were produced in four hours, with the consumption of 20. pounds of seasoned pine, a little wetted by lying out in a rain. This distillation was performed in one of the pots of a small Cabouse, with a tin cap luted on, and a strait tin tube instead of a worm, two feet of which passed obliquely through a Barrel of water.

On the 21st. of March from 32 pints of Sea-water *with Mr. Isaack's mixture*, 31 pints of potable distilled water were produced in 7 hours 24 minutes, with 51 pounds of hiccory which had been cut about six months. This was done in a furnace at the College, illy calculated to economise heat, and a five Gallon still and worm of the common form. A drop of the solution of silver in the nitrous acid was dropped into a glass of this water and produced a very slight milkiness, as it did in water distilled at the same time from Sea-water without any mixture[1] in a small retort, and also in the common pump water of Philadelphia: and in the last most of the three.

On the 22d. of March, from 32 pints of Sea-water *without any mixture* 31 pints of potable distilled water were produced in 7 hours 35 minutes, with 41 pounds of wood. This was done in the same furnace and Still, and under the same circumstances exactly as on the 21st. The saving of wood proceeded probably, not from Mr. Isaack's mixture rendering the separation of the water from it's salt more difficult, but from a more skilful management of the fire on the 22d. In the course of this operation the fire being once a little too much pushed, the violence of the ebullition threw about half a pint of salt-water over into the tube.

On the 24th. from 16 pints of Sea-water *with Mr. Isaacks mixture* 15 pints of potable distilled water was produced in 2 hours 55 minutes with 11 pounds of wood, 3 pounds of which were of dry hiccory and 8 pounds of seasoned and dry pine. This was done in a common iron pot of 3½ Gallons cased in brick and mortar, the flue passing spirally round the pot once, the same cap and pipe as on the 14th.

On the 25th. from 16 pints of Sea-water *without any mixture* 15 pints of potable distilled water were produced in 2 hours 56 minutes with 10½ pounds of wood, vizt. 3 pounds of dry hiccory and 7½ pounds of seasoned and dry pine in the same furnace and pot and all other circumstances the same as on the 24th.

It will be perceived that the experiment of the 22d. without a mixture was an exact repetition of that of the 21st. with the mixture, and that of the 25th. without a mixture an exact repetition of that of the 24th. with a mixture, and that the result is that[2] in both ways equal quantities of distilled water were produced from equal quantities of sea-water, in about the same time, and that less fuel was used in the simple distillation without any mixture: consequently that as far as these experiments justify a conclusion, Mr. Isaack's mixture does not facilitate the separation of sea-water from it's salt.

Given under my hand at Philadelphia this 26th. day of March 1791. Th: Jefferson

PrC (DLC); in clerk's hand except for signature and interlineations in TJ's hand, as noted below. Tr (MHi); incomplete. Not recorded in SJL or SJPL.

This affidavit was probably executed at the request of Isaacks. If so, the original must have been enclosed in TJ's letter to Isaacks of this date, recorded in SJL under 26 Mch. 1791 but not found. It is to be noted that TJ kept no record of this affidavit in his departmental files, evidently because the experiments were made not because Isaacks requested them but in order to enable TJ to report to the House of Representatives on the petition referred to him (see TJ's report, 21 Nov. 1791).

[1] Preceding three words interlined in TJ's hand.
[2] Preceding two words interlined in TJ's hand.

VII. Secretary of State to Isaac Senter

Sir   Philadelphia Mar. 26. 1791.

Congress having referred to me the petition of Jacob Isaacs setting forth his possession of a secret for facilitating the separation of sea-water from it's salt, it becomes necessary for me to know exactly the advances which have been already made towards obtaining that desideratum. I have reason to believe no body has carried them further than Dr. Lind. I possess his book on the diseases of warm climates, in which he has stated some general account of his method of distilling sea-water, and refers for more precise information to a pamphlet of his on the health and preservation of seamen. This pamphlet I cannot get. Besides this I understand there was another publication of his the object of which was to criticise Irving's method of distilling sea-water, and to prove his own right to what was useful in that. I am told you possess this, and perhaps you may possess also the former pamphlet. If you do, and will be so good as to send me both or either by post, they shall be most sacredly returned. They will come perfectly safe by the post. Your favor herein will much oblige Sir Your most obedt. humble servt,

Th: Jefferson

PrC (DLC); at foot of text: "Dr. Center." For what seems to have been TJ's real purpose in writing to Senter —which could scarcely have been to borrow Lind's work, already available to him in the edition he desired—see Editorial Note.

VIII. Isaac Senter to the Secretary of State

Sir   Newport April 13th 1791

I had the honor of receiving a letter from you yesterday, dated 26th March, desiring me to send you some writings of Dr. Lind's which you could not procure elsewhere, upon the subjecting of Distilling fresh water from that of the Ocean. It is Sir with the greatest pleasure that I embrace the first opportunity, by the post to comply with your request, as far as is in my power.

All the writings which I own of his are a copy of the volume you mention as possessing and the one which I now have the honor to inclose with this. In this you will find the paper which he so often refers to in the Volume on the Diseases of Warm Climates &c.

A new, enlarged and improved edition of the Volume I now send was printed in London, by the direction of Dr. Lind in 1774. In this is the criticism on Dr. Irving's method of Distillation which you mention in your letter. Dr. Irving obtained the Parliamentary reward of £5000 in 1772 and Linds *impeachment* of him was published two years afterwards. Dr. L. asserts in this edition of his work, his claim to priority in the discovery of sweetening sea water by distillation without the addition of any ingredients; and undertakes to shew that the alteration made by Mr. Irving was no real improvement. An account of which you may find in the *Monthly Review*, for Augt. 1774 p. 160. This I would send you, did I not presume it can be readily obtained in *Philadelphia*.

It has long since appeared to me that *Irving* obtained the parliament reward, merely by *Court favour*. Tho' Dr. Watson now Bishop of Landorf in the first Vol. of his Chemical Essays thinks that Irvings method was a real *improvement* upon Dr. Paissonnier's, without saying anything of Dr. Lind in the whole of the chapter which he imploys upon the subject of procuring fresh water from that of the Sea. As there is little which is either curious or useful, escapes your notice I have no doubt of your being acquainted with the chemical works of Dr. Watson. There appears to have been very little *useful* improvement in the Distillation of salt water into fresh, since the publication of Sir R. Hawkins in the reign of Queen Elizabeth, who with four billets and wood could distill a hogshead of fresh water from that of the ocean and dressed the Victules for the whole ships crew at the same time. This being a fact, I cannot see with what propriety Dr. Lind, Paissonier, or Irving could presume to claim the discovery.

Mr. J. Isaacks is an Inhabitant of this Town and early in his business of distillation he brought me a specimen of the water he procured from the ocean Water which he had distilled. I very readily discovered that he had made use of either alkaline Salts or calcarious substances in the process. I informed him, that they were not only unnecessary, but pernicious and that fresh water might be obtained from the ocean in great plenty by *simple* distillations as was practized both in the British and French navies. I heard nothing more of his *Supposed* discovery 'till Several months after when he presented me with a letter that he had just received from the late Governour *Boiden*, as President of the Academy of Arts and Sciences in Boston government. This was written in consequence of a Memorial Mr. Isaacks had presented to the Academy, accompanied with the certificate of several respectable gentlemen in this Town who had seen him go through the process and not knowing what had been done in Europe in this affair, supposed, it a *new* and usefull discovery of the Memorialist. In this letter the President treated the subject with that cautious scientific precision, which shew'd that he was well acquainted with the present State of this important part of Chemistry. Several other letters however passed between Mr. Isaacks and some of the Members of the Academy, by which, his expectations were very much raised.

Finally I was requested by a Committee of the Academy to attend his process and write them a true state of his proceedings. I did so and sent the Academy a particular account of it so much to their satisfaction that the matter was very little more noticed in this part of the Continent, and I thought that Mr. I. had given over the pursuit of a shadow, after the substance was *demonstrated* to be in the possession of other hands. But in this business he could not be brought to acknowledge that *two* and *two*, made *four*.

Mr. Isaacks can distill 8 pints out of 10, that might be used for any culinary purposes, where natural fresh water could not be gotten. But it has an unnatural soft tast, and upon being agitated exhibites more air bubbles than good water affords. I did not chemically analize it for I was very sure that what he could do this way was neither a *new* discovery, nor an improvement.

I hope Sir, that you will excuse my having written so much that may be thought foreign from your requisition. I thought it might possibly be of Some service in facilitating your report to know a little of the history of his proceedings in this part of the country. If you cannot obtain the Monthly Review and the Volume of Watson's Chemistry which I have mentioned, more handily and are desirous of seeing them they are at your Service and I will send them by the post as soon as you request them. This or any other Service that I can render you Sir, will add much to the happiness of your most obt. & very humble Servt.,   ISAAC SENTER

RC (ViW); addressed: "Honorable Th: Jefferson Secty State Philadelphia"; endorsed by TJ as received 26 Apr. 1791 and so recorded in SJL.

IX. Secretary of State to Isaac Senter

SIR   Philadelphia. May 10. 1791.

I recieved in due time your favor of April 13. together with Dr. Lind's book, which I now return you with many thanks. I had been able to get here the editions of 1774. and 1788. but not that of 1762. which was most important, as it was the best evidence of the time of his first publishing his idea of distilling seawater without any ingredient. The other peices you have been so kind as to mention on this subject, I had seen, except the Monthly review, which being in town I can procure. I shall be glad to see their criticisms on the pretensions of Lind and Irving. I confess the latter appears to me to have invented nothing. His still is Chapman's published in the Annual register of 1760. The idea of distilling without a mixture was Lind's, and of cooling by evaporation was Dr. Franklin's. The enlargement of the bore of the pipe is probably not advantageous.

I am to glad to learn that Isaacs either expected, or ought to have expected the disappointment he experienced here, because I am less uneasy for him. He made three experiments with his mixtures. We repeated two of them exactly, without mixture, and produced, as much and as pure water in as little time and with less fuel. Not that I believe his mixture requires more fuel, but that he managed it unskilfully. I am with great esteem, & thankfulness for your attention, Sir Your most obedt. humble servt,

TH: JEFFERSON

PrC (DLC); at foot of text: "Dr. Senter. Newport." The edition "most important" to TJ was one that he borrowed from the Library Company of Philadelphia (see Editorial Note).

X. Jacob Isaacks to the Secretary of State

HOND SIR   NewPort Novem. 1: 1791

I take the liberty to address You on the subject of taking the fresh water from the Sea Water, notwithstanding I met not with the encouragement by Some that attended at the time I made the tryall before you, tho' they were pleased to tell me that my method was not New, still it was their Oppinion that I was entitled to have some gratuity allowed me even for renewing the same, but I can say with truth, that I never read any book on the subject untill I had tried many experiments to bring it to pass. In many of them I fail'd, but have now to inform You that I can take off by calculation in 12 hours, with half the fire I did it at Philadelphia, and much less trouble, 60 Gallons of pure good fresh Water free from any Salt whatsever and on tryall will not be Milky or terbulent as Doct: Jeven was, as is said in the Book, that his best distill'd water on tryall proved to be Milky and terbulent and had a portion of sea salt, whereas this of mine has not any. I have some by me that I distill'd the 22d. July 1790, and is now clean and sweet without any Settlement in it. There is some gone forward to Europe, doubt not but it will meet with approbation, there, and as soon as I receive any Accounts from thence, I shall let Mr. Bourn know, and must desire you'll be so kind as not to make any report on my memorial, untill I have the answer from Europe, but I remain with much esteem, and have the honor to Subscribe Myself your Honors most hble servt.   JACOB ISAACKS

P.S. Please to take notice that I exceed my Memorial in taking off much more fresh Water then I mention'd in the said Memorial therein I say 8 parts out of 10, whereas I took 11 out of 12, and on the second tryall 23 fresh out of 24 salt.

RC (DNA: RG 59, MLR); endorsed by TJ as received 22 Nov. 1791 and so recorded in SJL. This letter, like Isaacks' letter to Washington, was written in an unidentified hand. The signature is clearly in the hand of Moses Seixas (see Editorial Note, note 7). See Document XII.

XI. Secretary of State to Jacob Isaacks

SIR   Philadelphia Nov. 23. 1791.

Your favor of the 1st. instant did not come to hand till yesterday 3. aclock. Unfortunately I had that very morning given in my report, which had been read in the house, and of which I inclose you a printed copy. That the discovery was original as to yourself I can readily believe. Still it is not the less true, that the distillation of fresh from seawater, both with and without mixtures, had been long ago tried, and that without a mixture, it produced as much and as good water as in your method with a mixture. Lind's and Irving's publications prove this, as also our experiments in your presence. As these were meant merely to be comparative with yours, we were not anxious to find what construction of a still would require least wood. It sufficed for our object to see whether, in the same still, it took less wood with a mixture than without one; because in that case your mixture would still have been of value, and afforded grounds for a favorable report. But it did not appear that the mixture economised wood. I am Sir your very humble servt,   TH: JEFFERSON

PrC (DLC). FC (DNA: RG 59, PCC No. 120).

XII. Jacob Isaacks to the Secretary of State

HONOR'D SIR   Newport Monday March 19th 1792

I recieved Yours with the Report, and was sorry to find You was so Hastity in Making the same so soon Publick, As it has proved greatly detrimental to my Interest. Altho' you were not in possession of my secret which I am fearful wou'd have shared the same fate, you must be thoroughly senceable of the injury that report has done me by making it of Publick use without any advantage to the Discoverer, and I am now deprived of Selling my secret to Private Persons many of whom had made me good offers before I presented my memorial, but have since withdrawn their proposals by your making the Discovery Publick, for which I must again entreat your aid and assistance in getting my Petition Granted and secure me such a Compensation as the Honble. Congress shall think just and reasonable. Having a large Family to support at my advanced time of Life will I hope be sufficient without any other motive to gain Your and the rest of my Good Friends' Interests for which I shall ever greatfully remember the Obliga[tion.] That I may succeed in my Petition is the constant prayer of Sir your most obedient Humble Servt, JACOB ISAACKS

RC (DNA: RG 59, MLR); endorsed by TJ as received 30 Mch. 1792 and so recorded in SJL. This letter is written in the same unidentified hand as that of Isaacks' letter to Washington of 17 Aug. 1790 (see Editorial Note, note 7); it, like that of Document x, has the signature in the hand of Moses Seixas.

From Joshua Johnson

London, 27 Mch. 1791. Before receipt of TJ's letters of 17 and 23 Dec. Purdie had told him of Capt. Young's mistreatment, but at the same time he found Purdie "more violent if possible against Mr. John Brown Cutting, charging him with motives that I was sensible never actuated Mr. Cutting, and making use of threats violent and dishonorable against him." He tried to get Purdie to return to America, offering him passage and employment on one of his own ships but this he rejected. He also refused choice of two other ships. "This conduct made me suspicious of his Justice and Integrity, and from inquiry I found him to be a profligate worthless Man." This is supported by enclosed letter from Cutting. He did not confront Purdie and Cutting, fearing that a few guineas might cause former to withdraw charges against Young and discredit Johnson. "Many others of our Country men have undoubtedly suffered but I have not heard of any of them being ill treated, and since . . . my appointment, I have met with every assurance and Friendly disposition in this Government towards that of the United States, and I am persuaded that there would never been cause for any complaint, had a Character been here to claim our Seamen and Citizens.—Taking a retrospective view of the whole, hoping that the appointment now about making from this Court to Congress, may define the rights of the two Countrys, and produce an Amicable liberal and Just understanding, *Considering your Letter of the 23d. December* gave me a discretionary Power to act as circumstances appeared, I trust that the Reasons which I have assigned will prove satisfactory to the President . . . for not carrying his command . . . into effect." If not, he will instantly pursue the matter on receiving further orders and will demand satisfaction.—Letters in TJ's of 23 Dec. were forwarded and all acknowledged save that to Willink & Co.

RC (DNA: RG 59, CD); endorsed by TJ as received 21 June 1791 and so recorded in SJL; at foot of text: "Thomas Jefferson Esqr. Secretary of the U.S. for the Department of State."

Dupl (same); in margin: "⚹ favor Colo. Smith ⚹ Packett." Enclosure not found. On Purdie's case, see Vol. 18: 310-42.

To George Washington

Sir   Philadelphia Mar. 27. 1791.

I have been again to see Mr. Barclay on the subject of his mission and to hasten him. I communicated to him the draught of his instructions and he made an observation which may render a small change expedient. You know it had been concluded that he should go without any defined character, in order to save expence. He observed that if his character was undefined they would consider him as an Ambassador and expect proportional liberalities, and he thought it best to fix his character to that of Consul, which was the lowest that could be employed. Thinking there is weight in his opinion I have the honour to inclose you a blank commission for him as Consul, and another letter to the emperor not otherwise different from that you signed, but as having a clause of credence in it. If you approve of this change you will be so good as to sign these papers and return them: otherwise the letter before signed will still suffice.

I inclose you a Massachusets paper whereby you will see that some acts of force have taken place on our Eastern boundary. Probably that state will send us authentic information of them. The want of an accurate map of the bay of Passamaquaddy renders it difficult to form a satisfactory opinion on the point in contest. I write to-day to Rufus Putnam to send me his survey referred to in his letter. There is a report that some acts of force have taken place on the Northern boundary of New York, and are now under consideration of the government of that state. The impossibility of bringing the court of London to an adjustment of any difference whatever, renders our situation perplexing. Should any applications from the states or their citizens be so urgent as to require something to be said before your return, my opinion would be that they should be desired to make no new settlements on our part, nor suffer any to be made on the part of the British, within the disputed territory, and if any attempt should be made to remove them from the settlements already made, that they are to repel force by force, and ask aid of the neighboring militia to do this and no more. I see no other safe way of forcing the British government to come forward themselves and demand an amicable settlement. If this idea meets your approbation, it may prevent a misconstruction, by the British, of what may happen, should I have this idea suggested in a proper manner to Colo. Beckwith.

The experiments which have been tried of distilling sea-water with Isaac's mixture, and also without it, have been rather in favour of the distillation without any mixture.

A bill was yesterday ordered to be brought into the H. of representatives here for granting a sum of money for building a federal hall, house for the President &c.

You knew of Mr. R. Morris's purchase of Gorham and Phelps of 1,300,000. acres of land of the state of Massachusetts, at 5d. an acre. It is said that he has sold 1,200,000. acres of these in Europe thro' the agency of W. Franklin, who it seems went on this business conjointly with that of printing his grand father's works. Mr. Morris, under the name of Ogden, and perhaps in partnership with him, has bought the residue of the lands held in the same country by Massachusets, for 100,000£. The Indian title of the former purchase has been extinguished by Gorham, but that of the latter is not. Perhaps it cannot be. In that case a similarity of interest will produce an alliance with the Yazoo companies. Perhaps a sale may be made in Europe to purchasers ignorant of the Indian right.

I shall be happy to hear that no accident has happened to you in the bad roads you have passed, and that you are better prepared for those to come by lowering the hang of your carriage, and exchanging the coachman for two postillions, circumstances which I confess to you appeared to me essential for your safety, for which no one on earth more sincerely prays both from public & private regard than he who has the honor to be with sentiments of the most profound respect, Sir, Your most obedient & most humble servant,   TH: JEFFERSON

RC (DNA: RG 59, MLR); at foot of text: "The President of the U.S."; endorsed. PrC (DLC). FC (DNA: RG 59, SDC). For the enclosed commission and letter of credence for Barclay, see TJ to Barclay, 13 May 1791.

From John Cooke to George Washington

Tipperary, 28 Mch. 1791. Understanding that regulation of weights and measures is one object of American government, he sends the enclosed "invention" from "a poor individual, in an obscure corner of a remote nation, as a mark of that universal esteem, which your Excellency's Merits have excited in all countries, and amongst every class of men."

RC (DNA: RG 59, MLR); endorsed by TJ: "To the President. Delivered to Th: J. Aug. 18." 1791 (so recorded in SJL). Enclosure: Cooke's "Description of a new standard for Weights and Measures," which began with the following premises: "The want of uniformity in weights and measures is a subject of general complaint at present; it is an infinite source of fraud, and the great obstacle to domestic and foreign commerce.—The first step necessary to remove this evil, is to appoint an universal, perpetual, and immutable standard, for length, superficies, weight, and capacity; whereby the instruments of measurement may be adjusted, and also whereby they may be described to distant countries, and to future ages.—Natural substances are incapable of furnishing one of this description. Every thing in the material world is in a state of gradual alteration, it differs from itself under different circumstances, and differs from every individual of the same species.—General and permanent immutability is to be found only in our abstract ideas; and none of these can define dimensions but our ideas of geometrical diagrams; therefore, if we could discover such relations or qualities in a geometrical figure, as are peculiar to it, and as would distinguish it from all other similar figures, we should have a correct standard; but as every attempt to accomplish this has failed, we are obliged to resort to these general qualities of matter which are the most durable and least variable. Of this class are cohesion, motion, gravity, &c. upon the last of which the following theorem depends, and from which also Mr. Huygens has deduced the pendulum standard." But Cooke rejected the pendulum for various reasons, substituting therefor a cube-shaped vessel having in its bottom an aperture in a given ratio to its base, so that "if the ratio between the weight of the water which this vessel contains when full, and the weight of the water discharged from it . . . in a given time be given, the cube itself is given" (MS not found; text from Am. Phil. Soc., *Trans.*, III [1793], 328-31, with an erroneous identification of TJ as the recipient).

Evidently neither Washington nor TJ responded to Cooke's letter. But on the day after TJ received it the enclosure was read at a meeting of the American Philosophical Society. The audience included TJ and Jean Baptiste Ternant, "Ambassador" from France (Minutes for 19 Aug. 1791, Am. Phil. Soc., *Procs.*, XXII [July, 1885], 195).

From Anthony Gerna

Dublin, 28 Mch. 1791. "It would be an insult to your goodness to apologize" for introducing the bearer, Robert Stafford, a skillful young apothecary, lately married, who is resolved to settle in America. Stafford will deliver "a small Parcel containing a new publication of the Dublin newspapers of this date." TJ's advice to him will "be an additional proof of that humanity and benevolence which characterise you."

RC (DLC); endorsed as received 21 June 1791 and so recorded in SJL.

TJ had known Gerna in Paris, having received through him a copy of Antonio Vieyra's work in linguistics (Gerna to TJ, ca. 8 Sep. 1787; Sowerby, No. 4743). The small parcel that Stafford brought has not been identified, but he probably presented also the printed announcement of Gerna's proposed establishment of a reading room in Dublin—"Gerna's Cabinet Litteraire, No. 31, College-Green, next to the General Post Office" —for French, Italian, German, Spanish, "and all English News Papers of known consequence . . . to which will be occasionally added those of the United States of America." Gerna also proposed to include for subscribers to the reading room all of the memoirs and publications of the various European learned societies and academies. The room was described as neat and commodious, with proper attendants, "and refreshments, if required," would be available from "Nine o'clock in the

Morning till Eleven at Night, Sunday Included.—*Subscription One Guinea for Six Months*" (broadside, dated "Febru- ary 1791," DLC: TJ Papers, 62: 10623).

To James McHenry

DEAR SIR   Philadelphia Mar. 28. 1791.

Having sent your letters to Mr. Short with a desire that he will, as far as is right, patronize the applications which shall be made to the minister on your demand, instead of destroying your first letter to Messrs. Le Couteulx, I have thought it better to return it to you, in proof that your desires have been complied with.—A murder of some friendly Indians a little beyond Fort Pitt is likely to defeat our efforts to make a general peace, and to render the combination in war against us more extensive. This was done by a party of Virginians within the limits of Pennsylvania.—The only news from Europe interesting to us is that the Brit. Parl. is about to give *free storage* to American wheat carried to Engld. in *British bottoms* for re-exportation. In this case we must make *British bottoms* lading with wheat, pay that storage here, in the form of a duty, and give it to *American bottoms* lading with the same article, in order not only to keep our vessels on a par as to transportation of *our own produce*, but to shift the meditated advantage into their scale. At least so say I.—I am with great esteem Dear Sir Your most obedt. humble servt.,   TH: JEFFERSON

PrC (DLC).

To William Channing

SIR   Philadelphia Mar. 29. 1791.

The recess of Congress now permits me to take up the subject of my former letter to you and to acknowlege the receipt of yours of Nov. 24. in answer, together with the laws you were so kind as to send forward. The M.S. copies of laws relating to British property, which you mention to be in hand, will be acceptable, as that subject will probably come under discussion some day. The perpetual occasions of turning to the laws of the states rendering it extremely desireable that our collection of them should be complete, I will still ask the favour of you to furnish any *printed* acts which may come in your way and assist to render our collection complete. It is not proposed to be at the expence of making M.S. copies for this purpose. Whenever you will be pleased to let me know your disbursements for what you have been or shall be so kind as to send, I will immediately forward to you a bank-post-note to the amount. Accept my thanks for your attention to this business & assurances of the respect with which I am Sir Your most obedt. humble servt,

TH: JEFFERSON

PrC (DLC); at foot of text: "Mr. Channing Rhode isld." FC (DNA: RG 59, PCC No. 120).

To Christopher Gore

SIR   Philadelphia Mar. 29. 1791.

The recess of Congress now permits me the honor of acknowleging the receipt of your favor of Sep. 27. together with the copies of the laws you were so kind as to send, for which be pleased to accept my thanks. Our collection now stands thus.
Laws from 1692. to 1772.
do. from Nov. 28. 1780. to July 6. 1781.
do. from Apr. 20. 1781. to July 2. 1785.
do. from June 16. 1783. to July 6. 1787.
do. from Nov. 16. 1787. to June 24. 1790.
The only chasm in this seems to be from 1772. to 1780. to which I will continue to ask the attention you are so kind as to promise, as occasions arise frequently of consulting the laws of the states so as to render it extremely desireable to have the collection complete of all the laws *in print*, for it is not proposed to go to the expence of making Manuscript copies.—Your observations on the several acts which might be objected as infractions of the treaty of peace will be our clue in that subject, whenever it shall be taken up. I do not think it necessary to have copies of any judiciary proceedings. As soon as you shall be so good as to inform me of the cost of what you have been so kind as to collect for the office and send forward, I will send you a bank-post-note for the amount.—I have the honour to be with great respect Sir your most obedt. and most humble servt,   TH: JEFFERSON

PrC (DLC); at foot of text: "C. Gore esq. Massachusets." FC (DNA: RG 59, PCC No. 120).

From Fenwick, Mason & Company

[*Bordeaux, 29 Mch. 1791*] Enclose duplicate of theirs of 10 Feb. and invoice for 14 cases of wine for TJ and 14 for the President as ordered by TJ 6 Sep. 1790, shipped on *Eliza*, Capt. Tilden, via Charleston, to Robert Hazlehurst & Co. with request to forward by first packet. "The proprietors of the Mirosmenil Estate . . . declined shipping the wine of Segur order for the President. We therefore have replaced it out of the wines of Lafite, the Estate of Mr. Pichard (formerly Segur) the growth of 1786. which we hope will prove perfect and give intire satisfaction. The white graves wine we have shipped you generally costs 500 or 600^{tt} per Ton at an age proper to bottle, is made on the Estate of Mr. Dulamont to whom you may in future apply for the same quality if it pleases. He may perhaps give it something lower.—We think the Comsse. de Lur Saluce has charged a very extraordinary price for the parcel shiped you. The same quality here never costs more than 600 @ 800^{tt} per Ton of 4 hogsheads and she we observe has charged you 30 Sols per bottle, glass included.— The carriage of the frontignac wine from Mr. Lambert also is at least equal to one third of the first price of the wine." They have asked him for better terms in future. They enclose account which will enable TJ to settle with President. Hazlehurst & Co. have been asked to pay freight there and draw on TJ for that and duties, if any.

RC (MHi); undated, but TJ placed the following at head of text: "[supposed Mar. 29. 1791.]"; endorsed by TJ as received 21 June 1791.

From William Jackson

Georgetown, 29 Mch. 1791. The enclosed papers "from the Secretary of the Western territory" were received by the President last evening. "His engagements with the Commissioners not permitting him to peruse them during his stay here, he commands me to transmit them to you for your consideration, and he requests, if you should think it necessary, that they may be reported on."

RC (DNA: RG 59, MLR); at foot of text: "Thomas Jefferson, Esquire, Secretary of State." FC (DNA: RG 59, SDC). Recorded in SJL as received 2 Apr. 1791. Carter, *Terr. Papers*, II, 342n, identifies the enclosed papers as the Journal of Executive Proceedings of the Northwest Territory from 1 Aug. to 31 Dec. 1790. This is no doubt correct. But the Journal alone would have taken Washington only a few minutes to read, since during the period covered the Northwest Territory was virtually without an executive and there were few actions to report (proceedings for this period are in Carter, *Terr. Papers*, III, 329-33). St. Clair did not arrive in the Territory until mid-September and Sargent was in the East attending primarily to Scioto affairs (see Editorial Note, proceedings in the Northwest Territory, 14 Dec. 1790). The enclosures must, therefore, have included other documents, though none has been identified and no covering letter from Sargent to the President has been found.

From James Monroe

Charlottesville, 29 Mch. 1791. When he left for Philadelphia last November he sought to place his brother "in a quiet good family and where he might pursue his studies to the best advantage." From general opinion of his friends he engaged lodgings for him with James Kerr, the more so because Monroe "had render'd him services, and had a claim to his attention." But to his astonishment he learned yesterday that his brother was married to Kerr's daughter. "I was informed . . . [t]hat by his managment the young man had been artfully kept from the society of any of my friends, and contrary to his own wishes, who urged the impropriety of it, had been precipitated into it before my return; although it was well known I should certainly be in by this time. As I have had the care of this youth since I have been able to take care of myself, have expended much money in the previous part of his education, and hoped whatever might be the indiscretions of his early life to make him at more mature age useful to himself and to others, and particularly if any accident should bereave my family of my support, to make him a parent to them as I have been to him, believe me this has been the most heartfelt and afflicting stroke I have ever felt. If his education had been complete and himself establish'd in life, able to take care of a family, to me it would have been a matter of indifference with whom he connected himself. But being yet a minor and quite unfinish'd in these respects the injury appears to be almost without remedy. It is likewise surprizing, considering . . . his minority, as that his guardianship was intrusted to me, who was daily expected, that the license was granted or that the clergiman Mr. Maury married him. However such have been the facts."—He heard on arriving yesterday that Mr. and Mrs. Randolph were well. He sets out in morning for Staunton court. Journey in was "slow and tedious beyond our expectation. Mrs. M. and child are at Fredbg. The latter by her indisposition detained us almost a week at Bal: I am dear Sir very affectionately yr friend & servant, Jas Monroe."

RC (DLC); endorsed by TJ as received 16 Apr. 1791 and so recorded in SJL.

To William Nelson, Jr.

DEAR SIR   Philadelphia Mar. 29. 1791.

Your two favours of Nov. 22. and that of Feb. 4. came to hand during the session of Congress, and making part only of a very extensive subject, I was obliged to postpone it till Congress had risen. The laws also which you were so kind as to send have been received. Our collection stands thus at present.

The Collection of 1732.
The Revisal of 1748.

The Collection of 1768-1769.
The Chancellor's revisal.

Laws of 1775. Dec.	1783. Oct.
1776. May and Oct.	1784. May and Oct.
1777. May. 5.	1785. Oct.
1778. May and Oct.	1786. Oct.
1779. May and Oct.	1787. Oct.
1781. May and Nov.	1788. Oct.
1782. May and Oct.	
1783. May	

Those of the first column were recieved from you, except the Chancellor's revisal. At present we want nothing but Purvis's collection, and perhaps some little chasms in the preceding list which you are so kind as to promise to fill up. I inclose you a Bank postnote for the amount, being 38½ dollars, which any collector will give cash for. I think it will be unnecessary to trouble you for the inquisitions, injunctions, judgments, decrees &c. or any thing else in manuscript. The observations you have been so good as to make on the whole will serve as a clue to us whenever the subject shall come on. There was more appearance of this some little time ago, than at present. However it must come on at some time, and the wish was not to be obliged to stop proceedings till the laws on the subject should be collected. There is moreover a constant occasion for turning to the laws of the several states, and the want of them hitherto has been very inconvenient.

Accept my thanks for the care with which you have been so good as to attend to this matter & assurances of the esteem with which I have the honour to be Dear Sir Your most obedt. & most humble servt,   TH: JEFFERSON

RC (NjHi); addressed: "William Nelson esquire Attorney for the U.S. Williamsburg"; franked; postmarked: "29 MR" and WMSBURG. April 6"; TJ's slip in addressing the letter to the former capital was corrected by the deletion of "Williamsburg" and the interlineation of "Richmond" in another hand. PrC (DLC). FC (DNA: RG 59, PCC No. 120).

To John Samuel Sherburne

SIR   Philadelphia Mar. 29. 1791.

The recess of Congress permits me now to acknowlege the receipt of your favor of Oct. 20. and also of the laws of New Hampshire from 1696 to 1773 and from 1776 to 1787. Should there by any other printed laws not in these collections I will avail myself of your kind promise to procure them for the use of my office, as it is very desireable to possess a compleat collection of every law that was ever in force in any of the states, and which can be had in *print*, for it is not proposed to be at the expence of making manuscript copies. Whenever you will be so good as to notify to me the cost of what you have sent, you shall immediately receive a bank postnote for it; in the mean time accept assurances of the esteem with which I have the honour to be Sir Your most obedt. & most humble servt, TH: JEFFERSON

PrC (DLC); at foot of text: "John Saml. Sherburne esq. New Hampshire." FC (DNA: RG 59, PCC No. 120).

From William Short

DEAR SIR,   Paris March 30. 1791

On my arrival here a few days ago I found your letter of the 23d. of January. The statement which you there give me of the reciept of my several letters is truly mortifying. They must necessarily have lost their principal merit by arriving so long after their contents had become known and given place to other matters of more recent date and greater interest. I had however followed the same mode of forwarding them which you had used—that is of sending them to Havre or any other port where I learned there were vessels about to sail for America. Before I went to Amsterdam I recieved your letter desiring I would write to you by the English packet. Since then I have done it regularly. I hope the letters which I sent from Holland by that conveyance will have been received in good time. The first of them is already acknoweleged in your letter. I know that those sent by the way of the Texel will have met with a delay almost without example on account of the contrary winds which prevented any vessel leaving that place during several months.

I have learned by some of M. de St. Triest's friends here that he has arrived in America. Of course you will have recieved my No. 44 which was sent by him and which was one of the three wanting at the date of your letter. The delay or loss of No. 45. gives me much mortification. It was a short letter written the morning after the English messenger arrived here from Madrid with an account that peace would not be interrupted. It was merely to give you that information, and was sent off in the instant to London in hopes of its carrying you the first certain intelligence on that important subject. A duplicate also was sent, so that I may consider myself as doubly unfortunate. No. 46 was sent by a young man going to settle in America. I shall be exceedingly sorry if it should be lost as it was very particular with respect to what I had done here relative to our commercial interests.

The situation of this country is much more quiet than I expected to find it—extreme agitation and calm have been for some time alternative here and have thus often deceived the best observers. This will probably last as long as the assembly; and my particular opinion is that that will be as long as they can support themselves.—As they have the means of making money and of exciting the alarms of the people with respect to what they call the *contre-revolutionaires*, it is difficult to say when their popularity will cease. I must add however that the opinion of all the most moderate and most enlightened persons with whom I have spoken here as well in as out of the assembly, is that the assembly is really disposed to end itself, and that letters of convocation for a new legislature will be issued before the 14th. of July. M. de la F[ayette] the Duke de la R[ochefoucauld] and M. de M[ontmori]n are of this number. I mention them because your personal acquaintance with them will enable you the better to appreciate the opinion. I think they decieve themselves by their wishes, and by the loss of influence which some of the leaders of the popular party have lately experienced in the assembly and particularly the La Meths and Barnave. This I consider however as only momentary, as they will always be the supporters of those principles which please the galleries who are the distributors of popularity and in general decide that of the assembly.

The decrees relative to the clergy give much uneasiness in the provinces and particularly those which diminish the number of parishes. On the whole the new constitution of the clergy formed by a committee of Jansenists, with the real intention of invigorating the Roman catholic religion, will probably turn out the most dangerous, as it always appeared the most useless and most improper operation of the assembly. It has in many places produced a conflict, in the minds of the people (of all classes but particularly of the lowest and most numerous) between their devotion and their attachment to the revolution, for which they were not yet ripe and which may end to the disadvantage of the latter.

The Cardinal de Brienne had written to the Pope to notify his having taken the new oath. The Pope in his answer passed such severe censures on his conduct and particularly with respect to what he said himself of this oath, as if he took it for form only and rejected it internally, that he has sent him back his hat as Cardinal which he refuses longer to wear. As their correspondence was in Latin it is not surprizing that there should be some misunderstanding as to the construction of a sentence which occasions the whole dispute. Some think it is the intention of the holy see to declare France schismatick. In that case the Cardinal would probably be made Patriarch. It would however create much uneasiness discontent and disorder, and this would be a reason the more with the Holy see.

The scene which passed at the Thuilleries in the King's apartment and of which you are already informed brought on an indisposition that was for some time alarming as he is essential to the preventing of intestine dissensions that would be immediately followed by civil war. He is at present recovered, but it would seem impossible that he should long support such agitation of mind and inactivity of body as he is now subjected to.

Since my arrival here nothing further has been done in such articles as concern our commerce. The diplomatick committee and particularly M. de M[ontmori]n desire much to obtain a change in the decree relative to tobacco so as to put the American vessels on the same footing with the French. I find many others well disposed also and it will certainly be effected with time. The duty also will then be reduced. In the beginning there would have been no possibility of getting them to listen to less than 5. sous a pound, for a variety of reasons with which you are already acquainted and which it is useless to repeat here.

I have an extract of the Procès verbal by which it appears that the American oils alone are admitted by the decree of the assembly which reduces the duty to 6.ᵗᵗ the quintal. I enclose you a note from one of the committee of commerce which shews that the duties and taxes to which these oils were formerly subjected amounted to the same less one sol and an half. Had the *arrêt du conseil* continued, the 10. sous per livre would have ceased with the last year. But the assembly refused to reduce the duties lower than 6.ᵗᵗ and this was done on account of the reclamations of some tanneries and the diplomatick committee. The same causes will operate with time to reduce it still lower.

I saw yesterday the member who is to propose the extension to the foreign possessions of France, of the decree for the abolition of the *droit d'aubaine*. The decree has already as I have informed you passed the several committees. He assured me it would be proposed to-day or to-morrow. He has no doubt of its passing without opposition at present. It is possible however he may be mistaken, though there is much more probability of success at present than formerly.

Ships and vessels built abroad are no longer to be sold here. This is a new and favorite idea with the assembly. They will not hear of modifying it at present, though some of the most enlightened of the committee with whom I have spoken are disposed to it. It may be found proper perhaps after a little while to propose some exceptions to the general exclusion.

I recieved and gave the supplement to your report on weights and measures to the persons you desired. The Bishop of Autun has been induced by the academy of Sciences to change his basis and to adopt a section of the meridian to be measured between Dunkirk and Barcelona. The assembly decreed this proposition a few days ago. The English Parliament having made no step towards meeting the advances of the assembly they have determined to proceed alone. M. de Condorcet promises to send me immediately a copy of the report of the academy which determined this change to be forwarded to you.—As the great object is to obtain a fixed standard the end will be answered although the means of execution are different.

Barnave has been for a long time and still is employed in framing the plan of connexion and dependence between this country and her colonies. From the interests which prevail at present there is no doubt it will be severely exclusive. Nothing will be decided probably until the new colonial assemblies shall have expressed their sentiments, but these sentiments will have little weight if they are not conformable to those of the national assembly and if the forces sent there should have a decided superiority.

Much is said here about the hostile intentions of the Prince de Condé and the French refugees who are with him or distributed on the borders of France.—Their wild projects and imprudent conversation will only serve as a support to the present assembly. I endeavoured to convince of this truth some of those whom I saw at Brussels, and particularly the Prince de L—— grandson to a lady of your acquaintance. He and others seemed sensible of it. Still they repeated constantly that it would take place—that Spain, Prussia, and the Emperor would act in concert to support them and other follies of the kind. It was evident to me that they decieved each other.—They think that three fourths of the people are against the revolution and that if an handful of good troops entered France they would be joined by a majority. It is possible they may make this experiment, taking care always to secure a retreat. It would probably produce much disorder and bloodshed here.

Preparations are making for hostile operations in the North with much activity and indeed every day which passes without bringing an account of peace renders war more probable. You will recieve the earliest intelligence from that quarter by the papers which you inform me M. Dumas sends you by the English Packet. The naval preparations of England go on also and must soon shew their real destination. It is even expected that the press will be renewed. When I left Holland that country was much embarassed by the anticipation of the effect of their present alliance. Several of the cities seemed disposed so to construe the present position as not to consider it the *casus fœderis*. There is no doubt however that they will definitely be forced to do whatever their allies may think proper.

The French Ambassadors at Rome and Venice having not complied with the new oath prescribed are recalled. Their successors are M. de Segur and Durfort lately at Petersburg and Florence. Several other nominations have taken place also, in which the minister trying to please all parties has pleased none. They are for the most part young men employed now for the first time in the corps diplomatique.

The newspapers which you supposed would accompany your letter have not come to my hands.—The letter from the Secretary of the Treasury has probably met with more delay than you expected. I have not recieved it although there are letters here as late as Feb. 10. My absolute ignorance of his views and intentions (having not heard a tittle from him since Sep. 1.) is embarassing, as it disables me from conjecturing what it is proper to say or do in certain cases which he must have foreseen. I take it for granted he has information of the letters you write, and particularly of the 7th. page of that of August 26. As yet no inconvenience has arisen but there may arise with time. Besides large sums of money lying idle at the same time that a double interest is paid, viz. on it and the debt it might extinguish, appears to me bad policy when it might have been so easily foreseen and prevented, whether it was destined to be called for in America or used otherwise.

I am much pressed now by those who wish to make a loan to the U.S. elsewhere than in Amsterdam, and which I have already mentioned to the Secretary of the treasury. I know nothing more than what I then communicated to him, except that they urge there being no time lost in commencing the business. The credit of the U.S. being thus favorably considered in several countries cannot but be an agreeable circumstance. Nothing of course will be done further, as he knows, until he expresses his sentiments.

I know not whether I am to construe your silence as to what was done in the business mentioned in the 6th. page of your letter abovementioned (Aug. 26) as approbation or disapprobation. I think there is room neither for the one or the other as there appeared to me no alternative. Still I should have been glad to have had your sentiments as they might have been a rule on a future occasion.

This letter will go by the English Packet. I will ask the favor of you to communicate to the Secretary of the Treasury such parts as relate to his department. I do not write to him at present that I may avoid repetition. I have the honor to be with the sincerest attachment Dear Sir, your most obedient humble servant,

W. SHORT

PrC (DLC: Short Papers); at head of text: "No. 62." Tr (DNA: RG 59, DD). Recorded in SJL as received 21 June 1791. Enclosure: Note from Roussillon, member of National Assembly from Toulon, 22 Mch. 1791: "Mr. Roussillon fait mille complimens à Monsieur Rainard. Il a l'honneur de lui envoyer l'extrait du procès verbal qu'il a demandé, et la note des droits que les amèricains payoient anciennement sur les huils de poisson.—Droit d'entree pour les huiles de poisson importées par les americains ⅌ q[uint]al 1 - 9 -

4-10 sous par livre	14 - 6
	2 - 3 - 6
Droit particulier des huils	3 -15 -
	5 -18 - 6

Le Droit principal etoit payé a raison

7ᵗ 10s ⅌ B[arri]que du poids de 520 [livres]" (Tr in DNA: RG 59, DD).

Short's dispatches Nos. 44, 45, and 46 were those of 21 Oct. 1790, 2 Nov. 1790, and 6 Nov. 1790, received respectively on 27 Jan., 9 Feb., and 18 Mch. 1791.—In the 7TH. PAGE of his letter of 26 Aug. 1790 TJ had authorized Short to assure Montmorin of measures taken to enable the United States to pay all arrearages of interest and principal due to France.—In the 6TH. PAGE of that letter TJ urged that the timing of the payment be used to influence the great object of introducing American grain, livestock, flour, fish, and salt provisions into the French West Indies, for which purpose the decision as to when payment was to be made was left with Short.

From William Short

DEAR SIR   Paris March 30. 1791.

Your letter of the 24th. (private) accompanied that of the 23d. and was received here on my return from Amsterdam. The commissions you there charge me with shall be attended to. Mr.

Fenwick writes me that he shall ship the wine you ordered, on a vessel bound to Charleston, despairing of finding an immediate conveyance before the warm weather.—Vernon was still there and he thinks has no intention of embarking. He has received the amount of the bill which his father sent me in order to get him out of Paris. He received the last of it at Bordeaux. I had much hopes in consequence of what he told me himself and Mr. Appleton also that he desired to return and would accomplish it. I know not whether Mr. Fenwick will make the experiment you recommended. I think it would be dangerous.

I am glad to hear of the arrival of your furniture. The carriages unfortunately got separated from it at Rouen. M. de la Motte informed me of his having since received them at Havre, and further I know nothing but hope they have long since left that place. It has been some time since he has written to me.—With respect to Petit, every thing will be terminated to your satisfaction. I sent him your letter after reading and sealing it agreeably to your desire. I received yesterday an answer from him in which he tells me that he is taking arrangements with his family and will be here in fifteen days in order to go and join you. He adds that you mention in the letter that I am to fix the terms with him. I think he will be very tractable, as the ennui he met with in the country has entirely changed his dispositions. Of this I informed you from Amsterdam by my letter (private) of Feb. 18.—I found by your letter to Petit that you supposed I had gone into a negotiation with him viz. made him greater offers. You observe that I do not give you the details. If you will advert to your letters of March 12. and April 6. you will see that I had not authority for any negotiation and consequently, there were no details to be given. He first hesitated about going. When your letter fixing the wages arrived and I mentioned them to him he decided. In that disposition it would have been improper to have tempted him by money even if I had been authorized. Finally he determined to remain for various reasons which he gave—relative to his family, aged mother, estate in the country &c. It was evident to me that he counted on being employed by your successor and I suppose it had weight.—I was never more surprized than when I received his letter written to the Secretary whom I left in Paris in which he supposes he had desired me to write to you to propose his going for an 100^{tt} per month. I wrote to him to know from whence he had collected that idea, letting him know that I would now inform you of it. He says that I told him I had written to you that he thought 72.^{tt} too little and that he asked an 100.ᵗ and that on my asking him if he would go for an 100.ᵗ he answered he could not promise it &c., but that *mourant d'ennui à la campagne* he wished much to go at present—that he should prefer much being employed at Paris by your successor &c. I shall propose to him at present 3½ Louis per month his passage and expences paid, and I think he will accept it. If not I will induce him to go and to fix the wages with you after his arrival. At any rate you may be sure of his coming in one way or another.

Tolozan is now at Dijon. I mentioned the subject of your letter to Sequeville who seemed well pleased with it. I offered him what you had desired. He insisted absolutely on it being deferred till after he had given me what he shall be charged to do. One he says is the necessary consequence of the other and can never precede it. Your wishes in other respects relative to this business shall be accomplished.

Among the letters which were inclosed in your last was one directed to the President of the assembly. I knew it was the hand-writing of the President and conjectured it was an answer to that formerly sent to him, and that was all I knew about it. I offered it to M. de M[ontmori]n, and mentioned this to him. He desired I would send it myself, which I did by the Duke de la R[oche-foucauld]. He was desired by the President to translate it that he might read it to the assembly. This he did but in such an hurry as to have made a very bad translation, and what is still worse to have used an expression with respect to the M[arquis] de la F[ayette] which bears a double interpretation that is by no means favourable. The enemies of the Marquis are much delighted by it and he much mortified. He complained that I did not have the letter well translated. I observed to him that it would have been somewhat difficult, as the letter was sealed and I had no copy of it and did not even know from whom it was except by recognition of the hand-writing, and of course could not have foreseen that he would be mentioned in it. The expression in English is as the Duke de la R. tells me *"May he* ever continue to have the public good in view &c."* In French it is *"Puisse-t-il &c."* Such impressions how-ever are only momentary, and this is already forgotten by all ex-cept the M—— is himself.[1]

I recieved your letter also one for M. de St Trys. I return it at present as I know he is in America.

In your private letter of Jan. 24. there was some mistake in the cypher which rendered unintelligible a sentence which I wished much to understand. I will thank you to examine it that you may

see whether it is an incorrection in the table. It is page 4. line 1.
—the four last cyphers of that line and the first cypher of the second
line. You acknowleged the receipt of my private of June 14. at
Monticello. My public of the same date and sent with it was not
received till some time after at Philadelphia. I cannot concieve how
they came to be separated.

Since my return from Holland I have lodged in an hotel garni,
the same where you were, Rue des Petits Augustins. In daily
expectation of being replaced I supposed it would be madness to
take an house or make preparations for stay. I have long prepared
myself for every event. I cannot deny my desire to remain but I
feel that it is not for me to judge how proper I may be. What
you mention at the bottom of the third page of your private letter
I had rather should take place than nothing, as I have reasons
which I have already mentioned to you for wishing to remain some
time longer yet in Europe.—Yet I wish most sincerely that circumstances had been such as to have admitted my return on the footing I desired some time past. I am sorry not to have studied
architecture fully so as to have contributed to the formation of
the new city on proper plans and principles. I hope it will be made
a monument that will do honor to the new world and far surpass
any in the old for beauty, simplicity, convenience &c. I think
frequently of it and generally end by determining that if I settle on
the Eastern waters that it shall be somewhere among the mountains
near the southern bank of the Potowmac. This however will depend
on circumstances which are not probable.—Parker has become
bankrupt instead of being a Croesus. I fear I shall suffer by him.
The money which had been remitted me from America and which
had long remained in Mr. Grand's hands was confided to him in
June 89. Adieu my dear Sir & believe me sincerely your friend &
servant,   W. SHORT

P. S. M[ontmori]n had frequently expressed his wish and his
hope that I should be named here. I always expressed my doubts
and particularly after recieving your letters. He added that [if]
it was not me he hoped it would be Car[micha]el. I mention this
is consequence of your last letter. M[ontmori]n is much and sincerely attached to him. He might certainly be rendered useful where
he is — or wherever he should have to treat with M[ontmori]n. I
hope his explanation will be satisfactory as to himself.

RC (DLC); endorsed by TJ as received 21 June 1791 and so recorded
in SJL. PrC (PHi). Tr of Extract
(DNA: RG 59, MLR); entirely in TJ's
hand, headed: "Extract of a private
letter from Mr. Short dated Paris. Mar.

30. 91."; docketed by Washington, in part: "from Mr. Short." FC of Extract (DNA: RG 59, SDC).

The difficulty Short had in decoding PAGE 4. LINE 1. of TJ's private letter of 24 Jan. 1791 is explained in note 7 to that letter. The statement made by TJ at the bottom of the THIRD PAGE of the same letter was that

Short might expect appointment to The Hague.

1 This paragraph constitutes the extract that TJ sent to Washington, in which he discreetly omitted the French *double entendre* (see Editorial Note, documents on the death of Franklin, 26 Jan. 1791).

To Pierpont Edwards

SIR   Philadelphia Mar. 31. 1791.

The recess of Congress now permits me to resume the subject of my circular letter of Aug. 12. which had the double object of procuring from all the states 1. a statement of their proceedings as to British property, and 2. a complete collection of their laws to be deposited in my office for the use of the general government. As to the first I am to thank you for the papers and observations you have been so good as to furnish in your letter of Oct. 28. and also for the statute books relative to the 2d. object which you were so kind as to send. You mention your purpose of sending on another volume of the laws as revised in 1702. which I shall be glad to recieve, as also any others which may hereafter fall in your way, and contribute to complete our collection, a thing extremely to be desired. Whenever you will be so good as to notify me what these things have cost I will immediately remit a bank-post-note for your reimbursement. With my acknolegements for your attention to this subject be pleased to accept assurances of the esteem & respect with which I have the honor to be Sir Your most obedt & most humble servt,   TH: JEFFERSON

RC (CtY); at foot of text: "Pierpont Edwards esq. Connecticut." PrC (DLC). FC (DNA: RG 59, PCC No. 120).

To Alexander Hamilton

SIR   Department of state Mar. 31. 1791.

The publication of the laws of the U. S. and the purchase of those of the several states call on us immediately for about five hundred dollars, for which sum I must ask a warrant from you to be accounted for. The contingent expences of my department to the 1st. inst. are now stated and will be settled with the Auditor tomorrow. I have the honor to be with great esteem & respect Sir Your most obedt. & most humble servt,   TH: JEFFERSON

PrC (DLC); at foot of text: "The Secretary of the Treasury." FC (DNA: RG 59, PCC No. 120). SJL entry reads: "Hamilton, Alexr. [for 500 D. contingt. money]."

From David Humphreys

Mafra, 31 Mch. 1791. He received packet last night from Mr. Bulkeley and information of a vessel departing for Alexandria in a few days, hence he sends this by a servant to Lisbon. Having accounts from America as late as 10 Feb. and not being advised by "the Department of foreign affairs" of receipt of any of his letters, he fears their detention or miscarriage. He gives their dates to show it was not due to negligence; his first of 14 Oct. 1790 from London was put in letter bag at New York Coffee House belonging to vessel bound for New York next day. Those of 20, 25, and 28 Oct. were delivered by Joshua Johnson to captains of vessels bound for different ports. That of 2 Nov. he himself gave to Jonathan Swift of Alexandria. His last from England, 4 Nov., from Gravesend, was sent through post office to Johnson. Those of 19 and 30 Nov. from Lisbon were given by him to Capt. Porter of New London, together with De Pinto's answer to TJ's letter of 7 Aug. last. Duplicate of that of 30 Nov. sent to G. Fox of Falmouth, who promises to send it by January packet. His first from Madrid of 18 Dec. was sent by an American vessel to Baltimore, and the two ciphered dispatches of 3 and 15 Jan. were also sent by American vessels from Lisbon. But the former was delayed by casualty and went by the same vessel carrying those of 6 and 12 Feb. written after his return to Lisbon. His 14th, dated Lisbon 6 Mch., was sent by Bulkeley in a vessel consigned to him from Virginia.

When he informed TJ in his last about American commerce at Lisbon and consular business being handled by Dohrman and Harrison under countenance of Portuguese government, he had not seen *Almanach* for 1791. He now encloses copy, listing former as consul general and latter as vice-consul of the United States. "This adds a fresh instance in support of a remark, which, I think, I have heard you make, on the numerous errors to be found in publications of this sort. I know not, however, any reasons why these Persons, residing on the spot, approved by the Government, and acquainted with the language, customs and offices, are not as competent to the performance of the duties as any other Characters would be." But, not having exchanged a word with either on consular appointments for Portugal, he can take no interest in the matter.

That our commerce with Portugal is important because of favorable balance for us cannot be doubted; it "merits to be cherished in the most discreet and dexterous manner." *Almanach* shows 85 American vessels arrived in Lisbon during 1790, a number equal to that of any foreign nation except Great Britain. But very few have arrived this year, which caused him to wonder because the last harvest was so uncommonly plentiful in the United States "and because the price in this Country . . . would yield a handsome profit," the last cargoes of wheat selling for 7/ stg. per bushel and great quantities more might have been sold at same rate. Many shiploads being expected from North, it is uncertain what price will be. "At present the prospect of the succeeding harvest here is extremely unfavorable. So great a Drought was scarcely ever known to prevail at this season. In short there has been next to no rain during the whole winter. Prayers have lately been offered in all the Churches of Lisbon for rain. In this place, Processions of Priests, People and Images have . . . been made, in three successive days for the same purpose. As yet the skies assume no appearance of relenting." But if rains come soon, crops may still be saved, as they were at a critical moment last year after orders were sent to America for a great supply of flour, under special license. "It is believed the unexpected restoration of the Crops at that time, was the real cause why that flour was rejected (to the ruin of the Shippers) by the Contractors; under, perhaps, a justifiable legal colour, as having been shipped after the day designated."

He is using his present leisure to get a just idea of the state of Portugal and to acquire competency in reading the language: the former will take time—the latter he has succeeded in to his satisfaction, being especially happy in his acquaintance with "several learned and respectable Characters in this College" to whom he is greatly indebted for many civilities. Through them he is able to see the *Courier de l'Europe* and other papers regularly received at the Convent. He has not neglected whatever other means available to get early and authentic intelligence of the general situation of affairs.

RC (DNA: RG 59, DD); at head of text: "(No. 15)"; endorsed by TJ as received 21 June 1791 and so recorded in SJL. Tr (same).

To Mary Jefferson

MY DEAR MARIA   Philadelphia Mar. 31. 1791.

I am happy to have a letter of yours to answer. That of Mar. 6. came to my hands on the 24th. By the bye you never acknowlege the receipt of my letters, nor tell me on what day they came to hand. I presume that by this time you have received the two dressing tables with marble tops. I give one of them to your sister and the other to you. Mine is here with the top broke in two. Mr. Randolph's letter referring to me the name of your niece was very long on the road. I answered it as soon as I received it, and hope the answer got duly to hand. Lest it should have been delayed, I repeated last week to your sister the name of Anne, which I had recommended as belonging to both families. I wrote you in my last that the frogs had begun their songs on the 7th. Since that the blue birds saluted us on the 17th. The weeping willow began to leaf on the 18th. The lilac and gooseberry on the 25th. and the golden willow on the 26th. I inclose for your sister three kinds of flowering beans, very beautiful and very rare. She must plant, and nourish them with her own hands this year, in order to save seeds enough for herself and me. Tell Mr. Randolph I have sold my tobacco for 5. dollars per C. and the rise between this and September. Warehouse and shipping expences in Virginia, freight and storage here, come to 2/9 a hundred, so that it is as if I had sold it in Richmond for 27/3 credit till September, or half per cent per month discount for the ready money. If he chuses it, his Bedford tobacco may be included in the sale. Kiss every body for me. Yours' affectionately,   TH: JEFFERSON

Tr (MHi).

To William Lewis

SIR   Philadelphia Mar. 31. 1791.

The recess of Congress permits me now to resume the subject of my letter of Aug. 12. and to acknowlege the receipt of your favors of Sept. 14. Nov. 25. and Jan. 1. with respect to British debts and property. It was thought possible then that they might come forward and discuss the interests and questions existing between the two nations; and as we knew they would assail us on the subject of the treaty, without our previously knowing the particular state or states whose proceedings they would make the ground of complaint, we wished to be in a state of preparation on every point. I am therefore to thank you particularly for having furnished us the justifications of this commonwealth in your letter of Jan. 1.—With respect to the more general object of my letter, that of making a very complete collection of all the laws in force or which were ever in force in the several states, we are now as to this state possessed of those from 1776. to 1790. I must still avail myself of your kind undertaking in your letters of Sep. 14. and Nov. 25. to continue your attention to this acquisition till we can have the whole. Indeed if you would order any bookseller to procure them according to such list as you should give him, it might greatly lessen your trouble, and he could deliver them himself at my office and recieve there his pay. Whenever you shall be so good as to notify me of the cost of those already furnished it shall be immediately reimbursed. I am sure you are sensible of the necessity of possessing at the seat of the general government a complete collection of all the laws of all the states and hope you will perceive there were no persons so likely to make the collection judiciously as the Attornies for the districts, which must be the apology for the trouble which has been given you on this subject by him who has the honour to be with great esteem & respect Sir Your most obedt. & most humble servt,   TH: JEFFERSON

PrC (DLC); at foot of text: "Mr. Lewis Pennsylvania." FC (DNA: RG 59, PCC No. 120).

Preliminary indexes will be issued periodically for groups of volumes. Indexes covering Vols. 1-6, 7-12, and 13-18 have been published. A comprehensive index of persons, places, subjects, etc., arranged in a single consolidated sequence, will be issued at the conclusion of the series.

THE PAPERS OF THOMAS JEFFERSON is composed in Monticello, a type specially designed by the Mergenthaler Linotype Company for this series. Monticello is based on a type design originally developed by Binny & Ronaldson, the first successful typefounding company in America. It is considered historically appropriate here because it was used extensively in American printing during the last thirty years of Jefferson's life, 1796 to 1826; and because Jefferson himself expressed cordial approval of Binny & Ronaldson types.

✧

Composed and printed by Princeton University Press. Illustrations are reproduced by Meriden Gravure Company, Meriden, Connecticut. Paper for the series is made by Curtis Paper Company, at Newark, Delaware; cloth for the series is made by Holliston Mills, Inc., Norwood, Massachusetts. Bound by the Maple Press Company, Baltimore.

DESIGNED BY P. J. CONKWRIGHT